12 95/AC

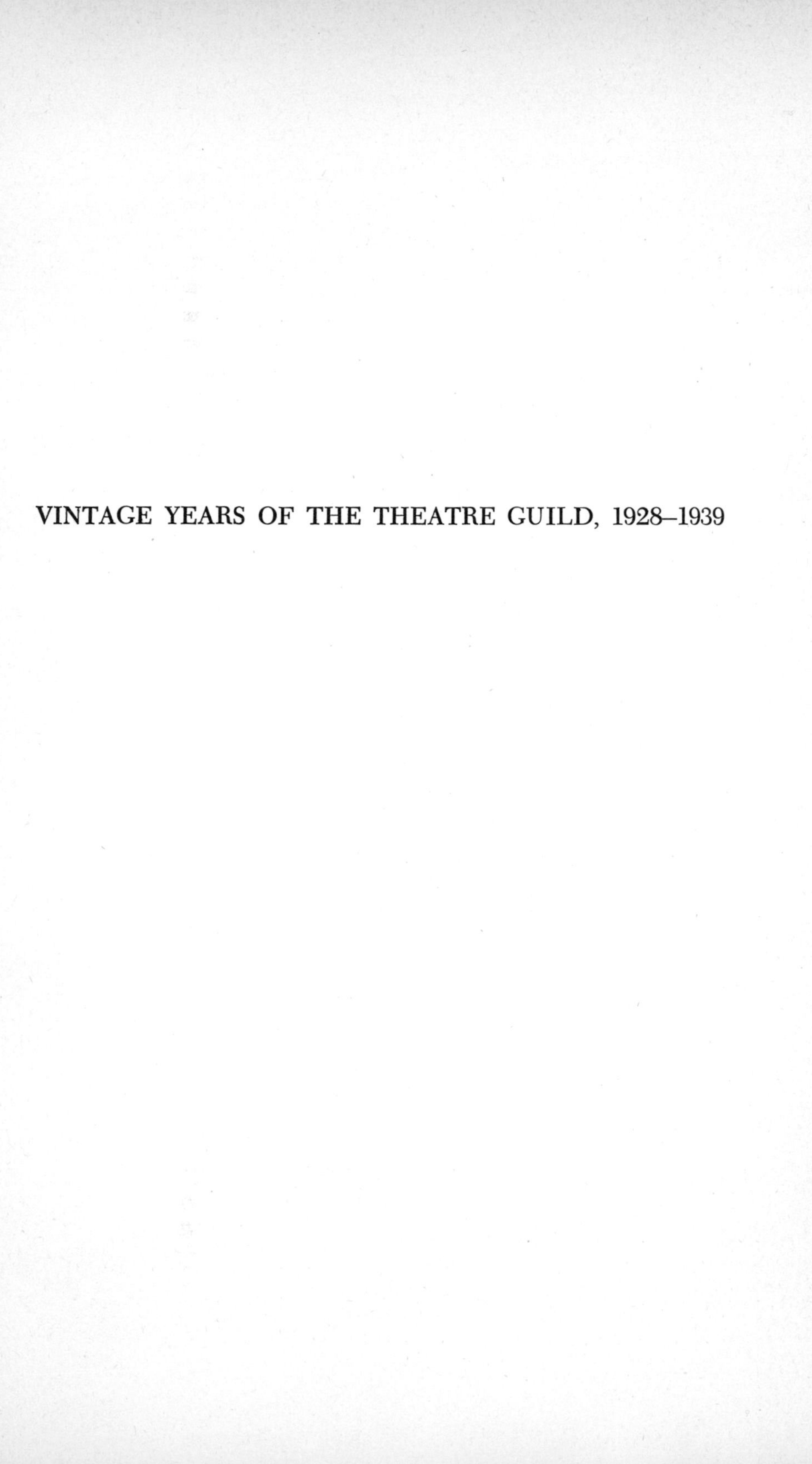

VINTAGE YEARS OF THE THEATRE GUILD, 1928–1939

VINTAGE YEARS OF THE THEATRE GUILD

1928 1939

ROY S. WALDAU

THE PRESS OF
CASE WESTERN RESERVE UNIVERSITY
CLEVELAND AND LONDON
1972

PN
2295
T5
W3

Copyright© 1972 by The Press of Case Western Reserve University,
Cleveland, Ohio, 44106.
All rights reserved.
Printed in the United States of America.
International Standard Book Number: 0–8295–0203–3
Library of Congress Catalogue Card Number: 79–141463

To the memory of my father and mother —both of whom loved the theatre much more than they cared to admit.

CONTENTS

ILLUSTRATIONS

PREFACE

My interest in the Theatre Guild began with its beginnings. In those days I was a professor in the drama school of the Carnegie Institute of Technology. As a lapsed Puritan, I had been a devotee of the stage since my adolescence, and, although never before had I been asked to prepare a course solely in dramatic literature, I accepted eagerly the opportunity to offer a survey of the contemporary drama—Continental, English, and American. Henceforth, till the fall of 1927, I alternated this hybrid compound with a hop-skip-jump series of lectures covering the entire field from the Greeks to Ibsen!

The Guild caught my attention with its first presentation, *The Bonds of Interest,* by the Spanish playwright Jacinto Benavente, who was enjoying a current vogue in America and on whom I was attempting to lecture. After this, I watched with increasing admiration the announcements of the Guild's productions and saw as many of them as possible during vacations away from academic duties. Upon my return from orgies of theatregoing in New York, I would report my experiences and observations to my class of aspiring "dramats," all of whom were dreaming of bright careers of their own on Broadway.

One gradually became well acquainted with the conspicuous personalities on the Guild's acting roster and observed with awe and delight the variety of roles which proved the astonishing versatility of such players as Dudley Digges, Helen Westley, Henry Travers, and, later, the incomparable Alfred Lunt and Lynn Fontanne. One can imagine my amazement when the Guild presented difficult and unusual plays that had never been done before in America but about which I wanted to say something pertinent to students. The selection was extremely wide in range: Tolstoy's horrifying tragedy *The Power of Darkness,* Georg Kaiser's expressionistic *From Morn to Midnight,* Franz Werfel's mystical *Goat Song,* Karel Capek's fantastic evocation of the future, *R. U. R.,* and Jacques Copeau's startling, brooding dramatization of Dostoyevsky's *The Brothers Karamazov.*

From 1919 to 1927 my interest in the Theatre Guild was most intense, and to that period my most vivid memories of its presentations belong: Joseph Schildkraut's and Eva Le Gallienne's sensitive playing in Molnar's *Liliom,* the lovely, ethereal Margalo Gillmore in Andreyev's *He Who Gets Slapped,* Winifred Lenihan's spirited creation for

America of Shaw's tomboyish *St. Joan,* even Alfred Lunt's making love to a sofa cushion in Molnar's *The Guardsman.* One remembers especially the splendid comedy ensemble portrayals in Stefan Zweig's adaptation of Ben Jonson's *Volpone,* and the consummate cast of O'Neill's *Strange Interlude* in which four men, Glenn Anders, Earle Larimore, Tom Powers, and Philip Leigh, were attracted and repelled in various ways by the fascinating Lynn Fontanne. The Guild was important to me as a teacher of the theatre's literature because it afforded outstanding samples of dramatic writing that could be experienced as they were meant to be experienced: on the stage, done by skilled performers who brought to them a good measure of the shadings and values their authors had intended. During its early years, the Guild's choice of plays seemed not only judicious but audacious—a joy to the dyed-in-the-wool drama buff. Then, several distressing things began to happen.

It would not be at all difficult to plot a curve showing the rise and decline in the fortunes of the Theatre Guild. The rising line would represent its modest beginnings, its acquisition of an increasingly impressive number of New York subscribers, and its education of certain metropolitan reviewers who had been elevated from lowlier journalistic assignments, such as sports writing and nightclub gossiping, to the lofty role of arbiters of drama, both commercial and noncommercial. This is reflected in a number of reviews quoted here which abound in "witty" observations, but indicate a deplorable lack of taste and a questionable set of standards—an outlook which suggests that when philosophy and poetic ideas appear, critical appreciation all but vanishes.

During the rise of the Guild's reputation, there were unfortunate occurrences within the organization that had the appearance of successes but actually were preludes to costly difficulties, if not disasters. The construction of the Guild Theatre had every indication of being a logical extension of growing plans; but in reality the burden of the debts it incurred became a weight that often threatened to topple the organization's slender financial structure. The recruiting of eager and demanding subscription audiences in several cities between Washington and Chicago was perhaps one of the Guild's major mistakes, because it proved to be impossible to provide enough worthwhile plays to keep promises made to these subscribers. Moreover, by its example the Guild prodded other producers who, as the years passed, exhibited the daring the Guild had seen fit to forfeit. These potential rivals began to stage quite successfully scripts the Guild's directors had considered and then rejected as being unsuitable for their new, burgeoning requirements.

The peak of the curve representing the Guild's fortunes probably occurred when the New York subscription lists were largest. Even this swelling audience, however, presented tremendous artistic problems, for it had been built on the assumption that six outstanding scripts could be found and produced every year—an overly optimistic expectation that could hardly be supported by the *entire* output of the American theatre during many of its seasons. From this peak of success on, as Mr. Waldau's book makes painfully clear, the Guild's directors were fighting a losing battle. They compromised with their earlier aims by offering plays they hoped would be financially rewarding but that were certainly not aesthetically satisfying. They felt threatened by the competition of the spectacularly active motion picture industry, and some of them succumbed to the lure of Hollywood, asking for longer and longer leaves from what many thought was their first and foremost obligation, the artistic guidance of the Guild. As time progressed, the directorate was inevitably disturbed by severe and often devastating responses from critics who had once been encouraging and friendly. Internally, there was devitalizing dissension among the directors, who in the beginning had worked together fairly harmoniously despite their varying theatrical preoccupations. The result was the breakup of the original Board of Managers.

Here, meticulously researched and recorded, is a saddening but highly provocative American story—the rise, decline, and artistic fall of the Theatre Guild.

Fred B. Millett
Wesleyan University

ACKNOWLEDGMENTS

This book is chiefly the product of several years spent poring over the Theatre Guild Archive, Collection of American Literature, Yale University Library. Access to this extraordinary compilation, now housed in the Beinecke Rare Book and Manuscript Library, was graciously granted me by Lawrence Langner. Included there are minutes of the Guild's Board of Managers' meetings, financial statements and account books, plus memos, letters, and articles written by various persons either employed by or otherwise interested in the organization. I am indebted to the collection's curator, Donald C. Gallup, Mrs. Anne Whelpley, and other members of Yale's library staff who were unfailingly helpful. Mr. Gallup was instrumental in securing permission to use certain portions of Eugene O'Neill's correspondence. Others, including William Saroyan and the heirs of Lee Simonson, have consented to the inclusion of personal letters and copyrighted matter.

The Research Library of the Performing Arts, New York Public Library at Lincoln Center, was also consulted; the personnel, especially Maxwell Silverman, have been generous with assistance. All illustrations except for the Robert Edmond Jones sketch for *Ah, Wilderness!* are Vandamm photographs from the Theatre Collection, The New York Public Library at Lincoln Center.

The late John Gassner, when reviewing a draft of the work, recommended the addition of material outlining the organization's beginnings as well as some suggestion of its course after Langner and Theresa Helburn assumed co-leadership. In following Mr. Gassner's recommendation, I found several volumes dealing with recent theatrical history useful. These include books written by the Guild's managers themselves: Lawrence Langner's *The Magic Curtain* and *G. B. S. and the Lunatic*, Theresa Helburn's *A Wayward Quest*, and Lee Simonson's *The Stage Is Set* and *Part of a Lifetime*. Also of interest were Mr. Gassner's own *Theatre in Our Times* and Norman Nadel's *A Pictorial History of the Theatre Guild*. Special note is made here of Walter Prichard Eaton's *The Theatre Guild: The First Ten Years*. I have mainly utilized the contents of this book, completed in 1928 under Guild auspices, to delineate the organization's first decade. My own principal concern has been the period of 1928 to 1939.

Of necessity, the opinions of New York drama critics have been constantly referred to, for they had a pronounced influence on the shaping of the Guild's policies. I have also depended to a large extent on what out-of-town reviewers thought of certain presentations, because the directorate paid careful attention to these hinterland voices, especially when productions were opening in tryout centers. These reviews, incidentally, now yellowing in dusty newspaper files, had a profound effect for better or worse on what we now know as final versions of many "classics" of American dramatic writing.

Finally, I would like to thank all the people who assisted me with their valued advice and special knowledge. My sincere appreciation goes to Miss Armina Marshall, one of the present Guild directors, and to Alfred Lunt for his critical reading of the final draft, as well as to Fred C. Blanchard, William P. Sears, and Miss Magdalene Schindelin, all of whom saw most of the productions mentioned herein. I have imposed on personal friendship to get editorial counselling from George P. Garrett, Kimon Lolos, Raymond E. Brown, Martin Sopocy, and Richard A. Patterson. As do most acknowledgments, this one concludes with a special word about a wife whose typing skill and knack of putting into workable English seemingly inexpressible ideas made the completion of this project possible. To these, and many others—heartfelt gratitude.

R. S. W.

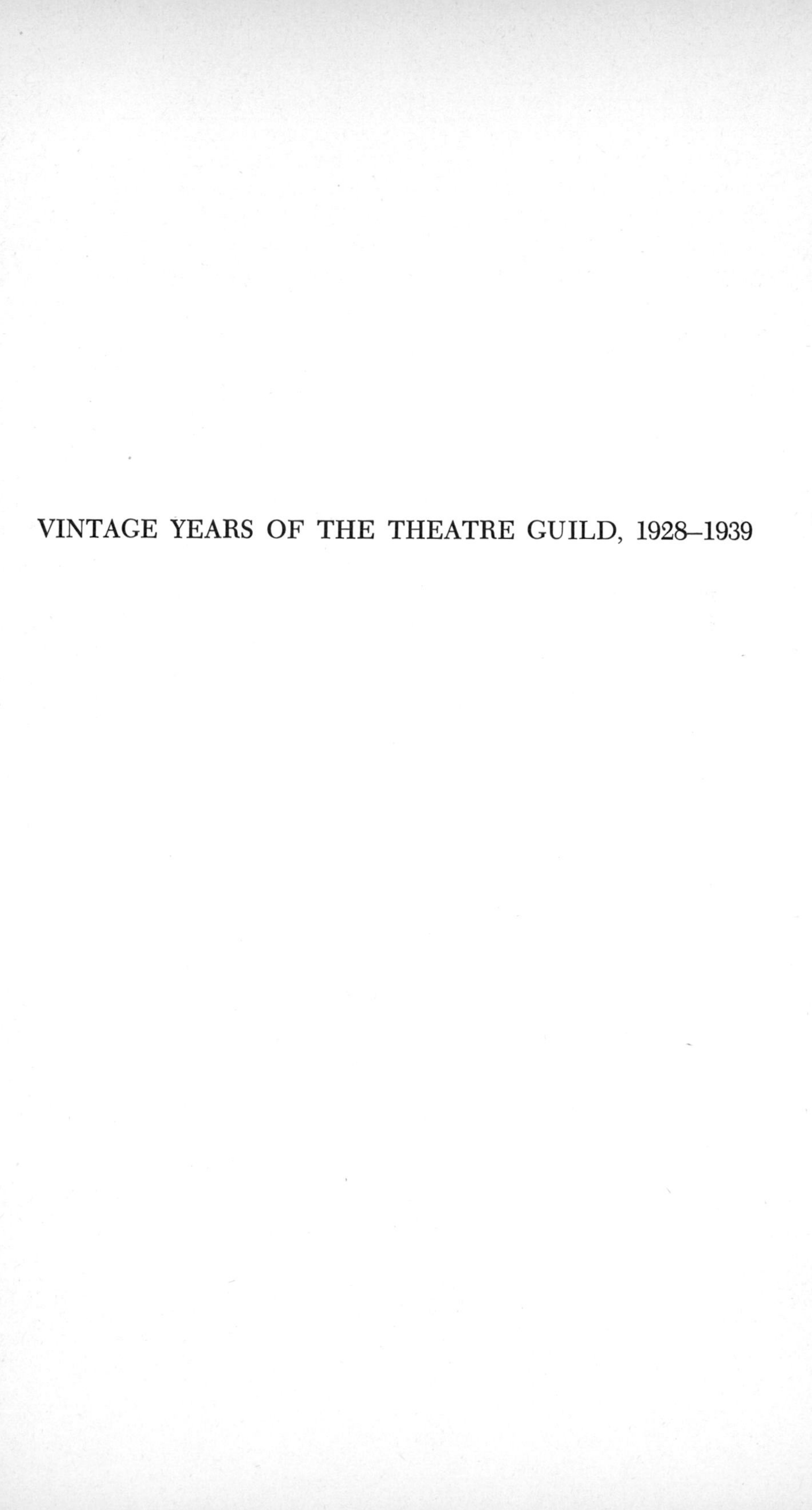

VINTAGE YEARS OF THE THEATRE GUILD, 1928–1939

CHAPTER 1 / Antecedents and Birth of the Guild

If the Theatre Guild had not come into being when it did, some similar organization undoubtedly would have been formed. The times were ripe for its inception.

From 1910 to 1915, increasing numbers of discerning people in the United States became aware of the challenges offered by innovations in older art forms that had been creating furors across the Atlantic. With the famous Armory Show of 1913, for instance, New Yorkers had their first full-scale look at what had been accomplished by such masters as Duchamp, Matisse, Picasso, and Rouault, and Post-Impressionism, as it was called, soon had its zealous and influential admirers. Even the beginning ferment of the First World War, which was naturally causing considerable excitement, too, did not seem to dampen the ardor felt for such dynamic new modes of artistic interpretation as Cubism, Expressionism, and a host of other "isms" then being imported.

Besides new techniques in painting and sculpture, advances in such fields as architecture, musical composition, and poetry were also being carefully scrutinized. Louis Sullivan and Frank Lloyd Wright insisted on the artistic possibilities of steel-frame construction, while Amy Lowell's *A Dome of Many-Colored Glass* (1912) and *Sword Blades and Poppy Seed* (1914) pioneered a new "Imagist" form of poetry. Others participated in the infectious "revival" of verse, such as E. A. Robinson, Vachel Lindsay, Carl Sandburg, Edgar Lee Masters, and Robert Frost. T. S. Eliot and Ezra Pound sought stimulation from expatriate existences. In music, inspired by Dvořák's use of folk melodies, Edward MacDowell worked with regional themes, while Arthur Nevin was influenced by the American Indian. It was a time when Freudian psychology gained its foothold in America (although it had appeared in Vienna some thirty years earlier) and drastically altered people's feelings concerning romantic love.

It was also a time when many "little magazines" and "little theatres" were organized—founded chiefly to circulate progressive artistic ideas.

One of the more prestigious magazines, *Poetry,* founded by Harriet Monroe in Chicago in 1913, served as a forum for innovations in verse. Another, *The Little Review,* begun by Margaret Anderson in 1914, gave encouragement to the early prose efforts of such writers as Ernest Hemingway, Ben Hecht, and Sherwood Anderson. Following the "little theatre" movement, then reaching this country from Europe, came Mrs. Lyman Gales's Toy Theatre in Boston and Samuel Eliot's Little Theatre in Indianapolis, among others. Possibly the first "little theatre" in America was begun in Chicago by an Englishman, Maurice Browne, who, with his wife Ellen Van Volkenburg, produced plays by Schnitzler, Shaw, and Strindberg in an auditorium seating less than one hundred people. Most of these "little" talent outlets, though toiled over as labors of love by their dedicated and certainly mercenary founders, unfortunately proved to be of an ephemeral nature. One, however, flourished, and grew to be one of the most important producing ventures in the history of the American theatre. It exists to this day, although in modified form. It became known as The Theatre Guild.

Following the trend toward things European, the period around 1910 was an era when certain foreign performing companies created a tremendous vogue in New York, and elsewhere, with their revivified productions of long-established works. For instance, deep feeling for classical dance forms had been stirred by a successful tour of Diaghilev's Ballet Russe which featured Nijinski in his most striking roles. Quite as impressive as this artist's astounding leaps was the imaginative use of color and design in the company's costumes and scenery, created by Léon Bakst, Alexandre Benois, and other European *décorateurs de théatre.* The legitimate theatregoing public, in its turn, had been surprised and stimulated by Harley Granville-Barker's carefully integrated repertory group, which offered brilliant innovations in staging and acting, and, above all, intelligently conceived interpretations of the spoken lines.

Clearly these new enthusiasms in the arts developed from an increasingly American aesthetic awareness. In architecture, change was fostered by dissatisfaction with oppressively ornate "Victorian" uses to which stone and mortar had been put. In poetry, there was a reaction against the pomposity of high-sounding cadenced, methodically rhymed verse. In drama, protests were voiced concerning the type of fare that had been surfeiting the nation's professional theatres.

Playgoing in the northeastern United States had been especially ready for some sort of rejuvenating influence. Earlier, a presentation of *The Playboy of the Western World* by J. M. Synge had caused scenes of riotous disorder when it appeared in Boston, New York, and Philadelphia. Typifying the era's critical standards, one theatrical magazine stated, "If Mr. Synge's intent was comedy, that comedy is too subtle for anybody of common sense or for Irishmen who attach importance to the decent sentiments of life. . . . The attempt to make a comedy out of the sayings and doings of a parricide fails. The effect is offensive."

Although offerings by Ibsen, Galsworthy, and Gerhart Hauptmann had made periodic appearances, and worthy experiments, such as The New Theatre, had elevated expectations, most "serious" plays presented by commercial managers at the time tended to be "real-life" melodramas, which paraded an unpalatably romantic set of ideas glossed over with a pseudo-realistic approach (like as not in direct imitation of David Belasco's painstaking dramaturgy). For example, one of the few claims to "realism" that the now-ridiculed *Governor's Lady* (1912) could make was its fully appointed Childs Restaurant set, complete with real flapjacks which were fried on a real griddle. Often, such "realism" was employed to enhance "highly moral" plots: e. g., a wayward son saves his father's fortunes, a corrupt woman reforms, a divided family reunites, or a girl, recklessly determined to sin, preserves her honor by marrying her seducer. Artistically, the resolutions seemed needlessly or hopelessly naive, and, of course, for discriminating theatregoers the results were too frequently lamentable. Another factor to be considered is that, with the changed acting style accompanying the advent of Belasco-like realism, the days had passed when seemingly breathtaking performances in quite ordinary plays, such as David Warfield's in *The Music Master* or Julia Marlowe's in *The Goddess of Reason*, could make thoughtful audiences feel that they had an inspiring theatrical experience.

There was indeed an understandable reaction against the stultifying influence of the theatre's businessmen. Gone was the day when managers with refined tastes, such as Augustin Daly or Lester Wallack, would offer fine companies in distinguished productions, and America unhappily had nothing to rival the brilliant ensembles of the Moscow Art Theatre, the Deutsches Theater of Berlin, or the Abbey Theatre of Dublin. Instead, during the end of the nineteenth century, the Klaw-Erlanger Theatrical Syndicate had been formed. Its purpose was control of an enormous chain of theatres in order to create a monopoly of available playhouses. Booking attractions through "the trust" became, in effect, a necessity. Despite the opposition of several managers and actors, the Syndicate largely dictated what plays the American public would or would not be shown. The ambitious actor or producer who might wish to present some important work limited in its appeal either had to do it at his own risk in a poorly located, outmoded theatre, or forsake the project entirely. Naturally, there were exceptions. Sarah Bernhardt, during one of her last American tours, defied the overlords by performing in a large tent, and artists like Richard Mansfield and Minnie Maddern Fiske, through great sacrifice, insisted upon high standards and good taste. But productions mainly had to conform to mass preferences (or what the magisterial group *believed* the public wanted). This iron-fisted control caused a severe setback to the development of modern American drama. Eugene Walter, Augustus Thomas, Percy MacKaye, William Vaughan Moody, and other serious playwrights in the first decade of this century had to accomplish what they did with no organized theatre to help them. Moody was least affected because he was not primarily a theatre man, and luckily his producer was a perceptive actor-manager named Henry Miller.

The grip of the Syndicate was finally broken about ten years after it began, but not by any resurgence of independent theatre owners. A rival chain of New York-controlled houses was built by the Shubert brothers, who were hardly gentlemen of great culture. Their foremost concern with a production was its box-office potential. This, of course, only caused the existing competition in mediocrity to become more firmly entrenched. About this time silent motion pictures also began to circulate widely their mass-oriented, crudely conceived "shadow dramas." The silent movies increasingly took from the playhouse its gallery audience because they could offer their competing banalities with the added inducement of low-cost admissions. They offered little, if any, of the intellectual stimulation accruing from the nuances of verbal satire, the lofty poetry, the social criticism, the finely edged emotions, or the other benefits furnished by spoken drama at its best.

It is not surprising that an important, if select, segment of the theatre-conscious public rebelled at this state of affairs. In 1914 the Washington Square Players, the spiritual predecessor of the Theatre Guild, was organized. Members of this organization included a representative sampling of New York's literati-intelligentsia set, including the publisher Albert Boni, the radical poet Max Eastman, and the novelist Floyd Dell, as well as Edward Goodman and his wife Lucy Huffaker, Lawrence Langner, Philip Moeller, Ralph Roeder, Daisy Thompson, the young actress Helen Westley, and Josephine A. Meyer, whose ill health did not prevent her from being an ardent supporter of the new enterprise. Poet and novelist George Cram Cook and his wife, the dramatist Susan Glaspell, also belonged for a time, but they soon left to nurture the Provincetown Players.

The underlying purpose of the Washington Square Players was to produce one-act plays, written by themselves and others, with the hope of bringing to them some of the fascination of the new European stagecraft techniques. An organizational notice sent out by the group underscored its praiseworthy intentions. An important part of this letter was devoted to a plea for necessary financial backing. It outlined a scheme for a "subscription series," an idea suggested to Lawrence Langner by a German theatre "entirely independent of political forces and springing from the people themselves," the Volksbühne. It was the first financing plan of this type ever offered in the United States. Admissions were fixed at fifty cents.

The Washington Square Players rented the little Bandbox Theatre on East 57th Street off Third Avenue, and on February 19, 1915, they presented an opening bill of one-act plays directed by Edward Goodman, whose *Eugenically Speaking* expressed advanced ideas on the subject of mating. Also included on this first bill was *Licensed* by Basil Lawrence (a pseudonym for Langner), from whose cast a young actress named Theresa Helburn reluctantly withdrew because of parental objections (the play has to do with restrictive marital conventions and contains a plea for more freedom in birth-control measures). *Interior*, by Maurice Maeterlinck, was also performed, as was *Another Interior*, a satire on Maeterlinck's symbolic piece in which the hero, Gastric Juice, runs amuck through an elaborately styled digestive system.

Promising actors soon joined the Players' ranks. Arthur Hohl, Frank Conroy, José Ruben, Elizabeth Patterson, Katharine Cornell, and Glenn Hunter all, in a sense, began their careers with the organization. The talented amateurs and professionals continued presenting their "off-beat" productions at the Bandbox and later at the Comedy Theatre for a total of only four years, but they performed over sixty intriguing plays. Some idea of their flavor and scope can be sensed from the list of dramatists they programmed, a list that includes such illustrious names as Andreyev, Benavente, Musset, Molière, Schnitzler, Wedekind, and Oscar Wilde. American writers such as Zoë Akins, Lewis Beach, Alice Gerstenberg, John Reed, Elmer Rice, and Eugene O'Neill were given a hearing, too. As time progressed the Players became quite daring, for they attempted such difficult programs as Ibsen's

Ghosts and Shaw's *Mrs. Warren's Profession,* and they gave Chekhov's *The Sea Gull* its first New York showing—with Roland Young portraying idealistic Treplev and Helen Westley as the self-centered Mme. Arcadina.

America's entry into World War I was the main cause for disbanding the Washington Square Players. This enthusiastic group, however, deeply influenced by the exhilarating artistic ferment of the times, had shown that intelligent productions of thought-provoking plays could, to a certain extent, compete with the largely uninspiring offerings of Broadway.

Helen Westley, Lawrence Langner, and Philip Moeller formed the nucleus for the organization of the Theatre Guild, which abandoned the name "Washington Square Players" mainly because it did not want to be held accountable for old debts. Almost before the Armistice had been put into effect, Langner contacted a number of his former associates, some in Army camps, some still overseas, outlining a *modus vivendi*: "It must be a little theatre grown up, and should be governed entirely by a Board of Managers, to which its director should be responsible. It should be a professional theatre, employ professional actors and produce only long plays, 'which should be great plays.'" The response was gratifying enough. The Guild's original Board included Rollo Peters (designated as director), Philip Moeller, Helen Freeman, Justus Sheffield, Lawrence Langner, Helen Westley, and Lee Simonson. Maurice Wertheim was made a member of the Board soon after the Guild's first production (he offered to help underwrite early losses), and Theresa Helburn was named "play representative" (her job being to recommend outstanding scripts for Josephine Meyer's consideration). Because of policy disputes Peters and Miss Freeman resigned their positions within a year, as did Augustin Duncan, who became a Board member for a time. Sheffield left to cultivate a growing law practice.

Walter Prichard Eaton, in his *The Theatre Guild, The First Ten Years,* likens the managers' get-togethers, which became the cornerstone of the Guild's administration, to a university faculty meeting—where many differing views are expressed, where the ensuing discussions may grow heated, but where, in the end, certain policies are decided upon in a more or less democratic fashion. Eaton's analogy to a university is an apt one, for if the Guild's managers had any one thing in common—besides a burning desire to promote worthwhile theatre and largely an amateur standing—it was their academic backgrounds. Philip Moeller, for instance, was an alumnus of Columbia, where he had remained after graduation to study with Brander Matthews from 1901 to 1908. Several of his one-act plays, including the delightful *Helena's Husband* and the satirical *Two Blind Beggars and One Less Blind,* had been presented by the Washington Square Players. Helen Westley was a graduate of the famous American Academy of Dramatic Art, and Rollo Peters had attended schools in Germany, England, and France. Lee Simonson, whose chief function with the Guild was as its scenery designer, had been graduated from Harvard, where he had attended George Pierce Baker's renowned "English 47." Maurice Wertheim, a banker, was also an alumnus of Professor Baker's courses. The Welshman Lawrence Langner, besides being a playwright, practiced international patent law. Theresa Helburn, who quickly rose from her position as the Guild's play reader to be titled its Executive Director, was an aspiring writer as well as drama critic for *The Nation.* She, too, had attended "English 47" while a graduate student at Radcliffe.

With limited capital (barely $2,000), but with impressive resources of imagination and a crusading zeal, the Theatre Guild's managers literally taught themselves the intricacies of stagecraft while garnering an appreciative audience for their efforts. Their first attempt at play producing was a *commedia dell' arte* costume drama by the Spanish Nobel laureate Jacinto Benavente, a charming bit of esoterica translated by John Garrett Underhill as *The Bonds of Interest.* It was clearly a venture none but the most wildly optimistic would have undertaken.

The Garrick, on West 35th Street, a small theatre that had previously housed Arnold Daly's police-troubled production of Shaw's *Mrs. Warren's Profession,* as well as the wartime visit of Jacques Copeau's Théâtre du Vieux-Colombier, was leased from the friendly Otto Kahn on a "pay-if-and-when-you-can" basis for the first performances. Philip Moeller supervised the rehearsals, and Rollo Peters, who played one of the principal roles, designed both settings and costumes using odd remnants of scenery left on the stage by Copeau's company. Lee Simonson helped paint the patched canvas to create a more or less Renaissance Spanish decor. Fellow board members, Helen Freeman and Helen Westley, learned interpretations of the ritualized heroine and dowager, while the experienced Amelia Somerville added a certain professionalism. It is reported that Miss Somerville's simulated brocade gown, constructed of black oilcloth dabbed with radiator gilt, had an unsettling tendency to disintegrate under pressure. The enterprise luckily attracted a remarkable character actor named

Dudley Digges, whose expertise, gained with the Abbey Theatre, was eagerly watched by the new producers. Digges' career was destined to intertwine with the activities of the Guild for the better part of three decades. An indication of the artistic aspirations of the Guild's experiment is that the poetess Edna St. Vincent Millay was persuaded to play its graceful Columbine. Unfortunately, *The Bonds of Interest,* which opened April 19, 1919, suffered from critical indifference, and was heartbreakingly unattended. Lawrence Langner and Maurice Wertheim defrayed its running losses for several weeks.

With two plays promised to at least 150 subscribers that first season, the managers decided, with some trepidation, to present a little-known piece of Irish realism concerning a debt-troubled family by a playwright whose works were almost unknown in the United States. When *John Ferguson,* by St. John Ervine, opened, the Theatre Guild had exactly $19.50 left in its coffers, but the play happily proved to be a success. It was a good play for a struggling group of beginners, and its emotional story appealed to the critics and general audiences alike, for its plot of a mortgage unpaid and a girl "in trouble" were easily comprehensible. As a matter of fact, it differed only in depth of treatment from what had come to be known as typical Broadway fare. It was staged by Augustin Duncan (the dancer Isadora's brother), and opened on May 12, 1919, with Duncan also playing the title role. Besides its familiarity, *John Ferguson* had another fortuitous circumstance working in its favor. The first important Actors' Equity strike closed all other legitimate theatres in New York City that summer; the cooperative nature of the Guild organization, however, met the approval of Equity, which saw in it a splendid example of how theatrical enterprises should be run. *John Ferguson* was thus the *only* play to be seen in New York at that time. The Garrick box office became so busy that the Guild found it necessary to hire a young man named Walter Wanger—who was to become a noted film maker—as business manager.

The neophyte producers, after financial near-extinction, had staged an embarrassingly popular hit capable of making respectable amounts of money, but for this they needed a larger theatre. One faction, namely Peters, Freeman, and Duncan, did not want the organization tainted with any hint of commercialism. They felt that the Guild had not been formed to compete in the show-business marketplace. Nevertheless, it was a comfort to meet expenses from profits for a change, and money in the bank would also ensure a more adventurous second season. In July, after hectic, tormented deliberations, the consensus was to move *John Ferguson* uptown to the much larger Fulton Theatre, where it played for the rest of the summer. Here, as later, the Guild pragmatically established a precedent: to move a remunerative presentation to a larger house to capitalize on its popularity while freeing the "working" house for the preparation of another production. The decision caused serious rifts in the managerial ranks, however. Justus Sheffield resigned as a Board member soon thereafter.

The 1919–1920 season found the organization pursuing its lofty ambitions at the Garrick, with little thought of recompense, apparently, because the first offerings lost all the capital that *John Ferguson* had made. Still, in terms of educating Guild audiences, which had increased to five hundred subscribing members, these productions hardly could be considered artistic failures. They included a verse rendering by John Masefield of a Japanese legend in the Kabuki tradition, entitled *The Faithful.* Lee Simonson was given his first chance as designer, and he prepared for the exotic piece delicately painted screens and elegant kimonos (which greatly exceeded the budget). Henry Travers and Erskine Sanford joined the company, which again was guided by Augustin Duncan, while Rollo Peters, Helen Westley, Walter Geer, and Henry Herbert gave the ensemble a sense of continuity. Disagreement continued to dominate the managers' meetings, this time over cuts in the Masefield script as well as over organizational matters. This was ended when Duncan and Peters left the group.

Possibly to replenish its roster of skilled performers, but more probably to guarantee large audiences, the Guild cast a long-established star, James K. Hackett, in its second attraction. This was *The Rise of Silas Lapham,* a dramatization by Lillian Sabine of William Dean Howells' novel about a self-made Boston businessman and his *nouveau riche* family. Hackett was a romantic actor who could not bring himself to fit satisfactorily into the realistic style of the Sabine adaptation. The two conventions collided, and the Guild was taught another costly lesson. It became the only time for many years that a player would be considered more important than the play. *The Rise of Silas Lapham* did set more precedents, nevertheless. It was the first modern story directed for the organization by Philip Moeller, and it was the first with a native American setting.

The third financial misadventure was a carefully considered presentation of Tolstoy's *Power of Darkness.* The Guild asked Emmanuel Reicher, a highly respected former director of the Volksbühne, to interpret the play's theme of redemption through deep suffering caused by ignorance, because the managers decided they had better entrust intense European realism to one equipped to understand its implications. They were certainly justified in this, but they also should have foreseen that *The Power of Darkness,* with its story of seduction and child-murder, would be nearly fatal for any organization that attempted it. It was not meant to be amusing; intensely spiritual statements seldom are. At the end of the short run there was approximately $100 in the bank with which to meet $200 worth of bills. Nevertheless, with *The Power of Darkness,* the Guild had provided America with a duplication of Europe's then progressive struggle for the acceptance of naturalism.

After three costly productions the Guild, although it had learned much, was again bankrupt, and yet another member of the Board, Helen Freeman, had resigned. Deciding to stick with a proven author, the Guild selected St. John Ervine's *Jane Clegg* for its next production. It is a touching domestic drama with a small cast, and its setting is modest. Futhermore, the British Isles brand of realism was regarded as rather more palatable to American tastes than the Russian. The critics loved the production, and especially Margaret Wycherly, who had joined the company to play Jane, the long-suffering wife. The Guild's second substantial success ran well into the summer months.

The final presentation that season was done for subscriber matinees only. It was a condensed version of August Strindberg's *The Dance of Death,* and it contained a memorable performance by Helen Westley as the shrewish, obsessed anti-heroine Alice. It is worth noting that this story of marital discord is considered so harrowing that until recently it could be offered New Yorkers only in the most obscure off-off-Broadway theatres.

For a number of years, the Theatre Guild directorate usually followed a policy of holding critical sessions, officially known as managers' rehearsals. These complete run-throughs of coming attractions took place on Sunday afternoons before the regular board meetings, during the last few weeks before an opening. The sessions came to be known unofficially by various actors as the "death watch," and it could hardly be considered morale-boosting to be required to give a performance in a role only partly learned and imperfectly rehearsed before an audience made up of one's employers, who were, to quote Theresa Helburn, "people already familiar with the material, impervious to the stimulus of suspense, sitting silent and apparently unresponsive," but armed with ever-ready pencils, scratch pads, flashlights or cigarette lighters, which flickered ominously in the darkened house, "to indulge in the menace of a critical note."[1] Then, after the cast had been sent home, the managers would converge and deliver their suggestions in no uncertain terms to the director involved (or to the playwright, if he happened to be around). Because these opinions often conflicted, this ritual tended to be heartrending, especially if the criticism was misinterpreted as being malicious or destructive. The managers' rehearsals, nevertheless, were an integral part of the Guild's collective production technique. Meager budgets, especially during the beginning years, did not allow for much hit-or-miss experimentation, and the "death watch" in many ways took the place of nonexistent previews or out-of-town tryouts. The managers' collective taste, they soon came to realize, was a fair cross-section of their audiences' likes and dislikes—honed razor sharp.

Early in its third season, subscription memberships had increased from 500 to 1,300 and the Guild began a long, pleasant, and, in most cases, estimable association with Bernard Shaw. It was given the opportunity to be the first to produce the cannily eccentric playwright's most recent effort, *Heartbreak House.* Shaw, just then, was finding it impossible to interest theatre managers in his work because of certain wartime sentiments concerning what he considered to be the idiocy of Victorian England's morality and mores that, characteristically, he had expressed quite indiscreetly. The Guild, possibly because it was not responsible to a British theatregoing public, entertained no such qualms, but rather felt flattered by the chance to do a world premiere for the famous iconoclast who enjoyed a worldwide reputation dating from before the turn of the century.

Heartbreak House, with its satirical if pessimistic theme "those who do not know how to live must make a merit of dying," requires slightly over four hours to perform. Having commissioned Dudley Digges to be director as well as actor, the Guild sought permission to cut the original script. Shaw flashed back that he had in mind, as an alternative to pleasing an audience for two hours, to strain their attention for three and send them away exhausted but inspired. New Yorkers apparently were impressed by *Heartbreak House.* It played 129 times—not bad at all for a lengthy play done "in the Russian manner" with a rambling plot notable mainly for barbed social and political insights.

Without a doubt, its Shavian premiere added enormously to the growing prestige of the Guild. Other noteworthy offerings were prepared during the third season as well. One was A. A. Milne's *Mr. Pim*

[1]Walter Prichard Eaton, *The Theatre Guild: The First Ten Years,* p. 133.

Passes By, for which actress Laura Hope Crews was fortunately rescued from retirement. *Mr. Pim*'s quaintly humorous premise of a long-forgotten husband suddenly believed to be alive proved Philip Moeller's abilities as a director of light comedy. Another great success was Ferenc Molnar's *Liliom,* the story of a no-account carnival barker who ultimately reaches Heaven. Joseph Schildkraut insisted the Guild do the Hungarian play, which the majority of the managers liked but somehow felt would not be popular. Nevertheless, they assembled a large cast, which included newcomer Eva Le Gallienne plus such regulars as Digges, Miss Westley, Sanford, and Edgar Stehli, and chose Emmanuel Reicher's son, Frank, as director. *Liliom,* playing through the summer for a grand total of 311 performances, broke all Guild attendance records up to that time. With *Mr. Pim Passes By* and *Liliom* the organization followed its established procedure of transferring commercial hits to other houses for the balance of the runs. It later allowed other managers, for a royalty, to perform them across the country.

Following *Ambush,* by Arthur Richman, which launched the Guild on its plan of providing a showcase for new American playwrights, and two French experimental imports—*Boubouroche,* by Georges Courteline, and *The Wife with a Smile,* by Denys Amiel and André Obey—the Guild began a series of more impressive productions. The first was the American professional premiere of Leonid Andreyev's *He Who Gets Slapped.* In the Guild production the hectic comings and goings in the robing tent of a circus were glamorously displayed by Lee Simonson's use of two scenic levels connected by a ramp stairway to prevent a sense of overcrowding. In the opinion of Walter Prichard Eaton, the script's philosophical overtones created problems: "Andreyev, [some persons] said, was writing realistic fantasy, whatever that is, and meant his tawdry circus as an ironic snarl at the cosmos he despised."[2] The audiences were frequently puzzled, and offered conflicting interpretations of what they had seen; but they seemed to enjoy being befuddled, for they rushed to see the play. Possibly the overt elements of sado-masochism and self-loathing had been softened purposely by director Robert Milton, remembering the tender sensibilities of many Americans.

The part of the embittered clown, He, who seeks a new life of being belted about by his fellow performers in a traveling show, was played by the famous actor Richard Bennett. Bennett gave a bravura performance, but apparently had little understanding of the character he

[2]Eaton, *The Theatre Guild,* pp. 55–56.

was playing. Lawrence Langner reports an incident connected with this phenomenon in his *The Magic Curtain:*

> During the rehearsals, the translator, Gregory Zilboorg, a Russian of formidable intellect who has since become a famous psychoanalyst, undertook to explain this complex Russian soul in detail to Bennett, who merely became more confused than ever. "Can I have lunch with you, Lawrence?" he asked one day during rehearsals, after having heard a long discourse from Zilboorg. We sat at a table in a small restaurant on Sixth Avenue. "Lawrence," said Dick, a troubled expression on his handsome face, "this high-brow fellow Zilboorg keeps talking to me for hours about the character's psychology, and I simply don't know where the hell I'm at, he confuses me so. Now, tell me simply: is this a Bassanio part or a Mercutio part?" I decided it was a Mercutio part, and as no one else could make Dick see otherwise, that is how he played it with enormous success.[3]

Along with Simonson's charmingly baroque *mise en scène* and Margalo Gillmore's moving portrait of little, tragic Consuelo, it is quite probable that Richard Bennett's failure to understand the main character made the 1922 production of *He Who Gets Slapped* so attractive. For a 1946 Guild revival directed by Tyrone Guthrie, in which the settings were made to seem soiled and sordid to reinforce the symbolic intent of Andreyev's masterpiece, audience apathy was most noticeable.[4]

The Guild's second astonishing undertaking of the 1921–22 season was the world premiere of Bernard Shaw's mammoth "metabiological pentateuch" concerning the length of time necessary for humans to become truly civilized, *Back to Methuselah.* When asked about contractual arrangements, the playwright had replied, "A contract is unnecessary. It isn't likely that any other lunatics will want to produce it." Nobody could disagree, for to stage this "Gospel of Creative Evo-

---

[3]Langner, *The Magic Curtain,* p. 161.

[4]In 1924 an adaptation of *He Who Gets Slapped* became the first movie begun and finished at the new Metro-Goldwyn-Mayer studios in Culver City, California. Under Swedish director Victor Seastrom, Lon Chaney starred as the disgruntled clown, and Norma Shearer as the pathetic equestrienne; John Gilbert played a handsome performer who loved her. Louis B. Mayer, however, insisted that the silent picture end happily for the little bareback rider rather than in suicide, consistent with the current fashion in films.

lution" the Guild had to split the play into three sections. Parts I and II (to include the "Gospel of the Brothers Barnabas") were given the first week, Parts III and IV (through "Tragedy of an Elderly Gentleman") the second week, and Part V ("As Far As Thought Can Reach") the third week—then the whole cycle would start again. Four different directors, including Alice Lewisohn and Agnes Morgan of the Neighborhood Playhouse, were used to stage the various sections under Moeller's leadership, and actors, Dennis King, Margaret Wycherly, A. P. Kaye, George Gaul, and Walter Abel, among others, performed as many as three different long roles. The Guild, of course, suffered through this method of production. A visitor to New York could not possibly see the whole triptych unless he stayed in town some part of three consecutive weeks; nor could anybody see it at all without paying much more than the price of one ordinary play, even at the reduced rates made for the complete cycle. This discouraged many who otherwise might have ventured to try it for a single evening.

The Guild, however, learned a great deal from producing *Methuselah*, which had the effect of three different plays done on a repertory basis. Simonson made the experiment, rare for the American theatre, of using a Linnebach projector, a type of magic lantern that uses glass slides, and concluded that because of the luminous backgrounds it creates its use must be sparing to be effective.

The complete three-weeks' *Methuselah* was presented only twenty-five times, and, as it had expected, the Guild lost money. Shaw later told the Shuberts, who were hesitating over whether to produce a translation he had done of a script by Austrian writer Siegfried Trebitsch, that they underestimated the commercial value of his hallmark. "The Theatre Guild," he said, "made $10,000 out of my name alone. They expected to lose $30,000 on their production of *Back to Methuselah*, and only lost $20,000." Following *Methuselah*, Shaw gave the Guild an exclusive American option on all his plays—a bright, prideful feather for its cap! Further, it was granted the right to release them for production by others, and this became a real source of income, although ultimately more was lost than was gained.

The third impressive presentation of the season followed a hurried showing of Arnold Bennett's story about "yellow journalism"—*What the Public Wants*—which, as a number of critics noted, did not live up to its title. Perhaps the Guild was too exhausted after struggling with *Methuselah* to do another play so quickly. Nevertheless, with limited funds it gave some performances, at first for its subscribers only, of Georg Kaiser's *From Morn to Midnight.* This product of German

Expressionism became an immediate success and was moved to a larger theatre to make money. One memorable sequence in the play depicted a bicycle race at a velodrome, but because of Lee Simonson's ingenious sets, all the audience actually saw was a box high up holding Frank Reicher as the larcenous bank clerk hero looking through binoculars into the middle distance. Yet that race was as real to those who saw the scene as if it were actually taking place.

Thus, at the end of four less than prosperous years (actually its third *full* season) the Theatre Guild could point to a number of accomplishments. The extreme difficulty of some of its scripts had forced the organization to solve intriguing creative problems not usually dealt with by ordinary staging techniques. It had given the world premieres of two Bernard Shaw works, one of which was perhaps its most impressive producing feat to date. True, it had not provided a hearing for many American playwrights, as had the Provincetown Playhouse, but it had given New York an opportunity to witness the new and rarely seen forms of drama involving Symbolism and Expressionism. Further, by demonstrating the drawing power of such frankly experimental fare as *Liliom, He Who Gets Slapped,* and *From Morn to Midnight,* it encouraged other producers to attempt "arty" plays of unusual quality. An illustrative instance might be its well-received production of *Mr. Pim Passes By,* which drew the attention of several managers to the work of A. A. Milne, whose scripts had been gathering dust on American shelves for a number of years. Also, chiefly because it had been unafraid to accept the challenges afforded by such an "unplayable" piece as the lengthy *Back to Methuselah,* it began gaining an international reputation as an art-conscious theatre of renown. Small wonder that it faced the future with its hopes more inflated than its bank account.

Its depleted financial resources were not a major concern, however, for as its fifth season opened, the Guild had over 6,000 subscribers paying nearly $60,000 in advance to see its promised series of "difficult" plays—an innovation in the American theatre. The managers of the Guild did not intend to disappoint such loyalty. On October 9, 1922, they offered an adaptation of Karel Capek's *R. U. R.*, a haunting satire concerning the future of the machine age. An example of the Guild's growing influence became apparent later that year when producer William A. Brady prevailed upon Owen Davis, a facile writer of "pre-modern era" melodramas, to try his hand at adapting the Capek brothers' particularly symbolic play, *The World We Live In* (*The Insect Comedy*). Simonson designed both Capek productions.

Earlier that year, the Guild had brought over from Europe the influential Russian director Theodore Komisarshevsky to mount several of its presentations. Komisarshevsky had conducted a theatre in Moscow named in honor of his late sister, the actress Vera, and he imbued this memorial with his aesthetic notions regarding "non-objective synthesis." Milne's *The Lucky One*, concerning the fortunes of two English upper-class brothers, was not a fortunate choice for the director's first American assignment. It failed to satisfy. The second offering he prepared, a sensitive if abbreviated translation from the French of Paul Claudel's inspirational *The Tidings Brought to Mary*, was better suited to his expressive Slavic talent. With Simonson as his collaborator, he provided a striking series of tableaux staged before a plain background under erected prosceniums resembling modified Gothic arches. The muted richness of the lighting, and the subtly theatrical groupings of players in loosely flowing costumes suggested church windows of stained glass—an effect wholly in keeping with the play's spirit of compassion and resurrection. As the acting had not been perfectly "synthesized," however, it was perhaps inevitable that, while many of the Guild patrons were enraptured by the spiritual quality of the play, others found the whole undertaking a disgusting exhibition of mystical sophistries.

Komisarshevsky made his third production for the Guild from a script based on William Archer's translation of Ibsen's *Peer Gynt*. It was to be the first revival of this unromantic romance in New York since Richard Mansfield had performed the title role some two decades earlier. Joseph Schildkraut, the estimable Liliom of the 1920–21 season, was recruited to play Peer, a man who aspired to be lord of the universe, only to find himself king of a dungheap. As too often happens in judgments concerning revivals, Schildkraut's performance unfortunately suffered by the older critics' recollection of Mansfield's seemingly transcendent portrayal and Komisarshevsky's representation of this sprawling drama sorely taxed the resources of the small Garrick Theatre. For instance, while he cut out the shipwreck scene in which the aged tragi-comic hero is tossed ashore on his homeland, he restored the traditionally abridged madhouse episode, where the inmates' antics are weirdly suggestive, and permeated the troll king's cave with supernatural grotesqueries of a lively sort (Helen Westley cavorted capriciously as the Troll King's Daughter).

When the Moscow Art Theatre visited the United States the same season, its director, Constantin Stanislavski, was invited to see *Peer Gynt*. His reaction was that it had been given only a surface interpretation. This gave the directors further cause to reflect on their need to form a company capable of the "ensemble" performances so much admired in the work of the Russian and of other foreign troupes.

Yet certain creditable players had become known as "Guild actors," because of their constant appearance in many of the organization's demanding roles. Several of them, including Louis Calvert and Margaret Wycherly, helped gain for their producer further recognition as one willing to experiment. Under Moeller's direction they performed Elmer Rice's model of American expressionism, *The Adding Machine*, in which Helen Westley played the nagging Mrs. Zero. The production sharply pointed up the script's treatment of American life, especially in its gamier aspects, and Simonson created startling effects, such as an infernally lighted "brainstorm" sequence and a monstrous platform-sized adding machine on which Mr. Zero is doomed to spend eternity.

The Guild's final offering that theatrical year, Shaw's *The Devil's Disciple,* invited further comparison with the late actor-manager Richard Mansfield, since he had appeared as Richard Dudgeon, the romantically inclined *diabolonian,* in 1897, and the performance of Basil Sydney was felt unequal to it. Memorable performances during this season had been Edward G. Robinson's Button-Molder in *Peer Gynt*—a production that ran for 121 performances, probably a longevity record for this particular Ibsen play; Dudley Digges' Mr. Zero, who was given a flesh-and-blood existence in a drama not notable for its subtle characterizations; and Roland Young's General Burgoyne in *The Devil's Disciple,* which turned out to be a crackling impersonation that undoubtedly helped the presentation run through the summer months and influenced the Guild's directorate to consider producing Shaw an annual necessity.

On the occasion of its fourth birthday dinner, held March 4, 1923 at the Waldorf Astoria, the Guild unveiled a plan to sell cumulative-interest bonds for the purpose of erecting a new playhouse. The limited facilities of the Garrick had become too cramped to accommodate the increasingly elaborate productions and to house the ever-swelling audiences. It had become impossible, the Guild also felt, to capitalize on deserving successes without dispersing actors to incommodious, high-rent theatres usually belonging to the Shuberts. The lack of an adequate headquarters left scant hope of building a permanent company—a circumstance which the leadership of the Moscow Art Theatre (which it hoped to emulate) suggested was a severe handicap; and this, of course, meant that the intoxicating dream of playing repertory would remain unfulfilled. Le Pétit Théâtre du Vieux Carré, an amateur organization in New Orleans, had sold bonds to its supporters when enlarged quarters were thought necessary. The Guild determined to follow suit. It recruited an impressive "executive committee" to enlist the aid of volunteer canvassers, including such luminaries as Professor George Pierce Baker, Mrs. August Belmont, Walter Prichard Eaton, Otto H. Kahn, Walter Lippmann, and Louis Untermeyer.

In the meantime, coupled with a time-consuming bond-promotion campaign, several new productions had to be readied for the coming season at the Garrick. John Galsworthy's *Windows*, staged by the actor Moffat Johnston, opened October 8, 1923, but its English sociological complexities did not prove particularly appealing, and it lasted only through the subscription series, which now numbered 12,000 members. A presentation of H. R. Lenormand's *The Failures (Les Ratés)*, as directed by drama critic Stark Young, was another enterprise hardly calculated to warm American hearts, for it depicted an unhappy group of postwar, middle-European nonentities of the theatre who agonized over sad psychological truths concerning the pervasive effects of evil and guilt. The cast included such earnest young members of the Guild's growing acting roster as Morris Carnovsky, Winifred Lenihan, and the artist Jo Mielziner. Besides, a promising Yiddish art theatre player, Jacob Ben-Ami, for whom the Guild held certain hopes, performed impressively as Lenormand's tormented protagonist; and while Stark Young may have been considered naive in the ways of producing, the keenness of his imaginative insights was never in question. So, although it lost money, the Guild never thought of *The Failures* as anything but an intriguing and wholly favorable undertaking. Still another bill of foreign origin, the atmospheric melodrama *Race With the Shadow* by Wilhelm von Scholz, about which the critic Alexander Woollcott was wildly enthusiastic, was prepared for matinee audiences only. Arnold Daly played a prescient writer, and Armina Marshall "walked on" as a maid.

Mid-season was approaching, without a substantial success; it was considered time for another Shavian excursion. When Theresa Helburn wrote the septuagenarian playwright that the Guild was going to use the French pronunciation of "Rheims" and "Dauphin" in its world premiere of his new *Saint Joan*, she received a whimsical reply:

> Terry Dear, you know but little of the world. The population of New York City is 5,620,048. The odd 48 know that the French

> call Rheims Rah'ce, and themselves call it variously Rance, Ranks, Rangs, Wrongs, Rass or Rams. The other 5,620,000 wonder what the 48 are trying to say, and call it Reems. The 48 also call the Dauphin the Dough-fang or the Doo-fong. The public laughs and writes to me about it. The 48 call Agincourt (an English word unknown in France) Adj Ann Coor. You had better do what I tell you every time, because I am older than you—at least my fancy pictures you younger, and very beautiful.[5]

Through an unfortunate misunderstanding, Moeller rehearsed *Saint Joan* using a manuscript which did not include all of the author's revisions. Hence the opening on December 23, 1923, ran well past midnight. Naturally, the critics bemoaned the play's great length, denounced the epilogue as being superfluous, and even suggested that Shaw had outlived his usefulness to the English-speaking theatre. The troubled Guild cabled the dramatist begging permission to make abridgments, giving as an excuse that suburbanites were all leaving before the end to catch the last train home. The reply came (as expected) "The old, old story. Begin at eight, or run later trains. Await final revision of play." A revised script arrived in due course, but by then *Saint Joan* was already a success (and was later instrumental in earning for Shaw a Nobel Prize). The production continued at the Garrick and then at the Empire for nearly a year, and later, with a different cast, it was wistfully turned over to other managerial hands for a protracted road tour.

By the end of winter, Moeller had put the finishing touches on the Guild's next presentation concerning a love affair between a young student and a bewitching married lady entitled *Fata Morgana* because of the leading character's resemblance to Merlin's pupil who created mirages more potent than reality. The managers secured the services of Emily Stevens, Mrs. Fiske's mercurial cousin, for the title role, and for settings Simonson created some of his tastefully correct interiors. The public relished this adaptation from the Hungarian of Ernest Vadja (although its implicitly sexy theme was quite unmemorable), and it ran for 249 performances. In the final production of the season Simonson evoked his impressions of a presentation in Germany of Ernst Toller's expression of working-class rebellion,

[5]Eaton, *The Theatre Guild*, p. 81. Reproduced by permission of the Public Trustees and the Society of Authors on behalf of the Bernard Shaw Estate.

Massemensch. Blanche Yurka appeared as the lady who spurs laborers toward proletarian revolt, and Simonson, with a designer's intuitions, reinforced the pictorial thrust of revolutionary crowds surging with arms upraised toward a dominating figure high above them. In prosperous, jazz-age New York, however, the underlying truth of imminent totalitarian reality could be but dimly surmised. *Man and the Masses,* as the translation was called, lasted but thirty-two performances.

Thus, at the close of the 1923–24 season the Guild found it had had only two financial successes—*Saint Joan* and *Fata Morgana.* While this was a decidedly better than average showing for a professional Broadway theatre, the Shaw play could scarcely be considered a gold mine because of the enormous costs of the production and the high royalties its author demanded. These two productions had to carry the Garrick Theatre, nevertheless, as well as pay interest on $600,000 which had been raised for constructing a new playhouse, and furnish working capital for the coming season. Only the Guild's subscribers, who were numerous enough now to reduce substantially any great loss on a failure, kept the organization solvent. Even so, it approached the 1924–25 season with just $1,000 in its coffers with which to defray operating expenses.

Clearly, the Guild was not in a position to weather much adversity. Yet, with the first production of its seventh season it appeared to be courting disaster, because it had chosen to do a revival of a Ferenc Molnar play that had been a dismal failure when first given on Broadway in 1913 under the title *Where Ignorance Is Bliss.* The managers, however, thought *The Guardsman* a more suitable name for their adaptation, and they cast it with Digges, Miss Westley, and newcomer Edith Meiser. Through Theresa Helburn's insistence, the leads were a young acting couple who had not yet appeared together professionally—Alfred Lunt and Lynn Fontanne. Lunt interpreted the title character as a Russian; with his performance, and settings by Jo Mielziner, as yet untried, that reflected the damasked and delightful depravity of Budapest, and Moeller's guidance, this play, with its contrived misunderstandings and transparent double identities, soared to the heavens. What is perhaps more important than the 271 performances it ran was the fact that *The Guardsman* marked the beginning of the most fruitful and compelling relationship between performers and management ever known in the American theatre.

The Guild's executive planning happily continued to pay dividends in other ways, for it next presented its first outstanding success with a native American work, Sidney Howard's *They Knew What They Wanted,* which featured Richard Bennett, Pauline Lord, and Glenn Anders, and which was awarded the Pulitzer Prize for drama. It, too, had to be moved to another theatre. Consequently, Guild productions were occupying two New York theatres, and presently the Garrick had to accommodate a third. This was John Howard Lawson's decidedly leftist version of American life, *Processional.* The story of a West Virginia coal-mining town in the grip of a strike, with its jazz-bitten cadences interspersed by vaudeville turns, it had its satirically theatrical setting executed by the promising Mordecai Gorelik. Its principal characters were played by June Walker and George Abbott, who later became a famous director and producer in his own right. *Processional* ran for 95 performances and became a milestone in the radical theatre movement, which with its dedication and energy, was to create partisan enthusiasms in the years to come.

Meanwhile, the cornerstone for the new Guild Theatre had been laid by Governor Alfred E. Smith on December 2, 1924, and construction had proceeded briskly throughout the winter and early spring. A. A. Milne's *Ariadne* was to be the last production made at the Garrick before the new building was inaugurated, but this inconsequential production failed to interest both critic and patron.

Most playhouses erected in New York's theatre district during the first decades of this century were built primarily as realty speculations. This usually meant maximum numbers of seats jammed tightly into whatever space was available with a resultant skimping on lobby and performing areas as well as inadequate backstage facilities. The Guild's directors were determined that their new building would overcome most of these inconveniences.

Constructed after plans provided by C. Howard Crane, Kenneth Franzheim, and Charles Bettis, in consultation with Norman Bel-Geddes and especially Simonson, the Guild's new quarters incorporated important innovations within its pleasantly eclectic Italianate architecture. The auditorium was built at a mezzanine level which was reached by broad stairways. This remoteness presumably would exclude all distracting noises from the lobby and the street. There were to be over 900 upholstered seats—more than double the Garrick's capacity—and these were arranged so that tall men would have enough knee room. There were no boxes, and the single balcony was hung without supporting pillars and well back of the accustomed position so that those seated under it did not feel as though they were in a deep cavern. The proscenium opening was nearly as wide and as high as the auditorium and had been kept free of the usual molded decorations (whose absence was regretted by some) in order to make for an increased sense of intimacy between stage and audience. Behind the scenes there was ample area to house two or more productions, ninety feet of fly space, an abundance of depth and side room, plus various machines, including stage wagons, and a range of lighting equipment that provided flexibility for experiments in stagecraft. Under the auditorium was a spacious lounge, while upstairs there were heated rehearsal halls for the company, a club room for the subscribers, a library, workshops, and offices. The newly projected Theatre Guild School was even to have headquarters there; and, although this undertaking was abandoned after a few seasons, it attracted a number of young enrollees, such as Sylvia Sidney, Romney Brent, Lucia Chase, and Arlene Francis.

Here, then, was a playhouse not constructed to prevailing Broadway standards, but instead designed to make its patrons comfortable, to afford working space for a repertory company, and, of equal importance, to provide adequate revenue to sustain the organization's efforts. It had cost well over a million dollars, which was much more than the initial sale of bonds had garnered, and regrettably a large mortgage had to be taken on the building. But no new theatre in New York for many years had opened with such high promise and such cheerful consent from the public.

The Guild *had* its theatre, but, unfortunately, it had nothing resembling a truly integrated acting company. With Moeller again in charge, Shaw's *Caesar and Cleopatra* was prepared to be the inaugural presentation on April 13, 1925. Helen Hayes, who won the coveted role of Egypt's queen, gives an amusing account in her autobiography, *On Reflection,* of what rehearsals were like in a theatre whose plaster was still damp. Bernard Shaw, whom the Guild now considered its patron saint, was invited to attend as guest of honor, as was President Coolidge, who instead pressed a button in Washington to start the festivities. The dramatist also declined to appear in person, with the quip that he was more accustomed to closing theatres than opening them. It is probably just as well he did not attend. The Guild's choice to play Caesar, Lionel Atwill, was found to lack a certain elegance in his interpretation of a Roman who could afford to be casual because he was so great. Likewise, several influential critics thought young Helen Hayes' kittenish Cleopatra was insufficiently equipped with either claws or teeth. Only a Guild regular, Henry Travers, was lauded for his thoroughly Shavian Britannus. So, despite all of Aline Bern-

stein's colorful costumes and the multiple scenic evocations of ancient Egypt by Frederick Jones III, the production was considered less than an artistic triumph. Enough people appeared to keep it running for 129 performances, but many came more to marvel at the plush and prideful theatre than at the production on stage. The relatively disappointing premiere at the Guild Theatre proved to be somewhat of a dark omen. The theatre's seating capacity was still not large enough to achieve full economic advantage from resounding hits, and the organization found itself offering most of its mediocre accomplishments there, while its outstanding attractions necessarily were housed in Broadway's cavernous halls, such as the 1,200-seat Shubert Theatre. The opening *was* an occasion to remember nostalgically, nevertheless—perhaps even with a touch of humor, for one wit-about-town was heard to exclaim when viewing the handsome tapestries which adorned the Italianate walls of the lounge's grill room, "The Gobelins will get ya, if ya don't watch out!"

In June, 1925, directly following the new theatre's opening, young members of the acting forces conceived a bouncy revue, which was originally prepared for one Sunday evening at the Garrick, as a fund-raising gesture (to help pay for the tapestries?). This intimate, highly irreverent romp, directed by Philip Loeb, with dances arranged by Herbert Fields, and stage-managered by Harold Clurman, was suffered as an indulgence by the various board members chiefly through the urging of Theresa Helburn, who was then offering encouragement to a pair of erstwhile contributors to Columbia University varsity shows. It was she who induced Richard Rodgers and Lorenz Hart to donate such songs as "Mountain Greenery" to the *Garrick Gaieties.*

The *Gaieties,* savored even today as a collector's item, enjoyed the services of such skit writers as a young lawyer named Benjamin Kaye, Morrie Ryskind, Newman Levy, Arthur Sullivan, and embryo actor Sam Jaffe, who happily provided takeoffs on *Fata Morgana* (as "Fate in the Morning"), *They Knew What They Wanted* (as "They Didn't Know What They Were Getting"), and amusing parodies of such current favorites as Michael Arlen's *The Green Hat*—all riotously performed by House Jameson, Betty Starbuck, Lee Strasberg, Hildegarde Halliday, and other youngsters. Old theatre buffs recall with pleasure singer Libby Holman's rendition of "Black and White"; Romney Brent in a burlesque of *The Guardsman;* "Manhattan," sung and danced by June Cochrane and Sterling Holloway; and Edith Meiser as "An Old-Fashioned Girl" who plaintively wondered what had become of old-fashioned men. The *Garrick Gaieties,* first intended

NMU LIBRARY

solely as a one-shot affair, ran for a year, with periodic shifts in its highly volatile material and personnel.

Elsewhere on the New York scene, it had beome increasingly apparent that more and more producers, notably Arthur Hopkins, Brock Pemberton, and Gilbert Miller among others, were willing to try unusual scripts which formerly would have been considered strictly Theatre Guild material. Thus, in 1924 the leathery realism of Laurence Stallings and Maxwell Anderson's *What Price Glory?* made mock of the sugary romanticism of most previous war plays. Well-received offerings produced by other managements also appeared, including George Kelly's *The Show-Off* and *Craig's Wife,* John Van Druten's *Young Woodley,* Philip Barry's *In a Garden,* Eugene O'Neill's expressionistic *The Hairy Ape* and experimental *The Great God Brown,* and Eva Le Gallienne's intensely moving revivals of Ibsen's works. Even the extremely commercially inclined Messrs. Shubert somehow convinced themselves to back *The Fall Guy,* which opened a few weeks before the Guild Theatre's inaugural presentation. It became the first Shubert-produced play ever listed as one of the year's "ten best" by serious critics.

The Guild, meanwhile, was learning something of the burdens connected with being the holder of taxable urban real estate. The bonded indebtedness of its new home, together with other inescapable expenses, required an annual outlay of almost $100,000—at a time when a theatre ticket cost about $2.50. This would obviously leave little margin for extravagant theatrical experiment, or for its long-promised repertory company, as several columnists noted.

Therefore, the second presentation at the Guild Theatre was a revival of Shaw's compact and relatively inexpensive *Arms and the Man,* given early in the eighth season as the last subscribed offering of the previous one. The Guild's cast was small but select, using such proven Shaw performers as Henry Travers and Ernest Cossart. Alfred Lunt played the pragmatic Captain Bluntschli, Lynn Fontanne was put-upon Raina, and Pedro de Cordoba, who had been trained in Winthrop Ames' estimable New Theatre company, was a convincingly blusterous Sergius. The playwright was still annoyed about liberties taken with his script when its edge had been blunted to accommodate Oscar Straus' lilting melodies for *The Chocolate Soldier,* but the new production reaffirmed Shaw's faith in the Guild's abilities. Moeller's deft touch helped the satire on wartime romance jell, and it was moved to the Garrick to make room for Molnar's *The Glass Slipper.*

This Hungarian version of the Cinderella story, with its prince a middle-aged cabinetmaker, irritated a number of the Guild's subscribers, who apparently misinterpreted the theme the production attempted to illustrate: that beauty can often shine forth from evil. The play, nevertheless, was moderately well attended, and as a result of this the next attraction, a twin bill consisting of Shaw's *Man of Destiny* and *Androcles and the Lion,* had to be put on at the Klaw Theatre. Some reliable players were used in these double casts, including Tom Powers, Clare Eames, and Edward G. Robinson. The acting, though, did not cause much excitement in the first play about what Napoleon *might* have been like, but in the second, Henry Travers delighted everyone with his humane portrayal of an early Christian, and the gaily exaggerated décor for *Androcles and the Lion,* designed by Miguel Covarrubias, is still remembered by stage designers. Thus, the Guild again had three productions running simultaneously, and if one or possibly two were considered less than artistically satisfying, at least they did not lose money.

The Guild Theatre did not play host to another production until mid-December 1925, when *Merchants of Glory* appeared. This sardonic French satire by Marcel Pagnol and Paul Nivoix concerning the hollowness of flag-waving political campaigns which benefit from the wartime sacrifices of others did lose money, and its visit was brief. On January 25, 1926, Franz Werfel's mysterious *Goat Song,* based upon sinister central European legends, could be presented at the Guild. This peculiarly symbolic drama was cast with the Lunts, Helen Westley, and many other players for whom the Guild had repertory ambitions. Jacob Ben-Ami directed it, paying attention to its moody overtones, and Simonson created some of his more atmospheric settings, built to suggest third-dimensional reality but removed enough from realism to reinforce an origin in superstition and to heighten its dark emotions. *Goat Song* left few people neutral. It bewildered many, revolted some, and filled others with awed enthusiasm for its accomplishment. The large cast was expensive and the physical production costs were staggering, and after a relatively brief run the losses incurred by Werfel's masterpiece were substantial. *Goat Song,* nevertheless, must be classed as one of the Guild's early successes, for with it the managers established themselves more securely as an organization able to cope with the most demanding of theatrical ventures, and through it they were able to assemble actors who could fill a large theatre with vibrantly projected portraits—a viable ensemble capable of stirring deep, if mixed, feelings.

The Guild, in fact, was so proud of *Goat Song* that it next attempted to lure customers with a Russian representation of the "inner entities" at work called *The Chief Thing.* Its author, Nikolai Evreinov, believed that plays should be simultaneous projections of various aspects of the same personality's multiple identities. Not too surprisingly, his "mono-dramatic" theories had been rather eclipsed by the advent of "social realism" in his homeland. As so often happens with attempts to duplicate the essence of uncommon theatrical feasts, the Pirandelloesque flavorings of *The Chief Thing* were considered completely unpalatable and were rejected by audiences.

Luckily, the Lunts became available once again and ended the season with yet another import—*At Mrs. Beam's* by C. K. Munro. For this more or less civilized British offering, somewhat in the drawing-room tradition, the Guild summoned actress Jean Cadell from England to reinterpret the role she had created for London's West End. The production reaffirmed Moeller's and the Lunts' superb control of fast, airy situation comedy: it contained the first of the couple's many knockabout stage skirmishes. *At Mrs. Beam's* ran through the summer, fortunately, because 1925-26 had earned for its producers a heavy percentage of financial misfortunes. The conclusion of the first full season at its new home found the Guild close to destitution once more, with a mortgage and other debts weighing it down, many of its subscribers apparently dissatisfied with the choice of scripts, and no feasible method yet found to keep its longed-for company together.

The Guild, nevertheless, determined to stretch its diminished financial assets by beginning the 1926–27 season with at least the nucleus of a permanent acting company. This move was partially motivated, no doubt, by the visit the previous year of the Moscow Art Theatre's studio group, and by Eva Le Gallienne's artistically satisfying repertory work "down on 14th Street." It might be added that the Guild's achievements thus far had given impetus to the formation of other seriously-intentioned groups, such as the Actors' Theatre, which, under the leadership of Clare Eames, Dudley Digges, Augustin Duncan, and others, had recently staged impressive revivals of Schnitzler's *Call of Life* and Ibsen's *The Wild Duck*. New York's ultra-liberal visionaries, too, had been effectively represented by such productions as John Howard Lawson's *Nirvana* and John Dos Passos' *The Moon Is a Gong*—samples of the type of theatre the left wing hoped would soon become the ultimate credential of the moment.

Following a year of relatively unpopular presentations, the Guild's subscribers now numbered nearly twenty thousand, surprisingly enough, and accommodating all these for each production made a nightly switching of plays in repertory virtually impossible. The managers, however, planned to adopt a compromise solution. First, they engaged ten actors as a permanent ensemble—as large a company as their slender resources would permit. Included, beside Board member Helen Westley, were Alfred Lunt, Lynn Fontanne, Ernest Cossart, Margalo Gillmore, Henry Travers, Edward G. Robinson, and the erstwhile directors of the Actors' Theatre, Dudley Digges and Clare Eames. Most of them were already quite familiar to Guild audiences. In fact, Clare Eames (Mrs. Sidney Howard) became a member of the Board for a short while. Earle Larimore, Edgar Stehli, Erskine Sanford, Morris Carnovsky, and Claude Rains, among others, later joined the group.

The enlarged Board of Managers proposed to lease a second theatre, the John Golden, to run two productions concurrently, hoping thereafter to add two more plays which would alternate with the first two at weekly intervals. With four plays offering a wider variety of parts, the odds were much better that everyone could fit in somewhere; also, if one or even two plays were successful, the runs could be prolonged using one of the two theatres with a resulting increase of box-office revenues. It was hoped that all actors would come fresh to their weekly assignments, and would have at least three roles a season.

The Guild decided that the first presentation to be made within its new scheme for altered repertory would be Werfel's poetic history play *Juarez and Maximilian.* In rehearsal, before costumes and scenery were ready, the acting, in street clothes on a bare stage, was deeply moving. The lavishness of the production seemed to inhibit the actors in the actual performance, however, and the work had an incredibly short audience interest span—so short, in fact, that the Guild did not dare to place it in repertoire. As a matter of record, it almost caused the whole idea of alternation to be shelved permanently, for another costly misadventure would have had ruinous consequences. With trepidation, the next try was also made at the Guild Theatre. It was Shaw's linguistic Cinderella story, *Pygmalion,* with Miss Fontanne cast as Eliza Doolittle. Dudley Digges directed the production, while Helen Westley played Mrs. Higgins, and Travers was Alfred Doolittle. Reginald Mason was brought in to portray Henry Higgins, and the veteran character actress Beryl Mercer played Higgins' housekeeper, Mrs. Pearce. *Pygmalion* was an immediate hit. Subsequently, a second repertory attraction was mounted at the Golden Theatre with Lunt, Robinson, and Loeb scheduled for an original comedy by Sidney Howard about conniving rumrunners being bested by native Yankee shrewdness. This production of *Ned McCobb's Daughter,* with Clare Eames in the title role, was lively, set in a contemporary American locale, with just enough underlying social awareness to satisfy prevailing tastes. Most importantly, it was superbly acted, and that assured its popularity. Later, its director, John Cromwell, took his prompt book to Chicago, where he played the production's leading gangster supported by Spencer Tracy as his bootlegger brother.

Soon, however, a thorny problem arose from the Guild's revised scheme of programming, namely, the selection of two more scripts of comparable stature that might work successfully with the two productions already running. The second attraction chosen for the Golden Theatre, entitled *The Silver Cord,* was also provided by Sidney Howard. Miss Gillmore and Earle Larimore were assigned principal roles, but because Miss Westley requested a "vacation from harridans and harpies," Laura Hope Crews took over as the self-centered, demanding mother, Mrs. Phelps.

The next play brought to the Guild Theatre was Jacques Copeau's adaptation of Dostoyevsky's *The Brothers Karamazov,* which allowed for a large cast; the celebrated French *régisseur* was brought to direct it. *Karamazov* was to take the place of *Pygmalion* when *Ned McCobb's Daughter* was not being given (both Lunt and Miss Fontanne were to play in the Russian work). Copeau's adaptation produced a disturbing theatre piece, and the actors involved, including Carnovsky, Robinson, George Gaul, and Lunt, who played the famous brothers, all benefited noticeably from the Frenchman's coaching. As with *Goat Song,* the public did not respond enthusiastically to the special appeal of the Karamazovs. Nevertheless, terrifying tensions crackled inside the production's murk-filled settings (designed by Raymond Sovey); and while the ugly father Feodor (played by Digges) gorged on his viands and relished his stew of distrust and hatred, the performers revealed through their characterizations startling passions.

Meanwhile Miss Crews and her companions were idle whenever *The Silver Cord* was not being presented. Miss Crews' freedom was utilized to stage special matinees of Luigi Pirandello's *Right You Are If You Think You Are* at the Guild Theatre and, when the Garrick became available, every other week in a revival of her earlier Guild success, *Mr. Pim Passes By.* During this period, of course, there was much shuttling from one role to another. For instance, Edward G. Robinson would be Ponza in *Right You Are* for an afternoon performance and *Karamazov's* Smerdiakov during the evening; or Morris Carnovsky would switch quickly from an Italian Commendatore to a Russian Aliocha with only supper in between. Keeping assignments straight made for a good deal of anguished bookkeeping and mix-ups sometimes occurred. For example, Theresa Helburn reports that Robinson was once scheduled to be in two different theatres at the same time, something even Little Caesar could not have done.

Since *Mr. Pim Passes By* could not be offered to old Guild subscribers as a new production, a new American comedy by S. N. Behrman was substituted in April 1927 when the Dostoyevsky had exhausted its drawing power. The intimate, sophisticated *The Second Man* concerns a writer's dual personality—opportunist versus idealist. It employed the Lunts, Miss Gillmore, and Larimore among the regulars, and played opposite *Pygmalion* on alternate weeks. Once again, the lure of the Lunts proved its potency. After the normal season ended, *The Second Man* continued through the summer.

Most of the managers, as well as many of the charter subscribers, felt that the ninth year had been the most rewarding thus far in the Guild's history. Of prime importance to Guild-watchers, however, were the premieres of three highly laudable American plays—occasions quite noteworthy if only for the fact that American dramatists are usually loath to have their newest works performed by repertory companies (the fractioning of royalties is generally considered unattractive). It should be noted, moreover, that both Behrman and Howard were alumni of Professor Baker's "47 Workshop" at Harvard, so doubtless their approaches to theatrical goals were much the same as those of the Guild's directors. Besides, by placing their scripts with the Theatre Guild, both writers had the opportunity of letting Philip Moeller, the Lunts, and others within the organization polish their efforts—no small boon, as Behrman especially was to find out later. Claire Eames resigned from the Board, incidentally, toward the end of the season.

Amusingly enough, one of the Guild's minor problems seemed to be that a majority of its current productions had been too popular to be used with good conscience in a repertory situation. (One producer once observed that the only sensible way to alternate plays is to mount sterling examples of dramatic art selected solely for their limited audience appeal, then one can shift them around without resentful tugs from one's purse strings because there won't be a purse left.) No doubt the Guild felt a twinge of embarrassment over the fact that its rather hectic scheduling, undertaken without benefit of a subsidy, had returned a handsome profit. By contrast, Eva Le Gallienne later found that her brave struggle to furnish Chekhov and Ibsen to the masses would cost her Civic Repertory Company a $200,000 fund-raising drive.

One promising script, however, would simply not fit into the Guild's system of repertory; this was Mrs. Du Bose Heyward's adaptation of her husband's novel *Porgy*. The Guild considered the script a distinct challenge to its resources and imagination, but obviously the predominantly Negro cast would be of little use in alternation for no other Negro drama was being considered.

Porgy, nevertheless, was the Guild's first offering of its tenth season. It opened at the Guild Theatre on October 11, 1927, with its striking sets representing Catfish Row painstakingly modeled by Cleon Throckmorton from observations he had made in Charleston, South Carolina. The Guild named as director Rouben Mamoulian, a young Moscow-trained Armenian, who had come from the American Opera Company in Rochester to the Theatre Guild School. *Porgy* emerged as a rare and memorable event in our theatrical history. Its haunting story of the sad love affair between a cripple and a beautiful but hopeless addict is now well known to everyone. While *Porgy* was being presented for the now 25,000 subscribers, the Board decided, after much debate and with many misgivings, to take their company outside New York until *Porgy* was ready to move to another house.

That season the Guild had also organized a secondary company headed by George Gaul and Florence Eldridge (whose husband, Fredric March, tagged along as a featured player) to take a repertoire of four earlier successes on tour. This caravan was booked through a road manager, with such oddly assorted stopovers as Chickashe, Oklahoma; Wingfield, Kansas; and Fairmount, West Virginia. The Guild had become extremely interested in such a cross-country adventure, for it explored fertile territory, so to speak, but felt it was quite another matter to risk the regular New York company in cities which might not be receptive to it. The season before, however, in answer to frequent offers from the Philadelphia Art Alliance, the organization had sent its principal company there for a one-week engagement of *Pygmalion.* The results had been so gratifying that it accepted an invitation to inaugurate a repertory season in Chicago that year. As the last play of this series, it decided to produce *The Doctor's Dilemma,* prior to its New York opening. Shaw's condemnation of the medical profession's ineptitude was led by Dudley Digges. It might be added that Shaw, when he had seen pictures of the production, did not share the critics' high estimate of the Guild's presentation.

Among the criticisms leveled at the Theatre Guild was the accusation that it had not paid sufficient attention to American playwrights in general, and to Eugene O'Neill in particular. The Board of Managers seemed to prefer the exotic products of the new European theatre to the largely drab fare offered then by most American dramatists—until some, like Sidney Howard, developed further. Charges of dullness, of course, seldom included O'Neill, for presentations of his works had been excitingly offered by the Provincetown Players and others, placing him among the foremost writers of his time. The Guild had rejected five of his scripts, though, including *The First Man, Welded,* and *The Fountain* (which it had originally intended to do). During its 1920–21 season the Board had offered to subsidize O'Neill while he wrote, but this met with a rather wry refusal:

> I'm in no dire straits for money, as you must know. Even if I were, my poverty stricken years of the past are proof enough that there is no danger of my streetwalking along Broadway. I simply ain't that kind of girl. . . . It is all very well to talk of my future work, but if everyone had done that I would have no past nor present to build upon. The only help I need or would accept from anyone is a hearing—a fair hearing as in *Jones* or *Anna Christie.* . . . So there you have my side of it; and it seems to me there is little else that can be said.[6]

It was not until January 1928 that the Guild produced a play by O'Neill—his epic satire on philistinism and Babbittry, *Marco Millions*—which turned out to be the most lavish presentation the playwright had ever been accorded. Once again, Rouben Mamoulian was given a directorial assignment of scope, and Lee Simonson designed the innumerable medieval and oriental costumes as well as the exotic settings, whose basic structures were ingeniously designed not only for *Marco Millions* but also for the *Volpone* being planned.

Marco Millions received mixed notices. Some loved what they saw, while others questioned what they heard and believed the whole undertaking nothing more than a vehicle for rather dated and humorless ideas. It was planned that on opening night Lunt, as the bumptious Marco, would walk through the audience in costume at the end of the play to the street where he would step calmly into a limousine, yawning along with the rest of the "tired businessmen." Many felt this diminished the stature of Marco Polo, who was, after all, one of the world's heroic figures. Nevertheless, enough glamor was connected with the mammoth production to assure its drawing power. Paren-

---

[6]O'Neill's letter, dated January 19, 1921, is quoted in Lawrence Langner's *The Magic Curtain,* pp. 230–31.

thetically, one of the slaves who carried the sedan of Princess Kukachin (Margalo Gillmore) was a young actor named Henry Fonda.

Two weeks after *Marco Millions* opened, the Guild presented a second O'Neill play at the John Golden Theatre—the much discussed *Strange Interlude,* a drama in nine acts, beginning at 5:30 in the afternoon with a dinner intermission for an hour after Act Five and continuing until past eleven. As soon as the play was put into rehearsal and the inevitable gossip about the novel technique it employed had circulated, the wags of Broadway had a field day. Many poked fun at the experiment, in which people speak their innermost thoughts out loud, thoughts that are not heard by the other characters. Many decreed for *Strange Interlude* the brief life afforded by curiosity.

Strange Interlude fooled the "experts." It played six performances a week—no matinees, of course—for a year and a half, without a vacant seat even during the hottest weather. Never has there been a more curious or unpredicted success in the history of our theatre. Alexander Woollcott christened it "The Abie's Irish Rose of the intelligentsia," possibly because of its unifying idea that only heartache can come from one's interference with other souls in their struggle for natural fulfillment—but more probably because its plot, stripped of its psychoanalytical trappings, would do quite nicely as a soap opera. The play, for all its excesses of length, overstraining to make a point, and lack of redeeming humor, was a moving attempt to find a dramatic form to express the emergent psychology of the times. Few can deny that it contains many moments of poignant emotion that only O'Neill could then create. The play was allowed to continue at the Golden uninterrupted. While this was a source of satisfaction to O'Neill, it succeeded in breaking down the system of repertory so lovingly nurtured.

The Guild prepared one more offering during the 1927–28 season, postponing its sixth bill till the next autumn. This was Stefan Zweig's *commedia dell'arte* farce freely adapted from Ben Jonson's famous satire *Volpone.* Zweig's work, which eliminates the Elizabethan subplots and ends by letting Mosca get away with his loot, had been translated from the German by Ruth Langner, Lawrence's sister-in-law, who earlier had performed the same service for Werfel's *Goat Song.* Again Moeller was named director, as he had been for *Strange Interlude,* and Simonson changed the oriental sets for *Marco Millions* into a colorful evocation of Renaissance Venice. The Guild's production did not emphasize the malice or the greedy corruption of the original; instead, the title role of the Fox was roguishly played by Digges, with Lunt as Mosca (the Gadfly), Travers as Corbaccio (the Raven),

Cossart as Corvino (the Crow), and Helen Westley as Canina (the Bitch). The public could not help liking this *Volpone,* and it was alternated with *Marco Millions* until summer; then it played alone.

The Theatre Guild's first ten years had obviously been a period in which a most remarkable balance between artistic achievement and financial returns had been attained. If the managers had been inclined to call it quits at the end of 1928, they would have done more than most other stage organizations had in the nation's history. *Strange Interlude,* which played 432 times in New York, won the 1928 Pulitzer Prize for drama. It was O'Neill's third such award; his previous ones had been for *Beyond the Horizon* in 1920 and *Anna Christie* in 1922. In addition, many critics felt that *Porgy* had been a far worthier depiction of the Negro than had Paul Green's *In Abraham's Bosom,* the Pulitzer recipient in 1927.

The 1927–28 season was, of course, an important milestone in the theatre as a whole, if only for the fact that the first "talkie" of consequence, *The Jazz Singer* starring Al Jolson, was released during that time. The talking motion picture, then only a squawking infant, would soon become lusty and ambitious enough to provide overpowering competition to the best the American theatre could provide. Legitimate plays would be increasingly sought for filming. For instance, M-G-M's dynamic production chief, Irving Thalberg, soon sought the screen rights for both *The Guardsman* and *Strange Interlude.*

The Guild had had the salutary effect of raising the level of expectations for New York's serious theatre public. Yet, it would be naive to suppose that the great majority of live-theatre addicts eagerly patronized the offerings of the Guild, or of any other art-conscious producer for that matter. Ironically, during the organization's outstanding 1927–28 season, far larger crowds attended such trivialities as Sigmund Romberg's operetta, *My Maryland,* with its hit song "This Land Is My Land," or the Gershwin musical *Oh, Kay!,* or *Luckee Girl,* featuring newcomer Irene Dunne, or *Countess Maritza,* in which Odette Myrtil played the role of a fiddling gypsy—all of which had been controlled by the Shuberts, it might be added.

The Guild had no intention of quitting just then, however. It was riding the crest of an unprecedented wave of creativity, while, much to its credit, good theatre had become an established part of the American scene.

CHAPTER **2** / 1928-29

Faust (Goethe), Graham and Tristan Rawson
Major Barbara, Bernard Shaw
Wings Over Europe, Robert Nichols and Maurice Browne
Caprice, Sil-Vara
Dynamo, Eugene O'Neill
Man's Estate, Beatrice Blackmar and Bruce Gould
The Camel Through the Needle's Eye, Frantisek Langer

The Guild, at the beginning of the 1928–29 theatrical season, had some sixty productions behind it—roughly half of them commercial, as well as artistic, successes. Because of its inspired tenth season, it began its eleventh with total assets of slightly over a million dollars. In the words of playwright-critic St. John Ervine, it was the best organization of its kind in the world. It was in a relatively good position, therefore, to indulge in one of its magnificent failures; although, as it turned out, the failure was to be something less grand than its earlier presentation of *Back to Methuselah.*

A production of Goethe's *Faust* (Part I) had been anticipated for fully a year. A version of the dramatic poem which had been produced at London's Old Vic during the 1924–25 season was to be used. But whereas the English presentation had included nineteen scenes, the Guild's performance was to cut two from the original. Advance publicity made much of the fact that Friedrich Holl was being imported from Berlin's *Volksbühne* to direct the production. Herr Holl had already mounted an impressive *Faust* in his homeland that removed most of the play's "operatic" elements; hence, his selection as *régisseur* seemed logical, and even intriguing.

From a scenic standpoint, this *Faust* was to be most impressive. Lee Simonson devised seventeen settings which were to utilize the unit frames already built and used for the previous season's *Marco Millions* and *Volpone.* This permanent structure ingeniously facilitated the rapid shifting necessary in such a multi-set show.

But when *Faust* opened at the Guild Theatre on October 8, 1928, it received devastating notices, although the reviewers seemed mixed in their opinions as to what went wrong. One found the adaptation "altogether mediocre, meant for nothing but mouthing," while another thought it "a good straightforward translation." Some critics liked Dudley Digges in the role of Mephistopheles; another found him to be "a trifle weary and over-comic at times." There was almost unanimous agreement that Simonson's sets were awesome to behold, but one commentator thought the scenic smoke, meant for brimstone, an ever-present reminder that "Faust's flue was faulty and his faggots wet." Brooks Atkinson of the New York Times found the "staccato scene changes visually enchanting"; while Burns Mantle, in *The Best Plays of 1928–29,* compared *Faust* unfavorably with *The Front Page,* Ben Hecht's and Charles MacArthur's cyclonic newspaper story, which had opened that summer under George S. Kaufman's hell-bent direction, saying that even the latter would have been boring if broken down into seventeen set pieces. And, while E. W. Osborn of the *New York Evening World* found the direction of *Faust* to his liking, John Anderson of the *New York Evening Journal* was bemused by the fact that a director who knew barely a hundred words of English was used to coach English-speaking actors in an unusually poetic drama, and felt this may have explained why George Gaul, who played the title role, turned "some of the most searching philosophical musings in dramatic literature into blank monotony and Saturday afternoon recitative." Nowhere in the performance, he concluded, did Gaul project the harrowing intensity of a mind willing to bargain with the devil for freedom, or the subtle curiosity of a man peering sensitively into the most refined of riddles, to be baffled at finding only himself. On the question of choreography, Robert Littell of the *New York Evening Post* wrote, "When we see the Guild's filmy bipeds galloping up and down we think, not of Goethe, but of the late Walter Camp and his daily dozen."

Nor did the costumes escape their share of censure. Gilbert Gabriel of the *New York Sun* averred that Goethe "left us no clue to his having conceived Dr. Faust as the dear old gentleman who lived just around the corner in a comfortable dressing-gown." And a look at one of the production's photographs partially substantiates this criticism: in a setting looking a bit like a seraglio devised by Bavaria's mad King Ludwig, one finds Faust replete with Beethoven fright wig, Mephisto resembling the trademark for the now-defunct Pluto Water, and two hexies looking "for all the world, like fugitives from one of the naughty scenes in most Cecil B. DeMille biblical melodramas."

FAUST — "Witches' Kitchen" scene, part of a larger setting designed by Lee Simonson. George Gaul as Faust stands at left, and Dudley Digges as Mephistopheles reclines in the background; in the foreground, Gale Sondergaard and Helen Ann Hughes.

Most of the reviewers, it should be noted, lauded the Guild's Shinto habit of occasionally worshipping its ancestors; although, in this instance, the rites seemed to be feeble and lacking in entertainment value. One thoughtful review, by Joseph Wood Krutch in *The Nation,* perhaps came closest to the reason for the play's failure when it suggested that "*Faust* is not supremely great drama. . . . We tend to think of it as such because we think of it not by itself, but in connection with all the greatness that was Goethe. . . ." It is true, of course, that Goethe himself thought of his fable as a poem, to be read rather than performed.

And what of New York's German-American population? Would it come to see this newest presentation of the Great Poet's masterpiece? One hardly finds that likely if one read a syndicated review then appearing in a number of German-language newspapers, which cried, "Der arme Goethe tat mir ordentlich leid. . . ." Unfortunately for the Guild, nationwide reports headed "Fans Find 'Faust' Fine Fizzle," in addition to the enormous size of the cast and the difficulty of hauling seventeen sets, tended to make a tour unfeasible. *Faust,* which ran for barely forty-eight performances, was truly doomed.

Beginning with this 1928–29 season, however, the Guild's Board of Managers decided to enlarge its playing company and to give a comparatively brief subscription series in several northeastern and midwestern cities, namely, Cleveland, Chicago, Pittsburgh, Baltimore, Boston, and Philadelphia. This decision was based, in part, on the experience of the previous year, during which a company had been sent out under the management of a concert bureau to give a repertoire of former Guild successes, including Milne's *Mr. Pim Passes By,* Shaw's *Arms and the Man,* Sidney Howard's *The Silver Cord,* and Molnar's *The Guardsman*—all of which, incidentally, were extremely easy to troupe. *Arms and the Man* and *The Guardsman* were five years old in the Guild's repertoire, a fact that was rather exploited in the advance publicity. The response to this tour, which began at Dartmouth College, had been gratifying enough to make the Guild willing to attempt a different method of producing than it had employed formerly. Subscription lists were sought in the above six cities, and a company, headed by Alfred Lunt and Lynn Fontanne, was rehearsed and sent on its way.

As soon as the Lunts and company had been launched, a second group was organized to start out with O'Neill's *Marco Millions* and the Stefan Zweig version of Jonson's *Volpone*—two shows not so easily trouped. Dorothy and Du Bose Heyward's *Porgy* with its all-Negro cast, which had played to great acclaim early in the Guild's previous season, was sent out as a third unit and "by popular demand" was induced to quadruple its originally scheduled two-week stopover in Chicago.

Late in October *Variety* leaked the news that the Guild's next proposed New York attraction, *Wings Over Europe,* had been temporarily sidetracked, and that Shaw's *Major Barbara* was to be done in its place. It gave as a reason for this the recent Equity ruling which restricted the percentage of foreign talent in any American production and consequently made casting the futuristic British play impossible. A day later a regularly scheduled release announced that Winifred Lenihan, headmistress of the Guild's acting school, who had given a memorable performance several years before as Shaw's *Saint Joan,* was to have the role of the disillusioned Salvation Army major. A subsequent news story revealed that the Guild was enlarging its acting company to fill gaps left by the departed members of the touring groups; among those added to the permanent acting company were A. P. Kaye, Percy Waram, Edythe Tressider, and Herbert Biberman.

An unofficial chronicler of New York's theatrical scene reminded his readers that *Major Barbara* had first been presented at the Court Theatre, London, in 1905—the year it had been written—and that Grace George had brought "Barbara's tambourine" into New York ten years later under the management of William A. Brady, Sr. (Miss George, incidentally, also happened to be Mrs. Brady). Even the cast of this earlier New York production was printed, to reveal a listing of some great theatrical names:

Stephen Undershaft	Clarence Derwent
Lady Britomart	Charlotte Granville
Barbara Undershaft	Grace George
Andrew Undershaft	Louis Calvert
Rummy Mitchens	Margaret Calvert
Morrison (butler)	Guthrie McClintic
Adolphus Cusins	Ernest Lawford
Bill Walker	Conway Tearle
Charles Lomax	John Cromwell

Bernard Shaw, always deeply interested in professional productions of his scripts, wrote Theresa Helburn a few words of caution regarding the play. Barbara was not to look "like a picture on the cover of The Maiden's Prayer," and he went on to advise that Lady Britomart should be played by the best grande-dame comedienne available, that Adolphus Cusins was easy for any actor who knew the prototype (Professor Gilbert Murray), or, failing this, he might be modeled after Harold Lloyd, and that Bill Walker should not be made up to look like a thug, but only as "an ordinary young workman excited by drink and a sense of injury." Shaw concluded with the enticing news that, if he lived, there might be one more play from his pen, but, he added, this should be kept a dark secret by the Guild.

When *Faust* closed, Digges assumed the role of Andrew Undershaft, one of the more demanding roles in modern dramatic literature—certainly, one of the longest. Philip Moeller, who had been responsible for readying the productions that were being presented on the road, staged *Major Barbara,* and when it opened on November 20, 1928 at the Guild Theatre, it received fairly good notices.

Most reviewers found the Shavian fable damning Holy Poverty a surprisingly up-to-date discussion of religion and morality. Howard Barnes of the *New York Herald Tribune* thought Moeller's direction was masterly enough "to dispel some of the mustiness that has gathered on the play with the passing of a quarter of a century." The acting was nearly universally praised. Some critics applauded the sure and satisfying work of Digges, while others felt that Helen Westley appeared as if she had been designed by fate for Lady Britomart. The *New York Evening Journal* found that Winifred Lenihan brought a quiet certainty to her role, although it might have been made to sparkle more.

But *Major Barbara*'s fourth act is an awkward hurdle in any production of this play. Stephen Rathbun of the *New York Sun* wrote that the Guild's production was a treat for any intellectual theatregoer, but concluded, "It is in the fourth act that the play drags a bit, being overbalanced with talk." The upshot of all this was that *Major Barbara* settled down to only a fair-to-middling run. It was moved in late December to the Republic Theatre to make room for *Caprice,* and there it peacefully expired after eighty-eight performances.

It became apparent, about this time, that the Guild was beginning to feel the competition provided by motion pictures. Earlier in the theatrical year Walter Prichard Eaton had observed that the comparatively certain daily revenue of the movies had proved more attractive to managers of theatres than the uncertainty of road bookings. In an attempt to explain this tendency, he suggested that the New York theatre usually favored plays of strictly urban appeal with a strong emphasis on sophisticated themes, which diminished their market value in large sections of the country. He also found that the "little theatres" had, to an extent, filled the gap left by the disappearing road companies and cited *Porgy* as a play which had stemmed directly from "little theatre" work.

Later in the year, Lawrence Langner, writing on behalf of the Guild and noting the extravagant use of adjectives in most movie advertising, scolded the competing flickers for their "stupendous fatuity," their "gargantuan insipidity," and their "elephantine inanity." He observed that the code of the Association of Motion Picture Producers would ban *Othello* and *All God's Chillun* because both deal with miscegenation, as well as *The Merchant of Venice* because it casts aspersions on a race or creed. He also pointed out that Shaw's *Saint Joan*, Ibsen's *Brand*, and even Sinclair Lewis' *Elmer Gantry* would be proscribed because they certainly would violate the code's "ridicule-of-the-clergy" covenant.[1]

Indeed, there was good reason for managerial concern; the first two offerings of the season had provided the Guild with losses of approximately $33,500. Nor was this trend toward deficit to end with the next scheduled production.

Wings Over Europe, which was to have been the second offering of the year, had been postponed because of casting difficulties (probably the failure to find a suitable percentage of American actors). Rouben Mamoulian was called upon to direct this new play by two Englishmen, one of whom, Maurice Browne, had earlier been the guiding light of an estimable "little theatre" project in Chicago. Browne had been doing well there until he told the Drama League of Chicago that its pet entertainment, George Arliss as Disraeli, was a disgrace to art, and that they laughed in the wrong places during *A Doll's House*. The co-author of *Wings Over Europe*, a prophetic play concerning the destructive power of atomic energy, was Robert Nichols, a respected poet who, at one time, had held the chair of English Literature at the University of Tokyo.

Wings Over Europe was an artistic success. The consensus of criticism termed it an engrossing and superbly performed work. Nichols and Browne were congratulated by Robert Littell for having contributed to the theatre "a vastly encouraging and exciting event . . . a bomb neatly exploded right under complacency's rocking chair." The

[1]Lawrence Langner, "The Morals of the Talkies," *Theatre Guild Magazine* (Dec., 1928), p. 11.

actors—especially Alexander Kirkland as the idealistic inventor Francis Lightfoot—received their share of accolades.

The reviews, however, while all favorable, were not what are known to the trade as "money notices." They described the play as appealing primarily to the intellect and doing credit to the authors' intelligence and vision. The *New York Herald Tribune* asserted that it was "written, perhaps, too learnedly for enjoyment by the outside throngs," but that it would still pleasantly stupefy those who ventured into it. Finally, said one review, possibly because of the presence of an all-male cast, "sex appealers are recommended to go elsewhere." Such praise was not calculated to provide a rich box-office bonanza. The size of the cast doubtless had a bit to do with the fact that, although *Wings Over Europe* ran for over ninety performances, it still succeeded in losing nearly $16,000 more for the Guild during its New York engagement. However, this compelling play, containing the threat of nuclear holocaust and a young messiah destroyed through the connivance of scoundrels, was chosen one of the year's "ten best."

It became evident quite soon that the Guild needed a financial winner—and quickly. Nor was the Guild alone in this. Percy Hammond, in summing up the first half of New York's 1928–29 theatrical season, observed:

> These are darksome hours for show-business and there is little, if any, dancing in the Broadway streets. Theatres that once were full of shoppers are now empty and their intake at the box offices is not commensurate with the overhead and upkeep. Where recently the Drama reveled in profits, it is at present prostrated by losses. [*New York Herald Tribune,* Dec. 30, 1928]

He attributed the surplus of playhouses to the meager supply of good scripts from the dramatists, and while he lauded *Wings Over Europe* as one of the few plays doing something to stem the wave of audience indifference, he cited *The Sign of the Leopard, Potiphar's Wife, One Way Street,* and *That Ferguson Family* as examples of the shoddy wares that were then being offered.

The day after Hammond's dour summation appeared, *Caprice* opened at the Guild Theatre. *Playing With Love* (the original title of *Caprice*) by Sil-Vara, a fashionable Viennese playwright, had already been abandoned for a season by the Guild. The Lunts, originally announced as leads in *Caprice,* had since been employed elsewhere—Lynn Fontanne in *Strange Interlude,* Alfred Lunt with *Marco Millions,* and later *Volpone.* Janet Beecher and Claude Rains were also announced for the cast, and Douglass Montgomery was to take over a role originally assigned to Robert Montgomery. But when first Richard Bennett and then Robert Milton, who was to have been its director, withdrew their association with the play, plans for the proposed production collapsed. Finally, the Lunts were again brought together. With Philip Moeller as director, and using his adaptation of *Mit Der Liebe Spielen,* they opened in *Caprice* at Boston's Hollis Theatre on December 17, 1928—the second time the Guild had previewed any of its attractions out of town.

After the opening, one Boston critic, Nicholas Young, seemed puzzled as to why such a trifling comedy, the theme of which might best be summed up as "sometimes much good can be accomplished by having your teen-age son seduced by your mistress," could work a first-night audience up to such a high pitch of exultation. But if he did not properly understand the Lunt-Moeller brand of magic, the Gotham critics did, for when *Caprice* opened in New York two weeks later, it became instantly obvious to all that the Guild had a solid hit on its hands. "As it skims across the stage it is piquant, sly, insinuating and frolicsome, and it's also touched with wisdom," mused Brooks Atkinson. John Anderson found that Moeller's adaptation had "the effortless sparkle of bubbles in clearest wine," while Percy Hammond thought his direction "almost feline, so velvety are the speeches and the action."

Not every Boston critic, it must be stated in all fairness, had been confounded by the players' adroit handling of their roles. One in the *Boston Globe* had written, "Mr. Lunt's impersonation of the man who loved well, if not wisely, is a masterly bit of characterization, quite irreproachable in every detail, make-up, speech and bearing"; while Philip Hale of the *Boston Herald* had been enchanted enough to utter, "Miss Fontanne is sparkling as the light woman with her emancipated ideas about love, marriage, and the home vs. freedom." Even Douglass Montgomery, who, as it had been noted, had played Valentine in *Faust* with a noticeable midwestern twang, apparently fitted a bit more easily into the Viennese drawingroom atmosphere of *Caprice.*

Caprice was thus termed "the soufflé in the six-course meal which the Guild serves to its subscribers," as the producers came in for their fair share of the general approbation. The Guild must have won the admiration of its bankers, too, after *Caprice*'s run, for in the twenty-one weeks it appeared in New York it showed a profit of nearly $75,000—which not only neatly recouped the season's previous losses, but overflowed the coffers as well. The delighted Guild sent the Lunts across the Atlantic with *Caprice* for a limited eight-week engagement at the St. James Theatre in London, sponsored by the American producers in association with Charles B. Cochran. It must be supposed that the Guild was not too dissatisfied when that enterprise ran about $5,500 in debt.

In February Langner wrote an article for the *Theatre Guild Magazine,* a periodical dedicated by the organization to the Broadway theatre in general, welcoming the 26,000 new subscribers the Guild had added to its paid membership by including the six new cities in its subscription series, asking "respect for the sincerity of our work, appreciation of its cultural value, and belief in our intention to steer the Guild in the course which it has followed since the days of its inception." He added, doubtlessly attempting to promote a possible tour for *Wings Over Europe,* that this play of the future had received a standing ovation its opening night, "the greatest since the almost forgotten days of *Liliom.*"

Immediately upon the completion of his work with *Caprice,* Moeller began preparations for directing possibly the most anticipated event of New York's 1928–29 season—the Theatre Guild's presentation of Eugene O'Neill's *Dynamo.* The theme of the play, as stated by the playwright, was "the passing of the old idea of a Supreme Being and the failure of Science, all-important in this day, to supplant it with something satisfying to the yearning soul of men permeated with the idea that the creations of Science are miraculous as the creations of the Supreme Being." This multi-pronged statement concerning man's spiritual emptiness contained probably too much philosophical speculation to be encompassed in a single play, but O'Neill had been wrestling with the problem for a number of years. As early as August 1927 he had written to Theresa Helburn from his home in Bermuda about the still unrealized script. Little had been done "in the way of actual dialogue" for *Dynamo,* but the scenes were completely planned. O'Neill, at the time, was finishing the final revisions of *Strange Interlude,* and of *Lazarus Laughed,* which was due to be published shortly. Earlier, in February, O'Neill had tried to interest the Guild in producing *Lazarus,* and he made several half-coaxing, half-teasing overtures to the Board about its possible production—a case of America's foremost playwright trying unsuccessfully to sell his wares.

In April 1928, when *Strange Interlude* was playing to capacity audiences, O'Neill wrote from France, where he had taken refuge from certain domestic difficulties, that he was "hard at" *Dynamo,* but that the writing would take much longer than expected because his original idea for the production was constantly developing in size. "I mean in imaginative flexibility," he added, possibly remembering a producer's abhorrence of excessive scenic costs.

Other communications concerning *Dynamo* followed. In June, O'Neill again wrote to Theresa Helburn, then touring Europe, inviting the producer to visit him, mentioning the uncertainty of his domestic affairs, and cautioning her to keep his whereabouts secret. Under the same cover as this letter the author enclosed another, with its March dateline scratched out, in which he stated he was doing the original writing of *Dynamo* with great care, "because I want the first draft as near to final form as possible and not have to go over it again and again as I did with 'Interlude'—work which is tremendously wearing and lacks the interest of first enthusiasm." There follows the first of O'Neill's explicit directions as to how he wanted his newest work presented, including a little essay on the use of sound in the modern drama:

> As an insufficient illustration I'd say the first part of the play derives from the method of simultaneous exterior and interiors I used with such revealing effect (at least, to me!) in "Desire Under the Elms." The second part—the hydro-electric power plant—derives its method (use of sounds) remotely from "The Hairy Ape." I use sounds very pronouncedly throughout the play as a definite dramatic motive—and, believe me, they will have to be done well and with crafty ingenuity. But nothing impossible! The trouble is we always let sounds go until the last minute and then throw them on, as it were, (boatrace scene, "Interlude") when they ought to be rehearsed weeks ahead. And thereby we throw overboard what could be one of the most original and significant dramatic values modernity has to contribute to the theatre. Believe me, I know, because I've always called for significant sounds in my plays and got insignificant ones which destroyed their meaning in my theme. Even the tom-tom in "Jones" has never been what I meant at all although with a little extra expense and trouble it could be done perfectly. . . . To return to "Dynamo" I warn you that there is a gradually approaching thunderstorm through the whole first part of the play that is a dramatic note in the composition and must be done as it *can* be done. Also during the second part we need in the background the continual metallic nasal purr of the generators—if you've ever spent a short time in a power house, you know how essentially symbolic and mysterious and moving this sound, (which is like no other sound but itself), is. And I speak with

> great seriousness when I say that whoever is to do the sets and noises ought to pay a friendly call on the General Electric people and get them interested in giving expert advice.
>
> . . . .
>
> As for the dialogue, it is Interludism. Thought will be as prominent as actual speech, probably, but there will be much less of the cutting-in of brief asides. "Dynamo" . . . ought to be done as "Interlude" and "Porgy" were—that is, as a separate thing in its own theatre. I feel it will be big enough and original enough to demand that—also that, if done right when written right, it can run a season at least on its own. There's one thing I think the Guild will have to face—that there are per se, plays for (original production in) repertoire and plays not for repertoire ("Marco," for example, is for r.)

In July, O'Neill again sent a progress report to Theresa Helburn, who was still in Europe. He was just starting the last act of *Dynamo*—what had been conceived as a two-act play had now grown to three. In this letter he warned the producer that he would be unable to attend any of the rehearsals for *Dynamo* in New York. He was determined to travel and had already booked passage for South Africa and the Far East, but he wished to have a conference with Moeller, whom he had chosen as director.

By early September O'Neill had finished *Dynamo* and had mailed the script to the Guild. The Board of Managers accepted it for production immediately—one of the few instances of their agreeing unanimously. The author had also drawn plans for the sets, and these were later reproduced in several New York newspapers. Although he would be absent from rehearsals, O'Neill felt that the subject matter of *Dynamo,* and its novel treatment, would stir up so great a controversy that the attendant publicity would more than make up for his being away. It was to be the first time the playwright had not been at hand during the preparation for one of his plays.

The original idea for *Dynamo* had apparently come to O'Neill while visiting the Stevenson generating station of the Connecticut Light and Power Company, and Moeller took his cast on a well-publicized field trip through this same plant to imbue it with the proper feeling for the play's super-charged, if gloomy, atmosphere. Lee Simonson also used the plant layout, along with the sketches O'Neill had provided, to design an imposing semi-constructive last-act setting for the production.

In articles preceding the opening, it was announced that *Dynamo* "in essence is a clearing ground for the erection of other structures," for the playwright had promised it was to be the first of a series of three plays, the others to be entitled *Without Ending of Days* and *It Cannot Be Mad.* When it opened, however, O'Neill's inquiry into the nature of a Science-God proved to be fairly disappointing. "To the end 'Dynamo' mirrors not only the obscurities of its theme, but further, and perhaps more lamentably, the uncertainty with which its author has formulated his own thoughts in regard to it," wrote Richard Lockridge in the *New York Sun;* and Percy Hammond felt that the play was "sometimes ludicrous, frequently raving, often encumbered with laborious 'interludisms,' and generally an entertainment for the rarer play-goer." One of the few favorable reviews appeared in the *New York Times.* Observing that "Mr. O'Neill reveals a drama of overwhelming stature," Brooks Atkinson concluded that "such broad and generalized plays as 'Dynamo' provoke endless discussion, and make enemies quite as violent as friends. For 'Dynamo' is violent, also. Writing on the most essential theme of modern life, Mr. O'Neill has strength and breadth, and a lashing, poetic fury."

The acting received mixed notices, too. While most critics found Glenn Anders as *Dynamo*'s hero, Reuben Light, and Helen Westley, as his mother, generally satisfying, Arthur Pollock of the *Brooklyn Eagle* thought Claudette Colbert, later a movie star, had "never exhibited so much poise and control of her modest talents." (Here it must be noted that Eugene O'Neill had slightly stronger and quite negative feelings concerning the young lady's poise and control.) Richard Lockridge felt that Dudley Digges gave a smooth performance in a role which permitted little more, while, according to Brooks Atkinson, Catherine Calhoun-Doucet sometimes lost the significance of her part in its farcical humor. Earlier, O'Neill had written to Theresa Helburn concerning this: "I have no suggestions—only a warning that if whoever plays it is ever conscious of being funny for even a moment or rides her lines for a laugh, I will swim back all the way from China with a kriss between my murderously gritted teeth and slay that actorine."

Simonson's set, "four rooms of two adjacent houses completely exposed," reminded some of the cutaway setting used in *Desire Under the Elms.* Most reviewers found the scene's strong and clear designs to be starkly expressive, more eloquent than the play itself. It has been suggested, however, that this early-act, skeletonized, constructivist representation in effect reduced the subtleties O'Neill wished to

DYNAMO — Eugene O'Neill first supplied rough sketches, then, at his suggestion, Lee Simonson visited the power station at Stevenson, Connecticut, before he started to design this atmospheric semi-realistic, semi-constructivistic setting.

L. to r. — Catherine Calhoun-Doucet, Claudette Colbert, Glenn Anders.

achieve in showing an old-fashioned New England house, with its "testaments of narrowmindedness, the distrust of industrial progress, the poverty, the piety of the Light family" compared to the "glaring newness" of the Fife family's home; for there was no difference discernible to the audience between the Lights' "faded wallpaper" and Fife's "too-shiny white" walls called for in the stage directions.

The majority of the reviews expressed the opinion that while *Dynamo*'s theme was a worthy one, technically at least, O'Neill had not written a very good play. The "inner voices out loud" device, which O'Neill later realized was mistakenly used in *Dynamo,* had been employed more lavishly, and with less reason than in *Strange Interlude.* He had used it to announce facts as well as to expose mental processes, and the characters were engaged in talking to themselves when they might better have been speaking to each other and the audience. By and large, the reviewers felt that quite a noteworthy play might still be forthcoming using *Dynamo*'s subject matter, and that "if Mr. O'Neill were a fine thinker instead of a man of feeling trying to think, he himself could write it."

Shortly after *Dynamo's* opening O'Neill became legally separated, and ultimately divorced, from his second wife, Agnes Boulton. Insofar as *Dynamo* is concerned, the Guild, of course, lost money—$12,761.23 to be exact—during the eight weeks it played; and O'Neill, according to Lawrence Langner, was never absent again from the rehearsals of any of his plays.

The Guild, having unsuccessfully tried its hand with an established playwright, resolved to try again—this time with two *un*established American playwrights. Bruce Gould and Beatrice Blackmar, a husband-and-wife team originally from Iowa, had never had a play produced before the Guild optioned their *Man's Estate.* Mr. Gould, it was noted, was employed as drama critic for *The Wall Street News.* Previously, Jed Harris had tried to work with the script but had found it unsuitable. It was decided to let Dudley Digges direct this homespun tale with its moral: "Youth, defiant and unashamed, fights the good fight. But nature, it seems, is on the old folks' side." More specifically, a young man, played by Earle Larimore (recently plucked from the cast of *Strange Interlude*), sacrifices his ambitions for a pregnant bride (played by Margalo Gillmore), and a cottage small (setting by Cleon Throckmorton). Mr. Digges, doubling in brass, played the domineering bourgeois father.

Some felt the offering was a quiet, quite cheerful play, but Gilbert W. Gabriel of the *New York American* wrote, "After reading all of

'Man's Estate' and seeing most of it, I must step out of the parade and wonder, was it worth the Guild's while . . . a play as unhappily ordinary, untidy and unhinged as this will be counted no credit to those who could pick and choose from the world's best." He went on to complain about the "reportorial Ladies-Home Journalese" flavor of the dialogue.

The most influential of critics found *Man's Estate* "a little clipped and thin, and as wanting in originality as a modern novel." Even Bruce Gould, reporting on his own handiwork in a review entitled "A Poor Thing—But Mine Own", candidly suggested that "surely the three or four critics who regarded our unpretentious and wholly American comedy as too simple and disjointed . . . cannot be entirely wrong, much as I believe them to be." (The Gould's autobiographical *American Story,* incidentally, contains a less-than-enthusiastic account of their relations with Jed Harris and the vituperative, debating-society production techniques used by the Guild.)

Surprisingly, *Man's Estate,* which featured a sensitive portrayal by Armina Marshall, did not lose money. Indeed, the modest sum it netted during its short run was much more welcome than the losses sustained by the organization's next offering, *The Camel Through the Needle's Eye.*

Rather grudgingly, the Guild had decided to perform another of its Hungarian rhapsodies (or middle-European light comedies) as its last bill of the 1928–29 season. Again, Philip Moeller directed his own adaptation of a tale the reviewers felt was quite insubstantial; nevertheless, few could restrain themselves from retelling, with relish, the "naughtily nifty" plot of *The Camel Through the Needle's Eye,* which has to do with a rich young man, bored into inarticulateness, becoming suddenly verbal under the kindly, dexterous ministrations of his right-headed little mistress.

Walter Winchell felt this a "rollicking play, lighter than a plum . . . chockful of highly amusing episodes, epigrams, and eppelsauce [sic]," a rather pleasant instance of the "cerebral Theatre Guild" in an inconsequential mood. *Woman's Wear Daily* agreed: "The Guild has been eminently more successful this year with the fluffy-feathery comedies than it has been with the more earnest plays probing the galactic schemes of the cosmos." Others, however, felt Moeller had possibly fortified and invigorated this import, originally from the pen of a little-known Czech army surgeon, Frantisek Langer, a bit *too* cannily: "Mr. Moeller knows Americans who buy seats for plays like to have something happening all evening, knows that a thin, light sentimental piece, slowly told, seems to them tiresome, though they like sentimentality well enough if it is thick and juicy. . . ." [Arthur Pollock, *Brooklyn Eagle*]. Helen Westley, as Stephen Rathbun stated, had contributed to *The Camel Through the Needle's Eye* "a veritable comedy triumph," and Miriam Hopkins, as the "little blonde flower of sin," was thought to be excellent as "one of those outstanding, wholesome young women who is always being cast as a sexily wild person." As for the script itself, the major portion of critical opinion seemed to stress that this Moeller-treated import from Prague was a diverting, if hokum-laden trifle; and that once again, as in the case of *Caprice,* a generous helping of fine-tasting technique by the Guild had overcome the lack of more nourishing intellectual fare. Here, it is only proper to mention that certain members of the Board were fully aware of the relative merits of the Guild's last two attractions. *Man's Estate* had been chosen specifically for Earle Larimore and Margalo Gillmore. These two members of the acting company were free and had to be used, and *The Camel Through the Needle's Eye* was at first considered as a vehicle for their talents. The minutes of the January 6, 1929, Board of Managers' meeting reports, "Mr. Simonson was asked by telephone for his vote and he said of two rotten apples he preferred THE CAMEL. There was a question whether this should be considered a vote in favor of THE CAMEL or not. . . ."

Percy Hammond, in a column designed to advise out-of-towners what to see when visiting the "big city," deplored the barren quality of the theatregoer's choices, but ended by saying:

> The best we can do now is listen to the call of the Theatre Guild. That organization, the most efficient of drama's aids, is offering at Martin Beck's theatre, a European entertainment entitled "The Camel Through the Needle's Eye" . . . a competent mediocrity from foreign parts. . . . I suspect that in its original performance [it] was a good gumdrop, approaching in palatability "Abie's Irish Rose". . . . Moeller, however, improves it in his merry adaptation and casts it with a competent company . . . making it another of the Guild's intelligent counterfeits. [*The St. Paul Pioneer Press,* April 28, 1929.]

Judging from its delightfully commercial notices, one probably would be justified in assuming that the banality of *The Camel Through the Needle's Eye* might at least turn into something of a gold mine. But at the end of the Guild's 1928–29 fiscal year *The Camel* was almost

$11,500 in the red, and after a decision to take losses within reason to keep the play running during the summer doldrums, this comedy tidbit cost its backers even more during the first five weeks of the 1929–30 season.

Elsewhere, the 1928–29 New York theatrical season had produced such Guild-like offerings as Tolstoy's *Redemption*, staged by Max Reinhardt and acted in his native tongue by the German actor Alexander Moissi; an English war play, *Journey's End*, which was produced by Gilbert Miller (by arrangement with Maurice Browne) and which enjoyed a long run with its all-male cast headed by Colin Keith-Johnson, Derek Williams, and Jack Hawkins. There were also showings of Ibsen's *The Master Builder*, Sierra's *The Cradle Song*, and Molière's *The Would-Be Gentleman*, which were staged successfully by Eva Le Gallienne's Civic Repertory Theatre. For the 1928–29 season the Pulitzer Prize was awarded to Elmer Rice's *Street Scene*, as produced by William A. Brady. The Guild had seriously considered, and had even held an option on, this notable example of American naturalism, but had decided not to produce it for aesthetic reasons—as Theresa Helburn explains in *A Wayward Quest*:

> I was partly responsible for the fact that the Theatre Guild did not produce *Street Scene*. When I read it I saw nothing but a cheap sex murder melodrama. At the time, I thought of it only in terms of its story value, I did not think of it in terms of production. Only when I saw it later did I realize that imaginative production had made it distinguished, had added another dimension. And yet, looking back, remembering that the Guild was founded on the idea "the play's the thing," I'm not sure I would change my original and spontaneous estimate of the play. It *was* a sex murder melodrama. The production, effective as it was, had been superimposed on an essentially sleazy structure. No, I'm not sorry we turned it down. [p. 108]

The Guild, apparently, had reason to feel that sexually suggestive situations treated lightly *(The Camel)*, or sentimentally *(Man's Estate)*, were quite acceptable to offer its customers, but that sex-laden situations treated realistically or melodramatically would not be especially good for them.

The 1928–29 season was a good one for the Guild financially. Although only one of its New York productions, *Caprice*, had proved lucrative, it finished the season with an increase in its total assets of more than $443,000—due principally to about $176,000 realized on its road productions, which included *Porgy, The Guardsman,* and *Arms and the Man,* almost $49,000 on *Strange Interlude* (a holdover still playing at the Golden Theatre with Judith Anderson replacing Lynn Fontanne), and $83,000 more from the touring company of that hit which starred Pauline Lord as Nina Leeds.

Artistically, though, the Guild had not fared as well as it had in the past, as George Jean Nathan perhaps too harshly observed when asking himself "What's happened to the Theatre Guild?" The production of *Faust,* he averred, "wouldn't have done credit to a Union Hill stock company"; *Wings Over Europe* was "an amateurish gimcrack," no matter how painstakingly it was presented, "in which the destiny of civilization was argued to be in the hands of a juvenile actor who had just discovered Shelley"; *Man's Estate* was a "cheap paraphrase of 'Hindle Wakes'"; and *Dynamo* was inferior O'Neill, carelessly prepared. When *The Camel Through the Needle's Eye* was produced, "even the Guild's staunchest devotees [had] to throw up their hands in dismay." Nathan was forced to conclude that unless the organization quickly took stock of itself it would not be long before it found its subscribers deserting it in favor of run-of-the-mill Broadway theatres where very much better plays "can be had for the same money." Somewhat less caustically, but in the same general tenor, Robert Littell appraised the Guild's situation by stating that the majority of recent productions had more or less been artistic failures. Possibly Whitney Bolton was fairer than either Nathan or Littell in hoping the Guild would soon restore itself "to vibrant and courageous activity."

While the quality of the Guild's choice of scripts had declined as the season progressed, it should be remembered that the country as a whole was reeling on the crest of a tremendous financial and spiritual binge; Black Thursday and Tragic Tuesday would not occur until later in October. Perhaps the mood of the times was one which needed a *Caprice,* a mood less amenable to the pessimistic *Dynamo.*

The Guild, of course, was aware of what its critics expected of it. It did not have what could be considered an impressive array of scripts on hand, however. Somewhat later, Langner wrote Miss Helburn a despairing memo, in which he outlined an unpromising prospectus:

> 1. A delightfully amusing play which our members will enjoy heartily, but which we do not yet possess.
>
> 2. THE COWARD, a play which will turn your stomach. The study of a disgusting character written by the author of THE FAILURES . . .

3. THE HOUSE OF CONNELLY, a gloomy tragedy, showing the utter hopelessness of the South.

4. DOG EAT DOG, a melodrama about a lot of disgusting people in a filthy hotel, with a few murders, and a great deal of seduction.

5. THE PARTY, another play about disgusting people, well written, but which we will never do.

6. THREE TIMES WATERLOO, a lousy farce, which we hope somehow, some way, to turn into a good one, possibly by the power of prayer.

7. THE SAILORS OF CATTARO, a stirring political document proving that sailors cannot run the fleet. Full of anguish and despair and the hopelessness of democratic institutions.

8. VERSAILLES, another cheerful little item, showing Wilson losing the Peace Conference. Might be educational if only the facts were correct . . .

The memo concluded with the suggestion that there ought to be a production of *Captain Brassbound's Conversion,* which would make Bernard Shaw once again the Guild's salvation, and an admission that even if "the above list looks pretty terrible," the Guild always had hopes that Eugene O'Neill, Maxwell Anderson, or Sidney Howard might provide it with a manuscript or two. Langner followed this by suggesting as the Guild's theme song "Tell us the old, old, story."

CHAPTER 3 / 1929-30

Karl and Anna, Leonhard Frank
Red Rust, V. Kirchon and A. Ouspensky
The Game of Love and Death, Romain Rolland
Meteor, S. N. Behrman
The Apple Cart, Bernard Shaw
A Month in the Country, Ivan Turgenev
Hotel Universe, Philip Barry
The Garrick Gaieties (3rd edition), Various Authors

As the 1929–30 season began, it became evident that the Guild had not been idle during the late spring and throughout the summer. Four new cities, Washington, Detroit, St. Louis, and Cincinnati, had been added to those six already included in the subscription series—Baltimore, Chicago, Pittsburgh, Philadelphia, Boston, and Cleveland. All these cities were promised productions of *Strange Interlude, Caprice, Wings Over Europe, R. U. R.,* and *Marco Millions,* as well as *Major Barbara* and *Pygmalion* during the coming year. Archibald Henderson, Shaw's official biographer, had been sent out by the Guild, perhaps to indoctrinate the hinterland with an appreciation for the last two offerings mentioned.

While Broadway had recently lost such stars as Ina Claire, Walter Huston, and Lenore Ulric to Hollywood and the talking pictures, the Guild's acting forces had remained remarkably intact. The organization was able to begin the 1929–30 season with an already impressive roster. Its only significant losses had been Edward G. Robinson, who went west as a result of a salary dispute, Clare Eames, who had left over a policy disagreement, and Margalo Gillmore, who had been signed by Gilbert Miller to appear opposite Leslie Howard in John L. Balderston's *Berkeley Square.* The Guild had added Sidney Greenstreet and Alexander Kirkland to its road acting company, and Otto Kruger, Alice Brady, and Frank Conroy for two projected New York productions. Kruger had already gained distinction in O'Neill's *The Straw* and Kaufmann's and Ferber's *The Royal Family,* and Conroy had been one of the original Washington Square Players. Alice Brady had almost been induced two seasons earlier to join the Guild's forces to play the part of Nina Leeds in the original production of *Strange Interlude,* but had declined the offer (to her ultimate regret).

The Guild promised New Yorkers a glowing season, part of which was to be selected from *The Genius and His Brother* by Sil-Vara, *Mirror Man* by Franz Werfel, *The Coward* by Lenormand, and *The House of Connelly* by Paul Green. Although none of these projects materialized that year, it is interesting to note that three foreign scripts were selected as opposed to one native playwright's work. The supply of worthwhile American pieces was still not abundant, apparently.

As early as the previous spring it had been announced that the Guild's opening production for the 1929–30 season would be the German Leonhard Frank's *Karl and Anna.* One critic was astute enough to observe that this wartime drama had appeared here as a motion picture only recently. It was also noted that *Karl und Anna* had played recently in Berlin and *Karl et Anna* was then enjoying a successful run at Gaston Baty's Théatre de l'Avenue in Paris. At least the Guild was going to be completely in fashion.

Leonhard Frank had written *Karl and Anna* first as a novel, and then had adapted it for stage presentation. The reviews which followed the opening of this Enoch Ardenish play, while hardly eulogistic, tended to stress the inadequacy of adaptation. Stark Young's began, "The Guild Begins With a Bad Play From a Beautiful Book." Another charged that in the dramatic version of the novel, "so much that is intended is left out . . . [that] the implied qualities, even, were lost most of the time. The framework of a pathetic depth is undoubtedly there in the last act of this play, but in the absence of any lines of much consequence or any compelling rhythm of dramatic themes and motives . . . only the most beautiful and intense innerness and spiritual resource among the players could create the necessary result." This resource was found lacking. Alice Brady as Anna, Percy Hammond felt, was rather hamstrung by the material with which she had to work. "But the last scenes give her a chance to display her notable knack for exhibitions of hysteria, and in one of these delirious eruptions she is aided by music from an off-stage gramophone . . . ."

A review appearing in the *New York World* about a week after the *Karl and Anna* opening was highly critical of the Guild, suggesting that it was betraying its reputation for high standards. No one would censure the ordinary producer for staging such a poorly written, drably acted failure, it stated; "we would say it was hollow to begin with . . . and let it go at that. But with the Guild one cannot let it go at that." Kruger and Conroy as actors and Moeller as director were politely scolded for having been in "something rather like a conspiracy to keep their several talents well out of sight." Possibly all that can be added to such a review is the fact that *Karl and Anna* lost $10,476.03 for the Guild. Courtenay Lemon, advisory play reader for the Guild, felt compelled to chide his employers with the following letter the day after *Karl and Anna*'s opening:

> I must confess that I have become really confused as to what is a Guild play. When the play was really the thing, I knew; but now I am uncertain as to what second-rate play you might eagerly do. The discussion I was in this afternoon made it plain that you are choosing plays according to the complicated necessities of finding roles for stars, and other actors, at just the right time for using them, which the policy of indefinite road expansion has made necessary. I predicted this, but didn't think its painful results would be apparent so soon.
>
> The Guild is suffering from over-organization and big business, at last in line with the usual American idea of size being more important than quality. Viz: the Guild should become a national theatre, not in the sense of a shrine to which dramatic enthusiasts might make a pilgrimage, but in an itinerant sense; it should restore and dominate the road; it should send out companies with the blind, unreflecting efficiency of a bee-hive—in short, the factory system and chain-store industry should be applied to art, with high-pressure salesmen, etc., all inducing delusions of grandeur based on the standardized products. But what the hell has all this to do with the delicate and imponderable values of art, the fine tendrils of thought and creativeness, except to coarsen and complicate your choice of plays, and to consume the energy of your Board with multitudinous considerations which have nothing to do with what the Guild was organized for.
>
> The logical next step would be to ask O'Neill or Werfel to write a play to order for some actress or actor to fit into the schedule. The dramatic poet should become a courturiere [sic] to measure, tailor and fit our superior actors and actresses. Also the Guild balcony subscriber, who has subscribed because of artistic and intellectual enthusiasm, should be content to watch accomplished actors making faces about nothing—all acting and no play.

> If the Guild commits itself still further to this policy, it will within a few years become so flabby that it might then as well change its name to Actors' Theatre and fade out of the mentally alive world like all theatres dominated by actors. The only salvation is to remember first, last and all the time that the play's the thing; that up and down, backwards and forwards and sideways, the play is forever the thing; and that without a sound play or a great play or a truly poetic or truly amusing play, no amount of acting can save you from deserved damnation.

It is interesting to note that Lemon, who was listed as advisory reader in *Karl and Anna*'s opening night program, had his name dropped from the program of the Guild's next two attractions. It was added again for the fourth, but vanished, seemingly forever, after that. It is still more interesting to note that the Guild was caught in the rather nightmarish situation of having hordes of actors on its payroll because of its expanding program of simultaneous road productions, and that these actors *had* to be kept working so as not to deplete the treasury.

Concerning the durable *Strange Interlude:* two companies had been sent out; one, headed by Pauline Lord, had been going continuously since the previous December, and after thirty-seven weeks of trouping netted $107,275. A second company, headed by Judith Anderson, Tom Powers, Glenn Anders, and Richard Barbee, played in Quincy, not Boston, Massachusetts, and made $103,230 during its thirty-four weeks on the road. A publicity release explained why this second company had to play in Quincy: the recent banning of *Strange Interlude* from Boston by the city's mayor, the climax of the Puritanical prohibition of a long series of plays and books. A parody of *Paul Revere's Ride* gained wide circulation:

> It was one by the village clock
> When he galloped into Lexington.
> "Get up!" he cried with accent rude,
> "Or you'll all get Strange Interlude."

All this, of course, did not hurt business—quite the contrary. Crowds arrived by the chartered busload, and feeding them during the dinner intermission helped finance the start of a nationwide chain for a nearly bankrupt Quincy restaurant owner named Howard Johnson.

Romain Rolland's *The Game of Love and Death,* it was announced, had been held by the Guild for two seasons "until a satisfactory cast could be found for its production." Rolland, best recognized in America as author of a best-selling novel, *Jean Cristophe,* was a well-known champion of libertarianism and pacifism in his native France. He was then hard at work writing a series of plays, or polyptich, dealing with the French Revolution. *The Game of Love and Death* was the last in order of historical chronology that he had finished.

Gilbert W. Gabriel predicted that the long-awaited *Game,* whose theme is the struggle between an individual's conscience and the public cause, was "apt to emerge in the rare light which only masterpieces can afford to wear." But, after his colleagues' opening-night reviews were in, it became evident he had not been quite accurate in his early appraisal. "Although my heart breaks as I write it, the Theatre Guild has picked a windy play for the second production of its twelfth season. . . . The trouble with 'The Game of Love and Death' is that it is made up of words, words, and yet more words," wrote Robert Garland of the *New York Telegram,* while Richard Lockridge found that "somewhere within its theme, as somewhere within its action, there lies undisturbed the material of drama." John Mason Brown felt that "M. Rolland's drama leads a strangely double life, because beneath all the literary and philosophic speeches which cross its surface lurks a romance of such a pasteboard kind that it seems built for music cues."

The acting in *Game,* with one notable exception, came in for mixed notices. Ruth Cambridge of the *Daily Mirror* found that "Alice Brady did the finest piece of subtle acting in her well-filled career of beautiful performing," while Richard Watts, Jr. of the *New York Herald Tribune* felt she "offers a performance that is probably the least convincing she has presented in the theatre." Arthur Pollock wrote, "To the beauty of 'The Game of Love and Death' Miss Brady adds immeasurably, and that beauty is a great, calm beauty"; on the other hand, John Mason Brown thought she "skimmed her way through Sophie, playing unevenly, and failing to give her the depth and credibility she posseses in the script." The one thing that all the critics agreed upon, however, was Claude Rains' absolute brilliance; but in giving such lavish praise, according to Whitney Bolton of the *Telegraph,* "they mistook the energy of the role for unusual resource on the part of the actor," and added, in defense of a much-maligned performer, that Frank Conroy, who "toiled with a somber, monotonous, unrelievedly dull role . . . had no chance to sparkle, no single opportunity to rise to dramatic heights and force." Here, one might note in passing that Claude Rains was at first very favorably considered for the role Frank Conroy ultimately played.

As it turned out, the French import lost slightly over $21,000 for the Guild. After two tries it had become evident that the Kruger-Brady-Conroy combination was not going to jell, and there was speculation in the press as to what would become of the cast's various members. One such article was headed "Tour For Miss Brady?" and suggested that there had been various guesses as to what the Guild would do with Miss Brady when *The Game* had run its course. "The puzzle may, perhaps, be solved by a report of the past week. The story has it that Miss Brady will play 'Strange Interlude' in some of the major cities during the Winter. . . ." And so she did, until a Milwaukee newspaper, under a headline that read "Nina Is Sick!" announced that, suffering from a nervous breakdown, she had been released from her contract with the Guild (a common ploy of actresses wishing to break an "onerous" contract) and had been replaced in the road show of *Strange Interlude.*

Of course, there were renewed flurries of criticism concerning the Guild's artistic plight. Richard Watts, Jr. bemoaned the production of *Karl and Anna,* which he stated had turned out "with much completeness, to be one of the least satisfactory of the Broadway year" and continued by adding that "when . . . with true international impartiality, there is provided a translation from the French of Romain Rolland's 'The Game of Love and Death,' and it proves to be an aesthetic loss, there is cause for anxiety." Indeed, after so much condemnation, he wondered, "does it sound like hedging to predict that the Guild's doldrums may be but temporary?"

It is interesting to note that in *The Game's* program Barrett H. Clark had been added to the roster of play readers after Courtenay Lemon's withdrawal. According to Burns Mantle, Clark would bring "a fresh and an intelligently penetrating mind to bear on what is currently the Guild's most desperate problem," namely, the discovery of an American play worthy of its effort and its earned reputation.

Although the Guild *had* an American play soon opening in Boston, its next New York offering, technically speaking, was *Red Rust.* This production of a modern Russian play by V. Kirchon and A. Ouspensky as translated by Virginia and Frank Vernon became a rather important landmark in the history of the American theatre, for it was the premier work of a young group known as the Theatre Guild Studio—later to become the Group Theatre.

The Guild had presented, in its earlier days, a special production annually for its subscribers—Strindberg's *Dance of Death* during its second season and Verhaeren's *The Cloister* during its third were examples of this "dividend" policy. At the time, however, the entire subscription list could be accommodated with two or three performances. During its twelfth season such a dividend would require a run of at least six weeks before it could be seen by all the Guild's New York subscribers. A publicity release stated that it was the lack of these special productions and the desire to give the younger members of the production department more actual experience and responsibility in the preparing of plays that prompted the Guild Studio project. The studio members expected to produce three plays that season. The first was to be presented at three matinees, but these plans were changed, and *Red Rust* was given as a subscription offering.

It was duly noted that *Red Rust* was but the second play to reach Broadway from Soviet Russia—the first having been *The First Law* which "went on one Monday night last May at the Masque and came off on Saturday." Concerning *Red Rust's* content, it was prophesied in the *Post,* somewhat prematurely, that American audiences would have little patience with propaganda drama, "for even our own native dramatists concerned with the evils of prohibition have received slight encouragement from the local public, which may account for the failure of Augustus Thomas' 'Still Waters' and Philip Dunning's 'Sweet Land of Liberty.' The eloquence which Maxwell Anderson put into the Sacco-Vanzetti drama, 'Gods of the Lightning,' went unheeded by the public, apparently because it was special pleading for an unpopular cause." (Anderson's revision of his *Gods of the Lightning* later became the record-breaking *Winterset.*)

The Guild Studio had as its managing committee three members: Cheryl Crawford, a recent graduate of Smith College, who was the Guild's assistant casting director; Harold Clurman, who in addition to possessing a "Jed Harrisish growth of beard" also held a Ph.D. from the Sorbonne—he was a member of the Guild's playreading department; and Herbert J. Biberman, the director of *Red Rust,* who was production stage manager for the Guild. He had attended the University of Pennsylvania and the Yale School of Drama, where he had played Machiavelli in Lemist Esler's play which was entitled *The Grey Fox* when it ran on Broadway.

Red Rust, which opened at the Martin Beck on December 17, 1929, ran for a total of sixty-five performances. The theme of this "authentic whiff of Moscow air" might have been stated as: no matter how uni-

RED RUST — Cleon Throckmorton designed this extremely economical setting for a Russian play written to depict the aftermath of the revolution. The cast contained many members of what later became the Group Theatre. Julian (John) Garfield is the more upright boxer at left, Luther Adler is about to leap (right center), Herbert J. Biberman, who also directed the play, flexes his muscles, and Lionel Stander reclines on the bench at right.

fied a front the Russian communists show to the rest of the world, they are far from being agreed among themselves; or, although a single doctrine has been set up in Russia, it has not evolved into a single mass which feels, thinks, and acts in unison. Some reviewers found it melodrama, but good melodrama. Over the presentation there seesawed an extraordinary debate which sooner or later brought in almost every important contemporary Soviet question on personal conduct, morality, and philosophy, "with enough ideas for ten plays and rather too many for one."

> "Red Rust" is in many ways a fair sample of books and plays about the younger Soviet generation. It is not a good play, it makes concessions to the sensational, and other contrary concessions to the Russian debating instinct, but it seethes with fragments, however curiously and clumsily assorted, from the lives that students and young party workers are living in Moscow today. . . . Here is dark and chaotic and fascinating ground which cannot adequately be covered in the tumble of first impressions after one of the Guild's most interesting experiments. [Robert Littell, *New York World,* Dec. 18, 1929]

Another critic, not a native New Yorker, found the play one of the best of the season, suggesting that if it had not been first produced in Moscow with the consent of the authorities, it might well have been viewed as an anti-Soviet tract. Instead, "the play becomes an authentic picture of a group of young men and women faced with a new burden and a new earth, and greatly bewildered by the chaos of creation." The acting as well was almost universally praised, with allowances made for the group's youthfulness. In addition to directing the piece, Biberman acted in it, playing the villain, and Arthur Ruhl of the *Herald Tribune* found him to be "relentless in making Terekhine as objectionable as possible." Franchot Tone and Luther Adler were effective as idealistic Communists. Gale Sondergaard, one of the host of *Strange Interlude*'s Nina Leedses that the Guild utilized as "interchangeably as Ford parts," was found to play the new Nina of *Red Rust* with "quiet skill."

Although many thought *Red Rust* furnished some of the "roughest language on any stage," and certainly provided one of the more bizarre settings then to be seen along Broadway, many persons found the presentation evidenced more than a trace of the vigorous youth which had characterized the earliest days of the parent organization.

But while in former years the Guild had allowed such young people only in the background of its presentations, or had let them try their wings in the *Garrick Gaieties*, now it was "letting loose the talents of these youngsters upon work which reflects the new expressions of any part of the world"—a great compensation for the failures of the season that had already received elaborate comment.

Less than a month after the opening of *Red Rust* a certain disquietude arose among the Guild's Board of Managers concerning the Studio Group "which were taking too many liberties with scripts." It was reasonable to suppose that during rehearsals some changes would be found necessary, but the Board agreed that the integrity of the plays should be insisted upon, that their original intentions not be changed simply for the sake of change. The principles of Studio productions were discussed, with Simonson seeming to feel that the Studio Board should be more or less autonomous, "that we should lean over backwards in leaving them freedom in the choice of plays." The others maintained that the Guild must exert its own powers of judgment because the Studio was "an intrinsic part" of it. No play, it was argued, should be staged to which the Board of Managers had not consented.

Insofar as *Red Rust* itself was concerned, Harold Clurman, who became co-founder of the Group Theatre in 1931 and its Managing Director in 1937, observed that the chief popularity of the Studio's initial presentation was among Soviet sympathizers "who showed themselves for the first time on Broadway":

> I remember being startled at the applause when the *Internationale* was sung before the curtain on opening night. The liberal intelligentsia, which had a goodly representation at that time on the large list of Guild subscribers, welcomed the play not for its message (it hardly had any) but for its tonic swing, which came as a relief in the Guild's now academic routine.[1]

This interesting experiment, dramatizing life in Russia after that country's recent overthrow of czarist power, had an encouraging eight-weeks' run. It lost $13,477.39 for the Guild, however, and after its close the Studio project was terminated.

About this time, nettled by the steady flow of criticism in the press about its script-selection policies, Lawrence Langner wrote on behalf of the Board:

[1]Harold Clurman, *The Fervent Years*, p. 25.

> The idea that the Guild sorts its plays on the basis that this play will make money, while that play will not, and thereupon selects the play which will make money, is arrant nonsense, and presupposes the Guild to be a good deal cleverer than it really is. All of our experience has gone to show that it is impossible to tell which play will make money, and which play will not . . . ."[2]

The truth of this statement is borne out by the following items from the minutes of the Board of Managers' meetings concerning a play which not only was awarded the Pulitzer Prize for that year, but played to sell-out houses for nearly 700 performances:

> Oct. 16, 1929—A preliminary discussion of GREEN PASTURES took place but no final decision was reached as Mr. Simonson hadn't read it. Mrs. Westley believed it would be impossible to produce a play that dealt in a comic vein with God. Mr. Moeller and Mr. Wertheim were inclined to agree with her. Mr. Langner and Miss Helburn did not. It was suggested that the substitution of an Archangel, or someone representing God, might be made to avoid the particular situation.
>
> Oct. 20, 1929—There was a discussion of GREEN PASTURES by Marc Connelly; considered for its value as a play, the vote—
>
> *In favor:* Mr. Langner, Mr. Moeller, Mr. Wertheim, Miss Helburn
>
> *Against:* Mr. Simonson, Mrs. Westley
>
> But those who were in favor of the play were not necessarily in favor of production, because of material which might be offensive to audiences. Miss Helburn was empowered to discuss the matter with Mr. Connelly and see if he had any ideas on the subject. Mr. Simonson thought the play was too repetitive after the first two scenes.

With its ultimate rejection of *Green Pastures,* the Guild lost its chance to do one of the most original plays ever to be produced on the American stage. It furthermore lacked the wisdom to stage Edwin Justus Mayer's *Children of Darkness,* to which it had held option; and now that it was turning again to S. N. Behrman for his new play, *Meteor,* its Board members could only remember having let his *Serena*

---

[2]Lawrence Langner, "The Guild Begs Leave to State," *Theatre Guild Magazine* (Feb., 1930), p. 48.

Blandish slip away earlier, to watch it be produced successfully elsewhere by Jed Harris in 1928.

One irksome question which confronted producers, as well as theatre owners during the 1929–30 season, concerned Sunday performances, which were expressly prohibited by New York City ordinances. "Movie houses find Sundays their most profitable days . . . . Why can't the theatre give up Monday and Tuesday nights, which are always slow in the theatre . . . ?" asked the *Theatre Guild Magazine* for January, 1930.

Another of the difficulties then confronting many Broadway managers was the problem of extortionate ticket speculation. Increasingly great numbers of the public, especially the suburban public, were patronizing the cinema instead of the legitimate theatre. One reason given for this was "their disgust at the prices charged by speculators for good seats—sometimes as high as $10 and $12." Certain managers were forcing brokers to take large blocks of tickets for their poorer offerings along with their popular ones. In order to cover themselves, the ticket brokers in turn had been forced to double, and even triple their prices on popular attractions. Many found this vicious circle to be "drawing tighter and tighter," as one producer claimed in February of that year. A Managers' Bureau was set up with a watchdog committee, which included Arthur Hopkins, Brock Pemberton, and Gilbert Miller—Lawrence Langner also became interested in this project. They proposed to establish a system of distribution and control which would prevent agencies from charging more than the box-office price, plus a service charge of not more than seventy-five cents. Hopefully, this would give the public the option of buying tickets at the box office whenever possible; for, according to the plan, all managers would agree to refuse to sell blocks of tickets to any broker after March 1st of that year. This, of course, was only one of many plans advanced over a long period of time. The problem of box-office "ice" is still with us, unfortunately, and "scalping" will continue so long as patrons feel they must attend a popular attraction as quickly as possible.

On May 23, 1928, the decision was made by the Guild to buy S. N. Behrman's *Meteor*. Three months later, Moeller expressed dissatisfaction with the script, saying it "lacked emotional grip and was not cumulative." The others agreed to reread the play even while Alfred Lunt and Lynn Fontanne were being considered as possibilities for the leads. In September, the Lunts attended a meeting of the Board to say that they would appear in *Meteor* only if it was extensively revised, but that they were not at all anxious to do it in New York. A bit later Gale Sondergaard was proposed for the leading female role, and a week following that, with the Board now unenthusiastic about doing the piece, Elliot Cabot was mentioned as a possibility for the leading man. There was a rumor that Jed Harris was interested in producing the play, and the Board was in favor of asking Harris to direct it for the Guild. Harris apparently demurred, and Rouben Mamoulian was offered the assignment. When Mamoulian showed little relish for the project, the whole idea was nearly dropped, but Moeller agreed reluctantly to assume the directorial chores himself, with the stipulation that the script be completely rewritten.

The following April Theresa Helburn reported that the Lunts, after reading the revised version of *Meteor,* were willing to appear in it, but that Miss Fontanne preferred to play it with *A Month in the Country* as an alternate rather than *The Game of Love and Death* because her two roles would be so much alike. After many false hopes and starts, including a great deal of tentative casting, Behrman's and Moeller's efforts were believed ready for the Board's inspection on November 12, 1929. After seeing them, the directorate considered "keeping *Meteor* away from New York as long as necessary." All thoughts of an alternating production had been abandoned, and the managers busied themselves making suggestions for the Lunts' *next* play.

Possibly the presentation of a realistic drama in which a Wall Street "Napoleonic general marshals his force of bulls against his enemy's bears, and terrible massacre results," was poorly timed. The great market crash had occurred during the period which had elapsed between the Guild's first receiving the script and its ultimate production, and although advertisements promised "even though you were ruined in the recent Stock Exchange landslide, you will still like this play," memories perhaps were too painful to make complete enjoyment possible.

As implied in the minutes, *Meteor*'s tryout period in Boston was especially nerve-wracking. The Guild's subscription list in that city had grown from about 5,000 the previous season to more than 7,500 paying members, and, because *Strange Interlude* had been considered "unacceptable" for a Boston presentation, *Meteor* was to be the first Guild production offered the ever-expanding list that year. It is questionable whether the Lunts had ever been wildly enthusiastic about the script, and a great deal of play-doctoring was thought necessary at the last minute. One anecdote tells how Behrman, when Lawrence

Langner asked him to strengthen the scenes of conflict and the scenes of tenderness, appeared the next day saying, "Here, Lawrence, are six pages of conflict, and here are three pages of tenderness."

When *Meteor* opened on December 2, 1929 at the Hollis Street Theatre, it received mixed notices. The Boston critics felt the piece well-acted, but, because of the repellent nature of its material, were reluctant about accepting it wholeheartedly:

> . . . an engrossing play, a strongly dramatic play; it holds the attention from the rising of the curtain to the final falling thereof; yet there is hardly a sympathetic character in any one of the three acts. Raphael, if he were not portrayed so admirably, with so great dramatic force, by Mr. Lunt, would be only a blatant, selfish, heartless egotist, an unendurable person. . . . The Theatre Guild is to be thanked for the production of this unusual play, unusual in the local history of the drama, but with a hero—for want of a better word—not unknown to the European stage, the Parisian stage especially. [Philip Hale, *Boston Herald,* Dec. 8, 1929]

When the play opened at the Guild Theatre on December 23, 1929, the New York critics, too, were bemused rather than beguiled by this delineation of "an extraordinary case of egomania—a man who would have been a splendid laboratory case for a psychiatrist." Bellamy Partridge of the *New York World* believed that "if S. N. Behrman, the author, had built a little more sentiment into his plot he might have made a great play of it. As it now stands the final curtain goes down on a meteor that has butted its head against a stone wall and is sputtering with the ineffectual gasps of a spent rocket." In Arthur Pollock's opinion, perhaps "it would be fairer to say that 'Meteor' is a play which, if it cannot convince by its ideas, does not care to draw its audiences along by affecting their feelings. My guess is that Mr. Behrman wrote the play the way he liked it best and during rehearsals it got in places to be something else."

Alfred Lunt's acting led Charles Darnton of the *Evening Sun* to evaluate *Meteor* as a character study rather than a play since in the "characterization of an arrogant and likable egoist . . . Mr. Lunt does a clever thing by giving Raphael a boyish quality [and] lets you see there is no real hardness in the man." *The Commonweal*'s Richard Dana Skinner was drawn to Lunt's portrayal of Lord "with just enough fire, intensity, and neurotic interest to give him the fleeting illusion of reality." Lynn Fontanne's performance, in what he called "the singularly difficult (because not obviously difficult) part of Lord's wife," was called admirable, and Philip Moeller's direction was considered "adroit and convincing." The principal regret was that with the brilliant possibilities of good writing, good acting, and good staging, the material of the play should seem so commonplace.

By the end of February came the first indications that *Meteor* had almost run its course. On March 16 the Lunts announced they were going on their first vacation in two years, Lunt complaining of acute bursitis that had necessitated his performing his role with his arm in a sling. Thus came to a close that season's first Guild offering by a native American author. *Meteor* lost slightly over $19,000 for the Guild during its unimpressive New York stay. The critical consensus, understandably, seemed to urge that "Mr. Behrman should return to his proper métier, which is pure comedy. . . ."

Elsewhere on the Broadway scene there were appearing, in highly successful runs, such Guild-like offerings as Frank Morgan in Marcel Pagnol's *Topaze* and Philip Merivale in the Shubert production of *Death Takes a Holiday*—both of which the Guild had optioned but later rejected. Katharine Cornell, whose services the Guild was most anxious to secure, was then appearing in Margaret Ayers Barnes' and Edward Sheldon's *Dishonored Lady*. Acting honors for the year might easily have belonged to Spencer Tracy, who was spellbinding audiences with his hard-fisted portrayal of Killer Mears in *The Last Mile* by John Wexley, a playwright whose work the Guild coveted. Two Guild alumni, Otto Kruger and Winifred Lenihan, had found profitable employment in Dana Burnet's *The Boundary Line*. A "direct competitor" of the Guild, the Civic Repertory Theatre, was then presenting "an intense pleasure"—Tolstoy's *The Living Corpse* (*Redemption*) with Jacob Ben-Ami, another Guild alumnus, who was most persuasive as the play's hero. The Guild had originally planned to present in February and March a Japanese troupe under the direction of famous actor Tokujero Tsutsui, which was then touring the States. The Guild relinquished its sponsorship after appearances in California before the Tsutsui Japanese Players had even crossed the country. Metropolitan areas on the East Coast had been playing host to the renowned Chinese actor Mei Lan-fang (and company) that season, so that New Yorkers were favored by having two distinguished Oriental theatrical groups performing for them at the same time, within a few blocks of each other.

Earlier in the year a press release had announced that Douglass Montgomery, who was originally scheduled for a *Meteor* supporting role, was leaving the Guild because it had "given him insufficient opportunity to develop his talent." In fact, various shifts in the Guild's acting personnel were frequently reported in the press:

> Certain cast changes impend in the Theatre Guild's production in and out of New York. Alexander Kirkland shortly goes into "Meteor" at the Guild, replacing Douglass Montgomery. Ernest Cossart will be in the new play, "The Apple Cart," and his roles in the repertory company now on tour playing "Marco Millions," "Volpone," and "R.U.R." have been taken over by Harry Mestoya. Frank Conroy will play in the "Strange Interlude" company now engaged in touring the East, replacing George Gaul, who shifts to another role in the same company. Ralph Morgan leaves this "Interlude" company to go into that now playing what appears to be a long engagement at the Blackstone, Chicago. He takes over the role of Marsden, which Tom Powers has been playing for more than two years. Mr. Powers comes to New York shortly and will appear in one of the Guild's coming productions. [*Women's Wear Daily*, Jan. 20, 1930]

It soon became apparent that the Guild was gathering its maturer acting forces in New York for a forthcoming presentation. Publicity leaked as to what this would be as early as January of the previous year, under various headings, one of which read: "Shaw Takes Rap At U. S. In New Political Comedy." The next month G. B. S. wrote to Theresa Helburn:

> By this time reports of my new play should have appeared in American press, as it is some weeks since I wrote a letter about it to a lady in Detroit to whom I wanted to do a good turn, authorizing her to communicate the relevant parts of it to the papers and telling her how to set about it. . . .[3]

He went on to outline the play's main action, which centers on a cabinet meeting at which the King of England is present. King Magnus of England, the pivotal character, was "the sort of part that George Arliss shines in." There were also four women's roles, "one of whom is a brilliant Millamant, one serious, one musical comedy," plus a young Princess. The letter ended by stating that this new play was to be as

[3]Langner, *G. B. S. and the Lunatic*, pp. 133-34. Reproduced by permission of the Public Trustees and The Society of Authors on behalf of the Bernard Shaw Estate.

unlike *Saint Joan* as anything could be. Following the typed portion of the letter, there is a postscript added in handwriting:

> P.S. The play will be produced in England next August at a provincial Bühnenfestspiel, with Methuselah, Heartbreak House, & possibly St. Joan; the particular Bayreuth in question being Malvern in Worcestshire, near the Welsh border. Reinhardt may produce it first in Berlin, but I am rather dissuading him, as the politics in the play are very English.

True to his word, Shaw did permit Sir Barry Jackson to produce *The Apple Cart* at a Shavian festival in Malvern, but not before it had been given its premiere performance in a Polish translation. The reports from Warsaw were not favorable:

> Mr. Shaw has disregarded most of the old stage tricks which gladdened the heart of the old stagegoer, has shunned fireworks, parody, and epigram, turned his back on cruel wit, and hardly used any of the usual finicky stage directions. It almost seems as though, now that he has the great public at his feet, he becomes the Fabian pamphleteer once more, sheer and simple. This new Shavian simplicity will not come as a surprise to those who have waded through the oceans of words of one syllable in "The Intelligent Woman's Guide to Socialism." This play is not a play—nothing more or less than a lengthy political two acts, without the comic quality of such a discussional play as "Getting Married." . . . [*Boston Evening Transcript,* July 6, 1929]

Shaw's fellow playwright, John L. Balderston, after having interviewed the world-renowned wit at the Malvern performances, reported him to be legitimately aggrieved by the reviews in the press, which, he suggested, had resulted from multiple language barriers. Some reviews, for example, had been written by Englishmen who did not understand the Polish text, "others written by Poles whose English was unintelligible." Balderston readily acknowledged the press's dilemma, even if Shaw, with his "counterfeited bitterness," chose not to. In Balderston's words, "the press might reply: Why have your play, which turns upon subtleties of English character and English politics, done for the first time in Polish?"

Through its magazine the Guild distributed an estimate of *The Apple Cart* by the respected British critic Ivor Brown—an estimate hardly calculated to whet the subscription list's sense of anticipation:

. . . to my own taste it seemed unworthy stuff and distinctly dangerous as an export to the politically embarrassed countries of Europe where defense of the Strong Ruler against elected statesmen simply gives a Shavian *imprimatur* to the claims of all budding Mussolinis, *Putsch*-promoters, bouncing parliament-smashers, and other nuisances whose forms of radio-activity are likely to endanger the lives of millions.[4]

Shaw, throughout, was busily obtaining as much free advertising space as possible, as the following London article, reprinted in several newspapers of this country, would indicate:

Bernard Shaw's next play deals with a conflict between a future Labor cabinet and a future king, including, according to the author, "a startling intervention by the United States, and . . . broken in the middle by a brief but intense sex interlude." . . . In regard to the complete edition of Shaw's works, which will be brought out shortly, it is revealed that the collection will include Shaw's first novel, called "Immaturity," which was written 50 years ago, and has never yet been published . . . . The edition will have an autobiographical preface, which Shaw says will describe "my condition in London when I wrote it, and the family life of the boy Shaw. The contrast between the jejune novel and this consummate preface makes me wonder whether the same people will be able to stand both." [Harry Cavendish, *Cleveland Plain Dealer*, May 12, 1929]

When the Guild's *Apple Cart* began its pre-New York tryout at Ford's Theatre in Baltimore on Monday, February 17, 1930, that city's Louis Azrael found it "all a bit disjointed . . . simply something upon which to hang his ideas," even if those ideas could be fascinating. *The Apple Cart* lacked the "lustre of the Shaw plays that have gone before. . . . It pays small attention to the so-called rules of the theatre," among which is surely one that insists a playwright not slander his audience's culture if it is foreign to that of his own country:

Many of the points dealt with require a knowledge of British customs, but not so the author's attitude toward the United

[4]Ivor Brown, "The British Stage," *Theatre Guild Magazine,* III:2 (Nov., 1929), p. 40.

> States. Mr. Shaw hates us and makes no bones about it. He makes the Queen say that an American is a wop trying to be a Pilgrim Father, and he slashes viciously at what he calls our lack of culture, manners and traditions. [*Baltimore Sun,* Feb. 18, 1930]

As might be expected, when the play arrived at the Martin Beck Theatre in New York one week later, the metropolitan critics displayed "enormous urbanity" in their approach to this work of a universally recognized theatrical genius. Burns Mantle wrote that *The Apple Cart* "is something like twice as wordy as was . . . 'Wings Over Europe' and something less than a third as exciting." Robert Garland claimed "from beginning to end . . . talk, talk, and yet more talk . . . in spite of Mr. Shaw's world-wide reputation as a wit, a seer, and a playwright. . . . Some of the talk is brilliant, some of the talk is politically important, some of the talk is commonplace and some of the talk is downright boring." John Anderson of the *Evening Journal* indicated that the play said nothing that had not already been said with greater dignity by such men as Dean Inge of St. Paul's; the playwright, Anderson charged, had used farce "to shirk a viewpoint, instead of driving it home . . . . Call it boob-baiting if you will, . . . it is more provoking than anybody else's boob-bait." Charles Darnton in the *New York World,* labelling the effort a travesty, could only offer in his anguish, "Maybe this sort of nonsense will be going on thirty years from now and maybe America will be offering to merge itself in the British Empire. But it will take more than 'The Apple Cart' to make us believe it."

Though hardly enthusiastic, other critics tended to be somewhat fairer. Robert Littell found *The Apple Cart* "highly satisfactory" as entertainment. Brooks Atkinson expressed the opinion that only Shaw "in the ripeness of his years" could write such enlightened theatre conversation and have "enough sense to make it sound like nonsense. With him intelligent conversation is cerebral horseplay. Of all the bad plays produced this season this is the best." Arthur Ruhl of the *Herald Tribune* insisted that while people who went to the theatre for stories of suspense and surprise would be disappointed, those "who are content to listen for an evening to the political table talk of the wittiest writer for the English-speaking stage—talk sometimes good, sometimes not so good, the average come-and-go of a brilliant playwright chatting on the subject of democracy," would find themselves quite comfortably entertained. And finally, what turned out to be the most eulogistic of New York's comments paid homage to both the Guild and Shaw alike: "This madcap and very shrewd political extravaganza of

THE APPLE CART – A setting by Lee Simonson for one of Bernard Shaw's innumerable discussions.

L. to r. – Morris Carnovsky, George Graham, Helen Westley, Claude Rains, Tom Powers, Eva Leonard-Boyne, Ernest Cossart, John Dunn, William Sams.

his not only discovers him offering the playgoers . . . as delightful and stimulating an evening as they have encountered in many a season, but also reveals the acting and producing forces of the Guild at their best. [John Mason Brown, *New York Evening Post,* Feb. 25, 1930]

In point of fact, the Guild's forces were unanimously lauded for having done a workmanlike job with uninspired, unlikely material. "Tom Powers played the King with skill, poise, charm, humor and understanding . . . . Claude Rains was particularly successful in bringing out the explosive vanity of the Prime Minister," felt Charles Darnton. John Anderson wrote that "Miss Kemble-Cooper . . . and Mr. Cossart proved as reliable as usual at their tasks, and the whole has been directed with much cunning and animation by Mr. Moeller," while John Mason Brown thought Helen Westley to be "at her most aggressive best" as Lysistrata, the Powermistress-General. Also admired were Lee Simonson's "modern settings of distinction," one of which is shown here, arrayed with sitting actors defining the "inadequacies" of all democracies.

The basic situation in *The Apple Cart* is one that Shaw uses time and again in his plays—namely, some person of exceptional gifts and personality (in this case, King Magnus) is surrounded by mediocre people with conventional standards and commonplace ideas. A fine defense of the play had been printed nearly a year before the New York opening in the *Boston Globe.* In summing up Shaw's contribution, "Uncle Dudley" concluded:

> The effect a century hence will be ironic. For when an age is past its little voices are stilled, but its great voices go on speaking. This leads later ages to infer that the great voices were typical and expressive of their time. Of course, they were not; often they were hardly heard. But the little voices die, the great ones live; so the age gets a better name than it deserves. Thus is history written. The perspective is false, but better than true.

Unfortunately, this article could not help the play's ultimate reception in America. It lost almost $21,000 for the Guild during the twelve weeks it played in New York.

Perhaps comparisons are odious, but worthy of mention here is an editorial appearing in *Theatre Magazine* for April of that year:

> *The Apple Cart,* as the work of a man acknowledged as one of our superior dramatists, is bound to take on an interest which, in this case, I fear, is greater than it deserves. *The Green Pastures,*

> coming into the Mansfield almost unheralded, has immediately revealed itself as a play whose deep sincerity and emotional beauty set it apart as the finest production our theatre has offered this season. And I think we may leave off the teaming of so ill-assorted a pair with that reflection.

Too bad the Guild had turned down *Green Pastures!*

The next scheduled Guild production, however, was destined to become one of acknowledged "emotional beauty." The name of Ivan Turgenev, renowned Russian novelist and playwright, had appeared but once before on New York theatre programs; this was during the first visit of the Moscow Art Theatre when his short play *The Lady from the Provinces* had been given as a curtain raiser to *The Brothers Karamazov.* Though well-known as a dramatist to Russian theatre-goers, he was a comparative newcomer to the English-speaking stage. His best-known play, *A Month in the Country,* had been seen in London only recently, and had never been given in America before the Guild's presentation.

Russian scenic artist M. S. Dobuzinsky had done the settings for the Moscow Art Theatre's production of *A Month in the Country* in 1909. When the Theatre Guild began making its plans for the local production of the play, it wanted to duplicate these settings. Dobuzinsky's sketches were secured and executed for the Guild by Raymond Sovey. Finally, Rouben Mamoulian was selected to direct the cast, headed by Alla Nazimova, recently liberated from "years of routine motion picture work."

A Month in the Country had its American premiere at Washington, D.C.'s National Theatre on March 10, 1930, and mixed notices were again the order of the Guild's day. John J. Daly of the *Washington Post* believed the Russian offering to be "one of the most unusual plays of the season," while Mabelle Jennings of the *Washington News* described the Turgenev book as "very much ado about very little . . . a pretty middling creaky gig." Of Nazimova's Natalia Petrovna, the *Washington Times*' Andrew R. Kelley wrote, "I could never become partisan to her misery"; however, Daly declared that "in a role somewhat different than those she has portrayed in her last appearances here, she proves herself to have mounted in stage stature; to have grown in her art—so that now she is the quintessence of artistry." The distaff side of the critical press shouted: "Ah, Nazimova, we have waited overly long for you!"

As expected, when *A Month in the Country* opened at the Guild Theatre a week later, the New York critics reacted in basically the same way as their confreres in Washington—some with enthusiastic praise and others with angry disapproval. While Robert Littell believed the play to be "fresher and more modern than dozens of plays born in 1929 or 1930," with its "delicate portraits of people unsuccessfully but not tragically in love with each other," Brooks Atkinson registered the dismay so many others already had felt that season in observing the Guild's frequent preference for producing bad scripts. After labelling *Month* "by modern standards a dull and maundering play . . . from a dramatic period hardly worth preserving," Atkinson states that, "especially in view of several good modern plays that the Theatre Guild has declined to produce, it is difficult to understand why they should go out of their way to produce this one." In contrast, Arthur Ruhl thought the play "had received at the hands of the Guild company about as perfect a performance as any American group of players could well be expected to give," while Gilbert W. Gabriel praised the uniqueness of Russian literary experience as its characters' "small lives weave lightly but ever grievously into some larger substance known as Life. The secret of this fine, brooding mood is a secret only the great Russian playwrights have learned. Perhaps Chekhov learned it from none else than Turgenev." Yet another reviewer, in taking up the Chekhov-Turgenev comparison, believed *Month* showed "clearly that Turgenev deserves to be remembered more as a novelist than as a dramatist, that he has not, for instance, Chekhov's gift."

One review in particular was a tribute to the Guild's acumen:

> It is enough that for once sunlight has been let into a Russian play. It floods a charming room and lights a pleasant landscape. As a rule, the American idea of producing a Russian play is to shroud it in gloomy shadows. Our eyes grope through it wearily and darkness settles heavily on our souls. All this is enough to make us suspect that the sun never shines in Russia. But Turgenev, with the sensible aid of the Theatre Guild, has dispelled this ridiculous notion. There is sunlight in Russia, and blessed be the Guild! [Charles Darnton, *New York Evening World*, March 22, 1930]

And finally, Burns Mantle wrote an article in which he attempted to analyze the Guild's position in the Broadway milieu that had emerged throughout the recent years. Professing sympathy for the Guild, which now had "another passive comedy success" even while it was issuing a statement as to the bigger things it hoped to do the following season,

Mantle expressed confidence that despite the Guild's failure to produce an outstandingly popular attraction that year, it would yet meet the demands of its newly acquired road commitments. The last paragraph in Mantle's article was an attempt to pinpoint the Guild's most recent failings:

> Having created . . . competition in its own field, the Guild has, I think, been slow in accepting and planning to meet it. It has held a little tenaciously to its earlier policy of continental importations, and these are no longer either as novel or as interesting as they were when their contrast was fresh. [*The Cleveland News,* March 30, 1930]

The nineteenth-century Russian drama had just cost its backers $14,519 during its ten-week New York run, and, although it was one of the few shows that the Board felt confident enough to send out on tour that year, one of its more practical accomplishments proved to be that it had introduced a young actress named Katharine Hepburn to Theatre Guild audiences when she was substituted in a minor role.

The Guild's next scheduled attraction was possibly calculated to dispel a bit of its reputation for being "the house of unimpressive importations." *Hotel Universe,* while having an exotic locale, was nevertheless the serious, experimental product of American playwright Philip Barry, who had earned a reputation as a writer of light comedies such as *Holiday.*

The *Hotel Universe* opening, as was the case with most Guild openings that year, was held out of town, with the critics' reports from Newark, New Jersey, foreshadowing the controversy which was to rage whenever and wherever the play was given. "Either you will be greatly intrigued with 'Hotel Universe' . . . or you simply will not care for it," wrote the *Newark Star-Eagle*'s reviewer Elizabeth Perkins, whose elaboration indicated that first-nighters were evenly divided between those who laughed in the wrong places and those who remained seated and applauded while the curtain was lowered and raised half-a-dozen times after the final scene. "It is all very strange, very beautiful, and very true," she concluded. Part of that strangeness was the method used by Barry to make "time stand still," reported Jerome Kurtz of the *Newark Ledger,* a method by which "his characters lapse into a reverie wherein they live parts of their lives over again." The *Jersey City Journal* considered it "the most unusual play . . . ever seen . . . . a queer mixture of fantasy, tragedy, comedy, philosophy, and poetry... with moments of grandeur, or boredom, of dramatic triumph, of an unusual type of comic relief, and of delicious satire." There is much beneath the play's surface, it was noted, enough indeed to make the shallow playgoer or critic treat humorously those serious moments which should be receiving the keenest attention. Unfortunately, "so many playgoers hate to make the effort... to see the beauty of its philosophy, and so many want to be constantly amused, that it seems doubtful as a hit."

An item had appeared in the *New York Times* on February 2 concerning Arthur Hopkins' initial reaction to Barry's proposed script. "I don't think there's a play in it," said Mr. Hopkins, whereupon the *New York Times* article concluded that a parting of the ways "so far as Mr. Barry and Mr. Hopkins are concerned" was nearing. This article prompted Hopkins' rejoinder which was printed two weeks later:

> Will you kindly say that there has been no estrangement between Philip Barry and myself? Will you also say that from the first I have been deeply interested in Mr. Barry's new play, "Hotel Universe"? In it he traverses new territory and shows definite growth—but I believe the play needs the early support that is assured it by a Theatre Guild production. No serious work into which an author has put himself unsparingly should be exposed to the hazard of sudden Broadway closing, such as befell Sidney Howard's play "Half Gods."

The Guild's managers next sent their controversial new product to upstate New York for a week. Possibly they felt more time to polish it was needed by the playwright, who was accompanying the troupe as it traveled. *Hotel Universe* thus started its second week at the Erlanger Theatre in Buffalo on April 7, 1930, and that city enjoyed "a mystical, unique and exciting drama which is the high point of our year of theater reporting in Buffalo.... It is propelled by an emotional stream, almost torrential... which must sweep aside the speculation of more materially-minded persons as to the meanings of this or that episode." In the same review by Ardis Smith of the *Buffalo Times,* there was a report on an interview with the author of *Hotel Universe*:

> Mr. Barry doesn't believe the legitimate play stands in slightest jeopardy through the weed-like growth of the talking picture. He is a bit snooty about this, it seems to us. For he said: "There's show business and there's theatre. The theatre will continue. It goes into doldrum, now and again, but it will survive. You know,

> I was very much interested in the moving picture before it took to sound. It really was beginning to be an art of exquisite pantomime. As for the talkies, I think their producers are too much inclined to adopt the theatre pattern."

The interview concluded by inferring that Barry had been a bit dissatisfied with the movie derived from his *Paris Bound,* which had starred Ann Harding; for, it seemed, the producers had held rather too closely to the original script for his taste.

Robert Garland, theatrical critic of the *New York Telegram,* alluded to this review in an article written a few days before the New York opening:

> Up Buffalo way Mr. Philip Barry's "Hotel Universe" is in process of being cheered. The critic for the Times goes so far as to admit that the Theatre Guild has every reason to be proud of its new production, although the words the critic used are "the plasticity of time," "the evanescence of reality" and "the concreteness of dreams."
>
> But perhaps these high and mighty phrases best not be mentioned . . . for what looks like a boost to a dramatic critic is frequently a boo to a press agent. Consider, as a genteel example, the case of Mr. Robert Sisk, the usually gracious and always gifted gentleman who writes little pieces about the Theatre Guild in the hope that they'll get into the paper. He and I have been known to differ where the infallibility of his Guild and his Guilders is concerned.
>
> Only last week, when Mr. Barry's latest dialogic endeavor was trying its wings in the presence of Newark's theatregoing intellectuals, I, out of the goodness of my heart, reprinted one or two of the next day notices. To these eyes, the reprinted notices were right smart swell. They came right out and admitted that Newark and the Newarkans were mystified—and what could be more heartening than a mystified Newark, unless it were a mystified Newarkan? . . . But Mr. Sisk was irked, irked as anything. And, when Mr. Sisk is irked, he doesn't mind saying so. In consequence, I was reached on the telephone and, metaphorically speaking, taken out behind the woodshed. It was, as you can see, in the spirit of nice, clean self-defense. Self-defense on the part of the Guild, I mean. So far this season, the Guild has been a wayward boy, and from afar I could sense the chip on the Siskian shoulder.
>
> . . . .

> Having seen "Hotel Universe" in Newark during its tryout period and admired it tremendously, I am well aware that when next Tuesday's review—in case you've not been notified, Mr. Barry's "evanescence of reality" comes to the Martin Beck this coming Monday—appears in print, praising the work prodigiously, the Telegram will be reinstated in the Guild's good graces and Mr. Sisk, himself, in person, will be happy to set them up when we meet at Tony's.

Garland's prediction, however, concerning *Hotel Universe*'s New York reception was only partially fulfilled, for after the play had opened in New York on April 14, 1930, the Guild was forced to use a rarely employed device in its "review" advertisements. Under the heading, "There Seems to be a Difference of Opinion," in one column it ran excerpts from the favorable notices—opposite this appeared bits from the unfavorable reviews. Such was the division of critical opinion that the raves and the adverse comments were about even. Conveniently, a reader could compare a judgment of his favorite reviewer with that of fellow critics. Such professional theatregoers as Robert Littell, Brooks Atkinson, John Anderson, John Mason Brown, Walter Winchell, and Charles Darnton stressed the play's deficiencies. For Littell, "the secrets of life and death" had come through "as thick and miscellaneous a fog as a dramatist ever spread on his own trail toward an inexpressible idea." Winchell, who found the proceedings "greatly fatiguing" and regretted the lack of intermissions, finally "limped away with a headache," so dispirited was he by this vehicle, "so glum and frequently given to the ravings of a crew of neurotics." Atkinson felt that "as far as characterization is concerned it remains very much on the surface. It is easier to make bricks without straw than it is to suffuse mental posturing with life." Anderson, recognizing Barry's capacity for what he called the "vaguely searching, very sensitive, and very glib," preferred addressing the play by such terms as "muddled and incoherent"—as though its altering moods were given no unity. John Mason Brown, after praising the accomplished direction of Moeller and Simonson's atmospheric setting, called the play itself a disappointment. And Darnton could only conclude that it was all "very strange and woolly and weird.... It couldn't have been harder to produce if it had been a dramatization of the Einstein theory."

On a more favorable side, the play did have stout champions: Bruce Gould, Stirling Bowen, Whitney Bolton, Gilbert Swan, Richard Lockridge, and, of course, Robert Garland. Garland could now say to his readers that "if the living, breathing, thinking theatre means anything to you, I advise you not to miss it . . . this is the sort of thing the Theatre Guild was created to achieve." Bowen praises the Guild's "hopeful and imaginative mood" in putting on such a production, "one of the most disturbing, or exciting." For Bolton it was "an earnest and beautiful play, a thing of blinding force and gigantic stature . . . moving across a trajectory that forces and holds unfalteringly every resource of the mind and eye." Swan chose to compare the play's importance with that of the playwright's earlier *White Wings* which, when about to close, brought half the "who's who" of the writing and art world together to publish a petition calling upon the public to keep it alive. Swan also wrote that for him *Hotel Universe* was far and away the most interesting thing the Guild had done. Percy Hammond, however, in trying to be sympathetic, could only believe the play to be far from his own grasp as well as that of most other playgoers: "I felt an embarrassed urge to cry out to Mr. Barry: 'Wait a minute! I didn't quite get that! Pray say it over again.' As it was, the night's pleasure was modified considerably by the feeling that I was but a yokel, astray in the court of Thespis, trying his best to join the proceedings and failing."

It is stale accusation that drama critics go into huddle to talk over new plays during intermission and thus arrive at an opinion. But, as Walter Winchell pointed out concerning *Hotel Universe,* "the most amusing comment is the N. Y. Amusement Guide's observation . . . . ''S funny that those widely diverted opinions occur over a play that has no intermission or chance for conclave.'"

Hotel Universe did run throughout the summer months, no doubt aided by the critical controversy which raged over it. It also succeeded in losing $16,433.06 for the Guild during the twelve weeks it played.

The final Guild-sponsored offering of the year was to be a new edition of the *Garrick Gaieties,* one that would be judged in comparison to the first two *Gaieties* of 1925 and 1926, which were characterized by the pertness of the preformances as well as the quality of the music and lyrics provided by the then unknown pair, Richard Rodgers and Lorenz Hart. Richard Dana Skinner of *Commonweal* focused on a number of these contrasts, remembering in the first "the magic of gay irreverent youth" pervading the air: "It was all deliciously fresh and spontaneous, rash in spots but clever nearly always." The new edition of the *Gaieties* had lost, according to Skinner, "the fresh audacity which breaks forth when a group of youngsters are on their mettle to do or die." Lost, too, were Rodgers and Hart, "although the metrical lyrics of Hart are freely copied throughout." Gone were Romney Brent, Libby Holman, Betty Starbuck, and June Cochrane. But while talent like Edith Meiser, Sterling Holloway, Philip Loeb, and Hildegarde Halliday had remained, "another element has entered in. There is now an increased undercurrent of false sophistication—of the kind, that is, which still believes that the only worthwhile form of wit is that which hovers around bedrooms." Skinner did, however, delight in one of what he called "those particular scenes . . . that merely indict the rest of the show the more heavily":

> *They Always Come Back,* easily the best comic-opera version of New York politics ever put into a review. This one number comes the nearest to catching the full magic of the old Garrick Gaieties and the Grand Street Follies rolled into one. It tells of the return of Grover Whalen to his great department store, and comes to a climax with a song, "Johnny Wanamaker," which emits nothing short of Gilbert and Sullivan genius. The music by Kay Swift and the lyrics by Paul James have the classic stamp. [*The Commonweal,* June 18, 1930]

Percy Hammond also commented on this same sketch, and upon the angry reaction it caused from ex-police commissioner Whalen, the target of the ribbing: "The Guild makes sport of Mr. Whalen's abdication, and pictures his return to Wanamaker's in a cruel cartoon in which he is represented as something of a stuffed shirt, applying the law's iron hand to the gentle ways of commerce." It was a caricature, brutal and amusing, successfully portrayed by Philip Loeb. The former commissioner, now weak without his power, could only rage at the Guild's showing, which a month before he could have closed down "as an infraction of the laws prohibiting indelicacy." As Hammond put it, the Guild was honor-bound to comply with Mr. Whalen's desire to have the offensive sketch eliminated from the show in order to obey some unwritten rule which "protects ex-celebrities with oblivion."

The Guild, however, did not remove the skit from its revue. In fact, it was one of the few pieces retained in the revamped fall edition of the *Gaieties,* which featured, among other additions, much-needed material by Rodgers and Hart, Herbert Fields, and the debuts of young comediennes Rosalind Russell and Imogene Coca. For the present, however, the *Gaieties* clung to all manner of amusing snippets to entertain its audiences: a sneer at a Chinese Julian Eltinge and at the blue-blooded ladies "who glorify mattresses and cosmetics with their aristocratic hallelujahs in the magazines."

Despite a few obvious triumphs, the Guild had hardly achieved a remarkable record during the 1929–30 theatrical season, as indeed the press attested to by such samplings as an interview with Lee Shubert or some waggish dactyllic verse published in the *New Yorker.* Lee Shubert, after a moment's pensiveness, told his interviewer that in the past the Guild had had good intentions with its policies, "good things in the theatre, big things, and not just to make money." Shubert continued:

> The Guild gets actors cheaper than do the other fellows. Why? They do it on the assumption that the organization is uncommercial. They get their actors that way and their subscriptions that way. But the Guild, in spite of its greed, has had its share of bad plays and will continue to have them. I'm tired of its "king-can-do-no-wrong" attitude. The Guild is money-mad and should admit it. [*The New York Sun,* Feb. 24, 1930]

A poem in the *New Yorker* written by Arthur Guiterman was called "Plea to the Theatre Guild":[5]

Hope of the Drama in Gotham's locality,
Cease to forget your presumed nationality!
Say, is the world of the playwright a semisphere?
Isn't there anything good in this hemisphere?
May not Peorians, even Bostonians
Prove as exciting as Czechs or Livonians?
Banish the plays of the cultured Bulgarians,
Fathoms beyond our untutored barbarians!
Garnish your stage with indigenous scenery,
Village, metropolis, office or beanery;
There let explorers of human inanities
Show us our manners, futilities, vanities,
Social, domestic, commercial, political,
Viewed with an eye sympathetic though critical.
We've had enough of the grim Bolshevistical,
More than enough of the talky and mystical
Magyar, Bohemian, Norwegian, Batavian
Even the British including the Shavian.
Give us no more of the deep sophomorical
German verbosities called "allegorical,"
Pale Celtic moonshine and such esoterica!
Be a Columbus! Discover America!

[5]Reprinted by permission; copyright 1930, 1958 by The New Yorker Magazine, Inc.

Understandably, the members of the Board of Managers were becoming increasingly nettled with what they construed to be anti-Guild propaganda. One meeting, apparently, had been given over completely to a discussion of adverse reactions in the press. The Board was especially concerned about a recent article by George Jean Nathan—possibly because it implied charges of commercialism—which came on the heels of a financially most unsatisfactory season, in which almost $112,000 had been lost. This article, appearing in the *New Freeman,* assailed the Guild on a number of sensitive points. The six-director system, according to Nathan, had "become a group of talents pulling against one another," and that, in turn, had created an indecisiveness as to the nature and quality of plays to be presented. Nathan went on to list some of the finer scripts the Guild had turned down, while "the more individualistic American commercial theatre produces the new plays of such men as George Kelly, Vincent Lawrence, Elmer Rice and George Kaufman." Even in its chosen field of offering predominantly European imports, the Guild, Nathan felt, had failed to scout the field adequately to find the best available, but rather had chosen such a museum piece as *A Month in the Country* to cash in on a vogue for the Russian, instead of selecting one of Chekhov's works "which has all the elements of modernity and sound dramatic worth that the antecedent play lacks." The Board of Managers' reaction to this article was recorded in its minutes: "It was felt that Nathan's last article in the *New Freeman,* attacking the Guild, could be answered out of his own mouth but the wisdom of this was dubious." Certain measures, however, were advocated to stem this tide of fault-finding in the press, namely:

1. Use of the Guild magazine to answer charges.
2. The securing of special articles in favor of the Guild's production policies by well-known writers—for which they would be willing to pay.
3. Occasional large parties for the press.
4. Lecture propaganda in New York and in subscription cities.

Later in the year George M. Cohan, acknowledged dean of America's actor-producers, was interviewed concerning the Guild's position in the theatre. He gave the following laudatory account of its accomplishments—without thought of reimbursement (as far as can be ascertained):

The Guild has had and is having a bitter fight. I think no single organization ever aroused such jealousy along Broadway, but sensibly enough, its managerial board has seemed to take no notice of these things. . . . From the Guild I have gathered its subscription figures, which show something of its growth.

It started with 150 subscribers. Now there are 34,000 subscribers in New York and about 45,000 on the road. In Chicago alone, where the Guild plays a regular winter season, it had 15,000 subscribers last year; in Philadelphia about 10,000; in Boston about 8,000. In a one-week stand like Baltimore, which has been considered a poor show town at various times, the Guild has about 5,000 followers and slightly more in Pittsburgh. Its growth, then, has been phenomenal.

The reason I am interested in the Guild is that it is the kind of theatre we didn't know in this country when I was growing up. We had, of course, the fine stock companies and there was Augustin Daly's troupe, but in this country we have the Guild to thank, I believe, for the somewhat international aspect of New York as a play producing center. There have been many who have claimed that the Guild should have produced more American plays and the Guild answers that a search of the records will reveal that they have produced more plays by Americans than by authors of any other nationality. When Eugene O'Neill had signed to let the Guild do some of his plays, among them "Marco Millions," there was an effort to get me to go into the role that Alfred Lunt later played.

I couldn't see my way to do it. . . .

But it brought me into my first direct contact with the Guild and its people interested me. I found, for one thing, that Miss Helburn was an intelligent and shrewd woman and that her associates also knew their way around. They are peculiarly stubborn people and often will produce a play they know is going to lose a lot of money simply because they think it ought to be produced, and they are as independent as theatrical firms come. During the past year I think this was sweetly demonstrated.

. . . .

The serious talkers of the stage often say that the Guild has improved audiences in New York. I believe this and I do know that it has helped the road enormously. Its strength outside New York is widespread and growing all the time. One reason for this, I figure, is that when they announce a series of plays they deliver what they announce.

> In 12 years the Theatre Guild has gone through its pains and aches, but it now seems firmly established. It has its own fine theatre on Fifty-Second Street, built by a popular bond issue which was over-subscribed in two ways, subscribed by people who were willing to take income bonds, meaning that they would only draw a dividend if the theatre earned one. No dividend has ever been skipped and I'm told that the Guild has bought back many of the bonds long in advance of their redemption date, so that it practically owns the theatre now.
>
> Its subscriptions lists in New York vary but little. For one thing, the books are closed in June for the season to come and because it has never put on whirlwind campaigns for its subscribers, those it has are faithful and renew from season to season. Where actors are concerned it hires them for long terms and keeps them working. Actors like this. And the Guild apparently likes it, too, for the same actors appear continually in their casts. . . . [Springfield (Mass.) *Evening Union*, Aug. 2, 1930]

During the year various directors of the Guild had been engaged in altercations other than those directly concerned with their productions. For instance, Theresa Helburn had had it out with John S. Sumner, secretary of the New York Society for the Suppression of Vice, over censorship matters connected with the stage in general, and Lawrence Langner had argued with Jed Harris over the proper way to end ticket speculation along Broadway. Harris proposed establishing a central ticket agency to take orders from people who lived too far away from the theatre district to obtain their tickets directly. Langner countered by pointing out such a plan had been vetoed previously by the smaller producers, and offered instead a plan whereby ticket sales would be handled by an "impartial committee" composed of representatives from Actors' Equity, the Dramatists' Guild, theatre owners and producers, the ticket agencies, and the public—represented by former Governor Alfred E. Smith. Meanwhile, Rouben Mamoulian had rather peevishly quit the Guild to start producing on his own, about which more will be said later.

Two of the 1929–30 Guild productions, *Red Rust* and *Hotel Universe,* were included in several of the year's "ten best" lists compiled by New York drama critics—although, interestingly enough, the Guild usually had held options, at one time or another, on well over half of the honored scripts. One observer, summing up the year's outstanding achievements, cited a fair share of the Guild's performances:

. . . the unforgettable scene in "The Green Pastures" of the march of the Hebrew children . . . the conversation of the char angels who cleaned up the Lord's office, the entrance of Jericho, the characters of the Lord, Noah, Gabriel and Hezdrel, and the work of the actors who played those noble parts . . . Mr. Jed Harris's magnificent production of "Uncle Vanya". . . . Alfred Lunt in "Meteor". . . . The scene in "Hotel Universe" in which the men return to the games of their childhood and then slowly begin to take them as the most important problems in all the world. Edward J. McNamara's engaging, if realistic, portrait of a policeman in "Strictly Dishonorable." The hearty, slightly ribald humors of "Children of Darkness," a literary play that acted, and the valor and dramatic incisiveness of the significant and critical drama from Soviet Russia called "Red Rust." The comedy of Helen Broderick, as the bored American tourist, in "Fifty Million Frenchmen." The assistance supplied current musical comedies by Cole Porter's willingness to write musical scores for two of them. . . .

The acting of Claude Rains in two Theatre Guild productions, "The Game of Love and Death" and the garrulous Shaw editorial, "The Apple Cart". . . . The fascination of Katharine Cornell in the cheap, but compelling, "Dishonored Lady". . . . The lyrics of "June Moon" and the deceptively engaging hilarity of the Lardner-Kaufman play, which apparently hides from so many people the essential bitterness and contemptuous viewpoint of the comedy about song writers. . . . [Richard Watts, Jr., *New York Herald Tribune,* May 9, 1930]

The Guild's managers, incidentally, continued to think highly enough of the Philip Barry play to include it in their *Anthology* (published in 1936) where it shares space with thirteen of the organization's other stellar accomplishments, including Werfel's *Goat Song,* Shaw's *Saint Joan,* and O'Neill's *Strange Interlude.*

Some of the bonuses the Guild was justly proud of having offered its New York subscribers during the 1929–30 season, besides the "extra" play, *Red Rust,* were admission at reduced rates to the *Garrick Gaieties* and to three of its road shows, *R. U. R., Marco Millions,* and *Volpone,* which it brought into the city for one-week stands. A special performance of Sue Hastings' Marionettes and a talk by Mrs. Patrick Campbell on the art of beautiful speech, as well as free admission to other lectures and symposia, had also been included.

In May Theresa Helburn went to Europe on a "working vacation" to scout for available manuscripts. In June the Guild announced a list of plays from which it would choose six of its productions for the 1930–31 season. These included *Elizabeth the Queen* by Maxwell Anderson, *Green Grow the Lilacs* by Lynn Riggs, *Roar China* by S. M. Tretyakov, *Distant Drums* by Dan Totheroh, *The Genius and His Brother* by Sil-Vara, *The Lonely Way* by Arthur Schnitzler, *The Good Soldier Schwejk* by Jaroslav Haschek (as produced by Piscator), *Spiegelmensch* (Mirror Man) by Franz Werfel, *Much Ado About Nothing* by Shakespeare (to be produced and designed by Robert Edmond Jones), *The House of Connelly* by Paul Green, *The Coward* by Lenormand, *Lysistrata* (a modern version of Aristophanes' play), *Dog Eat Dog* by Katherine Clugston and Hamilton Crook, *In The Meantime* by Claire and Paul Sifton, and *Conjur* by Margaret Freeman.

The Guild next announced that its Saturday night prices would thereafter be no higher than its week-night admissions. It was the general custom along Broadway then to add fifty cents, plus tax, to box-office scales on Saturday night. In most instances the Guild had maintained a week-night top price for its attractions of three dollars, and the reasons it gave for the change of policy were: 1) because of the government tax of 10 percent on tickets over three dollars, the added revenue from the increased Saturday night scale was slight, and 2) the computation of tickets on the same basis for all nights simplified the handling of the extensive subscription lists, both in New York and out of town.

In an interview, Theresa Helburn was quoted as saying that the Guild feared no competition from sound films. She pointed out that the Guild had produced some seventy-four plays since its inception, and of that number not more than four or five had been sold to the picture makers. Their audiences' expectations were just different. She concluded by saying, "The men who are interested only in the commercial side of the theatre seem to be turning to pictures—and they should. They can make much more money." Interestingly enough, Miss Helburn later became a motion picture producer herself.

Other managers, notably the Erlanger offices, were refurbishing their far-flung road theatres with the idea of following the Guild's example of sending out companies to present their better productions. They promised that "these companies will play authentic New York hits at sensible prices and the actors will be selected for talent rather than an ability to ride day coaches without a murmur." Taking such emulation as a form of flattery, the Theatre Guild clearly faced its 1930–31 season more concerned with artistic problems than with either the Great Depression, then barely a year old, or the potential competition presented by the omnipresent talkies.

CHAPTER 4 / 1930-31

Roar China, S. M. Tretyakov
Elizabeth the Queen, Maxwell Anderson
Midnight, Claire and Paul Sifton
Green Grow the Lilacs, Lynn Riggs
Miracle at Verdun, Hans Chlumberg
Getting Married, Bernard Shaw

According to at least one competing producer, Gilbert Miller, the Theatre Guild was largely responsible for the influx of artistically satisfying productions which had become a substantial part of the Broadway scene. An informal poll taken at the close of the 1929–30 New York theatrical season revealed that of the thirty-eight non-musical plays then appearing, the greatest number of financial successes, about 90 percent according to the gross box-office receipts as listed in *Variety* (the recognized authority on such mysteries), were those which might be termed highbrow by the Shuberts. It was also noted, however, that at least twenty theatres were dark along the Great White Way at the end of this Depression-ridden fiscal year, presumably because the theatregoing public had less money to spend on entertaining itself and was either going to the movies or staying at home with the radio. Undeniable, too, was the fact that few good scripts had been available for production, and those that had "caught on" had become so highly prized by the ticket scalpers that the prices for hit attractions had become almost unmanageable for the average legitimate theatre buff.

The Guild, which had just weathered a generally poor season, editorialized in its magazine about an accepted phenomenon in Broadway producing practices, possibly forgetting its own slenderly financed beginnings of a decade before: "An industry in which a penniless man can produce a play with ten thousand dollars of borrowed money with the chance of making some hundreds of thousands of net profit, is obviously one which attracts all sorts of speculators and parasites." The writer added that the *Theatre Guild Magazine* would record with relish the woes of those producers "who endeavor only to suck the maximum amount of money out of the public without undertaking to guarantee real value in return," suggesting that the public could be fooled into buying spurious theatre much more readily than it could be induced to invest in, say, inferior real estate, and that the Guild's publication would gladly undertake the role of playgoer's guardian.

In July, Lawrence Langner replied in the *Theatre Guild Magazine* to a letter asking about the adverse criticism the Guild had sustained in the New York press. This letter contained a query as to whether the Guild's relatively small advertising budget had anything to do with this seemingly undeserved and harsh censure. Langner, naturally, assured the letter writer that this belief was groundless, remarking that the New York critics had been the Guild's enthusiastic supporters in former years. He pointed out, also, that expectations for the Guild were so high that "we are apt to be blamed for what we do not do, just as much as for what we do." His reply concluded with the prediction that the pendulum of critical opinion would swing the other way before too long, and with a parting crack at George Jean Nathan, asserted that certain reviewers, because they were unable to praise, felt they must chastise "for the same reason that some husbands beat their wives."

Needless to say, the Guild's directorate keenly felt the need to reassure its subscribers concerning its artistic policies, and, responding to a demand for worthier offerings, presented a list prepared by its publicity director of the New York season's most anticipated productions, with the Guild's coming attractions slightly underscored. This cataloguing, which included plays to be produced by Arthur Hopkins and Sam H. Harris, among others, announced the Guild's determination to present several premieres of rising American playwrights' works with Maxwell Anderson's *Elizabeth the Queen* first, to be followed by Paul Green's *The House of Connelly* and Lynn Riggs' *Green Grow the Lilacs.*

Early in its planning for the new season the Guild had announced its intention to open more of its new attractions outside of New York City, following its recent experience with *The Apple Cart* in Baltimore, as well as with *Hotel Universe* in Newark and Buffalo. In keeping with this policy, the Lunts had been sent to Philadelphia late in the summer to prepare for the premiere of *Elizabeth the Queen* there; shortly following this, the show was to be brought into New York as the first attraction of the 1930–31 subscription season. It became obvious, however, that more time-consuming rewriting than had been believed necessary was going to be required from Maxwell Anderson. It was decided, therefore, that New York's opening presentation would be a modern melodrama by a little-known Russion playwright, S. M. Tretyakov.

Roar China, which had been originally produced at the Meyerhold Theatre in Moscow some four years before, had been in rehearsal with the Guild only since September 29, less than a month from its opening date. Herbert Biberman had been selected to direct this semi-propaganda piece, much to the dismay of Rouben Mamoulian who argued that his prestige in Russia would suffer if he did not prepare the production. The Board sustained its decision, a decision which troubled Mamoulian to such an extent that he asked to be released from his contract. Later in the year, Mamoulian's defection would loom large in disputes which aroused all the managers' passions enough to threaten the group's solidarity.

The Guild's board, having decided to limit carefully all 1930–31 production costs, assigned a budget of $12,305 for *Roar China,* to cover costumes, props, and scenery. Considering this restriction, Lee Simonson must have performed near-miracles in designing *Roar China*'s unique setting, which he described, with understandable pride, in a later article:

> Biberman then conceived the idea of using sampan sails as a scene curtain. They floated in a tank behind the front stage ramp. The tawny, interlocking sails formed a curtain which almost hid the gunboat; only its topmast was dimly visible. At a cry of "Sampan, sampan" they parted, gliding with incredible grace to stage right and left, where their sails in shadow gave the suggestion of a river front harbor. As they opened the warship was dramatically revealed, in towering, menacing silhouette. . . . The device provided me with one of the most beautiful theatrical curtains I have ever seen in the theatre.[1]

A goodly number of *Roar China*'s pre-opening night press releases, as well as its producers' jitters, were occasioned by the fact that Chinese actors were to comprise almost 80 percent of the production's large cast, of which about half were amateurs. Indeed, ten of the players spoke no English whatsoever. This, undoubtedly, made it necessary for

[1]Lee Simonson, "Settings and Costumes of the Modern Stage," *The Studio* (Winter, 1933), p. 98.

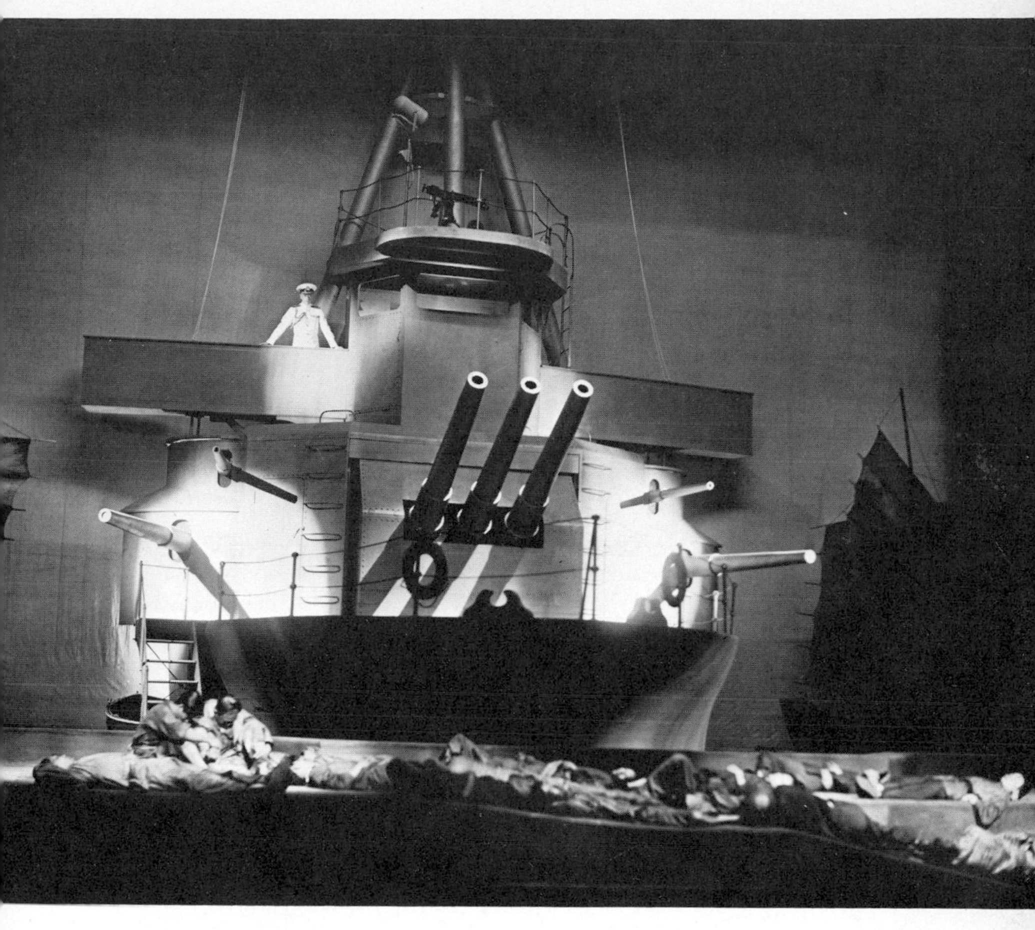

ROAR CHINA – Lee Simonson considered this striking set one of his finer accomplishments. The sampan sails at either side literally floated in to serve as a scene curtain. Edward Cooper is on the bridge as captain of the symbolically named "H. M. S. Europa."

Oppressed "coolies" lie in the foreground.

Biberman to assume the role of an authoritarian director who acted out every key scene and insisted it be slavishly imitated. Because of this, disagreements arose among the Board members concerning interpretations of the European roles and whether or not this was a proper method to assure artistic integrity for the production.

Roar China opened at the Martin Beck Theatre on October 27, 1930. The reviews the next morning, although slightly tongue-in-cheek, tended to praise the Guild for its willingness to experiment, but deplored the fact that a melodrama, with unquestionable propagandistic overtones, was the opening fare offered New York by its first theatrical organization. Percy Hammond compared it with *Uncle Tom's Cabin,* while Gilbert Seldes thought the message of proletarians versus an oppressor out to exploit their heritage was not even good Marxist doctrine. All the criticisms, however, were enthusiastic about the scenic designer's resourcefulness, which featured extending the stage's playing area out to include Row A of the orchestra.

According to at least one modern theatre historian, Communist Party leaders had realized that theatrical ventures in New York City could assist them in influencing the masses. They therefore seized on any production which seemed to illuminate or foster the struggles of the proletariat as worthy of their careful attention. *Red Rust,* and now *Roar China,* both fell into this category.

> The Marxist press complained that the Guild had once again distorted a Soviet drama. The reviewer for the *Daily Worker,* Myra Page, provided a long list of deviations from the "original text." The producers, she said, failed to refer to the Soviet Union by name; they prohibited the cast from waving a red flag in the finale; and they blurred class distinction within China. The critic for *New Masses,* Leon Dennen, added that the Guild's directors had shortened the part of the Communist organizer and that they had substituted final prophecy of world peace for the original prediction that the Chinese would soon destroy the English. Despite these changes, both reviewers commended the play for its anti-imperialistic plot and for the sincere acting by the untrained Chinese cast. The sight of real Chinese proletarians on the stage was especially thrilling to Communists. If you were unable to see the original Moscow presentation, the *Daily Worker's* critic advised, the Guild's production was worth seeing in spite of its many errors. . . .[2]

[2]Morgan Y. Himelstein, *Drama Was a Weapon—The Left-Wing Theatre in New York,* 1929–1941, p. 128.

Later in the season, the Theatre Guild's managers turned down an offer from Freiheit, a leftist organization, to guarantee thirty performances of *Roar China* for New York and elsewhere, because they felt they could not permit themselves to offer one of their attractions solely for propaganda purposes.

Although *Roar China* ran for seventy-two performances, it lost a great deal of money for the Guild, over $31,000 according to one estimate. This was undoubtedly due in part to the enormous size of its cast, but more probably because the public at large somehow did not evince an overwhelming interest that year in Oriental impoverishment or enslavement, no matter how urgently it may have been touted in the leftist press.

Even if the slim possibility of Broadway's being taken over by the Communists was suggested, a more immediate concern to producers of "highbrow" stage plays at the time was the increasing scope and maturity of the cinema. More and more the talkies were being dignified by serious criticism in many publications. The exodus of acting and producing talent from Broadway to Hollywood often took on alarming proportions: George Arliss, Ruth Chatterton, Basil Rathbone, Roland Young, Joan Bennett, Ann Harding, Chester Morris, Raymond Hackett, Sidney Blackmer, Paul Muni, Jack Oakie, Robert Armstrong, Marguerite Churchill, Claudette Colbert, and Eddie Cantor had all succumbed to the golden lures of the California movie lots. Who could blame them? Few summer jobs were offered in legitimate productions, and the periods between Broadway engagements forced even the most popular theatrical personalities to supplement their theatre work with motion-picture activity.

Although one of the great stage hits of the 1930–31 season was George S. Kaufman's and Moss Hart's *Once in a Lifetime*, "a classic flaying that not only strips the hide in neat ribbons from the Cinema City, but has the added exquisite torture of salting the open wounds left by this stripping," a number of talking pictures were more than holding their own artistically. *All Quiet on the Western Front*, adapted from a German war novel, was being compared favorably with *Journey's End*, which had shortly preceded it, and was considered to be the first example of the talkies' using a staccato style of cross cutting with a "ruthless insistence on realistic detail." George Arliss had also enriched "both the cinema and the drama, as well as the historical record," when he brought to the screen his outstanding characterizations in *Old English* and *Disraeli*. Even the British movie makers were doing notable work with such plays as *Juno and the Paycock*.

In fact, the most successful talking pictures were usually those based on stage plays, although few Theatre Guild scripts had been used. The apparent reason for this was that most Guild plays just were not the type of fare usually sought out by movie producers for a mass audience.

Deploring the drift of talent to Hollywood, the Guild had editorially suggested a plan to keep the best playwrights working in the theatre:

> It would actually pay the theatre as a whole to support ten of our worthiest dramatists with an annual contract guaranteeing them at least twenty-five thousand dollars a year, provided that the theatre had the benefit of their work. For without the work of the dramatists, the investment of millions in theatre buildings is just so much money lost. Yet not one of the so-called brilliant commercial managers has ever thought of the theatre in terms of continuous employment to a dramatist, who must either write hits or nothing, and if he cannot write enough hits to subsist upon —well then, he is welcome to take himself off to the talking pictures, which know how to appreciate talent and pay for it.[3]

A recent returnee from Hollywood, Maxwell Anderson, was the next author produced by the Guild. Because of the less-than-thrilling notices *Elizabeth the Queen* had received when it opened at the Garrick Theatre in Philadelphia on September 29, 1930, the Board of Managers decided to send the production to a number of its "outer fringe" subscription cities to give the playwright an opportunity to make some needed revisions. A few of these reviews stated that "there is no dash, no sparkle, no lustiness whatever" in this "cold historical romance"; that *Elizabeth*'s second act was old-fashioned, stagey, and episodic; and that the all-over impression created by the over-blown costume drama was "unmistakably draggy and unenthralling."

The first stop for *Elizabeth the Queen* after Philadelphia was Ford's Theatre in Baltimore, where it began a week's engagement on October 13. The critics of that city were somewhat kinder to the play, although they indicated that there was still room for improvement. Gilbert Kanour of the *Baltimore Evening Sun* felt that it had a certain distinction, "but not of the kind out of which masterworks are evolved." Baltimore reviewers, nevertheless, were among those who sung the praises of Lynn Fontanne's brilliant acting in the title role:

---

[3]Lawrence Langner, "Hit It or Miss It," *The Theatre Guild Magazine* (May, 1930), p. 14.

> Tender, hard, wise, crafty, selfish, forgiving—Elizabeth is all these as portrayed by Miss Fontanne. She dominates Maxwell Anderson's drama at every turn. She overshadows everybody and everything. True, the Guild has selected an excellent cast, as usual, and the production shows the same upper-strata stamp that marks all this worthy New York organization's work, but Lynn Fontanne's projection of Elizabeth is what will carry the play to whatever measure of success it reaches. [Norman Clark, *The Baltimore News,* Oct. 14, 1930]

After Baltimore *Elizabeth* travelled to Pittsburgh's Nixon Theatre for a week, where it appeared that the script had been further strengthened as the Lunts' famed ensemble playing became ever richer in its refinement. When the company reached Erlanger's Grand Opera House in Cincinnati on October 27, most of the wrinkles had evidently been ironed from Anderson's historical-dramatic fabric. The reviewers in that city were unanimous in approval of the Guild's latest achievement. Several dwelt on Miss Fontanne's unflattering makeup, which consisted of a crimson wig, unmistakable folds of flesh, a putty nose, and shaved eyebrows that suggested perfectly the unattractive Elizabeth of several seventeenth-century prints. Others spoke of the sumptuousness of the court setting and the costuming, all of which had been budgeted at a mere $13,525.00. At last, the Guild felt, *Elizabeth the Queen* was ready for its New York debut.

A number of metropolitan critics were unhappy, however, with what they saw when the long-awaited *Elizabeth* opened at the Guild Theatre on November 3, 1930. John Mason Brown of the *New York Evening Post* thought the piece as a whole "somewhat negative and negligible." Gilbert Seldes was a bit more specific, finding that the last act was unsatisfactory, while the Philadelphia reviewers had thought that the second act was weakest. Richard Dana Skinner, on the other hand, claimed that the *opening* scene was the worst—"stiff and awkward." Seldes also felt that Anderson had failed to personalize his characters enough, "to put them into our skins and us into theirs." Robert Littell found fault with the play's "humdrum, flat language," while others thought that most of the dialogue had a "distinctly Shakespearean flavor." Robert Garland applauded the script after it had appeared in book form: ". . . it seems that Mr. Anderson has written more worthily than he has been given credit for . . . a flight of imagination in which the English language leaps and glows."

ELIZABETH THE QUEEN – Alfred Lunt and Lynn Fontanne.

Despite these conflicting opinions regarding the merits of the play, the one undeniable fact was that the Guild's first actress was close to the peak of her considerable powers in the role of Elizabeth. "One of the greatest exhibitions of histrionic skill in recent years. . . . Lynn Fontanne is ever dynamic, interpretive, and magnificent," wrote Thomas R. Dash, and Burns Mantle agreed completely: "Miss Fontanne's performance . . . has taken the town. In every way it is her greatest personal triumph."

Elizabeth the Queen made money for the Guild during its 147 New York performances plus those elsewhere—about $45,000 according to the conservative estimate of the Guild's business manager. It is obvious, of course, that whatever success the production attained would be due to Miss Fontanne's virtuoso performance—which became *the* thing to see—instead of the sterling qualities of the play itself.

In December, during the run of *Elizabeth the Queen,* the Guild began rehearsals on a production of *Much Ado About Nothing,* which Robert Edmond Jones was to direct as well as design. Lunt was scheduled to play the haughty Benedick, and Lynn Fontanne was to be the caustic Beatrice. Other members of the *Elizabeth the Queen* company were to perform important roles, and it was announced that this attraction would alternate weekly with the Anderson play. Jones, however, experienced unexpected difficulties, as related by Theresa Helburn in *A Wayward Quest:*

> In *Much Ado About Nothing* he had started with what he believed would be a tremendously effective and different way of presenting Shakespeare. On either side of the stage, Bobby had the respective dressing rooms of Lynn Fontanne and Alfred Lunt. As he had supposed, the audience watched in fascination while the famous couple changed costume and put on make-up. What he had overlooked was the simple fact that he was not merely exploiting the Lunts, he was producing a play, but with the audience's attention riveted on two characters who were "off stage," the main action might as well have been taking place in another theatre. Bobby finally realized this staging was untenable, changed his mind, and ended with a totally different idea. [p. 190]

The producers halted Jones' *Much Ado* before its promised New York opening. Langner later referred to this ill-conceived attempt to capitalize on the Lunts' popularity as one of the Guild's greatest artistic defeats, this "failure to stage decently one of the simplest plays of Shakespeare." He suggested various reasons for the collapse of the enterprise. One, of course, was that the Board had been misled by Jones' novel "production scheme." Another was that the organization's acting company had become so dispersed, and its level of competence so questionable, that Jones' presentation had been miscast in some instances and poorly acted in others. A third reason Langner gave was that the Board, contrary to its customary and primary function, had either been unable or unwilling to help Jones when he was in obvious trouble. These contentions, along with others, caused serious rifts among the managers.

Other practical considerations offered by Board members for not going ahead with the *Much Ado About Nothing* production included Maurice Wertheim's feeling that, because losses for the season had already been so heavy, it would be prudent to continue uninterrupted the profitable run *Elizabeth the Queen* was enjoying. Anderson's historical drama still had eleven weeks to play on the road to fulfill out-of-town commitments, and the twenty-odd weeks left in the Lunts' New York engagement, Miss Helburn reminded her colleagues, had better not be dissipated by the couple's indulging in an untried offering—which could not possibly be shown for more than eight weeks, no matter what its reception. For a time the Board thought there might be a way of salvaging or modifying Jones' original idea, for reasons of prestige. Langner recommended turning the direction over to one of the Board members, but Philip Moeller insisted it would be impossible for him to do it. Finally, Equity began demanding an increased salary for the cast because of the extra rehearsal time it had been required to spend on *Much Ado*. Regretfully, the decision was made to abandon the project, which would have been the Lunts' first attempt at classical comedy. In March, *Elizabeth the Queen* left New York to play Boston, Washington, and other stopovers along the subscription route, while what had promised to be an intriguing Shakespearean performance, along with the revival of one of the Guild's pet undertakings—alternating repertory—was shelved after costing its producers nearly $23,000.

On December 1, 1931, the organization's next offering, under the working title *In the Meantime*, was to have its premiere at Ford's Theatre in Baltimore. This Moeller-directed "melodrama of ideas," as it was to be advertised, had been written by a husband-and-wife team, Claire and Paul Sifton. Sifton was feature editor of the *New York World*, and he and his wife, apparently, were deeply interested in current social problems.

In presenting a play with social overtones—the theme of which was that capital punishment is never a crime deterrent, that it hardly upholds the majesty of the law, and that when the law and practical politics come into conflict, political considerations eventually are victorious—the Guild was quite in step with a recent tendency in the American theatre "to take shots at some of our national customs, foibles and idiosyncrasies."

After the opening in Baltimore, all the reviewers commented on the play's lack of polish. Norman Clark of the *Atlantic City Union* found it a novelty to hear a "prompter's voice crying in the wilderness offstage" in a Theatre Guild production, while Louis Azrael of the *Baltimore Post* thought the Siftons were "poor dramatic economists. . . . If the business of the theatre could permit it—and it can't—the thing to do would be to hand the play back to its authors for a few months, so they could re-work it entirely."

The production's next stop was Washington. From there it moved to Pittsburgh, where George Seibel of the *Sun-Telegraph* considered *In the Meantime* a confusing study in conflicting styles: "The architecture is by Sardou, but the atmosphere is by Ring Lardner, and the moral is by H. L. Mencken."

The less-than-enthusiastic press reception *In the Meantime* had received caused the Guild's Board of Managers to doubt seriously if it would be wise to let New York see it. Moeller, its director, thought it would be better to bring in another production, *Green Grow the Lilacs,* then in preparation. This substitution was vetoed, however, when it was pointed out that rushing through its necessary script and cast changes might prove fatal to that production. Wertheim was opposed to showing New York anything that was not going to raise the Guild's artistic reputation, and Simonson suggested that the city's critics probably would be harder on *In the Meantime* than the road's critics had been. But Langner felt that, while the Sifton's melodrama might not be a particularly good play for the road, it might have a good chance in New York. Besides, there was the very real financial consideration of having the Guild Theatre dark for an extended period if there were nothing to fill it. So, it was decided to continue with the production as scheduled. It was sent to the Court Square Theatre in Springfield, Massachusetts, on Christmas day—with its name changed to *Midnight.* Less than a week later, on December 29, 1930, *Midnight* opened at its producers' headquarters to be judged by its first New York audience.

As Simonson had feared, Gotham's critics hardly found *Midnight* a vehicle to bolster Theatre Guild prestige. The kindest of them felt that, as melodrama, it was sometimes exciting; another thought it was "soundly acted"; but the majority shared John Mason Brown's opinion that *Midnight* found the Guild at anything but its best, doing rather badly a play it should never have bothered doing in the first place.

Having moved to the Avon Theatre on January 26 for the balance of its run, *Midnight* closed after its forty-eighth performance. This melodrama of sorts lost slightly more than $17,000 for its producers. This comparatively modest figure was due, no doubt in part, to its having been done in modern dress and with a conventional setting.

With the 1930–31 theatrical season half completed, it would have been quite in order to speculate whether or not the Guild's Board of Managers were going to produce anything of merit that year. As had happened before, worthwhile scripts had been scorned only to be sensitively and successfully produced by other managements. In December, for instance, Eva Le Gallienne and her Civic Repertory Company opened in an original American play instead of their usual classical revival. This was Susan Glaspell's *Alison's House,* which purportedly told the story of Emily Dickinson's family after her death, and which the Guild had turned down the year before. *Alison's House,* "full of ideas and perceptions," succeeded in capturing the Pulitzer Prize for the 1930–31 season.

The members of the Guild's management, meanwhile, had been concerned with wondering if poorly written experimental plays could be brought to life with exciting, original staging techniques; or, if it would be wise to extend its list of six promised productions to include as many as its budget would allow, as extra nonsubscription programs.

After repeated frustrations the Guild's directorate soon became involved in internal bickerings, not uncommon in an organization where carefully nurtured projects are constantly going awry. A case in point was the Board members' censure of Maurice Wertheim for being absent from certain rehearsal meetings. Wertheim countered by noting that such criticism probably arose from monetary considerations, "because these objections were never raised during the years while I was taking no compensation from the Guild." Since he felt, however, that his major concerns lay outside the Guild, he was willing to have his rate of compensation changed. As it is recorded in the minutes for December 23, 1930, Moeller, Langner, and Simonson resented Wertheim's imputations and said their criticism was based solely on the fact that Wertheim had overstepped his bounds in discussing the state of Guild productions in rehearsal when he had not attended any rehearsals. Wertheim missed few managerial meetings after that. Such fault-finding, however, would become more pronounced among the Board members as the theatrical year progressed.

In the meantime, a new Guild production opened under Herbert Biberman's direction which once again revived interest in its producers as a vital force in American experimental theatre.

Lynn Riggs' *Green Grow the Lilacs* had its premiere at Boston's Tremont Theatre on December 8, 1930, and the critics were universally captivated by this long-considered presentation featuring real rodeo performers in its cowboy roles. "Frankly, this . . . is for the most part so fresh and natural that it is easy to enjoy" was the enthusiastic first reaction of E. F. Harkins of the *Boston Record,* while Katherine Lyons of the *Boston Traveler* felt that "talented Lynn Riggs, who if failing as a playwright would have his poetic gifts to rely on, has written more play than plot." Philip Hale of the *Boston Herald* came closer to the truth than he even suspected in suggesting that Riggs' script might serve as a libretto for an opera or operetta, since "the chorus is already introduced, and there are cowboy songs for genuine cowboys brought on to give 'realism' to the scenes."

Only the acting, in some important instances, was found to be ragged. The authentic Westerner, in the role for which baritone Lawrence Tibbett had first been considered, was found "plainly remembering and accomplishing what Mr. Biberman had schooled him to feign and suggest." In a meeting at the Ritz Hotel in Boston the day after *Green Grow the Lilacs* opened, the Board of Managers decided that several changes ought to be made. For instance, they suggested that the play should be rewritten with more emphasis on comedy and less on the sadism of the shivaree scene. This "would avoid the overstressing of the neurotic note that has crept in . . . . The shock of the girl should come from the death of Jeeter rather than from the brutality of the men." More importantly, when the play reached Ford's Theatre in Baltimore on January 12, Franchot Tone had been substituted in the role of Curley McClain, the romantic cowhand, and from the reviews that appeared in the Baltimore papers one gathers that the production was in fairly good shape.

When Riggs' play of the Oklahoma Territory opened at the Guild's home theatre on January 26, the consensus of Gotham's criticism seemed to be pleasant surprise that folk drama could be so much fun. Most of the reviewers felt that the Guild, accused the previous season of having been a house of imports, had now presented the American scene with heartwarming alacrity, without ostentation, and with definite poetic charm. "Clean gusts of prairie wind blow through it. White moonlight gleams on its haystacks. The odor of crumbly black loam is in it," wrote Baltimore's Louis Azrael.

There was, as might be expected, quite a lot of good-natured ribbing done at the expense of this "ruralized" production, but, on the whole, critical reaction was entirely favorable—even if it did not indicate a smash box-office success. The Guild's managers, nevertheless, had proven again that, when given to honest experimentation, they worked as a team to make a *succès d'estime,* and even a modest financial gain, from a poetic American folk play which included such "untheatrical" elements as a loose story line, cowboy ballads, and amateur actors.

Finally, of course, *Green Grow the Lilacs'* most important contribution to Theatre Guild history was that it provided the book for Rodgers and Hammerstein's first musical play, *Oklahoma!,* which the Guild later produced with such overwhelming success.

Even with the brief lift that the satisfying reception of *Green Grow the Lilacs* must have afforded the Guild's Board of Managers, they soon realized that Riggs' type of play would not be good for much more than a run of eight weeks in New York. They had been preparing Arthur Schnitzler's *The Lonely Way* under Moeller's direction, with a tryout period in a few of their subscription cities. But it became increasingly apparent that the production would take a good deal longer to get into shape than at first thought necessary. In fact, there were serious doubts whether it would be wise to show *The Lonely Way* to New York at all. As it turned out, after costing the Guild more than $18,000, it never was "brought in."

To fill the gap, it was suggested that Shaw's *Getting Married* be put immediately into rehearsal using a director from outside the Guild's ranks. Helen Westley, who was appearing in *Green Grow the Lilacs,* objected to this, feeling that the Guild should not do a Shavian comedy without her portraying one of the principal roles. Lee Simonson seconded these feelings, but Langner objected to the Guild's doing plays for the benefit of its Board members, saying that it was contrary to the spirit of the organization. He said, furthermore, that Moeller, Simonson, Miss Westley, and Biberman were constantly making decisions which were influenced by possible opportunities for themselves. This accusation, of course, was resented by the four, but Langner refused to retract his statement and indicated he would try to sort out his feelings and present them to the Board in the form of a memorandum.

Trouble also arose over a proposal by Simonson concerning the management of Guild funds. Wertheim believed this indicated an attack on his financial acumen, and Simonson unsuccessfully tried to make it clear to the banker that the proposed changes were based on a desire to safeguard him from any needless imputations by relieving him of much undue responsibility. With such unfortunate animosity, possibly a trifle humorous when viewed in retrospect, the Guild was preparing for its next New York attraction—one which would all but bring it to the verge of bankruptcy.

This fifth and ill-fated production was Hans Chlumberg's *Miracle at Verdun,* for which the Guild's publicity drums had begun beating early in the winter. The press provided appetite-whetting articles concerning this last work of this Austrian poet-dramatist who had died at one of the rehearsals for his play in Germany two years before. *Miracle at Verdun* concerned the resurrection of countless soldiers from that great battlefield's international cemetery and ironically showed the unenthusiastic reception they received upon returning to their former homelands. Advance opinions from the continent rated *Miracle* as something of a masterpiece. "Herr Chlumberg's name promises to be among the most widely discussed of next season's playwrights in New York," wrote John Mason Brown in the *New York Evening Post.*

The Guild made staggeringly extensive preparations for this antiwar play's American premiere. For example, talking pictures were used as an integral part of a legitimate stage presentation for the first time, not as an adjunct but as a part of the storytelling process. Three separate screens were employed, with different pictures projected on each, "to achieve a contrapuntal dramatic effect." John E. Otterson of Electrical Research Products and Joseph Coffman, of the Audio-Cinema Corporation, helped the Guild prepare these filmed scenes, for which Aaron Copland composed a special musical score. Four major film corporations also cooperated with the Guild in securing the films for other sequences. The libraries of the Fox Film Corporation, Paramount, Universal Pictures, and Kinograms were opened to the Guild and their officials aided in assembling the materials for the experiment.

When *Miracle at Verdun* opened at the Martin Beck Theatre on March 16, 1931, without having previously appeared on the road (possibly because of the highly technical nature of the production), the critical reactions were mixed, but few could be considered enthusiastic. One of the most devastating reviews was by Dorothy Parker; it appeared in the *New Yorker,* where she was substituting for Robert Benchley, the regular drama critic. Miss Parker found the Guild's production "pompous, pretentious, pseudo-artistic, and stuffy":

> The acted scenes of the play are alternated with moving, and occasionally, talking, pictures; but even had they been good, or at least not terrible, I cannot see how they could have added anything but confusion. Possibly it is considered that there is something pretty doggy, something Continental and *moderne,* in doing a piece in more than one medium, but, as worked out by the Guild, there is little to the notion—perhaps it is essential that at least one medium be happy. [March 28, 1931]

In contrast to Miss Parker's tartly amusing article, there was another written for the more austere, religiously oriented periodical, *The Commonweal,* which also tried to decide what was wrong with the latest Guild presentation. It found that the real trouble with the play "lies deeper than its experimental combination of sound screen and stage, and deeper than its loose-jointed dramatic construction. The trouble is in the color and emphasis and direction given to the theme itself by the author—in the attitude it presents toward the meaning and purpose of life and death." Richard Dana Skinner continued by taking the Guild to task for not having noted the script's lack of "universal significance . . . of any deep poetic feeling and sense of universal drama." He suggested that the animated corpses should not have wandered back to their graves beaten and discouraged, but should rather have laughed with knowledge founded on the release they have won from this "valley of tears."

Because of *Miracle at Verdun*'s less than enthusiastic notices, the Board held council a few days after the play's opening to discuss what they could do to salvage the production from predicted artistic and financial devastation. Theresa Helburn and Langner criticized Herbert Biberman's direction, stating that they thought the acting possibilities had not been realized because the director had projected his interpretation arbitrarily upon the actors. Biberman defended his methods by comparing them to those of Max Reinhardt in that the director knew in advance exactly what effect he wanted, and therefore should be free to project his interpretation literally rather than wait for an actor to catch it himself and possibly miss it in the process. There was also a discussion of possible promotion angles for the

MIRACLE AT VERDUN – Lee Simonson designed this set so that the monument at left yawned back to disgorge its "corpses" during the Resurrection scene.

On steps, left of center, Claude Rains.

seemingly moribund production. Among the several suggested were the soliciting of opinions from well-known people, a debate between members of the press and members of the Guild concerning the merits of the play, and the sending out of a form letter to the Guild's membership incorporating selected quotes in the play's favor.

Then, if their woes were not piled high enough, the Board ran into a possible suit concerning the movie rights to Chlumberg's script, which they had not acquired, and which they presumably had violated when including filmed material in their presentation. It soon became apparent, however, that the Guild was not the only organization to lose money on *Miracle,* for Joseph Coffman of Audio-Cinema sent a plea regarding his company's expenditures, asking that the Guild help out with costs that ran well above the original estimates. The Board refused this request on the grounds that their own losses had been excessive.

Despite attempts at resuscitation, *Miracle at Verdun* lasted only forty-nine performances, even though Lee Simonson's unique settings had been an outstanding accomplishment, and several members of the cast had received excellent reviews. For instance, Claude Rains as the Belgian minister gave "one of his electric performances, biting his way into the play like etcher's acid," and Germaine Giroux was "all vivacity in less important roles" (there had been much doubling of parts).

It is also interesting to note that even if the orientation of *Miracle at Verdun* was slightly left of center, its presentation was not widely heralded by the Communist press. Some believed, though, that the play, with its episodic structure, its device of resurrection, and its sentiments against war, was the forerunner of Irwin Shaw's more radical drama *Bury the Dead.*

It had been decided early in March that Clare Woodbury should replace Helen Westley in the role of crusty Aunt Eller on the road tour of *Green Grow the Lilacs.* This would allow the Board's actress member to be on hand for important Guild meetings—and, incidentally, free her to play the part of the Mayoress in Shaw's *Getting Married,* which was to be the organization's last offering of the year.

Shortly thereafter, Lawrence Langner offered a set of proposals to the Board of Managers that was headed, for reasons to become apparent, "Strictly Confidential." In it he charged that the artistic orientation of the Guild had changed over the years from a group of individuals working for a group ideal—"the best plays to be done in the best possible way"—to a set of personalities—three artists, and three "business minds." Also, he asserted, a policy of "asking" had become established among the artistic members—asking to direct, asking to design, asking to act—and other gifted artists outside the Board were never considered to fill these roles if a Board member, specifically Moeller, Simonson, or Mrs. Westley, wanted to occupy them. Langner went on to charge that this took any inspirational value out of Guild work for the three "non-artistic" members of the Board, and, quite possibly, had led to a decline in the artistic capabilities of the group as a whole. There also seemed to be no direction to the work the Guild was attempting, but rather a simple process of parceling out the work to the artists, Biberman included, who felt, because they had "enthusiasm" for a particular script, that they could turn in an exceptional production. Langner reasoned that the Guild was being held down to the level of how far its two staff directors could progress.

He then began to quote instances: Moeller, he admitted, was a good director of comedy, but when it came to scripts of deep emotional values, or experimental American scripts, or scripts where he did not respect the author's capabilities, or indeed, even Shavian comedies, his contributions were limited. He also charged that Moeller had no interest in developing the talents of new actors but could only use actors of proven talents, such as Lunt and Fontanne, to advantage. Thus, *Midnight* and *The Lonely Way* had both been killed by Moeller's inability to instruct tyro cast members in their business. Langner also mentioned Moeller's patronizing attitude toward American authors, such as S. N. Behrman, Philip Barry, and Maxwell Anderson, and his attempts to "rewrite" their scripts, which had infuriated them. Unfortunately, it had become a matter of course for over 50 percent of the Guild's productions to be handled by Moeller, so the Guild as a whole had to suffer for his defects as well as benefit from his strengths. Langner suggested Moeller do some directing away from the Guild to alleviate some of his weaknesses.

Next, Langner mentioned Lee Simonson, who "time out of time remarked that he would keep Mamoulian off the Board because he could not work with Mamoulian, and this would result in his doing less scenic work for the Guild." Langner then charged that talented designers such as Robert Edmond Jones, Norman Bel Geddes, and Jo Mielziner were given little or no opportunity to work for the Guild because it was considered as settled that Simonson would have first pick of any shows he wanted to design, and those he didn't were given to men of "lesser importance." Langner concluded that Simonson should not be given a series of plays to do for the Guild, but should be considered along with other designers for each production as it came along.

Herbert Biberman was the next to receive Langner's censure. He, apparently, also had fallen into the policy of having preferences and of "asking." Langner stated that Biberman's directorial results all came from having actors imitate him, which was perhaps all right with amateurs, but not with professionals, for it did not make use of their hard-won technique or their creativity.

Helen Westley was the last "artist" mentioned in Langner's missive of discontent. He objected in general to her implied feelings that productions should be rescheduled until she could conveniently appear in them; or, even that certain plays should be done so that she might star in them. Langner's opinion was that while she was a first-rate character actress, she could not be counted on to put across a play by herself. In other words, she was not the sort of actress that Ethel Barrymore, Katharine Cornell, or Lynn Fontanne were, meaning that she did not have the following necessary to "carry" a production. Langner concluded that if other actors could not ask for parts in Guild productions, Mrs. Westley should not be allowed to either, even if she was a member of the Board of Managers.

Another complaint that Langner made concerned Theresa Helburn's being mentioned in the press as "the ruler of the Guild, and the person responsible for its work." Here, he felt, the existing policy should be enforced that no personal interviews should be granted unless it was promised that first they would be submitted to the person involved for verification before publication. In Miss Helburn's case, however, he felt that perhaps her ego demanded some sort of acknowledgment for services performed as the "artists" in the group were seldom willing to give her a fair share of recognition or credit. Langner felt certain that changes in the policies would have to be made to insure the continuation of the Guild as a united theatrical producing organization.

At the end of March, with the strong feelings of restlessness that Langner's memorandum must have engendered, the Guild was about to produce its sixth and final New York presentation for the 1930–31 subscription season. The managers decided to give but one out-of-town performance of Shaw's *Getting Married* before "bringing it in." This was to take the form of a one-night stand at the Playhouse in Wilmington, Delaware, on March 26, 1931. The opinion of one reviewer the next day was a mild indication of what was in store, for he wrote that

> perfect candor compels the confession that . . . the Guild has done its task in a capable, though at times uninspired, manner . . . . Whatever faults may be indicated, and they are numerous . . . should be placed at the doorstep . . . of Mr. Shaw himself. Even he would cheerfully admit that he has violated all the classic tenets of dramatic technique by writing a play that has little plot to speak of, no action, no character development, and hardly any love interest. He has made mere mouth-pieces of actors and actresses who have achieved a great distinction on the American stage and each, burdened like Atlas with the weight of the playwright's ideas, was obliged to forego any histrionic attempts at characterization . . . . [I. B., *Wilmington Journal,* March 27, 1931]

Four days later, *Getting Married* opened at the Guild Theatre in New York. The play's theme might be stated as "the boundaries of marriage should be circumscribed or amplified now and then, as the occasion demands, especially in the matter of divorce as a means of escape." Or, "the rules and regulations that govern a conventional marriage are childish, and adult people should be able to negotiate a more ideal contract to suit their personal tastes." The Guild's production included charming settings by Aline Bernstein. The critical opinion concerning the presentation, however, was not kind. "The Theatre Guild adds another quaint item to the relic-drama," wrote Percy Hammond (the play had been first performed in 1908), "and affords its subscribers an evening of inspection rather than entertainment." John Mason Brown was even more devastating: "the melancholy fact is that *Getting Married* is . . . one of the most trying and interminable bores that the present season has produced." The review also criticized Moeller's direction, saying his pace was slow, his touch heavy, and his casting, in some instances, unfortunate.

In all fairness, it must be stated that not *all* the New York press notices were this discouraging. One generally favorable report by Robert Garland had some complimentary things to say about a number of the actors. For instance, he felt Henry Travers made his points in an engrossingly subtle and sustained manner, "well-rounded and constantly delectable." Margaret Wycherly, an actress of standing and distinction, brought "humor and humanity to a role which, without them, would be deplorable," and Helen Westley's Mayoress was thought to be "Miss Helen Westley on a holiday."

Getting Married, of course, was hardly the prestige item or box-office bonanza that the Guild had hoped it would be. It lasted forty-

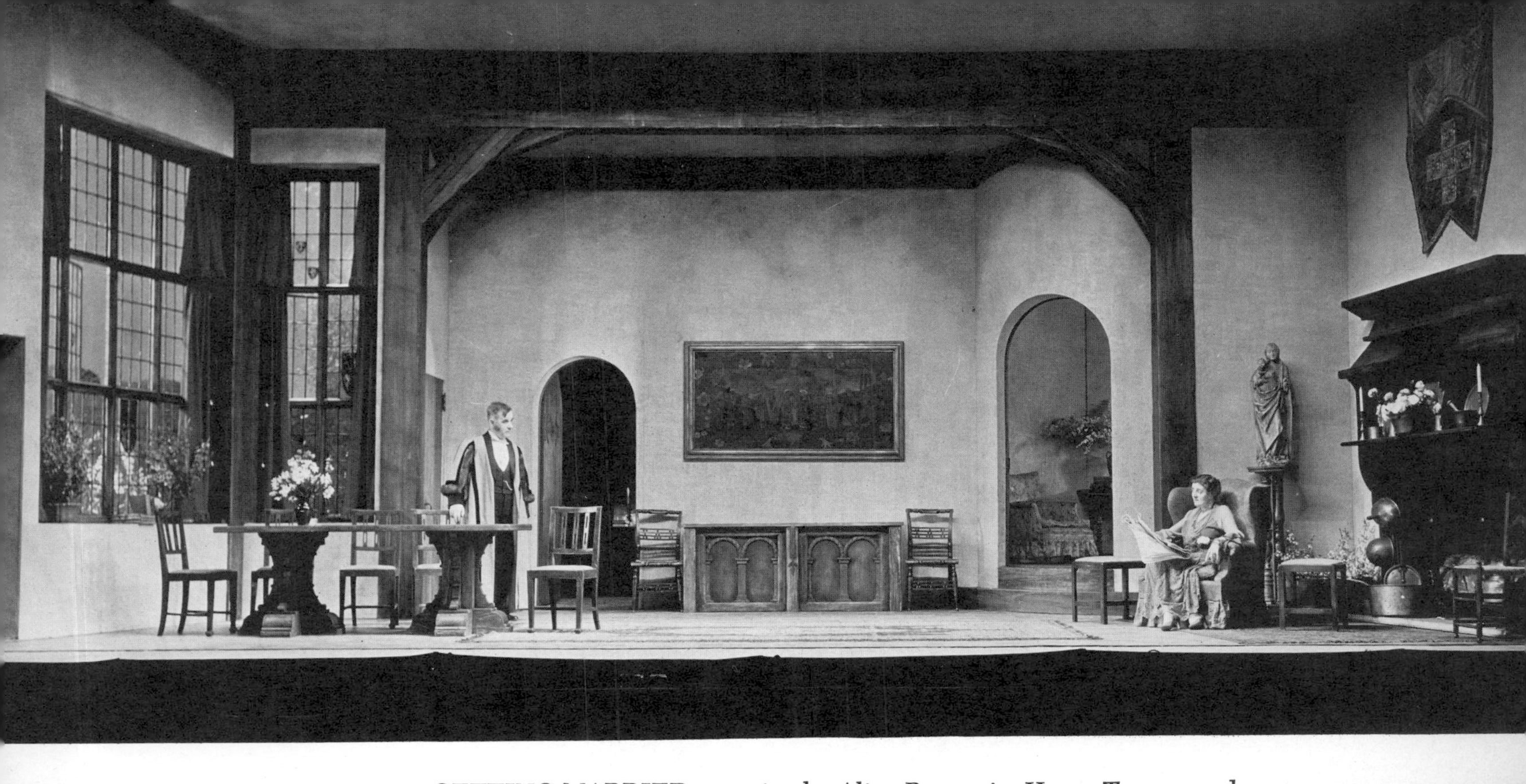

GETTING MARRIED – setting by Aline Bernstein. Henry Travers and Margaret Wycherly.

eight performances, accommodating the subscription list, and then departed, leaving an estimated $8,000 deficit in its wake.

A few days after *Getting Married* opened, April being the "cruelest month," the second of Lawrence Langner's memorandums was delivered to the members of the Board of Managers. In it he made rather specific recommendations for the future of the Theatre Guild in general and of the individual Board members in particular. Not too surprisingly, this document called for a complete reorganization of the Guild, its policies, and its method of operation. Comparing the present 1930–31 season with those of the past, he recalled that on the average four out of six productions had been at least artistic successes, of which at least two had been lucrative enough to carry those that had made little, if any, money. The present season, he maintained, had netted but two productions of any artistic merit out of eight attempts. On the financial side, the losses for the year had run well over $180,000, with *Elizabeth the Queen's* profits the only ones of any consequence.

Harking back to the Guild's former glory, Langner stated that after a disappointing season—the year they had moved into their new quarters—the formation of the Guild's acting company had led to a series of outstanding successes with the alternating repertory system, which culminated at the end of two seasons in the stunning renown of *Strange Interlude*. Once the Guild began to send its shows to a number of subscription cities (solely nourished, incidentally, by accomplishments of the acting company), this talented group slowly dispersed, with the resultant lowering of the Guild's acting standards. Gone was the famed ensemble playing; in its place was the foolish notion that retaining a few of the original players, with fumbling attempts to "scratch up" the balance of Guild casts, would result in maintaining a true acting company; whereas, in reality this led to nothing but miscast plays and generally bungled productions.

Langner went on to call attention to the notion that the debacle of the present season had left the Guild with few scripts of merit for the following season, and that he seriously doubted if it would be prudent to send a "substantial number of plays" on the road at all. He proposed reassembling the acting company, as far as possible, to do three plays in New York utilizing the alternating repertory system; then, to send this group, with their productions intact, to the subscription cities the following year. Another series of three plays could then be done with "outside guest players of the very highest calibre" to fit in with the schedule of promised offerings.

Shortly after Langner's second memorandum had been delivered, the three "non-artist" Board members presented an eight-point outline for operations, to the "artist" members of the Board. The ceremony, as recorded, consisted of Wertheim's offering, on behalf of Langner, Miss Helburn, and himself, a proposed *modus vivendi* to the Board's "artist" members. Simonson and Moeller evidently resented this proposal being presented to them as an ultimatum, but it was explained that, as the three "non-artists" had made up their minds, they wished only for acceptance or rejection of the points outlined. If accepted, the proposals would be put into effect; if rejected, "the Guild would have to discontinue."

After some discussion, Simonson, Moeller, and Helen Westley asked for a week to consider their position. Their answer took the form of two letters, dated only "April 1931," which expressed their belief that future Guild productions would have to be considered in the light of the Guild's slender financial resources, that an all-inclusive budget should be prepared indicating revised fees and salaries for everyone working for the Guild; that one of the Guild's problems in the past had been that it had not drawn up budgets for whole seasons, but instead had improvised financial arrangements from one production to the next; that this budget was imperative for future clarification of road policies as well as planning for the permanent acting company; that fixed fees should be assigned for directors, scenic artists, costumes, and for actors, as far as possible; and that fees for all managers should be kept at a minimum, which meant an abolition of the percentages now paid the Board. It was also maintained that this budget should be based upon the "normal expectation of failure, or artistic successes which show no profits, and not on the expectation of continued or inevitable successes which no theatre management has ever enjoyed."

The "artist" Board members then gave assurances that they would subscribe to a production committee-of-two scheme, whereby two managers would be assigned the primary responsibility of each offering in subsequent seasons, and that they individually would not seek to fill any of the creative jobs involved in the Guild's work, but would be content with whatever tasks they were asked to do by vote of the entire Board. Simonson, however, had reservations about the production committee-of-two scheme because he did not feel he had "the specific managerial ability called for and at no time has the Board convinced me that I had it"; also, he doubted if he would be able to design any of the Guild's shows during the coming year "for several personal reasons."

At a closed meeting held on April 12, 1931, after Moeller had read the memorandum signed by himself, Helen Westley, and Lee Simonson, and after Simonson had read the memorandum concerning the reservations he entertained, eight main points were adopted as guides for future operations:

1. All titles of members of the Board of Managers were to be abolished.
2. A production committee of two members of the Board would be selected for each play by a majority vote of the entire membership.
3. Biberman's contract for next season would not be renewed.
4. The abolition of percentages to members of the Board, and the substitution of a maximum fee of $100 per week for forty weeks for each Board member for attending meetings and rehearsals when called, and for reading plays; and an extra fee of $500 per play for each member of the production committees—flat salary to Miss Helburn (if she were secretary) and to Mrs. Westley (if she were under contract) on a replacement basis—flat compensation to Mr. Moeller and to Mr. Simonson per play, on a replacement basis, when they do plays, with neither being excluded from outside work.
5. No advance commitments would be given to members of the Board for production or scenic work.
6. At Board meetings, members were to conduct themselves in parliamentary and gentlemanly fashion, as freedom of discussion does not involve the use of offensive and insulting language.
7. A definite agreement by all on basic principles of Guild policy in accordance with a budget for operations would be drawn up.
8. Reduction of employees' salaries would be considered.

In addition, the Guild's managers, of course, did not exclude entirely the possibility of their receiving a cash dividend at the end of a season, if the working capital of the organization were not "reduced below a safe minimum."

Several other policy matters were discussed at this meeting. For instance, Moeller voiced a protest concerning Biberman's contract not being renewed, but realized a full-time director's rehiring "would be impossible under the revised conditions of our operations." Besides, it was explained, the refusal to renew Biberman's contract did not necessarily mean that Biberman would not be asked to direct for the Guild at some future date.

Cheryl Crawford's and Harold Clurman's plans for a "group theatre" as an independent yet auxiliary producing organization were also discussed. The Board went on record as wanting to know specifically what kind of cooperation this new organization would require from its Guild affiliation. Another point discussed was the possibility that the Guild would be unable to supply an entire subscription season outside New York City from its own output of productions. The "road," it seemed, was asking for offerings of proven substance. Langner and Miss Helburn therefore suggested that the Guild's repertoire outside of New York be augmented by productions made by other managers, such as Arthur Hopkins and Gilbert Miller. It was also suggested that a proposition be made to the Erlangers to combine the Guild's road attractions with those of other producers, especially those utilizing the Klaw-Erlanger road facilities.

And, finally, there was a discussion of Langner's pet idea for revitalizing the Guild's acting company, which, of course, would affect all future New York operations of the Guild. This led to the possibility of reviving outstanding Guild successes of former years. Wertheim went so far as to suggest that the Guild consider experimenting with genuine repertory. Miss Helburn and Simonson both concurred that true repertory would be the only possible method of developing an acting company of any real consequence.

The meetings immediately following these basic policy agreements were given over almost exclusively to hearing recommendations and proposals for desperately needed frugality measures. For instance, the managers felt that all percentages should be done away with, except for actors' percentages, which were somehow indispensable. They also discussed the possibility of not paying any interest on outstanding Theatre Guild bonds for the following season (an option the Guild was allowed by the farsighted nature of its income bond issue). It was decided not to renew the lease on the Martin Beck Theatre, but to hire it only when needed. Other measures included eliminating the technical and casting departments, reduction of salaries for business manager Munsell, and Miss Helburn as executive director, the last giving rise to some heated discussion:

> Mr. Simonson objected to the item of $11,000 for Miss Helburn, stating that he felt that the executive work might be done as a half-time job, even though this work included the casting. Mr. Moeller agreed with this and that the casting might and should be done by the director with a secretary in charge of the cards. Miss Helburn felt that this suggestion came with rather bad grace from Mr. Moeller and argued an ignorance of the amount of work done by the department in his behalf. Mr. Simonson stated that he felt it would be better not to have a member of the Board an executive as that made for inequality of power and consequent trouble in the board which could be avoided by the appointment of an executive secretary from outside the board.

Apparently Miss Helburn had foreseen this wrangle and had her resignation as executive director already prepared. It was unanimously accepted. Cheryl Crawford was then approached to undertake all executive duties for the following year, and she filled this position until conflicts with her Group Theatre work caused her to withdraw. Langner requested $4,000 to develop the acting company. If this were refused, he said, he would carry out his ideas elsewhere, even if it meant leaving the Guild. The play-reading department was cut; the telephone operators, as well as other office personnel, were cut; there was even talk of cuts in the publicity department. A number of actors' contracts also were terminated, and the Theatre Guild Studio was dissolved. The Guild was tightening its belt and digging in after the internal and external buffetings it had taken during what was undoubtedly one of its poorer seasons.

Only one Guild offering, *Elizabeth the Queen,* was mentioned in some of the "ten best" lists issued at the end of the 1930–31 season. A sampling of one such roster, compiled by Ward Morehouse for the *New York Sun,* named Lynn Fontanne's Elizabeth and Alfred Lunt's Essex as especially memorable. Other actors who received honorable mention (incidentally giving an indication of the range of fare offered New Yorkers during that Depression-ridden Broadway season) were

> Siegfried Rumann as the gross business magnate, Sam Jaffe as the dying bookkeeper having a fling, Hortense Alden as the desirable travelling companion-typist, Henry Hull as the desperate and bogus baron and Eugenie Leontovitch as the dancer in "Grand Hotel," the season's outstanding success.... Webb-

> Holman-Allen, that irresistible trio, in "Three's a Crowd" . . . . Granville Bates as the Bishop who plays the horses, Hugh O'Connell as the light-brained and nutcracking Dr. Lewis, Jean Dixon as his wise-cracking Hollywood associate, Leona Maricle as the world-weary reception room attendant and George S. Kaufman as the unhappy dramatist in "Once in a Lifetime" . . . Elissa Landi, an actress from the London stage, as Catherine Barclay in "A Farewell to Arms" . . . Herbert Marshall as Nicholas Hay and Zita Johann as Eve Redman in Philip Barry's strong and disturbing "Tomorrow and Tomorrow" . . . Ethel Merman as the throaty crooner of "I've Got Rhythm" in "Girl Crazy" . . . .

The Guild did allow another management to produce *Elizabeth the Queen* "west of Denver" to boost its earnings for the year. Pauline Frederick was seen in the title role of this Belasco-Curran production, with Ian Keith as her fiery and ill-fated Essex. William Keighley, then a Broadway director, was responsible for the new staging.

Thus, the Guild closed its 1930–31 season, a season which had not added much to its stature artistically—and certainly was a disaster financially—but which had been important for its reappraisals, its retrenchment, and its readjustment of policies.

CHAPTER 5 / 1931-32

He, Alfred Savoir
The House of Connelly, Paul Green
(A Group Theatre Production)
Mourning Becomes Electra, Eugene O'Neill
Reunion in Vienna, Robert E. Sherwood
The Moon in the Yellow River, Denis Johnston
Too True to be Good, Bernard Shaw

The Theatre Guild's first production of the 1931–32 theatrical year had appeared on stage the previous season, although not in New York. Alfred Savoir's *He,* which under its French title *Lui* was produced in Paris and had also been shown in London for a single performance at the Arts Theatre, was to be given in a new adaptation by Chester Erskin, a young director who produced for the Frohman organization, and who was subsequently hired by the Guild to direct this newest attraction. After one performance, presented at the McCarter Theatre at Princeton University on April 25, 1931, the production moved to Philadelphia's Garrick Theatre to open on April 27. Paul Muni was originally slated to play the title role of a lunatic who thought himself to be God, but the actor was not considered completely suitable, and Tom Powers, a veteran Guild performer, substituted. Powers was to have appeared in the late-lamented *The Lonely Way,* "but suffered a fractured leg," conveniently "forcing" the Guild to "postpone" the production.

The scheduling of theatre space in Philadelphia proved to be a tricky business, and for the last three days of its Pennsylvania visit *He* had to be moved to the Broad Street Theatre to permit *The Band Wagon,* a Max Gordon musical revue, to arrange the Garrick stage to suit its peculiar demands, which included installing a revolving stage (the first in American theatrical history), "and several other unique appliances, necessitating extensive alterations to the theatre before it can open." In the cast of *The Band Wagon,* which was to become one of the bright stars of that season's musical firmament, were Fred and Adele Astaire, Frank Morgan, Helen Broderick, and Tilly Losch.

The notices *He* received from Philadelphia's professional playgoers were anything but encouraging. Some believed the play, which had to do with a person claiming divinity suddenly appearing in a modern milieu, in this case a Swiss hotel, was treading on the toes of such venerable relics as *The Passing of the Third Floor Back.* Moreover, Savoir, usually a writer of airy and sophisticated comedy, was accused of delving into spiritual and theological premises with much the same frothiness that characterized his lighter work. J. B. Keen of the *Philadelphia News,* for instance, found the piece to be of little worth and instead, only a "psychological artifice concerning the unknown that has no more relation to dramatic literature than the hocus-pocus of sawing a woman in half has to surgery."

With such generally discouraging notices given its tryout attempt, the Guild received support from a totally unexpected source. As previously noted, George Jean Nathan had been anything but enthusiastic about the Guild's policies, but he liked *He*, and berated his Philadelphia confreres for having missed what he considered to be the thoughtful ironies, the satiric thrusts, and the sprightly handling of rather shopworn material that the production afforded. Having taken the Philadelphians to task, Nathan went on to laud Savoir's accomplishments:

> Instead of handling the whiffle in the habitual whifflish manner, with the quasi-divine character comporting himself after the mien of Forbes-Robertson dressed up for a funeral or after the basso elocutionary fashion of Walter Hampden, Savoir goes at the business with wit, and not only spoofs his characters but his audience and even himself. Yet what makes his play the entertaining job it is, is not this mockery so much as the critical intelligence with which, like some boozy boulevard Pirandello, he gives it a measure of body and substance. Burlesque Pirandello—that is perhaps the best way to describe "He." And burlesque Pirandello, take this department's word for it, makes pretty amusing theatrical fare. . . . The idea advanced by the Philadelphia boys that Savoir's point of view is lamentably blasphemous is perfumed with imbecility. "He," even to an unduly sensitive pew-holder, isn't—or at least shouldn't be—one-tenth so blasphemous as "The Servant in the House," "The Passing of the Third Floor Back" or any other such solemn theatrical cheat. . . . [*Judge,* May 3, 1931]

The production next moved to Boston's Colonial Theatre, and the critics of that city, possibly intimidated by Nathan's article, were rather noncommittal in their appraisal of the religiously colored satire and asked only if Savoir had not, at times perhaps, lost control of his theme in the welter of talk "about the nature of the Deity, and his traditional or hypothetical dealings with mankind."

Hard put for "road fodder," the Guild had been under criticism by its Chicago subscribers for not presenting its plays there in a continuous season. *He* was probably sent to Chicago for that reason, then held in abeyance until it opened September 21, 1931 at the Guild's home theatre. The New York reviewers, apparently not in the least impressed by Nathan's springtime defense of *He,* had hardly a kind word to say for the Guild's first Gotham offering of the new season. Thomas R. Dash of *Women's Wear Daily* thought the much-traveled, much-criticized attraction "not likely to add to the lustre of the Guild's scintillating record" and deplored the "academic exercise" quality of the offering. Only Claude Rains' impersonation of a Napoleon-aping hotel flunky roused any critical admiration for fine acting. Richard Lockridge thought the "fabric of the play not only thin, but full of holes," and found the presentation, on the whole, self-conscious, precious, and "no niggard at giving itself airs. It contains many of the vices of the Pirandello play—philosophical hollowness and pseudo-profundity, for example—without the dramatic power which is never absent from a Pirandello drama. . . . "

One of the few votes of confidence accorded *He* was printed in an unidentified French language newspaper. Unfortunately, there were not enough theatregoing Frenchmen living in New York to keep *He* running. It closed after its fortieth performance, which apparently did not aggrieve its producers greatly. The Guild actually needed its theatre empty to accommodate preparations involving the next attraction—one which must unquestionably be called one of the Guild's outstanding accomplishments with one of the masterpieces of the American theatre.

In tracing the various developments in the planning for the opening of *Mourning Becomes Electra,* as recorded in the minutes of the Guild's Board of Managers' meetings, one should keep in mind, of course, the arguments concerning artistic and financial policies that had shaken the Board during the closing weeks of the previous season. Some of the *Electra* planning had taken place even as early as the previous April.

On April 19, for instance, Langner offered two resolutions calling for reassembling the members of the old Guild acting company to rehearse three plays that could then be presented the following season. He knew, however, that his proposals would be affected by the Board's accepting O'Neill's Aeschylean trilogy—which meant that the Guild Theatre would be occupied for most of the season. Also, the casting of the O'Neill opus required personalities other than those the old acting company could provide. One solution seemed to be a repertory company, headed by the Lunts, to be housed at the Martin Beck, with the O'Neill presentations to be done at the Guild's home on 52nd Street using an outside cast.

On April 22, there was a discussion appraising O'Neill's script. While some criticized the play for its lack of subtlety and overtones and because, as Moeller phrased it, it was too big for its size, it nevertheless was considered to be extremely good theatre. After a decision to buy the script, Helen Westley suggested Alfred Lunt and Lynn Fontanne's appearing in it would make the play a definite "commercial asset." Lunt, she felt, should play both the parts of Ezra and Orin, the Mannon father and son.

On April 26 a new comedy by Robert E. Sherwood, entitled *Reunion in Vienna,* was voted upon. The Guild decided to buy the script immediately although Simonson had reservations, "feeling it very superficial." It was also decided by consensus that *Reunion* would be a perfect vehicle for the Lunts, and plans were at once formulated to discourage their consideration of O'Neill's manuscript, even if it might prove embarrassing if they should find *Mourning Becomes Electra* especially attractive and completely to their taste.

Discussion arose concerning possible directors for the two pending productions. According to Langner, Miss Helburn, and Wertheim, Moeller would be the ideal director for *Reunion in Vienna.* Hearing this, Moeller made it clear that he preferred doing the O'Neill cycle. This, of course, was a classic example of the conflict that had split the Board into "artist" and "non-artist" factions only a short time before. By vote, according to the basic agreement, Moeller was offered *Reunion* or nothing. He asked for time to consider his answer to this ultimatum. Thereupon discussion was held concerning possible directors for *Electra;* George Abbott, Rouben Mamoulian, and Jacob Ben-Ami were being considered. Moeller and Wertheim were chosen as production committee, and Cleon Throckmorton was selected to design the settings.

O'Neill, it is reported in the minutes of May 24, did not seem to be in favor of either Ben-Ami or Abbott. He suggested Chester Erskin as a possibility, "but wanted Mr. Moeller to produce the play." O'Neill's vote, apparently, was a decisive one in Moeller's favor.

When Eugene O'Neill met with the Board of Managers on May 24, there was talk about a possible cast. He approved the selection of Alla Nazimova as the mother, and Earl Larimore as the son, but disapproved Larimore's doubling as both the son and the father. Then, to everyone's surprise, O'Neill recommended Lillian Gish to be given a trial as the vengeance-obsessed daughter. Moeller and Helen Westley were quickly appointed a committee of two to audition Miss Gish at Bad-Neuheim, where the actress was vacationing. In June, Moeller wrote the Guild concerning his appraisal of Miss Gish's qualifications:

> She is marvelous in type but practically inexperienced as an actress—but very, very intelligent and with marvelous pantomimic projection which of course was to be expected. Her voice while somewhat monotonous in range I think could be worked and what encouraged me particularly was the amazing way in which she understood and reacted to the directions I gave her . . . . would obviously prefer [Judith] Anderson because I know her work and what she could do but Gene seems opposed to her and calls her a "ham." Gish won't be this though it will take everything that's in me to bring her up to the mark as she will have to be coached in every "if" "and" and "but"—but a very sensitive instrument is there and in "atmosphere" and years and type she's very fine for it.

Early in July Jed Harris approached the Guild's Board with a proposition for presenting a season of O'Neill plays. He was turned down since the Board felt they might adopt the repertory company idea later in the year and so would need O'Neill's plays themselves. They also told O'Neill that they would prefer his not making any specific arrangements with Harris just then. Obviously, their exclusive contract with O'Neill was one of their more valuable assets.

By August 26, Robert Edmond Jones had been ultimately selected as the production's set and costume designer and was instructed to keep his proposals within a maximum budget of $20,000. O'Neill, in his preliminary drafts, had toyed fleetingly with a number of non-realistic stage effects which he had used earlier with success. At one time he believed it might be truer to the Aeschylean original if the actors wore masks. This, of course, would have made Jones' task much more difficult.

Once he had discarded the idea of using masks, and the *Strange Interlude-Dynamo* devices, the author decided to employ almost complete realism as his technique. There were, however, other remnants of Greek formalism, such as a chorus and the setting of the trilogy occurring chiefly in one locale. But the chorus, composed of townspeople, is colloquial, never speaks in unison, and the setting varied, primarily alternating between the exterior and interior of a house. This last constituted another problem that Jones had to solve.

All during the spring and summer months various players were suggested and rejected as being either unsuitable or unavailable. Finally, the final cast selection was announced, and with it the decision to present all three parts of *Electra* in one day, starting in the late afternoon, rather than splitting up the trilogy between two consecutive evenings as originally planned. It was almost at the last moment, however, that the Guild decided that *Mourning Becomes Electra* should be given all in one evening instead of in the manner O'Neill had conceived of its being performed. Hence, on October 26, 1931, at the Guild Theatre, an opening night audience experienced a dramatic presentation which lasted slightly longer than seven hours—including a supper intermission allowed between the second and third parts of the trilogy. The next day, while several of the unanimously favorable reviewers noted in particular *Electra's* considerable length, not one complained of it. Instead, such phrases as, "a story of majestic proportions," "has grandeur and ecstasy to offer its patrons," "bears the mark of true and enduring greatness," and "it may turn out to be the only permanent contribution yet made by the twentieth century to dramatic literature" were the order of the day. One review by Gilbert Gabriel, typical of many, concluded:

> The three plays march with inexorable interest. Discarding all asides and familiar formulae of the O'Neill stages of the past, they capture a firmness of wording, a litheness of incident, a burning beauty, which insure them rightful place among dramatic masterpieces of the world today . . . this "Mourning Becomes Electra" bulks as the major event in the history of the Theatre Guild. [*New York American,* October 27, 1931]

Briefly, nearly everything about *Electra's* production was termed a triumph by the New York critics: Robert Edmond Jones' atmospheric

MOURNING BECOMES ELECTRA — Robert Edmond Jones' famous set designed after several New England town houses. Alice Brady (seated) and Alla Nazimova. This photograph became a trademark in the production of publicity; various actresses' faces were substituted as the cast was changed.

settings, Moeller's perceptive direction, and especially the splendid performances of Miss Nazimova and Alice Brady as the fate-bedevilled Mannon women, all received press ovations which were like cooling draughts after a long dry spell for the masterpiece's producers. One of the seemingly few reservations was voiced by Joseph Wood Krutch, in *The Nation,* one of O'Neill's more ardent champions, who compared the play rather flatteringly with *Macbeth* and *Hamlet,* only to find that the dialogue's colloquial-speech patterns did not possess the necessary poetic intensity to rival the greatest of classical dramas:

> Here is a scenario to which the most soaring eloquence and the most profound poetry are appropriate, and if it were granted us we should be swept aloft as no Anglo-Saxon audience since Shakespeare's time has had an opportunity to be. But no modern is capable of language really worthy of O'Neill's play, and the lack of that one thing is the penalty we must pay for living in an age which is not equal to more than prose.

Electra's after-opening ferment included O'Neill's picture gracing the front cover of national magazines and awed newspaper interviews with various cast members. It also gave the Guild an opportunity to recircularize its subscription lists with pamphlets filled with eulogistic critical blurbs. Particular attention was paid to those who, for one reason or another, had not renewed their series memberships for that season.

In January the Guild announced that final preparations were being made for a road company of its great attraction. Among the members of this special company, which was bound for Chicago, were Judith Anderson, Florence Reed, Walter Abel, and Crane Wilbur. This decision to travel had been reached in order to capitalize on the New York press ovation of *Electra,* for it had soon become apparent that after its first flush of success the O'Neill tragedy was not going to do the land-office business the Guild had expected it would. The minutes of the Board of Managers' meetings suggest that reductions in performance prices and in the number of auditorium seats to be used for weekday presentations began as early as November. On January 31 the entire New York company was faced with a cut in salary. *Mourning Becomes Electra* undoubtedly must be considered a landmark in the American theatre, and its 150 performances during its maiden New York stay were quite a respectable showing for an offering of such length, and of such gloomy intensity. Its lift to Guild prestige and morale was tremendous, although benefit to the Guild's exchequer was not quite so gratifying.

The Theatre Guild's second great triumph of the 1931–32 season had its premiere about two weeks before *Mourning Becomes Electra* opened, at Pittsburgh's Nixon Theatre, with the enthusiastic support of the city's Drama League. Pre-opening night publicity included scraps of "little-known" biographical information about *Reunion in Vienna*'s stars; one concluded:

> It was at the performance of *Outward Bound* that some of us, however, saw in Alfred Lunt for the first time the power to dominate the spirit of a role and project its essence in terms of suggested emotion within the glamorous spell of the theatre. The Moscow Art Theatre had just departed from these shores, and one suspected that here was the American counterpart to the spiritualized realism in the acting of the Russians.

Another scrap, lauding the production's other star, stated that Miss Fontanne's emergence as New York's top dramatic actress the season before in *Elizabeth the Queen* should have been no surprise to anyone who had noted her grasp of character and the undertones of her playing.

After a highly successful week in Pittsburgh, *Reunion in Vienna* moved to Buffalo's Erlanger Theatre, where upstate New York critics expressed delight even though they realized that beneath the script's surface brilliance "there probably isn't much profundity." One Buffalo reviewer, Ardis Smith, even went so far as to make a prediction, which later proved to be quite accurate, that *Reunion* would be playing in New York, "when the current theatrical season is wrinkled and senile. So if you don't avail yourself of the two nights and one matinee remaining, you're going to be a miserable, apologetic figure when your friends haul off and talk of this year's drama." When *Reunion in Vienna* did finally open at the Martin Beck Theatre on November 16, the Lunts had already been "appearing" in New York for a month and a half—their talking picture, *The Guardsman*, had been playing since September 9 at the Astor.

As expected the New York newspapers gave Sherwood's comedy an adulatory reception, giving ecstatic praise both to the leading players and to Worthington Miner's adroit direction. They also felt that the producers had mounted a perfect foil for their deeply tragic *Electra*. That season the Guild seemed to be busily supplying something for everybody:

REUNION IN VIENNA — Lynn Fontanne, Alfred Lunt, and Minor Watson in a modernistic setting by Aline Bernstein meant as a contrast to the faded Imperial Suite of the Hotel Lucher, in which the reunion of Austria's bygone aristocracy takes place.

> It is as light and frisky as one always believes Viennese comedy should be, and as one so seldom finds Viennese comedy is. It needs, apparently, an American to write it—and a couple of Americans to play it. It needs Miss Westley to bite her words and the end of her cigar; Henry Travers, to wander, with innocent eyes through its delicious pungency. . . . it needs those actors and actresses the Guild calls on to play the funny, rather pathetic relics who stage a reunion in the Imperial Suite of the Hotel Lucher clad ludicrously in the finery of a long-dead court. . . . The Guild has made it one of its happiest excursions into comedy. The direction and the playing keep their banners flying even on those rare occasions when Mr. Sherwood falters. [Richard Lockridge, *New York Sun,* Nov. 17, 1931]

Reunion, obviously, was set for a long and profitable run, but a certain uneasiness plagued the Lunts' association with the Guild. In October, Wertheim and Theresa Helburn reported that they had talked with the Lunts about a contract for the next season but found them unwilling to sign anything at that time. In general, the Board felt it would be wise to wait until *Reunion* opened in New York, or until the Guild had another good Lunt script ready, before bringing up the matter again. Hence, at the end of November, Moeller and Helen Westley again approached the couple, only to find that they had stuck to their decision not to sign and that they were planning to take a long vacation.

Taking a "long vacation" at the peak of a phenomenal career might have seemed a bit pointless but, as the Guild was to learn later, its stars had been in touch with a certain British actor-producer-playwright and were actively engaged in the process of making "other plans."

Nor was the Lunts' unsigned contract the only worry besetting the Guild's managers. At the end of September the newly formed Group Theatre, headed by Harold Clurman, Lee Strasberg, and Cheryl Crawford, had presented Paul Green's *The House of Connelly* at the Martin Beck Theatre under the "auspices" of the Theatre Guild "by fusing the technical elements of their crafts with the stuff of their own spiritual and emotional selves," according to Clurman. Much had been written about the conditioning to which the Group's members subjected themselves: the director's attention devoted to the individual actor's needs, a summer's intensive training in the art of interpretation and ensemble playing, and constructive criticism from the Group as a whole on all phases of production. This unique preparation drew such rave notices for their work in *The House of Connelly* that they decided to quote the metropolitan critics verbatim in advertising their maiden effort. A throw-away pamphlet issued the week following the opening contained in toto the comments of Gilbert Seldes of the *Journal,* Gilbert W. Gabriel of the *American,* Percy Hammond of the *Herald Tribune,* John Mason Brown of the *Evening Post,* Arthur Pollock of the *Brooklyn Daily Eagle,* Ed Sullivan of the *Evening Graphic,* John Anderson of the *Evening Journal,* and Brooks Atkinson of the *Times.* The tenor of all these reviews was that the Group had been "arrogant enough to regard acting as an art" and had profitted handsomely thereby.

All this furor must have been ironically noticed by the Guild's managers, especially Langner, who had pleaded for a properly trained company of actors to represent the Guild the year before. Here was a splinter organization, composed mainly of younger Guild talent, doing almost precisely what the Guild had projected but had been prevented from doing by its presentation of *Mourning Becomes Electra,* which required personnel not available in the proposed acting company. The repertory idea, which was to have revolved about the Lunts, was also unavoidably shelved because the great popularity of *Reunion in Vienna,* with the resultant surge at the box office, justifiably alleviated the Guild's serious fiscal losses. The Guild had its badly needed artistic and financial successes, although, paradoxically, it had realized few of its projected goals.

The Group Theatre was proving to be embarrassing to the Guild in a number of other ways. Clurman, who had been one of the Guild's play readers, offered his resignation. Cheryl Crawford, who had taken over many of Theresa Helburn's administrative duties, was making artistic contacts for the Group at the same time she was making similar contacts for the Guild. For instance, a number of Guild-produced authors, including Maxwell Anderson, John Howard Lawson, Lynn Riggs, and Sidney Howard, had become so interested in the exceptional production possibilities offered by the emerging Group that they had promised it their newest scripts, much to the annoyance of the Guild's managers. There was an obvious conflict of interests in this situation, and Cheryl Crawford was asked to decide which of two masters she wanted to serve. Shortly thereafter she dropped her affiliation with the older organization, stating, "I feel there is more creative work for me to project and accomplish within the Group. I think it is a shame that the organization which brought me up should not have the benefit of what I might do but I have puzzled and found no solution within the Guild." Needless to add, the Group's umbilical connection with its Guild parentage became increasingly tenuous as time wore on.

Another nettling matter the Guild's Board had to thresh out was that late in August it had been confronted by the possibility that Langner might start a theatrical enterprise of his own, quite apart from the Guild. He proposed using the Guild's subscription-season apparatus, as well as many other of its methods, and a number of his fellow managers felt this made him a potential Guild rival. A memo dated August 24, 1931, from Lee Simonson to the Board, protested Langner's advance publicity using the phrase, "Lawrence Langner, Founder of the Theatre Guild." Simonson claimed that this was not only grounds for possible confusion in the public's mind, but also "invidious, derogatory, and in bad taste," particularly since Langner remained a director of the Guild. The next day, in a closed meeting, the following conclusions were reached:

1. That all of us at the meeting appreciate the necessity of Mr. Langner's self-expression;
2. That we hope he succeeds;
3. That we would regret it deeply if developments make his resignation necessary in our opinion;
4. We believe that only time can prove whether this is necessary or not;
5. Mr. Langner states that his resignation, according to the terms of the financial agreement between us, is in our hands whenever we all feel it necessary to act on it;
6. Mr. Langner suggested the possibility of cooperation between the two theatres. . . .

Moeller, who undoubtedly had been stung the previous April by Langner's expression of rather candid views concerning his directorial abilities, made it known that he felt Langner's plan to open his own theatre "was in the nature of the strongest possible move that could be made toward the disintegration of the Guild." Langner did not see it this way, but maintained that the Guild would benefit from the experience this new theatre would afford. The following week, however, either for financial reasons, or from a sincere desire to continue in Guild work, Langner tentatively withdrew his statement of resignation. This was frowned upon by Wertheim and Simonson, who stated he was not in favor of "cold storage" resignations. Langner then hedged and asked for copies of the corporation's by-laws and all bondholder's agreements, and in the flurry of excitement caused by impending productions, the incident seems to have been forgotten. But Langner's discontent possibly resulted in his founding of the Westport Country Playhouse that summer.

As early as November the Theatre Guild's 1931–32 subscription schedule called for only two more productions. Four offerings had already been accounted for: *He, Reunion in Vienna,* and the marathon-length *Mourning Becomes Electra,* which, understandably, had counted as two. Broadway columnists in the know were betting that the first of the remaining shows would be a play by a little-known Irish playwright, Denis Johnston, that had already been playing that season in North America:

> The Irish Players are now trouping through Canada, offering it to audiences in that something less than arid territory. . . . The Guild directors have an excellent idea as to what the drama appears like on stage, for they journeyed up to Montreal a few weeks ago and saw the Irish production. [Ward Morehouse, *New York Sun,* Jan. 9, 1932]

The Guild's production of Denis Johnston's *The Moon in the Yellow River* opened in Philadelphia on February 15, 1932, and two weeks later, on February 29, it was brought to the Guild's home theatre to replace *Mourning Becomes Electra,* then giving its last performances.

The Moon in the Yellow River's notices the next morning were so mixed that the Guild again felt it necessary again to run an advertisement beginning "There Are Differences of Opinion!" What followed were excerpts from the New York papers—the *Times, Herald Tribune, World-Telegram,* and George Jean Nathan being for; the *American, Post, Journal,* and Ed Sullivan being against.

The Moon in the Yellow River has to do, roughly, with attempts made by a group of resurgent Irish nationalists to frustrate the erecting of a much-needed power plant by a German engineer. The word "roughly" is used because *Moon* does not have a clearly defined plot line, but instead is filled with poetic and philosophical talk—as reflected in the equivocal tone of some of the critical judgments that tried despairingly to cope with the curiously anomalous script. Thomas R. Dash called it a "frustrated play, yet one shot through with fulgurous moments of beauty . . . and transient moods. Now it seems droll, now in dead earnest; now it is discursive and again it bristles with action; now it is matter of fact and suddenly it becomes poetic."

Stark Young admitted *The Moon in the Yellow River* was difficult to discuss, but that the Guild "should be honored for producing it," adding that no other management in New York would have done so. His article concluded that *Moon* was a deliberately and subtly elusive piece of theatre writing "in which lies a rich, vagrant content, and through which beat certain wild wings that we have heard before in the Celtic drama, legend, poetry and politics. . . ."

It is doubtful whether such a conglomerate offering as *The Moon in the Yellow River* would ever break Broadway attendance records. Although Claude Rains reported that he learned a great deal from his role in it ("I simply can't tell you about working in a part that so completely dominates me as this. . . . To explain it or discuss it would take something away from its integrity and intactness"), Johnston's obscure play about thwarted rebellion, which can be classed as one of the organization's minor artistic accomplishments, closed after a mere forty performances—in plenty of time to make room for the perennial Shavian charade at the Guild Theatre.

In the spring of 1931, George Bernard Shaw had written to the Guild, addressing his letter to "The Secretary" and, doubtless because he had heard of Miss Helburn's resignation as executive director (the position having been abolished), his salutation read, "Dear—whoever it is:" The text of this letter told briefly of a script he was just then finishing, and concluded "My new play will not, I am afraid, please everybody. It is not meant to. So do not expect another Apple Cart or St. Joan."

It was rumored about the middle of January that the Guild still had not received Shaw's final draft for *Too True To Be Good,* but a few weeks later it was announced that they expected to open with it at the end of February. Somehow, the Guild managed to meet their deadline. They persuaded Leslie Banks, then appearing in *Springtime for Henry,* to be the director, and musical comedy star Beatrice Lillie to be principal player. On February 29, 1932, the Guild presented the world premiere of George Bernard Shaw's latest creation at Boston's Colonial Theatre.

The reaction of Boston critics suggested that *Too True To Be Good* was rather better than the previous season's *Getting Married,* but hardly in the same category as, for example, *The Doctor's Dilemma.* Although the presence of Miss Lillie, Hope Williams, and a giant microbe tended to enliven matters somewhat, there was still a basic pessimism inherent in the play that had been absent from Shaw's other works, a feeling concerning the "futility of hoping for anything but the worst . . . ." One speech in particular was commented upon by Nicholas Young of the *Boston Evening American.* It is uttered at the close of the play by Shaw's mouthpiece, played by Hugh Sinclair, who must "explain, preach or perish":

> The negative-monger falls before the soldiers, the men of action, the fighters, strong in the old uncompromising affirmations which give them status, duties, certainty of consequences, so that the pugnacious spirit in them may reach out and strike death blows, with steadily closing minds. . . . Their way is straight and sure; but it is the way of death, and the preacher must find the way of life. Oh, if I could only find it!

Apparently, the stage directions, imperfectly realized in this first performance, emphasize the point: "There is nothing left but fog. The gap is lost to sight. The ponderous rocks are hidden in wisps of shifting white cloud. Impenetrable fog. . . ."

Much to the Guild's dismay, *New York Times* critic Brooks Atkinson journeyed to Boston to watch the premiere, only to fill his column the following Sunday with his derogatory reactions, which stated, in part, that if Shaw had been an unknown playwright, very probably *Too True To Be Good* would never have reached the professional theatre's stage. He inferred that "Shaw's weakness for chatter seemed to be getting the better of his theatrical judgment."

In finding fault with a production before its official Broadway opening, Atkinson apparently violated an unwritten rule which forbade New York critics to review plays in advance of their opening in the city. Langner and Miss Helburn, therefore, felt justified on behalf of the Guild to complain to Arthur Hays Sulzberger, the president of the *New York Times,* about Atkinson's conduct, an action which may not exactly have endeared the Guild to one of the nation's more powerful theatrical observers. In the meanwhile, *Too True To Be Good* was going the rounds of certain Guild subscription cities, where the critical reaction implied that if Shaw's loquacity, and especially his stirring valedictory as the curtain fell, was "the symbol of waning powers, may senility overtake more of our modern dramatists!"

Shaw's "Collection of Stage Sermons," as he had subtitled his play, mounted before slightly impressionistic stage settings by Jonel Jorgulesco, opened in New York at the Guild Theatre on April 4, 1932. The morning-after reviews tended to yawn politely at these sermons, which jibed in an all too familiar way at Shaw's pet hates (inoculation,

TOO TRUE TO BE GOOD – setting by Jonel Jorgulesco depicting a desert outpost.

Ernest Cossart (seated), Hugh Sinclair, Beatrice Lillie, Hope Williams.

meat eating, and the British army), but most of the reviews insisted this need not have deterred anybody from attending, for Shaw stale and sometimes flat was seldom unprofitable:

> It represents Mr. Shaw vivaciously removing from their pigeon holes the odds and ends of his traditional philosophy, and holding them up to view again with a mischievous pride dulled a little by the years. He talks as well as ever and, it seems, at greater length, about topics once refreshing but now tinged with a suggestion of monotony. The story is only a wisp, and the people in it the usual contrasts of character and thought "without action and without appeal to the emotions." As the microbe says, the play is over at the end of the first act. "The characters," he adds, "will continue to discuss it for two acts more, and the exit doors are all open." And it is discussed brilliantly, so far as the actors are concerned, until long after Mr. Shaw's bedtime. [Percy Hammond, *New York Herald Tribune,* April 5, 1932]

It soon became apparent that once again Shaw had failed to provide the Guild with a real triumph with which to end its season. Even with such favorites as Bea Lillie and Hope Williams in its cast, *Too True To Be Good* was given only fifty-seven performances in New York. It was then replaced at the Guild Theatre by the only remaining production, *Reunion in Vienna,* which, fortunately, ran on into the summer months.

Elsewhere along Broadway, the 1931–32 theatrical season had been responsible for such "serious" offerings as Norman Bel Geddes' production of *Hamlet* starring Raymond Massey. This presentation with Celia Johnson as Ophelia and Colin Keith-Johnston as Laertes, made "a thoroughly good play out of that compendious and cluttered prompt book." Also, monologist Cornelia Otis Skinner appeared in her *The Wives of Henry VIII,* "as good dramatic entertainment as anything you are likely to find on Broadway." Paul Muni received rousing critical acclaim in ex-Guild playwright Elmer Rice's *Counsellor-at-Law.* Also appearing was former Guildite Philip Barry's *The Animal Kingdom,* which starred Leslie Howard. The Guild had not been offered either of these scripts, something that usually occurred when neglected writers found eager acceptance elsewhere from discriminating theatrical managers.

Lighter Broadway fare of the season included the work of authors that had been previously produced by the Guild. For instance, there was S. N. Behrman's new play, *Brief Moment,* which offered as a novelty Alexander Woollcott in a spoof-laden appearance as an actor. Ferenc Molnar's *The Good Fairy,* with Helen Hayes and Walter Connelly, also had a successful run.

Farces and musicals, too, made well-received appearances that season. There had been Benn W. Levy's *Springtime for Henry,* which starred Leslie Banks, Nigel Bruce, Helen Chandler, and Frieda Inescort. Ed Wynn, "the perfect fool," was capering in his production, *The Laugh Parade,* "the most successful musical revue in New York." In January the New York new year was greeted with the finest American musical satire ever: George S. Kaufman's and Morrie Ryskind's *Of Thee I Sing,* with words and music supplied by the Gershwin brothers. The cast included William Gaxton, Lois Moran, and Victor Moore who is still remembered as that do-nothing Vice President Alexander H. Throttlebottom. The entire production had been directed by Kaufman, and never had more honors been accorded to a presentation of this type—honors which included a Pulitzer prize, in a season that had offered Eugene O'Neill's *Mourning Becomes Electra!*

The 1931–32 theatrical year had been a better than average one for Broadway as a whole, as well as for the Guild. At the end of its previous season the Guild's fortunes had sunk to a dangerously low level both artistically and financially—a situation which had been growing steadily, with few reversals, ever since its road commitments began to demand a greater number of quality productions than the organization was equipped to furnish. The various cities involved wanted to see outstanding New York shows, and the Guild was not producing them. In order to satisfy this demand and to bolster its sagging road attendance, the Guild attempted to substitute, for part of its outside New York season, successes produced by other managements. An arrangement was worked out with the Erlanger office, which controlled the out-of-town theatres the Guild used, whereby Guild subscribers were offered certain "hit" plays booked through the Erlanger chain at the same prices the Guild charged for its own productions. Later, the Guild and the Shuberts pooled their road membership lists, combined their subscription cities, and called the controlling office the Theatre Guild-American Theatre Society. This partnership then combined with the Klaw-Erlanger organization and formed the United Booking Office—to supervise engagements, and, incidentally, to prevent damaging road competition. As it turned out later, this arrangement was not without some drawbacks.

Most theatrical managers were fighting desperate rear guard actions hoping to maintain their positions in the battle with Hollywood and the Depression that year. The Guild was no exception. It was forced by circumstances to make a number of adjustments in its operational methods. For instance, during this season it cut its personnel and discontinued the publication of its magazine, mainly for reasons of economy.[1] Stricter controls were put into effect, both in the area of production cost and in the type of artistic management. With committees of two responsible for each offering, there was greater authority exercised by the Board of Managers over all phases of its endeavors.

The emergence of the Group Theatre had cost the Guild some key people, and a bit of reshuffling was found necessary. Harold Clurman's resignation was followed by the Guild's appointing John Gassner as play reader. Cheryl Crawford, who had been acting as the Guild's secretary, also resigned. Theresa Helburn had refused categorically to resume any executive duties, so Warren Munsell took over this job. Several members of the Guild's hoped-for acting company had joined the Group's forces, Franchot Tone and Morris Carnovsky among them. After the Guild sponsored the Group's *The House of Connelly,* it released another of its properties for production by its offshoot. *Son of God* (ultimately entitled *1931*), by Claire and Paul Sifton, became the Group Theatre's second presentation. It opened at the Mansfield Theatre on December 10, 1931, and closed in nine days—"a total failure." Clurman stated, however, that "the Guild trusted our abilities enough to contribute $5,000."

The "defection" of the Lunts was another occurrence the Guild had not counted on, and, naturally, with that team went the nucleus of the anticipated acting company. The Lunts, their contract expired, refused to play the entire road engagement of *Reunion in Vienna,* and replacements were hurriedly sought, with Mary Ellis, Basil Sydney, Melvyn Douglas, and Helen Gahagan receiving prime consideration. (Ina Claire finally took over as Elena.) The Guild tried everything conceivable to bring its top actors back into the fold. Attempts were made to induce Noel Coward to let it manage his new play in which the Lunts were scheduled to appear, but Coward refused, and according to Alfred Lunt told Miss Helburn why "in a most violent manner." (Max Gordon finally produced it.) Offers were made of tempting scripts with juicy parts in them, such as *The Taming of the Shrew* and

[1]The *Theatre Guild Magazine* became *The Stage* beginning with the May 1932 issue, which was "published on behalf of the Theatre Guild" by John Hanrahan Publishing Company.

Shaw's *Captain Brassbound's Conversion,* as showcases for the pair's talents. There was mention of a London season for *Reunion in Vienna.* The Lunts were also advised that the publicity given their leaving the Guild's aegis had brought many inquiries from subscribers asking if it were true, and if so, when they would return. The Lunts finally intimated they would in all probability be back with the Guild at the end of the season, but the Guild kept its fingers crossed.

Although it enjoyed a financially profitable season for a change, the Guild was kept aware of the ever-present "wolf at the door" whose snarling affected all segments of the American economy that year. The Guild's employees were constantly solicited to contribute to the Emergency and Unemployment Relief programs by Arthur Hopkins, Broadway's chairman. The Guild organization gave Sunday night benefit performances of its shows to add to these contributions, and put on several of its productions, notably *Reunion in Vienna,* for special Actor's Fund matinees to help alleviate the plight of destitute actors, as well as other poverty-stricken theatrical workers. So while the nation had suffered a financially ruinous year, the Guild had enjoyed a comparatively remunerative one, and three of its productions, *Electra, Reunion,* and *Too True To Be Good* had been mentioned on several "best of the year" lists. At the end of April the Board was in the enviable position of being able to vote an additional $8,000 to each of its members, with Munsell receiving a goodly advance on his percentage of the profits. Thus, everyone concerned benefited, at least substantially if not exceedingly, in the Depression-dominated period.

CHAPTER 6 / 1932-33

The Good Earth (Pearl S. Buck), Owen Davis and Donald Davis
Biography, S. N. Behrman
American Dream, George O'Neil
Both Your Houses, Maxwell Anderson
The Mask and the Face (Luigi Chiarelli), W. Somerset Maugham

Apparently delighted and made optimistic by the success of the 1931-32 season, Helen Westley suggested in the latter part of March 1932 that the Guild immediately stage John Howard Lawson's play *The Pure in Heart.* It would be done as economically as possible, using makeshift scenery culled from the Guild's warehouse, and sent to one or two of the organization's western subscription cities for a trial run. Finally, it was decided to postpone the presentation until the fall because the cast might grow stale, as it had with *He.* Also, the Guild felt it would be unfair to ask Lawson, who was working in Hollywood, to come east for rehearsals then and in the fall as well.

During the planning session, several possible directors were discussed for the Lawson script, George Abbott and Worthington Minor receiving initial consideration. A controversy later ensued concerning whether or not Theresa Helburn and Langner should be given an opportunity to direct a play for the Guild. At the end of this meeting Miss Helburn was named director for *The Pure in Heart* (Moeller's was the one contrary vote) and Langner and Wertheim were designated to act as its production committee. At last, the Board's three "non-artists" were going to work as a team! In this production, Elia Kazan—the stage manager—began his long career.

After a summer of planning, *The Pure in Heart* made its debut at Ford's Theatre in Baltimore under the sponsorship of the newly formed American Theatre Society. Lawrence Langner had been named the Society's president.

After the October 3 opening night, *The Pure in Heart* was found to be awkwardly constructed and badly written. Furthermore, the situation and the characters were not considered sufficiently interesting to overcome this handicap. "There are long scenes in which the dialogue is painfully stiff. There are scenes in which the melodrama creaks," wrote Louis Azrael of the *Baltimore Post*, who also found that Osgood Perkins, one of the better actors on the American stage, was decidedly cramped in a role both too small and too static for his talents.

Langner, who, of course, had a big stake in this production, was quoted in the *Baltimore Post* as predicting a great future for the play:

> This is very much the kind of play New York likes. . . . It's a hard-boiled picture of theatrical life in New York today and New York will always like that. . . . It's full of strong dramatic situations. . . . It has poetry, beauty and strong psychological development. I call it a fairy tale told by a man who doesn't believe in fairies. . . .

Langner went on to compare the present offering with Lenormand's *The Failures,* whose theme was also defeat in the theatre, a Guild production which had been poorly attended in New York during the 1923-24 season, only to have been well received abroad.

Langner's optimism, possibly a trifle forced, was not shared by critics in some of the Guild subscription cities that *The Pure in Heart* visited. For instance, in Pittsburgh, where the play opened at the Nixon Theatre on October 10, critic Harvey Gaul felt that "the author has never made up his mind which way he is going . . . *in toto* it seemed like early Belasco, dateline 1915, influence Hollywood." After its opening at Cincinnati's Shubert Theatre a week later, Frank Aston found it to be "a hearty admixture of melodrama, comedy, sentimentality and that intangible property known rudely as hokum." When taking stock, the Guild decided that rather than risk a critical flaying in New York where, incidentally, the Group Theatre was then presenting Lawson's *Success Story* at the Maxine Elliott Theatre, they would relegate *The Pure in Heart* to Cain's storehouse for defunct theatrical enterprises.

Unfortunately, Lawson's forgettable epic had been shown to a number of road customers under the Guild's banner. This caused discontent, as evidenced by a message received by Anita Block, the Guild's play reader, from a friend who had seen *The Pure in Heart,* and called it "to my unprofessional mind . . . the cheapest kind of drivel." Mrs. Block then circulated a copy of her friend's note to the Guild's Board with an accompanying memo, which said, in part:

> I am sending you this letter in no trivial spirit of I told you so. Although you will remember that I fought the Guild's production of THE PURE IN HEART steadily and consistently from the time I first read the original script. I am sending it because it seems to me to put a larger issue directly before the Theatre Guild, and that is, exactly what does the Theatre Guild stand for today and what type of plays does it today want to present?

Obviously, the Guild's play reading department still had the same critical intelligence necessary for honest evaluation that it possessed when Courtenay Lemon wrote a similar, but somewhat stronger, memo to the Board of Managers in October of 1929. One might wonder why the Guild ever bothered with such mediocre fare to begin with—whether it needed to renew its option on Lawson's output, or whether there were just not enough decent scripts available for production.

As early as the preceding April the Guild had been offered $40,000 by a representative of Metro-Goldwyn-Mayer for the motion picture rights and a 25 percent interest in its coming production of Pearl Buck's *The Good Earth* as dramatized by Owen and Donald Davis, a father and son team of playwrights. By the end of May, after a month of bargaining, the selling price had been increased to $75,000 cash, plus $1,500 weekly during the run of the play until the total earned was $150,000—with a guarantee that the amount would not be less than $100,000, regardless of the length of the run. Here, at least, was one offering that would not ruin the Guild financially, even if it indulged somewhat its predilection for a *Miracle at Verdun* sort of grandeur.

Alla Nazimova was the unanimous choice for the leading role of O-Lan, the salvaged slave-turned-wife of the farmer, Wang Lung, and she was put under contract early in the spring. The rest of the casting was uncertain. The Davises all but insisted that Moeller direct their adaptation and that Simonson design its scenery. After a summer's work, the Guild was ready to let the public see its evocation of agricultural China.

On September 20, 1932, the Buck-Davis-Metro collaboration, *The Good Earth,* had its premiere at Philadelphia's Chestnut Street Opera House. Arthur B. Walters of the *Public Ledger,* although giving credit to the team of adaptors for having carried the modern classic "over to the footlights with a maximum of honesty and understanding," thought they somehow missed "the supreme authority and intense human appeal of Pearl Buck's book." He thanked the Guild for "as rich and yet as tasteful a production as could be asked"; although the constantly descending curtain interrupted the illusion of continuity that the performers created, "each time forcing the theatregoer to regain that sense of inevitability so vital to a proper appreciation of the story." Only Madame Nazimova, "that pale genius of the stage," won universal praise as she brought to her role "all that dark and brooding passion that she has worn for so many years as her own particular mantle of illusion."

Several reviewers on the road, such as George Seibel of the *Pittsburgh Sun-Telegraph,* referred to an unnecessary glibness and an overall unevenness in Earl Larimore's portrayal of the Chinese peasant, Wang Lung. "Larimore became a conventional American villain when he fell in love with Lotus. . . . Perhaps he talks too much to be creditable as a Mongolian." On October 4 it was announced that Larimore was being replaced by Claude Rains. Finally, after being nearly a month on the road, the production made its way to New York and opened at the Guild's home theatre on October 17.

Brooks Atkinson, perhaps still smarting from his disagreements of the year before with the Guild's managers concerning his reviewing their out-of-town efforts, curtly wished to know why "every year our foremost drama organization opens, by special arrangement with God, on a rainy night, and every year it begins with a bad play." He went on to assert that *The Good Earth* was a complete failure on the stage, adding that Nazimova's acting as O-Lan in the first part of the play had "an interior image of the dumb, clumsy peasant that goes straight to the heart of that magnificent character." But it seemed that in the second half her acting subsided "into torture-some grimaces and her speaking becomes a series of primordial sounds."

As for the visual aspects of the production, John Mason Brown found it ". . . dragged indoors; played by white actors with English accents and Occidental hearts, who wear pigtails and Chinese costumes; set before a wrinkled cyclorama that is supposed to represent sky, and acted in rice fields that are about as luxuriant as a youngster's beard," *The Good Earth* did little more than demonstrate the limitations of the theatre as a story-telling medium. Little fault was found with the Davises' adaptation, "except insofar as it is a fault to attempt the impossible," wrote Richard Lockridge, "—to attempt, in this instance, to picture through the necessary chatter of the stage the slow, inarticulate minds of the Chinese farmers who are the characters; to attempt with a few highlights to illuminate the slow endurance of a life in which occasional melodrama is only an incident."

The Guild's after-the-event apologia for *The Good Earth*'s capital if grim example of good intentions gone awry, stated:

> This play met with one of those fatalities that sometimes overtake an opening night. Nazimova, in her nervousness, slowed up her performance and added nearly twenty minutes to the playing time. The play never recovered from the newspaper notices the next morning.

The dramatization of Pearl Buck's famous novel closed after only seven weeks in town. It was a miracle it ran that long; it probably would not have done so if movie money had not been backing it. On December 26 the play was slated to start a three-week stand in the Midwest. Ashton Stevens, dean of Chicago's drama critics, wrote in the *Chicago American* that he did not feel quite comfortable at *The Good Earth*'s opening: ". . . it was the play that contributed most to my discomfort. . . . I tried to be 'fair' to it. And that was fatal. . . . The theatre is supposed to do things for you, not you for it." He found, however, that Nazimova had added new dimensions to her already considerable abilities:

> Nazimova was—well, if not another woman, at least another actress. Her every deep-mouthed and reluctant word was no longer a Cesarean operation. She was stepped-up, if not indeed from grave to gay, at least from Grave to Andante. Her self-consciousness had largely given way to something like characterization. Her superb technique was no longer to be denied, and there were even sly, shy, charming and furtive little souvenirs of humor. But when I go to my tomb still loving this splendid lady of the theatre, the portrait on my breast will not be of Alla Nazimova as the Davis boys' O-Lan.

Perhaps a brilliant performance from its leading actress would have made a difference on *The Good Earth*'s New York opening night. Be that as it may, the Guild pioneered a new phase of its operations with *The Good Earth,* that of sponsoring scripts primarily intended for movie use. There can be little doubt that Pearl Buck's saga made a greater and more forceful impression as cinema than as a play. The well-remembered multimillion dollar feature starring Luise Rainer and Paul Muni earned numerous awards. However, that the country's foremost theatrical producer would allow its facilities to be utilized for motion picture purposes was a notable and disturbing change of policy.

The sale of *The Good Earth* was only the first of the Guild's dealings with motion picture companies that year. In the autumn it authorized the immediate release of a production still running on the road, *Reunion in Vienna,* so as to "secure the film money." The organization's next New York offering of the 1932–33 season, a distinct popular success, was also destined to be snapped up by the monied masters of Hollywood for a goodly fee.

The Guild acted with far greater haste between the buying and the production of *Biography* than it had with its last S. N. Behrman script, *Meteor,* which had been two years getting before the public. On October 21, the decision to purchase *Biography* was made, and the sifting of leading ladies took place during the same Board meeting. Star quality actresses such as Laurette Taylor and Jane Cowl were considered, but the Board of Managers' first choice was Ina Claire, if she could be signed. Her request for $1,500, or even $1,000, per week against 10 percent of the gross was substantially more than the Guild was paying any of its other performers, but then, the hiring of star quality actresses has always been an expensive proposition.

During rehearsals for *Biography* several of the cast members, including Earle Larimore, were found to be considerably under the mark, although when the production opened at Pittsburgh's Nixon Theatre on December 5, reviewer Harvey Gaul thought the Guild's casting department had "hit it off in every corner." This "best comedy of the season" was found to be both "stimulating and intelligent," if perhaps not quite of epic proportions. Following such praise, the Guild rushed Behrman's latest effort into New York to replace *The Good Earth* at the Guild Theatre on December 12—in plenty of time for the Christmas rush if notices held true to form.

The Guild need not have worried about its leading man, nor anything else for that matter. The press' observations following *Biography*'s New York opening, if not superlative, at least did little harm to the box office. Ina Claire (whose return to Broadway after being away for four years was somewhat stressed in the Guild's advertising) played an artist about to seek aid in writing her autobiography which intimately characterized all the famous men in her past—one of whom happened to be a United States senator. Brooks Atkinson, after calling Guild first-nighters "disdainful," grudgingly admitted that if *Biography* was not top-flight Behrman, at least it was "one of his maturest revelations of character. . . . When Mr. Behrman comes to grips with his people in the last act his characters stand fully revealed," and this third act was thought to have "taken his full measure as a modern playwright. He has a height and a depth, to say nothing of a skill, that few of his colleagues can encompass."

It is apparent, too, that others had helped Behrman's writing along the way, for in April it was recorded that a dispute arose with Metro-Goldwyn-Mayer, which was to pay $30,000 for *Biography's* screen rights, because it refused to honor its contract unless permitted to film the play without payment to either Moeller, the director, or the scenic designer. Moeller, especially, thought he was being undercut because of his extensive contributions during the rewriting process:

> The Board supported Mr. Moeller's request for compensation even though, according to the Basic Agreement with the Dramatists Guild, such changes and additions as he has made in the script belong to the author. It was suggested that he agree to take $1,000 for such interest as he may have in the play. If necessary it was agreed that half of this could be paid by Metro-Goldwyn-Mayer and half by the Theatre Guild.

Moeller must have been appeased by this, for later in April the Guild granted the necessary permission to film its production of *Biography.*

Among the cordial New York notices accorded *Biography,* not one critic complained about the acting. Ina Claire was found to have made a triumphant return to the stage as Behrman's heroine, "bringing with her the high comedy aptitudes that have been so useful to her before this." It was her performance, undoubtedly, that kept the comedy before the public for 283 performances, one of the more successful runs of that Broadway season. It also heralded another departure from the Guild's usual practice of casting an acknowledged star in a part that seemed tailored rather precisely to her measurements. Whitney Bolton in the *Morning Telegraph* recalled the rumor that implied Behrman had written his comedy expressly for the Lunts, although he expressed his disbelief at it: "Miss Fontanne could have played with great distinction the role of Marion Froude, but I doubt that Mr. Lunt could or would have been either happy or genuine or even agreeable in the role of Richard Kurt, which Mr. Earle Larimore plays so successfully."

Concerning the Lunts: the Guild lost their services for the year on December 3, the end of their enormously successful tour in *Reunion in Vienna.* On December 5, they began an "association for a season" with Noel Coward, which culminated in Max Gordon's production of Coward's latest comedy, *Design for Living.*

On February 20, 1933, *Biography* was moved to a slightly larger house, the Avon Theatre, to make room at the Guild's home for its next New York venture, a trilogy entitled *American Dream*. Attention was called to the fact that *Biography* had opened on the same night that Eva Le Gallienne's Civic Repertory offering, *Alice in Wonderland,* had been scheduled; consequently, Miss Le Gallienne, who naturally wanted the first-line critics to pass on her endeavors, had "to invite the sage gentlemen to a dress rehearsal the night before, at considerable inconvenience to all." The Guild was about to do the same thing again. Early in the season Katharine Cornell had announced that she would bring Sidney Howard's *Alien Corn* into the Belasco on Monday, February 20. The Guild chose the same evening to open its newest attraction, *American Dream* by George O'Neil. This time it was the Guild that gave ground. It previewed its new production on Monday for selected subscribers only, with the official opening for the press on Tuesday. Katharine Cornell, after all, *was* Katharine Cornell!

The Guild had previously accepted another of O'Neil's scripts, *Something To Live For,* but because of delays it never found its way before an audience. *American Dream* had a better fate; the Guild placed it in rehearsal as soon as it was acquired. In three episodes the play attempts to trace an American family from its Pilgrim beginnings in 1650 to its riotous end in 1933, focusing on the theme of America's lost ideals. O'Neil had written this trilogy to be played in reverse chronological order; Moeller, the director, decided to play it in a normal chronological order. It might just have happened, though, that O'Neil was right and the Guild was wrong, for the critics were all impressed with O'Neil's style of writing but not especially with his narrative technique. One critic, however, felt that O'Neil's first effort was not without a certain degree of merit:

> The first two scenes have a rather genuine if conventional literary quality; the last, which goes modern with a vengeance, is competently written in the manner, somewhat flashy and somewhat splashy, of the contemporary playwright; but the confusion of intention is almost as marked as the confusion of manner, and the result is a collection of shreds and patches. . . . Indeed, the change in both style and mood is violent enough to arouse the suspicion that the author underwent a change of heart between the time when he began and the time when he finished his work. . . . [Joseph Wood Krutch, *The Nation,* March 22, 1933, p. 327]

Krutch went on to assert that a playwright had every right to change his outlook on life, but that conversion should take place *between* works. If there is evidence of it in the middle of a play, "the result is likely to be more than a little bewildering to an audience which finds it difficult to shift its allegiance during a ten-minute intermission." Robert Garland of the *World Telegram* found it to be "a finely wrought, beautifully written, genuinely perturbing play" while Percy Hammond thought it "brief, inert and incoherent. . . . The first part is slow, the second slower, but the third, representing the wild practices of the present generation, is an orgy of champagne, lust, and loose talk about communism and the several genders. In this section the play bulges almost to the bursting point with bizarre characters and hysterical notions. . . ."

O'Neil's maiden offering may very well have been provocative, serious, and important, as some of the critics thought. The Guild surely gave it their finest team of talents. The production ran only a total of thirty-nine performances, however, something of a Guild record for brief runs. O'Neil's premise had certainly been up-to-the-minute for 1933. Cynicism toward the greed a postwar prosperity had engendered and the contamination of idealists in the world-numbing despair of the Depression were popular themes with many young men of letters. George Jean Nathan later took the Guild to task for its "damaging" rearrangement of the script. Critical opinion seemed to stress that if O'Neil's first Broadway play was no knockout, it was no disreputable failure, either. Perhaps the Guild learned a lesson—namely, to leave a playwright's original scheme alone, no matter how new he might be to the ranks of the profession. Unfortunately, O'Neil's promising career was halted by his untimely death.

As short-lived as the run of *American Dream* would prove to be, its presence at the Guild forced the Board of Managers to hire John Golden's Royale Theatre to house their next New York attraction, Maxwell Anderson's *Both Your Houses.* There had been a split decision among the Board members to buy Anderson's script, yet if his script was not accepted they might possibly lose the playwright's services entirely. After all, had he not let the Group Theatre produce his *Night Over Taos* the previous season without even offering it to the Guild beforehand?

It soon became apparent that the plot of *Both Your Houses* very closely resembled a movie called *Merry-Go-Round.* The Guild's counsel, Charles Riegelman, warned that the Guild should not produce the play without some definite agreement or understanding with Columbia Pictures or without a guarantee against possible damage charges by Anderson should a suit for plagiarism result. By the middle of January the Guild felt that the releases they had acquired were sufficient to justify going ahead with their plans. And after sifting through its usual choices, it finally selected Worthington Miner as director and Arthur P. Segal as scenic designer.

When *Both Your Houses* premiered at Pittsburgh's Nixon Theatre on February 27, 1933, the critical reaction, while noting the similarity to the recent film, proclaimed that Anderson had fashioned a work of "deep meaning, forthright courage, savage vigor and enlightenment." *Both Your Houses* tells the story of a bill passed by Congress over a presidential veto that starts out as a mere $40,000,000 appropriation and ends up as an omnibus pork barrel with dozens of "riders" amounting in all to over $400,000,000. A young freshman Congressman from Arizona tries to kill the bill only to be defeated himself in the process. Obviously still another thwarted idealist had reached the boards that season.

While the treatment of the play's theme might not have been exactly new ("sometimes in the committee room there seems to be a quote from *Wings Over Europe,* and often the dialogue sounds as if Anderson had decided to go George Kaufman's *Of Thee I Sing* one song and two parodies better"), on the whole the Pittsburgh reviewers were not timid in expressing their distinct approval "minus any attempt to guess what the New York wiseacres will say about it." George Seibel of the *Pittsburgh Sun-Telegraph* termed it "well-constructed, full of uproarious characterizations, spiced with epigrams worthy of Shaw, and acted with great gusto. . . . The country needs a strong dose of this sort to purge it of its poisons."

A week later, sensing it had something of a winner, the Guild brought *Both Your Houses* into New York, incidentally again stepping on the toes of the Civic Repertory Company, which was opening that same evening with Nazimova in a revival of Chekhov's *The Cherry Orchard.* The Gotham critics, on the whole, were a bit more reserved than their Pittsburgh confreres had been concerning the merits of *Both Your Houses.* Robert Garland found that the message of the play was slightly dated. A "lame duck" Congress, which had failed to pass *any* noteworthy legislation, much to Roosevelt's disgust, had just been adjourned, and the country was experiencing the New Deal. "Mr. Anderson was all for blaming Mr. Roosevelt for Mr. Hoover's shortcomings," Garland thought, and quoted Richard Lockridge's remarks: "Circumstances quite foreign to the drama have worked against the play, reducing it to a minor footnote on a page just now prodigiously crowded with more relevant excitements." The majority of the New Yorkers' votes, nevertheless, were in the affirmative. Brooks Atkinson found that Anderson had been "sufficiently pragmatic to write a lively, funny, persuasive play. During the course of the discussions he finds several occasions to deliver fighting statements, but in the interest of good dramatic sportsmanship he gives his opponents certain enjoyable assets."

Not the least of such assets was one positive delight cited by all the reviewers. In an inspiration of casting, the Guild had chosen a professional storyteller, Walter C. Kelly (known to vaudeville audiences as "The Virginia Judge"), to play the part of Congressman Solomon Fitzmaurice, who in his thirty Washington years had "never stooped to do an honest deed." As Fitzmaurice, Kelly, the brother of playwright George Kelly and uncle of the future Princess Grace of Monaco, stole the show and the critics' hearts.

In the middle of April Thomas R. Dash nominated what in his opinion were the outstanding contenders for Pulitzer Prize honors. *Both Your Houses* headed his list, followed by *Dinner at Eight* by Edna Ferber and George S. Kaufman, *When Ladies Meet* by Rachel Crothers, *20th Century* by Charles MacArthur and Ben Hecht, *Alien Corn* by Sidney Howard, and *Run, Little Chillun* by Hall Johnson. Not eligible, because of their foreign genesis, but nevertheless considered outstanding, were Sidney Howard's adaptation, *The Late Christopher Bean*, and *Design for Living*, by Noel Coward, who, besides doing well on Broadway, was captivating motion picture audiences that season with his *Cavalcade*.

Early in May the forecast proved to be correct. *Both Your Houses* was awarded the Pulitzer Prize in drama for the 1932–33 season. The following week it was shunted to Philadelphia's Shubert Theatre for two weeks to fulfill subscription commitments there. Afterward it returned to the Guild in New York and continued a goodly run—104 performances in all.

As early as January the Board of Managers had begun asking themselves, "Whither the Guild?" Theresa Helburn suggested that because there were really so few decent scripts available, they might do well to produce only five instead of their regularly-promised six attractions, carrying the sixth play over to the following season. In March the decision was made—the Guild subscribers would see only five plays for the 1932–33 season. Instead of a sixth offering they would be allowed a credit applicable to their next year's subscription payment. It was felt that this was more advisable than carrying the sixth play over to the following season, which would require the Guild to do seven productions.

It could be debated whether or not decent scripts were available to the Guild. Had not play reader Anita Block made a number of suggestions along this line in her memo to the Board earlier in the year? Records indicate that the managers turned down quite a few scripts for one reason or another that rival managements later offered with sterling results. These included *The Green Bay Tree, Turn of the Screw, Little Old Boy,* and *Present Laughter.* Sidney Howard's *Alien Corn,* which Katharine Cornell brought to the stage with distinction, had been rejected by the Guild, and his *Yellow Jack,* which the Guild considered promising, was later done by another organization. As late as May, Judith Anderson let it be known that she was anxious to do *Medea,* but the Board decided not to attempt it. Shortly after this one restless critic, Richard Dana Skinner, asked the Guild some pointed questions about its policies:

> Surely somewhere between San Francisco and Moscow the Guild ought to have been able to find a new play worthy of its last offering of the season—a play of some substance, at least, if not of brilliancy. What of Dan Totheroh's unproduced play on the Brontë sisters? Or are there not plays by Sidney Howard, Elmer Rice, George Kelly or other likely playwrights which might have been produced? The Guild would probably answer that its play committee has searched high and low throughout Europe and America and found nothing. But what has been the quality of the search? Has it been open-minded, willing to accept an unpretentious play if it be good, just as a play? Or has the Guild been searching too hard for the bizarre and so missed the obvious? At all events, it is very sad that our premier producing group should present anything so puerile and shop-worn as a new translation of a play that was unsuccessfully produced some years ago. [*The Commonweal* (May 26, 1933), p. 107]

Skinner's observation was provoked by the Guild's fifth production of the theatrical year which seemed to have an unsettling effect on most of the critics that saw it. Normally, the Guild ended its seasons with a play by Bernard Shaw, but in March the Anglo-Irish wit, who was to pay the United States a visit early that spring, cabled the Guild an affirmation of former instructions: "Unchanged. Play nothing until I leave." This order, it may be added parenthetically, came as something of a relief to the Guild's Board. So the Guild reluctantly made a decision to present W. Somerset Maugham's translation of Luigi Chiarelli's *The Mask and the Face* as their fifth and final production of the 1932–33 New York season.

The Mask and the Face is a rather important milestone in the history of the drama. Chiarelli never referred to this work as a "play," but rather as a "grotesque," a special sort of comedy where illusion and reality intertwine and become confused with mordant results. Its importance lies in the fact that it is the springboard that Pirandello used for his later experiments with "seeming and being," the obvious mask and the not so obvious face behind it. Unfortunately, the grotesque blend of the real and unreal, the comic surface concealing tragic depths, as worked out by Chiarelli, is not always pleasing to American audiences. The theme of the play might be "humiliation is harder to bear than outright sin." The plot is labyrinthine and contains many odd little vagaries such as an older husband who pretends to snooze while his philandering young wife is flirting rather than acknowledge his horns; or a hero, who is on trial for doing away with an unfaithful wife (whom he has actually sent out of the country), being eloquently defended in court by the wife's lover. The hero is acquitted of murder, but when an unrecognizable corpse is "positively" identified as his spouse he must sit through the funeral with a long face. Finally, when the wife returns to her husband from exile unharmed, the hero ironically is imprisoned for making a mockery of the law.

Much was made of the fact that *The Mask and the Face* was to be Philip Moeller's fiftieth directing assignment for the Guild. Maugham's translation of Chiarelli's "grotesque" had its world premiere at Boston's Colonial Theatre on May 1, 1933. The reviews that appeared next day were barely calculated to add lustre to the Guild in Boston's eyes. Some compared it to Chester Baily Fernald's adaptation of the piece put on by Brock Pemberton in 1924, which, despite the acting of William Faversham and Robert Montgomery, had been a miserable failure. The kindest review, which appeared in the *Boston Globe*, stated that "in both atmosphere of incident and portraiture of character it is distinctly European," and probably a bit too much so for complete appreciation by Yankee playgoers. The unkindest review, by Philip Hale in the *Boston Herald*, frankly asked, "Was the comedy worthy of the Theatre Guild?"

A week later, on May 8, the Guild opened *The Mask and the Face* at its home theatre in New York, and one of its erstwhile friends, Gilbert Gabriel, wondered if the city's foremost producing organization was so filled with "spring languors that it needs must fall back against a mossy milestone" for its last offering of the season. He further suggested that *Cyrano* or *Camille,* "or any other of the pseudo-romances which Maestro Chiarelli thought to kid, is still a livelier and lovelier

THE MASK AND THE FACE – one of the less impressive investitures.
Critic Stark Young complained of it, "The décor that Mr. Lee Simonson has supplied for the play could not, with the arches, walls, doorways et cetera used, be called extravagantly costly; and certainly any producer has a right to economize on settings nowadays. But the room is in all respects stupid and without distinction, banal and semi-vulgar would be descriptive also; and the scene . . . outside is drab and lighted without any sort of imagination or even realistic beauty. The sophistication implied in the drama was not in the room, and the dreams or erotics implied in the world outside were not in the scene displayed. None of this is a question of cost; it is a matter of taste and dramatic design" – *New Republic,* May 24, 1933, p. 46.

In foreground: Leo G. Carroll, Judith Anderson, Dorothy Patten, Shirley Booth, and Stanley Ridges. Standing in background: Humphrey Bogart.

last resort." Of the grotesque comedy itself, "an old futility clings to its flights. Its alternate atomizings of the perfumes of the boudoir and the graveyard still refuse to mix well—for American nostrils, anyway . . . ." Most other reviewers saw little if any improvement over the former Fernald-Pemberton version, and although the actors, many of whom later gained stardom, especially Judith Anderson and Stanley Ridges, were complimented for "nothing much done nicely," the Guild's beacon was regarded as having flickered noticeably with this presentation. Even Lee Simonson, who usually received nothing but critical approbation, was scolded for his less than adequate setting. The play closed after a disappointing forty performances.

During the tryout week in Boston, Theresa Helburn, as well as others connected with the production, had been rather lionized by the press and various civic groups. In an interview with Elizabeth Bordon of the *Boston Herald,* Miss Helburn had been quoted as believing that what the American theatre needed were better trained actors, better political and social satires, but most especially, better audiences. Implied, of course, in Miss Helburn's statement was a promise that the Theatre Guild would do its utmost to keep supplying the theatrical sustenance necessary for these drama enthusiasts.

The Guild's dealings with motion picture concerns became an accepted fact during 1932–33. *The Good Earth* had been produced with Metro-Goldwyn-Mayer's backing, and *Biography* was sold to the same company shortly after it opened. During the course of the year Metro was also authorized to release its version of *Reunion in Vienna,* starring John Barrymore, Diana Wynyard, Frank Morgan, and featuring Henry Travers, on leave from the Guild, in the role he had originally played with the Lunts. The reason the Guild approved the showing of this picture while its own stage version of *Reunion* was still on the road was obvious. Also, there had been negotiations with Columbia Pictures to secure releases necessitated by the close similarity of *Both Your Houses* to Columbia's *Merry-Go-Round.* The Guild apparently was becoming increasingly Hollywood-conscious.

The spectre of the Great Depression, of course, haunted many theatrical enterprises that year. In February the Guild decided to drop its prices for the following season from $3.00 to $2.75 top for all evenings, with the subscription price at $2.20. At the same time the American Theatre Society was closing down several of its cities because of its inability to secure productions that people would pay to see. Two months later the Shuberts were reported anxious to discontinue the Society, and the Guild authorized Warren Munsell to dissolve the partnership as quickly as possible. In May, however, the minutes record that this decision had been rescinded and that the Board agreed to present three plays in association with the American Theatre Society on the basis of a modified plan. This decision to keep the road subscription series going by increasing the number of commercial "hits" supplied it by other managers, while economically sound, meant that in the future the Guild would find it necessary to compete with this type of entertainment—a practice it was not designed to follow. Such a decision implied a downgrading of standards—possibly one of the more damaging mistakes made by the organization in its middle years.

CHAPTER 7 / 1933-34

Ah, Wilderness!, Eugene O'Neill
The School for Husbands (Molière),
Arthur Guiterman and Lawrence Langner
Mary of Scotland, Maxwell Anderson
Days Without End, Eugene O'Neill
They Shall Not Die, John Wexley
Jig Saw, Dawn Powell

Late in the summer of 1933 the Guild's Board of Managers decided to feature certain star performers in a number of their coming attractions. The ranks of the Guild's original acting company had diminished considerably since the halcyon days of 1928. Such players as Edward G. Robinson, Dudley Digges, and Richard Bennett were no longer available, and the Board was faced with the problem of increasing its talent pool to cast future productions. The idea of offering featured billing was reinforced by the success of Ina Claire's appearance in *Biography* the previous season. Although Miss Claire ostensibly had been just another member of the cast, quite in keeping with the long-held Guild tradition of the play first, the actors second, the Guild nevertheless had made her stellar presence known and felt through its advertising. Now, the Board decided, there were definitely going to be guest *stars,* and no hedging about it. Henceforth, it would be "George M. Cohan in *Ah, Wilderness!* by Eugene O'Neill"— instead of the play's title having top billing and Cohan's name appearing along with others in the cast. In keeping with this new policy, Helen Hayes, Fay Bainter, and Elizabeth Bergner had been contacted as possibilities for important roles, as had Philip Merivale and Mary Pickford, whom the Guild was considering for a part in *Sarah Simple.*

The Board believed it was showing sound business sense in altering a policy to accommodate an obvious need for success. *Biography* had been something of a box-office bonanza, and principally because of this production's financial success both in town and on the road, the

Board was able to vote a $2,800 increase in salary for five of its members. The Board's banker member, Maurice Wertheim, was pointedly left out of this augmentation. Wertheim, in fact, had been receiving no weekly salary since February because he could not or would not attend meetings, although his financial advice was still sought by the Board. Now, at the beginning of the 1933–34 season, a resolution was passed making the nonpayment penalty for missing meetings applicable to everyone.

The Board, as it happened, had been functioning without the services of either Helen Westley or Lee Simonson since the end of August. Mrs. Westley had accepted a Hollywood offer and would not be back until the end of January. Simonson, busy elsewhere, would not return until the first weeks of November. All things considered, it seemed good judgment to suspend action on the salary-withholding resolution; both Mrs. Westley and Simonson were paid their full fees from the beginning of the season. Wertheim, however, offered to waive his, "on account of ill health and an inability to attend meetings regularly." His offer was accepted. These absences, of course, left many artistic and financial dilemmas to be solved by the few Board members remaining on the job.

One of the pressing problems with which the Board had to contend was attempting to lure the Lunts back into the fold. It became obvious that Alfred Lunt felt the Guild just did not have the proper scripts in hand for him and Miss Fontanne to appear in with distinction. He approved of the suggestion made by Langner and Helen Westley (before she had gone to Hollywood) that the Guild get in touch with playwrights and advise them of the deplorable shortage of plays for the Lunts so that they might work with the pair in mind. He also promised that Miss Fontanne and he would be combing Europe for Guild-sponsorable plays in which they could star, and which might possibly be done on a repertory basis with a new acting company. The Board then hastened to notify Behrman, Howard, O'Neill, Anderson, and Sherwood that if they had anything promising for the Lunts, they should send it to the Guild by all means—and quickly. It was soon apparent, however, that the talents of America's first acting couple were going to be lost to the Guild for at least another season.

Another set of problems facing the Guild's reduced Board involved the extensive rewriting they felt was necessary on several of the scheduled offerings. John Wexley's *They Shall Not Die* was considered to be in imperfect shape, and a representative of the Board was named to discuss script changes with the author. Also, Moeller had several suggestions to make for Eugene O'Neill's *Days Without End.* Langner said that earlier drafts of the work had included elements now believed missing, and that O'Neill would in all probability be willing to rewrite along the lines Moeller recommended.

O'Neill, who had been pushing the religiously-oriented *Days Without End* through several revisions, awoke one morning with a completely formulated idea for a comedy. He was quoted by Richard Watts, Jr., as stating that "only once before, in the case of 'Desire Under the Elms,' has a plot idea come to me so easily, so I put aside the graver drama and went to work on the new plot. I wrote it more easily than I have written any other of my works and then went back to 'Days Without End.'" This inspiration, entitled *Ah, Wilderness!* after Omar Khayyam's *Rubaiyat,* promptly became the Theatre Guild's first offering of the season.

Most of the news stories that preceded the opening of O'Neill's play concerned the announcement that "America's first actor," George M. Cohan, would appear in it. O'Neill was apparently delighted by the prospect, since he had wanted Cohan for *Marco Millions* some years earlier. Cohan's father and O'Neill's father had been the best of friends during their trouping days, and a fine rapport developed between the two illustrious sons during the rehearsals. Much was made of the fact that the incomparable actor-dancer-tunesmith-producer for the first time in his life was appearing in a theatre piece he had not personally written and directed. He expressed dismay at having to rehearse for more than two weeks: "I suppose the Guild has a reason for the way they do it. They want to go slow and finish the job right. . . . But it's funny for a guy like me to be sitting around all afternoon, just reading my part."

Another circumstance that pleased O'Neill about the production was that the Guild had induced his old collaborator, Robert Edmond Jones, to design the sets. Jones' faithful rendering of the "medium-priced tastelessness" O'Neill called for captured the essence of turn-of-the-century stodginess in a middle-class Connecticut "large-small town."

O'Neill had not been greatly pleased by the failure of the Guild to revive any of his plays during the year following *Mourning Becomes Electra* when he had urged the producers to offer any one of six previous works. He was also unhappy about the Guild's opening *Ah, Wilderness!* in Pittsburgh, the first out-of-town tryout ever given an O'Neill play. During rehearsals in New York the playwright had been in constant and enthusiastic attendance. In Pittsburgh he could only bring himself to watch certain scenes, never a complete run-through.

The notices following the *Ah, Wilderness!* premiere at Pittsburgh's Nixon Theatre on September 25, 1933, were kind, but not ardent. All expressed the opinion that *Ah, Wilderness!* was a decided departure from the demon-driven processes of O'Neill's previous works, but that a departure did not necessarily signal an arrival. One reviewer commented on the accuracy of O'Neill's homey portraits which reminded some of those popularized by Booth Tarkington:

> Oh yes, it's true enough; so true that sometimes, at odd isolated moments you forget that you're at a play. You're in the sitting-room, "squabbling," or in the dining room interrupting each other. You are eavesdropping upon the past—YOUR past—your heart all swollen and funny! And then, all at once, the play sags and caves in—and that, too, I dare say, is Life. Life isn't dramatic, or even interesting all the time, you tell yourself. So maybe this stage record is faithful and fetching, and a disarming kind of art. At least, that's what you feel you should say . . . that Eugene O'Neill wrote it, that great dramatist, and so it HAS to be right! I dare say if someone else had written it, you'd have shuffled and squirmed in your seat. You'd have said to each other: "Yes, that's all very well, but NOW WHAT?" [Florence Fisher Parry, *Pittsburgh Press,* Sept. 26, 1933]

Other Pittsburgh reviewers found that O'Neill spent far too long developing his folksy characters while letting them bask in the mellow richness of 1906. There was also general critical bewilderment over a proper method to evaluate this kind of O'Neill play. If it were satire, it lacked sharpness, but if it were a simple comedy, it lacked suspense and conventional plot complications. Most agreed, however, that young Elisha Cook, Jr. displayed a disturbing tendency to steal the show from his famed superior.

The Guild brought *Ah, Wilderness!* into its home showplace on October 2, and featured a star's name on its marquee for the first time in its history. As John Mason Brown noted, the first-night audience, usually "notoriously indifferent . . . remained to cheer Mr. Cohan until, after twelve curtain calls, he stepped forward to express his thanks in his customary little speech."

The critics' reactions to the play were mixed, but Cohan's creation of small-town editor Nat Miller inspired these same critics to write all sorts of complimentary niceties:

AH, WILDERNESS! — Robert Edmond Jones' original sketch for the Miller dining room, which, according to Brooks Atkinson, recognized "the humor in the stuffy refinement of 1906." (Courtesy, Miss Elizabeth Jones and Theatre Arts Books. (Copyright 1933 by Robert Edmond Jones; all rights reserved.)

AH, WILDERNESS! — A scene as played in R. E. Jones' set for the Miller dining room.

(Clockwise from head of table) George M. Cohan, Eda Heinemann, Elisha Cook, Jr., Gene Lockhart, Marjorie Marquis, Walter Vonnegut, Jr., Adelaide Bean.

He creates a living portrait of the man. He casts off entirely the clear line, the sharp active rhythm which have been the familiar marks of his stage personality, and, with only his spectacles for make-up, he builds the slightly stooped, hesitant, wise, kindly *paterfamilias*. . . . Nat Miller is an easy part to play but what Mr. Cohan does to it is a lesson in the art of acting. [Edith J. R. Isaacs, *Theatre Arts Monthly* XVII (Dec., 1933), p. 909]

Other members of the cast, notably humorist Don Marquis' wife, Marjorie, and Gene Lockhart as amiable, alcoholic Uncle Sid, gained recognition for their portrayals; Elisha Cook, Jr., as the pivotal character in the play, Richard, won major praise as a poetry-quoting, teenage radical. Only one reviewer, Percy Hammond, was not enchanted by this adolescent's depiction. But then, the *Tribune*'s man considered *Ah, Wilderness!* the worst of a series of bad plays in which the great Cohan had appeared.

If the critics did not all find *Ah, Wilderness!* to their liking, the public certainly did not share this lack of enthusiasm. The homespun comedy became one of the first Broadway successes of the 1933–34 season. George Jean Nathan, to whom O'Neill had dedicated the play, voiced his approbation in such a way as to squelch all captiousness, and audiences kept coming and coming, and cheering at the end of performances.

At the beginning of the season the Guild had decided to increase the top box-office price for *Ah, Wilderness!* to $3.30, leaving the equivalent subscription price at $2.20. The plan proved successful. The total of New York subscriptions was well over 15,000 by the middle of October, a decided decrease from its peak in 1928, but a definite increase from the preceding season. In November the Guild concluded the sale of *Ah, Wilderness!* rights to Metro-Goldwyn-Mayer for $75,000. In the spring a West Coast *Wilderness* company, produced by Henry Duffy under a Guild franchise, opened in San Francisco and later in Los Angeles. This company starred Will Rogers in the role of Nat Miller. California loved O'Neill's story of "sweet-scented youth" tripping over New England's mores.

It is easy to assume that O'Neill's nostalgic evocation of youth's vicissitudes could not fail to please the public wherever and whenever it was presented. The fact is, however, it did not rouse much enthusiasm when it was revived by the Guild in 1941 with Harry Carey as Nat Miller. In the thirties, though, the innocence of *Ah, Wilderness!*

with its remembrance of things in the untroubled past, together with its gaiety and tender charm, was most appealing to a Depression-troubled public.

Meanwhile Lawrence Langner had been exceedingly busy with theatrical enterprises unconnected with his Theatre Guild duties. During July and August a revamped version of Strauss' *Der Fledermaus* by Robert Simon and Langner had been readied at Langner's Country Playhouse in Westport, Connecticut, and was presented with Peggy Wood as its lead, Jo Mielziner its designer, and Monty Woolley in charge of its staging. In the fall, producer Dwight Deere Wiman brought the offering, its name changed to *Champagne Sec,* into town. It gave a good account of itself. A bit later Mr. and Mrs. Langner's reconsideration of "bundling" as a practice, *Pursuit of Happiness*—another alumnus of the Connecticut establishment—was being offered at the Avon with its original Country Playhouse stars, Peggy Conklin and Tonio Selwart.

Finally, the Guild suspended its house rule against producing the work of one of its Board members, to present another product of Westport summers, Molière's *School for Husbands* as adapted by Langner and magazine rhymester Arthur Guiterman.

The details involved in preparing *School for Husbands* for its New York debut were impressive. Langner was to direct his adaptation, and Charles Weidman, who earlier in the year had created dances for Marilyn Miller, Clifton Webb, and others in Moss Hart's and Irving Berlin's *As Thousands Cheer,* was called upon to choreograph and later to dance with his partner, Doris Humphrey, in the offering. Composer Edmond Rickett had fashioned a score heavily dependent on old French madrigals and folk tunes, and Lee Simonson executed a baroque setting along with a variety of *commedia dell'arte* costumes. With the exception of *Volpone,* the Guild had never done well with its rare classical revivals. Would it be different this time?

The School for Husbands opened at the Empire Theatre on October 16, 1933. The majority of Manhattan's professional playgoers tried their utmost to be kind:

> The Messrs. Langner and Guiterman rhyme marvelously; they rhyme wit with wisdom. . . . They make it a veritable frolic of words, but words are not strong enough by themselves to hold Molière in the magic of the modern theatre. [John Anderson, *Evening Journal,* Oct. 17, 1933]

SCHOOL FOR HUSBANDS — Lee Simonson's imitation of a Renaissance setting using heightened perspective.

Osgood Perkins and June Walker in foreground.

> The Guild's production . . . is a thing of beauty and a joy for sixty minutes. The second hour is a little less thrilling, as second hours so often are . . . a little hard to take by reason of repeated themes and situations. I think perhaps there are a few too many songs. [Burns Mantle, *Daily News,* Oct. 17, 1933]

> . . . it is charming, which is obviously what the Guild intended it to be, and nothing else than what the Guild could hope it to be at best. It is sometimes stilted, but purposely so. It is often thin, but unavoidably so. It is occasionally a Dresden-china bore, but forgivably so. [Gilbert W. Gabriel, *American,* Oct. 17, 1933]

> It was all pretty, tinkly, light and fantastic, but somehow, I wanted to go home. And I was ashamed of myself, of course, because I should have been grateful to the Guild for reviving Molière. [Bernard Sobel, *Mirror,* Oct. 17, 1933]

The School for Husbands is not one of Molière's more widely known comedies. Its theme might be stated as "women respond to kindness, abiding faithfully with those who trust them and deceiving those who rely on locksmiths." It is a proposition which should be presented with a certain finesse. Of the cast only Osgood Perkins, who had distinguished himself on Broadway in varied roles, gained acceptance as the suspicious Sganarelle with acting that was a good-natured compromise between the antique and modern. June Walker, as Sganarelle's ward, Isabelle, was awarded honorable mention, though some reviewers found themselves doubting if enthusiasm could legitimately be substituted for elegance. It seemed that throughout the undertaking the elusive quality known as "style" was lacking—elusive, that is, to most American players not trained in the European tradition. "You cannot make a silken actor out of a seventeenth-century wig," wrote Richard Lockridge in the *Sun,* "or capture the informality of a Fête Champêtre in the labored cavortings of a modern dance-vaudeville."

One of the few things most reviews agreed about was the fitness of Simonson's setting, even though Stirling Bowen of the *Wall Street Journal* thought that the designer once again gave the impression that "a clear primary color would blind him." The incidental dances by Humphrey and Weidman also received favorable comment, although the second-act ballet was believed to be "cluttered."

The Guild had taken pains in reviving Molière and enhanced the season more than, say, *Let 'Em Eat Cake,* which opened the same week, and was supposed to be a sequel to the highly regarded *Of Thee I Sing*. *Cake* had the same authors, composer, lyricist, players, and producer as *Of Thee I Sing*, but still managed to be unalluring when compared with the original. Another play that opened the same week did make something of a name for itself, however. This was a Guild reject, *The Green Bay Tree*, by Mordaunt Shairp. Directed by Jed Harris, this production featured Laurence Olivier, Jill Esmond, James Dale, O. P. Heggie, and Leo G. Carroll, with settings by Robert Edmond Jones. *The Green Bay Tree*, produced by Lee Shubert, was a "different" kind of drama, and proof again that even a Shubert would now rush in where the Guild feared to tread.

The School for Husbands had a respectable New York run of 116 performances. After January it was sent the subscription route to Pittsburgh, Philadelphia, and Washington, to be shown thirty-two more times before it finally closed.

Barely a week after *The School for Husbands* opened in New York, the Guild's next play had its premiere in Washington, D. C. In September, Theresa Helburn had been appointed the director for Maxwell Anderson's *Mary of Scotland*, since Moeller was busy with O'Neill's *Ah, Wilderness!* and Langner was staging Molière. Miss Helburn thus became one of the few women stage directors in the history of the American theatre who was not first and foremost an actress.

Casting the role of Queen Elizabeth in *Mary of Scotland* was a headache from the beginning. Phyllis Povah had been considered, as had Fay Bainter, but the characterization called for "keen intelligence and iron-willed restraint." Helen Menken was approached and soon decided she liked the role, especially after being offered featured billing. There was one drawback, however. Miss Menken had already begun rehearsals with George Abbott and Philip Dunning for their production of *The Drums Begin* by Howard Irving Young, and she had a "verbal agreement" in lieu of a formal contract with these two producers. After several lengthy conferences at the Actors' Equity offices, and some bad feeling, Miss Menken was allowed to remain in Anderson's play.

Other troubles were plaguing the Guild, having to do with certain theatrical artisans, scenery builders, costume makers, and scene painters. Word had gone out that the Guild was going to do two period productions, and when various houses asked to bid on the costume and scenic work all turned in identical estimates, collusion was obvious. Then Eaves Costume Co. underbid its competitors for the

Mary of Scotland costuming, but after they had been selected, Brooks Costume Co. offered to do the job for half of any other bid. The Guild honored their agreement with Eaves, although a union official threatened he would not allow the costume house to deliver the costumes because overtime had not been paid for the work.

From the first, the Guild had wanted Helen Hayes to take the title role in *Mary of Scotland,* but problems arose concerning her motion picture contract as well as her contract with Gilbert Miller. When the play opened in Miss Hayes' home town, Washington, D. C., she was appearing locally at first-run picture theatres, along with John and Lionel Barrymore and Clark Gable, in Metro-Goldwyn-Mayer's *Night Flight.*

Preparations for the play's out-of-town openings were complex and varied. Howard Wicks, the Guild's chief technician, wrote to Herman Bernstein, who was responsible for the production's scenery, costumes, and props, that "this road experience sets a new high for volume of correspondence between technical department and any company manager." The hundreds of messages exchanged before the curtains rose on the Guild's reanimation of sixteenth-century Scotland bear this out.

The world premiere of *Mary of Scotland* in Washington was an exceptionally brilliant affair in every particular. A fashionable audience, headed by the country's first lady, Eleanor Roosevelt, "remained to give round after round of applause, the best testimony that the New York Theatre Guild has wrought another magnificent achievement . . . staged in its finest tradition."

The *Washington* Post invited the chairman of the Pulitzer jury, Clayton Hamilton, down from New York to write its criticism of prize-winner Anderson's latest offering. Hamilton extolled the play's virtues so unrestrainedly that the Guild was delighted to use quotations from his remarks whenever it ran "review" ads. This august dean of critics clearly preferred Anderson's *Mary* to Schiller's, and in lauding Anderson, quoted the author's precepts for memorable playwriting: "All great plays I can remember were in verse. If we are going to have a great theater in this country, somebody has to write verse, even if it is written badly. It is at least a beginning." Hamilton concluded by commending Anderson's and the Guild's contribution to America's heritage: "In recent years we have not been burdened with an overplus of reasons to be proud of the United States. We may be proud this morning. Our country has given to the world a great and noble play."

In large part the critical reception of *Mary of Scotland*'s pre-Broadway openings in Washington, Pittsburgh, Baltimore, and Boston compared Anderson to Anderson, for apparently in the field of historical drama written by Americans he could be discussed only with the classics or with himself. A Boston reviewer remarked that *Elizabeth the Queen* was a more striking play with its bullyings, gesturings, and splendor, whereas *Mary* had more heart, more smoldering passion, and a truer tragic sense emanating from a deeper despair. Another found that *Elizabeth the Queen* had depended upon one magnificent performance, Lynn Fontanne's, whereas *Mary of Scotland* contained not one but four striking characterizations, and this contributed to the newer play's greater depth and dramatic range. George Seibel of the *Pittsburgh Sun-Telegraph* voiced the opinion that Schiller's *Mary* was superior, but added that Anderson's was more "vibrant and tender." All in all, such critical quibbling could only whet the appetites of potential audiences.

In addition to the three stars, Helen Hayes, Helen Menken, and Philip Merivale, most of the early notices praised Fritz Leiber who played fiery, pulpit-hammering John Knox. During the Baltimore run, however, Leiber announced he was severing his connection with the show. It appeared that when he had signed his contract he was under the impression that he was to be featured along with the other three, and "after fourteen years" in starring roles, Leiber did not feel he could continue under the existing arrangement. Burns Mantle felt Leiber was making a mistake. He was not as well known in New York as elsewhere, and a fat Broadway part would have added to his professional stature. But Leiber withdrew anyway and Claude Rains was first considered as his replacement. Moroni Olsen was finally chosen, however; he played the role as a "bellowing, parable-reciting, biased critic of everything that Mary does."

After two weeks in Boston under American Theatre Society booking, with seat prices "no higher than $2.75 and low as fifty-five cents," *Mary of Scotland* moved to New York, and opened at the Alvin Theatre on November 27. The New York reviewers were just as impressed as those in the preview cities had been. A few noted that the historic Mary Stuart and Anderson's Mary were two quite different personalities. It seemed that the poet-dramatist had made the tall, impetuous, heedless Mary of history completely over into a pocket-sized darling, England's dupe, Bothwell's faithful wife, and posterity's handmaiden. Other critics felt that in the last act the author's rhetoric became relatively less convincing, especially in the debate at Carlisle Castle.

While the settings met with universal approval, there were mixed reactions as to the appropriateness of the costumes. Brooks Atkinson

MARY OF SCOTLAND — In contrast to the historical Mary, who was over six feet tall, Miss Hayes' diminutive stature made it necessary to elevate her whenever possible, accomplished here naturally with a dais.

In foreground: Philip Merivale, Helen Hayes, Ernest Cossart, George Coulouris, and Wilton R. Graff.

found that the suits and dresses designed by Robert Edmond Jones visually sharpened the alignment of forces: "In the last act the simple black costume he has fashioned for Mary and the regal gold of Elizabeth's sweeping raiment pointed up with great brilliance the opposition of will and the inequality of power that set the tone of that encounter." Stark Young, on the other hand, was at a loss to understand the monotony of texture and intention in a good deal of the costuming:

> In the scene where, after their defeat, Mary visits Bothwell, her habit is a sparking new red-leather jacket and cap or "bonnet," with modern gloves—though gloves were endlessly meaningful in those days and astonishingly varied—where we might have some costume of escape, some cloak, perhaps, or some fine gown whose state might tragically express her circumstances.

Although there were isolated instances of cavilling, in the main the notices were worshipful. The play was shrewdly built with scenes that had been chosen for their pictorial effect as well as their dramatic value. Reviewers found that Anderson's language not only had exceptional poetic imagery, but was also charged with the excitement of deep emotion. In short, everything connected with *Mary of Scotland* became something of a triumph. All the actors, especially Miss Hayes, Merivale, and Miss Menken, were thought to be excellent. Even Anderson's son Quentin, who played a warder, gained his share of recognition.

With three hits playing simultaneously in New York, the Guild felt it could loosen its purse strings. It voted to pay off the interest on its theatre-building bonds for the preceding year, deducting the payment from current profits. It also decided to pay its behind-the-scenes personnel a Christmas bonus of approximately $1,500. The financial picture had not looked so bright for some time.

Two producers were anxious to produce *Mary of Scotland* in England, and the Guild was able to ask a substantial royalty. Persistent rumors arose in many news stories on the play that Helen Hayes would leave before it had run its course, claiming possibly another "act of God" as she had in the past. In Boston it was primarily Helen Hayes movie fans who had cued up around the block, and not Theatre Guild admirers or those rejoicing at the return of poetic drama. The same was true to a considerable extent in New York. It was not until June, however, that press releases confirmed that Miss Hayes had to give up her part, for the time being, to fulfill motion picture commitments, and that Merivale would go to England for a vacation. The Guild decided to try a summer run with its popular attraction, then playing to capacity houses. They called on two of their more talented and dependable players to fill the leading roles. Margalo Gillmore, who earlier in the season had appeared in Alexander Woollcott's and George S. Kaufman's mystery melodrama, *The Dark Tower,* took over the part of Scotland's queen. Stanley Ridges played Bothwell. Although the pair received very creditable mention, during the first week of their reign the box-office receipts fell off about $15,000, and the second week brought in approximately $20,000 below the closing week of the Hayes-Merivale engagement.

Even with Helen Menken still in the cast, poor business left the Guild no recourse but to close *Mary of Scotland* for the remainder of the summer. A West Coast company, offered by producer Homer Curran with the Guild's authorization, directed by José Ruben and featuring Helen Gahagan as Mary, Ian Keith as Bothwell, and Violet Kemble-Cooper as Elizabeth, played in San Francisco and other West Coast cities. Miss Hayes and Merivale were scheduled to rejoin the original company in September to begin an extensive tour which the Guild hoped would last well into the coming year.

In spite of the success that *Ah, Wilderness!* was enjoying, the Guild's managers had never been completely convinced of the merits of O'Neill's other play, *Days Without End.* As early as September it was the subject of disagreement among the members of the Board, with the dominant sentiment being that even if the managers were not wholeheartedly in favor of doing the play, the Guild was definitely committed to stage it if only to maintain amicable relations with its foremost dramatist. It came as something of a relief, then, when O'Neill promised to stop work on *Days Without End* until after *Ah, Wilderness!* had opened. But, almost immediately after that, O'Neill again took up *Days Without End,* which was conceived as a spiritual sequel to *Dynamo,* and the Guild began to ponder the problems of casting. One possibility considered for the leading woman's role was the German actress Elisabeth Bergner, "if her accent were not too pronounced." Others thought about were Ina Claire, though "it was felt she would not be interested in the part" and Jane Cowl, whom Langner induced to read the script.

Earle Larimore, who had been the unanimous choice for the role of the hero, was summoned from the touring company of *Biography,* then in St. Louis, to start rehearsing, and Sheppard Strudwick was sent out to take his place. O'Neill, who paid the closest attention to the selection of players, insisted that even the smallest bit part "needs to be out of life, and not an old theatrical type." The biggest casting problem, however, was the role of the hero's long-suffering wife:

> A star might overshadow the lead, yet the role needed an actress who could act and who, at the same time, had personal charm, and audience appeal—not too much to take sympathy from the lead, but enough to make "Elsa" attractive and believable—in other words with star quality but one without star mannerisms and attitudes. . . . [Mary Hedwig Arbenz, "The Plays of Eugene O'Neill as Presented by the Theatre Guild," pp. 386–87]

Finally, Earle Larimore's wife, Selena Royle, was chosen.

Moeller, who had been selected almost against his wishes as director, was far from happy about the state of the script, but the Guild decided to defer to O'Neill's wishes concerning the premiere's timing. In a memo to Theresa Helburn, O'Neill wrote: "Open it as *immediately after* Christmas Day as possible! You see the point, of course—it is in sense a Christmas play—that is, a lot of people are (if ever now) pyschologically tuned in on a religious aspect of life then. Don't you agree?" The opening of *Days Without End* was finally set for December 27 at Boston's Plymouth Theatre. The press duly reported on the Guild's new husband-and-wife team, "who have signed a joint contract . . . similar to the one given Alfred Lunt and Lynn Fontanne," and on Stanley Ridges, who had been seen by Boston audiences only a few weeks before in a minor role during the *Mary of Scotland* tryout. O'Neill was scheduled to arrive in Boston in the company of his good friend Noel Coward, whose romantic operetta *Bitter Sweet* was opening at that city's Shubert Theatre on Christmas Eve.

The *Days Without End* final rehearsal period was beset with difficulties. The Guild, besides being confronted with a union demand that only relief men instead of department heads be sent as light operators, ran into director trouble. Moeller, experiencing resistance from the author over additional cuts he believed necessary, was on the verge of resigning, but was persuaded to stay on at least until after Boston, or until such time as "Mr. O'Neill should express dissatisfaction with the cast and production."

O'Neill's script called for two actors to play contrasting portions of the hero's personality—one to be conventionally made up, the other, representing his baser nature, to wear a grotesque semi-mask. O'Neill had used masks before; so, not too surprisingly, the Boston critics did not respond aversely to this somewhat novel device. They all seemed to be rather taken by the play with its frankly Roman Catholic overtones. Helen Eager of the *Boston Traveler* thought, "America's foremost dramatist has delved deeply into the mental anguish of a man torn between the peace remembered in a religious childhood, and a mind blackened with atheism, born of tragedy." Elinor Hughes of the *Boston Herald* felt that while the masks used in *The Great God Brown* had obscured meanings, making them needlessly bewildering, the same device used in *Days Without End* had clarified the contrasting "static quality of this visualized spirit of denial with the desperate, agonized, emotional side of the same man . . . . one of the most adroit theatre strokes we have ever seen."

The third act of the play, in which the two sides of John Loving have it out before a huge crucifix, was found by George Holland of the *Boston Evening American* to be "one of the best . . . ever written for the stage. No play's beginning and middle could cope in strength with that climax." The sum of Boston's critical opinion was that O'Neill's latest contribution to morality drama would be warmly welcomed by the orthodox everywhere for its emphasis on domestic and religious regularity.

Moeller's doubts seem to have subsided, judging from an interview granted a few days after the play opened. He had only glowing things to say about script and dramatist (at least, for public consumption). O'Neill, he stated, was a quiet man, saving his communications for the play form, and was an author who never made suggestions about how to stage or how to act various scenes. Also, though he always had a final word on casting, he seldom forced any change in personnel. Moeller then went on to analyze *Days Without End:*

> This play of his is almost static. There is no motion in it. It is musicianly throughout, as O'Neill is always. His writing is truly contrapuntal. He takes a theme, devises its answer, and plays around it, in different keys, building up complexities of counterpoint until the whole thing resolves in a magnificent climax. [Philip Moeller as quoted by Elizabeth Borden, *Boston Herald,* Dec. 31, 1933]

Moeller discussed his own technique for handling actors. He always worked out a pattern for a play, "curves and graciousness for comedy; angles and stark monotonous levels for tragedy." He also encouraged his players to contribute as they worked, to give their conception of how to communicate their roles to the audience. Moeller said he knew from experience when an idea would work and when it would not, although he could never indicate how to change it. He explained, "I am like a conductor who cannot play the oboe, nor teach it, but who knows when it is played ill or well, and what its uses are."

Because of Boston's enthusiastic critical reception, church sources implied that a special performance of *Days Without End* might be given in the auditorium of Saint Patrick's Cathedral for New York's Cardinal Hayes. The Guild was delighted by this special recognition, and unhesitatingly offered that the performance could be presented at the Cardinal's convenience. There was, however, still the New York opening to reckon with; so, the publicity mill, under Russel Crouse's control, continued to grind.

In a pre-opening night interview for the *New York Times,* O'Neill mentioned his utilizing of masks for "psychological characterization." The playwright went on to discuss the uses masks might be put to in other plays:

> Masks would liberate "Hamlet" for example . . . from its present confining status as a "star vehicle." We would be able to see the great drama we are now only privileged to read, and to identify ourselves with the figure of Hamlet as a symbolic projection of a fate that is in each of us, instead of merely watching a star give us his version of a great acting role.

O'Neill openings have usually been occasions of deep interest on the part of New York's theatregoing public, and *Days Without End,* opening at Henry Miller's Theatre on January 8, 1934, was no exception. The Guild, alert to this special excitement, made a strong bid in its programs for season's subscriptions, offering good seats for six productions for as little as $6.60. Then the play opened.

The kindest of reviewers said that the playwright was apparently furthering his quest after the religious meanings in life:

> As for the play as a play, it is only very partially successful. One must assume, I think, that it was deeply felt, but the deepest feelings do not, unfortunately, always receive the most adequate expression, and the fable suffers from the fact that it can hardly mean much to those who are not themselves half prepared to join the hero in his leap. [Joseph Wood Krutch, *The Nation,* Jan. 24, 1934]

Most of the reviews, however, were not so sympathetic. John Anderson accused O'Neill of having gone on an emotional binge in which he unreservedly championed the old-time religion. Richard Lockridge found that O'Neill's means of telling his story had "seldom laid him more open to travesty." Brooks Atkinson was of the opinion that the play offered no suggestion of "the nervous drive with which he can usually give his thoughts stature and force in the theatre."

Nevertheless, Moeller's direction won universal approval, as did Simonson's settings—especially his use of lights and the crucifix in the third act. Earle Larimore was thoroughly complimented for his sensitive portrayal, and other members of the cast were singled out for praise. But John Mason Brown in the *Post* summed up most of the reactions:

> . . . the sorry fact remains that, in spite of the Guild's first-aid treatment, and the script's obvious sincerity of purpose, this latest drama of Mr. O'Neill's must take its place along with "Dynamo" and "Welded" among the feeblest of his works. . . . It is as heavy-handed and pretentious as only its author can be in his less fortunate efforts. Indeed so static is most of its tricky writing and so trite is the conclusion toward which it labors that one hates to think of what a first-night audience would have done to it if the program had not carried Mr. O'Neill's name.

The day after the reviews appeared, Moeller announced at a Board of Managers meeting that O'Neill had stated he was prepared to keep *Days Without End* running indefinitely. Faced with the playwright's determination, the Guild engaged Helen Hoerle to do special publicity work on the production's behalf. She arranged to speak before numerous church groups, and the Guild in its turn would invite about 1,400 priests, ministers, and rabbis to the performances as its guests. Although he approved the play, Cardinal Hayes now sent word, however, that he did not sanction a special performance to be given for himself and the clergy. Apparently, there would be no official endorsement of a turkey, be it ever so pious.

Valiant attempts at stimulating general participation did not keep the production from closing after fifty-seven performances. It was the last new O'Neill work the Guild's managers, or the playwright, were to offer the public for more than twelve years.

If *Days Without End* had dealt with the realm of the spirit, the Guild's next New York production pondered more mundane matters. The organization held an option on *They Shall Not Die* by John Wexley, a "journalism playwright," whose burning indictment of capital punishment, *The Last Mile,* had profoundly stirred Broadway audiences two seasons before. The script of *They Shall Not Die* more or less accurately reported on the famous Scottsboro case, involving nine Negro youths who were tried for raping a white woman hobo on a freight train traveling through Alabama in March, 1931. In spite of the fact that the International Labor Defense Committee had thrown its weight behind the accused, and chief defense counsel Samuel Leibowitz had fought a brilliant court battle, two of the boys had been sentenced to die in the electric chair. Wexley felt it important that his piece be staged while appeal petitions were actively being sought.

On September 6, 1933, a reduced Board of Managers voted two to one to do the play—Moeller and Miss Helburn for, Langner opposed. On September 20, the managers decided they could not schedule the production until after the first of the year, and Miss Helburn was authorized to tell Wexley that the Guild was inclined to release the script if he felt such a late production date would impair the play's propaganda value. Other producers were interested, but Wexley decided to stay with the Guild. On October 10, play reader John Gassner, who had been in touch with the playwright, reported that Wexley was most anxious to start work on a final version of the script. Simonson, who had returned from other work to take up his Guild duties, and Moeller were named a committee to suggest whatever revisions were believed necessary. At the same time, Moeller announced that he would be quite interested in staging the production.

The Guild's managers apparently were not completely convinced of *They Shall Not Die's* artistic merits nor of its marketability, although the International Labor Defense Committee had indicated its willingness to buy out a number of performances. The Guild even entertained the idea of presenting the play for two weeks only as a special nonsubscription bill, offering its regular subscribers reduced rates. Thus, losses would not be so great if the attraction should receive bad notices and fail completely.

On November 20 the managers considered delaying *They Shall Not Die's* production date indefinitely: "It was felt that this play should not be produced until after the current trial because if the Negroes were acquitted the play would not be so vital whereas if they were convicted or lynched the play would be of tremendous interest."

By the beginning of December the Guild had warmed a bit to its task. The size of the cast of *They Shall Not Die* and its four different settings made for an unusually costly production. Yet, the Guild did not renege on talent, and considered the best available players for important roles, though it had been decided no one was to be featured. Paul Muni and Ruth Gordon were approached to play leading parts, and, when Muni could not join, Claude Rains, in what was to be his first stage appearance since portraying *The Invisible Man* in the movies,[1] was given the assignment of defense attorney Nathan G. Rubin. Helen Westley, who had also just returned from Hollywood after playing Constance Bennett's maid in *Moulin Rouge* and George Arliss' mother in *The House of Rothschild,* was assigned to the cast because she did not want to break her record of appearing in at least one Guild play during the season. Later, Linda Watkins, Dean Jagger, and Thurston Hall were also selected.

During the early weeks in February, with rehearsals already well under way, the Guild became apprehensive. Its legal representative, Charles Riegelman, suggested the possibility of libel or slander suits initiated against the Guild because *They Shall Not Die* adhered so closely to actual personalities and events. Wexley reported that his attorneys had advised him no basis for a suit existed. Riegelman, nevertheless, believed otherwise, stating that the Guild's directors individually would be liable if such suits were instituted. The Guild requested its counsel to go over the script with Scottsboro defense counsel Joseph Brodsky to confirm Wexley's opinion that, even if the content of the play were libelous, it was a fair statement of the case based on the evidence, the testimony, and the affidavits of various witnesses. Following this meeting, Riegelman suggested the deletion of certain lines to which the Board agreed.

The Guild at first toyed with the idea that all returns from the presentation of *They Shall Not Die* would be donated to the defense of "the Scottsboro boys." It was decided, instead, that "a substantial sum" would be proffered, if the production were to show a profit. It was also decided that a benefit performance for the National Committee for the Defense of Political Prisoners would be given if the actors would agree to forego their salaries for the occasion. The actors refused, and the indignant Guild sent letters to Actors Equity, the Stage Relief Fund, and the Actors Fund concerning its cast's refusal to participate in this worthy act.

From the very start, the Guild had planned an out-of-town premiere for *They Shall Not Die.* First Philadelphia had been considered, then

[1]Other Guild alumni, such as Henry Travers and Dudley Digges, also played in James Whale's *The Invisible Man.*

Washington was decided upon, and the Board voted that Clayton Hamilton, "or some other suitable person," should be sent there to enlist the interest of prominent people on the play's behalf. A short time later the opening was announced for the week of February 19—then, under a Washington dateline, the story broke that *They Shall Not Die*'s first showing had been cancelled at the National Theatre "because of the District of Columbia laws preventing the appearance on the stage of anyone under sixteen." Racial considerations, however, were believed to have contributed heavily to the decision. It was recalled that the playing of *The Green Pastures* in Washington had occasioned many protests and had run afoul of the same minimum-age requirements. A special performance had to be given for Negroes, who were not permitted to attend the production's regular showings. The Guild sent its *School for Husbands* to fill the gap left by the cancellation.

Another play concerned with the Scottsboro case, called *Legal Murder,* was scheduled to open just before the Guild's premiere date. The Guild decided to do nothing to oppose this production, but it must have felt relieved when the *Brooklyn Times* claimed that *Legal Murder,* which opened at the little President Theatre on February 15, "although . . . not altogether devoid of merit," had to be classed as crude melodrama. It was also felt "that a more pretentious effort could have been made if the idea was to sway public sentiment in behalf of the convicted colored men." The Guild was sure *They Shall Not Die* would succeed where *Legal Murder* had failed.

John Wexley's *cause célèbre* opened at New York's Royal Theatre on February 21, 1934, with Samuel Leibowitz, Mayor LaGuardia, and other dignitaries in the audience. Toward the close of the evening, as the spectators began to be gripped by the effect of the play's argument, "there was applause and occasionally hisses, both expressing not so much the feeling of the audience toward the work of the players, as such, as toward the personages and proceedings of the story."

The next day the reviews all admitted that Wexley had written another powerful stage piece, although there were some questions raised as to whether it could be called art:

> For the most part its frank propaganda makes stirring and effective use of the stage, and the Guild has given it a production that is at least flexible and swift. . . . But taken as propaganda or not, "They Shall Not Die" does make up a play that is steadily engrossing, a painful play, no doubt, but exciting, and something to

get hot about these cold nights, which are not so cold, it seems as a court can be. [John Anderson, *New York Evening Journal,* Feb. 22, 1934]

John Wexley, who once wrote a good play entitled "The Last Mile," and then a second one entitled "Steel," which was better than most people believed it to be, has now written one that will send a shiver of apprehension across the country. . . . It was played at the Royale Theatre last evening by one of the most stirring casts the Theatre Guild has assembled. It is Mr. Wexley's declaration of his belief that the Scottsboro Negroes have been sentenced to die when grave doubt as to their guilt exists. Under Philip Moeller's resourceful direction it is a play of terrifying and courageous bluntness of statement—thoughtfully developed, lucidly explained and played with great resolution. None of the great causes of the last decade has received in the theatre such a calmly worded and overwhelmingly forceful defense as this. For once good works match the crusader's intentions. [Brooks Atkinson, *New York Times,* Feb. 22, 1934]

Often he has lessened the impact of what he says by the excited manner of the saying. . . . Where Mr. Wexley has overwritten, several of the actors badly overplay. One must wish it were all more surely done—and be glad of its violent sincerity, and that it was done at all. [Richard Lockridge, *New York Evening Sun,* Feb. 22, 1934]

Acting honors in *They Shall Not Die* were many and varied. Claude Rains was judged to be magnificent in the closing courtroom scene in which Wexley had "evaded nothing—Jew baiting, sectionalism, political rancor, bloodlust or mob rule for Negroes." Rains had seized upon this challenge "with all the conquering power of his voice and dynamic force. It is a passage of brilliant inflection, sharply defined and deeply felt, closing its heated logic in the startling, cool, and majestic prayer at the end. . . . " How did Rains, an Englishman, act with such skill the part of a Jewish-American lawyer?

He watched Samuel Leibowitz, upon whom the character is based, in court. He visited East Side restaurants and listened to Jewish lawyers talk. . . . His greatest difficulty was with words such as "produce." The American pronunciation is not quite the King's English. . . . The opening night he considers one of his real victories in the theatre. For in all the reviews of the play the following day not one word could be found which referred to his English accent or even to the fact that he is an English actor. That is what pleased him most. Evidently it pleases audiences, too, for he never fails to win applause and even cheers when he finishes his great speech in the play, the courtroom speech, which, incidentally, he considers the finest speech he has ever had in the theatre. [*New York Evening Post,* Feb. 28, 1934]

Ruth Gordon as Lucy Wells, one of the girls who presses rape charges, also won praise, as did Helen Westley and Dean Jagger. One comment came from Ruby Bates, the actual girl who recanted her testimony during the Scottsboro trial, and whom the International Labor Defense Committee brought to New York to see the play:

> "Well," she said, pausing to choose her words, for she isn't, by training, an articulate person, "It's pretty much like what happened to me. And the girl that takes my part [Ruth Gordon]—she's very good in that. I liked that part best. I guess I would, it being supposed to be me. Where Russell Evans [Dean Jagger] comes in and makes love to the girl, that's pretty much what happened. Only, instead of bringing me those dresses, he brought me two pairs of stockings. The woman who is supposed to be my mother [Helen Westley], she takes off the part real well. She doesn't look like my mother, but I guess that would be pretty hard to do on the stage, but what she says and all was like my mother."
>
> The interviewer wondered whether Miss Bates had any objections to that part of her characterization which has its sordid side. Mr. Wexley has been brutally frank in places.
>
> "Why should I object?" she said, simply. "That's what happened. Why shouldn't people know about conditions down there that make those things happen? Maybe it does make me look kinda not so nice in places. I was making only $2.75 at the most in the mills, and after the trial I was making less than that. We had to pay $9 a month rent, and we had to have some money. Besides, all that is past now, and I don't think of it so much as myself when I look back, but as some other girl. I just try to forget it." [*New York Herald Tribune,* March 4, 1934]

There was also considerable interest aroused by *They Shall Not Die* below the Mason-Dixon line:

> Indeed, a pretty picture is presented with the various scenes of this play. Obviously written to shock, it is as close a parallel of

> the unfortunate Scottsboro case as could be made without mentioning actual names and without damaging the evidence in favor of the accused. In the first act practically every white is represented as a Simon Legree with a fowling piece instead of a bull-whip, the Negro boys as objects of profound pity (and all of them potential Uncle Toms). As the play unwinds black is found to be no less white and white no less black. Then to color up the piece a bit a dash of red is introduced with the advent of the International Labor Defense's legal Lochinvar, who comes out of the North. [Leo Hershfield, *Chattanooga Daily Times,* Feb. 28, 1934]

The foreign-language newspapers of New York—Greek, Russian, German, Chinese, Lithuanian, Italian, etc.—gave special and complete coverage to the Guild's production of *They Shall Not Die.* The Jewish press ran stories about playwright John Wexley, "the nephew of Maurice Schwartz of Yiddish Art Theatre fame." The play's verisimilitude was attested to by *New York Times* reporter F. Raymond Daniell, who had been present at the actual proceedings. He did not recall one important line in the play he had not heard before in the Alabama courtroom, although he suggested that the dramatist's imagination may have roamed a bit at the play's opening, which undertook to convince audiences that the defendants had been "framed" by the public officials involved. *World-Telegram* critic Robert Garland, however, in post-opening write-up seized on the Daniell article to score *They Shall Not Die* a bit. Two days later, Richard Watts, Jr. of the *Herald Tribune* wrote an answer to Garland's column defending the production and scoring Garland!

One might suppose that, after so much give-and-take concerning *They Shall Not Die,* curious New Yorkers would make a special point of seeing just what all the controversy was about. The fact was that New York playgoers, by and large, remained aloof and stayed away, flocking instead to *Dodsworth,* a play by Sidney Howard based on Sinclair Lewis' novel, or patronizing *Men in White* by Sidney Kingsley, which the Group Theatre was presenting with marked success.

The Guild had partially foreseen public indifference, however. Before opening *They Shall Not Die,* it had scheduled a discussion forum for its members, and anyone else interested, to publicize the case and, incidentally, the play. Maurice Wertheim acted as moderator, and Samuel Leibowitz and Joseph Brodsky, defense counsels for the Negroes, William Patterson of the International Labor Defense, and Scottsboro witness Ruby Bates shared the Royale Theatre stage with

Elmer Rice, Ernest Boyd, H. V. Kaltenborn, Wexley, and Moeller. Rice, called upon to sum up the findings of this symposium, said, "We have tended to be pretty critical of the Hitler regime, of Mussolini, even of Russia, but right at our doorstep lies something which overshadows anything being done in Europe."

Reviewers of the intellectually-oriented periodicals found *They Shall Not Die* stimulating and worthwhile. Stark Young thought it "racially socially significant . . . tragic material for drama." Joseph Wood Krutch voted it one of the "ten best" of Broadway. Samuel Leibowitz even offered to play Rains' role for one performance to awaken interest. Nevertheless, the public preferred not to be harrowed by plays about social injustice, and serious patrons of newer Broadway productions found a Guild reject, Sidney Howard's and Paul DeKruif's *Yellow Jack,* more to their liking.

By the beginning of April, with the National Association for the Advancement of Colored People insisting that certain portions of the play be emended, the Guild decided to conclude *They Shall Not Die*'s run. Hope for survival, however, came from an unexpected source. Left-wing journalists began exhorting the faithful with "any money to spare for the theatre" to see this "real" drama:

> The old Theatre Guild, which has wasted so much fine talent and technique on feeble costume plays, and the senilities of Shaw and O'Neill, and similar "spiritualities" of the empty and pretentious bourgeoisie, has exhibited a kind of second youth in this production. . . . It was almost taken off last week, but was continued for a while. Prices have been slightly reduced, to put the seats within reach of a proletarian pocket. Go and see this play. Don't let your prejudice against the Theatre Guild or Broadway hold you back. If you can keep this play alive for six months on Broadway, it will be a great victory for revolutionary culture! [Michael Gold, *Daily Worker,* April 11, 1934]

They Shall Not Die closed after its sixty-second performance.

It is doubtful whether the Guild was able to make much of a contribution to the Scottsboro defense fund from *They Shall Not Die*'s profits. The size of the cast drained any substantial return from the offering. And, as Brooks Atkinson pointed out, most plays written concerning current controversial issues rarely became Broadway hits. The Guild's *Both Your Houses,* for instance, had not been a success until the Pulitzer Prize drew attention to it. No matter how well it was produced, nor how well it was received, *They Shall Not Die* was still social propaganda. The Theatre Guild was not set up in principle, nor equipped by temperament, to offer this kind of *engagé* theatrical fare, which could have been better left to the Theatre Union or some other group dedicated to displaying and exploiting the political passions and struggles of the times. Yet, with its very next production the Guild offered its customers yet another look at contemporary problems.

About the middle of December the Guild decided to buy a script that was both an anti-Nazi and an anti-racial discrimination treatise. Its author, Ferdinand Bruckner (real name: Theodor Tagger), had been a stage director of some note at the Renaissance Theatre in Berlin before he turned playwright, but he had had to leave Germany to live in Vienna and Paris when Hitler rose to power. His play, *Races,* had been given first in Zurich to considerable acclaim, and the Guild wished its translator, Ruth Langner, to polish her adaptation so that it might be submitted to the Lunts, who were enjoying a successful season in England. The Lunts were not interested, however. Theresa Helburn and Lawrence Langner were then appointed a temporary production committee to begin tentative casting procedures. Franchot Tone, Judith Anderson, Walter Slezak, Dorothea Wieck, Sam Jaffe, Elisabeth Bergner, and Zita Johann were all considered at one time or another, and Jacob Ben-Ami was thought of as a possible director. Mordecai Gorelik put in a bid to do the scenery, but Simonson was selected as designer, and Miss Helburn as director, with Langner and Simonson to act as the permanent committee.

Guild actors Earle Larimore and Stanley Ridges, who were terminating their run in *Days Without End,* were assigned to *Races,* but it became obvious the most important member of the potential cast was a young Viennese actress by the name of Mady Christians. Indeed, when the Guild faced the possibility of being denied Miss Christians' services, it agreed to cancel the production rather than do it without her.

In January the Guild's managers decided to pay Bruckner's passage to America and his living expenses so that he might help to publicize *Races,* and also help "to clarify its obscure points." A symposium was arranged, similar to the one held for *They Shall Not Die,* in which Bruckner was to address the Guild's subscribers in German. The managers also hoped to give a benefit performance of the play for the American Committee for the Relief of Victimized German Children, a charitable gesture seemingly a necessity with plays of this nature. They decided upon an out-of-town opening.

Ferdinand Bruckner's *Races* made its American début at the Chestnut Street Opera House in Philadelphia on March 19, 1934. Although its credentials were impressive the Guild's latest offering was not found to be too inviting by Philadelphia's professional playgoers. All felt that the production displayed the Guild's usual technical adroitness, but that the play itself left much to be desired:

> Too often it loses sight of its story to become a one-sided debate. Too often characters theorize under the stress of emotions. Bruckner has called upon every device to achieve his effects. He has used the colloquy, and the hidden voice which is a man's soul speaking to him. When he reverts to the dramatic, Bruckner is most effective [and] his theories become believable. When he allows characters to become involved in debates . . . he sacrifices drama. [Peter Stirling, *Philadelphia Record,* March 20, 1934]

> . . . the play is better propaganda than theatre. One feels that unless the spectator takes into the playhouse a desire to see the Nazi government "exposed," he will not find the proceedings absorbing. [Odell Hauser, *Philadelphia Evening Ledger,* March 20, 1934]

Such warnings were ominous, and, as the out-of-town performances limped along, Bruckner expressed his utter dissatisfaction with the way Miss Helburn had changed his "spectacular" play into an "intimate" production. He was also dissatisfied with certain cast members, Mady Christians included, and suggested that directors be changed. The estimated cost of such adjustments was exceedingly high. One actor, Clarence Derwent, sent a letter to the Guild, stating that the cast members would play cooperatively if the Guild would pay all other expenses and bring the show into New York. The Guild resolved, however, that rather than risk a debasement of its reputation on Broadway, it would quietly close the offering at the end of its two-week Philadelphia sojourn. Bruckner was sent back to Europe, and the play was shelved "perhaps until next season."

Thus, the Guild had learned again that a sermonizing and proselytizing play, no matter how worthy its cause, usually does not make for very rewarding theatre. The producers also had learned that they could not sustain enough interest with this kind of production to satisfy their regular patrons, who were unquestionably used to a more sophisticated set of values in character and situation than these special "pleading dramas" afforded.

The sudden out-of-town demise of *Races* left a sixth play missing from the Guild's New York schedule. There were hurried conferences about whether to produce a final play or to make ticket refunds to subscribers—as the Guild ignominiously had been forced to do the previous season. Warren Munsell pointed out that refunding admissions was not a good policy; several thousand patrons had already renewed their subscriptions; also, since bills to some had been sent, corrected ones would have to be made out and over 10,000 checks returned. It was decided to do a three-week rush job on a light comedy entitled *Jig Saw,* which the Guild had hoped to do only "as an extra production with a limited commitment in case it did not succeed." The Board, indeed, had been sharply divided over whether or not to do this trifle. In any event, Moeller's directorial touch was believed necessary to bring novelist Dawn Powell's *Jig Saw* up to stageworthiness.

Earlier in the season, Alice Brady had been considered for *Jig Saw,* and Ina Claire had been sent the script, but returned it saying it was unsuited to her talents. Finally, only Fay Bainter and Spring Byington were being considered as possible leading ladies, and when Miss Bainter became involved with *Dodsworth,* the role fell to Miss Byington.

Miss Powell had had some success with her nondramatic writings before her play *Big Night* was produced by the Group Theatre during the 1932–33 season. An earlier play, *Walking Down Broadway,* had been made into a movie. At college she had been a member of a class in dramatic technique taught, incidentally, by Eda Heinemann, then appearing in *Ah, Wilderness!*

The Guild opened *Jig Saw* on April 30, 1934, at the Ethel Barrymore Theatre. The reviews were more or less typified by that of Percy Hammond in suggesting that, while Miss Powell had a flair for breezy patter and a rakish sort of sophistication, "there are indications at times that . . . the actors have to stoke the play to keep it burning. Its humor and observations are industriously deliberate, even forced now and then." *Jig Saw* concerns a fluttery, amoral divorcée "who hums as she opens packages from the shops, and who worries in fear that some day she will enter a restaurant and that men present will not stop eating." This lady lives in a penthouse atop a comparatively smart Central Park hotel, an arrangement provided "by a frigid sweetheart, wise, witty and sardonic. . . . This dominant and understanding person is acted by Ernest Truex, hitherto famed as a portrayer of sturdy Casper Milquetoasts," Hammond wrote. Complications arise when the divorcée's sixteen-year-old daughter appears.

Jig Saw was barely distinguishable from the majority of commercial entertainments that Broadway provides yearly for its customers:

> Miss Powell has learned her craft by close attention to the accepted patterns. She knows when to be daring, when to be perverse, what foibles are most risible and how to twist lines into laughs. . . . "Jig Saw" may be dull under the surface, but it is bright on top, where facile humors are displayed to best advantage. [Brooks Atkinson, *New York Times,* May 1, 1934]

The consensus on *Jig Saw* was that, while its naughty sophistication was well inside the Broadway bailiwick, it might have become a trifle monotonous were it not for the deftness of its cast and the cunning of its director. It lasted for forty-nine performances.

In October 1933, *Time* magazine compared the depressed beginning of the 1933–34 season to 1929–30, when roughly 30,000 people had made their living as actors in burlesque, vaudeville, and stock companies, as well as in first-run legitimate dramas and musical presentations. The doleful fact was that since 1930 paid-up memberships in the Actors Equity Association had declined by 70 percent and a number of relief organizations in Manhattan, such as the Actors' Fund, "and the benignantly tactful Actors' Dinner Club—where nobody knows who pays for two dinners and who pays for none,"—had spent almost $300,000 yearly to temper the blight of hard times on the profession. Two-thirds of the theatres along Broadway had been dark at the close of the previous year.

Although at mid-season the *Daily News* could boast, "We're having a perfectly grand theatre season in New York!" (besides the Guild's two hits, other productions, such as *Men in White* and *Tobacco Road,* were doing exceptional business), there were rumblings from legions of unemployed theatrical artists. This unrest was influential in producing the restrictions set forth in the Dickstein Bill, a proposed piece of legislation that would have curtailed the use of foreign acting talent in American productions even more.

Frank Gillmore, president of Actors Equity, upheld passage of the Dickstein Bill:

> The [American] actors feel that they should be permitted in their own country to make their art a national one without the undue

> influence of foreigners. My people feel that the individual alien actor of no standing should not be permitted to take the place of our own; those who are longing to express themselves in the profession to which they have devoted their lives. [*New York Evening Post,* March 3, 1934]

The Guild, however, was opposed to it, since a number of their employees—Merivale, Coulouris, Rains and others—could have been affected if such legislation were passed. Miss Helburn stated the Guild's position:

> One of the most valuable elements in the American theatre is that which is contributed by the infusion of foreign actors. Type casting and the absence of established companies in America have limited the range of our acting technique. The foreign actor is still essential, especially in view of the raid constantly being made on the theatre by Hollywood. Therefore, any movement to limit the acting profession to Americans exclusively, such as the Dickstein bill, is dangerous.

Other stage luminaries, notably Helen Hayes (who was then working with a large group of Englishmen), and Tallulah Bankhead (whose career had been enhanced by appearances in England), were opposed to the Dickstein provisions, while some, such as Katharine Cornell and Clifton Webb, lent their qualified support to the bill. Finally, George M. Cohan noted a similar ruling in force on the other side of the Atlantic:

> I feel that we should have a corresponding law here to offset any law they now have in England governing alien actors. . . . They'll soon discover, however, that placing restrictions on the art of acting will not work out successfully. They need American actors and we need English actors in order to cast our respective plays properly. My honest conviction is that for the good of the English-speaking drama it should be free to all and the whole idea called off both ways.

Ultimately, Equity became the regulating agent in all such matters.

Despite the possibility of losing some of its more talented players because of pending legislation, the Guild had treated its subscribers to a rather remarkable season. Success had caused a number of interesting propositions to be offered the organization. For instance, Rouben

Mamoulian had suggested the possibility of directing a play for the Guild with Greta Garbo as its star, and the play department sought vainly for a vehicle worthy of the actress' talents. Fritz Kreisler had written a Viennese operetta he thought the Guild might be interested in presenting. Al Jolson approached the Guild with an offer to star in a musical version of *Porgy,* for which he had lined up Jerome Kern and Oscar Hammerstein to write the music and lyrics. Later, George Gershwin expressed a desire to work on a score for the Du Bose and Dorothy Heyward play, and he was granted tentative approval by the Board of Managers.

The various Guild managers also had pet projects which they wished to have produced. Theresa Helburn, for instance, was very keen on presenting a German comedian, Max Pallenberg, in the title role of *Good Soldier Schwejk,* to be directed by Piscator. Langner thought the Guild should bring over John Gielgud as *Hamlet,* and Wertheim believed *King Lear* with either Charles Laughton or Edward G. Robinson (with *The Tempest* as an alternative) would help alleviate the Guild's long neglect of Shakespeare. Simonson was enthusiastic about doing *Antony and Cleopatra* with the Lunts, while Moeller suggested mounting a production of *The Sea Gull* with Claude Rains and Nazimova.

Such intriguing plans would not materialize until some time in the future; still, the Guild could happily look back on the events of their noteworthy sixteenth season. For a fair part of the theatrical year the organization had four Broadway playhouses operating simultaneously. Things had not all gone as expected, to be sure (*Days Without End, Races, Jig Saw,* and *They Shall Not Die* could be called flops), but *Ah, Wilderness!* and *Mary of Scotland* had been among the major successes of the year for many months, and *The School for Husbands* had been at least one of its minor triumphs. Any commercial manager would have been more than happy with such a record. Only Max Gordon had surpassed it with a series of hits which included *Her Master's Voice, Roberta, The Shining Hour,* and, finally, *Dodsworth.*

There was no denying the impression, however, that the Guild had reached more-or-less comfortable middle age. *Jig Saw* had been something of a milestone in its career—its hundredth major presentation. The production policy of the organization had seemed to answer most of its critics of the past by obliging them. Once it had been criticized as indifferent to American drama, but during 1933–34 all but one of its offerings were the works of American authors, and Arthur Guiterman's humorous couplets had given *The School For*

Husbands an unmistakable American flavor. At one time the Theatre Guild's lack of interest in O'Neill had infuriated such critics as George Jean Nathan, but during its latest season the organization had demonstrated a willingness to produce O'Neill as uncritically as it had once produced Shaw, whose query concerning the staging of his *On the Rocks,* incidentally, had been gracefully sidestepped by the Board of Managers during the course of the year.

Naturally, the absence of Alfred Lunt and Lynn Fontanne had not gone unnoticed, and reportedly both Anderson and Behrman were working with the pair in mind. Although the Guild had cast its shows with many talented actors and had given George M. Cohan and Helen Hayes what many believed to be their greatest roles, the absence of the Lunts, who had been performing *Reunion in Vienna* for delighted London audiences, continued to be a very real concern to the Board. During its second year without them, however, the Guild had proven itself to be enormously able. Its standards of production were still as high as ever. With Lee Simonson on its Board and Robert Edmond Jones available for assignment, it had not once bungled its scenery or its costumes. On the contrary, both men had received praise for all their work. As a director, Philip Moeller had demonstrated he could master the details and motives of plays as remote in rhythm and feeling as *They Shall Not Die, Days Without End,* and *Jig Saw.* The Guild's level of craftsmanship seemed as high as that of any comparable organization in the United States, possibly even in the world. Brooks Atkinson, however, questioned whether superb technical skill was sufficient for a vigorous producing organization which was dedicated to artistic pursuits:

> Enthusiasm, exuberance, enterprise–these are the essence of a living theatre. Although the Guild has seldom been gay, it was once more aggressive and alert and it was once bursting with original ideas. Now it is giving sanctuary to authors who have already made their mark under different auspices, and it has concluded its season with a bright, clever, wicked little comedy that is indistinguishable from the primrose dalliance of Broadway. Although this has been one of the most successful seasons the Guild has ever had, it lacks advancement. . . . The Guild needs the tonic of a bold experiment. [*New York Times,* May 6, 1934]

Bold experiment probably would have been damned by the Guild's many critics, but it would have been encouraging to know that the foremost theatrical organization in America was still interested in such adventures as advancing the cause of the legitimate drama.

For the most of the 1933–34 season, Helen Westley, busy in Hollywood, had been excused from her more arduous Guild duties. A number of former Guild actors—Miriam Hopkins, Richard Bennett, Claudette Colbert, and Lionel Atwell among others—had, with varying success, ventured out to the West Coast. Mrs. Westley was the first of the Guild's Board to be so tempted. Her movie experience led her to seek a return engagement, starting a trend in which she was followed by first one, then another of her fellow Board members during the coming year.

CHAPTER 8 / 1934-35

A Sleeping Clergyman, James Bridie
Valley Forge, Maxwell Anderson
Rain From Heaven, S. N. Behrman
Escape Me Never, Margaret Kennedy
The Simpleton of the Unexpected Isles, Bernard Shaw
Parade, Various Authors

At the end of the 1933–34 theatrical year, Moeller announced to his fellow Guild managers that, following Helen Westley's lead, he would like to go to Hollywood to make a picture. There was no objection to this proposal, and in the early summer he left for the Radio-Keith-Orpheum lots in California. Several months later, in the early fall, Lee Simonson reported that he also had had a motion picture offer beginning in December, which would require about eight weeks of his time. The Board felt it would be good for him to have this opportunity. Sooner or later, thought Langner, the Guild itself would have to begin making movies of some of its own plays in order to hold any sort of acting company together; hence, the more Guild directors who became acquainted with the techniques of picture-making, the better. In fact, he suggested that feelers be put out to possible backers to finance a Guild picture unit. A bit later Maurice Wertheim stated to the Board that it would not be entirely impossible to finance a Theatre Guild picture outfit independently. In the meantime, it was necessary to begin seriously considering what the main business of the Guild was supposed to be.

Lawrence Langner, who was going to be abroad during the summer months, was appointed a committee of one by the Board of Managers to see the long-running London production of *A Sleeping Clergyman* by a Scottish physician named O. H. Mavor, who wrote for the stage under the pseudonym James Bridie. Being interested in the play, the Board gave Langner recommendations to Bridie concerning some rewriting they believed necessary for an American presentation. In September, Philip Moeller returned from Hollywood, where he had just finished directing the film *Age of Innocence,* to begin rehearsing the Bridie hit immediately.

A Sleeping Clergyman concerns the unpredictable nature of genetically determined qualities; as Joseph Wood Krutch stated it in *The Nation,* "There is no way of foretelling the slight twist which can turn a hereditary trait from virtue to vice or from vice to virtue."

The opening scene of *A Sleeping Clergyman* takes place in a London club where two doctors discuss various impulses attributed to heredity, while nearby a clergyman snoozes, symbolizing the dormant powers of the church. Unfortunately for the Guild, this snoring figure became a convenient vehicle upon which many clever reviewers rode, stating that they envied the churchman his noisy slumbers. Stark Young in *The New Republic* wished to know if the Guild's workers were worn out by the summer chores of "mounting plays in barns and sweeping wharves into immortality. If not, what else could account for the fatigue so evident in this event, [and] why should subscribers and critics be subjected to this banality, chitter and sloppiness?" The consensus indicated that Bridie the playwright might well acquire a few pointers from such former medical men as Schiller, Chekhov, Schnitzler, and Maugham. Yet, few reviews of *A Sleeping Clergyman* suggest that the play is devoid of ideas or markedly lacking in substance. Krutch became a Bridie champion, declaring that, while the playwright may not have mastered the essential art of compact dramatic construction,

> his characters stand on their own feet, are unmistakably themselves, not traditional figures of the drama. His passion is real and articulately communicated. Moreover, many individual scenes are written with the finest dramatic instinct, so that whatever has been said about a certain cumbersomeness in the organization of the whole does not apply to the movement of most of the parts taken by themselves. Some of them are, indeed, very nearly unforgettable, and they make the play by far the most worthwhile which this season has offered. [*The Nation,* Oct 24, 1934]

Several of the reviews noted Ruth Gordon's ever-increasing skill as an actress in her three roles, as well as Ernest Thesiger's perfectly enunciated King's English. Both Moeller and the Guild were complimented for general effectiveness. But the box office languished even so. The Guild cast about for various methods to promote their imported attraction. One attempt was to publish letters from Krutch,

Alexander Woollcott, and others attesting to the play's "passionate idealism" and "vividly alive" characters. Nothing lessened audience apathy, however, and the production closed after forty performances —almost as short a run as any Guild subscription offering could attain. Helen Westley returned to Hollywood as soon as her chores in *A Sleeping Clergyman* were finished. Theresa Helburn followed the actress' example shortly thereafter.

A Sleeping Clergyman closed so abruptly that the Guild was able to bring its second presentation of the 1934–35 season into its home theatre instead of having to hire another. This was Maxwell Anderson's *Valley Forge,* and the playwright was very anxious to choose its designer as well as to have a hand in its direction. The Guild, however, did not take kindly to his proposals, stating that if he wished to proceed along these lines he might obtain a half interest in the venture if he were willing to pay the entire production cost.

Since the tour of Anderson's *Mary of Scotland* was being delayed because of Helen Hayes' motion-picture commitments (much to the Guild's consternation), Philip Merivale, who was under contract to the organization and marking time in order to play Miss Hayes' Bothwell, was cast as General George Washington in *Valley Forge,* although it was felt that Lionel Barrymore, if available, would draw "bigger grosses."

Valley Forge had its out-of-town premiere at Pittsburgh's Nixon Theatre on November 19, 1934, with Anderson and John Houseman listed as co-directors. Although the critical reaction was encouraging, one reviewer, who had seen Anderson's script prior to opening night, felt that *Valley Forge* was better literature than theatre.

Valley Forge was moved to New York on December 10. Maxwell Anderson had been replaced as co-director by Herbert Biberman to improve the offering's timing and pace, and the entire production was critically well received—especially Merivale's acting. John Mason Brown felt that if Anderson's newest effort lacked some of the glamour and romantic sweep of *Mary of Scotland,* it evidenced other more important elements from some of his better earlier work:

> The starved frontiersmen who serve in his revolutionary army have much of the same vitality to them that belonged to the doughboys he once created with Laurence Stallings in "What Price Glory?" His representatives from the Continental Congress are treated with the same acid disrespect that he brought to the later-day legislators with whom he dealt in "Both Your Houses."

> And his language, in all his bigger moments, is possessed of the same loveliness and distinction that turned the verses of "Mary of Scotland" and "Elizabeth the Queen" into verbal music. [*New York Post,* Dec. 11, 1934]

Anderson had tried to tuck in a "silly and completely unnecessary former sweetheart of Washington's who visits his headquarters dressed as a Redcoat," but few critics were fooled into believing this character integral to the plot. *Valley Forge,* nevertheless, was considered to be a stirring theatre event by many. Grenville Vernon of *The Commonweal* thought it more deserving of a Pulitzer award than the ultimate 1933–34 recipient, *The Old Maid,* a dramatization by Zoë Akins of an Edith Wharton story which had been unanimously turned down by the Guild's Board earlier in the year. At least one critic, John Anderson, believed it to be one of the organization's all-time great presentations and recommended its inclusion in the Guild's 1936 anthology.

But in 1934, *Valley Forge,* an expensive show to run, failed to attract numerous patrons, and the Guild's managers doubted whether they could afford to keep it playing until the national tour began in the spring of *Mary of Scotland,* which used many of the same actors. *Valley Forge,* with its evocation of America's ideals in that year of general financial depression and threats from abroad, lasted fifty-eight performances. Theresa Helburn, however, acting in her new capacity as film producer, entered an inquiry concerning *Valley Forge*'s picture rights. It was decided to accept a $25,000 offer.

The Guild's next presentation also contained a strong statement in defense of human rights. S. N. Behrman had patterned the male protagonist of his newest play, *Rain From Heaven,* on a German literary critic, Alfred Kerr, who had lost his position in Nazi Germany because he was not farsighted enough to exclude some Jewish forebears. The play condemned Hitler's outrageous treatment of Jewish intellectuals, although the tone was almost one of high comedy.

The chief female character in *Rain From Heaven* is an English noblewoman of deep humanitarian convictions. The Guild and Behrman very much wanted Ina Claire to be their Lady Violet Wyngate; but because she was busy elsewhere, they obtained the services of Jane Cowl instead. The music critic in the play, Hugo Willens, was played by suave, Brooklyn-born John Halliday, and the usual rewriting necessary for a Behrman presentation took place after the premiere date of December 10 at Boston's Plymouth Theatre.

Rain From Heaven moved to New York's John Golden Theatre on Christmas Eve, where it was paid several graceful compliments by the local reviewers. One professional theatregoer could "recall no American play of recent years which contains . . . more sensitively drawn, civilized men and women." Robert Garland called *Rain From Heaven* "Behrman's most reflective composition," while Brooks Atkinson thought it had "the beguiling brilliance of a finely mitered work of art." Gilbert W. Gabriel registered his approbation by stating that the play needed none of its Shakespearean title's plea for mercy:

> It must be recognized as Mr. Behrman's finest work. . . . Finest, in this sense; his most thoughtful, his most positive and cleanly probing into the complex innards of those curious creatures, eternal man and modern woman. Finest, too, in its almost aromatic graciousness of wit and well-distilled wording. Full of his finest things to say, and of valor and of sleight-of-pen to say them. [*New York American*, Dec. 26, 1934]

Of course, not all the reviews were favorable:

> "Rain From Heaven" is a drama which is neither fish, flesh nor fowl. It has moments of Mr. Behrman's expected dialogic felicity. It is at most times warmed with ideas—even if they prove to be ideas that Mr. Behrman is unable to cope with. But it is more talky than is good for it and more confusing than is comfortable. [John Mason Brown, *New York Post*, Dec. 26, 1934]

Brown continued, though, to praise the Guild's production, Moeller's fit direction, Simonson's comfortable setting, and the fine nuances of Halliday's and Miss Cowl's acting.

Brooks Atkinson was perceptive enough to see in *Rain From Heaven* a second theme partially hidden under the dominant one of Nazi injustice. This had to do with civilized people who meet on congenial terms in the ordinary course of events, but who are enemies at heart. Social usage keeps their meetings pleasant, but, if they ever discussed seriously their private convictions, they would be astonished by the distances that divided them and the antagonisms that would result.

Rain From Heaven ran longer in New York than any Theatre Guild show that year, having ninety-nine performances. Toward the end of March it moved to Philadelphia, Pittsburgh, and the other Guild subscription cities. Moeller in the meantime had reported that a tentative offer had been made to him to direct another picture during the winter months. Therefore, he requested a leave of absence, with the proviso that he return in time to do his third contracted production for the Guild. The remaining managers had no objection.

Because of their growing preoccupation with the business of making Hollywood films, the Guild managers were quite glad that their next New York stage production was already made and needed only the proper theatre for its presentation. This offering was tailored to the famous German actress Elisabeth Bergner, who was to be introduced to American audiences.

This dramatic sequel to Margaret Kennedy's novel, *The Constant Nymph,* was described by Burns Mantle as a "spotty play, cut into eight scenes" called *Escape Me Never.* It had already played a highly successful season in London under the aegis of producer Charles B. Cochran, and the Guild, with Cochran as co-manager, brought the entire English production to New York intact. The organization hoped to make much of Miss Bergner's international reputation which included, among other things, her performance in a number of the Guild's plays in Germany. She had appeared as Nina in *Strange Interlude,* for instance, and as Joan in Shaw's *Saint Joan* and had played many classical roles such as Ophelia in *Hamlet* and Goethe's Iphigenie. Miss Bergner received good publicity when she arrived in this country by granting absolutely no press interviews. The Guild was to present its imported star's "limited engagement" at the Shubert, a large theatre mainly used for musical comedies.

The reviewers were, for the most part, enchanted by Miss Bergner's performance, but her vehicle left them a bit cold. Burns Mantle compared the foreign star favorably to Laurette Taylor in *Peg-o-My-Heart.* John Anderson wrote:

> It is neither the play nor the theatre for her, for the play is too small and the theatre is too large, but Miss Bergner triumphs over both of them to establish herself in her own right as an actress of uncommon power and distinction. By the skill and persuasion of her performance she almost makes even such stuff as "Escape Me Never" worth seeing. [*New York Evening Journal,* Jan. 22, 1935]

Some commended Komisarshevsky, who directed and designed the production, for having extracted just about everything that could be wrung from the sentimental script:

> Miss Bergner . . . is an elfin actress versed in all the pixie magic of the stage. In the beginning scenes she plays a blonde Topsy with a Jack Pearl Dialect. . . . She is addicted to scratching herself from head to heel and otherwise to be gamine and all that sort of thing. . . . There is nothing in the reservoir of a keen mime's devices that does not come to her when she summons it. She haunts a ramshackle play hauntingly. [Percy Hammond, *New York Herald Tribune,* Jan. 22, 1935]

The *Escape Me Never* reviews tended to stress the script's rather obvious appeal to those whose eyes moisten readily and the Guild's seeming willingness to secure a monetary triumph from Miss Bergner's American debut by displaying her talents in an over-large house:

> As a result the audience feels that something of importance is going on but cannot get the whole drift of it and goes away irritated. If you can't afford a front-row seat you will have a pleasanter reaction if you remain at home. You will unless the Guild's wise directors tell Miss Bergner she must talk loud enough to be heard at the box office. [Arthur Pollock, *Brooklyn Daily Eagle,* Jan. 22, 1935]

The inference that the Guild had raised its admission prices and had used a huge theatre in order to make a killing, however, was a trifle unjustified. The Shubert's management had demanded a huge percentage of the gross as its rental fee. Added to that, Cochran had asked for a dark theatre for two weeks in order to rehearse the large cast, on top of which the Gaige-Selwyn interests, who apparently owned a piece of the production, had to be guaranteed a $500 weekly payment. Hence, the Guild's portion of the Bergner pie was to be rather thin, but not so thin as to be unattractive (about $3,500 a week).

Escape Me Never did little to enhance the Guild's prestige. Elisabeth Bergner, whose cries in some performances could not have been heard in an off-Broadway house, while her whispers would easily have filled the Hippodrome during others, became offended by the reviews which stressed her spritely fey quality and wanted to show American critics what she could do in a truly demanding role. She persuaded Cochran to approach the Guild's Board with a proposition to revive *Saint Joan.* The Board refused. The actress then inquired about the possibility of appearing in *As You Like* It, to which the Board was a bit more receptive, especially in the event that *Escape's* business dropped off. Fortunately, business held steady and the Margaret Kennedy play filled its three-month engagement. Not too much later New Yorkers were favored with the movie version of *Escape Me Never,* which Miss Bergner had made earlier in England. It opened amid dignified fanfare at the Radio City Music Hall.

Several amusing incidents developed during *Escape Me Never*'s New York stay. The Guild was intrigued by the possibility of presenting Miss Bergner in a new James M. Barrie play, and then allowing Cochran to take the production back to London with him. It was pointed out, however, that if the Guild wanted Miss Bergner for any more plays the managers had better call on her individually and ingratiate themselves, for the actress liked attention and flattery. In fact, it was rumored, Cochran kept her happy only by acting as a combination factotum and nursemaid. A visiting schedule was therefore set up by the male members of the Board to facilitate the necessary veneration. It was also reported that Merivale was very much annoyed with the various members for not having come near him during the run of *Valley Forge,* and it was suggested that this seemingly impersonal treatment of important actors was one of the Guild's glaring weaknesses. George M. Cohan and the Lunts, too, (whose offering that year was Noel Coward's *Point Valaine*) apparently resented the distant attitude of the Guild's directorate toward its principal players. Immediately assignments were made putting into effect this back-patting routine throughout the various productions in New York and on the road. The Guild was learning a bit late what the employing of great stars entails.

During this period two authors, Paul Sifton and Virgil Geddes, began picketing theatres that housed the several Guild attractions and distributing pamphlets proclaiming themselves to be "The Provisional Committee of Unproduced Theatre Guild Playwrights." It seemed that together Sifton and Geddes had written some eight plays on which the Guild had accepted options, but that only one had been produced. The Guild chose to remain aloof in the face of such irritating behaviour. The press, however, was delighted to play up this tidbit, and John Gassner suggested that the Board's silence was being misconstrued as guilt or shame in some quarters. To alleviate this impression, the managers held serious deliberations to find a proper way to reply to the newspaper articles, as well as to answer the numerous letters that had come to the Guild's offices—some of which the managers felt had been "directly inspired" by the playwrights themselves. Business manager Munsell and press representative Crouse were appointed a committee of two to deal with any further trouble from peevish playwrights.

The Sifton-Geddes incident, however, served to point up a legitimate grievance younger playwrights entertained in regard to the Guild, for it usually took many months for the six managers to read a proposed script. Then, if it were accepted, there would often be no production arrangement for several years, if indeed a production ever did materialize. Certain scripts were accepted immediately and rushed onto the stage, of course, but usually these came from established authors such as Maxwell Anderson or Robert E. Sherwood. The Guild's Board, whose policy in the past had been to encourage newer playwrights, now believed that a reading option entitled it to ask for extensive revisions with no commitment whatsoever on its part made for a forthcoming production. This arrangement was bound to be considered unsatisfactory by any writer, as the Guild was to learn later, to its regret.

The Guild's most firmly established playwright, then in his eightieth year, had sent a new script to the organization which the managers surmised could not make money. But, since the Guild considered Bernard Shaw to be its patron saint, and because it rather shamefacedly failed to produce his *On the Rocks* the previous year, it decided to present his new offering using an inexpensive stylized setting, and otherwise cutting corners. Dudley Digges was approached to act as director for *The Simpleton of the Unexpected Isles,* but because he demanded an "exorbitant fee," several alternatives were considered, including Worthington Miner, Robert Sinclair, and Antoinette Perry. Finally, Harry Wagstaff Gribble, who had demonstrated a flair for enlivening unusual scripts, was selected, and rehearsals began, with Nazimova and Romney Brent in the leading roles. The Guild asked Shaw's permission to abbreviate the offering's title to facilitate advertising procedures. The producers should have known better. Shaw defended his title beautifully.

When *The Simpleton of the Unexpected Isles* opened at the Guild Theatre on February 18, 1935 (the organization's fifth Shavian world premiere), the superannuated wit was celebrating his fiftieth year of drama writing. The Guild had presented fourteen of his works, from which it had gained a good share of its renown. Financial considerations aside, Shaw, without a doubt, had served the organization well.

The next-day notices for *The Simpleton,* however, were unreclaimably bad. "Mr. Shaw, whose imagination has never been his peculiar

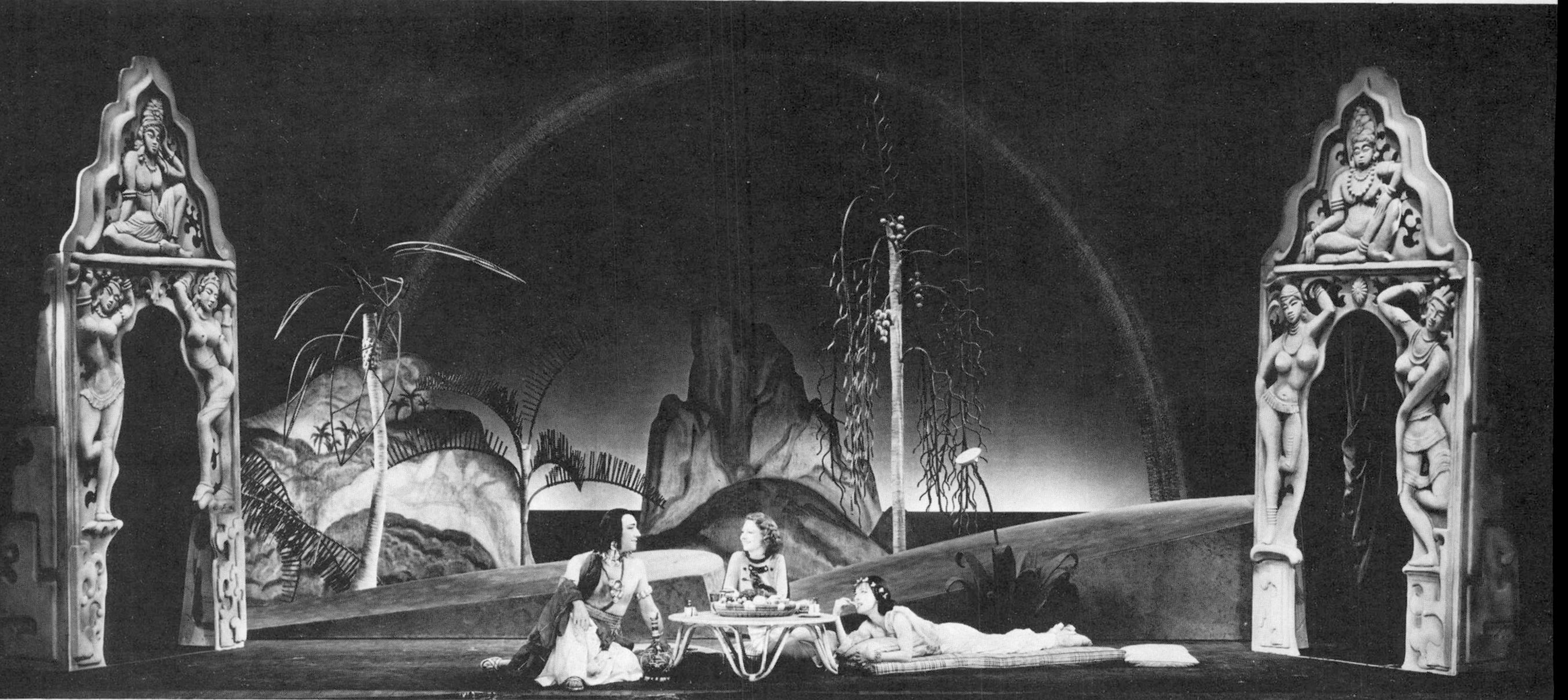

THE SIMPLETON OF THE UNEXPECTED ISLES – Lee Simonson's inexpensive, yet exotic depiction of a never-never land.

L. to r. – McKay Morris, Patricia Calvert, and Nazimova.

genius, has tried to write a serio-comic allegory or fantasy. It turns out to be labored, loquacious and soporific," Brooks Atkinson wrote. Romney Brent, who played the addlepated Reverend Mr. Phosphor Hemmingtap (originally "Hummingtop"), was thought admirably expert in his delivery of the seemingly endless Shaw dialogue, and Nazimova had never appeared to be more beguiling. Many said Gribble squeezed as much action out of the static script as possible, and Simonson's exotic settings, some of his most colorful, were considered to be as provocative as any to be then viewed along Broadway. General critical condemnation of the talkfest, however, continued unabated:

> The play is a collection of Mr. Shaw's favorite museum pieces posed in a gallery located on an island in the Nightmare Sea. He makes that atom of mythical geography the forum for a rambling discussion of what's-it-all-about. . . . The conclusions, and the events which lead up to them are, to batter a down-and-out adjective, Shavian. Like a dignified monkey he climbs a tree and pelts us with edifying cocoanuts—an experience that frequently becomes exceedingly onerous. [Percy Hammond, *New York Herald Tribune,* Feb. 19, 1935]

Despite a few half-hearted Guild salvage attempts, *The Simpleton of the Unexpected Isles* closed after forty performances.

The Guild's none-too-plentiful patrons of the Shaw failure had been promised that the organization's final play of the year would be chosen from a list that included *Native Ground* by the recalcitrant Virgil Geddes, *Storm Song* by Denis Johnston (author of *Moon in the Yellow River*), *The Last of the Equipajew,* a play from Soviet Russia written by Valentina Katajev, and *The Postman Always Rings Twice,* adapted by James M. Cain from his best-selling novel. The faithful subscribers instead were offered *Parade,* a satirical musical originally intended for presentation by the Theatre Union.

The prime attractions of *Parade,* as far as the Guild was concerned, included the exciting hope that the show seemed to be in fair working order with its cast mostly selected and rehearsed. Could it be put on the boards without too much managerial effort required? It seemed it could. And yet the Guild's Board, which had been operating at half strength for a good deal of the season, found time to tinker with the sketches, songs, and other arrangements submitted to it by Paul Peters and George Sklar, the piece's principal writers. The Guild after all would be gambling much more money on a politically oriented revue than it would have spent on, say, Edith Hamilton's version of Euripides' *The Trojan Women*—still another possibility for the year's last offering. *Parade* was selected, after considerable deliberation, because the satire seemed to have a better chance for a summer run than did the classic.

The "socially conscious" *Parade,* with Jimmy Savo as its star, opened at the Guild Theatre on May 20, 1935. It was not exactly a joyous occasion. Its biting thrusts at the often misdirected efforts of the New Deal might have been diverting had they been viewed from the vantage point of 14th Street. Uptown, under the Guild's banner (and after a bit of Guild tempering), its various insubordinations and "come-the-revolution" banterings seemed self-conscious and a trifle hollow. Percy Hammond found that the whole had "little gaiety and less beauty, though it is brimming with gaudy show-stop rebellion." Brooks Atkinson, a Savo buff of the first order, felt the show's comedian would have been shown to better advantage under less pretentious auspices:

> But give him a collection of gadgets as a background for his pantomime, starve him and wheel a hot-dog stand up to him, strike him down with appendicitis in a feverish clinic, or translate him into a bogus Indian—and the sheer good humor and gleam of Jimmy's comic dance will shatter your risibilities and open your heart at the same time.

Parade's main contribution to Broadway that year was presenting the musical-theatre public with the talents of such newcomers as Ezra Stone, Jack E. Leonard, dancers Dorothy Fox and Charles Walters (who had played the young son in *Strange Interlude*), as well as Eve Arden, "a versatile, good-looking and intelligent satirist," and singer Avis Andrews, "a lady of color who sings dark songs explicitly, and with better than the usual Harlem taste." But *Parade* never had the remotest chance of a summer sun. It closed after thirty-two performances and lost close to $90,000. The pink radicalism of the Guild's directorate, whose combined annual income (even excluding Wertheim's) ran well over $100,000, was a touching phenomenon of the times. In the case of *Parade,* however, it had warped managerial judgments. It should be added, nevertheless, that John Gassner always believed *Parade* was an important attempt to fill one rueful void in our culture's patterns, namely, the dearth of political satiric revues, long a staple of other countries' theatrical diet.

With *Parade,* the Guild brought to a close one of its less distinguished seasons. On the surface, the organization appeared to be keeping very much abreast of the cultural and social milieu of the period. It had demonstrated an awareness of conditions abroad as well as at home with its three best offerings: *Valley Forge* had called upon America to remember the convictions and the moral climate that existed during a distressed period of its past; *Rain From Heaven* had been an earnest appeal for the intellectual, as well as others who were tyrannized by Fascism, and its presentation of *Escape Me Never* had extended America's hospitality to Elisabeth Bergner, then a refugee from Nazi Germany. With its last and least successful offering the Guild had "paraded," often humorously, the clouds of protest then drifting across America's horizons. *The Simpleton of the Unexpected Isles* had offered rather a compendium of the wit and wisdom accumulated by one of the era's more important philosophers, as well as its most illustrious playwright. *The Sleeping Clergyman* had given the country a look at a highly regarded work by a promising Scottish dramatist. Furthermore, not one of the Guild's offerings had been darkened by the utter pessimism or the psychological malaise that was reflected in other plays on Broadway that year such as Sherwood's *The Petrified Forest,* Hellman's *The Children's Hour,* and Coward's *Point Valaine.*

Yet, the Guild's behavior had vexed a number of people along the way. The organization had turned down Odets' *Awake and Sing,* which the Group Theatre then had proudly presented together with his widely-acclaimed *Waiting for Lefty.* Hollywood had beckoned more invitingly that year and most of the managers had spent at least part of the year on the Pacific coast, forsaking their Guild duties for extended periods. There was a great deal of managerial deliberation as to the division of the prospective profits from the forthcoming folk opera based on *Porgy,* with no definite decision as to which manager was to get what percentage, and with some managers or other Guild workers not included who thought they should be. Such bickering was a new twist in Theatre Guild production preparations.

The Guild was by now very much in the habit of hiring stars, but one of them, Jane Cowl, possibly because she was not receiving enough personal attention, began demanding that the Guild make greater publicity efforts on her behalf. Another star, George M. Cohan, had definitely refused to continue his tour in *Ah, Wilderness!,* and O'Neill was annoyed because the producers would not continue the tour, replacing Cohan with Fred Stone or someone else as Nat Miller. The Guild believed, however, that neither Stone nor any other replacement would make enough money. It had also turned a deaf ear to O'Neill's agent's request to revive some of his other plays. Yet it was most eager to see a *new* play from him, which he, in turn, did not care to send. And Maxwell Anderson was unhappy with the arrangements accorded his *Valley Forge,* although Theresa Helburn was offering Hollywood gold for the rights to his *Mary of Scotland.*

One bright spot in the future, however, concerned the Lunts, who at last decided to do a production for their former employers. The Guild was delighted, although they would now be more partners than bosses. When Langner urged that he be made a member of the team's production committee, he was restrained in order to avoid conflicts, "especially as Mr. Simonson felt that Mr. Langner's preconceived ideas of a Shakespearean production might not work smoothly with the Lunts who had already conceived their [own] ideas."

Finally, throughout the year, the Guild, with its spotty showing, had annoyed a number of critics. Brooks Atkinson was one who had several uncomplimentary things to say:

> May it never have another season so desultory. . . . Never before has the Guild looked so much like a routine organization that has lost interest in the current theatre. . . . Most of the directors of the Theatre Guild have given the impression this year of running private property with their left hands. Some of them have entered into specious bargains with Hollywood which distracts them from a job big enough to take their whole minds. [*New York Times,* May 26, 1935]

CHAPTER 9 / 1935-36

If This Be Treason,
Rev. John Haynes Holmes and Reginald Lawrence
The Taming of the Shrew, William Shakespeare
Porgy and Bess
Du Bose Heyward, George and Ira Gershwin
Call It a Day, Dodie Smith
End of Summer, S. N. Behrman
Idiot's Delight, Robert E. Sherwood

By springtime of 1935 the Guild's managers realized that the current season was going to be as disappointing financially as it had been artistically. The only appreciable income had come from the sale of motion-picture rights for some of its plays, and the heavy losses to the Guild's prestige as well as to its bank balance, caused by *Parade* and the year's other short-run presentations, seemed to call for drastic changes in existing producing procedures.

Lawrence Langner issued a memorandum outlining the Guild's more pressing problems. First, he asked that revised methods of operating be adopted when two or more managers were to be absent for extended periods of time—remembering that Miss Helburn, Mrs. Westley, and Moeller had been away for a great portion of the season. In addition, he asked that plans approved by Board members left on the job be adhered to, "not toppled by those returning from long leaves." He suggested that lack of suitable manuscripts had made the task for the remaining managers doubly difficult since no adequate planning to meet such a possibility had ever taken place. Enlarging on this, he maintained that the Guild was badly in need of contact with playwrights other than those who regularly submitted work—newer European authors as well as some vigorous, promising Americans.

Langner further urged that no manager leave for Hollywood in the future until at least four of the year's productions had been staged—the earlier in the season the better, since this made possible a longer run if one or two caught on. He also deplored the practice of postponing until the last minute a decision concerning the final offering of a season. Such delayed decisions in the past had resulted in productions like *The Mask and the Face, Jig Saw,* and *Parade,* fare that left a bitter aftertaste for potential subscribers.

Langner's memo included a reference to the Guild's most urgent need of the moment. Criticism of the organization pointed to its being out of touch with theatrical trends being explored by the younger generation. Specifically, Langner wanted a few bright young people—"individuals who have something to contribute to the theatre"—to take the place temporarily of Board members who requested protracted leaves of absence. These people would be asked for opinions on the selection of plays and casts, and on production policies generally, Langner explained, noting: "Such younger persons may ultimately be our successors." Later, a tentative list was submitted which included the Guild's casting director, Margaret Linley, as well as Carly Wharton, Bretaigne Windust, Norris Houghton, and Donald Oenslager (at Wertheim's suggestion).

The Board as a whole was against the formation of a second group within the Guild, possibly recalling its less than satisfactory Studio Group experience. It decided, however, to ask the young people if they would like to act as production committee assistants, and if they would be willing to give their reactions to various scripts then being considered. After the more compatible members were discovered they could be retained and the others eliminated.

The managers did consent, nevertheless, to the selection of one other Board member. The gentlemen to be so favored was Alfred Lunt, who did not exactly constitute "new blood," and who, one gathers, was elected more from expediency than from managerial necessity, a possibility the actor rather wryly noted in his letter of acceptance in which he wondered if he would have "voice enough and stamina" to be any use. The Guild, however, had yearned for its stellar team's return through too many seasons, and now the Lunts had mounted a ripsnorting version of *The Taming of the Shrew,* which was being played at a number of road stopovers before its New York appearance. The Guild wished to make certain of the pair's services for the future. Lunt requested that his appointment not be publicized until the fall.

The internal bickerings that seemed to become more prevalent after lacklustre seasons appeared again as the managers sought solutions to their financial and artistic problems. One suggestion considered was a proposal by Worthington Miner for the formation of a "loyal" acting company. Another resolution was that Board members should receive only fifty dollars weekly beginning in the fall, and this to be paid by promissory notes. If not precisely attractive, this offer was at least acceptable to those managers who had outside incomes; but Simonson, who depended on his theatre earnings exclusively, stated he would have to secure a year's work in Hollywood or elsewhere "so that he could build up a reserve." Simonson was later guaranteed $12,000 for forty weeks, provided he devote his full energies to Guild assignments. Simonson countered by requesting a dispensation which would allow him to design outside theatrical productions without in any way impairing his guarantee. The Board agreed.

As precarious as the Guild's financial position was, however, the situation was more than overshadowed by its need for worthy scripts. During the summer, play reader Anita Block had been instructed to review some of the Guild's former rejects. She submitted a list which included French, Hungarian, German, and Russian works, but not one was deemed usable. The fact had become all too clear that the best new plays were just not reaching the Guild's offices. The Guild had not been notified about the potentialities of *Victoria Regina,* for instance, which had played successfully in London. When a rival Broadway manager presented it later, it was widely acclaimed. Maxwell Anderson had a revision of his Sacco-Vanzetti drama, *Gods of the Lightning,* on hand; but he wanted the Group Theatre to produce *Winterset,* not the Theatre Guild. When the Group turned down the script for various reasons, it was given to Guthrie McClintic, much to the Guild's chagrin. Alfred Lunt urged that *Ethan Frome* be secured when another manager's option expired, but when the Guild's Board initiated inquiries, it was told by adaptor Donald Davis that he and his father were very much disappointed that the Guild did not get the play, but they could not do anything to prevent its transfer to Max Gordon. Thus, fine scripts, which at one time would have been considered exclusively Theatre Guild material, were now bypassing the organization as the abler playwrights placed their choice items with other, more hospitable managements.

The Guild continued in pursuit of star performers. Leslie Howard had expressed a desire to do *Hamlet,* for example, and when the Guild's plans for bringing John Gielgud to Broadway in the part had failed to materialize, the organization was anxious to put Howard under contract. Simonson sought out Howard and interested him in a production scheme, but Lawrence Langner resented this because some three years before *he* had prepared a scheme for *Hamlet,* which he felt the Board should reconsider if Howard were agreeable. Later, it was decided to postpone plans for *Hamlet.* The Guild was committed to one Shakespearean production already with the Lunts. There were discussions of a new play for Helen Hayes, who had concluded her sporadic *Mary of Scotland* tour. The Guild had shelved Edith Hamilton's version of *The Trojan Women* after acquiring a modern Greek tragedy called *The Daughters of Atreus* by Robert Turney. Miss Hayes was actively sought to play Klytaemnestra in this new drama, but then so were Nazimova, Edith Evans, and Sybil Thorndike.

The Guild was overjoyed when Ina Claire agreed to join it on a partnership basis, and its scrambling for a fit vehicle for her was rather hectic. A quickly written Moeller adaptation of Ladislas Fodor's *Love Is Not So Simple* finally was decided upon, but after a less than promising road experience, other settings were examined for displaying Miss Claire's talents. These included *As You Like It,* revivals of *The Circle* or *Captain Brassbound's Conversion,* and even a reworking of the Fodor script by the current Pulitzer Laureate, Zoë Akins.

Theresa Helburn, in the search for Ina Claire material, talked to Sam Harris about the possibility of co-producing one of his properties as a showcase for Miss Claire. There was an embryonic work by S. N. Behrman, in whose *Biography* Ina Claire had starred, but the Board did not like the new Behrman play and voted against it. Miss Helburn later offered to help Behrman rewrite *End of Summer* if the Guild were allowed a first reading of it. In the meantime, Behrman suggested he might be willing to make a version of Molnar's *Great Love* for Miss Claire's use. The brooding over Miss Claire continued for more than half a season.

The Guild was more than a little disconcerted that an adaptation of a novel *(The Old Maid)* had been chosen by the Pulitzer committee that year, especially since the managers felt that at least one of their offerings, *Valley Forge,* had been more deserving of the honor. They therefore lent their moral support to a plan for the New York theatre critics to bestow a prize for "year's best." This plan was adopted for the first time during the 1935–36 season, and came to be known as the Critics' Circle Award.[1]

[1]The original Critics' Circle was composed of Kelcey Allen, John Anderson, Brooks Atkinson, Whitney Bolton, John Mason Brown, Rowland Fields, Gilbert Gabriel, Robert Garland, Percy Hammond, Richard Lockridge, Burns Mantle, George Jean Nathan, Arthur Pollock, and others.

Another cause for Guild concern came from the announcement that Katharine Cornell planned to appear in a revival of Shaw's *Saint Joan.* The Board of Managers had not been informed of this possibility by the playwright, whose American representative it was supposed to be, and the knowledge that it might be losing one of its more renowned assets, the right to license all Shavian performances in the United States, plagued it more than it cared to admit.

Amid such slings and arrows the Guild readied its initial offering of the 1935–36 season. Dr. John Haynes Holmes, a New York minister of pronounced pacifist leanings, and Reginald Lawrence, a playwright of similar persuasion, had fashioned a script "admittedly not easy to perform" concerned with averting impending war by the simple method of having the President of the United States approach and reason with the premier of Japan. In Japan the jubilant masses force their government to consent to a peaceful settlement of the quarrel. Lawrence Langner had been willing to accept the challenge presented by Holmes' and Lawrence's "mad, idealistic melodrama," and the Guild suggested that Walter Huston play President John Gordon at the Westport Country Playhouse during the summer. The role eventually was given to McKay Morris for the pre-Broadway tryout, however, with Langner's wife, Armina Marshall, playing Mrs. Gordon.

Although Moeller and Mrs. Westley had been against presenting it in New York, *If This Be Treason* inaugurated the Guild's eighteenth season on September 23, 1935, at the Music Box Theatre. Many of the actors retained the parts they had played in the tryout.

On the whole, the press was quite responsive to the timeliness of the play's message, which was greeted "with much tumult and hurraying by its audience." Brooks Atkinson found himself "terribly persuaded last evening to believe in what the peace prophets had in mind." Robert Garland thought the Guild's opening production "transcends the showshop." Only Percy Hammond had serious misgivings concerning pacifist propaganda parading as a theatre piece:

> . . . it is as impious a desecration of the Theatre as Broadway has ever reveled in. The play is a greasy extravaganza, loud, boisterous and unreal. It tells the truth in the egregious manner of a lie, and cheapens it by its exaggeration. . . . It is a bad and blowsy play about a good idea. . . . [*New York Herald Tribune,* Sept. 24, 1935]

If This Be Treason, as it turned out, was prophetic to an extent, although it obviously was less than accurate in its major premise. The Japanese people were eventually forced to outlaw the waging of war (as they do in the play), but not until most of the world had been put to a great deal of inconvenience. The generally kind critical reception accorded *If This Be Treason* in 1935 unfortunately did not help it to last much longer than the subscription period minimum. Toward the end of its run Dr. Holmes found himself the target of a threatened plagiarism suit, and the Guild's attorney, Charles Reigelman, was engaged to represent him in the matter. Perhaps symbolically, the Guild decided to destroy most of the production's scenery after its closing.

The Guild's next New York presentation was to be the organization's as well as the Lunts' first Shakespearean production. It was the pair's first appearance under Guild auspices in nearly three years, and the first performance of Shakespeare in "circus trappings," at least in the United States:

> With three acrobats, four dwarfs, a steed that was more than human, being doubly so, with a real snowstorm, and moving scenery like "Parsifal." . . . It was not a departure from tradition—it started from scratch. . . . About the only traditional things in the production are the whip of Petruchio, and the revival of Christopher Sly as an important commentator from a side-box. [George Seibel, *Pittsburgh Sun-Telegraph*, April 23, 1935]

The Lunts had not been over-anxious to attempt a Shakespearean revival. The Bard had never done particularly well on Broadway, although *The Taming of the Shrew* was better known to American audiences than some of his other works. Edwin Booth and others had included it in their repertory as *Katherine and Petruchio*. It was acted as a modern comedy by Sothern and Marlowe; Walter Hampden and Mary Hall did it with Elizabethan scenery; Basil Sydney and Mary Ellis even did it in modern dress. Some recalled seeing Charles Richman play it with Ada Rehan, and many more remembered the picture made by Mary Pickford and Douglas Fairbanks, with "additional dialogue by Sam Taylor."

In February Helen Westley had been sent out to urge the reluctant stars to do their *Shrew*, for which Lunt had conceived a veritable "screeching parrot" production scheme and a plan that called for playing numerous out-of-town engagements before bringing the extravaganza into New York. The Guild had been anxious to present it as its sixth New York bill of the previous season, but Lunt demurred, probably hoping for a smoother production and a longer run if it were offered locally early in 1935–36. Lunt also wanted a young designer, Claggert Wilson, to do the scenery, but since Wilson was not a member of the Scenic Artists' Union, it was necessary for him to associate himself with a recognized professional. Simonson suggested either his wife (Carolyn Hancock), or Raymond Sovey for this assignment. The Board decided it preferred Mrs. Simonson.

The Guild's production of *The Taming of the Shrew*, presented in association with John C. Wilson, had its première April 22, 1935, at Pittsburgh's Nixon Theatre. There was nothing but praise for the entire undertaking. The Lunts, who with Noel Coward had made in *Design for Living* "an incomparable trio of delightful decadence, faintly touched . . . with the faraway tincture of decay," now were thought by Florence Fisher Parry of the *Pittsburgh Press* to "fill the eye, pierce the ear, engage the risibilities and invite the brain." Compared to Julia Marlowe, whose Kate had been a "modified Delilah . . . lovelights instead of lightning flashing from her eyes," Lynn Fontanne was found to rant, to tear, to mock and to spit. Prominently engaged in the supporting cast were "the admirable Helen Westley, on a short holiday from Hollywood . . . the always excellent Stanley Ridges as the careless wooer, Hortensio," the "decorative" Edith King and Rex O'Malley, whose roles were later taken by others for the New York opening.

Following the initial engagement in Pittsburgh, the Lunts began to barnstorm their *Shrew* through Cleveland, Cincinnati, Detroit, Dayton, Indianapolis, Rochester, and Buffalo, sometimes merely a one- or two-night stand, sometimes staying as long as a week—operations, incidentally, which only served to whet New York's appetite. After a rest for the summer, they played Philadelphia for two weeks to hone their performance before opening at the Guild Theatre on September 30, 1935.

The honing process left Lynn Fontanne with a badly wrenched knee—a painful circumstance that did little to lessen her trepidation before the Gotham opening. It continued to plague her through the balance of the presentation's run in New York and later on the road. In recent years Shakespearean productions had been relatively scarce, though the season before Katharine Cornell had appeared in a rather well-received *Romeo and Juliet*, and the fall of 1935 brought

THE TAMING OF THE SHREW – Curtain call for a pre-Broadway opening; setting by Claggett Wilson and Carolyn Hancock.

In center foreground: Edith King, Alfred Lunt, Lynn Fontanne, and Sydney Greenstreet.

Philip Merivale and Gladys Cooper in *Othello* and *Macbeth* to Broadway, where both received a rather apathetic response. Hollywood was about to release Max Reinhardt's three-hour film version of *A Midsummer Night's Dream,* and there were several projected plans for *Hamlet* in the wind. Shakespeare was being dusted off, and Miss Fontanne's infirmity was more or less mollified by the reception the metropolitan critics accorded *The Taming of the Shrew,* "a pleasant comedy to bar a thousand harms and lengthen life."

> It you complain that you cannot hear the lines nor decipher the Bianca plot, you are well within your rights. There is no time for clarity or exposition when the comedians are riding the whirlwind. Since he was an actor, Shakespeare will not object to a brace of good actors using his cluttered script for a public holiday. After all, lines are a nuisance. Pantomime is a sounder comedy medium. What you are offered by way of compensation is Richard Whorf's seedy Christopher Sly, who is as drunk as a waterfront stew, and a rag-tag and bobtail of prancing performers in a costume antic. . . . All Shakespeare needs at any time is actors. He has them here. [Brooks Atkinson, *New York Times,* Oct. 1, 1935]

Another supporting player singled out for commendation was Sydney Greenstreet, who performed an "admirable" Baptista, according to Stark Young, "a new drawing that brought the character into interesting lights." In most respects, however, the evening belonged to Alfred Lunt, whose Petruchio

> takes its place among his most distinguished performances. It misses no chances, finds him reading Shakespeare with surprising ease, is richly humorous, has tremendous drive and variety, benefits by an unfailing invention, and is a memorable achievement in acting. [John Mason Brown, *New York Post,* Oct. 1, 1935]

With Lunt on the Board, discussions were begun again concerning assembling a new permanent Guild acting company. Lunt suggested that with this group he and Lynn Fontanne might produce two plays a year of the Guild's scheduled six. Whorf, Greenstreet, and Tom Powers were considered possibilities for this new ensemble. Toward the middle of November the *Shrew*'s box-office receipts began to drop, and Lunt told the Board that he and his wife were prepared to take cuts in their salaries in order to keep the expensive production running.

In January, *The Taming of the Shrew* traveled to Boston, and two weeks later it opened in Chicago.

At the end of December Lunt announced to the Board that he had bought a new script by Robert Sherwood, and that he and the playwright were more than willing to present it in conjunction with the Guild, but that it had to be done that spring. The directorate, who had been dickering for revisions on another Sherwood comedy titled *Acropolis,* were surprised by Lunt's announcement, but the Board quickly affirmed that it "would be glad to associate itself with anything Mr. Lunt and Miss Fontanne wanted to produce." Thus, during their Midwest engagement, it was announced by Ashton Stevens in the *Chicago American* that the stars were "working on another production that must go on before this season goes off. . . . It is Robert E. Sherwood's 'Idiot's Delight,' a very frivolous comedy framed within a play that is not so frivolous."

One further word about *The Taming of the Shrew.* In the fall of 1939, four years after their initial success with Shakespeare's comedy, the Lunts resurrected their "sumptuous circus" to open formally a new theatre building being erected at the University of Wisconsin. This revival played in Washington, D. C., before the dedication ceremonies at Madison, then went on to Milwaukee (Lunt's birthplace) and elsewhere.

The Guild's next New York presentation of the 1935–36 season apparently had been conceived nine years before, when a young composer of musical comedy scores wrote to a young novelist asking if it might be possible to do an opera based on his most sought-after book. George Gershwin had been jarred into activity by Al Jolson's suggestion that Oscar Hammerstein and Jerome Kern turn *Porgy* into a musical vehicle for his talents.

As early as the previous autumn the Guild had been aware that producing George Gershwin's folk opera would require outside financing. One hope was that the Philadelphia Orchestra would be able to absorb part of the total cost if the opera were presented in Philadelphia under the orchestra's auspices. Another plan was to ask the Juilliard Foundation to sponsor the New York showing. When neither of these proposals worked out, Maurice Wertheim agreed to buy a 20 percent interest in the production, provided this was based on a $40,000 overall budget (seemingly small today, but substantial then). In the meantime, tryouts for a few of the principals went on even before the Guild had secured the necessary backing, because even if the Guild decided not to do the play some other management would undoubtedly want to use the same people. Eva Jessye, the conductor of a Negro choir, was called upon to assemble the "extras" in the cast, and Alexander Steinert was to begin coaching them about the middle of June. Full rehearsals would start by the middle of August.

It was considered poor policy to have word circulate that the Guild was selling shares in one of its offerings (although it had already produced "in association with" on several occasions). Finally, Gershwin decided he would be willing to take 25 percent of the risk, but that he would sell 10 percent to a Mr. Mossbacher. The Guild asked the composer not to sell to an outsider, with Simonson, Warren Munsell, and Russel Crouse all agreeing to take 5 percent apiece if Gershwin did not want to keep all his shares.

For one reason or another, few of the Guild's managers were willing to serve on the *Porgy and Bess* production committee. Wertheim and Langner both declined, and Moeller said he expected to be in Hollywood during the summer rehearsal months. Theresa Helburn was away. Helen Westley therefore suggested that the Guild's business manager, Warren Munsell, an early booster of the enterprise, be given a chance, and the Board agreed.

Casting was a slow proposition, since singing voices were to count as heavily as dramatic skill, and several judges had to pass on each applicant's suitability—Gershwin, director Mamoulian, voice coaches Steinert and Jessye, casting director Linley, as well as the production committee. Alexander Smallens was selected as conductor in his second opportunity to work with Negro singers (his first had been the Gertrude Stein-Virgil Thomson offering, *Four Saints in Three Acts*). Georgette Harvey was the only member of the original *Porgy* company to be reemployed. During this period the Guild had numerous well-intentioned suggestions from outsiders; one was to use Ethel Waters and Paul Robeson in various roles. Casting procedures were slow, sometimes fruitful, but seldom dull.

Another inconvenience to be faced was the hiring of a large New York theatre with adequate acoustics. Gershwin's first choice, the Hollywood, was going to be used by the Warners for their *A Midsummer Night's Dream*; the next choice, the Imperial, would also be unavailable. Finally the Alvin was settled upon.

Before the opening in September, a $100,000 offer for the *Porgy and Bess* movie rights caused a flurry of excitement, especially in view of the impending financial difficulties. The Guild, however, had not realized that the silent-movie agreements Du Bose Heyward had made for his original novel would be the obstacle they were. These would have to be purchased for an estimated $15,000 and even then, the arbiter might not allow them to be resold before the opening. A week later, through Munsell's efforts, the Guild had obtained the troublesome silent picture options.

A number of Boston newspapers took no chances when *Porgy and Bess* had its premiere at that city's Colonial Theatre on September 30, 1935. They sent their music critics as well as their drama critics to cover the event, a practice generally followed whenever the presentation had a first showing. After all, what came to be regarded as Gershwin's masterpiece had been announced as "an American folk opera," a designation the composer insisted on retaining—possibly to prove to everyone that he *could* write an opera.

Drama critic Elliot Norton was impressed by what he saw and heard:

> It is a huge venture, in the physical sense as well as in the musical and theatrical. There are more than 70 actors and actresses—all colored but four—and the way in which they have been instructed, directed, molded into a vast, responsive unit is little short of thrilling. For Mr. Gershwin, the composer, the whole verdict cannot yet be read. . . . What he has attempted is too big and too new to be completely and casually weighed after two or three hours of watching at an opening night. This much can be said: He has written much beautiful music; some of it so melodic and inspired that it will positively be included in the best-seller lists. That best sellers could come from any opera is a miracle. . . . Considering the opera as a whole—and considering it strictly from the point of view of popular entertainment—it is a little uneven. When it hits the clouds—and it does time and again—it is definitely exciting and even thrilling. [*Boston Post*, Oct. 1, 1935]

Norton's musical counterpart, however, had a number of reservations:

> The sophisticated atmosphere and idiom of opera scarcely suits the protagonists of "Porgy." . . . In the first act Mr. Gershwin began ambitiously. Even if his score almost never rises above the level of incidental music, this music is well contrived, it displays craftsmanship which we would not have expected from the Gershwin of a few years ago, and if it never adds materially to the atmosphere created by play and production, neither does it seriously interfere with nor dissipate it. That this music scales tragic heights may hardly be said. It is not yet within Mr.

> Gershwin's power to write significantly. [Warren Storey Smith, *Boston Post,* Oct. 1, 1935]

Other Boston critics, however, were not so restrained in their appraisals. E. F. Harkins of the *Boston Record* concluded that *Porgy* was "one of the best plays ever written in this country, and Gershwin has given it a magnificent musical setting, matching the play's well-nigh infinite variety of moods and glorifying the loves and hates, tragedies and comedies of Catfish Row." Music critic Moses Smith of the *Boston Transcript* complimented the composer on his unsuspected depth and versatility:

> . . . when he needs to, for his purpose, he can write an aria almost in the accepted tradition. If a fugue will serve better, he can write one—and an effective one, whatever the academicians may say. He can write single-lined melody, with a simple tonic-dominant kind of harmonic support, throwing in a few barber-shop chords for color. Or he can set two score of voices singing in a rich polyphonic music in the best vein of the Negroes—music that sounds spontaneously from the singers' throats, yet which only a composer who knows his craft can write. He can make music even out of street cries.

The Boston opening-night audience stood and cheered all who were associated with the production, and if there was ever a show-stopper that evening it was vaudeville performer John Bubbles who played Sportin' Life (a role originally conceived for Cab Calloway), the character who casts good-natured aspersions with "It Ain't Necessarily So" on the "William Jennings Bryan version of Holy Writ."

The Guild decided to run *Porgy and Bess* only one week in Boston instead of two, and then to open in New York after giving the cast a few days' rest. The Sunday before the New York opening, however, music critic Irving Kolodin wrote a "preface" to the opera in the *Brooklyn Daily Eagle* in which he disapproved of Gershwin's love songs:

> His most heroic effort in that direction (the second act duet of "Porgy and Bess") is contaminated by echoes of Leoncavallo, Mascagni, et al; and the later bit in the same act ("I loves you, Porgy") is pure musical comedy—and not particularly good

> musical comedy at that. It is rather paradoxical that Gershwin could triumph over most of the lacks of his early training and yet be fettered by something which has actually been one of his strongest attributes in the past. Whether this weakness will adjust itself as Gershwin devotes himself with more regularity to a less meretricious form of writing than is involved in musical comedy one cannot, of course, say, but the composer will have to make up his mind which God he is going to serve—for he cannot hope to be considered by the musical world as an artist, and yet turn out "commercial" music on the side. As it is, Gershwin's talent is one that can lend itself to a very happy adjustment between God and Mammon—if he can content himself with a somewhat leaner version of Mammon than he has known previously.

When *Porgy and Bess* opened at New York's Alvin Theatre on October 10, 1935, it missed by one day the eighth anniversary of the original *Porgy*'s premiere. Both Todd Duncan as Porgy and Anne Brown as Bess received considerable recognition from the press for their portrayals of the title roles. This was not too surprising. Duncan, a baritone, had been head of the music department at Howard University, and Miss Brown had been a graduate student on scholarship at the Juilliard School of Music. Warren Coleman, who played Crown, was also singled out for lavish praise, as were most of the others in the supporting cast—Ruby Elzy, Georgette Harvey, Abbie Mitchell (all respected singers) and most especially the irrepressible Bubbles. Mamoulian's staging was again considered superb, and Sergei Soudeikine's settings, though reminiscent of Cleon Throckmorton's original *Porgy* designs, were admired, as was Alexander Smallens' handling of the large, forty-five piece orchestra—large, that is, for any legitimate theatre presentation.

The only fault the drama critics seemed to find concerned the recitative passages Gershwin had provided whenever actual song did not seem proper or fitting. In a generally favorable review, Brooks Atkinson remarked:

> Turning "Porgy" into an opera has resulted in a deluge of casual remarks that have to be thoughtfully intoned and that amazingly impede the action. Why do composers vex it so? "Sister, yo goin' to the picnic?" "No, I guess not." Now, why in heaven's name must two characters in the opera clear their throats before they can exchange that sort of information?

PORGY AND BESS – "Catfish Row" as conceived by Sergei Soudekine reminded some of Cleon Throckmorton's settings for the antecedent *Porgy*.

Henry Davis (kneeling); Warren Coleman (arms raised); John W. Bubbles (wearing derby); at extreme right, Anne Brown and Todd Duncan.

The music critics were a bit more rigorous with Gershwin's work. The *New York Times'* Olin Downes, for instance, was appreciative yet cautious:

> He is experienced in many phases of the theatre, and his work shows it. His ultimate destiny as an opera composer is yet to be seen. His native gifts won him success last night, but it appears in the light of the production that as yet he has not completely formed his style as an opera composer.

John Mason Brown, however, was completely captivated:

> Unless my untrained ears deceive me, it contains some of the loveliest music he has written. Its idiom is the idiom of the spirituals and of Harlem. But he has crossed them so that regardless of what qualities his score may or may not have from the technical standpoint of opera, it succeeds at most times in being compellingly dramatic. [*New York Post,* Oct. 11, 1935]

Yet, his musical colleague at the *Post,* Samuel Chotzinoff, was reserved almost to outright chilliness:

> As entertainment it is a hybrid, fluctuating constantly between music-drama, musical comedy and operetta. It contains numerous "song hits" which would be considered ornamental in any of the composer's popular musical shows. A few of these tunes are elaborate in treatment and verge on the character of operatic arias, but they do not rise to the emotional stature of the traditional aria, nor to its melodic dignity. . . .

Interesting in hindsight is this gentleman's appraisal of what came to be among America's best-loved songs:

> Such a song is the duet between Porgy and Bess in the first scene of the second act, "Bess, You Is My Woman Now," a fine tune that is on the threshold of passionate expression but which is kept from passing over it by obvious melodic and harmonic resolutions. In themselves, "A Woman Is a Sometime Thing," "I Got Plenty o' Nuttin" and "It Ain't Necessarily So" are admirable examples of Mr. Gershwin's knack for the wistfully humorous in music. Yet they are too "set" in treatment, too isolated from the pitch of opera for us to accept them as integral parts of a tragic music-drama.

All things considered, even the severest critic had to admit that in general effectiveness *Porgy and Bess,* with all its real or imagined defects, as an integrated work was several cuts above Louis Gruenberg's *Emperor Jones,* which had recently made its debut at the Metropolitan Opera with Lawrence Tibbett in the title role. The major trend of opinion, however, indicated quite plainly that during its eighteen-year history the Guild had produced few events more stirring or satisfying than this musical folk tale, or completely-scored play, or, if one preferred, this "first American opera of any real importance."

With such a lift to its prestige, the Guild was anxious to suggest other libretto possibilities to the Gershwin brothers. The former sale of motion-picture rights, however, created obstacles. For instance, RKO was unwilling to hold up its filming of *Green Grow the Lilacs* for any reason, and M-G-M would have to stop its production of *Reunion In Vienna,* "if we are to make an opera." Theresa Helburn finally recalled a "very amusing . . . and charming" Guild reject, *Memorandum for Kings* by Philip Goodman. It was decided to get this manuscript back from Goodman for the Gershwins' perusal.

The Guild ran into a number of unexpected labor difficulties with *Porgy and Bess.* Equity refused to grant extra rehearsal time after the preparations had arrived at the blocking stage. This, of course, did little to facilitate coaching the huge, and largely inexperienced, cast. The Guild advised Equity that if it could not be granted the same privileges accorded managers who closed flops at the end of one week, thereafter it would also arrange its season so that it could close at the end of a small token period and thereby cut losses, which consisted chiefly of actors' and stage hands' salaries in the case of failures. Another difficulty arose after the show opened when the musicians, who had been hired according to a wage scale approved for grand opera, felt that they should be paid according to the considerably higher stipends set for musical comedy. The Guild countered by offering to keep the full orchestra on during the New York run if the minimum rate were maintained. In December Equity reported that exorbitant commissions were being paid by members of the *Porgy and Bess* cast to unauthorized agents. The Guild wisely urged that the cast cooperate with Equity in eliminating nonaccredited agents, and that no one in the company should fear losing his position if he did so. This placated Equity and also took some of the sting out of the cast cuts which began happening after the first month.

At the end of January *Porgy and Bess,* its company now reduced to forty members, moved to the Forrest Theatre in Philadelphia after a run of 125 consecutive performances in New York, reported to be the longest uninterrupted run ever achieved by a serious opera in the history of music. Three weeks later it was playing in Chicago, where the Guild wondered if it should cancel the remainder of the planned tour unless business warranted continuing it beyond the next week.

The disheartening fact was that the Guild, having produced three extremely well-received attractions in less than three weeks' time (two of which might easily be classed as milestones in the American theatre), began to lose money on all of them after the opening surge at the box office began to level off. Much to the organization's credit it may be said that although it had begun the year in strained financial circumstances, the Guild had not cut corners on any of its commitments. On the contrary, although quite aware that well-produced Shakespeare and opera had seldom shown appreciable profits in New York, or anywhere else in the United States, the Guild had put all its resources behind securing suitable casts, as well as outstanding musical facilities, costumes, and scenery. Incidentally, without the Gershwin name behind it (as well as some Gershwin backing), it is doubtful whether *Porgy and Bess* would ever have been produced, professionally or otherwise. Needless to say, the Guild's financial situation soon became calamitous. The Lunts, the Gershwins, and Heyward all agreed to take cuts in their stipends in order to reduce losses. But, even so, the Guild was forced to take further measures to insure its continuation. Discussions took place as to whether to pay the interest on the Guild Theatre bonds. Although the managers decided to pay, a letter was prepared to be sent to bondholders stating that the Guild was operating at a loss partly because of "excessive" Guild Theatre rent, and asking for a retroactive adjustment. Further discussions entailed a plan to readjust the interest payment on bonds: "The interest rate is to be reduced to 4 percent per annum; the bonds to become non-cumulative; interest to be payable only to the extent earned in any year and if no profit is made and therefore no interest paid, the interest for that year is to be forgiven." Even then, a certain amount had to be borrowed. Miss Helburn, Langner, Moeller, Wertheim, and Mrs. Westley provided a total of $30,000 from their personal funds, hopefully to be paid back from future Guild profits. Later, $50,000 was secured as a loan from the banking concern of Wertheim and Company.

Prior to this spate of borrowing, Langner and Miss Helburn reported that they had been in touch with a Mr. Holman of Paramount Pictures who had made them a tentative proposition; namely, that a finance company could be formed to back four of the Guild's productions during the coming season. $100,000 would be advanced to finance these plays, in addition to which the Guild would be paid $25,000 as a bonus. Further, the financing company would have no control over the sale of picture rights, but would, of course, own a half interest in the managers' profits, if any. Wertheim took exception to the fact that Langner and Miss Helburn had approached anyone in this manner without his knowledge, and he hastily excused himself from the Board meeting. At the next get-together, he appeared with a memorandum which stated that he had formerly believed large financial matters involving the Guild to be within his province, that his long association with the directors of Paramount had hardly been made use of by Langner and Miss Helburn in their peremptory actions, that no organization could function effectively if one or two members took it upon themselves to reverse authorized procedures simply because they believed their handling of a situation to be better, and "through this method of approach the value of my large acquaintance with the major executives of the Paramount Company has been lost to the Guild and the strong approach I had planned made impossible."

Toward the end of January a synopsis of a tentative agreement with the "financing corporation" was drawn up for approval by the Board of Managers. It included, among other things, the stipulation "In case the Guild suffers running losses, the Guild is to be repaid these running losses out of the picture [sale] money, such payment to be pro rated in proportion to the losses of the finance corporation." In other words, the Guild was actively engaged in adopting a plan practiced by certain other Broadway managers, Gilbert Miller among them, which depended on the motion picture interests for a large portion of future financing. The plan was perhaps helpful in insuring the continuity of an organization in those troubled times, but included the risk of having outside interests dictate production policies, including the selection of manuscripts. The paradoxical situation was that in gaining a great deal the Guild was in danger of losing a great deal more. There was, however, an escape clause proposed for the agreement: "The option to renew for another season is to be reciprocal and exercisable before February 1st, 1937, or March 1st, 1937, at the latest, and is to be subject to the Guild's continuance for another season."

In the midst of these hectic deliberations the managers prepared to present their next attraction—one of those "in association with" ventures to which the Guild had been increasingly drawn. Lee Ephraim, an enterprising English producer, had acquired the script of Dodie Smith's domestic comedy *Call It a Day* in London and was offering it there to great acclaim. Convinced that the play would make money in the United States, the Guild invited Ephraim to "associate" himself with the organization for the American presentation, and Alfred Lunt suggested as director a young man named Tyrone Guthrie, "scion of one of the royal families of the English stage." Recent "Shakespeareans" Philip Merivale and Gladys Cooper were chosen to be the stars of the comedy. The rest of the cast included Miss Cooper's son, John Buckmaster, actor Ralph Morgan's daughter, Claudia, as well as Glenn Anders, and a teen-age girl named Jeanne Dante.

When *Call It a Day* had its out-of-town tryout in Washington, D. C., reviewers, though delighted, found it necessary to use oddly assorted comparisons to describe it. Nelson B. Bell of the *Washington Post* thought it might "be said to possess something of the sophisticated comedy of a Noel Coward, a little of the dramatic forcefulness of a Benn Levy and a bit of the introspective psychology of a John van Druten." Andrew R. Kelley of the *Washington Times* felt it had "much of the delightful charm of Drinkwater's 'Bird in Hand' and more of the genuine and wholesome domestic quality of 'Laburnum Grove.' "

The New York critics were equally titillated by this English import ostensibly describing one day's happenings in the "ordinary" lives of an "average" British family by portraying their crotchets, love affairs, likes, and dislikes. As Joseph Wood Krutch suggested, this "slice of life" was surely cut where the raisins were thickest:

> . . . it is actually about as artificial as a play can well be, but it is blessed with the priceless gift of universal appeal, and only the veriest Scrooges of criticism will succeed in concealing their delight. Simpler souls may take it for a miracle of realism—which it isn't—but even those not unaware of the wheels going round will join in the laughter and applause, for "Call It a Day" is, to an extraordinary degree, neat and witty, lovely and gay. [*The Nation*, Feb. 12, 1936]

In his American debut, Guthrie had handled *Call It a Day's* cast so that it gave a performance, in Percy Hammond's appraisal, "out of the Theatre's jewel box, so beautifully does it ornament the comedy." Miss Dante became one of the town's reigning darlings, and Simonson's eight settings (changed by use of a revolving stage) were all lauded. It is well-nigh impossible to find one censorious word written about this dexterous comedy concerning "life's little fires that are quickly trodden out," which played 194 times in New York and then began an extensive tour. Almost a year after its Washington opening, a professional playgoer in Chicago could still write praising it:

> The Theatre Guild has given this delightful trifle a brilliant production. . . . The casting is perfect beyond the wildest dreams of the most optimistic . . . from the famed and glamorous Gladys Cooper-Philip Merivale combination to the lowly charwoman who mournfully predicted that nothing good would come of a day so fine—"it lets people in for things." [Carol Frink, *Chicago American,* Nov. 10, 1936]

With its next offering the Guild would be responsible for yet another example of "perfect casting," although the repetition of this rarity was arrived at in a most imperfect and haphazard manner. As noted, one of the organization's knottier problems that season concerned what to do with Ina Claire, who was still being carried on the payroll as an associate to insure her stellar presence. At the beginning of the 1935–36 season the Claire-Moeller version of Fodor's *Love Is Not So Simple* had proved to be too difficult and tedious in its tryout stage to be brought into New York. A number of "play doctors" had been asked to revise the script, including S. N. Behrman, who had a new but imperfect manuscript of his own the Guild was considering. Theresa Helburn had offered to work with Behrman on his latest drawing-room comedy, and by December it was thought to be in more acceptable shape, although the Board wanted a conference with Behrman to "see if he couldn't quickly clarify its obscurities." Meanwhile, frantic searchings for Ina Claire material continued. The Board agreed to lend her to the Shuberts for their coming production, *Sweet Aloes,* if they "would take her for a minimum of five weeks." The Shuberts politely declined the offer. Other possibilities were then considered, including *Eastward Ho!* and *Madame Sans-Gêne.* Brian Aherne had suggested he would like to do *The Beaux Strategem* with Miss Claire, but she preferred *The Way of the World* in the cut version Langner had submitted. Finally, after rejecting or exhausting most of the other solutions, Miss Claire was cast in Behrman's *End of Summer* almost by default.

In a slight departure from its by then accepted tryout ritual, the Guild held its premiere of Behrman's barely completed piece at a new stopover, the Bushnell Memorial in Hartford, Connecticut. Osgood Perkins had been cast as co-star to Miss Claire, and Doris Dudley, daughter of New York's radio drama commentator, Bide Dudley, played the role of her daughter. One respected Hartford critic, H. T.

Parker, delivered a not overly ardent verdict on the play. He stated that the difference between this and other plays by Behrman lay in what advance publicity had called the "added thoughtfulness." He believed he personally preferred Behrman in a less "thoughtful" mood:

> It seems to me that a deal of platitudes, commonplaces, arrantly stock ideas, and sententiousness are scattered about in Mr. Behrman's comments of life, 1936 A.D., however scintillating the verbal form in which they are served up. . . . More motion, less discussion, will help "Summer" to end more pungently and to the point. [*Hartford Daily Courant*, Jan. 31, 1936]

Parker added that with work *End of Summer* would undoubtedly improve. He glowingly praised the star's adroitness, however.

> With her brilliant rattle of lines, the splendid skill with which she tosses out smart phrases, her compelling personal charm, the vividness with which she melts or freezes emotionally, Miss Claire simply repeats all the elegances of her past performances, absolutely the actress for the part in every way.

End of Summer moved next to Boston, where its first two acts were thought to be "priceless," while the third was found "unconvincing." George Holland of the *Boston American* refused to discuss the plot, "because Mr. Behrman is going to be forced to find a new conclusion for it. . . . When (and if) he does, the Easter season in New York will be taken up with Ina Claire (how *does* she do it?) . . . ."

Behrman, who was traveling with the company, must have worked prodigiously in concert with director Moeller and "general supervisors" Miss Helburn and Langner, for when *End of Summer* opened at the Guild's home theatre in New York on February 17, 1936, the reactions in the press were extremely cordial. Miss Claire was singled out for special praise and, according to Brooks Atkinson, "as the psychoanalytical charlatan, Osgood Perkins honors an unpleasant part with some of his most expert and unflinching acting." Other members of the cast, including Van Heflin, Mildred Natwick, and Tom Powers, were all believed excellent. But, it was Behrman's dialogue, as usual, that provided special delight:

> It may have been that I was in a listening mood, but it seemed to me that Mr. Behrman has here done his best job of making

> long talk sound true. Not being intent on getting a lesson from any play, I didn't mind the fact that his characters end up right where they were when they started talking. Possibly that was Mr. Behrman's idea. At any rate, it is a pleasure to hear them and it is a great satisfaction to know that Mr. Behrman can still be counted upon to give us a play every year or so. We need him. [Robert Benchley, *New Yorker*, Feb. 29, 1936]

Behrman's newest hit, hailed as a worthy successor to *Biography* in every way in its "fluent and sunny performance" (even if it lacked a unifying thesis), played through the summer months.

The Guild's long-term champion of the 1935–36 season, however, was to be its next and final presentation of the year. Whereas *End of Summer* had been totally a Theatre Guild effort, with four of the original managers actively engaged in shaping it (as well as casting director Margaret Linley serving as its stage manager), the guidance of the forthcoming attraction was all but divorced from the control or possible interference of the organization. The original managers resented this somewhat, as can be sensed from the muted language used in the minutes of the Board of Managers' meetings—a copy of which was undoubtedly supplied to Alfred Lunt:

> Mr. Langner felt that the Guild's cooperation was not wanted in the sense that we had formerly cooperated in productions with the Lunts, and since it seemed impractical to restore the old relationship, he suggested that it might be desirable to establish a separate unit for them which would be more or less self-contained. . . . [January 15, 1936]

The Guild's original managers were very much aware that, although Lunt was allegedly an active member of the Guild's Board, he and his wife could take any production they cared to do to any management in town—which would gladly pay them attractive percentages without any investment required on their part. Consequently, the Guild had not held the Lunts accountable for defraying any of the organization's overhead, apart from a $250 weekly sum their productions were to be assessed.

In January, while *The Taming of the Shrew* was completing its run, the Lunts and their company had begun rehearsals on an anti-war comedy destined to win that year's Pulitzer award. Robert E. Sherwood had requested a larger percentage for *Idiot's Delight* than the Guild was accustomed to paying its authors (save Bernard Shaw).

The Board felt that if it consented to this requirement, his payments should be divided with the Lunts "since they had contributed the idea of the play and were continuing to create a great deal of valuable material." He also stipulated that *Idiot's Delight* be shown at the Shubert, a house with one of New York's larger seating capacities. Although Sherwood's relations with the Guild had rarely been very cordial, his close association with the Lunts, as well as personal feelings, may have led to their seconding his predispositions.

Be that as it may, when *Idiot's Delight* opened at Washington's National Theatre on March 9, 1936, its mixture of tragedy and humor, plus its large number of characters and problems, had its audience frankly puzzled at first. But, observed *Variety*, "early in the play [this tendency] is overcome by permitting none of the lesser threads to become more than atmospheric complications. Granted that it is a Herculean task, Lunt and Fontanne keep their roles, upon which the structure of the play depends, always dominant." The production was remarkably free of "first-night trouble," despite the fact that only one of the original managers, Lee Simonson, had been invited to participate in its creation, and he had been asked to design its setting solely for reasons of economy. The Board felt frustrated, and the Administration Committee (an innovation that year composed of Miss Helburn and Langner) received permission to have a meeting with the Lunts to arrange and possibly conciliate their artistic and business relationship for the rest of the year and for the season to come.

In the meantime, Sherwood's pacifist theatre piece moved on to Pittsburgh, where Kasper Monahan wrote:

> Without the Lunts "Idiot's Delight" would suffer tremendously. It would, I fear, collapse under the sheer weight of its high and honest intentions. However, Mr. Sherwood undoubtedly fashioned his play with the Lunts in mind—so he knew precisely what he was doing. . . . If anyone else but Lynn Fontanne played the role of the bogus Russian woman, I'd shudder for the role and the play. . . . Quite deliberately, I suspect, she copies nobody else but the Great Garbo. . . . But there's enough Lynn Fontanne left, never fear, to bring a vitality and exuberance . . . we rightfully expect when she's before us. [*Pittsburgh Press*, March 17, 1936]

Other members of the cast were also thought to be uncommonly good. Particularly noteworthy was Sydney Greenstreet's portrayal of the German scientist and the ranting pacifist played by young Richard Whorf.

IDIOT'S DELIGHT – Lynn Fontanne and Alfred Lunt.

"Then there is the piano which Mr. Lunt plays in 'Idiot's Delight.' It is stunning, and not at all bizarre. However, it was designed ten years ago . . . and at that time was considered so daring that no one would buy it. It was Mr. Simonson's idea that a piano could be made without legs. 'Piano legs' have become something of a joke. . . . Instead, it has a metal truss construction and is built something on the formula of a bridge" – Russel Crouse, "The World Is Just Catching Up With Simonson," *New York Herald Tribune,* May 24, 1936.

As the date for its New York opening approached, the grapevine designated *Idiot's Delight* "as the show in which Alfred Lunt plays a third-rate vaudeville hoofer and Lynn Fontanne wears an exotic blonde wig." And so the attraction became *the* thing to see, not so much for its intrinsic worth as an anti-militarist tract, as for Lunt's song-and-dance man antics in the second act, which brought on what might be termed "Intelligentsia's Rapture"—the same sort of hosannas that later greeted Laurence Olivier's music-hall turns in Osborne's *The Entertainer*—not because it was especially well done, but because a highly respected legitimate actor did it at all. The spectacle of the Lunts squandering their talents on low comedy was extremely diverting.

Regarding the play, Sherwood's theme might have been uttered by his star hoofer, Harry Van, who says, "no matter how much the meek may be bulldozed or gypped, they will eventually inherit the earth." Brooks Atkinson, waxing philosophic, felt that the technique employed to demonstrate this prosaic point of view resulted in scattering the force of Sherwood's liberal argument:

> . . . his last scene is considerably on the maudlin side. More than that: liberalism, as we are beginning to find out, is a weak force in a world that quivers with fear and suspicion. . . . Meanwhile, the power and ruthlessness of reaction, which is consolidating everywhere, and the fervent, self-confident dogma of communism are concrete schools of thought that are much more resourceful in an emergency. If liberalism is to have any influence on the trend of world affairs it will have to find something more coherent to stand for than a compassionate and open-minded vocabulary. [*New York Times,* April 12, 1936]

Atkinson closed by stating that *Idiot's Delight* as a protest against war could not compare with Irwin Shaw's *Bury the Dead* (an offshoot of the Guild-produced *Miracle at Verdun*) which was "one long act of horror, loathsomeness, stink and rebellion." Shaw's macabre method, he felt, would surely secure more anti-carnage converts than Sherwood's ever could.

John Mason Brown, always a Sherwood partisan, compared the author of *Idiot's Delight* to another, better-known Shaw. Although he did not go so far as to label Sherwood's efforts "half-Shavian, half Hasty Pudding," as did some, he did compare the "justification for existence" speeches of Weber, Sherwood's munitions manufacturer, to those uttered by Andrew Undershaft in *Major Barbara.* He concluded that Sherwood's arguments were decidedly less profound. Perhaps the comparison was unjust. Weber, after all, is Sherwood's villain, and as such had to be cut up a bit, whereas Undershaft is treated as the "hero" in Bernard Shaw's play. *Idiot's Delight,* nevertheless, was published that spring by Scribner's after it had received the Pulitzer accolade:

> As might be expected, Mr. Sherwood's text is not given the same protection in the library that it is at the Shubert. His final curtain, his resorting to "Onward Christian Soldiers" while the din of "bombs, gas-bombs, airplanes, shrapnel and machine guns" is heard, emerges in the reading room as an even more obvious and second-rate bit of hokum irony than it does on the stage. [John Mason Brown, *New York Post,* April 23, 1936]

Idiot's Delight proved to be so successful that it continued playing to packed houses into the summer months; then, after a vacation, it reopened in September. Certain updating had to be done as changes in world affairs made new allusions necessary. Lines about the situation in Ethiopia, for instance, were changed to include the more topical "Spanish business." On February 1, 1937, *Idiot's Delight* began two weeks in Philadelphia, and from there it went on tour, lasting until late spring. It was an instance of perfect mating between vehicle and star performers, and almost everybody believed Bretaigne Windust when he said he had had a minimum to do in "directing" the production.

Idiot's Delight brought to a close the Theatre Guild's eighteenth year of playmaking, a year that had been obviously one of the more satisfying it had yet offered its subscribers. But then, it had been a dazzling theatrical year all around. It was a year that had seen a number of America's better actresses in some of their more memorable roles. It had, for instance, provided Helen Hayes with *Victoria Regina,* Katharine Cornell with Shaw's *Saint Joan,* Jane Cowl with *First Lady,* and Pauline Lord with *Ethan Frome.* The Guild had also added to this honors list by presenting Ina Claire in *End of Summer,* and by reaffirming the range of Lynn Fontanne's acting prowess as both Shakespeare's virago Kate and Sherwood's part-time Russian, Irene. The Guild had offered some fine male performances, as well. Alfred Lunt had leaped astonishingly from a resourceful Petruchio to a small-time American song-and-dance artist, and Richard Whorf had portrayed with distinction a delightfully inebriated Christopher Sly as well as *Idiot's Delight's* ardent, yet tragic, idealistic communist. In addition, Sydney Greenstreet had won the critics' plaudits with his varied interpretations, and Osgood Perkins, Philip Merivale, and Gladys Cooper had all been favorably noted. Newer directors, such as Tyrone Guthrie and Bretaigne Windust, had demonstrated their capabilities; Rouben Mamoulian, moreover, had been induced to return to New York from Hollywood to guide a largely inexperienced cast through the intricacies of a memorable *Porgy and Bess.* The scene designing talents of John Root, Claggett Wilson, Carolyn Hancock, and Sergei Soudeikine had been displayed. It seemed that the Guild had done well in every one of its production departments.

The financial crisis that had threatened the organization after the presentation of its first three efforts early in the season had been dispelled by its last three money-makers, although as Langner noted, principally because of the high cost of star-laden casts, profits were not so large as might reasonably be expected. Nevertheless, enough box-office income had accrued by the beginning of April to pay off the emergency loans the Guild had been forced to negotiate, and to increase a bit the Board members' nominal salaries. At the end of the month, however, Miss Helburn, Langner, and Wertheim appointed themselves the organization's financial committee with the right to veto any future planning which in their opinion would be financially unwise. This veto power was to be theirs for a period of five years.

The Guild's incessant search for worthy manuscripts continued unabated, of course. During the year it had acquired James Bridie's adaptation of Bruno Frank's *Sturm in Wasserglas,* and had seriously considered an adaptation of Charlotte Brontë's *Jane Eyre* as a possible vehicle for Ruth Cordon and Brian Aherne, or Fredric March. It had also been interested in Sinclair Lewis' *It Can't Happen Here,* if Laurence Stallings or Sidney Howard could be prevailed upon to do the stage version. In the spring, Theresa Helburn had visited Eugene O'Neill in Georgia in the hope of obtaining some new material *not* in adaptive form. O'Neill, at work on a cycle of plays tentatively titled *A Tale of Possessors Self-Dispossessed,* had nothing new to offer the Guild except vague promises. These inconclusive pledges were eagerly grasped by Miss Helburn, whose bread-and-butter letter to the playwright stated that the Guild would be more than willing to devote all its energies to an "O'Neill season" and present exclusively anything he could provide.

Although it was eagerly seeking new and exciting scripts, the Guild's relations with its other playwrights were none too happy. Robert E.

Sherwood's aversion to the Guild's interference and apathy has already been noted. Another case in point was Maxwell Anderson, who that year received the first Critics' Circle award for *Winterset.* Anderson possessed a number of scripts which supposedly were contracted to the Guild, but which, for various reasons, the organization was finding terribly elusive. For example, the Board of Managers wished to obtain his *Wingless Victory,* but in conference with Miss Helburn and Langner, the author had "wondered" about the casting. Rouben Mamoulian, a friend of Greta Garbo, was asked to suggest someone for the female role who might be acceptable to Anderson. But, Anderson wanted Katharine Cornell, who, though asked, apparently wanted nothing to do with the Guild.

The Lunts, too, had expressed an interest in Anderson's play. Their presence had made what ordinarily would have been a fine season into a sparkling one. According to opinion, neither the Guild nor the Lunts were ever quite so good as when they were working together.

The collaborative efforts of the 1935–36 season had placed the Guild ahead in such current fashions as "toward Shakespeare" and "toward pacifism"—but not, as some noted, very far in a direction "toward experimentation." Critics recalled that during its early years the Guild had offered some of its better-remembered inspirational pieces, one example being its 1922–23 presentation of Claudel's *The Tidings Brought to Mary.* During the previous season, though, a script dealing with Christ's formative experiences, *Family Portrait,* had been thought unsuitable. The Guild also had rejected scripts of such exciting potential as Jean Cocteau's *The Infernal Machine,* T. S. Eliot's *Murder in the Cathedral,* and Jean Giraudoux's *The Trojan War Will Not Take Place* (later called *Tiger at the Gates*). Even Chekhov's *Three Sisters* was considered to involve "too much risk." Indeed, the experimental scripts it had been actively considering, Edith Hamilton's version of *The Trojan Women* and Robert Turney's *The Daughters of Atreus* for instance, were soon released, only to be produced by others. Perhaps the Guild's uncertain financial state precluded experiments. If that were true, however, it had definitely ceased to be the force it still considered itself to be, according to its press releases.

The theatrical year had brought a few changes in Guild personnel. Carly Wharton and Margaret Linley had filled new roles within the organization, although, when Donald Oenslager inquired concerning an announcement to engage production assistants he was told that the original plan had been somewhat "deferred and modified"—a possible instance of "don't call us, we'll call you." For the first time within memory, too, neither Helen Westley nor Claude Rains had graced any of the organization's New York presentations. But, as the end of the season neared, with three hits playing on into the summer months, the fruits of a highly productive aesthetic labor were sweet to harvest. For instance, Random House had expressed a desire to publish an anthology of great Theatre Guild plays, and critics, both professional and nonprofessional, were asked to help in the selection. A few had objected to the inclusion of *Hotel Universe,* but the Board overruled this, believing that Philip Barry's fantasy demonstrated the organization's zeal for the experimental. Shaw had characteristically objected strongly to the inclusion of his *Saint Joan,* but in the end he was mollified and gave the project his blessing. Bennett Cerf, editor-in-chief of Random House, had wanted the managers collectively to write an introduction to the volume, but ultimately Russel Crouse acted as their ghost, while the seven managers proudly affixed their signatures.

CHAPTER 10 / 1936-37

And Stars Remain, Julius J. and Philip G. Epstein
Prelude to Exile, William McNally
But for the Grace of God, Leopold Atlas
The Masque of Kings, Maxwell Anderson
Storm Over Patsy, Bruno Frank
Jane Eyre (Charlotte Brontë), Helen Jerome

One would suppose that the latter half of the Theatre Guild's 1935–36 season had been sufficiently successful to allow the Board of Managers a certain latitude in its selection of offerings for the new theatrical year. True, it did not own a *Tobacco Road* (which was then playing well beyond its thousandth performance, posing a threat to the old endurance records set by *Abie's Irish Rose* and *Lightnin'*), but the Guild did have *Call It a Day* and *Idiot's Delight,* which were both attractive enough box-office draws to guarantee the organization a safe margin of working capital. Furthermore, there are strong indications that Paramount Pictures had agreed to finance four of the Guild's 1936–37 productions to the extent of $90,000—two at $25,000 apiece, and two at $20,000 each—plus an added "second capital loan" to be allocated at the rate of $12,500 per play to be paid to the Guild as a fixed amount for overhead.

Langner and Miss Helburn had also arranged the Board members' salaries for the coming year, with those bearing the heavier responsibilities to receive the greater rewards. Wertheim was to receive nothing, and neither was Helen Westley until her return from Hollywood to a more active participation in Guild affairs made paying her practicable.

Visiting Europe during the summer, Miss Helburn had paid special attention to the English theatre in the hopeful search for new Guild material. She had seen Bridie's adaptation of Bruno Frank's *Storm in a Teacup,* and had gone so far as to invite the Irish actress Sara Allgood over for the Guild's production in New York. The other managers, however, did not feel they could produce this play before February. Miss Helburn had also seen Helen Jerome's version of *Jane Eyre* in its premiere at Malvern and had made suggestions to her for rewriting parts of it. The Guild sent out publicity releases announcing Katharine Hepburn's proposed appearance in this adaptation of Charlotte Brontë's novel later that year. Miss Helburn reported that among other projects she had discussed Shaw's *The Millionairess* with Edith Evans.

The Guild's need for suitable manuscripts was a matter of deep concern. Several of the works the Board of Managers had rejected the previous season, however, had been produced by others with substantial critical acclaim, with the knowledge, it should be added, that they would lose money. Eliot's *Murder in the Cathedral,* one case in point, had been given its first American production in March of 1936, by the WPA-sponsored Popular Price Theatre, an organization seemingly dedicated to short runs, "with surprising and frequently rather startling results." Another case was "one of the finer failures of the year," Robert Turney's *Daughters of Atreus* as produced that October by Delos Chappell, an "angel" who frequently backed worthy theatre projects. Comments on this modern play based on ancient Greek tragedies ranged from its being named an event of the first magnitude to the witty, but banal, "a thing of beauty but a bore forever." It was generally agreed, though, that without the support of a superlative cast, such as the one the Guild had envisioned for it, Turney's poetic evocations would have had a difficult time of it during any Broadway season. Hence the federal government and a modern Maecenas had taken over a playmaking function that once would rightfully have fallen to the Guild.

The Guild instead began its 1936–37 season with an offering that involved little risk. Twins Julius and Philip Epstein, twenty-seven year old Hollywood script writers, had fashioned a comedy concerning the conflict between liberalism and conservatism, hoping that it was both brittle and clever. One thing that appealed to the Guild was that *And Stars Remain* required only one modern setting and a relatively small cast. When this simulation of S. N. Behrman's techniques opened in Pittsburgh, George Seibel of the *Pittsburgh Sun-Telegraph* felt it was an attempt to apply the methods of Noel Coward to a plot conceived by Clifford Odets, all of which was "about as close to real life and actual politics as the game called Monopoly is to Wall Street finance." One ray of sunlight filtered in, though, through Clifton Webb's deft performance, which another Pittsburgh critic, Florence Fisher Parry, found made the evening endurable:

> . . . the play almost justifies itself in having given us the opportunity of seeing this suave and elegant fellow in a full-bodied parlor role, sans music, sans dance routine, sans everything which has furnished . . . a graceful career for so many charming years. . . . He is, to speak quite crudely, The Whole Show. [*Pittsburgh Press,* Sept. 29, 1936]

Two weeks later, on October 12, 1936, the Epsteins' semi-sophisticated comedy opened at the Guild's home theatre. For the first time within memory, critics called Moeller's staging inept, and Aline Bernstein's setting mediocre. Furthermore, Helen Gahagan's talents were believed wasted on a largely unrealized role. Gilbert W. Gabriel, searching for the play's theme, offered as a possibility, "bedfellows make strange politics." Except for Webb's adroitness, the reception accorded *And Stars Remain* was on the whole several degrees cooler than lukewarm:

> It is thin, it is tangled, it is a crankily phony little affair. But there's an occasional cleverness to it which should have been met with a thrice quicker, lighter, livelier playing. The Guild makes funeral meats of it. [*New York American,* Oct. 13, 1936]

Only the *New York Times'* Atkinson was not discouraged, for he had been through it all before:

> After long years of patient servitude, this column has learned never to take the Theatre Guild's first play seriously. . . . Sometimes it is a little embarrassing to see actors dutifully picking their way through the mazes of a silly play. . . . As for the rest of us, we know that the Theatre Guild is opening a new season with the usual bit of balderdash.

This "bit of balderdash," however, did achieve a slightly longer run than the Guild's second offering, which was considered by a few to be a more adult undertaking in every particular. The play's subject matter, unfortunately, did not have wide popular appeal.

Playwright William McNally had fashioned *Prelude to Exile* with scrupulous attention to historical data concerning Richard Wagner's stay with the Wesendonck family in Zurich, a stormy period that had culminated in the completion of *Tristan and Isolde.* The Wagner descendants looked with favor on this project and even offered a fair amount of their supervision, should it be needed. The Guild, therefore, considered carefully its selection of an actor to portray the composer. Pierre Fresnay, Cedric Hardwicke, and Paul Muni were suggested and rejected; Claude Rains indicated he would be glad to accept the assignment if it could be made to fit with his motion-picture commitments. When this was found to be impractical, Wilfred Lawson was given the role under Moeller's direction. Eva Le Gallienne, Lucile Watson, and Evelyn Varden were to play several of the ladies who hovered about the eccentric musical genius.

Prelude to Exile had its premiere in Philadelphia on November 16, 1936, with four of the Guild's managers actively engaged in its preparation. On the whole, Philadelphians felt they had experienced a leisurely, but satisfying, evening's entertainment. They liked Lawson's portrayal of Wagner as an "egotistical, petulant, unscrupulous and inconsiderate man who is a hero to everyone except, for very good reasons, his wife." They believed that *Prelude to Exile* had succeeded "where most biographical plays fail, by neither seeking to eulogize nor to debunk its central character or, for that matter, to explain him." Only Peter Stirling of the *Philadelphia Record* was antagonistic. He stated that the Guild, "the one-time theatrical champion of champions," was becoming flabby and feeble. He still felt cheated by the previous season's *Love Is Not So Simple,* the short-lived Moeller adaptation, and thought the present offering only further evidence of directorial hardening of the arteries:

> . . . a long-winded, pretentious collection of theatrical bunkum which the Guild would have audiences believe is ART . . . an atrociously written play with bad dialogue, worse motivation and absolutely no reason for production. . . . Mr. Moeller's position does not give him the right to do such a sloppy, inartistic piece of direction as he did in "Prelude to Exile." Even Mr. Moeller can't have two actors sit down opposite each other and talk and talk and talk. . . . Looking over the program, I notice that the "Prelude to Exile" production is under the supervision of the Guild's three horsemen, Helburn, Moeller, and Langner. When you mention the names of this trio to a New York actor, his knees begin to tremble. It's about time the knees of these three began to tremble. Because they are slipping. They are slipping fast.

Two weeks later *Prelude to Exile* opened at the Guild's home theatre. The metropolitan critical reaction was mixed, but the stimulating excitement that had greeted other Guild openings was definitely lacking. One gentleman thought the Guild had fashioned "a decent enough theatre evening for any literate adult," while another found it "a good though by no means brilliant study . . . a sound piece of play-making," adding that if one were expecting riches he might be a trifle disappointed. On the other hand, Gilbert W. Gabriel condemned it as being "an embarrassingly bad play. I am just as willing as you are that great figures should have feet of clay . . . but why the grease-painted toenails?"

Indications at the box office suggested that *Prelude to Exile* would shortly expire. In an attempt to pump life into the moribund production, the Guild induced the Metropolitan Opera's famed *Heldentenor*, Lauritz Melchior, to visit Lawson in full Wagner makeup backstage—while flashbulbs popped. This, seemingly, was not enough. Brooks Atkinson, however, once again felt optimistic for the Guild's chances as he concluded that *Prelude to Exile* was "so vast an improvement upon the first play of the season that patient subscribers may now logically look forward to a third play that will be not only respectable but exciting."

Meanwhile, the Guild had sent a memorandum to the holders of Guild Theatre bonds to the effect that it requested a reduction of the rental it had to pay for the use of the theatre. In the past, the organization maintained, it had been too generous in its percentage payments to the point of draining its own resources by renting the theatre (incorporated separately from the Guild) when cheaper auditoriums were available elsewhere along Broadway. The Guild claimed a steady revenue loss since 1929, reaching $92,721 in 1934, as a result of continuing its lease on the theatre—its only conceded obligation to the bondholders. Other modifications in the terms would make the bondholders' interest noncumulative, set up a working capital of $100,000 prior to interest payments to the bondholders, and allow the Guild to renew its lease on an annual instead of a five-year basis.

In December, the bondholders, headed by the largest investor, violinist Jascha Heifetz, replied that they would like to see a detailed accounting of the Guild's finances, that $600,000 worth of Guild Theatre bonds had been sold in 1923–24 with the blessing of the late Otto H. Kahn, who urged the public to support the American theatre through this "safe investment," but that this investment had become practically worthless—with bids of $150 currently being offered for $1,000 bonds. They pointed to the Guild's report that the present year represented its second largest popular subscription season—with subscriptions totalling only 4,500 less than the 1929 peak of 64,000. The

Guild could only indicate the losses it had sustained on its first two productions of the year, for it seems it was pledged to secrecy concerning its underwriting arrangement with Paramount Pictures.

Hoping to recover lost prestige, the Guild determined to try yet another script by a young American dramatist, and chose for its third presentation *But for the Grace of God* by Leopold Atlas, an alumnus of George Pierce Baker's playwriting classes at Yale. Previously, Atlas had written a poignant study of a boy torn between divorced parents titled *Wednesday's Child* that had been well-received some three years earlier. His newest work had to do with children forced by the Depression to support families, and with the brutalizing effects of slums and sweatshops on these youngsters. James Bell, one of *Tobacco Road*'s several Jeeter Lesters, played the principal indigent parent, but, necessarily, the play was mainly concerned with the young turning toward robbery and violence. Thus, it was compared, unfairly perhaps, with the previous season's long-playing *Dead End.* Whereas the "Dead-End Kids," as they were later billed (ad nauseam), had been made to exude a certain hang-dog charm, Atlas' children had been created for sociological purposes rather than for their titillating pranks and scruffy sayings. The Guild had obtained the Yiddish Artef's Benno Schneider to direct the production, and a young designer, Stewart Chaney, to execute its expressive settings. The *New York Times*' critic was again disappointed. Atkinson admitted that the play's melancholy theme of juvenile degeneration was certainly a worthy, if tragic, one:

> Mr. Atlas has patiently followed it through the streets and tenements and once he takes it into a miserable machine shop where boys and girls are engaged in dangerous labor. Nor has he left out any of the horrors, including a harrowing accident to one of the boys in a deadly machine. But the writing is monotonous, the course of the story is familiar, and the spirit is apathetic. . . .

Robert Benchley was another of the many who were sympathetic to the playwright's attempt to point up a frightening situation: "Not that 'But for the Grace of God' is a grade B play in its intent, scope, or even in its performance. It simply gives off a grade B impression."

Only Charles E. Dexter, critic for the *Daily Worker,* was wholly in favor of the Guild's latest effort to document prevailing social ills, but his approbation had little to do with the offering's artistic horizons:

> . . . a scathing picture of what child labor and unemployment do to life, liberty and the pursuit of happiness. The core of capitalist rottenness is exposed. Skilled labor tossed upon the rubbish heap . . . despair . . . loss of self-respect . . . finally a bitter pessimism . . . because this play cuts with scalpel deep into a wound, it is worthy of support. The Theatre Guild has wavered hither and yon in recent seasons. Here it swings leftward–and if not too far, far enough for us to cry: "Howdy, friends . . . sit down and we'll talk things over!"

Nevertheless, shortly after *But for the Grace of God* opened, and the dispiriting reviews were counted, the Guild seriously considered closing the production and bringing in *Jane Eyre,* already playing on the road, to fill the vacancy. Munsell, the Guild's business manager, argued against this merciful disposition, however, by pointing to the play's running expenses, which were small because of the largely teenage cast in which no "name" performers were featured. He suggested that, even if there were few attending the performances aside from regular subscription patrons, the Guild would suffer only moderate rent losses; whereas, if *Jane Eyre* proved successful, the organization would make a great deal more money by presenting it at the Imperial, with its expansive seating capacity, which would soon be available. Even if the Guild Theatre were dark for several weeks before the final production, Bridie's *Storm in a Teacup,* could be made presentable, it would still be financially feasible, he thought, to let *But for the Grace of God* run its course. Sidney Harmon, the Guild's co-producer for this venture, requested Atlas and Schneider to rework portions of the play to make it more palatable to the public, hoping that if the revisions were major enough some of the critics might see the play again and perhaps comment on it more favorably. As it turned out, this plan caused the Guild a number of regrets, but possibly the biggest losers were subscription patrons who were asked to sit through this "singularly lifeless" study of depressing circumstances.

Having fared none too well with the creations of newer American playwrights, the Guild next presented the work of an established one, Maxwell Anderson, who had been already represented on Broadway that season by two productions, *High Tor* and *The Wingless Victory.* His new offering had as its climax the still unsolved mystery surrounding the Mayerling "suicide pact" of Crown Prince Rudolph of Hapsburg and young Baroness Mary Vetsera. Negotiations had begun even before the Guild's casting was complete to sell the movie rights of *The Masque of Kings* to Warner Brothers, for a version in English of the famous French film *Mayerling,* which starred Charles Boyer, was to be released as soon as the play was produced. Leslie Howard was anxious to do the Warner Brothers film and they wanted to have him make the picture and publicize it so that the other movie would lose its sale value.

Casting continued at a brisk pace with the usual flurries of rejected suggestions. It became evident the richest role was going to be that of Franz Joseph, and Claude Rains was contacted—but was found to be unavailable—for this important assignment.The Guild was fortunate, however, to find one of its original acting company members momentarily between engagements. The portrayal of the enfeebled emperor, "given to Polonius-like sayings," became one of the finer achievements of Dudley Digges' varied and distinguished career.

The Masque of Kings had its initial presentation on January 18, 1937, in Montclair, New Jersey, under the sponsorship of the Montclair Junior League, which used the Guild premiere to raise money for a Montclair building fund. Conditions at the cramped Montclair Theatre for the event proved to be far from favorable. Two of Simonson's plush settings could not be fitted on the suburban stage, and the distinguished cast, which contained among others Pauline Frederick as Elizabeth and Glenn Anders as Koinoff, struggled to make themselves heard above "an unusually croupy audience." Henry Hull, who had played the first of *Tobacco Road*'s Jeeter Lesters, was Crown Prince Rudolph, and Margo, who the season before had charmed audiences as Anderson's pathetic Jewish waif in *Winterset,* portrayed Baroness Mary Vetsera. Hull's son also had been given a small part as one of the court's retinue.

Although the Guild wanted to keep *The Masque of Kings* away from New York as long as possible, out-of-town bookings were difficult to secure that season because so many shows were traveling; hence, after appearances in Baltimore and Boston, Anderson's re-creation of the Hapsburg tragedy opened at the Shubert on January 18, 1937. The following critical notices, while basically respectful, were not ardent. Most reviewers thought the play was by far the best Theatre Guild presentation of the year, but Anderson's poetry was largely considered too abundant:

> . . . when Mr. Anderson finishes with his characters his audience knows everything about them. He lays bare their hearts and minds

> by the thoroughness of his analysis. But Mr. Anderson is not yet as ruthless with himself as he is with the people he writes about—or rather, the people he overwrites about, for that is his stage infirmity. He turns every action into a full-length speech. His revolution is chiefly a prolix conversation between garrulous opponents. In moments of action his style is heady and dynamic. In moments of meditation it is verbose . . . a respectable piece of academic playmaking now; someone might make it also stimulating by hacking away its excesses. [Brooks Atkinson, *New York Times,* Feb. 9, 1937]

John Anderson of the *Journal* thought the play's theme, "the power within the crown corrupts its virtues," a bit dated, and concluded:

> Whatever value the original story had as a melodrama of sex and mystery on royal proportions is deadened in the author's attempt to give it larger significance; what's left is merely a full dress parade which takes too long to pass a given point.

Preparations for *The Masque of Kings* had been the first that season to employ the services of all seven Guild managers—Mrs. Westley having returned for a time to actual participation. Many rehearsals were held on the *Idiot's Delight* set, then still being used at the Shubert. Some, like Arthur Pollock, felt, however, that the production lacked the organization's sure touch of old, believing it indicated, among other failings, that "Philip Moeller cannot stage a Maxwell Anderson play so well as Guthrie McClintic," even if the overall effectiveness was better than average.

In March, rumblings were heard concerning Anderson's license to twist certain historical events and personalities to suit his purposes. The Archduke of Tuscany, one of Anderson's villains, for instance, had a son living in New York who protested the conspirator's role his father was assigned in the play. The actual Countess Larisch was another who felt her image distorted and her privacy violated by Anderson's vivid imagination. She demanded $25,000 damages, although it was suggested that the suit might be settled if she would accept a few hundred dollars.

Also during March Dudley Digges, who had walked away with most of *The Masque of Kings'* acting honors, played his three thousandth performance for the Guild. It was a sentimental occasion. His current role was his twenty-third portrayal for the organization, and his career closely paralleled that of his employer. His first Guild play, *Bonds of*

Interest, for example, was also the organization's debut presentation in 1919, while the second, *John Ferguson,* established not only Digges' reputation as a character actor of the first rank, but also the Guild as an art theatre of prominence and permanence, and many remembered the actor's superbly controlled performances. Between his appearance in *Marco Millions* and his assignment in *The Masque of Kings* he had appeared in approximately thirty-five motion pictures including *Mutiny on the Bounty, The General Died at Dawn,* and *What Every Woman Knows.* He had also staged four productions for the Guild, *Heartbreak House, The Doctor's Dilemma, Pygmalion,* and *Man's Estate,* appearing in them as well. Small wonder that the Board of Managers was pleased to present so gifted a protégé with a gold pencil as a remembrance of the milestone.

For its next offering, the Guild turned from Anderson's tale of dynastic doom to a story that contained no earth-shaking involvements. That, in fact, was the point made in *Storm Over Patsy,* which had been adapted by James Bridie from Bruno Frank's 1929 comedy *Sturm in Wasserglas*—i.e., a tempest in a teapot. The tempest was over an independent woman's refusal to purchase a dog license for her beloved mongrel, and a young journalist's making a *cause célèbre* of her skirmishes with the law. Although the script was about trifles, the Guild did not trifle with its preparation. The play, in various adaptations, had already been shown over 6,000 times in various parts of the world, and it had been translated into seventeen different languages. Bridie could not see the sense of coming to the United States to rework his manuscript, since his adaptation had already run a year in London. The Guild would just have to do its own revising.

As previously noted, the Guild had already signed Sara Allgood for *Patsy* in the hope that she would repeat her London triumph as Mrs. Honoria Flanagan. The managers were also anxious to employ a young British actor, Roger Livesey, who had played the journalist in London. Livesey earlier that season had made his American debut as Horner in Gilbert Miller's production of *The Country Wife.* Because of this, the performer ran afoul of the ruling of Actors' Equity that foreign actors could not play another role in the States within six months after their previous vehicle closed. Wilfred Lawson, incidentally, was another to be troubled by this rule, for when his assignment in *Prelude to Exile* ended he was cast too soon afterwards as Benedict Arnold in *A Point of Honor.* Livesey's case was appealed several times by Miss Helburn, Munsell, and Langner, the Guild's managers arguing that a previous version of *Storm in a Teacup* (as it was then called) had been presented by producer Harry Moses, only to be withdrawn after a tryout proved it unsuitable Broadway fare. The Guild, therefore, felt it important to retain as much of the successful London cast as possible to help ensure success in the States. Equity finally relented in Livesey's case.

Storm Over Patsy had its American premiere the evening of March 1, 1937 at Washington's National Theatre, and the critics were quite satisfied with this intelligent and unostentatious little comedy, this "delectable theatrical confection." Moeller's direction, this time, was believed "spirited and entirely in keeping with the spirit and pace of Mr. Bridie's lively charade. . . ."

A week later, *Patsy* opened at the Guild's home theatre, and, again, the critical reception was most cordial. The players were all happily complimented by critic Stark Young:

> They all seem to enjoy themselves and to be reaching after the laurels of character acting—no harm in that. You get the sense of nice people behind the footlights, people too used to the amenities to be overanxious, and too pleasantly nurtured in this world to be hard-driven. The final result is not unlike certain situations in life: you are not bothered about the crux of events because you enjoy the company of the agents involved. [*New Republic,* March 24, 1937]

According to Richard Lockridge of the *Sun,* being patient with *Patsy*'s leisurely meanderings was more than rewarded by the final courtroom scene. "It remains quiet, even there, but its very sedateness enhances the tickle and makes the whole long act bubble with comedy. . . . Actors in holiday mood make pleasant evenings, and this is one of them; no great shakes, except for Patsy's tail, but always quietly engaging." Patsy, as portrayed by a hirsute specimen named Colonel, was the biggest scene stealer in the cast. Leo G. Carroll, however, received unanimous approval for his drily humorous and resourceful playing, as from Stark Young:

> For fifteen years, at the Neighborhood Theatre and elsewhere, not to forget that brilliant performance of the butler in "The Green Bay Tree," Mr. Carroll has been giving performances in New York, none of which that I have seen has been anything but excellent. His portrayal of the judge is now one of the finest things of this season. Watching his beautiful shadings and perfect vagary of picture, I found myself wondering if Mr. Carroll

should not be a bit more vulgar, and so get on faster. Or more stage piggish. Who knows?

Despite its charm and latent appeal *Storm Over Patsy,* possibly because Sara Allgood became ill and had to leave the cast, was nowhere nearly as popular an attraction as was a production the Guild's Board of Managers decided *against* bringing into New York. This decision resulted in Gotham subscribers' being denied their sixth promised performance of the year.

The Guild had acquired an adaptation of Charlotte Brontë's *Jane Eyre* by writer Helen Jerome, whose version of Jane Austen's *Pride and Prejudice* had been successfully produced by Max Gordon the previous season. After a premiere tryout in England, Helen Jerome and her *Jane Eyre* manuscript were brought to the States. Casting then took much of the Guild's time and ingenuity. For Mr. Rochester the managers had considered, beside Fredric March and Brian Aherne, such players as Raymond Massey, Colin Keith-Johnston, Basil Rathbone, Henry Hull, Philip Merivale, Eric Portman, Wyndham Golding, and Basil Sydney, while Moeller, who was *not* to function in his accustomed capacity for this production, thought Nicholas Hannen a good choice. Katharine Hepburn had already been signed for the title role, but she was reported to be considering another play with director George Cukor. The actress was put on notice that *Jane Eyre* rehearsals would definitely take place, so there was no question of her not reporting as scheduled by her contract.

In December, with preparations under Worthington Miner nearly completed, Langner said that he understood Lloyd's of London would insure a theatrical production, and he urged that the Guild take out such a policy on *Jane Eyre.* The Board of Managers approved. Within days, the Jerome adaptation's American debut took place at the Shubert in New Haven, with Viola Roache cast as Mrs. Fairfax and Dennis Hoey playing Rochester. *Variety*'s out-of-town reporter wrote that this dramatization would "probably not be rated as a great play, nor even an outstanding one, but it does make good entertainment . . . and serves as a not-too-strenuous test of Katharine Hepburn's worth as a legitimate actress."

After New Haven, the *Jane Eyre* company began a tour which took it to Boston, then to numerous points west. The original plan called for bringing the production into New York's Imperial Theatre the latter part of February. But, while the attraction was popular in the Midwest, it had not been garnering an outstanding set of critical notices. Furthermore, some metropolitan reviewers, Brooks Atkinson and George Jean Nathan included, had seen the show on the road and had panned it in their reports. Nathan, for instance, had written that "as a play in the modern theatre *Jane Eyre* is impossible of serious acceptance. Even as a curio, interest in it evaporates after the first act." This Olympian disapproval, however, did not lessen the reception accorded movie star Katharine Hepburn (who was being "secretly" courted enroute by millionaire Howard Hughes) in such stopovers as Milwaukee, Toledo, and Kansas City, where business was marvelous:

> "Jane Eyre" woke this town from a legit slumber with triphammer alacrity during a three-day dusting at the Music Hall Feb. 15–17. Hepburn piece grossed fine—approximate $10,000 at $2.20 top. Press, while courteous, judged that a rewrite was in order if and when it hit Broadway. [*Variety*, Feb. 24, 1937]

The rewriting hinted at was something that had been going on incessantly in an attempt to strengthen the title role, for in the reviews Hoey, Viola Roache, and young Barbara O'Neil had received most of the commendations. This plagued the Guild. In March, the producers called on Sidney Howard to see if he could further bolster the script. Howard believed he could, if Helen Jerome consented, stipulating further that he wanted no credit on the program or elsewhere for his participation, but that he did want a royalty. The playwright also wondered if this work should take precedence over his doctoring of *The King of the Mountains* and the revising of his own script, being written with Ethel Barrymore in mind, which was already contracted to the Guild for the following season. The managers decided *Jane Eyre* should come first. Finally, with Miss Hepburn's other commitments threatening to take her out of the cast, Helen Jerome decided she had had enough and asked that her script be returned. During the latter part of April *Jane Eyre* closed in Baltimore, but hopes were kept alive that it might be re-cast and revived during the coming year.

As soon as news that the Guild had no sixth play to offer its subscribers circulated, the organization was beset with intriguing alternatives offered by eager actors. Ruth Gordon, for instance, suggested that she be featured in a revival of *A Doll's House*. Philip Merivale and Gladys Cooper, too, thought they might appear in *Man and Superman*. The Guild, however, was not too interested in the latter, since with Shaw's royalties of 15 percent, and two actors taking percentages plus the heavy cost of the sets, it would be too risky a venture.

With a final production for the year not forthcoming, it became obvious to all that the Guild had treated its road patrons to a much better theatrical season than it had offered its home subscribers, for, in addition to *Jane Eyre, Idiot's Delight, Call It a Day,* and *End of Summer* had all toured extensively. Under the aegis of the American Theatre Society such non-Guild attractions as *The Children's Hour, Lady Precious Stream,* and *The Two Mrs. Carrolls* had also been offered subscribers in Boston, Chicago, Philadelphia, Pittsburgh, and Washington. The Guild hoped to extend its 50,000 road membership in the near future.

New Yorkers had been exposed to many delightful presentations, however. Maxwell Anderson, whose *High Tor* was the Critics' Circle choice, had not been the only playwright responsible for several offerings. George S. Kaufman, collaborating with Edna Ferber, had produced the successful *Stage Door,* and then had seen his and Moss Hart's *You Can't Take It With You* win the season's Pulitzer award. This was also the year of Broadway's simultaneous *Hamlet* productions, with John Gielgud's acclaimed presentation arriving in October and Leslie Howard's, believed "interesting" but less aesthetically incisive, coming a month later. Max Gordon, who offered Clare Boothe's *The Women* in December, followed this festival of feline hair-pulling with Robert Edmond Jones' festival version of *Othello,* which featured Walter Huston as the Moor and Brian Aherne as Iago. Katharine Cornell, who had portrayed an exotic princess in *The Wingless Victory,* changed her costumes, makeup, and acting style to play Bernard Shaw's *Candida.* The Group Theatre had done Paul Green's critical success, *Johnny Johnson.* Even a lacklustre revival of *Abie's Irish Rose* had outdistanced some of the Guild's carefully prepared presentations.

The Guild's outlook, then, both forward and backward, was anything but sanguine. For the first time within memory it had not been offered even a chance to refuse prize-winning manuscripts. There had been a discussion of turning *Liliom* into a musical play with Kurt Weill to write the music and Arthur Guiterman, the lyrics. But, when inquiries were made, Ferenc Molnar's agent informed the managers that the Hungarian author showed no enthusiasm whatsoever for sanctioning a musical version of his script as proposed by the organization. More often than not during that year, the Guild's productions had evolved into showcases for clever actors, with Clifton Webb, Wilfred Lawson, Dudley Digges, Leo G. Carroll, and, to a lesser extent, Dennis Hoey and Katharine Hepburn, receiving somewhat more critical attention than the plays in which they had appeared. The Lunts, again, held out the best possibility of Guild resurgence, for during the coming season it was hoped the pair would present two offerings, with "possible repertory to follow." For the subscription patrons, many of them reluctant to renew, this half-promise was one of the few prospects of excitement the Guild could provide.

CHAPTER 11 / 1937-38

To Quito and Back, Ben Hecht
Amphitryon 38 (Jean Giraudoux), S. N. Behrman
Madame Bovary (Gustave Flaubert), Gaston Baty
The Ghost of Yankee Doodle, Sidney Howard
Wine of Choice, S. N. Behrman
The Sea Gull (Chekhov), Stark Young
Washington Jitters, John Boruff and Walter Hart
(with the Actors Repertory Company)

The Theatre Guild's frustration at not having a sixth production thought promising enough with which to conclude its 1936–37 New York season was heightened by the fact that its backlog of suitable scripts was far from impressive. There were scattered intimations that Ben Hecht's *To Quito and Back* or Sidney Howard's newest effort, as yet without a title, would be rushed in to fill the gap. The Lunts, on tour with *Idiot's Delight,* were said to have had a retelling of the Amphitryon legend in rehearsal since February. In addition, Lunt had suggested that Alice Duer Miller or Ruth Gordon be approached to do an adaptation of Birabeau's *Dame Nature* after Robert E. Sherwood had refused the commission, and the Guild's play department was instructed to secure a copy of a newly rhymed *The Misanthrope,* recently produced abroad, as well as a translation of the Moscow Art Theatre's acclaimed presentation of Gogol's *Dead Souls.* Negotiations continued, moreover, for Flud's *The King of the Mountain*—the Guild wanted the Abbey Theatre to attempt a production of the experimental play before it tried the production itself. The Guild was also in the process of acquiring the American rights for Isherwood's and Auden's tragedy concerning an Himalayan expedition, *The Ascent of F 6.* Nevertheless, the fact remained obvious to many that the Guild had really nothing to offer its New York subscribers, when the run of *Jane Eyre* was terminated before its appearance in New York. Many theatregoers were annoyed by this, for they felt they had been refused the Guild's only decent offering of the year, and quite a few wrote the Guild expressing their displeasure.

Hopes had not died for salvaging *Jane Eyre* for the 1937–38 season, however, for it had been a great money-maker on the road. In November, Helen Jerome wrote to Theresa Helburn:

> I have heard from what may be a fairly authoritative quarter that RKO are afraid to let their Duse [Katharine Hepburn] play Jane Eyre—(in which they show a certain amount of sense). It seems all her costume pictures have been flops—and her Stage Door affair, being modern and requiring no poetic feeling or artistic invention, has brought her back to screen popularity. Therefore, I suggest that you not be fooled by RKO as Arthur Hopkins was when he foolishly wanted her for *Pride and Prejudice* (which God saved me from)—It is my opinion they will stall and delay until we lose the season.

Miss Jerome went on to suggest Luise Rainer, or Janet Gaynor, who, she felt, could be directed by a proper director, and mentioned as a third possibility Heather Angel, who was both "ideal and English." Jerome then alluded to her recent adaptation of Somerset Maugham's *Theatre*. Producer deLiagre, it seemed, had tried in vain to cast it, but John Golden was "wildly enthusiastic" if the authoress was willing to wait until Gertrude Lawrence, then playing in Rachel Crothers' *Susan and God*, was free. Miss Jerome offered to let the Guild see her Maugham adaptation, while admitting, "there's only Leontovitch for it —outside Lawrence—Jane Cowl has gone virtuous—says she 'smells success' in the script but wouldn't dare present such a naughty actress." Later, the Guild, still hopeful for a *Jane Eyre* revival, rejected *Theatre* as a possible offering.

The Guild had magnanimously offered preferential treatment to the remaining subscribers of the left-wing Theatre Union, which had been lately disbanded. Even with its subscription lists filled, however, the Guild's financial picture had not by any means been enhanced by the relative failures of the 1936–37 season. Because the organization had no new exciting fare to offer its road patrons (with the possible exception of *Storm Over Patsy* and *The Masque of Kings*—expensive shows to troupe, even after omitting several of the sets), it agreed to allow Tallulah Bankhead's *Antony and Cleopatra* and Jed Harris' production of *A Doll's House* to be included in the American Theatre Society's road subscription series. The Bowery Savings Bank also was increasing its pressure for a substantial reduction of the Guild's mortgage commitments, and the bondholders' committee was still registering an oppressive dissatisfaction. The Guild's managers decided, therefore, to exercise their option for extension of an underwriting agreement with Paramount Pictures similar to the one drawn up in 1936. This meant further reliance on movie-oriented material.

Possibly to cater to its new Theatre Union clientele, but more probably to please its motion-picture backers, the Guild was in the process of preparing its first offering of the 1937–38 season, under Moeller's direction, an offering which "glibly and artfully spread a communistic gospel." Ben Hecht, reportedly the highest paid motion-picture writer in the world, had written *To Quito and Back* to woo the legitimate theatre public once more. In the past, he had been rather a respected author of novels, short stories, and several substantial comedies, including *The Front Page* and *Twentieth Century* (done in collaboration with Charles MacArthur). His motion-picture credits were impressive, and included *Topaze, Scarface, Viva Villa, Design for Living, Nothing Sacred,* and *The Goldwyn Follies,* as well as *Crime Without Passion, Soak the Rich, The Scoundrel,* and *Twentieth Century,* again with MacArthur. Now, however, Hecht was quoted as having forsaken the West Coast although his contract with Samuel Goldwyn reportedly still had a time to run: "Yes, I will start all over again. Once, in my youth, I wrote books with some mental content. Now I am going back . . . and see if it's any fun to be a writer again." Continuing, he spoke endearingly of *To Quito and Back*: "This play . . . contains so many of the subjects and situations that are absolutely taboo in Hollywood that I'll promise you one thing, anyhow . . . they'll never be able to turn it into a motion picture!" [*New York Times,* Sept. 19, 1937]

The Guild offered the Shuberts, who originally had held an option on Hecht's script, part of *To Quito and Back,* providing they finance the production at the rate of two to one. It was the first time the Guild was managerially allied with the rival organization, although it had been using Shubert houses on the road and in New York City for years. But, it was not the first time the Guild had others financially interested in its productions. John C. Wilson, a member in the Lunt-Noel Coward partnership, for instance, had been associated with the organization for the presentations of *The Taming of the Shrew* and *Idiot's Delight.*

Casting procedures for *To Quito and Back* began as early as February with Joseph Schildkraut and Elia Kazan being considered for the important role of a South American rebel leader. *Quito's* featured players, however, were Leslie Banks and Sylvia Sidney. Miss Sidney, a movie star, had been away from the legitimate theatre for more than seven years, but it seemed that no recent film concerning rebellion, social or otherwise, would have been complete without her. She had, for example, just finished playing the lead in Samuel Goldwyn's picturization of *Dead End,* and was scheduled to return to the Coast, as soon as she finished in Hecht's play, to do a picture about the Spanish struggle. Her only other association with the Guild had been when, as a youngster of fifteen, she attended the acting school run by the organization and had been dismissed by headmistress Winifred Lenihan for some minor infraction of the rules. Banks, too, was not unfamiliar to movie patrons, although his association with the theatre, and the Guild, had been a good deal more extensive than Miss Sidney's. He had directed the organization's production of Shaw's *Too True To Be Good* in 1932 and was remembered by many for his adroit playing in Benn W. Levy's farce, *Springtime for Henry.*

When *To Quito and Back* had its premiere at Boston's Colonial Theatre on September 20, 1937, critical reactions seemed to indicate that Hecht's script contained the seeds of a good play, and there was a possibility that with rewriting and much pruning, a commendable presentation might emerge; as the *Christian Science Monitor* observed: "If he begins by cutting out the profanity he will reduce his running time by about one half. This is by all odds the most blasphemous drama to reach the boards within memory." Top acting honors for the evening had been carried off by an émigré actor, Joseph Buloff, who had played the revolutionary Zamiano with zest and authority. Walter N. Greaza was also complimented for having done well by some of Hecht's funnier lines, as was Evelyn Varden, who played a wise-cracking nymphomaniac. There was not much said about either of the leads, however.

Three weeks later, when *To Quito and Back* opened at the Guild Theatre, it appeared that Hecht had been too enamoured of his characters' philosophical discourses to do the much needed tightening. New York's critical reception was most uncordial:

> It has become one of the quainter rituals of the Theatre Guild to open its season by rushing out upon its 52nd St. stage and falling flat upon its annually astonished face. This peculiar ceremony was efficiently managed last night at the Mother House with the aid of Ben Hecht's first solo play. . . . [John Anderson, *New York Journal and American,* Oct. 7, 1937]

> Mr. Hecht has been mixed up in so many robustly humorous American sagas with low comedy gibes bouncing off the heads of giddy characters that the second phase of his career begins on

> a flat note. As a leader of the people's revolution and the physician of love he gives off a sound that is perilously close to quack. . . . In his brooding mood he has complicated love and the revolution a good deal. They were hard enough to understand before he took pen in hand. [Brooks Atkinson, *New York Times,* Oct. 7, 1937]

Most reviewers believed Moeller's handling of the players displayed its usual competence, but there were those who thought it "a little confused," or that "half-hearted direction . . . accentuates the play's defects of design and does nothing to conceal its verbosity." Aline Bernstein's settings and costumes were felt to be colorfully appropriate, and minor characters played by Horace Sinclair and Harry Bellaver were recognized felicitously. It was suggested, however, that Sylvia Sidney, while physically very attractive, had failed to adjust her vocal delivery to the requirements of the stage and either ran her words together monotonously or mumbled them incoherently. Critics also noticed that she registered emotion with a certain frozen-faced lack of variety. Banks, on the other hand, was thought to give a good account of the vacillating, not overly sympathetic character of Alexander Sterns, a liberated Hollywood writer groping toward fulfillment. It was his unhappy lot to carry many of Hecht's weighty utterances.

Interestingly enough, Richard Watts, Jr., of the conservative *New York Herald Tribune,* preferred *To Quito and Back* to Crothers' "overly competent and slick" *Susan and God,* for it "deals, however badly, with one of the most vital and provocative of present-day problems: the plight of an unstable intellectual liberal in a world of violently shifting social forces." The reviewer for the ultra-liberal *New Masses,* however, loved *Susan and God,* a play surely predicated upon bourgeois values, while he felt apathetic toward the dilemmas of *To Quito*'s leading character:

> Sterns' emotional vagaries are never properly integrated into the revolutionary part of the plot; the conversation shifts arbitrarily from society to love and back, and the play languishes. . . . The production is below the usual Guild standards, crude and halting.

George Jean Nathan summed up the general feeling that Hecht's allegiance to Hollywood had lasted just a bit too long, and now there was no turning back:

> Hecht returns to the theatre with an exhibit desperately calculated to persuade us that Hollywood hasn't made the slightest dent in him. With this purpose ferociously in view, he superciliously adjures the straightforward drama of conflict and action as something suitable only to the lowly screen and permits himself the treat of going on an intellectual bender. The result is a play that, while a teetotaler in the matter of drama, is so boozy with rhetoric and Brown Derby animadversions on love, life, sex, politics, religion, and what not that even the most loyal theatregoer suffers a painful ringing in the ears before the evening is half over and battles with an impulse to get out, run around to a film parlor, and seek some less pretentious, less verbose, less postureful, and more relieving entertainment in one of Hecht's old melodramatic Hollywood movies. [*Newsweek,* Oct. 18, 1937]

Barely a week after *To Quito and Back* opened, Federal Theatre ironically offered a well-received, vigorous revival of John Howard Lawson's *Processional,* which the Guild had initially produced during its 1924–25 season. The Guild's managers had often spoken of staging a few of their former critical triumphs, and if they had been overly concerned with liberating the proletariat or economic injustice, they might have reconsidered Lawson's work, which dealt with a West Virginia coal strike, instead of airing the Marxist views of a writer whose salary at the time was approximately $6,000 a week.

Within three weeks of *To Quito and Back*'s New York appearance, the Guild's second offering of 1937–38 made its well-publicized arrival at the Shubert. As early as 1935, a script by France's Jean Girardoux concerning Jupiter's dalliance with Alkmena, the wife of a Theban general named Amphitryon, had been considered by the Guild as a possible vehicle for the Lunts. During their coast-to-coast tour with *Idiot's Delight,* the pair had rehearsed this fable with their company, using S. N. Behrman's sophisticated, epigrammatic adaptation. At the close of the tour on the West Coast, the Lunt-Fontanne troupe completed its preparations for *Amphitryon,* preparations which included settings by Lee Simonson, costumes by Mme. Valentina (whose striking gowns had adorned Miss Fontanne in *Idiot's Delight*), and incidental music composed by Samuel Barlow, a native New Yorker whose reputation had been enhanced abroad.

In April, the proposed production was rechristened with its original title, *Amphitryon 38,* which was Giraudoux's whimsical assertion that his was the thirty-eighth reappraisal of the story; hence, a fair portion of the pre-opening press articles were devoted to futile attempts to uncover the previous thirty-seven versions.

Lunt realized *Amphitryon 38* would not use all the members of his company; nevertheless, he wished to keep the organization intact, for it contained the seeds of a well-integrated ensemble. One progress report was written to Theresa Helburn from Detroit: "We have, by the way, an interesting understudy system . . . Barry Thompson (who plays Amphitryon) understudies me—and I understudy him—It's a neat trick if we can pull it off—"

While the preparations for *Amphitryon 38* were hectic and exhausting, the end product was seemingly worth all the pains. When the production had its premiere at the Curran Theatre in San Francisco on June 23, 1937, the first-night audience loved it, and all the reviews were favorable. John Hobart's reaction in the *San Francisco Chronicle* was typical: "In S. N. Behrman's translation, the exquisite flavor of the original French has been magically preserved—this limpid, finely filtered prose has the bloom of poetry upon it. . . ." All commented upon the witty prologue, which had been staged to employ a delightful scenic innovation. Two heroic-sized figures, fitted with the heads and arms of actors Lunt and Richard Whorf, reclined, legs in the air, on a bank of fluffy clouds, while they discussed the foibles and persuasions of the mortals who passed below. All agreed the prologue was grand. There were some reservations concerning the rest of the play, but the entire company was complimented by Claude LaBelle in the *San Francisco News*, including Sydney Greenstreet, who played a philosophic, if impudent, trumpeter; Hope Williams, who contributed "a slyly humorous sketch of a regal and slightly pompous lady who could never forget that she was once courted by a swan"; and Richard Whorf, who made a "marvelously unctuous Mercury (the play, based on Greek antecedents, employs Roman names!)." The greatest promise *Amphitryon 38* held, however, deservedly belonged to the Lunts.

Costumes, music, and Bretaigne Windust's direction were all praised, and Simonson's settings were especially lauded. It was obvious to the management, however, that *Amphitryon 38* needed work. Even after another opening two weeks later at Los Angeles, where the movie colony turned out en masse to greet the Lunts with twenty-one curtain calls, doubts still persisted concerning the second and third acts. Behrman, who had been deeply troubled by the recent deaths of Osgood Perkins and George Gershwin, and by personal illness, had gone to Europe. Theresa Helburn, who had attended the Los Angeles opening with Langner, wrote to Lunt asking about the rewriting believed necessary, and also whether the star would consider trying out Robert E. Sherwood's *Acropolis* during the *Amphitryon* run. Lunt replied: "We haven't read Bob's new version of Acropolis, but two

AMPHITRYON 38 – The heads of Alfred Lunt and Richard Whorf animate Lee Simonson's models of "Jupiter" and "Mercury." This picture became almost as famous as the production. It was used on the cover of *Life* as well as in other periodicals and newspapers.

Greek plays in succession doesn't sound too interesting at the moment. We would rather do The Last of the Turbins or the new Max Anderson play, and then probably Acropolis following them." Interestingly enough, plans for the formation of the Playwrights' Company were being furthered by Sherwood, Anderson, and Elmer Rice during this same period.

The imminent arrival of a Lunt-Fontanne production in New York was always newsworthy, especially after the grapevine reported their stunning success on the West Coast, assuring the public that something very special was in the offing. Covers devoted to the presentation appeared on such magazines as *Life* and *Time; Theatre Arts Monthly* included stories concerning Behrman and Giraudoux, and the press continued its attempts to uncover Amphitryon 1 through 37:

> By the time Molière wrote his version the historians had lost track of the number of Amphitryon products. Although he had been turning to Spanish and Italian playwrights for material, Molière in this case went directly to Plautus, making use not only of the original Latin text, but also of a clever translation by Rotrou. He himself enacted the role of Sosie. . . . John Dryden's version, entitled "Amphitryon: or the Two Sosias," went far toward lewdness. It is not one of his best works, although it is probably the most outspoken; it was a failure even in his own day. Sir Walter Scott, comparing this play with Molière's says: "Dryden is coarse and vulgar where Molière is witty, and where the Frenchman ventures upon a double meaning the Englishman always contrives to make it a single one." [Helen Deutsch, *New York Herald Tribune*, Oct. 31, 1937]

Amphitryon 38's eastern tour took it to Baltimore, Washington, and Cleveland before it headed for New York. Its reception enroute was cordial, though some reviewers were still not unduly impressed. Louis Azrael of the *Baltimore News*, for instance, thought the play had two parallel themes: that real friendship can be a substitute for love, and that there can be achieved, at times, a kind of marital perfection. He found, however, that too little time was devoted to exploring these basic ideas, and too much was devoted to keeping the production's "gleaming bubble" aloft by trickery.

The same week that *Amphitryon 38* was due to open on Broadway, incidentally, any number of heralded attractions were also scheduled to make their appearance. There was to be, for instance, a revival of *As You Like It* with a ready-made reputation; a satirical musical from

AMPHITRYON 38 – Richard Whorf, Alfred Lunt, Lynn Fontanne, and Barry Thomson.
"Lee Simonson's opening setting, which reveals Jupiter and his son Mercury perched on a cloud looking down on their favorite planet, will be the talk of the town from now on. But his other settings, although less audacious, are to my mind much better . . . the white house framed against the deep blue sky, the billowing rococo clouds, wittily reflect in their artful artlessness, the spirit of the play and at the same time their purity of form and simplicity capture the essence of Attic beauty" – John Hobart, *San Francisco Chronicle*, June 24, 1937.

the famed team of Kaufman, the two Harts, and Rodgers entitled *I'd Rather Be Right,* in which George M. Cohan played the part of President Roosevelt; a new play by Clifford Odets called *Golden Boy* to be presented by the Group Theatre; and a modern-dress version of *Julius Caesar,* created by Orson Welles for the Mercury Theatre (formerly The Comedy—where the Washington Square Players had once held forth). It was felt, however, that perhaps it was not a good thing for productions to be praised too widely before they opened, for the town's reviewers were likely to be led to expect too much, and to react adversely.

This sense of over-anticipation possibly worked to the detriment of *Amphitryon 38*'s critical reception, for with all the revising and refurbishing, the New York notices found fault with pretty much the same things that had been lightly criticized on the road—they just bore down a bit harder. Richard Watts, Jr. wrote that it was nothing short of churlish to be disappointed by the Lunts' latest presentation, and then, after praising all its external values, suggested that it lacked "a fairly continuous flow of lively and ironic wit." There were suggestions that Behrman's adaptation of Giraudoux's text was sufficiently inventive to deserve the numerical designation of "39":

> But with all the grace and sensitiveness of the writing, Giraudoux's play seems to leave Mr. Behrman at something of a disadvantage. It is said to be Mr. Behrman's fate as a dramatist to be praised always for his play before the last, but surely he shows here very little of the glinting humor . . . of his usual trademark. The lines have no sting in them. They merely accompany a sort of scenic festival with appropriate, but not very striking conversation. [John Anderson, *New York Journal and American,* Nov. 2, 1937]

The consensus, then, seemed to stress that *Amphitryon 38* could hardly be called an immortal comedy, or even a very good one. Brooks Atkinson believed that the indigenous bedroom joke upon which the action had been based was possibly more durable than most bedroom jokes; still, the play really provided only one joke for the space of three acts, and it had not been juggled with inexhaustible brilliance, "playing all the changes that might be gaily rung on a god's night out among the gullible mortals." The deftness of the peerless Lunts, however, was thought as near to perfection as it had ever been. Stark Young of the *New Republic* was but one of many who attempted to capture and define their magic qualities:

> With patience and taste Mr. Lunt and Miss Fontanne have slid over places that might have passed for wisecracks and even been guffawed upon as such. To have been salacious, smarty and buffo would have been only too easy. They have preferred to seek instead dignity, a genuine inner rhythm, and distinction, and have accomplished a degree of profound meaning beyond any play I have seen them do. Only those, perhaps, who know the theatre could know with what work and consideration many of their readings have been discovered and given so secure a projection. At the same time the basis of ironic farce also is maintained throughout the performance. Through skill and repeated experiment and genuine professional conscience there has been achieved a sense of constant struggle between the story's deeper implications and its farcical rebound, and from our sense of this struggle arises a dramatic quality, as well as cerebral kick and entertainment, that is brilliant and expert. It is, however, a quality that is special to the methods of Mr. Lunt and Miss Fontanne, as they approach and develop the production of a play.

Despite the comedy's lack of enthusiastic critical acceptance, *Amphitryon 38* became a hit, mainly through its stars' performances, just as *I'd Rather Be Right,* which the critics thought turned out to be neither very biting nor very inventive, also sold well chiefly because of George M. Cohan's charming persuasiveness. Jean Giraudoux, who had come unannounced to see the American presentation of his play, thought those critics who demanded a more hilarious evening had somehow missed the whole point. He was quoted as saying that *Amphitryon 38* was something of an experiment in the theatre, and in no sense a farce or madcap jest. "The closest designation I can think of, for it is one used by Mr. Lunt, is 'a gentle philosophic comedy.' " Giraudoux continued by stating that he had great faith in the public, but very little in professional critics. These, he felt, fell into two categories: those who went to a play with a sympathetic attitude and a genuine desire to understand what an author was trying to accomplish, and the other sort, who attended the theatre with almost an attitude of antagonism. They approached a play with the sole intention of ridiculing what was wrong with it, "or of showing how much cleverer they are than the theatregoers, the actors, the playwright, and the other critics." The playwright thought it unfortunate that the latter group usually managed to be more conspicuous and more frequently amusing. Giraudoux, also, had been captivated by the Lunts' methods:

> They have some of the freedom of improvisation and the accuracy of gesture that exists in commedia del arte. That to me is the best kind of theatre. I think a playwright should write for publication and permit the actors to do as they please in the way of interpretation. Elisabeth Bergner's production of my "Amphitryon 38" in Germany was different from the Paris production, but it was extremely satisfying. . . . [*New York Herald Tribune*, Nov. 7, 1937]

The French author had a graceful compliment for S. N. Behrman, too:

> I write for the French theatre, where conditions differ materially from those that occur on the New York stage. For instance, I assure you that to write a successful French play one need only to write a very long play. If you are sufficiently discursive, they will love it. The original "Amphitryon 38" was full of philosophic dissertations. I find the speedy American version, which Mr. Behrman has made, thoroughly exciting and extremely provocative.

In January, word went out that the Lunts were holding talent auditions, and numerous stage-struck youngsters flocked to these informal tryouts for what they hoped would be the opportunity of a lifetime. It was also reported that the gifted pair was well advanced with plans to offer Chekhov's *The Sea Gull* in repertory, alternating it with *Amphitryon 38*. Later, they decided they would present the Giraudoux-Behrman comedy for a short season in England, a decision that would necessitate opening *The Sea Gull* for a regular uninterrupted run to accommodate subscription audiences before the troupe sailed. This decision must have been painful to the rest of the Guild's managers, for, after more than five months, *Amphitryon 38* was still one of the better-attended shows in town.

In May, the Lunts' company opened to encouraging notices at the Lyric Theatre in London, and at the end of July the couple visited Scandinavia. Lunt, in a Swedish newspaper interview, graciously suggested that he had long considered presenting some of Strindberg's works in New York, and that he was particularly attracted to doing *The Father*. This could not have been more than idle musing, however, for, with the possible exception of *The Sea Gull*, the Lunt-Fontanne type of play had already been pretty well set, and *The Father* surely was not the sort of fare the pair's numerous admirers would have accepted with relish.

Lunt wrote Warren Munsell from Finland in August concerning a projected fall tour of *Amphitryon 38,* which he felt would have limited appeal. The actor-producer was more interested in reviving *Idiot's Delight* for the road, despite the fact that a picture starring Clark Gable and Norma Shearer was ready for release, and that Phil Baker had been hoping to troupe the show in short road engagements. The Lunts' *Idiot's Delight* was a sure drawing card in the hinterland, whereas *Amphitryon 38* was not. In September, the pair returned to the states on the *Normandie,* glad to come home "to a land removed by many miles of water from a world where the atmosphere is so tense and ominous that 'one can scarcely breathe.'" In October, *Amphitryon 38* had been prepared for a short tour which took it to "relatively sophisticated" eastern seaboard cities.

At precisely the same time that *Amphitryon 38* was being readied for its New York opening, the Guild was preparing another vehicle, for which Lynn Fontanne had once been considered. In fact, the Guild had bought the English-language rights to *Madame Bovary* with the Lunts' talents in mind. In Paris, Maurice Wertheim had been favorably impressed upon seeing Gaston Baty's version of Gustave Flaubert's realistic nineteenth-century novel concerning the downfall of a callow Normandy farm girl who become a bourgeois housewife and who longs to become the heroine of every romantic tale she reads. Baty, a sort of French mélange of David Belasco and Max Reinhardt, a noted scenic designer and dramatist, had obtained consent from Flaubert's heirs to adapt the famous novel, which had been the woe of French censors when it was first published. Baty's production, as presented in his Montparnasse Theatre, had run successfully for over a year. For a long time, the Guild was troubled by finding a proper translator for Baty's adaptation; first Julian Leigh and then John Gerard were asked to submit versions. Possible casting for the title role again indicated the Guild's complete acceptance of the star system, for the names of Greta Garbo, Luise Rainer, Ann Harding, Tallulah Bankhead, Judith Anderson, and Miriam Hopkins were all mentioned. The Guild followed up a suggestion made by Wertheim that Katharine Cornell might be interested in the part as well. In May, even though Ina Claire was interested in the title role, the Board decided that playwright Benn W. Levy should adapt as well as direct the production as a vehicle for his wife, film star Constance Cummings. Levy, an Englishman, began to cast several English actors for the more important roles including Eric Portman, Carl Harbord, and Ernest Thesiger, who had appeared for the Guild once before in *A Sleeping*

Clergyman. It was also decided that Baty's staging had been "exactly right" for showing off all the adaptation's potentials; so, the Guild began negotiations for the privilege of copying exactly the French production.

As rehearsals progressed, it became apparent to the Board members that *Madame Bovary* was not shaping up the way they had hoped. Levy had been tinkering with the script in order to make it more playable, and in the process he removed some things the Board felt made the play intelligible. When the presentation had its American premiere on October 5, 1937, at the National Theatre in Washington, D. C., it received mixed notices; but, surprisingly, several were no less than adulatory:

> Benn W. Levy's adaptation of Gaston Baty's dramatic version of Flaubert's great novel does honor and reverence to this finest of all studies of the beastliness possible in beautiful ladies. The interpretation of Madame's mad career of romancing is in the accomplished hands of Constance Cummings. Her playing of it left little to be desired, little that cannot be realized when she has built up her endurance to sustain the burden of one of the largest tasks ever thrust upon any actress. . . . She earned the ovation she received at the end. [Jay Carmody, *Washington Evening Star*, Oct. 6, 1937]

> And what a fitted and finished and fine show it is as done by the Guild's other actors! . . . Lee Simonson, adapting the original production from Gaston Baty, has mounted its 16 scenes perfectly, costumed its players delightfully, rightly, and the stage hands and electricians have worked overtime. . . . All in all, the Guild gets the 1937–38 legitimate season off to its real start. . . . [Maybelle Jennings, *Washington Herald*, Oct. 6, 1937]

Madame Bovary's next stopover was Pittsburgh's Nixon Theatre. The critics there largely liked what they saw, yet seemed to be disturbed by what they believed to be illustrations of motion-picture techniques being used in the theatre—"voice-over" explanations delivered by six young ladies situated in the loges who were supposed to be Emma's school companions, for instance, or the multitudinous, tricky scene changes thought necessary in telling a melodramatic story on stage.

Madame Bovary was scheduled to play Cleveland after its stay at Pittsburgh, but it was sidetracked, possibly to help celebrate "Go To The Theatre Week" recently proclaimed by Chicago's mayor. The

Madame Bovary company must have given a superb opening-night performance, for Chicagoans, who had recently turned up their collective noses at such high-powered musical comedies as *Red, Hot and Blue* and *The Show Is On,* turned out in record numbers for the Guild's newest offering. They undoubtedly also came to witness the ascension of a new stage star.

> Dark, big-eyed, full-figured, Miss Cummings suggests the rose in the muck Emma fancied herself to be, and also suggests the overblown quality of the fancy. She has power, this girl, an ability to hurl herself into emotion, a gentle quality that rivets attention. Perhaps the stage has a very young actress, after all. . . . [Claudia Cassidy, *Chicago Journal of Commerce,* Oct. 19, 1937]

This same review complimented the playing of O. Z. Whitehead, who evidenced "a quickness of response, a swift accuracy of effect, that makes one say 'born actor.' "

Despite the fact that *Madame Bovary* was a box-office bonanza during its Chicago engagement, the Guild's managers were not blind to the show's deficiencies. They made long, fruitless telephone calls to Levy requesting the restoration of material that was being cut, including a scene featuring O. Z. Whitehead which they felt was important. Levy also wanted the pharmacy set "lightened," but the Guild refused to do this for it would mean complete rebuilding. After two weeks the presentation moved to Philadelphia, where the critics were far less kind than previous ones had been. Even the once-heralded acting now failed to impress completely:

> It is the same problem in performance that confronts Constance Cummings in the title role and her associates in the cast. Persuasive in appearance and pleasing in personality, Miss Cummings is beyond her depth dramatically. And that isn't only because her skill has not grown sufficiently in stage stature for the part she plays, but because some of the inner aspects of the role apparently cannot be caught and conveyed convincingly. [Linton Martin, *Philadelphia Sunday Inquirer,* Nov. 6, 1937]

The Guild's Board of Managers had serious misgivings about bringing *Madame Bovary* into New York, but because of obligations to the Broadhurst Theatre, and many other financial ramifications, the play opened there on November 16 as scheduled. Unfortunately, the Gotham reviewers, if they could not decide exactly what was wrong,

MADAME BOVARY – Lee Simonson's 19th Century Apothecary Shop setting.

L. to r. – Harold Vermilyea, Constance Cummings, Ernest Cossart, Eric Portman, O. Z. Whitehead, Viola Roache, Valerie Cossart.

"A program note says that the sixteen scenes were adapted by Lee Simonson from the original production of Baty in Paris. Whoever deserves the credit for them, it is an approximate certainty that one shall not look upon their effective and varied like again this season" – Jay Carmody, *Washington* (D.C.) *Evening Star*, October 6, 1937.

did decide with unusual unanimity that they did not find the Guild's offering very stageworthy:

> It makes a sweetly sad, rather slow play, sentimental to its pretty fingertips. . . . This prettying up of the character does, obviously, a good deal of violence to the original conception. . . . Flaubert was serenely objective as he pictured her, and he did not sob over her sad lot [however] there is enough of the book's plot left in to stand in the way of any other interpretation. . . . I should suppose that anyone seeing the play, without having read the book, would be a good deal puzzled to understand Emma's reactions. It may be this lack of sustaining motivation which makes the episodes seem so spotty, makes the action jump uncomfortably and leaves the way clear for growing tedium. [Richard Lockridge, *New York Sun,* Nov. 17, 1937]

> One of the things wrong with the dramatization, it seems certain, is the use of those girls in the boxes. They are good-looking young women and its is a pleasure to the eye to watch them, but I fear that they get in the way of what is passing for drama on the stage. Just what they are supposed to represent I never could quite figure out. Part of the time they seem to stand for Emma's conscience; sometimes they are her tempters, and then, again, they merely repeat to you actions that have taken place offstage. In the end you come to the conclusion that they are chiefly an author's confession of failure. Since he couldn't tell the story of the novel in straight dramatic terms he had to fall back on a clumsy device to carry him over the tough spots. But, unfortunately, the chief result is that the naturalistic mood of the drama is thrown out of key. . . . "Madame Bovary" is, I fear, not one of the Guild's triumphs. [Richard Watts, Jr., *New York Herald Tribune,* Nov. 17, 1937]

Simonson's many settings, as well as the direction and acting, were generally well received, especially Ernest Cossart's effectively humorous portrayal of the apothecary Homais, Harold Vermilyea's skillful drawing of Emma's lumpish husband, Charles, and Ernest Thesiger's fastidious rendering of the miserly L'Heaueux. "But," concluded the *New York World Telegram*'s Sidney B. Whipple, "they cannot persuade anyone that, after the first act, it is not time to turn off the reading lamp and go to sleep. You have had all you can stand of the novel."

In rebuttal, the Board of Managers rushed a special edition of the *Theatre Guild Bulletin* to its subscribers. Under the heading "The Guild's Puzzle Page," this document sampled some of the diametrically opposed verdicts that had been delivered on *Madame Bovary* by various critics as it had played throughout the country. This issue of the Bulletin became something of a collector's item, for it was referred to in several newspaper articles—pointing out that however violently the New York critics had disagreed about certain details, they were right in one respect—namely, that the presentation had been vastly disappointing—and this is what really disturbed the Guild.

The organization announced that early in December it would give a "curtainless" performance of *Madame Bovary* for students of stagecraft who wished to see its "marvels of rapid scene transformation, and also some of the costume changes which take place on the stage." Later in the same month, lack of business caused *Madame Bovary* to close its curtains forever.

The production had become something of an example for moneywise theatrical producers, seeming to reinforce the lesson learned by such offerings as *Doll's House* with Ruth Gordon and Paul Lukas, *Yr. Obedient Servant* with Fredric March and Florence Eldridge, and the Nazimova repertory company of the previous season, to wit: if successful road productions opened in New York and received poor notices, they were not only doomed on Broadway but quite likely had small chance for continued success throughout the rest of the country, even though *Madame Bovary* had broken attendance records in Chicago. There was general agreement, too, that productions could do well on the road if there were Hollywood names associated with them; whereas, New Yorkers were not too impressed by "personal appearances" and demanded substantially more of their theatre.

Shortly before *Madame Bovary* began its death throes, another adaptation of a novel appeared on Broadway. The acclaimed *Of Mice and Men* by John Steinbeck had been originally written with the theatre in mind, however, and it possessed an economy of story line, a unity of mood, as well as compact, pungent dialogue that *Bovary* lacked. The novel *Of Mice and Men* was implicitly dramatic and not really "theatre at second-hand," even if it did not presume to the same stature as literature that Flaubert's work had attained.

With the tragic Emma Bovary behind her, Constance Cummings immediately began preparing for her next appearance. This time it would be in a farce, *If I Were You,* again written and directed by her husband. The playing of farce was a bit closer to what Miss Cummings had done in her many escapist movie roles. There was to be no escape for the Guild, however, for the organization was left with sixteen handsome *Bovary* settings on its hands, as well as a huge *Bovary* deficit—both critical and financial.

Even though the Board of Managers had thought of Sidney Howard as a possible candidate to help strengthen *Madame Bovary* before it opened on the road, Howard was busy with his own script, belatedly retitled *The Ghost of Yankee Doodle,* and could ill afford time for more play-doctoring. As early as the previous February the Guild had considered Howard's newest offering as a possible vehicle for its winning Gladys Cooper-Philip Merivale combination and had wanted to produce it as the sixth play of the 1936–37 season, but it was far from being in presentable shape. By June, Howard had rewritten great portions of the script with Ethel Barrymore's talents in mind.

Sidney Howard, newly returned from Hollywood, had gained a sizable share of his reputation through such Guild productions as *They Knew What They Wanted, Ned McCobb's Daughter,* and *The Silver Cord.* Later, he had successfully adapted for other managements such varied works as *Yellow Jack, Dodsworth, The Late Christopher Bean,* and *Paths of Glory.* Upon his return from the West Coast he had submitted a draft of *The Ghost of Yankee Doodle* to the Guild. It would be his last original play. When the production was being tried out, Howard had been asked if he intended *Yankee Doodle* to be in any sense a propaganda piece. The playwright replied in the negative, but stated that most of his work did deal with social themes:

> In this play, for instance, I am discussing the problem of the poor liberal, caught between the ultra-conservative, die-hard philosophy and the radical philosophy. I am not interested in the die-hards nor in the radicals—the showy extremes—but I am intensely interested in the plight of the true liberals who are not showy and are in a fair way to being crushed by the bombastic extremists. [*Buffalo News,* Oct. 29, 1937]

The Guild prevailed upon one of the great ladies of the American stage, Ethel Barrymore, to forego retirement to play in Howard's tailor-made vehicle. It had also succeeded in getting another Hollywood returnee, Howard's friend John Cromwell, to act as director for its new presentation. Cromwell agreed but somewhat angered the Guild by trying to direct two plays at once. He guided *The Ghost of*

Yankee Doodle up to its out-of-town opening, then rushed back to New York to work with Fredric March and his wife in *Yr. Obedient Servant,* due to reach Broadway the week before Christmas. Because the Guild quite properly expected Cromwell to stay with *Yankee Doodle* during the all-important tryout period, it was strongly in favor of the idea that "appropriate reduction should be made in Mr. Cromwell's compensation."

The Ghost of Yankee Doodle premiered in a one-night stand at the Auditorium in Rochester, New York. A Rochester reviewer the next morning predicted its unqualified success during the current season, but *Variety's* out-of-town reporter was less sanguine, for while admitting that Howard's opus had "a notable cast and strong material for a great play," he also felt it contained "a lot of talking and rushing about," and inferred a vast amount of rewriting had to be done before a metropolitan opening would be feasible.

The following day, Woodman Thompson's elaborate single setting, decorated to provide "an excellent background for the Barrymore gowns," was moved to Buffalo, and four days later to Boston, where the representative of the press seemed to be wholly in favor of what they saw and heard. Elliott Norton of the *Boston Post* thought *The Ghost of Yankee Doodle* "a bruising, brutal, powerful and sometimes brilliant piece, expertly written and admirably acted. It is the first significant new drama of the season, something to be enthusiastic over, something to cheer about, to stir staid playgoers to dance in the aisle." Robert E. Roberts of the *Boston Evening American* commented on the novelty of the play's construction—two long acts, each with five or six scenes separated only by a brief lowering of the lights—while Helen Eager of the *Boston Traveler* found the piece symbolic in that its family of liberals mirrored civilization, existing at a time when "rumblings from the outside world which seep through the walls are not pretty sounds." All welcomed veteran actors Ethel Barrymore and Dudley Digges for their professional adroitness as well as for their engaging qualities, and Louise Mace of the *Springfield Republican* wrote that she found ex-Hollywood player Russell Hardie the most acceptable juvenile to haunt the stage that season. She continued somewhat more soberly concerning the presentation's other merits:

> . . . it is loaded with enough ideas for a couple of other plays. Mr. Howard is unable to control his fevered rebellion at the world's selfish rush into expediency. So he develops his subject wordily while technical directness, vital to stage fulfillment, gets

> out of hand. This deluge of ideas, idealism and earnest moralizing clutters the course and leaves the whole business becalmed.

She did conclude, however, that if necessary trimming and tightening were accomplished, *The Ghost of Yankee Doodle* might well become "one of the important plays of our time."

There was to be only a week's stopover in Washington before *Yankee Doodle*'s New York opening, but the critics in the nation's capital, which had already seen *Madame Bovary, Amphitryon 38,* and *Tovarich* during the 1937–38 subscription season, hospitably received the Guild's latest presentation with such phrases as "a most enjoyable session with the adult drama," and "one of the season's most thoughtful and most significant exhibits." There did not seem to be much to worry about as the production headed for its most important opening.

A number of reviews on the road had commented on the similarity of themes in *The Ghost of Yankee Doodle* and *To Quito and Back,* the much-abused offering that Howard's play was to replace at the Guild Theatre. Both scripts dealt with the plight and the problems of liberals whose professions did not always match their practice; yet, it was felt, if all the tangles and uncertainties which seemed somehow inescapable whenever the Guild tried to deal with liberalism and war in a serious way were straightened out, *Yankee Doodle* had a better chance at success than *To Quito* ever had.

Alas, the New York critics were unimpressed and turned thumbs down on Howard's prolix if ardent arguments. Richard Watts, Jr. wrote that the play was "as confused as the liberal mind it attempts to fathom," and Brooks Atkinson thought it resembled "a dramatization of spare parts in a playwright's tool shed." Reviewers recalled that Sidney Howard was one of America's more competent writers, but John Mason Brown waxed indignant over his seeming ineptitude in *Yankee Doodle:*

> Mr. Howard's arguments are for the most part stale ones, stalely stated. They lack the passion one hoped he would bring to liberalism's defense. They lack the logic, too. What they say is what everyone knows. In getting even this said they tend to run away from the drama that is latent in them. Worse still, they lead to a last-act curtain which, however hopeful it may be as a prayer for the world's remote sanity, shows that Mr. Howard has not thought his plot through to any consistent or satisfactory conclusion. [*New York Post,* Nov. 23, 1937]

Reviewers for periodicals were also confounded by Howard's latest dramatic miscue. George Jean Nathan, in a *Newsweek* article entitled "A-Riding on a Phony," snorted, "The play in its entirety indicates anew that the place for playwrights who have been spending most of their time in Hollywood is still Hollywood"; and Stark Young wrote:

> The best way, perhaps, to describe Mr. Sidney Howard's new play would be to say that if you read it in book form you would find it a smatter of numberless topics, ideas, allusions, incidents, casual or grave, and [you] would resent the presence of such literate facility amidst such lack of gestation . . . . [*New Republic,* Dec. 8, 1937]

The poor Guild! In less than two months the organization had given New York four productions which, taken at face value, represented the finest the American theatre had to offer. It had presented the efforts of three of America's more important playwrights, one a former Pulitzer award winner, in addition to two of France's more illustrious literary figures, one modern and one a giant of the past. It could hardly have been accused of neglecting contemporary trends or ideas, for two of its presentations had dealt more or less exhaustively with the pressures applied to the liberal philosophy during those years of deepening uneasiness abroad. Moreover, the organization had employed the creative energies of a number of respected artists in theatrical production—the considerable talents, for instance, of Moeller, Benn W. Levy, John Cromwell, Aline Bernstein, Woodman Thompson, and Valentina, among others, and it is needless to underscore that Lee Simonson had distinguished himself by providing the amazing settings of *Amphitryon 38* and *Madame Bovary* that quite understandably were the talk of the town.

Furthermore, the Guild had given its audiences an opportunity to enjoy such established stars of the stage as Alfred Lunt, Lynn Fontanne, Ethel Barrymore, Dudley Digges, and Leslie Banks, and had displayed in good faith such renowned younger players as Sylvia Sidney and Constance Cummings. Added to this galaxy it had offered the highly diversified talents of Evelyn Varden, Richard Whorf, Sidney Greenstreet, Edith King, Ernest Thesiger, Harold Vermilyea, Eric Portman, Viola Roache, Ernest Cossart, Frank Conroy, Eliot Cabot, and many others. It had also enhanced the reputations of such promising newer actors as Joseph Buloff, O. Z. Whitehead, Valerie Cossart, John Drew Devereux (a Barrymore nephew), Marilyn Erskine, and Richard Carlson.

And yet, the disillusioned Guild found itself in the midst of an artistic and financial morass that must have been heartrending to contemplate. By the first week in December, *To Quito and Back* and *The Ghost of Yankee Doodle* had lost about $15,000 apiece, and *Madame Bovary* was a staggering $33,111.07 in the red. The only production to show any profit had been *Amphitryon 38,* but then the Guild's share was only one-half of the net, the other half going to pay the Lunt-John C. Wilson-Noel Coward "outside investor's share."

Nor were the Guild's pangs of frustration helped any by the sniping of the New York press in general, and of George Jean Nathan in particular. This gentleman, in one acid article, suggested that the Guild's Board of Managers resign in a body and turn the running of its affairs over to a "younger, and more intelligent directorate," or follow the dictates of some imaginative play reader. John Anderson was the next to take up the gauntlet flung at the Guild's feet by "El Georgio":

> Mr. Nathan implies that the low humming noise we hear in 52 St. is the Guild rejecting masterpieces. If Broadway were blooming with magnificent plays, all of which had been turned down by the Six Characters in Search of an Author, it would cinch the argument. Mr. Nathan might then go so far as to prove that the Guild can't even read. But neither Mr. Nathan nor I have seen any Broadway productions this season that would have added to the Guild's reputation, except possibly the Mercury Theatre's "Julius Caesar," the Group's "Golden Boy" and Sam Harris' "Of Mice and Men." [*New York Journal and American,* Nov. 30, 1937]

Anderson went on to point out that the Guild had had little chance of securing any of these productions for itself, since *Julius Caesar* was solely the product of a vigorous new producing organization, that John Steinbeck's hit had been nurtured by the old partnership of Sam Harris and George S. Kaufman, and that obviously Odets was "the Group's own Golden Boy."

> Well, then, we might all ask, why produce anything? . . . Why not revive "R. U. R." or Shaw's neglected "Heartbreak House"? Or wangle the American right to the Soviet production of Gogol's "Dead Souls." Why not give Mr. Nathan some Strindberg or

> Hauptmann? The answer presumably is that the Guild promises its customers . . . a series of new plays. If they aren't plays, the Guild can say truthfully, at least, that they are new—if that makes any difference. Personally I don't think it does, because I would rather see one old, good play than all the poor new ones in the world, and I think the Guild's subscribers could be bullied into the same viewpoint. . . .

Lawrence Langner immediately wrote a reply to Anderson, although *not* mentioning that the Guild had tried unsuccessfully to secure the American rights for the Soviet's *Dead Souls,* nor that Orson Welles and John Houseman of the Mercury Theatre had already entered into direct negotiations with Shaw concerning a revival of *Heartbreak House.* He did state what seemed to him to be the theatre's most persistently annoying problem of the moment—that of gifted and trained theatre personnel being unavailable because of various motion-picture commitments, thereby making it next to impossible for the theatre to secure the sustained services of its best actors, directors, and dramatists. When playwrights did return to the theatre briefly, they seemed to be interested only in sociological subjects, denied to them by movie censorship, and thus this type of play had glutted the theatrical market. Because of this, Langner suggested, Broadway seemed to be turning toward "actor's theatre," in which revivals were becoming increasingly seductive through novel production ideas coupled with skilled acting. He concluded this letter with a playful allusion to George Jean Nathan:

> You mention in your article a suggestion made by Mr. Nathan that the answer to all the Guild's problems is the retirement of its directors to Hollywood. You even speak of this as a war between Mr. Nathan and the Guild. I think you have entirely misunderstood Mr. Nathan. He is at heart a kindly and whimsical fellow who has for years bombarded us with a pea-shooter, under the mistaken impression that he was handling a machine gun. Having watched magazine after magazine with which he has been associated (from "The Smart Set" to "Vanity Fair") fold up and disappear gracefully into the past, I can quite understand how retirement of any sort, even to Hollywood, must express a profound wish-fulfillment on his part.

The Guild, naturally, was nevertheless deeply concerned by its diminishing artistic and financial returns in a situation where apparently it could do nothing right. These circumstances obviously called for drastic measures, and so the odious machinery of curtailing Board members' salaries was again set in motion, although Lee Simonson strongly objected to this stopgap arrangement, at least, as far as he was to be affected. In a letter to Lawrence Langner he stated his objections:

> On last year's arrangement I was the only member of the board that was judged of no executive value. You (as well as Terry and Phil) took $20,000 salary out of the Guild (or twice mine). This difference was defended on the ground that you and Terry, beside contributing more to the success of the Guild, took a risk and I didn't, my salary being guaranteed. Well, you have taken out $20,000 and I can hardly be expected to sacrifice my salary and be subject to a risk now that my lower scale of salary was to insure me against. If I had $20,000 in my hip pocket I could also afford to take my salary at present on the cuff.

Simonson continued by pointing out it was quite evident that salaries of $20,000 could not justifiably be paid, especially by an organization which had lost about $120,000 of its subscribers' investments and roughly $85,000 of its working capital in the first thirteen weeks of the current season. Shortly thereafter, Simonson also forwarded to the Board a succinct memorandum (Appendix, pp. 495–97), in which he placed most of the blame for the Guild's recent failures on artistic misjudgments, miscasting, and mismanagement in general, and on the "Steering Committee" system in particular.

Langner and Miss Helburn, who had taken over an ever increasing share of the Guild's administrative duties, were desperately attempting to find solutions to such problems as averting total disaster for the organization's latest offerings, while attempting to explain away the embarrassing circumstances of being picketed by the Theatrical Managers, Agents and Treasurers Union for not hiring union personnel. Feverish efforts were also initiated to chart the Guild's future course. John Gassner, at Langner's insistence, submitted recommendations. These included the fostering of a better image in the press through offering several experimental productions, as had been done by the Group and Mercury Theatres, both of which enjoyed the enthusiastic support of New York's theatre journalists. Gassner also suggested the Guild inexpensively present adaptations of such masterpieces from the past as Molière's *Tartuffe*, Webster's *The White Devil*, Goethe's *Eg-*

mont, or Ibsen's *Brand*. He thought, too, that Strindberg's *Miss Julie* had more to offer thoughtful audiences than the current *Of Mice and Men*, and that Marlowe's *Edward II* could be adapted to stir up even more interest than the experimental production of his *Dr. Faustus* had the previous season. Also considered were such Greek classics as *Agamemnon* and *Antigone*, as well as Edith Hamilton's translation of *The Trojan Women*, on which the Guild had once held an option. He also advocated the exciting possibilities of presenting a bill of novel one-act plays. He thought the Guild would need a group of young actors for such presentations—hordes of whom were then hungrily hovering around Broadway—and Gassner wrote that a number of them could be integrated into a more or less permanent company (the Group and the Mercury's forces were hardly as permanent as was advertised), with the Guild gaining the valued publicity such youthful groups invariably received. This younger body, of course, would do away with the necessity of forever using established stars in "svelte" productions, because this group, employing a little more than "a plank and a passion or idea," could be used to educate the Guild's road subscription audiences to appreciate a different kind of fare than that which the American Theatre Society's bookings through the years had led them to expect from New York companies. He felt, too, that the Guild was not capitalizing on its greatest resource, the prestige connected with its productions of former years, which could be fruitfully reexamined for revival possibilities. One suggestion was that the *Theatre Guild Bulletin* should be less "an announcement and apology leaflet," and given more to heralding the arrival of important theatre books, as well as providing analyses of technical problems of the theatre such as those encountered in directing and in scenic design. Gassner also stressed the necessity of the Guild's finding a way to keep a talented small circle of new playwrights constantly encouraged, "because dissatisfied authors have a way of dinning their chagrin into critics' ears."

However seductive these proposals may have seemed, some of them had been apparent to the Guild's Board for years, and, as Gassner well knew, most organizations in the past that had followed policies similar to those he advocated (and there had been a fair number), were no longer producing plays of any sort. His plan for a future modus operandi, with its plea for the formation of another studio group and possible additional revivals, such as *Arden of Faversham* and Thomas Heywood's *A Woman Killed with Kindness*, apparently arrived too late to become a basis for discussion at a special meeting held to reassess the Board's myriad problems. At this get-together, though, the Board agreed henceforth to avoid any "congestion of production"; a plan offered by the Lunts to revive some of their old hits in repertory was favorably considered. The formation of a temporary advisory committee to bring fresh ideas to the Board was suggested by Langner, and it was proposed that such guests as Donald Oenslager, Worthington Miner, Armina Marshall, Bretaigne Windust, Rouben Mamoulian, and Theodore Komisarshevsky be invited to attend the "artistic policy" board meetings. Following a request by Simonson, it was decided that he should not be granted complete authority over all the Guild's scenic work—this might be resented by outside designers—but it was voted that he should be allowed, as an advisor, to see all blueprints for projected settings. Wertheim believed that *Jane Eyre* should definitely be produced in New York that season, "with or without Miss Hepburn" (who was then persistently trying to sell the Guild on a script called *Amstel*), and Theresa Helburn said that Leslie Banks was most anxious to play the title role in *Richard III*, in which "he felt he would give a very excellent performance." Miss Helburn also suggested that everyone read Langner's combination version of *Love for Love* and *The Way of the World*, in which Ina Claire might or might not be interested. Even with all the hue and cry for great policy changes, the Guild's thinking still seemed inextricably linked to the whims of its stars.

Nor does it appear that much attention was paid to the trenchant comments Simonson had laid before the Board in his most recent memorandum, comments which pointed to the Guild's seeming inability to judge competently the dramatic and theatrical values of the scripts it selected, as well as an inability to oversee the rewriting of these manuscripts to eliminate their basic weaknesses as plays. He had also mentioned the Guild's distressing habit of using "star" actresses who did not possess sufficient ability or experience to carry demanding roles by themselves, and the hiring of directors whose ideas concerning script revisions were at odds with the Board's own views.

While deliberations concerning possible future policies were taking place, the Guild was at work on its next production, which would become known as one of the more bedevilled presentations of its career. In early December, as previously noted, the Guild had furnished its subscribers with a special edition of its *Bulletin* that attempted to explain, in solicitous terms, just why it was doing what it was doing. The organization seemed embarrassed that so few of its recent offerings had been free of strong ideological overtones:

> With so many of our authors engaged for a considerable part of the year in Hollywood, the number of worthwhile manuscripts to choose from has been somewhat reduced during the past few years. This has made our selection more difficult, but it has not caused us to change our policy. Many of our leading authors are deeply concerned with the political and social changes which are taking place in the world today. It is impossible to find vital plays of contemporary life which do not take cognizance of these facts.

This was fair warning that the organization's next work would contain more of the same liberal versus reactionary plot elements. The *Bulletin* also announced that another film star, Miriam Hopkins, would grace this new attraction.

An ever-increasing stream of Hollywood luminaries seemed to be flooding the legitimate theatre. Some of these people possessed little basic talent, and some, like Fredric March, who possessed a good deal, were doing anything short of murder to obtain fat Broadway parts. This influx of movie stars was attributed to a number of causes. For one thing, Hollywood producers were financing movies in which prized stars under long-term contract were exhibited with the idea of enhancing their reputations. The actors themselves, those whose public appeal had been faltering, needed to boast of New York theatrical successes to give a boost to their sagging screen images. Then, too, the plots of nearly all motion pictures were being patterned more and more closely on legitimate theatre material, and these "screen plays" required a more legitimate sort of acting for which the stage was obviously the only classroom. Another reason was always tactfully omitted in "personal appearance" announcements. The hard-eyed motion-picture camera, working at close quarters, had a tendency to pierce the illusion of youth, and movie stars, especially the women, were considered old at thirty. Many of them were too old to continue as romantic leads, and too young, not to say quite unwilling, to be relegated to character parts. Stage appearances helped such actors enormously.

Miriam Hopkins, a Samuel Goldwyn protégé, must have felt fortunate in her choice of Guild vehicles, for S. N. Behrman had the habit of furbishing feminine lustre in the theatre. Ina Claire owed him a great deal for both *Biography* and *The End of Summer,* and Jane Cowl was still remembered for her appearance in his *Rain From Heaven.* The part that first displayed the scope and variety of Ruth Gordon's talents had been his *Serena Blandish,* and *Brief Moment* had helped establish Francine Larrimore's acting career. Even the Lunts had him to thank for *The Second Man* as well as their current success, *Amphitryon 38.*

Behrman had staked out as his special province a tricky and elusive genre known as the comedy of manners; this type of play was rare in recent American dramaturgy—although twentieth-century England had provided a few practitioners such as Frederick Lonsdale, Somerset Maugham, and possibly Noel Coward. Behrman was quoted as saying that, in the past, comedies of manners had needed an entrenched aristocracy for a target, and that America had never produced such a phenomenon, except possibly a quasi-aristocracy based primarily on economic advantage. Thus, he had decided to use conflicts over current ideologies as the basis for *Wine of Choice,* as he had to a degree in his other comedies. The Guild felt it necessary to issue statements that his latest effort would not concern itself so much with the etiquette and follies of genteel society, but rather

> . . . with the mental attitudes of cultivated men and women as they face, or fail to face, the social adjustments necessary to the swift changes of the modern world. What the author has in common with other writers of comedies of manners is his command of epigrammatic wit, and his belief that what people say is often immeasurably more important than what they do, or even what they are. Since manners in this country have not yet been crystalized into a code, it would be better to call his goal high comedy, comedy which appeals more to the mind than to the emotions.

Besides Miss Hopkins, rumor had it that director Philip Moeller wanted film celebrities Herbert Marshall and Peter Lorre for important parts in *Wine of Choice,* but Leslie Banks, under "featured-player" contract to the Guild, had been without work since *To Quito and Back* had closed, and he was naturally chosen to play the role of a liberal senator from New Mexico. Ex-Hollywoodite Donald Cook and ex-Guildite Harry Wagstaff Gribble were also in the cast.

The Montclair Junior League had become the envy of New Jersey the year before when it had presented the premiere of Maxwell Anderson's *The Masque of Kings,* "with such success that it carried the financial end of its philanthropies" through an entire season. The Junior League approached the Guild again to help its treasury with another "first night." Thus, *Variety*'s out-of-town reviewer saw the first showing of Behrman's *Wine of Choice* at the Montclair Theatre on December 11, 1937, and, for the most part, he liked what was offered—especially Banks, who, to explain away his British accent, had to confess to being a Rhodes scholar: "This sounds like a neat last-minute trick on the part of the author when he found the Guild had cast the popular Englishman." Paul Stewart was brought in to fill the abandoned role of a disillusioned movie director in what was to be the first of numerous personnel changes. Miriam Hopkins, it was felt, seized "every moment the author gives her," but one of the play's weaknesses was that there were too few of these moments. Harry Wagstaff Gribble was also applauded for his playing of "an unctuous Alexander Woollcott."

It was not too surprising, therefore, that Alexander Woollcott himself was haunting the Erlanger's orchestra seats a few days later when the presentation took up residence in Chicago. Woollcott, who possessed a reputation for being a literary gadfly and witty raconteur, also possessed some theatrical ability, for he had appeared in character in Ben Hecht's picture *The Scoundrel* as well as in Behrman's *Brief Moment*, and for several seasons he had acquired a national following as the "Town Crier" of radio. Not too surprisingly, Woollcott was playing the role of Binkie Niebuhr when *Wine of Choice* moved from Chicago two weeks later.

Undoubtedly remembering *Madame Bovary*'s road reception, the Guild anticipated that Chicago would welcome *Wine of Choice* with hosannas and long queues at the box office. Chicago's critics, unfortunately, found Behrman's newest comedy, if not totally illiterate, at least ill-assorted and ill-assembled. Lloyd Lewis of the *Chicago News* wrote that it was

> rich with epigram, hammered thought and searching comment upon the state of the modern world's spirit. But the pleasures of the library are one thing and the delights of the drama are another. . . . The heroine fights for the right to choose in life, as the hero, the liberal senator from the desert, fights the Communists for the American right of free choice in politics and economics . . . when he warns the hard-eyed radical, "We democrats have guns, too, and will fight for our system," he has a trigger line that should have brought a bang of applause, but last evening's audience was, by that time, smothered in literature.

Charles Collins of the *Chicago Tribune* felt that the whole undertaking had been ill-advised at best, and that the contrivance of the starring role was particularly unrewarding:

> This play buries Miriam Hopkins' talent in a vaguely conceived and thoroughly uninteresting character. Girls of this type can be found perched on bar stools in almost every tavern. The flood of talk about her glamour carries no conviction, and her sudden leap into bed (off stage) with a communist writer (her only dramatic moment) calls for harsh descriptive words that may be tolerated in the stage speech of this loose era, but which are still barred from the newspaper vocabulary. My opinion of Mr. Behrman's Wilda Doran can only find private expression, and I feel that Miss Hopkins' Chicago debut as a dramatic star has been made in unfortunate circumstances.

Only the usually acerbic Claudia Cassidy found much to admire in the Guild's most recent production. While admitting it was not Behrman's best play—as a dramatist he had the weakness (a strength in most men) of invariably discerning merit in both sides of a controversial situation—still it had more to offer than the radical one-sided arguments of "a complete left-winger like Odets." *Wine of Choice,* she thought, was more in the Guild tradition than such "amiable fluff" as *Call It A Day*. The Guild, after all, had been established to give unusual plays a hearing, and for it to risk box-office disaster in that day of staggering theatrical investments was admirably in character. She suggested that well-made plays, "slicked up by the gifted Mr. Kaufman, with every 2 and 2 making four," could very well be presented by others, but that she would not trade a *Wine of Choice* "for a baker's dozen of inconsequential 'Yes, My Darling Daughters,' much as I like them in their place."

The upshot of *Wine of Choice's* Chicago engagement was that, with all of Behrman's feverish rewriting, Miss Hopkins became increasingly dissatisfied with her part. Moeller had worked with Miss Hopkins about ten years before when she had played the "little blonde flower of sin" in his adaptation of *The Camel Through the Needle's Eye,* but that had been a decade earlier when she was making something of a name for herself on the stage "as a sly and saucy 'soubrette' type of comedienne." Now she was a Samuel Goldwyn movie star who could afford to express opinions, although these might have been questioned, for she had turned down the leading role in *It Happened One Night* which had won an Academy Award, and at one time had led the field in the "Who's to play Scarlett O'Hara?" sweepstakes, but had lost out because of "other commitments." The Guild, however, listened to her, since it probably had no other option. Soon it was rumored that Moeller was being replaced as director of *Wine of Choice,* and Sidney

Howard and Worthington Miner were called in to assist in the reworking of the production.

After *The Ghost of Yankee Doodle*'s demise at the Guild Theatre, the Board of Managers expected to fill the vacancy with *Wine of Choice,* but with the fortunes of Behrman's comedy so uncertain it was decided to rent the empty house to its first outside guest, Delos Chappell's production of *Father Malachy's Miracle,* which was then occupying the St. James Theatre. Later, the St. James' management instituted a suit to keep the profitable presentation from moving.

Meanwhile, the wires from the organization's publicity department were kept humming:

> The Theatre Guild's official "Wine of Choice" bulletin for today confirms the report that the play, now in Pittsburgh, will be idle next week, re-opening in Baltimore on Jan. 24 for a week. Thereafter: Wilmington, Jan. 31; Princeton, Feb. 1; Hartford, Feb. 2; New Haven, Feb. 3–5. At Pittsburgh's Nixon on Wednesday afternoon it played to capacity, plus standees. . . . Another bulletin, this one informal, is the result of a telephone conversation yesterday between this column and Miriam Hopkins in Pittsburgh. She said: that S. N. Behrman will arrive there with a new version of the play; that if she likes it, she will continue in the cast; that Herman Shumlin may re-stage the play, but will not be interested in doing so unless Miss Hopkins continues in it; that the critics have written the truth about the show thus far; that Alexander Woollcott is excellent in his role, and audiences like him; that she alone in the company had a run-of-the-play contract, which expired last Saturday, and she is appearing this week as a "gesture." [*New York Times,* Jan. 14, 1938]

Other bulletins stated that Hopkins' latest husband, famed movie director Anatole Litvak, whose acclaimed *Mayerling* was then making the rounds, was also in Pittsburgh trying to whip *Wine of Choice* into shape. Apparently, all efforts were not overly productive, for the next bulletin stated that Hopkins was "amicably but firmly" withdrawing from the cast, and that the Guild was considering as a replacement Kay Johnson, Martha Sleeper, or Tallulah Bankhead, whose *Antony and Cleopatra* had recently closed. Equity kindly allowed the Guild to pay the company half salary during the proposed layoff while readjustments were being made. When the production began traveling once more, with Herman Shumlin as its director and Claudia Morgan as its new Wilda Doran, much reshuffling had been done, but obviously much more was needed, for even an amateur reviewer, a Princeton undergraduate, could pick out the play's basic weaknesses when it played in that town: "It is a literate play. It is also an urbane play and an amusing one and an interesting one . . . [but] it is not a very good play. . . . It is a confused . . . comedy of manners. . . . Like the liberal mind . . . it is inchoate and undecided." Even Simonson's generally admired blue-and-white setting came in for its share of censure.

More *Wine of Choice* cast changes were contemplated by the Guild, and the advisability of exchanging Leslie Banks (a candidate for Rochester in *Jane Eyre*) for either Earle Larimore or Frank Conroy was discussed. However, when *The Ghost of Yankee Doodle* closed, Conroy found employment in Paul Osborn's *On Borrowed Time.* Another *Wine of Choice* possibility, Dudley Digges, followed Conroy —he replaced ailing Richard Bennett as *On Borrowed Time*'s affectionately remembered Gramps. Meanwhile, under Shumlin's direction, the role of Cleo Hackett had been eliminated from *Wine of Choice;* he also ordered the building of additional scenery, which was to be added to the show as it traveled.

By the time *Wine of Choice* reached Boston, the emphasis of advance publicity had shifted to the eccentricities of Alexander Woollcott, who made Binkie amusingly into "an overstuffed elf—an old, placid, pudgy pantywaist, part Cupid, part Elsa Maxwell." Newspaper handouts told gleefully of gourmet Woollcott's gaining fifteen pounds during the production's tribulations because he insisted that real caviar and paté de foie gras be served on stage. George Ross of the *New York World Telegram* observed:

> As playwright Behrman now has revised the part in "Wine of Choice," the Theatre Guild wonders if Maurice Schwartz shouldn't be drafted to coach Alexander Woollcott. Over the week-end actor Woollcott acquired a sheaf of Yiddish lines to learn, since he is portraying a Lithuanian Jew who has grown affluent in the United States. When last heard murmuring he was struggling over the exact inflection of "Olev Hashalom." The Town Crier, incidentally, becomes fairly steeped in his stage work; when a visitor went back to see him the other night he found the portly Mr. W. correcting proofs of a magazine article with an eyebrow pencil.

Film hopeful Claudia Morgan, who had played with distinction in several Guild productions, did not radiate the same glamour that Miriam Hopkins possessed, but as much as possible was made of her

WINE OF CHOICE – "Mr. Simonson's setting is charming, but is in many ways impractical. The stairs go up in a strange manner to rooms that would need to be situated on the roof which slopes down over the doorway to a garden, a handsome fireplace is in a peculiar corner, and a large bell cord is conspicuous for its lack of use, everybody apparently preferring to call the efficient Jap servant by his name, Togo" – J. B. T., *Hartford* (Conn.) *Times,* February 3, 1938.

L. to r. – Leslie Banks, Herbert Yost, Alexander Woollcott, Donald Cook, Claudia Morgan, Theodore Newton, Paul Stewart, Akihiko Yoshiwara.

family affiliations (her father, Frank Morgan, and her uncle, Ralph, were both famous actors). Then, during the production's Boston residency, Miss Morgan, who reportedly was exasperated by the numerous script changes, also became plagued by marital difficulties and separated from her third husband, Charles Hornburg—all of which was duly reported in news stories throughout the country. With few good road notices to work with, the Guild's new press representative, Helen Deutsch, was using anything possible to make *Wine of Choice* newsworthy.

All efforts, rewriting, redirecting, recasting, redesigning, and good press relations were to no avail. *Wine of Choice,* which had undoubtedly become better during its many trials on the road, was still considered not good enough. When it opened at the Guild Theatre on February 21, 1938, it ran into a solid wall of critical indifference:

> "Wine of Choice," in sum, is an intelligent though unexciting discussion of political systems. Doctor Herman Shumlin, called in to administer a blood transfusion to the anaemic script, hasn't been altogether successful with his treatment. We doubt that the patient will survive long past the Guild's subscription limit. [Robert Coleman, *New York Daily Mirror,* Feb. 22, 1938]

> If there is little to blame at this stage in the comedy's fortunes there is little to praise beyond a taut and sparkling performance by a band of first-rate professional actors with the portly Alexander Woollcott tossed in for groaningly full measure. [Brooks Atkinson, *New York Times,* Feb. 22, 1938]

> It takes Mr. Woollcott several scenes to begin acting and abandon protective mannerisms, but he is always engaging to watch . . . just a wee bit like a captive balloon. The acting all seems to improve tremendously in the last act. This is probably a matter or perspective, due to the sudden emergence of drama in the play. [Richard Lockridge, *New York Sun,* Feb. 22, 1938]

> . . . the result is a conversational evening among the usual Behrman characters, light, humorously intelligent, and mildly interesting, which is all by way of saying evasively that it is disappointing. The more Mr. Behrman seems to have on his mind the less he gets on the stage. [John Anderson, *New York Journal and American,* Feb. 22, 1938]

It appeared that the Guild had failed once again, as Simonson had charged, to judge the "dramatic and theatric" values of a script and, though it had called in a host of "experts" to remedy the weaknesses (weaknesses the Board of Managers would themselves have attempted to strengthen in former years), Behrman's liberal versus authoritarian arguments had remained for the most part intractable. Theodore Newton, who played the unyielding Communist Dow Christophsen, had been picked out for special plaudits from the production's fine cast, although the New York leftist press did not particularly like the tone of the lines Behrman had given him:

> Judging from the fact that there is usually a Communist in Mr. Behrman's plays, the subject of Communism has long been haunting him. Yet he shows no advance in his understanding of it. Evidently he has no wish to learn. Dow, in the present play, is a cold, almost inhuman, fanatic. [John Cambridge, *Daily Worker,* Feb. 24, 1938]

Leslie Banks, another actor generally admired, had not been having a very rewarding season with the Guild. He asked to be released from his contract as soon as *Wine of Choice* had run its course. The Board reluctantly granted his request.

The Lunts, as was their wont, had been having a good season with *Amphitryon 38.* From the beginning of December, however, they had been rehearsing scenes of *The Sea Gull* with their company for a proposed presentation in the spring. Plans called for Chekhov's impressionistic masterpiece to be done in repertory with *Amphitryon,* with each play being offered for an entire week.

Advance publicity stressed *The Sea Gull*'s historical importance—it had been instrumental in the founding of the Moscow Art Theatre in 1896 after a disastrous first performance at St. Petersburg's Alexandrinsky Theatre, and it had been the first full-length play presented by the old Washington Square Players, with a cast that included Helen Westley as Irina supported by Roland Young, Mary Morris, and Frank Conroy. Philip Moeller had acted as property man for this production. Other items supplied by the Guild's press department recalled the play's few American professional presentations, one of which was by Eva Le Gallienne's Civic Repertory Theatre in 1925 featuring Josephine Hutchinson as Nina, Jacob Ben-Ami as Trigorin, and Le Gallienne herself as Masha. She revived her production again in 1929. Leo Bulgakov also revived the play that year; in April he staged a production at the Comedy Theatre, with Walter Abel as Trigorin, Dorothy Sands as Irina, and Barbara Bulgakova as Nina.

In 1932, Bulgakov's Theatre Associates toured with *The Sea Gull*, this time offering Morris Carnovsky as Trigorin, J. Edward Bromberg as Shamraev, Sheppard Strudwick as Constantine, Phoebe Brand as Nina, and Mme. Bulgakova as Irina. A more recent *Sea Gull* had been presented in London two seasons before with John Gielgud as Trigorin, Peggy Ashcroft as Nina, and Edith Evans as Irina. There had also been much talk of Guthrie McClintic's bringing Miss Evans to the States to play the "shallow, cruel, vain actress-mother," and George Abbott was supposed to be making plans for a production with Joyce Arling portraying Nina. All this is only by way of showing the various talents that had been attracted to this relatively difficult, but rewarding, play. It is extremely doubtful, furthermore, whether any of these productions had made any money.

Be that as it may, the Lunts forged ahead with their planned presentation. Early chitchat by Broadway columnists speculated about the possibility of at least three actors from outside the *Amphitryon 38* company being needed to fill some of *The Sea Gull* roles, and a number of actresses were auditioned for the part of Masha. The biggest casting problem, however, concerned finding the "sea gull" herself:

> . . . we can't help wondering which of the younger actresses in town will have the opportunity of playing Nina, a part that is faintly Ophelian in character and can easily be done so kittenishly that drowning would seem to be the only remedy for most of the ingenues who take on the role. [Wilella Waldorf, *New York Post*, Jan. 15, 1938]

As previously noted, the Lunts held well-publicized, well-attended talent hunts, and finally selected Uta Hagen, who had made her first professional appearance in Eva Le Gallienne's *Hamlet* at Dennis' Cape Playhouse the previous summer.

Robert Milton, who had directed the Guild's *He Who Gets Slapped* in 1922, had recently approached the Board with plans for a revival of Andreyev's symbolic circus story. The Board felt it would be unwise to revive *He Who Gets Slapped* that spring, however, as there was a possibility that the Lunts might want to present a repertory of their former hits in the near future. Milton, whose father had been a director for the St. Petersburg state theatres, was considered something of an expert on Russian dramatic methods. In the middle of February, Lunt announced that he wanted Milton to take over as director of *The Sea Gull*.

THE SEA GULL – Alfred Lunt and Uta Hagen.

"Uta Hagen, who is considered by the Lunts to be the acting discovery of the season . . . is receiving special coaching from them – with pay – while rehearsing in 'The Sea Gull' " – George Ross, "So This Is Broadway," *New York World-Telegram*, March 24, 1938.

Early rehearsals of *The Sea Gull* had been held using the available English language versions of the play. Erstwhile drama critic, essayist, and novelist Stark Young had been working on a new translation himself, which he let the Lunts have even before it was fully completed. Its presumed superiority to existing texts caused it to be immediately adopted.

Lunt also prevailed upon Robert Edmond Jones, who, excluding his work with Walter Huston's *Othello,* had not been represented on the Broadway stage for five years, to develop a production scheme for the projected Chekhov opus. Jones' glorified versions of the original Moscow Art Theatre's designs added greatly to the presentation's effectiveness. Immeasurable pains—a Lunt hallmark—were evidenced in the preparations for this newest *Sea Gull,* and the estimates of cost submitted to the Guild's Board were high. Lunt, however, proposed that he and Fontanne receive reduced salaries during the run to help eliminate some of the expected deficits.

In March, Lunt surprised the Board with the announcement that he and his wife wanted to take *Amphitryon 38* to England for a six-week stay in the late spring. He also wished to know if the Board would be amenable to forming a Guild partnership for this London engagement. The managers, who had not been having a particularly remunerative year, decided that, unless such aid was really needed, they preferred not entering into any overseas financial arrangements. This sudden change of plans, however, necessitated abandoning the idea of presenting *The Sea Gull* in repertory with the French comedy, as all available time would be consumed fulfilling the New York subscription commitments.

When the Washington Square Players had presented *The Sea Gull* in 1916, one reviewer, in his opening remarks, stated that "Theodore Roosevelt would undoubtedly be intensely annoyed. . . . Its people, with a single exception, are stand-patters . . . pussy-footers, who see a dread fate catching up with them and yet make no effort to escape it." Another reviewer pointed out that the play was "very un-American," while a third called it "an interesting novelty," but added that it was "a gloomy, static, drooping, badly-constructed play." Subsequent productions had fared better with the critics. Brooks Atkinson, following the Civic Repertory Theatre's 1925 presentation, had written that it was "a less tangible play than 'The Cherry Orchard,' more difficult to press into shape." He pointed out that it is "an exercise in the overtones of acting," and spoke of "the strangeness of the form and the sensitivity of the impressions." Such reminders from the past, needless to

THE SEA GULL — setting by Robert Edmond Jones.

L. to r. — John Barclay, O. Z. Whitehead, Uta Hagen, Edith King, Harold Moffet, Lynn Fontanne, and Sydney Greenstreet.

say, were hardly calculated to cause the Lunts to wax sanguine over the potential drawing power of their experiment. On the closing night of *Amphitryon 38,* when the packed audience called the pair back for numerous curtain calls, a few standees began to shout, "Speech, speech!" Lunt had stepped forward, thanked them for their hearty reception, and added, "We'll be back in two weeks with *The Sea Gull.* Heaven help us all." He was probably quite serious. Interviewed in his dressing room later, he was quoted as saying:

> "The Sea Gull" is much too good for us! I don't see how actors can ever exhaust or reach the bottom of its subtleties, its complex meanings, its unspoken emotions. The longer we rehearse the more amazing things we find in it. It is the most difficult and wonderful play I ever read; it is tender and human and profound, and ah, so difficult to play! The values are all there, but so elusively, so delicately expressed! [*New York Journal and American,* March 27, 1938]

When *The Sea Gull*'s road bookings had been discussed, Lunt confessed that the company preferred playing split weeks to facing half-empty houses. Journalists in Baltimore, however, recalled that it had been their reception of *The Doctor's Dilemma* ten years before that had prompted the Guild's road policy:

> The success of that enterprise encouraged 2,000 Baltimoreans, according to the Guild, to write in requesting more plays. One of them, printed in *The Sun,* read, 'The Guild has an extensive repertoire. It has been touted all over the country as the foremost American theatre, so if we can possibly insure its return to Baltimore, let's do so!' . . . Principally because of this city's encouragement, the Guild got to work and eventually built up the largest road subscription organization in the world. [*Baltimore Sun,* Feb. 27, 1938]

Other articles deplored the Guild's seeming neglect of Baltimore in recent years. Baltimore demanded, and got, a full week of *The Sea Gull.*

The night before the opening in Baltimore, incidentally, there was a flare-up between Lunt and the Guild's press agent, Helen Deutsch, who, it must be admitted, had been given fairly lacklustre wares to hawk since she joined the organization. Reports of the quarrel over the taking of publicity pictures immediately found their way into the columns of *Variety*, and eventually into the minutes of the Board of Managers' meetings. Although the disagreement was patched up, the Guild also had a new press agent the following season.

On the whole, Baltimore responded enthusiastically to the first professional production of Chekhov ever given in the city. Ticket sales were brisk, if not overwhelming, and the reviews all extolled the haunting, almost baffling qualities of *The Sea Gull*:

> The fascination of the play indeed rests on the infinite variety of human experiences compiled in Chekhov's document. His unobtrusive technique resembles that of a symphony, with major and minor themes developed, embroidered and intermingled, and finally resolved in an inevitable climax. . . . Above all, Chekhov wrote with a compassionate understanding of the frailties of human nature. [Donald Kirkley, *Baltimore Sun*, March 17, 1938]

Another of the paper's reviewers, Gilbert Kanour, found it to be gloomy yet strangely stimulating:

> A pretty generous dose of Russian pessimism . . . with its collection of wasted or empty or ruined lives, its futile failures and its futile successes and its forlorn lovers . . . it should have sent last evening's audience to their homes depressed and disheartened. Yet, as we say, because the cast is at all times unfalteringly the master of the play and of themselves the outcome is just the contrary, and the theatregoers enjoy a feeling of elation and, when the impersonations are taken into account as histrionic feats, even exhilaration.

The same type of reaction was felt in Boston the following week when the play moved to the Colonial Theatre directly prior to its Broadway appearance. Oddly enough, although its title and author had been clearly announced in the newspapers, some of Boston's citizens mistook *The Sea Gull* for Ibsen's *The Wild Duck*, while others thought they were going to spend a jolly evening enjoying *Amphitryon 38*. Nevertheless, such was the Lunts' box-office potential that, "sight unseen," the Colonial's facilities were swamped with mail orders demanding tickets, a phenomenon in the American legitimate theatre only Katharine Cornell (who, incidentally, was not appearing that season) could duplicate.

There were good reasons for the Lunts' popularity on the road, of course. Besides a knack for anticipating trends in theatrical tastes, they had the reputation of surrounding themselves with the finest production facilities available. Furthermore, their road patrons realized, as they did with Katharine Cornell, that they would see skilled actors, well-rehearsed in support of the stars—not casts scratched together at the last moment solely for purposes of touring. Thus it was that *The Sea Gull's* ensemble was complimented fully as much as were the Lunts, who, many felt, were "subordinating themselves" in minor roles. Acting company regular Sydney Greenstreet, for instance, lent "his hearty authority to the role of Sorin, the actress' brother, who wanted to write, to be a good speaker, but who never did nor was; who wanted to marry, but remained a bachelor; who wanted to live and die in the city, but who is spending his last days in the country, which he loathes." Helen Eager of the *Boston Traveler* also claimed that Richard Whorf made "the idealistic son [Constantine] a pitiable figure of restlessness. . . . at his best in his hysterical scene with his mother and his final scene with his erstwhile sweetheart." A newcomer to the Lunts' multi-talented group, Margaret Webster, the enterprising daughter of Dame May Whitty, had already directed Maurice Evans' production of *Richard II* that season, as well as *Young Mr. Disraeli*, in which her father, Ben Webster, had appeared. Elinor Hughes of the *Boston Herald* thought that Miss Webster, as the steward's young daughter, Masha, who "drags her life behind her like an endless train," contributed "a masterpiece in little, a beautifully spoken performance, aptly mingling the tragic and the ludicrous." Edith King as Pauline, John Barclay as Doctor Dorn, Harold Moffet as Shamraev, and O. Z. Whitehead, who earlier that year had distinguished himself in *Madame Bovary*, playing the role of Madvedenko, all won plaudits from the Boston critics.

Variety's out-of-town reviewer, while admitting *The Sea Gull* offered proof of the Lunts' almost limitless versatility and hinting that students of Chekhov would thrill to this newest interpretation of one of his great plays, also suggested that Lunt admirers, "who are used to their comedy, will be disappointed in varying degrees. And playgoers, who don't like to wrinkle their brows in thought, will be dismayed at the sombre circling of the 'Gull' and its relentless descent to a tragic end." E. F. Harkins of the *Boston Daily Record* even felt a bit disgruntled with this melodrama in which the "bad guys" win:

> It is hardly the year to revive so scathing and cynical a tragedy, in which the flamboyant ham actress and her darling novelist, as shallow and brutal a wretch as ever escaped the whip, triumph at the expense of almost everyone else. . . . "The Sea Gull" is a good vehicle for so competent a company, but as diversion it is no dish of bonbons.

On March 28, 1938, *The Sea Gull* opened at New York's cavernous Shubert, possibly not the best theatre to house so intimate a play. As grounds for this contention, one might point to John Gielgud's 1966 production of *Ivanov,* which received excellent notices in Boston and elsewhere on the road, as had *The Sea Gull,* but which was evidently considerably coarsened when the company tried to project Chekhov's understated introspective themes into the vast reaches of that theatre. *The Sea Gull,* actually, did not fare too badly. Robert Milton, who had directed Lynn Fontanne's early success, *In Love With Love,* as well as Alfred Lunt's in *Outward Bound* and *Banco,* was congratulated for expertly guiding their *Sea Gull.* Pre-opening news stories had questioned how Uta Hagen would handle her assignment as Nina, a role that had in the past added impetus to the careers of Mary Morris, Josephine Hutchinson, and Peggy Ashcroft. It turned out that Miss Hagen utterly captivated the New York critics, who found her "beguiling in her early scenes and direct, forceful and magnetic in her great scene," "grace and inspiration incarnate," "lovely, sensitive, impressionable . . . something to cherish." Only George Jean Nathan felt it necessary to point out that Chekhov made the part practically actress-proof by supplying Nina with ingratiating qualities which could not help but be interpreted attractively by a teen-age neophyte.

Most reviewers viewed their colleague's efforts at translation with praise and gratitude:

> Mr. Young has laid a solid groundwork for complete exposition of the play by rendering it at last into sensible working English, freed from the cumbrous phrasing, and often actual evasion of Mrs. Garnett's well-known translation. . . . By going back to the original, he has recaptured what must have been the author's intent in the repetition of words, sharp commentaries themselves on the lives of the characters. And he has enhanced greatly, with fastidious precision, the quality of the lines for stage speech. It is an excellent version which authoritatively makes the play a

> part of the English-speaking theatre. [John Anderson, *New York Journal and American,* March 29, 1938]

Curiously enough, Stark Young himself published several articles concerning the succinct beauties of his "literal" translation.

Unfortunately, the Lunts, and especially Miss Fontanne, did not receive the same critical approval which embraced Greenstreet, Webster, and Whorf, in particular. Brooks Atkinson, for instance, found Lunt to be "a little obtuse to the spiritual solitude of the play as a whole." He was, nevertheless, lauded for his rendering of Trigorin's long speech in which the novelist discourses on the pangs of literary composition in particular, and upon the sterility of his existence in general. As a star, Lunt was also complimented for his display of artistic integrity, "by burying himself in the ensemble, and giving a passive performance of a passive role." Miss Fontanne, however, was to bear the brunt of critical disapprobation. This might have been because she tried performing unsympathetically a basically disagreeable role. Be that as it may, John Mason Brown felt her Irina was "a totally external creation; a noisy, blatant road company Queen Bess." All the reviewers remarked disdainfully about the vibrant, carrot-colored wig she had chosen to wear, but Eva Le Gallienne, who "loved" the whole undertaking, emphatically guarded against attacks on her choice of color: "Nonsense! . . . It was just the sort of color a woman like Irina would achieve when she dyed her hair!" Miss Fontanne, too, added her own defense:

> Irina was a woman no longer young. . . . Her hair was dyed. In those days dyes were not what they are now, and she would have had little choice in the matter of color. The red hair which she chose was certainly to be preferred to the awful, dead-black, varnished-looking locks which were the most common result of hair dye in that era. Another color which she might have had for her money was a terrible peroxide blonde, but Irina would have chosen the nice bright orange, I think. [*New York World-Telegram,* April 23, 1938]

She reasoned that since Aubrey Beardsley had caused hennaed hair to become extremely fashionable at the turn of the century with his drawings of strange, vermilion-tressed women, heroines of popular novels of the period would all have acquired the modish tendency to become red-headed, and Irina would have copied them.

A more fundamental complaint concerned the Lunts' inadvertently injecting humor into a presentation where humor seemed largely uncalled for, and George Jean Nathan, characteristically, felt called upon to chide the stars for seeming to have confused Chekhov with Molnar, for having unwittingly portrayed Trigorin and Irina in too sparkling a manner:

> The Molnar impression is induced . . . and helplessly, by the apparently increasing inability on the part of the Lunts to suppress those acting idiosyncrasies which have so joyously in the past embellished the lighter plays that have been their greatest successes. These idiosyncrasies, both vocal and deportmental, have become so deeply ingrained in them that, try as they will, they cannot conquer them in the interests of the more sober and serious drama, and the result in a play like "The Sea Gull" is that the characters they are playing become to a considerable degree disturbingly Lunts.

In his article, Nathan also deplored the increasing habit of imposing theatrical modernity on more and more of the current revivals, "by lightening . . . sombre aspects, or at least gingerly avoiding a complete and thorough statement of the author's full-blooded tragic intention." It was observed by some, however, that reviving a classic put a special strain on its interpreters, for there was always a tendency on the part of the critics to reflect with nostalgia on past performances, so that any departure from what was considered to be an ideal was apt to be resented and resisted. New productions of *Hamlet,* for example, were seldom enthusiastically received in New York, and a previous adaptation was usually thought superior to a newer one: "When John Gielgud played the Dane here a season ago most of the critics harked back to the golden days of John Barrymore. Then along came Leslie Howard, and Mr. Howard's reviews were the best notices Mr. Gielgud received in New York." [Wilella Waldorf, *New York Post,* April 9, 1938]

On the other hand, one worthwhile accomplishment of *The Sea Gull*'s revival was the desire it engendered in several of New York's theatrical columnists to employ deeper critical techniques. It had been altogether obvious, one supposes, that "criticism" in the metropolitan dailies, and elsewhere too, very often consisted of highly personalized opinions, the more cuttingly expressed the better, and too often these essays contained merely a recital of a production's plot or peculiarities, or a subjective judgment as to what portion of the director's work appeared to be most competent, or which performer seemed the least capable. All this had very little to do with true criticism, or even objectivity. Following *The Sea Gull's* opening, however, Richard Watts, Jr. was led to explore the affinities between a "sense of the mystery and wonder of life" found in Chekhov's feelings about hopelessness and Shakespeare's "lovely paeon to the idea of defeat" expressed in *King Richard II.* Arthur Pollock of the *Brooklyn Daily Eagle* noted that both Behrman's *Wine of Choice* and *The Sea Gull* presented singular pictures "of men and women faced by a consciousness of their own perplexity and the confusion and meaninglessness of the world about them." In both plays he found "a girl who was once caught by the glitter of life," a facile man "who can take things as they come because nothing touches him deeply," and a discontented intellectual, "who wants new forms, sees the idiocy of things as they are, and wants to do something definite about them." Similarly, John Anderson was taken with the appropriateness of comparing such Chekhov dramas as *The Sea Gull* and *The Cherry Orchard* with such Shavian plays as *Heartbreak House* and *Too True To Be Good;* perhaps they could be produced as a tetralogy illustrating current fears and disillusionment. The Guild's re-examination of *The Sea Gull* unleashed something resembling a more rewarding critical apparatus, one that employed thought-provoking comparisons for the benefit of New York's newspaper readers.

A curious phenomenon which plagued *Variety's* financial experts during closing months of the 1937–38 theatrical season was that *The Sea Gull,* with all its tidings of despair and futility, became the best-attended legitimate attraction in town. There were several reasons given for this. One was that the ever-popular Lunts had announced a strictly limited five-week engagement in order to allow time to fulfill their London commitment with *Amphitryon 38.* Another was that Guild patrons, who had been hoarding their subscription stubs through the bleakness of the Guild's winter, suddenly cashed in their remaining tickets to avail themselves of the Lunts' spring sunshine. So even if the stars were not highly gratified by the critical appraisals accorded them personally and would never again use their facilities to mount other revivals (though they definitely lacked suitable new scripts), they nevertheless had succeeded in proving that Chekhov could get an enthusiatic reception in the United States' commercial theatre if enough pains were taken to give his "epics of melancholia" superlative productions.

In May, the Lunts took *Amphitryon 38* to England for a limited engagement, but *The Sea Gull* was kept intact in their repertoire and scheduled for a fall showing in Philadelphia. Undoubtedly, a further result of the Guild's Chekhovian experiment, which had turned in handsome box-office receipts on the road as well as in New York, was that other managements were encouraged to present more revivals. However, *The Wild Duck* and *The Merry Wives of Windsor* both failed because of insufficient preparation, although the Mercury Theatre's *Heartbreak House* and William A. Brady's brilliant resurrection of Maugham's *The Circle* added distinction to Broadway's noteworthy 1937–38 gallery of restorations.

Besides its flurry of revivals that season, Broadway was also playing host to two well-received political satires, the aforementioned Kaufman-Harts-Rodgers musical, *I'd Rather Be Right,* which starred George M. Cohan as FDR, and the impudent *Pine and Needles,* as conceived and produced by the theatrically inclined of New York's Garment Workers' Union. The success of these two long-playing satirical fantasies probably led the Guild to consider plans concerning a similar venture for itself, at first thought of as an experimental offering for which Maurice Wertheim proposed his financial support.

The Actors' Repertory Company, a group of young hopefuls, was organized in 1935 when most of its members were appearing in the Theatre Union's production of Albert Bein's *Let Freedom Ring.* The following year they attracted favorable attention with their presentation of Irwin Shaw's anti-war drama, *Bury the Dead,* and during the 1936–37 season they had offered E. P. Conkle's *200 Were Chosen,* a play about American farmers who were moved to a government settlement in Alaska as an experiment. The Guild, which owed its New York subscribers one extra production to compensate for having failed to bring in *Jane Eyre* the previous spring, decided to join forces with Actors' Repertory, which already had a script written by collaborators John Boruff and Walter Hart based on a novel satirizing the government, *Washington Jitters,* by left-wing oriented Dalton Trumbo. The Guild's Board possibly felt it had spent enough after the enormous failures with *To Quito, Madame Bovary, Yankee Doodle,* and *Wine of Choice,* so that utilizing the boundless, inexpensive energy of the youthful Actors' Repertory Company seemed both a feasible and practical solution. It might have recalled its unhappy experience with the late Theatre Union's *Parade,* but memories involving theatrical fiasco are characteristically quite short-lived.

Washington Jitters tells of a mild mannered, rather stupid sign painter named Henry Hogg, who, because a reporter mistakes him for the "coordinator" who is to receive one of his nameplates, becomes an important figure in the bureaucracy of alphabet-ridden New Deal Washington. It appeared obvious rather soon, however, that *Merely Henry Hogg* (the working title of the Boruff-Hart adaptation) was far from stageworthy. The members of the Guild's Board, therefore, began tinkering away—as they had in the case of the lamented *Parade*:

> Mr. Langner thought the play needed more humor and that someone like Newman Levy or Howard Brubaker should work on the script. Mr. Lunt thought the play would be better developed as a comedy melodrama. At present it lacked wit. He also suggested that the play be called *WASHINGTON ZOO*. . . . Ernest Truex, Leo Carroll, and Roland Young were suggested for the leading role. It was decided to wait until Worthington Miner had read the script and then have a conference with him concerning this play.

In the course of many sessions the working title changed frequently—to *Simply Henry Hogg, Simple Henry Hogg,* and *What Happened to Henry?* to *Alphabet Jitters,* and finally back to the original name of Trumbo's novel. In a seemingly endless cycle, Boruff and Hart contacted Hollywood-bound Trumbo, whom they had never met, to ask for more workable ideas, Wertheim withdrew his promised support from the project, both Moeller and Worthington Miner tried their hands at script doctoring, Walter Hart was dismissed as the principal director involved, and finally it was decided not to let the critics see *Washington Jitters,* if possible, because the show was in such a wretched state. In desperation, the Guild sent messages to Ernest Truex, who had been unavailable, pleading with him to consider playing the lead—although, amusingly enough, he was later found to be "unsuitable." As its only recourse, the Guild was forced to extend the rehearsal period one week, or even two in order to give the members of the cast, which had been padded to include such seasoned players as Harry Shannon, Francis Pierlot, and Will Geer, more time to add polish and authority to their performances.

The story given to the press was that the early showings of *Washington Jitters* were to be presented solely for the benefit of subscribers to fulfill overdue Guild commitments, but that there was nothing particularly "unusual" in this. Subscribers' previews had been a part of past policies, the Guild maintained, citing such examples as *The Dance of Death* during 1919–20, *John Hawthorne* during 1920–21, *The Race with the Shadow* during 1923–24, and *Right You Are If You Think You Are* during 1926–27. The press, however, was not satisfied by such evasions, and there were dark mutters of "secret show business," and "theatre on the Q.T." Helen Deutsch, the Guild's harried press representative, was kept busy explaining matters, while Brooks Atkinson was openly troubled and perplexed by the Guild's policies. The Guild, however, used every excuse to delay its opening for general public consumption: "An April 18th premiere date for William A. Brady's revival of 'The Circle' caused the Theatre Guild and Actors' Repertory Company to again postpone the debut of their 'Washington Jitters.' Previews for the latter play began Monday but the formal premiere will be announced later."

Finally, three weeks after its first showing for subscription audiences, *Washington Jitters,* had its official "first night" to which the New York critics were all "cordially invited." The notices accorded the Guild-Actors' Repertory joint effort predictably were not too laudatory. Most of them unflatteringly compared its bumptiousness to George M. Cohan's smoothly-running vehicle, then playing way past its two hundredth performance just across the street from the Guild's Theatre. A few of the kinder comments were "a couple of scenes do manage to be passably amusing in an A-B-C sort of way," "the idea is fantastically entertaining for a half hour, but fades out after that," "the authors of 'I'd Rather Be Right' got there first, I'm afraid, and with bigger guns. They had music, too, which is always a help, particularly when wit dries up a little." One of the more caustic reviews was contributed by Wolcott Gibbs of the *New Yorker;* it was perhaps more merciful than damning by faint praise:

> For them [Boruff and Hart] the political situation is no more subtle than it would appear to be from the cartoons in the Hearst papers and so what we get at the Guild is not satire but burlesque, applied with a stuffed club. . . . It is my own opinion that "Washington Jitters" is as dismal and irritating a way to spend an evening this side of picking oakum, but I am aware that it has its supporters. The night I was there it was greeted jubilantly by many of the Guild's most fashionable subscribers, one woolly imbecile even going so far as to say that it was the wittiest thing he's seen in five years. I guess it will just have to be my word against his.

The Guild, nevertheless, achieved certain Broadway records in fulfilling its responsibilities with *Washington Jitters,* which was allowed to run at a loss because there was last-minute evidence of "picture interest." One was that the presentation had twenty-two scenes calling for more than 250 varying cues—an unprecedented number for a non-musical offering, which made stage manager John Haggott, who earlier in the season had attended to *Madame Bovary's* multitudinous shiftings, the champion backstage man along the Great White Way. Another record concerned the number of preview performances the Guild had scheduled, and these included several pre-opening "benefit performances" business manager Munsell had arranged, gambits which presaged current New York commercial theatre practices. A third near-record had to do with the amount of paid rehearsal time the organization was forced to use to compensate for its improper preliminary preparations.

Almost simultaneously with the announcement of its alliance with the Actors' Repertory Company, the Guild issued bulletins concerning arrangements "to sponsor" a Shakespearean presentation to be undertaken by the Mercury Theatre for a fall showing. Many wondered whether this was a portent, this trend toward participating with others in play producing, of radical changes in the Guild's twenty-year-old organization. It was also true that during the course of the year the Guild's Board had seriously considered the advisability of acting as co-backer for an enterprise titled *Charles the King* with Maurice Colbourne and Leslie Howard, as well as entering into a co-producing arrangement with Maurice Evans. Ashley Dukes also had offered to present jointly with them Isherwood and Auden's *Ascent of F 6* and T. S. Eliot's *Meet at Wishwood Manor* (a working title for *The Family Reunion*).

Throughout its troubled 1937–38 season, the Guild for the first time tried to lease its West 52nd Street home to outsiders. When difficulties arose over the proposed tenancy of *Father Malachy's Miracle,* the Board instead planned to allow Paul Vincent Carroll's *Shadow and Substance* to occupy the theatre, but decided against it when the play's future seemed uncertain before its opening. *Shadow and Substance* later won the first Critics' Circle Award ever bestowed on a foreign offering.

Other critical accolades that year included the Pulitzer prize for drama being awarded to Thornton Wilder's *Our Town,* presented by Jed Harris. Theresa Helburn extracted a half-hearted commitment from Wilder "that as soon as he finishes the next two plays which he has promised to others, he is going to write a play for the Theatre Guild." The organization was happy even to receive this crumb of encouragement for an indefinite tomorrow, since during the year a number of its erstwhile star dramatists had formed what was to be in effect a rival producing group. Robert E. Sherwood, Maxwell Anderson, Elmer Rice, and Sidney Howard—none of them too pleased by treatment received from the hand of the paternalistic Guild—had banded together to form the Playwrights' Company. These four were soon joined by S. N. Behrman.

Early in February, Alfred Lunt had informed his fellow Board members that Sherwood had just finished a script believed superior to E. P. Conkle's *Prologue to Glory,* which was to be given that spring by the Federal Theatre—both concerning Lincoln's formative years. The Guild contacted Raymond Massey concerning a possible joint presentation of the Sherwood play, but was rebuffed. The newly-organized Playwrights' Company was actively making plans of its own to present *Abe Lincoln in Illinois.* Soon afterwards, Miss Helburn approached Behrman, who was contemplating writing a new script for the Lunts, for there were fears that Behrman too would turn any completed play over to his Playwrights' Company companions, in which case the Guild would not only lose the production but the services of its star actors as well.

Superior, skillfully managed revivals had been one mainstay of the season, as was generally recognized. Besides the Guild's presentation of the Lunts' acclaimed *The Sea Gull,* there had been the Mercury Theatre's updating of *Julius Caesar* as well as its highly regarded versions of Dekker's *Shoemakers' Holiday* and Shaw's *Heartbreak House,* which had been given its world premiere earlier under Guild auspices. Other managements had been responsible for such presentations as Ibsen's *A Doll's House,* which featured Ruth Gordon's controversial portrayal of Nora. Maurice Evans had played superlatively in what was really a revival of a revival (for touring purposes) of his *King Richard II.* Dublin's Abbey Players made another pilgrimage to America, and had offered New Yorkers such classics in their repertoire as O'Casey's *Juno and the Paycock* and *The Plough and the Stars* as well as Synge's *Playboy of the Western World.* There had also been brief presentation of *As You Like It,* which was much admired by some.

In addition, the first important revival of an American play that year had been the Federal Theatre Project's re-examination of Lawson's *Processional,* which also had been originally produced by the

Theatre Guild. Later, the government-sponsored organization had reviewed such varied American classics as Fitch's *Captain Jinks of the Horse Marines* and O'Neill's *S. S. Glencairn* cycle. It had also presented a stirring *Coriolanus.* All this purposeful activity caused the Guild, and other commercial managers, to send protests to the WPA concerning its supposedly non-competitive theatrical group's leasing houses in the heart of New York's theatre district. A year later the project was disbanded by Congress for being "Red-dominated."

Not all the 1937–38 revivals had been resounding successes, of course. There had been a restaging of *Antony and Cleopatra* for the talented Tallulah Bankhead, and this had been generally regarded as a disaster. Bankhead redeemed herself, however, with a "vibrant" portrayal of restive Elizabeth in William A. Brady's production of Maugham's *The Circle,* which also featured, as the déclassé Lady Kitty, Grace George in one of her great interpretations; she played "a Dresden-china caricature of a pretty woman grown old." Earlier, when approached by Theresa Helburn concerning a revival of *Mrs. Warren's Profession*, Mae West had replied, "I'll tell you, dear, I feel I owe it to my boys not to play the part of a mother."

This spate of restorations led the Guild seriously to ponder the suggestions made by John Gassner concerning a possible classical repertoire. Several Greek classics, such as *The Trojan Women* and *Agamemnon,* were rather soon rejected, but the Board appeared quite interested in the possibility of Francis Lederer being used in one of Schiller's plays, if Gassner could find a good version of *Don Carlos.* Later, Langner sent a copy of the play he had obtained to Maxwell Anderson for possible improvement; however, it was annoyingly reported that Robert Turney was making a version for Guthrie McClintic, presumably also for Lederer.

Other European and English plays of the past were further discussed, such as *The Sheep Well, The Duchess of Malfi, The White Devil,* and *The Beaux Stratagem,* which was considered as a vehicle for Cornelia Otis Skinner and Brian Aherne. A version of *The Changeling* was especially prepared for Alfred Lunt, and the star was toying with a revision of *The Guardsman,* for which Richard Whorf was designing a basic unit set that could be used for any play. Another possible revival suggested by Gassner, Massinger's *A New Way To Pay Old Debts,* also received intensive attention from the Board.

The Guild had not precisely added to its diminishing prestige with its presentations of *Madame Bovary* and *Washington Jitters* because it apparently had failed to perceive what other managers had; namely, that if a stage adaptation of a novel is prepared it had better first possess the quality of a unified, dramatic story which, ideally, would also appeal to movie makers. Interestingly enough, the Sam Harris-George S. Kaufman offering of Steinbeck's hybrid *Of Mice and Men*, first written as a novel, won the Drama Critics' Circle Award for 1937–38, and Dwight Deere Wiman's presentation of Paul Osborne's *On Borrowed Time*, based on a novel by Lawrence Edward Watkin, was one of the major successes of the season. *Father Malachy's Miracle* had been adapted by Brian Doherty from a book by Bruce Marshall; and when Ethel Barrymore had finished in the Guild's poorly received *The Ghost of Yankee Doodle*, she began a tryout tour with Mazo de la Roche's dramatization of her own novel, *The Whiteoaks of Jalna*. Her performance in *Whiteoaks*, which opened on Broadway in March, became one of the things to see in the waning theatrical year.

Another novel's adaptation had caused the Guild a certain amount of vexation all season long. Katharine Hepburn's road appearances in Helen Jerome's dramatization of *Jane Eyre* had been among the organization's more important money-makers during the 1936–37 season—before Miss Hepburn had felt disposed to stop touring and return to Hollywood. The Board of Managers, much to Helen Jerome's disgust, had sent several pleas to the star to consider reviving Charlotte Brontë's heroine for Gotham theatregoers, or, barring this (because of threatened New York critical annihilation), to play a number of short engagements in Philadelphia and elsewhere. By the middle of January, the Board had been informed that Miss Hepburn did not intend to play *Jane Eyre* in Philadelphia or anywhere else on the road. So, other actresses were considered for the assignment, including Peggy Conklin and the British Jessica Tandy, whose eligibility to appear in another American production that year, under existing regulations, was questioned. Miss Jerome, who had been continuously revising her script, increased her agitation to have Margaret Webster redirect the planned New York showing, and for Miss Tandy to perform the title role. Ultimately, the Guild decided to cancel plans for *Jane Eyre* entirely; although it would continue to be hounded about possible future performances by agents, and by requests for the amateur acting rights, licensing powers the organization had not definitely earned.

When it appeared unlikely that a production of Katharine Hepburn as Jane Eyre would materialize, the Guild began dickering to put the reluctant movie star under *some* kind of contract for the following season. It was believed Miss Hepburn's presence would provide enough lift to brighten dismal prospects, as well as to insure much-needed revenues. The problems were, however, *first* to get her to sign, and then, what to do with her *if* she signed, problems similar to those that had perplexed the Guild in Ina Claire's case during 1935–36. By the middle of February, they had sent her a script entitled *Gallow's Orchard,* even before she had agreed to appear for the organization. Following that, movie magnate Howard Hughes was contacted concerning possible conflicts with her RKO motion-picture contract, as were several representatives from Equity; finally, Leland Hayward was urged to bring his good offices to bear on the matter. In the meantime, more scripts were sent to the star as possibilities, including *The Corsair, The Wayfarer,* and later, during the summer, the sentimental *Morning Glory,* a script felt to be inferior, but one which was considered a better than average vehicle for her abilities.

It must not be supposed, however, even if a stream of manuscripts did flow toward Miss Hepburn, that the Guild's storehouse was bursting with marketable new material. Quite the contrary. The organization had nursed along several projects during the year, only to have them evaporate for one reason or another. These included Flexner's *Marie Antoinette,* thought of as a possibility for the Lunts, Ervine's *Robert's Wife,* Matson's *The Lunatic From Boston,* Hemingway's *Working, Do Not Disturb,* and the previously mentioned *Ascent of F 6* among others. There was also some interest in Molnar's *Delilah* as a vehicle for Ina Claire, Romney Brent, and Dorothy Gish, and in Jeffers' *The Tower Beyond Tragedy* for Judith Anderson, if she was at all enthusiastic. The Guild had also received a few off-beat proposals from eager agents, such as to be the first to produce professionally *Aaron Slick From Punkin Crick.* All of these turned to dust, however, despite the Guild's earnest efforts.

The sad truth, apparent to anyone remotely concerned, was that the Guild had encountered few causes for rejoicing during its twentieth year of playmaking. It had had to engage legal wizard Arthur Garfield Hayes as advisor when difficulties arose between the organization and the Theatrical Managers, Agents, and Treasurers Union and with New York State's Labor Relations Board. It had been forced to cut Board members' salaries when financial straits seemed unavoidable, and Wertheim, Jeremiah-like, prophesied that the Guild would run at a deficit the following season on the basis of its average fiscal expectations.

To help offset its monetary woes, which surely were not alleviated by the increased clamorings of its bondholders, the Guild set about trimming its staff of once essential personnel. For instance, in the future there was to be but one person in the casting department, and this was to be solely a part-time assignment. Only one stage manager would be retained, and even the Guild Theatre's custodian would be required to take a leave of absence, without pay, during the summer months. There were discussions about the selling of the motion-picture rights to scripts that had been lying dormant on the organization's "possibility" shelves for several seasons, and Munsell wrote to agents Swanson and Orsatti to see whether they would be interested in promoting these properties. Feasible methods for financing forthcoming Guild productions with outside capital were also appraised, and for the first time the Guild's management was forced to contemplate borrowing from theatrical "angels." There were further thoughts concerning leasing the Guild Theatre to accommodate other managers' productions, a plan that had been unfruitfully attempted that year. Another idea was to use other managers' independent offerings to fulfill the Guild's New York subscription obligations. After all, the organization had been using such a system on the road for years!

The last proposal, of course, was the most dispiriting of all the alternatives the Guild had yet been compelled to face. Nevertheless, there was no denying the evidence, rather undiplomatically pointed out by George Jean Nathan, that a certain vitality, or spark, or whatever, had been sorely lacking in the Guild's directorate for quite some time. Its only taste of success had been provided by productions over which the original Board of Managers had had little control. It was true that Simonson had designed the striking settings for *Amphitryon 38*, but *The Sea Gull* had been a Lunt-Fontanne undertaking from first to last, and it had not escaped the notice of many that the six parent managers shared negligible responsibility for these two critically and financially rewarding presentations.

There was no glossing over the facts, moreover, that Helen Westley had attended very few of the Board's meetings during the course of the year, and that Moeller, after directing one failure—*To Quito and Back*—had been ignominiously asked to relinquish the guidance of Behrman's *Wine of Choice*, another stage director's salvage efforts being regarded with greater trust. The whole Board, for that matter, had either lost interest, or, as Simonson put it, had lost the knack of "tricking them over . . . in the manner of Messrs. McClintic, George Kaufman or George Abbott." Therefore, more difficulties and changes faced Miss Helburn and Langner, the Guild's steering committee, as they formulated plans for the future.

Movie sponsorship had necessitated utilizing scripts and performers of questionable stageworthiness (as various critics from Nathan to Walter Winchell vexingly had surmised). Langner, however, still envisioned building an acting ensemble, similar to the Lunts' troupe, with which he hoped to perform tryouts of several of the Guild's hardier projects at his Westport Country Playhouse that summer, even though Equity disallowed the Guild a season's option on any of the actors' services. Worthington Miner, who had been granted a year's contract with the Guild during the run of *Washington Jitters,* was asked to handle the directorial chores connected with these fledgling offerings. The company, which consisted of such veteran performers as Theodore Newton, Charles Bellin, Francis Pierlot, Harry Irvine, Jessie Royce Landis, Onslow Stevens, and Glenn Anders, as well as a younger group composed of Montgomery Clift, Lois Hall, Hugh Marlowe, Rosemary Ames, Morgan James, Alfred Ryder, and Kathryn Grill, began a straw hat season in the latter part of June to put on *Fool's Hill, Dame Nature, Mirror for Children,* and *Inner Light,* only one of which *(Dame Nature)* was deemed sturdy enough to be included in the Guild's fall roster.

Later in the summer, during these subsidized Westport tryouts, Langner wrote to Eugene O'Neill about unsettling articles then appearing in some newspapers to the effect that the playwright planned to lease the Broadhurst Theatre during the coming year to present a series of revivals of his own plays. This was truly a shocking disclosure, for one of the few intangible assets of any worth that the Guild possessed was the right it had assumed to perform professionally any or all of O'Neill's output. The semi-retired author answered to reassure Langner that such news items were nonsensical, but he continued by suggesting that the critical broadsides the Guild had sustained during the course of several seasons had been more than partially deserved:

> Ever since several Guild directors got bored with 52nd Street and went Hollywood, you have been steadily getting farther away from the spirit of all the old Guild represented, all that made it a distinctive and distinguished leader in the American Theatre—all that made it a commercial success, for that matter! You became in spirit and intent—to all appearances, anyway—just another manager star-casting with an eye on the box office and playing the racket according to the stale old rules that the mere existence of the Guild in the old days had proved shoddy and

> stupid. I think the feeling behind all the adverse criticism was one of being betrayed—that you'd sold out on them—and of resentful disillusion.

The dramatist even went so far as to propose that the Guild drop all its entangling alliances with motion pictures and concomitant "movie-casting," with bondholders, with other theatrical managements, even with the road, to begin all over again at the Garrick as a "fresh adventure." Needless to say, the organization was much too deeply involved with these restrictive elements to make any such "regenerative" move possible.

CHAPTER 12 / 1938-39

Dame Nature (André Birabeau), Patricia Collinge
The Merchant of Yonkers,
Thornton Wilder (A Herman Shumlin Production)
Jeremiah (Stefan Zweig), Eden and Cedar Paul
Five Kings, Part I, Orson Welles (A Mercury Theatre Production)
The Philadelphia Story, Philip Barry
My Heart's in the Highlands,
William Saroyan (A Group Theatre Production)

An unending, agonized search for manuscripts for the 1938-39 season continued to annoy and frustrate the Guild's already harassed managers. In August, Alfred Lunt sent word from Europe that he kept "waking up in a cold sweat having had some horrible dream" concerning the season's selections. He promised to examine in detail the Parisian theatre's most recent output.

As one of the 1938 summer offerings at his Westport Country Playhouse, Lawrence Langner had provided the first public showing in America, or England, of Bernard Shaw's *The Millionairess* with Jessie Royce Landis playing the title role of Epifania. The production was not thought stimulating enough, however, to warrant inclusion in the Guild's winter prospectus. Shaw had suggested that the actress needed for Epifania should have something resembling Katharine Hepburn's dominating personality, but Miss Hepburn did not like the script and rejected it. Several months before, the Guild had received an announcement that a new play by Shaw called *Geneva* was to be presented at the 1938 Malvern Festival. When reading the unedited prompt copy Shaw had provided, Langner became distressed by what he conceived to be anti-Semitic overtones in the writing, and he notified the dramatist to that effect. Although Shaw later revised the offending portions, it soon became apparent that Shaw's latest works would not be suitable for the Guild's 1938–39 season.

As September approached, Langner was asked to write to Theodore Dreiser concerning a playscript the novelist was supposedly preparing; at the same time rumors flew that Jed Harris and Thornton Wilder had amicably concluded their play producing relationship. Theresa Helburn, therefore, quickly contacted the Pulitzer laureate to inquire about his newest efforts, only to learn that Wilder had already turned *The Merchant of Yonkers* over to the Herman Shumlin offices. Helburn had hoped to interest Max Reinhardt, already named *The Merchant*'s director, in a proposition to include Wilder's farce as one of the Guild's subscription programs for New York. But in the meantime, Shumlin had entered the picture, and his terms were not found to be attractive enough to justify "sufficient interest for the Guild to proceed," as Miss Helburn told him. According to her, there was some discussion of the play's merits, and extensive differences of opinion developed concerning the advisability of doing it at all, especially when it was brought to the Board's attention that one of the Guild's newly acquired flock of "angels," Mrs. Vivian Spencer, was not too enthusiastic about advancing money for a production of *The Merchant*. This seemed to curb the Guild's ardor for Wilder, although the pros and cons of presenting his version of *Hedda Gabler* with Tallulah Bankhead were strenuously debated. After all, Wilder's re-examination of *A Doll's House* had provided a stunning showcase for Ruth Gordon's talents the previous season.

It was learned, too, that S. N. Behrman had finished his promised vehicle for the Lunts, and the Board of Managers was faced with a decision concerning its possibilities. Behrman had stated his willingness to wait indefinitely, or at least until the Lunts were available, for a proposed production by the Guild. However, it appeared that the Lunts, who were busily making plans for an extensive cross-country tour, were not too keen about spending time on Behrman's drama. The Guild, therefore, considered casting the comedy with other actors, although it was hesitant about even undertaking the production. Shortly thereafter, Katharine Hepburn intimated that she was enthusiastic about appearing in *No Time for Comedy*, and the Guild, delighted that the actress had at last evinced an interest in something, quickly arranged a meeting between her and Behrman, but indecision concerning the treatment of the play dragged on for a good part of the year.

The Board of Managers, continuing its relentless search, urged its new director, Worthington Miner, to make an assessment of Robert E. Sherwood's *Acropolis*, on which the Guild still held an option and, as it was rumored that Eugene O'Neill was completing the fourth play of his projected cycle, he was asked to submit whatever he had available. Several of the Board members thought that Robinson Jeffers' *The Tower Beyond Tragedy* was the most promising work the organization had at hand (if only Judith Anderson would make up her mind). Otto Preminger sent a suggestion that the Guild do the thirteenth-century Chinese *Circle Of Chalk* with Luise Rainer—if it were possible to have an adaptation prepared by a poet, perhaps Edna St. Vincent Millay.

These conjectures and fruitless scramblings after worthy offerings were accompanied, and to a large degree influenced by, the most stringent economy measures. For instance, in the spring the Guild had had to barter one of its prime assets, its road subscription lists, to a few rival managers at a fixed fee per city, and when the opportunity for establishing a subscription season in Cincinnati came along, the Guild lacked enough funds even to promote its initial appearance, and hoped that Lee Shubert would offer to provide additional finances since the program would be presented in his theatre. Hence, when its reduced personnel made the offer to take a voluntary no-pay vacation one week in every five, the Guild's administrators, who could ill afford to have operations grind to a halt every fifth week, countered that they were willing to have the staff take three weeks at full pay and two weeks at half pay, if possible. Alfred Lunt, who would be away from New York for a major portion of the season, was asked to waive his stipend as a member of the Board of Managers, and both Munsell and Gassner received no salary one week every month.

The previous spring, John Hanrahan, who had taken over the *Theatre Guild Magazine* in 1932 and continued publishing it as *The Stage,* was so beset with monetary difficulties that he wondered if the Guild could either increase its subsidy (insuring its productions' favorable mention in the magazine), or drop out entirely as one of *The Stage*'s benefactors so that he might interest other investors in underwriting it. As an alternative he offered to pay the Guild for any subscriptions secured from its members. The Board was forced to accept this proposal. It meant, however, that the Guild would need another organ to issue statements concerning its future intentions in promoting its highly esteemed services to theatregoers. A revamped version of the Guild's *Bulletin* was therefore projected, to include "most of the following . . . articles or squibs":

> Announcing the Season of Plays for New York and On Tour;
> Explanation of Last Season (there was some opposition to this);
> Book Reviews on Theatre Books;

Subscription Columns with Letters from Subscribers;
Announcement of the Christmas Entertainment [a program conceived by Will Geer called 'Elizabethan Jigs'];
Article About the Lunts' Tour;
Announcement of the Theatre Book Club with One-Third Off the Price to Guild Members;
Some Notes about the American Theatre Council and the Ticket Code;
Announcement of Burgess Meredith and Orson Welles in FIVE KINGS;
Discussion of the Repertory Company;
Articles by Actors;
Items Concerning Robinson Jeffers, Tony Miner, Norris Houghton;
Something about DAME NATURE and children in the theatre.

John Gassner was named the editor for this revised scheme, which embodied a number of his ideas, anyway. The *Bulletin* was to be produced on a tight budget, for when the editor-elect requested a minimum of eight large-sized pages, he was told that the format had to be kept about the same size as in the past—not exceeding four ordinary-sized pages.

Amid such pressing pecuniary and artistic problems the Guild planned to present the first offering of its twenty-first season. For several years the organization had been holding a script by André Birabeau, a French author of novels and light comedies, for whom Alfred Lunt in particular showed a marked enthusiasm. As early as 1936, the actor had suggested that either Alice Duer Miller or Ruth Gordon might do a worthwhile translation of *Dame Nature,* after Robert E. Sherwood had turned down the assignment. When it was realized that neither of the ladies wanted to work with Birabeau's script, the Guild tried to interest Philip Barry; Miss Helburn also reported that Marc Connelly appeared "very interested" in its possibilities. However, neither Connelly nor Barry saw fit to pursue the commission, and the Guild considered the translating abilities of Otto Preminger and Samson Raphaelson, while Theresa Helburn was authorized to approach Rachel Crothers. When none of these accepted the job, she called on Patricia Collinge, an actress then in self-imposed semi-retirement after having played mostly sugary roles, Pollyanna among them. But she had also contributed occasional witty pieces to the *New Yorker, Stage,* and the old *Vanity Fair.* This time, Miss Helburn's entreaties were more fruitful, for Miss Collinge said that though she had never done an adaptation, she was quite intrigued by doing one for *Dame Nature* and would talk to Miss Helburn again after reading the script. Two weeks later, she was hard at work on some trial scenes for Birabeau's comedy, which she planned to submit for the Board's approval.

Advance publicity stressed that *Dame Nature* was one of the more successful plays to have been produced in France for many years:

> It had its world premiere at Paris' Théatre de l'Oeuvre. . . . after 75 performances there, it was moved to the Théatre de l'Etoile, and in December of the same year it was passed on to the Théatre Mogardor. It finally terminated its elongated career with 400 performances at the Théatre Bonau in 1937.

Miss Collinge's version of Birabeau's long-playing Parisian hit, depicting thoughtless parental reactions toward "innocent" teen-agers begetting offspring, was included in Langner's summer tryout series at Westport. Several critics found its prospects for commercial success excellent. *Variety* considered the members of a projected Guild Repertory Company, especially Montgomery Clift, Lois Hall, and Jessie Royce Landis, to be "brilliantly effective in the central roles." Articles appearing prior to the opening gave information concerning the much-traveled Norris Houghton, *Dame Nature*'s scenic artist, as well as references to the varied career of director Worthington Miner, who was to become more and more involved in Theatre Guild affairs as time went on. Alas, the potential that had been indicated during *Dame Nature*'s early showings never materialized. When the Guild opened it at the Booth Theatre on September 26, 1938 (the Board had decided to rent the Guild Theatre to other managements during the greater part of the year) the more hospitable reviews were scarcely calculated to bring forth avid *Nature* lovers. Some of the less complimentary included musings by Ruth McKenney:

> The Theatre Guild used to produce New York's significant drama, years ago. But progressive ennui has overtaken the art-loving ladies and gentlemen of Broadway's subscription drama, reaching its climax (I hope) in this week's trivial little play, *Dame Nature* . . . [which] is hopelessly and irrevocably dull. Of course, I find whimsy embarrassing and perhaps people who like gentle little items about fifteen-year-old children having babies will simply adore *Dame Nature*. Personally, the idea of a young father trying to get a 10 percent reduction on a baby carriage

via his Boy Scout's card makes me look for the nearest exit. [*New Masses,* Oct. 11, 1938]

George Jean Nathan was another of several dismayed by the editing *Dame Nature* had sustained:

> The pall that latterly and relentlessly seems to hover over the Theatre Guild's productions is again in evidence. . . . I reported in this place after witnessing its summer tryout that the play, provided it were properly nurtured in the meantime, indicated considerable possibilities as light diversion. In point of fact, even in its unprepared state, it was promisingly droll. . . . But now that it has been brought to town and as it is unloaded on the Guild's storm-tossed subscribers, it only goes to prove again that for sheer theatrical ineptitude the once-esteemed Guild presently hasn't a rival this side of an Arkansas little theatre. [*Newsweek,* Oct. 10, 1938]

Nathan went on to state that necessary alterations, obvious to "anyone who knew the least thing about the stage," had not been made:

> . . . not only did the Guild not make them; it actually—as in the case several years ago of Savoir's potentially jovial "He"—monkeyed what other values the exhibit already had right out of it. . . . Worthington Miner redirected what is essentially a comedy of juvenile sexual infraction in the oversentimentalized spirit of a mother-love and father-love tearbräu. . . . The pace is so slow that the little girl of the play seemed to have ample leisure in which to have not only the single baby she had, but several sets of quintuplets.

Even Montgomery Clift, admired by most, did not escape Nathan's wrathful indignation:

> The innocent little boy's role was cast with an actor tall enough to light Gary Cooper's cigar and so clipped-British in speech and so sophisticated in manner that Noel Coward in comparison seemed like Peter Holden [a child actor portraying Pud in *On Borrowed Time*].

Several other reviews stressed not only *Dame Nature's* inappropriateness, but more especially the further evidence it provided of the Guild's slowly dwindling managerial powers.

The performers appearing in *Dame Nature* were purported to represent the nucleus of a revitalized Guild acting ensemble, and Miner was instructed to keep them working on a list which included a special adaptation of *The Birds, Romeo and Juliet,* Hauptmann's *Hannele,* and Anouilh's *Traveller Without Baggage.* Pirandello's *Henry IV* and one of the Guild's former successes, Andreyev's *He Who Gets Slapped,* were actually put into rehearsal, however, hopefully to be performed in repertory with *Dame Nature.* Shortly afterwards, when the Board saw run-throughs of the Pirandello and Andreyev plays, there was little enthusiasm to include either of them in a series of special matinees.

Another possibility for the new repertory company was a script dealing with the loneliness and guilelessness of adolescence—Merrill Rogers' *Mirror For Children*—for which Maurice Wertheim evinced a particular fondness. Rogers' play had been one of those shown Westport audiences during the summer, and it represented an investment of $1250 for the Guild, as well as a loss of $750 for Langner. Wertheim had enough faith in the script, nevertheless, to offer to pay half of its production costs. The other managers felt, however, that the subject matter of *Mirror For Children* was too similar to that of *Dame Nature* to allow its inclusion in the 1938–39 New York series. Early in November, *Dame Nature* was sent to fulfill subscription commitments in Chicago, and there it expired, as did hopes for a new Guild repertory group.

With its hopes for a permanent acting ensemble dashed, the Guild once again grappled with the problem of what to offer its New York patrons. Theodore Dreiser's dramatic effort, as yet untitled, was obtained, but the Guild found it to be "too old fashioned for production." Pulitzer-award dramatist Sidney Kingsley submitted a new work he had adapted from a novel called *The Outward Room,* but the Guild thought it inadequate. The following season this play, its title changed to *The World We Make,* was produced by Kingsley himself at the Guild Theatre and was selected as one of the year's "ten best." At the Guild's request, S. N. Behrman had talked with Katharine Hepburn regarding *No Time For Comedy,* but the Guild came to think that Behrman was stalling until Ina Claire's newest vehicle opened, to see whether she would be available. In the spring, Behrman's fellow dramatists in The Playwrights' Company induced Katharine Cornell to break her two-year sabbatical from the stage to appear successfully with Lawrence Olivier in this long postponed comedy.

Katharine Hepburn, meanwhile, was asked to think about appearing in *The Tower Beyond Tragedy,* which the Guild hoped to produce with a cast picked from among Ruth Gordon, Winifred Lenihan, Kathryn Emery, Wendy Hiller, Margaret Rawlins, Jessica Tandy, and Margaret Webster, in addition to Judith Anderson. Margaret Webster was also considered as a possible director of the play. Worthington Miner regarded Edmond O'Brien as a likely prospect for the leading male role, but through indecision the Guild lost out on the actor's services. A work entitled *Mrs. Lincoln* was also considered as a vehicle for Miss Hepburn, possibly to compete with the glowing spectacle of Sherwood's *Abe Lincoln in Illinois* which the Playwrights' Company had provided, but she informed the Guild that her friend Philip Barry was putting the finishing touches on a specially tailored work to which she had pledged her talents. The star was willing, however, to give the Guild first refusal on this new script, possibly as a reward for its perseverance and patience.

Word spread quickly, of course, that the sorely tried Guild was contemplating using others' productions to fulfill its New York subscription program, circumstances that elicited "co-producing" proposals from a number of interested managers. The first presentation made by an outsider to occupy the Guild Theatre on a non-subscription basis had been Gilbert Miller's production of J. B. Priestley's *I Have Been Here Before,* directed by Lewis Allen, which opened on October 13, 1938, and lasted for twenty performances. Miller believed that he had other properties in which he might persuade the Guild to join with him, such as a project he had in mind of doing a play based on Tolstoy's *War and Peace.* Another proposal concerned Emlyn Williams' *The Corn Is Green,* for which an English manager owned the American rights. Actor-manager Philips Holmes suggested this Englishman might be persuaded to bring over his London production intact for the Guild's series. The Guild, it must be remembered, had already signed an agreement to sponsor a Mercury Theatre amalgamation of Shakespeare's chronicle plays with Orson Welles, who first wanted to put on a production of Georg Büchner's *Danton's Death,* much to the Guild's chagrin. The organization agreed to offer its members reduced rates for his poorly received revival, however, even if it did not feel inclined to include it as a subscription presentation.

Actor-manager Eddie Dowling was another who wished to become allied with the Guild. During the summer, he had suggested his coming attraction, *Madame Capet,* as a possible occupant for the Guild Theatre, but the Board declined. He later offered his presentation of Philip Barry's *Here Come the Clowns* as a co-produced subscription venture, but the Guild's managers did not find this "weird, inspirational" play to their liking, either. So Dowling presented his metaphysical Barry production elsewhere, and although the work's ambiguities confounded several of the New York critics in the course of its fair-to-middling run, Barry's symbolic attempt would be among the *succès d'estime* conversation pieces in the theatre world for some time to come.

Impresario John C. Wilson's production of Dodie Smith's *Dear Octopus* was also considered by the Board, but the Guild chose instead for its second non-subscription theatre rental Leonard Ide's melodrama, *Ringside Seat,* as produced and directed by Rufus Phillips. The Guild was even required to post a portion of Phillips' Equity bond to guarantee his actors' salaries. *Ringside Seat* opened at the Guild Theatre on November 22 and departed after seven lean performances.

As Langner ruefully observed, the Guild's career as a real estate agent catering to non-subscription clients during 1938–39 was to cost it a good deal of money. In the face of continued financial distress, a meeting of the Guild's business faction was called to discuss whether or not the Guild should continue as a theatrical producing organization after the current season ended. Wertheim was in favor of dissolving the Guild, and Miss Helburn seems to have been noncommittal. Langner and Munsell, however, argued against such a move, Langner feeling that it would be an unfortunate thing to happen, and that if the bank gave them relief from paying interest on the mortgage and taxes they could probably survive. Munsell pointed out that the Guild still had several worthwhile assets, including the services of the Lunts, its option on O'Neill's plays, as well as the good will of its subscribers—especially those outside of New York. The minutes continue:

> There was then discussed a proposition to arrange for the plays of other managers to be presented on the Guild program in New York next year. It was decided to try to find one more suitable play this year produced by an outside producer to give our New York subscribers. The discussion extended to the road and Mr. Munsell explained that as the American Theatre Society had had such a splendid response from outside managers this year, plans

were being considered to have ten plays on the road subscription program next season in groups of 5 and 5 or 6 and 4. He said he had already had inquiries from John C. Wilson, Eddie Dowling and many others which indicated we would have no difficulty in getting plays. The main problem now is to build up the New York subscription list so that we will have an inducement for other managers to come under subscription in New York. Mr. Langner felt that this could not be done in one season but that perhaps during the season 1939 and 1940 the subscriptions could be increased in New York and the number of plays on the program be increased with the help of satisfactory outside plays so that the subscription program would pay for itself and insure employment to our subscription staff regardless of what happened to the Theatre Guild as a producing unit.

After the meeting it was obvious that survival, in one form or another, would be the goal of *any* Theatre Guild policy in the future.

The Guild increased its efforts to secure a fitting presentation provided by another manager to flesh out its New York subscription series. Earlier in the year, it had evaded an offer from the annoyingly successful Playwrights' Company to use Elmer Rice's *American Landscape,* for early reports concerning the play were not too encouraging. As it turned out, *American Landscape* was the one failure the Playwrights produced that season—its successes being Maxwell Anderson and Kurt Weill's *Knickerbocker Holiday,* as well as the previously mentioned *Abe Lincoln in Illinois* and *No Time For Comedy.*

Now, however, the Guild faced dire problems, such as the Bowery Savings Bank's refusing to accept a suggestion made by Langner, Munsell, and attorney Charles Riegelman to waive the interest charges on the Guild Theatre, as well as reduce its back taxes. The bank promptly issued an ultimatum that its Board of Directors had no recourse but to proceed to foreclose the mortgage on the property. Added pressure came from the Guild's membership secretary, Addie Williams, who urgently stressed the difficulties she was experiencing because of the long period between subscription plays. Hence, through necessity, the Guild was forced to accept its first New York subscription offering made by an outsider—Herman Shumlin's production of Thornton Wilder's *The Merchant of Yonkers,* which the organization had rejected several months before. A number of Shumlin's terms were onerous, such as his demand for so many opening night complimentary tickets that there were none left for the Board of Managers, and his refusal to allow his actors to perform before the

Guild's traditional first-night audience, which usually consisted of a rather blasé coterie. These differences were undoubtedly ironed out to everyone's satisfaction before the New York opening, but the Guild also wondered whether it had been worth all the fuss. *The Merchant of Yonkers,* a fanciful comedy which very few of the critics fancied, an offering "that even the art of Jane Cowl could not hold up," closed after the minimum subscription period of five weeks. Some years later, in 1955, Wilder revised *The Merchant of Yonkers* and retitled it *The Matchmaker.* The Guild invested some money in this production. Still later, *The Matchmaker* became the basis for the bonanza musical, *Hello, Dolly!,* but by that time the Guild had lost all interest in its amusingly adaptable potentialities.

Because of its financial straits, the Guild was forced to withdraw its projected Christmas offering to its subscribers, the *Elizabethan Jigs,* just as it had had to cancel its employees' Christmas bonus. It was faced with mortgage foreclosure on its home, in anticipation of which the house was to be rechristened the 52nd Street Theatre, to relieve some of the onus connected with foreclosure proceedings. And yet, in a rash manner (rather magnificently, under the circumstances), the organization resolved to try to recoup lost prestige with one lavish production. The time that elapsed between the first thoughts of presenting Stefan Zweig's monumental *Jeremiah* and its opening performance was remarkably short by Guild standards—barely four months—especially so when one considers that various "acting versions" had to be first prepared by two of the organization's personnel, Worthington Miner and John Gassner. The option for Eden and Cedar Paul's translation was originally owned by an emigré entrepreneur named Halevy. At first, the Guild's Board was sharply divided over whether to produce *Jeremiah* or not: Moeller, Langner, and Miner were for; Simonson, Westley and Lunt against; others were for parts of it. The final decision could not be reached, however, until it was known whether Halevy would be agreeable to the Guild's terms, which included billing as co-director. It soon became apparent that Halevy wanted complete control of the production, which he hoped to use as a stepping stone to other directorial activities in New York. The Guild decided to cable Zweig advising him that it could not agree with Halevy's proposals and asking whether the play was free for them to produce without Halevy. Zweig must have answered affirmatively.

During the Guild's "golden era," Stefan Zweig's version of Ben Jonson's *Volpone* had been one of the organization's noteworthy critical and commercial successes, but *Volpone* had been sustained by the performances of such outstanding talents as Alfred Lunt, Dudley Digges, Ernest Cossart, Margalo Gillmore, Henry Travers, Albert Dekker, Morris Carnovsky, Sanford Meisner, and other members of the Guild's famed acting ensemble of that period. Furthermore, the direction had been Moeller's with settings executed by Simonson. It is even conceivable that Helen Westley, who had contributed a "delightfully bitchy Canina" to the 1927–28 *Volpone,* could have handled one of *Jeremiah*'s dozen or more women's roles, but, cannily, she had acquired a juicy part in George Abbott's forthcoming production of *The Primrose Path,* and so would be "unavailable." As evidence of his good faith, however, Moeller agreed to work on *Jeremiah*'s production committee.

The Guild's thoughts on casting *Jeremiah* included Maurice Evans' being approached to essay one of the leads. A script was also sent to Paul Muni, who had expressed an interest in the production. Miner even decided to try to cast *The Tower Beyond Tragedy* at the same time that he held readings for *Jeremiah,* hopes for repertory not being completely dormant, but Gassner was of the opinion that if this scheme did not work out the Guild should relinquish its option on *Tower Beyond Tragedy* because Max Gordon wanted to present the play. Langner suggested that Munsell ask Gordon if he would like to present it in cooperation with the Guild. Their juggling act was to become even more involved as plans for *Jeremiah* progressed.

When the erudite Helen Deutsch had announced at the end of the previous season that she was resigning as the Guild's press representative, several respected press agents, such as Charles Washburn, Oliver Saylor, and Elmer Kenyon, had applied for the job. Brooks Atkinson had also suggested the name of Philo Higley to Langner. The Guild decided, however, that one of the junior members of its publicity staff, Joseph Heidt, should be given an opportunity to see what he could do. For the forthcoming production, though, it was decided that Heidt, whose ideas for the promotion of *Dame Nature* had included a series of verses descriptive of certain characters in the play, and "that individuals such as Larry Hart, Russel Crouse, George Kaufman, and others be asked to write limericks," should not be entrusted to provide all the copy for such an "important" offering as *Jeremiah,* but that he should approach better qualified people to provide special stories and other materials. The Guild went all out in its promotional efforts on the play's behalf, especially in regard to New York's Jewish community. Zweig was brought over from Europe for special interviews, and much was made of his request that the Guild pay his share of *Jeremiah's* royalties for relief of German and Austrian refugees. The Jewish Publicity Service wrote special material for the Jewish-language newspapers throughout the country. One article about the play appeared in the Yiddish Art Theatre's program:

> Of all of Stefan Zweig's works, his great drama "Jeremiah" . . . has a unique claim on his own affections. Written during 1917, when the world was drunk with war, Zweig knew that there would be no other way to give expression to a pacifist attitude in Austria, a country then at war, than by the symbolic form of poetry. . . . He hesitated a long time between Cassandra and Jeremiah for the leading character in his drama, before finally deciding on the latter. Both had suffered a tragic fate, both were universally derided and persecuted for their prophetic visions. He finally determined upon Jeremiah "because he was inwardly closer to me, more familiar through Biblical tradition." [Program for week of Jan. 27, 1939]

The article continued by stating that although *Jeremiah* was considered to be "one of the four great dramas of modern times," already "presented in all the important capitals of Europe," the Guild's production, including "more than sixty actors and nine scenes," was to be the play's American premiere. Reference was also made to Chemjo Vinaver, *Jeremiah*'s musical director, "the greatest living authority of Hebraic music," as well as a note about set designer Harry Horner, "an Austrian Jew, who has been making quite a name for himself since coming to this country three years ago."

When looking at photographs taken of *Jeremiah*, one is struck by the difficulty of identifying individuals in its fairly interesting cast because festoons of crepe hair hang from most of the actors' faces. When the play opened at the Guild on February 3, 1939 (after several sold-out previews), a majority of reviews noted this hairy quality, adding that the whole undertaking seemed similarly moss-covered. Atkinson wrote that *Jeremiah* had been given an eye-filling production, and that veteran Arthur Byron as King Zedekiah and Kent Smith as the mournful prophet were both responsible for notable performances. He went on to say, though:

> But with all proper respect for the admirable motives of the drama and the Guild's recognition of it in the angry world today,

> "Jeremiah" seems like ponderous and hackneyed drama to this playgoer. . . . When a dramatist attacks a Bible theme, he generally throws the craft of modern drama out the window and imagines himself a prophet . . . when he has a Bible on his desk a playwright generally feels superior to the lay necessities of the theatre. In the present instance it is a case of crying, "Play, play when there is no play." [*New York Times,* Feb. 4, 1939]

Richard Watts, Jr. was similarly impressed by the Guild's motivations in presenting Zweig's symbolic anti-war offering. Unfortunately, to him it just never seemed to come alive:

> . . . it is, I am sure, a lofty and dignified narrative, filled with a valuable lesson for all of us and replete with significance for those who will hear. . . . There is earnestness and a high idealism about "Jeremiah" and the Guild has cast and set it with proper regard for its virtues. Nevertheless, it remains a verbose and ponderous play, overrun with a pompous air of profundity and bowed down under the weight of its elocutionary excesses. Nor do I think that its message to the effect that war takes its cruel toll of those who bring it about is as valuable to us as it might be in other quarters. [*New York Herald Tribune,* Feb. 4, 1939]

With its nine scenes, a huge cast, its music and dancing, *Jeremiah* closed after being presented fewer times than the subscription minimum allowed. Obviously it had been an extremely expensive undertaking. The Guild, which had been debt-ridden before the production, was financially devastated after it. Five of the managers, Wertheim, Miss Helburn, Langner, Moeller, and Mrs. Westley, had to dig into their own pockets to cover a $60,000 deficit, with Wertheim providing the largest share. Despite the sentiment expressed by both Moeller and Langner that *Jeremiah* "had been a worthwhile production," its failure led directly to important changes in the Board of Managers' executive alignment.

In all fairness, it must be stated that the Guild was having a far better year out of town than it was experiencing at home. For one thing, the number of road subscribers was advertised as being "substantially higher" than that of the previous season, and although half the offerings provided by the Guild-controlled American Theatre Society, including *Golden Boy, Our Town,* and *Of Mice and Men,* had been produced by other managements, the Guild's share of the profits was undoubtedly high.

Added to this, the Lunts, who had been touring the country since October with a repertory that included *Amphitryon 38, The Sea Gull,* and later, *Idiot's Delight,* played all the Guild's subscription cities with heart-warming success. The trouble was that the Guild urgently needed three more presentations to satisfy its New York patrons, presentations that it hoped would contrast markedly with the three mediocre ones it had already provided, *Dame Nature, The Merchant of Yonkers,* and *Jeremiah.* Plans called for one of these to be the Lunts' trouping "Festival of Comedy," due to arrive in New York in the spring with *Reunion In Vienna* and *The Taming of the Shrew* added to the repertoire. Robert Milton's plans for *He Who Gets Slapped* had been sidetracked because the Lunts' festival was to include five revivals of former Guild hits. A production of *A New Way To Pay Old Debts* was considered with Dudley Digges' talents in mind, but Digges soon decided that he did not want to attempt Massinger's classical comedy. Uta Hagen had been released from the Lunts' ensemble when she was forced, for personal reasons, to forego further one-night stands, and both Olive Deering and Eugenia Rawls were considered to play Nina in *The Sea Gull.* Miss Hagen was hastily sent a copy of *The Tower Beyond Tragedy,* though there was still no change in the Board's decision about producing this play, especially since Judith Anderson was to be occupied in Cheryl Crawford's memorable Lenten presentation of *Family Portrait* (another Guild reject).

Richard Rodgers and Lorenz Hart had proposed doing a musical for the Guild if the managers would suggest a compatible book for their purposes. Moeller immediately seized on the play *Sophia,* while Langner thought either *Lysistrata* or *The Way of the World* would be better material. Theresa Helburn was of the opinion that *Marco Millions, Memorandum for Kings,* or *Reunion In Vienna* would be more suitable, all things considered. This possibility of a musical based on an unadulterated dramatic work had long been one of the Guild's pet ideas, of course. In the spring, Miss Helburn wrote to Bernard Shaw about commissioning a musical adaptation of *The Devil's Disciple.* The playwright replied that, after his distasteful experience with *The Chocolate Soldier,* nothing would induce him to allow another of his works to be set to music "except his own." In Moscow he had seen a modern version of *The Beggar's Opera* (probably *Die Dreigroschenoper* by Kurt Weill), and was determined that neither Weill nor any other composer should touch *The Devil's Disciple.*

Parenthetically, arrangements for turning *Pygmalion* into *My Fair Lady* could be made only after the dramatist's death. Be that as it may, Shaw's note concluded with a query as to whether or not the Guild was still alive (bad news travels quickly), as well as a query about a possible future production of *Geneva,* then "painfully approaching its sixth month in London." Langner had already vetoed the presentation of *Geneva,* however.

Other Guild considerations included Charles Morgan's *The Flashing Stream* as a possible subscription bill. Munsell reported that Richard Madden called to suggest that they write O'Neill urging him to submit two or three of his manuscripts so that plans could be made for casting and production. Langner agreed to take care of this. Miss Helburn reported that she had had a conversation with Sidney Howard, reminding him that he had promised the Guild his next play. Howard admitted it, but said that in the meantime he had committed himself to the Playwrights' Company. He made a counter proposal to have the Guild and the Playwrights' Company jointly produce his next two plays instead of giving the Guild his next one outright. The Board thought this satisfactory, and Miss Helburn confirmed this to Mr. Howard in writing. Unfortunately, Howard died before this plan could be put into operation. Mrs. Westley volunteered that *The Primrose Path* might be available for subscription, as well as *The Corn Is Green* for the following season, although manager Stephen Mitchell had caused the Guild to bridle because he was so adamant in his insistence that Peggy Wood be given the principal role of Miss Moffat. Munsell also reported that the Group was talking of moving *The Gentle People* or *The Quiet City* into the Guild Theatre. However, it was decided that there was no point of putting on any of these plays in their theatre unless they were assured of compensation for the expenses involved.

All this presumably necessary backing and filling still left the Guild shy at least two promised New York offerings. The organization held distinct hopes, though, that the Mercury Theatre's condensation of several Shakespearean chronicle plays, titled *Five Kings,* would help fill this hiatus. Had it not contracted with the Mercury with this end in mind? Seven classics for the price of two? Orson Welles, Mercury's "Wunderkind," assumed the major responsibility for this impressive undertaking; but Welles was never one to channel his enormous energies into any one project. During the summer, besides assembling a number of straw hat theatrical projects, he found time to produce the radio series that included his famous dramatization of H. G. Wells'

The War of the Worlds, which, because of its "realistic" qualities, had badly frightened numerous Americans. Welles later frightened the Guild more than a little, too.

Early in the season, the Guild believed that after Welles had his way with *Danton's Death,* rehearsals for *Five Kings* would start in earnest not later than November 7, to open in New York on January 16, after tryouts in Boston, Philadelphia, and Washington. This schedule allowed a little more rehearsal time than a normal production would require, but *Five Kings* as conceived, directed, and performed by Welles was to be anything but normal. First, it would be presented in two parts: Part I containing portions of both *Henry IV* plays and *Henry V,* Part II to contain Shakespeare's recounting of the careers of Henry VI, Edward IV, and Richard III in bits and snatches. To bridge the gaps, Welles wrote in the part of a chorus, who would fill in the narrative with material from Holinshed's history. By the end of November the Guild had seen little more than a basic script; the Board began to feel apprehensive. It was the Mercury's show, however, and the managers held their tongues. Suddenly, Burgess Meredith, who was scheduled to play Prince Hal and then become Henry V, was available sooner than expected. So, rehearsals for Part I began, and Part II was sidetracked. The opening date in Boston was advanced to January 9, and the production routed to come into New York the first week in February. By the first week in December, Welles had announced that his cast would contain such luminaries as Walter Hampden and Walter Abel, and also announced that the Mercury Theatre was considering doing an American opera in conjunction with *Five Kings.* The Guild asked him to clarify this surprising turn of events. Langner also sought assurances from Mercury's co-director John Houseman that the Guild need not take Part II of *Kings* on subscription unless it turned out satisfactorily. This proved a wise move, since Part II never turned out at all.

By the end of January, *Five Kings'* novel scenery was nearing completion. One of the few settings in the history of the American theatre up to that time to be made exclusively of wood, it consisted of a series of platforms joined by ramps or stairs, the whole being mounted on a large revolving stage. Various scenes were to be pinpointed by use of a complicated light plot. The Guild, alarmed by mounting costs, forced Mercury's management to sign a statement to the effect that the Guild's "sponsorship" would be strictly limited to $10,000 before the premiere. It also required Mercury to include an "obligatory" declaration in all its scenic and costume contracts to protect the Guild against attachment in case Mercury could not pay its bills, possibly remembering its earlier experience with the cavalier management of *Ringside Seat.*

Another unpleasant complication was added to *Five Kings'* labor pains when Maurice Evans, having just completed his acclaimed presentation of an "un-cut" *Hamlet,* decided to don enough sponge-rubber padding to revive his portrayal of the fat knight Sir John Falstaff in *Henry IV* at New York's St. James Theatre in late January. Unhappily, Falstaff also happened to be Orson Welles' own particular province in *Five Kings.*

After a great amount of extra rehearsal time that the two casts required (much to the Guild's annoyance), Welles' amalgamation finally opened in Boston on February 27, two-and-a-half months behind its original schedule. The critics for the most part were gracious. Elliot Norton wrote that Part I of *Five Kings* was

> an extraordinary and exciting adventure in drama. It is not yet, for various reasons, a perfected piece. It is overlong, by at least an hour. . . . But it has on it the mark of magnificence. It has beauty, power, some excellent acting, and potential greatness. [*Boston Post,* Feb. 28, 1939]

Welles' Falstaff was universally admired, but Burgess Meredith, whose last Boston appearance in Maxwell Anderson's *The Star-Wagon* had been distinguished, was found wanting in the *Henry V* episodes.

The production, with its heavy paraphernalia, next moved to Washington, where its reception was also cordial. Critic Nelson Bell of the *Washington Post* was especially impressed by all the moving scenic devices:

> The genius of Orson Welles in the theatre was demonstrated again last night. . . . Departing radically from the stark severity of his modern-dress version of "Julius Caesar" . . . "Five Kings" presents a contrasting and equally novel form of stagecraft. By use of a revolving rostrum, which, for the greater part, is kept in motion in full view of the audience, he has found it possible to adapt a strictly motion picture technique to the requirements of a sound and comprehensive interpretation of Shakespeare. The mobility of the settings and the movement of characters has been devised in such a way that the effect is one of continuous action and dialogue, with a revolutionary blending of scenes that is the equivalent of the screen's "dissolve."

Despite its better than average notices, *Five Kings* unfortunately kept sinking deeper and deeper in debt. For one thing, extra paid rehearsal time had drained the Mercury Theatre's financial resources to a dangerously low point; for another, the size of the cast almost guaranteed a running deficit. The platoon of back stage personnel needed to keep all the moving parts moving was also large. The drayage alone must have been staggering. The Guild determined it had better close the show after the Washington stay ended. The decision was altered, however, with the following understanding:

> The Booking Office will guarantee that the show will receive $17,000 on the two Philadelphia weeks. The Mercury Theatre will pay $1500 and Welles will waive his salary except $150 weekly for living expenses on the two weeks. Under the circumstances it was decided to play the two Philadelphia weeks in order to give the Mercury time to raise the necessary capital for a possible New York engagement.

The Guild should have stuck to its guns, for nearly everything possible went wrong in Philadelphia. The complicated lighting arrangements malfunctioned, and the great turntable had to be rotated by hand. The presentation, which seemed overlong to begin with, stretched into the wee hours of the morning. The critical view, understandably, was dim:

> In spite of its occasional resourcefulness, its color and the lavishness of its production, we do not like the drama's scheme. It has more pace than poetry, more action than expression and, except for possibly three or four portrayals, too little of the Shakespearean play of character. . . . In addition, it is played false by its revolving-stage production, designed to speed the story but actually hampered it by reason of its mechanical squeaks and groans and its wooden staircases and battlements, which suggests nothing so much as a spot for a Bill Robinson tap dance. Besides, there seems an inordinate amount of motion to the stage, it being frequently revolved for no apparent reason whatever. [Henry T. Murdock, *Philadelphia Evening Public Ledger,* March 21, 1939]

To make matters worse, Philadelphians had already seen the Maurice Evans production of *Henry IV* the previous season, and Welles' troupe suffered in the inevitable comparisons:

> As an experiment, "Five Kings" (Part I) is an interesting undertaking. As an entertainment, it is an unfortunate offering. And, at that, not so much on the score of Mr. Welles' ambitious and enterprising attempt to jazz up genius for playgoers who may be in a hurry to have their history wholesale, but because of the obviously and incredibly amateurish aspect of the acting. . . . To compare Orson Welles' Falstaff to Mr. Evans' Falstaff, John Emery's Hotspur to Wesley Addy's Hotspur, Burgess Meredith's Prince Hal to Winston O'Keefe's Prince of Wales [Edmond O'Brien played the part in New York], or Mr. Welles' coarsely keyed direction to the electrifying direction of Margaret Webster would be unconscionable as it would be unkind. [Linton Martin, *Philadelphia Inquirer,* March 21, 1939]

It is probably unnecessary to add that news items appeared shortly thereafter announcing that the "unwieldy" *Five Kings* was being cancelled, although Welles stoutly maintained that he had plans to restore it for New Yorkers the following year. By that time, however, Welles was pursuing his mercurial career in Hollywood.

Soon thereafter other items appeared to the effect that the Lunts were deferring their planned New York showing of the "Festival of Comedy":

> The arduous tour which has occupied the couple all season has been a tiring one, and Mr. Lunt especially is in need of a rest to recuperate from an arthritic infection which has been troubling him. . . . Now in Minneapolis, the stars will carry on through Milwaukee, Cincinnati, Indianapolis, Columbus and Pittsburgh, winding up the season's activities on April 29. [*New York Post,* March 23, 1939]

This unheralded postponement, plus *Five Kings'* out-of-town closing, left the troubled Guild late in the spring still owing its Gotham subscribers half of their promised offerings.

Even before Philip Barry had finished the play he was writing for Katharine Hepburn's talents, Langner and Miss Helburn agreed it should be presented under the Guild's aegis. They were the ones who had been chiefly responsible for the *Jane Eyre* road venture, which had amply proven Miss Hepburn's potential drawing power. Experience had shown, however, that the actress could never be induced to make a New York appearance in anything that did not represent almost sure-fire success, possibly to avoid repeating the unfortunate impression caused by her maladroitness in *The Lake,* a 1933 misadventure that occasioned Dorothy Parker to observe that the actress had run the gamut of emotions from A to B. Furthermore, Hepburn had acquired the reputation among motion-picture producers of being "poison at the box office," a circumstance that might have given rise to the rumor that she had bought back her RKO movie contract at considerable expense in order to be free to refurbish her dimming lustre on the stage. Philip Barry, moreover, had not had a truly commercial windfall in the theatre for many years, a fact that had not exactly enhanced his value in the eyes of his recent movie employers; and the Guild's achingly acute financial problems are already well known. Obviously, much depended on an enthusiastic response from theatregoers to Miss Hepburn's unique qualities as an actress in Barry's latest Broadway bid. With this in mind, Langner and Miss Helburn decided to bring *The Philadelphia Story* along slowly, giving it plenty of time to mature on the road before having it face Broadway audiences.

At the beginning of January, the Guild's Board determined that since funds for producing both *Jeremiah* and *The Philadelphia Story* were being advanced by the managers themselves "they should be considered as a joint investment and if one made money and the other didn't the profits from the money-maker should be applied to reimburse the investors (if Theatre Guild directors) for losses on the other play." This new method of financing, of course, had to be explained to the Guild's bondholders, who would naturally be especially affected by this novel "problem of compensation." By the end of January, the "smell of success" had already crept to interested nostrils, and the Guild, for once, was to experience the gratification of being courted by an offer for the sale of motion-picture rights to *The Philadelphia Story* before the play opened. The plan of sale included a down payment and weekly payments for the duration of the play's run. The producers insisted that able and personable actors support Miss Hepburn's and Barry's anticipated critical redemption, such as Van Heflin, Shirley Booth, and Nicholas Joy, who had worked before in Theatre Guild presentations. From the Mercury Theatre they borrowed the services of Joseph Cotten, who had appeared with distinction the previous season as Rowland Lacy in *The Shoemakers' Holiday.* Barry had stipulated that Robert Sinclair direct his comedy, and the Guild secured the services of Robert Edmond Jones once again to design the conventional drawing room settings.

The Philadelphia Story opening took place at New Haven's Shubert Theatre on February 16, 1939, and all the huzzahs that followed were typical of the reception accorded all subsequent road appearances:

> Rollicking, gay, spicy, racy—last night's audience laughed from beginning to end at Mr. Barry's light, sophisticated comedy and the delightful Miss Hepburn. This very lovely actress seems at last to have a vehicle that sets off her different and charming personality to the fullest extent. [*New Haven Journal-Courier,* Feb. 17, 1939]

The Guild's publicity sense almost demanded that *Story* be displayed to the theatre patrons of the play's namesake, and the critics in Philadelphia, including those who could be so cruel to *Five Kings* exactly one month later, were nothing less than adulatory:

> To put it in a palindrome and for the enlightenment of those who must run as they read, the verdict this morning is . . . WOW! . . . It is an unqualified joy to hail a play that calls for a little hat tossing, bell ringing in the belfry, dancing in the streets, and confetti throwing. [Linton Martin, *Philadelphia Inquirer,* Feb. 21, 1939]

Edwin Schloss, of the *Philadelphia Record,* who had been threatened with exclusion from all Shubert Philadelphia showings because of his unusually caustic comments, proved he could be highly appreciative of anything as attractive as Barry's workmanship:

> . . . an expert piece of stage carpentry executed in the finest satinwood. There is one rickety leg (the last act) but that will be glued up in time for the Broadway opening, no doubt. . . . one of the author's lightest essays in thistle-down comedy. . . . melts quickly on the palate but the flavor lingers.

Two weeks later, the critics in Washington wrote opinions that had come to be expected, using such phrases as "crisp, slightly daring, most agreeably amusing," or "witty, captivating, and dramatically sparkling." Boston, too, reacted about the same way: "Light, pleasant, not particularly consequential, but very agreeable entertainment", "very brightly and effectively done. More than that, it is the funniest show in months." All this, of course, was accompanied by the most flattering publicity for Katharine Hepburn (often on the front page), as well the other members of the cast and production team. The Guild was learning all over again that the world can be a jolly place—if you happen to have a hit on your hands.

New York's reception of *The Philadelphia Story* was no less ecstatic than the road's had been, for here was a superb omelet that contained a little something for everybody: a little titillation of the libido, a little satire at the expense of Henry Luce (of *Time* and *Life*), a little tug at the heartstrings, a little philosophy concealed in sophisticated banter, an uncle who likes to pinch fannies a little too well, and a kid sister who is a little too precocious (played to fare-thee-well by Lenore Lonergan, daughter of a well-known theatrical family). Added to this, there was Beauty (dubbed a "frigid goddess") saved by two Princes Charming from marriage to a working-class chap socially beneath her (in reality, an ogre): this amid small-talk calculated to tickle everyone's funny bone concerning divorce, cocktails on the veranda, midnight swimming in the nude, and the exotic qualities of champagne (do the gentlefolk *really* live that way?). There was much more; there was Katharine Hepburn (*in person,* as the Guild felt it necessary to advertise) garbed in gowns and play clothes designed by the famous Valentina, all set in a gracious suburban mansion designed by Robert Edmond Jones. What if Robert Sinclair's direction made all this seem much more important than it really was, and if the level of writing was inconsequential or not quite up to Barry's *Holiday* or *Paris Bound*? You could have seen his *Here Come the Clowns* earlier in the year if substance is what you wanted. Hadn't *The Philadelphia Story* caused the forgotten adjective "yare," to regain currency in the language? Perhaps all that need be added is that Barry's delightful comedy packed the Shubert for two straight years, and its sale to the movies was negotiated for an enormous sum. More significantly, the $60,000 worth of indebtedness the Board members were forced to cover after the failures of *Jeremiah* and *Five Kings* was paid back by the Guild barely two months after *The Philadelphia Story* opened, and new notes for $30,000 were issued, a profit of 50 percent on the joint "investment."

The organization still owed its New York patrons two productions, of course, but after the box-office miracle of *The Philadelphia Story*, it could well afford to *buy* productions ready-made, if necessary. This, in effect, is what it did for its next offering.

As previously noted, the Group Theatre held two plays by Irwin Shaw, *The Gentle People* and *Quiet City*, with which it hoped to interest the Guild, but Miss Helburn and Langner chose instead from among the Group's options *My Heart's in the Highlands,* the maiden dramatic effort of William Saroyan, a startling new writer aggressively proud of his Armenian heritage. Frankly experimental, the Group-produced *My Heart's in the Highlands* was presented as the Guild's fifth subscription bill of the year. It received a mixed reception. "Those who found it poetically and symbolically inspired liked it very much.

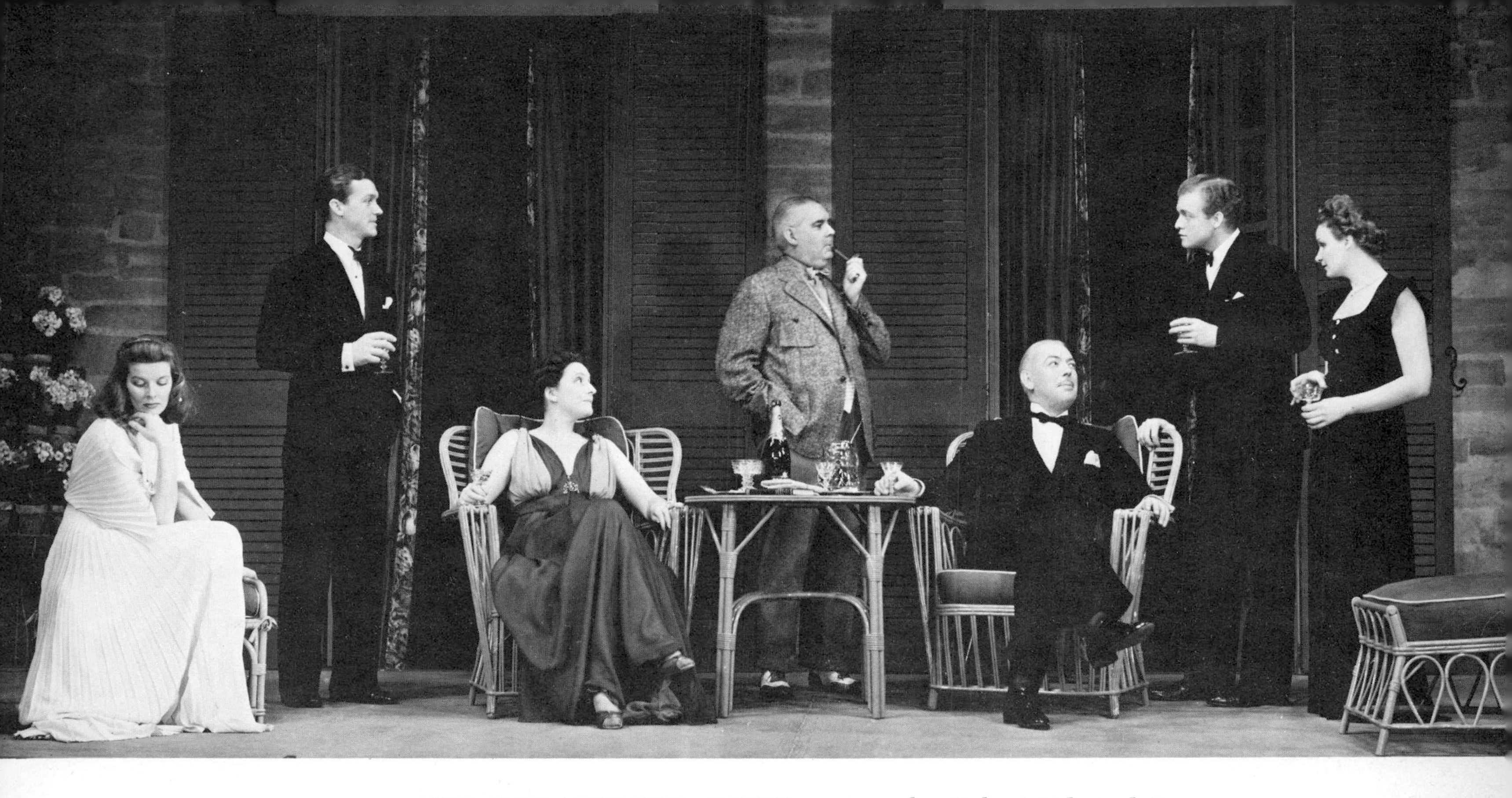

THE PHILADELPHIA STORY — setting by Robert Edmond Jones.

L. to r. — Katharine Hepburn, Dan Tobin, Vera Allen, Forrest Orr, Nicholas Joy, Van Heflin, and Shirley Booth.

Those who did not thought it formless, purposeless and lacking in all the basic qualities necessary to legitimate drama."[1] *My Heart's in the Highlands* did, nevertheless, serve to introduce the unconventional Saroyan to the Guild's management, who would make important use of his talents the following season. The Guild, however, closed its bedevilled 1938–39 theatrical year still owing New Yorkers one production.

Following the 1938–39 season, Lawrence Langner and Theresa Helburn were responsible for all Theatre Guild policy determinations, with Maurice Wertheim, still a member of the Board of Managers, acting usually only as an advisor. Alfred Lunt tendered his resignation shortly thereafter. The other three "artist" managers, Lee Simonson, Helen Westley, and Philip Moeller, were sometimes called into consultation on script selection, although rarely allowed to participate any more fully than this. Simonson, evidently, would have consented to remain an active partner if allowed to function in his usual capacity as design director, but this apparently was denied him.

There are several versions of how this ultimate allocation of responsibility took place. One is the supposedly official version, which states:

> By 1939, however, the governing board system of operation had become impractical and was divorcing from the Guild some of the best American playwrights, who preferred to deal with one or two persons rather than six. Hence, The Guild was reorganized with Lawrence Langner, who called it into being in 1919, and Theresa Helburn, for fifteen years its executive director, remaining as directors in charge of all its artistic activities.[2]

Then there is Simonson's version, which is included in his book, *Part of a Lifetime*:

> The waning of the Guild's creative powers as a producing organization coincided with growing personal friction that split us into separate production and finance committees so that we no longer functioned as a whole. A struggle for power was quietly begun on the part of the executive group to discredit the other board members who were practicing artists. Langner and Helburn convinced each other that they alone knew how to cast a

[1]Burns Mantle, *The Best Plays of 1938–39*, p. 12.

[2]*The Story of the Theatre Guild—1919–1947* [a souvenir booklet], p. 4.

play, select a director, supervise him, run a theatre, and manage its finances, although every season we continued to lose money, prestige, or both on productions that missed fire and for which they were no less responsible than any other members of the Board. Their assumption of superior theatre wisdom seemed to them so self-evident that they were astounded on finding it aroused any animus; they saw themselves more clearly with every season as the predestined Sheridans, always dashing up in the nick of time to save the author, the director, the Guild itself from imminent catastrophe.

Much of this may have been a compensation for their failure to develop as artists. Their continued and successful attempts to grasp more and more managerial power were perhaps unavoidable in the Guild's struggle to survive by adopting the methods of Broadway. The ability to negotiate became the essential talent. In every field of American effort it is the executive rather than the executant who becomes the indispensable personage both in public estimation and his own. Workmen, artists, inventors, in every field continue to abound and at the first sign of waning powers are easily replaced. But those who can assemble them, organize them, negotiate, make deals, set up and finance systems of production, are, to judge by published income tax returns, so exceptional as to merit the highest remuneration and have become a ruling class whether they turn out steel plate or produce plays, manufacture machinery or administer moving picture companies, run railroads or theatrical enterprises.[3]

There is also Langner's version of the Board's dissolution, contained in a memorandum to Theresa Helburn, which was occasioned by what Langner believed was a slurring innuendo of their "subordinating artistry to the dollar sign." He wrote:

After the production of *Jeremiah,* Moeller and Simonson participated in none of the subsequent productions, and, indeed, Westley had been inactive for years before. Helburn and Langner produced *The Philadelphia Story* of Philip Barry, Saroyan's *The Time of Your Life,* Hemingway's *The Fifth Column,* etc. etc., during the time that Moeller and Simonson were inactive. Helburn and Langner, bearing the brunt of the work of the Guild, were, nevertheless, in the minority and refused to continue unless the Guild was reorganized to recognize their contribution. The reorganization took place with Moeller, Simonson, and Westley

[3]Lee Simonson, *Part of a Lifetime,* pp. 85–86.

> resigning as directors and changing their common stock into preferred stock, which they still hold.
>
> Now, you can't get all this into an article, but it is the true story. How can we circulate it? [Memo dated Sept. 15, 1948]

It is actually unimportant to know which of these versions is most accurate—there is probably more than a little truth in all of them; the significant thing is that after the 1938–39 season the "original Guild" ceased to exist.

CHAPTER 13 / What Went Wrong? What Went Right?

The story of the Theatre Guild's vintage years is a curiously paradoxical one: some of its failures were engendered by its oustanding successes, while its overall success, as a phenomenon in the American theatre, came about through many of its failures. Its six managers were, in the main, intelligent, dedicated idealists who, through careful deliberations, tried to shape the Guild's policies with aesthetic discrimination and foresight. Yet, they were criticized for being practical in the wrong way, given to easy solutions, being guilty of nearsightedness, or for having too complacent an attitude. When they failed to provide the very best, they were accused of being artistic malingerers or dilettantes. When they were forced to retrench to make ends meet, they were accused of being niggardly; and when they provided too lavishly, they were considered to be either inept or improvident. Predictably, their detractors multiplied as their managerial powers waned —an occurrence not uncommon in the professional theatre.

It is doubtful whether the protean propensities of the Theatre Guild, once regarded by many as the world's major art theatre, can be attributed to any one cause. One of its great problems, however, appeared to be a problem of size. In the beginning, the relatively tiny Garrick Theatre had been spacious enough to house the early and largely experimental offerings. The subscription list was also small and, if a production proved lacking in general appeal, it could be easily taken off and another substituted without undue bother or expense. Conversely, if a production proved to be commercially successful, it could be transferred to a larger theatre for the balance of its run. Within a few years, however, with its subscription list grown into the thousands, and its production standards steadily increasing, the Guild felt the walls of the Garrick too confining, and in 1925 it opened its new million dollar base of operations, The Guild Theatre, on West 52nd Street. But, the successful productions still had to be sent into other houses, a burdensome mortgage had to be met, and the Guild's new home, by Theresa Helburn's admission, again became too confining because playwrights demanded bigger royalties, various theatrical unions asked for larger compensations, and across-the-board costs of producing also mounted.

During the 1927–28 season the decision was made to send the Guild's most successful productions on the road (following a trial session in Chicago and Baltimore the year before) in an effort to reach potential audiences outside New York City who had shown a genuine interest in good theatre. As more cities were added to this subscription series, however, the annoying problem of size again became acute. Facilities had to be expanded in every department and, as payrolls swelled, the logistics of keeping everyone gainfully occupied created continuing frustrations. The Guild became hampered in its choice of scripts as more and more attention was given to which personnel under contract were working or not working—for inactivity caused them to become nonproductive overhead. Evidence shows that a number of scripts were selected to accommodate the talents of idle actors rather than to insure intrinsic artistic merit.

When the decision to supply road shows was made, the Guild could boast a backlog of an unprecedented number of artistic successes, a backlog which included such outstanding presentations as *Pygmalion, The Silver Cord, Porgy, The Second Man, Volpone, and The Doctor's Dilemma,* as well as *Marco Millions* and *Strange Interlude.* With such a record, it was reasonable to suppose that more of the same excellence would be forthcoming. The sad fact is that, following its series of successes, the Guild produced a succession of near misses or outright misses, which road subscription audiences were not at all anxious to see; neither was anyone else, apparently. Such fiascos as *Faust, Man's Estate, Karl and Anna,* and *The Game of Love and Death* did little to promote the Guild's reputation, and certainly they could not be exhibited nationally after they had been ridiculed by the New York critics. Playwrights—O'Neill and Shaw included—were not providing the type of awe-inspiring material that had earned the Guild its renown. Such lightly regarded examples as *Dynamo, Days Without End, The Apple Cart, Getting Married,* and *The Simpleton of the Unexpected Isles* were carefully rendered, but did not excite much enthusiasm in New York or, understandably, on the road. The Guild, following current fashion, also produced such "socially conscious" proletarian-oriented fare as *Red Rust, Roar China!,* and *Parade* which, while considered "interesting," were not productions that could safely be sent traveling.

For a time the road policy produced appreciable revenues, fed mainly by the glowing successes of former years, but when these were used up there was little of value with which to keep the promises made to thousands of paid-up subscribers who had to be provided dramatic fare, six plays a year, hit or miss. The point had obviously been made that increasing size and frantic activity were not calculated to produce excellence, especially in the art theatre realm. The Guild's play reading department was well aware of the decline in the Guild's standards. First Courtenay Lemon and later Anita Block sent letters to their employers deploring the types of scripts they had been asked to examine and then to recommend for the Board's consideration. Harold Clurman, too, entertained strong doubts about the Guild's selections. But, production quotas had to be maintained, even at the expense of quality and, when the first rate was unavailable or unsuitable to its needs, the Guild had to settle for the second or even third rate to meet its commitments.

Rather than abandon the road with its undeniably lucrative income, the Guild attempted to keep it primed by various means. Thus, out-of-town tryouts which, before *Caprice,* had been the exception, became the rule as the Guild, reverting to established Broadway techniques, hoped to have as many of its road customers as possible see a production before the metropolitan reviewers delivered their irrevocable verdicts concerning an offering's merits or demerits. These untried works were hardly as satisfying to its national subscribers as were the superlative productions with which the Guild had inaugurated its road policy. Quite soon after the creation of the American Theatre Society, the Guild was forced to use this hybrid agency to augment its own output for the road with proven presentations provided by other managements.

Attention should be focused on the fortunes of the Guild's acting company, which shortly before, during, and after 1928 could boast an array of performers who were not only exceptionally talented, but who, in the main, were dedicated to the Guild's principles. This meant, in effect, that none of them were billed as featured players or stars, that the play rather than the performer was the thing. Most of these actors were happy with the opportunities the Guild afforded them to appear in a broad spectrum of roles in concert with others whose work they respected. In other words, flexibility and ensemble playing were stressed with the result that performers had a chance to grow as artists. With the inception of the road subscription series, however, this finely trained company was soon scattered in assignments away from New York. The Guild's system of "alternating repertory," which allowed many actors to perform two or perhaps three roles simultaneously in several productions, was abandoned, for it could not be made to pay its way on the road, and in New York rising producing costs as well as specialized scripts such as *Porgy* and *Strange Interlude* also made its use unfeasible. Repertory usually is an extremely expensive method of theatrical exhibition and, therefore, has seldom been employed extensively in the recent American theatre (witness the demise of such organizations as the Civic Repertory Company and the A.P.A.). Most of the world's theatrical institutions that utilize the repertory system are subsidized by state grants. Thus, they can afford to fail financially if they remain successful artistically. Losses are underwritten by governmental offices grateful for the cultural resources their nations undeniably gain. Repertory audiences of the state theatres of Europe and elsewhere expect and are given a diet of dramatic fare that, more often than not, comprises the best of what the past has to offer. The Guild had no financial guarantor of this type, and its policy chiefly was to produce new works. The brilliant acting company of the 1926–28 era began to disperse for one reason or another, especially drawn by the golden lures of Hollywood or by interesting propositions from other Broadway managers. For instance, such Guild stalwarts as Edward G. Robinson, Claire Eames, Henry Travers, Margalo Gillmore, Dudley Digges, Judith Anderson, and Richard Bennett all heeded calls to greener fields from which they sometimes returned briefly but seldom stayed. Morris Carnovsky, Franchot Tone, and later Alexander Kirkland, among others, threw in their lot with the Group Theatre which proposed to train an acting ensemble. The Guild watched and applauded but made no such schooling provision for itself. Then, a most devastating blow seemed to fall when Alfred Lunt and Lynn Fontanne left to become associated with Noel Coward. When these star performers returned, they formed an autonomous organization within the Guild, with absolute authority concerning the selection of scripts, players, and production personnel.

The original acting company members who remained under the Guild's aegis were frequently out on the road performing in one or another of the Guild's subscription cities, making them often unavailable when they were needed to fill new roles in New York. Once again the Guild acquired the typical Broadway habit of casting from scratch for many of its coming attractions, and of featuring certain "name" players, a system it had for a long time been loath to imitate after the failure of *The Rise of Silas Lapham* in 1919 with an established star in the title role. This padding of its company with guest stars who had little loyalty to the original Guild doctrines and precepts had the effect of damaging the Guild's *esprit de corps* and coarsening the level of its performances, no matter how hard the Board tried to carry out policies of improvement.

During its first years the Guild had felt free to provide its patrons with a number of unusually experimental works, all done on small budgets. Kaiser's *From Morn to Midnight,* Strindberg's *Dance of Death,* and Rice's *The Adding Machine* were examples of this willingness to experiment and, in one season, the Board of Managers also thought it quite in keeping with its commitments to produce a short play such as *Boubouroche* as well as the marathon length, three-week cycle *Back to Methuselah.* As time went on, however, this willingness to experiment lessened, probably because of such costly failures as *Miracle at Verdun,* where experimentation had been confined to expensive technical gimmickry rather than to offering an exploratory or novel form of dramatic literary expression.

One must naturally infer that the Guild's increasing conservatism led it to turn down such scripts as Elmer Rice's *Street Scene,* Marc Connelly's *The Green Pastures* and Susan Glaspell's *Alison's House,* all of which won Pulitzer awards. It also undoubtedly caused the Guild some embarrassment to watch other managements (including the rapaciously minded Shuberts) mount well-received productions of many of its other rejects, like Edwin Justus Mayer's *Children of Darkness,* Marcel Pagnol's *Topaze,* and Mordaunt Shairp's *The Green Bay Tree,* to name a few. The Guild was justly proud that its pioneering efforts had proved that thought-provoking dramas, which were more than a trifle "different," could find a ready and even eager market in New York and elsewhere in the United States. But even so the record indicates an ever-increasing reliance on the commercially acceptable rather than on the extraordinary.

Naturally, this dour appraisal is not meant to imply that the Guild did not have its resounding triumphs along the way. During its "vintage" years it brought to the stage such milestones in the American theatre as *Mourning Becomes Electra* and *Porgy and Bess.* It was also responsible for producing such outstanding theatre pieces as Maxwell Anderson's Pulitzer Prize-winning play, *Both Your Houses,* as well as his historical romances, *Elizabeth the Queen, Mary of Scotland,* and *Valley Forge;* for presenting such civilized high comedies as S. N. Behrman's *Biography, End of Summer,* and *Rain From Heaven;* for such dissimilar Philip Barry offerings as *Hotel Universe* and *The Philadelphia Story,* as well as Robert E. Sherwood's *Reunion in Vienna* and *Idiot's Delight,* or O'Neill's *Ah, Wilderness!*. A record like this would indeed be unexcelled if it were not for the failures or, perhaps, more lamentably, those *Camel Through The Needle's Eye—Escape Me Never* "almost-hits" of little aesthetic worth.

The Depression had no more dire effect anywhere than it had on the Broadway theatre. Professional theatrical artists of all types suffered the blight of unemployment as fewer and fewer productions were scheduled in New York's showcases and substantially less personnel were being used to mount those that were performed. Equity's rolls steadily decreased as its economic demands, and its charities, increased. With the rise of the talking picture to something resembling an art form, legitimate theatre patrons found that they would rather see a good movie than a mediocre play—for, above all, it was a far less expensive indulgence. So, the staple of the theatre, the good-for-three-month-run production, began to disappear, and job volume suffered. Naturally, there were always regular theatre patrons eager for the exceptional, as the Guild proved by having financially as well as artistically noteworthy seasons during depression-ridden 1933–34 and 1935–36. But, when its quality was only average, the Guild found its income falling way below average. Gifted younger playwrights, who rebelled against the Guild's highhanded treatment of their work, were no longer considering the organization their first and only outlet. Sidney Howard, whose Guild-produced plays won early critical acclaim and box-office success, looked to other managements, as did Elmer Rice. Later they joined with Maxwell Anderson and Robert E. Sherwood, also Guild-harassed over script revisions and casting arrangements, to form the Playwrights' Company. For the same reasons, S. N. Behrman also became a member.

As outstanding new scripts failed to find their way to the Guild's offices, there were proposals to exhibit one or more of Shakespeare's works, long considered anathema along Broadway. However, the Lunts first failed with Robert Edmond Jones' scheme for *Much Ado About Nothing,* which was withdrawn, and later they were unwilling to commit themselves in anything as tricky as *Antony and Cleopatra.* Productions of *Hamlet, King Lear,* and *The Tempest* were also considered by the Guild's managers, but all were shelved for one reason or another. At last, in 1935, a rousing, if rowdy, version of *The Taming of the Shrew,* in which Shakespeare was "unfettered," was created by and for the Lunts.

The Lunts have always been potentially the finest acting team America has produced. After their initial success in *The Guardsman,* they were cast together by the Guild in a broad range of productions which included *Arms and the Man, Goat Song, At Mrs. Beam's, The Brothers Karamazov, The Second Man, The Doctor's Dilemma,* and *Elizabeth the Queen,* and separately in plays of such varied mood as *Pygmalion, Ned McCobb's Daughter, Volpone, Strange Interlude,* and *Marco Millions.* But, after the bubbling success of *Caprice,* in which the team's flair for light, sophisticated froth was established, the Guild quite possibly made a serious blunder matching them in *Reunion in Vienna* rather than in *Mourning Becomes Electra* as was originally contemplated. The overwhelming acclaim accorded their clever work in the Sherwood comedy put the stamp on their careers, and this tendency toward the trivial was further fixed by their association with the witty Noel Coward, not to overlook their comparative failure in his disagreeable *Point Valaine.* The Guild, eager for the pair's return, had to offer them a free hand to choose their own *Taming of the Shrew, Idiot's Delight,* and *Amphitryon 38* sort of romps, which, although delightful, hardly stretched the Guild's or the actors' abilities beyond certain well-defined, coterie-inspired limits.

For a number of years the Guild had been known as a house of imports, but in 1930 it was chided by George Jean Nathan for letting the better European plays, such as Marcel Pagnol's *Marius* and R. C. Sherriff's *Journey's End,* escape them because of managerial disagreements. What they had presented were the results of compromises reached after listening to less than competent European play agents rather than scouting the field for themselves. Nathan also accused the Guild of having ignored such outstanding European playwrights as Sean O'Casey, John Drinkwater and, of course, Chekhov. Another of the Guild's critics, Harold Clurman, implied that the managers were people of little philosophic consistency or ideological cohesion who selected plays in a random manner simply because they were "interesting" or "intriguing," with little thought given to a unifying direction to govern or guide what was presented. These men were but two who found fault with the Guild during these years; there were numerous others.

The Guild's level of physical production during its "vintage" years was equal to any here or abroad. With as consummate a scenic artist as Lee Simonson on its Board, and with such other designers as Robert Edmond Jones, Cleon Throckmorton, Jo Mielziner, Aline Bernstein, and Raymond Sovey available when needed, the Guild's scenery, lighting, and costumes were rarely challenged for being either inappropriate or slapdash. On the contrary, the Guild undoubtedly set standards with its scenic investiture that were envied by many in the professional theatre. Notable also in the total picture of the Guild's *mise en scène* were the adroitness and general effectiveness of its staging. Philip Moeller was unquestionably one of the top directors in American theatrical history. His range was exceedingly wide, as is shown by the variety of productions he guided during his many years as a member of the Guild's directorate. Other fine stage directors from outside the Guild's ranks, including Worthington Miner, Rouben Mamoulian, and Tyrone Guthrie, also put their personal stamp on some of the Guild's more noteworthy offerings.

Perhaps the finest achievement of the Theatre Guild, however, is that it proved American theatre audiences respond to and, therefore, deserve high standards of aesthetics and a good measure of artistic accomplishment. Before the Guild came into its own, usual professional theatre offerings had been quite one-sided in the sense that they stressed the sensational but not the thoughtful—all show and little substance. Several sporadic attempts had been made to cultivate excellence, as in productions prepared by Mrs. Fiske, Winthrop Ames' New Theatre, the Neighborhood Playhouse, the Provincetown Players, and in a few avowals of faith made by Arthur Hopkins; but the patrons of most professionally produced plays were required to endure the traditional happy endings. The Theatre Guild materially changed this state of affairs by proving that taste and discrimination could be cherished commodities and that, above all, this could be done profitably.

With the inauguration of their subscription policy, the first in American theatre, the Guild had secured a reliable financial footing from which to launch its operations. By 1930 it had about 35,000 paid-up subscribers in New York and about 45,000 on the road—a solid basis for its continuity. And it undoubtedly felt flattered as other organizations used similar procedures to maintain financial and audience levels.

Americans have the Guild to thank, at least in part, for the truly international aspect of the American theatre. The Guild was responsible for enormously enhancing the reputations of such foreign playwrights as Franz Werfel, St. John Ervine, and Ferenc Molnar among others. It also let New Yorkers experience at first hand the work of such distinguished foreign directors as Emmanuel Reicher, Jacques Copeau, Friedrich Holl, and Theodore Komisarshevsky. In addition, the Guild helped open this country's doors to new developments in European stagecraft with such examples as Tolstoy's *Power of Darkness* (Naturalism), Toller's *Man and the Masses* (Expressionism), Andreyev's *He Who Gets Slapped* (Symbolism), Pirandello's *Right You Are If You Think You Are* (Illusionism), and Ibsen's *Peer Gynt* (Mock-Romanticism).

Mainly because the Guild had shown the way, more and more American theatrical managements displayed greater willingness to gamble on this same unconventional type of stimulating fare from abroad. But, perhaps more importantly, American playwrights, who before had written mainly according to formula, began to find new direction and purpose in their work, until during the late twenties and thirties, the finest playwriting in the world was being done chiefly by American dramatists. It is true that England could boast of Shaw (whose best work was behind him) and possibly Noel Coward; that Ireland had Synge, O'Casey, and possibly Lady Gregory; that Spain had Benavente and possibly Lorca; that Germany had Hauptmann, Werfel, and possibly Georg Kaiser; that Italy had Pirandello and possibly D'Annunzio; and that France had Giraudoux and, a bit later, Anouilh. However, during this period, Americans enjoyed the work of such native craftsmen as O'Neill, Rice, Odets, Anderson, Sherwood, Behrman, Paul Green, Thornton Wilder, Sidney Howard, William Saroyan, Philip Barry, and a number of others, most of whom had Theatre Guild experience. This categorizing is only to suggest that the Guild played a supreme role in this resurgence of native drama to which Americans owe so much.

Unquestionably the American stage has lost something of the eminence and lustre that these playwrights gave to their theatre. One realizes, too, that during this period the Theatre Guild had at least one and usually two or three serious dramas playing in several New York houses at the end of most seasons, and that it was not uncommon for rival managements to have produced fifteen or twenty legitimate theatre attractions that were considered sturdy enough to brave the summer months. And all these plays were given in times when relatively few potential patrons could afford the luxury of theatre tickets.

The period of the 1930s was a time of steady drain by various motion-picture companies on the resources of the American theatre in general, and on those of the Theatre Guild in particular. All of the major studios maintained New York offices staffed by competent talent scouts who constantly watched Broadway productions for the evidence of salable qualities. Few stage directors, theatrical designers, or other behind the scenes craftsmen who were summoned to the fabulous "back lots" felt that they could refuse the enormous monetary rewards being offered. Such playwrights as Maxwell Anderson, Ben Hecht, S. N. Behrman, Sidney Howard, and Philip Barry, among others, did stints for varied lengths of time and in various capacities for the movies. The most important drain on the theatre's resources, however, was the stream of acting talent which flowed toward Hollywood, a stream that carried with it such occasional Guild players as Claudette Colbert, Humphrey Bogart, and Helen Hayes, or such traditional Guild performers as Claude Rains and Helen Westley. It is revealing to scan the Guild's programs for such a typical season as 1935–36 to compile a listing of personalities who ultimately made the West Coast their home, a talent pool that included such performers as Tom Powers, Rita Johnson, Tom Neal, Richard Whorf, Gladys Cooper, Sydney Greenstreet, Thomas Gomez, Philip Merivale, Shepperd Strudwick, Doris Dudley, Minor Watson, Van Heflin, and Edgar Barrier. The sturdiness of a "fabulous invalid" that could sustain such a depletion of its lifeblood is quite astonishing. The dissipation was felt too often by theatre managements which were forced to postpone productions, or cancel them entirely, because the right personnel for their proposed offerings were unobtainable. They usually gave up trying to cast their attractions around the omniverous demands of Hollywood's shooting schedules. The Guild, however, made intermittent attempts to reverse this trend by using established film stars in several of its plays, with Helen Hayes appearing in *Mary of Scotland,* for instance, and Katharine Hepburn in *Jane Eyre.* The organization also produced scripts submitted by Hollywood writers, namely, Julius and Philip Epstein, authors of *And Stars Remain,* and Ben Hecht's *To Quito and Back,* for example. Alas, the stars could not always remain for the whole run; besides which some of the attractions proved to be distinct disappointments. There were, of course, other examples of the Guild's managers trying to cope or to coexist with the opulent and ever eager movie industry. Helen Westley was the first of the Board's members to venture into the "celluloid jungle," but was soon followed by Moeller, Simonson, and Theresa Helburn, who served their Hollywood employers in a variety of short-lived capacities.

Other film involvements followed. There was talk of starting a semi-independent Guild motion-picture unit, using adaptations of the organization's old hits for vehicles, in the expectation of luring lost players back into a Guild acting company. It should be noted, too, that as time went on the Guild relied more and more upon revenues brought in through the sales of its properties to the movies. Before 1929, very few of the Guild's presentations, with the notable exception of *He Who Gets Slapped,* had been considered usable, for the Guild's type of intellectual experimentation was usually not the sort that would be found acceptable by the majority of film fans. Slowly, however, the sale of motion-picture rights increased as *Strange Interlude, Reunion in Vienna, The Good Earth* (Guild-produced with Metro-Goldwyn-Mayer backing), *Biography, Ah, Wilderness!, Mary of Scotland, Porgy and Bess, End of Summer, Idiot's Delight, Juarez and Maximilian, Elizabeth the Queen* and others were bartered for ever-expanding prices, until, in the forties, Eugene O'Neill, through the Guild, could ask $150,000 for the rights to such unlikely movie material as *Mourning Becomes Electra.*

Other Broadway managements had, for a number of years, been involved with the motion-picture industry through various semi-secret subsidy plans, because the industry believed, quite rightly, that the theatre could try out a script, a production idea, or an actor for far less than it would cost to organize, build, and photograph the same material in Hollywood. Such arrangements cut down the possibility of film failures; for the industry, this was simply a matter of sound economic practice. Trial runs in the theatre undoubtedly raised the artistic horizons of the movies, too, although at the same time they often tended to have a depressing effect on the level of the theatre's output. Be that as it may, the Guild concluded a number of dickers, financial and otherwise, principally involving Paramount Pictures (with Samuel Goldwyn represented to a lesser degree). Several well-publicized Hollywood stars, such as Sylvia Sidney, Constance Cummings, and Miriam Hopkins, were given the opportunity to appear in Guild productions, which indubitably provided these ladies with invaluable live-theatre experience, but which, unfortunately, did little for the Guild's reputation as America's premier art theatre. What happened, too, is that the Guild began to sanction potential motion-picture material, and even motion-picture production techniques, being used in its stage presentations, in such plays as *And Stars Remain, Prelude to Exile,* and *The Masque of Kings,* or the seventeen rapid scene shifts of as many settings and the voice-over bridgings of narrative gaps in *Madame Bovary,* or the brief lowering of lights to represent the passing of time and mood in *The Ghost of Yankee Doodle.* The employing of such Hollywood apparatus, as well as the using of Hollywood stars, proved to be effective and popular on the road. The Guild, however, did not seem to be doing quite the same job of education for its national subscribers that it had once done for its New York audiences during its early years. Instead of being offered thought-provoking scripts, intelligently produced on an experimental basis, the road subscribers were led to expect ornate productions involving pedestrian material which, more often than not, featured leading motion-picture personalities. Unfortunately, these exquisite concoctions became thought of as being the last word in "New York theatre." Alas, too few road presentations strove primarily to deliver basic dramatic and theatric excellence.

During its 1937–38 season the Guild boasted of having nearly 45,000 subscribers on the road, a total which surpassed the peak year, 1929, and the following year (1938–39) this number was announced as being substantially higher. Through the Guild-controlled American Theatre Society, attractions provided by other managers, such as Gilbert Miller, Alfred deLiagre, and Jed Harris, were included in the road subscription series also, so that there were few gaps in the supply of "Broadway hits." Road audiences sometimes had to be content with second or third "national" companies, of course, but, by and large, they were given their share of stars and "all New York casts."

The Guild, following increasingly the production policies of other managers, used its out-of-town subscribers as guinea pigs for testing untried presentations moving toward hoped for New York openings. The road, oddly enough, began to look forward to this peculiarly insulting treatment, and, in many cases, felt slightly "honored" that it was considered worthy to witness the agony of playwrights, directors, and casts laboring to give birth to Broadway's anticipated offsprings. If an infant proved to be malformed or defective enroute, however, this ugly duckling was usually mercifully exterminated before its off-key quacks had to face the taunts and derision of a big-town critical assassination. The Guild contributed a number of these oft-lamented mercy killings with such examples as Moeller's version of Schnitzler's *The Lonely Way* during 1930–31, John Howard Lawson's *The Pure in Heart* during 1932–33, and Ferdinand Bruckner's *Races* during 1934–35, the last two directed by Theresa Helburn. Other road fatalities included Moeller's adaptation of Ladislas Fodor's *Love Is Not So Simple* during 1935–36, Helen Jerome's dramatization of Charlotte Brontë's *Jane Eyre* as directed by Worthington Miner during 1936–37, and Orson Welles' Shakespearean amalgamation,

Five Kings, during 1938–39. In most cases, professional critics on the road tended to be more lenient in overlooking a fledgling's awkwardness than would their New York colleagues, and they often played a silly game in which they tried to predict a work's chances for success once it reached Gotham. They even tried to be helpful by suggesting the addition of a scene or the deletion of an unessential character or a piece of business. This game had its curious aspects; it very often seemed that the critic in a road show city was more interested in enumerating a production's potentialities for New Yorkers than with insisting on some sort of standard's being maintained for his own readers. In other words, tryout audiences, who very often had paid for their tickets in advance, seemed more than content with their lot of being used as testing laboratories.

This state of affairs quite naturally led to the rise of a certain cynicism among workers in the professional theatre, an attitude that suggested "anything goes" in Buffalo, or that Chicago "loves that sort of thing." There was always the further danger of productions being tailored, unconsciously perhaps, to exhibit those qualities that had proved reliably popular with out-of-town patrons. Examples of this tendency might include the Guild's presentations of *Jane Eyre* and *Madame Bovary.* Here were adaptations of important novels in which beautiful film stars were swathed in beautiful costumes, then surrounded by beautiful settings—almost to excess. Both offerings presented heroines from a misty past who became involved in various affairs of the heart. Strangely enough, such an anti-romantic tract as the novel *Madame Bovary* became heavily weighted with all the external trappings of *Camille*-like romanticism when prepared by the Guild for the stage. Both *Jane Eyre* and *Madame Bovary,* it might be added, did excellent business on the road.

The road provided other inherent disadvantages, too. One was that certain tremendously popular Guild productions had the effect of trapping their leading players in much the same way that James O'Neill had been trapped by *The Count of Monte Cristo* or Joseph Jefferson III had been trapped by *Rip Van Winkle* in the course of touring the country during the latter part of the nineteenth century. Thus, Alfred Lunt could have easily surrendered to Harry Van in *Idiot's Delight* with Lynn Fontanne ever his bewigged Irene, Ina Claire could have developed portraitist's elbow as Marion Froude in *Biography,* or George M. Cohan could have been appreciated for many more folksy performances of Nat Miller in *Ah, Wilderness!,* and Katharine Hepburn might have grown old as Tracy Lord in *The*

Philadelphia Story. As it was, these performers gave almost too many years of their collective professional careers to portraying these popular characters. Needless to say, actors supporting these luminaries were often similarly entangled. Lunt, as noted, attempted to break the pattern by alternating Harry with other roles in his road repertoire, but not all were so lucky or had so much foresight—consider Frank Bacon in *Lightnin'* or Edward Everett Horton in *Springtime For Henry*. Countless repetitions scarcely produce professional growth, although the acquisition of road commitments had much to do with the Guild's forsaking its system of alternating repertory where this stultifying situation had been effectively circumvented.

It is also questionable whether any of the parts or plays just mentioned can really be classed as imperishable artistic achievements, despite their élan. The American Theatre Society's bookings, more often than not, featured delectable gumdrops provided by the various producing organizations along Broadway. Quite naturally, road audiences enjoyed such frankly commercial tidbits as *The Two Mrs. Carrolls*, *Yes, My Darling Daughter*, and *Tovarich*, which were offered the road subscription clientele by outside managements, just as they did such Guild productions as *Caprice*, *Call It A Day*, and *The Philadelphia Story*, even though this was not the type of dramatic sustenance the Guild originally provided its patrons. It is possibly not too farfetched to suggest that the recent steady rise of professional resident companies in Seattle, Minneapolis, Houston, San Francisco, Washington, Milwaukee and other metropolitan areas throughout the country was more than partly occasioned by these communities being surfeited by the typical road offerings that many managements (the Guild included) increasingly supplied. As theatregoing tastes became more refined, civic leaders sensed a need and furnished facilities for the presentation of repertories of great plays which they had learned not to expect from touring New York companies. In all probability, this was inevitable, for American legitimate theatre audiences usually register uneasiness and long-range dissatisfaction with the second rate or the gaudy. Over the years, Broadway playmakers failed to keep up with the increasing expectations of their road patrons, with the result that New York lost much of its importance as the center of America's theatrical universe.

No appraisal of the Theatre Guild's early and middle years would be complete without taking into account the resources and ingenuity of the organization's original Board of Managers who, for over twenty years, collectively or individually remained pillars of strength in the buffeting the professional theatre invariably sustains. One might not always agree with the decisions they made, nor with all the divergences in the course they plotted. One must always keep in mind, however, that second-guessing armed with hindsight is infinitely easier than arriving at a correct determination between several alternatives in the heat of the moment. One must remember, too, that these six individuals of widely varying temperaments remained together through years of financial distress, devitalizing personality clashes, and pressure from criticism often merited, but sometimes applied needlessly or recklessly. One cannot help marveling that mutual loyalties lasted so long in a super-charged milieu where associations have been known to dissolve almost before they begin, usually for the pettiest of reasons.

Consider then the energy, creativity, and drive of these six individuals, most of whom had important interests away from the Guild that would have kept lesser people fully occupied. Maurice Wertheim, for instance, was the senior partner of a New York banking house, and Lawrence Langner, besides being the author of several books and plays and running outside theatrical enterprises such as the Westport County Playhouse in Connecticut, was the founding member of the flourishing patent law firm of Langner, Parry, Card, and Langner. Theresa Helburn, for a time an executive for Columbia Pictures, served on several theatrical committees, and was the director of the Bureau of New Plays under the joint sponsorship of major motion-picture studios; Lee Simonson did interior decorating and fine arts painting, and designed modern furniture as well. Philip Moeller, besides directing over seventy productions in twenty years, was a practicing writer employed as the adapter of a number of the Guild's productions by foreign authors, and Helen Westley appeared in over a score of motion pictures while she served (possibly not overattentively) as a member of the Board.

These six were responsible for carefully scrutinizing an average of fifteen to twenty scripts a month. They oversaw an organization that included many departments, such as those concerned with technical aspects, including lighting, scenery, and costumes; with play reading, casting, business and legal matters, as well as the subscription secretariat. Over the years the managers selected a staff of behind-the-scenes personnel which contained many gifted theatre artisans, a number of whom later became well known in several allied fields: John Gassner, Anita Block, Russel Crouse, Ruth Benedict, Cheryl Crawford, Harold Clurman, and Kate Drain Lawson. Other members of the Guild, some of whom served the organization from its inception, were Joseph Heidt, Sara Greenspan, Lucille Lutrell, Michael O'Connor, and Addie Williams, to mention only a few. One should not forget that the original managers were responsible for selecting and presenting such "glorious failures" as Paul Claudel's tender *Tidings Brought to Mary*, or the *succès d'estime* of Franz Werfel's *Goat Song*, which received unrestrained praise couched in lyric prose from critics, but which cost the Guild $28,357.24, despite the fact that its cast included many in its famed acting ensemble including the Lunts and Helen Westley. Or, the presentation of *Juarez and Maximilian*, which caused the discriminating few to become wildly enthusiastic about its superb literary qualities, but which also lost money although acted by such skilled performers as Edward G. Robinson, Dudley Digges, Claire Eames, and Alfred Lunt. *Wings Over Europe* and *Hotel Universe* are two more plays which rightfully deserve to be classed in the "glowing failure" category, for, although they turned in deficits, they undoubtedly increased the Guild's stature, as well as raised the standards of playgoing throughout the United States.

It must never be forgotten either that the redoubtable six were responsible for what is probably the closest thing America has ever had to a national theatre, if such criteria as providing a set number of plays each year, as well as possessing an institutional character, maintaining a history of continuous operation, and the sending of productions of certain recognized standards to audiences throughout the nation are taken into account. There have been other experiments along this line, it is true. There was, for instance, during the depression decade of the 1930s, the government-sponsored Federal Theatre, but this interesting enterprise was regrettably short-lived. There is also the American National Theatre and Academy, with a Congressional charter, but this institution has been unable to accomplish much more than sponsoring experimental productions on a small scale, housing certain foreign and commercial offerings in its theatres (one of which happens to be the Guild's old home), and encouraging certain community ventures into the field of production. Their record, however, is scarcely as dazzling as the Guild's.

If, as Moss Hart declared, a major test of any theatrical enterprise, either individual or institutional, is *survival*, then the Guild's managers fully proved themselves. One is reminded of the producing organizations which came into being and faded while the Guild endured, many using roughly the same precepts as it did. Such little-known organizations as The Little Theatre Players, The American Show Shop, The Stagecrafters Association, or such relatively important undertakings as The Theatre Union, The Actors' Repertory Company, and The Mercury Theatre—even such a steadily productive organization as The Group Theatre—all suffered defeat and dissolution for one reason or another (usually monetary). The list is as long as it is varied. Perhaps it is not surprising, then, that the Guild's business manager, Warren Munsell, became more and more important in the managers' policy meetings. (He acted as their recording secretary.) Heeding the tunes of various pipers, the managers were forced, or found it convenient, to become followers or fellow travelers where once they had been the leaders. They followed a trend toward the portrayal of social protest or leftist revolt, and as others were presenting such exciting yet artistically limited sociological tracts as *The Last Mile* and *Stevedore,* Odets' *Awake and Sing* and *Waiting for Lefty,* or Kingsley's *Men in White* and *Dead End,* the Guild's managers decided upon *Roar China!, Midnight, Both Your Houses, They Shall Not Die, But For the Grace of God, Races,* and *To Quito and Back.* They also selected a number of amusing situation comedies such as *Call It A Day, Escape Me Never, Storm Over Patsy,* and *The Philadelphia Story,* as well as spicier or racier comedies, such as *Caprice, The Camel Through the Needle's Eye,* and *Reunion in Vienna.* The shift, noticeable to many, was that the managers allowed the Guild, which was conceived as a theatre for the intellectual elite, to drift slowly away from experimentation and artistic excitement that characterized its early days toward a more popular type of theatre which invariably must cater to mass tastes, employing all the paraphernalia of compromise: big stars, big productions, and the inevitable big budgets, with the expectation of big returns. In the end, the six managers suffered a chronic inability to adjust their sights to the dramatic possibilities of the exceptional or the unexpected. Their collective vision, which had been quick to distinguish true dramatic values in the past, had been dimmed by time, by captious criticism, by financial pressures, by ill-advised collaboration with the motion-picture industry, and by attempting to adopt the methods of big business to an art form—"bigger and better for the greater public"—until the Guild, under their guidance, seemed to be producing chiefly for another group of patrons than the one it had served at its outset. Its presentations became more and more conventional and platitudinous; they entertained; they restated the familiar. It is revealing to note that one of the ills Broadway experiences today—openly catering to benefit audiences—had early beginnings, arranged by Munsell, during preview performances of *Washington Jitters, Jeremiah,* and other Guild offerings.

The Guild's directorate, then, listened to real or imagined pipers who played on brass rather than upon silver instruments, and their perceptions as well as their critical balance faltered. The managers intuitively realized this, and from time to time tried to bring new blood and renewed creativity to the organization but, for one reason or another, these efforts were never overly successful. Other Broadway directors and producers who had, in one way or another, surpassed the original six managers' various theatrical abilities, naturally were quick to sense the uncertainty that accompanies waning powers, and eagerly brought forward their own productions to take advantage of the hard-won shelter of the Guild's organization.

CHAPTER 14 / Toward *Oklahoma!*-and Beyond

The 1939–40 theatrical year began with the team of Theresa Helburn and Lawrence Langner wholly in charge of the Guild's fortunes. They had been the ones chiefly responsible for the organization's one gratifying achievement of its nearly fatal twenty-first season. Like blessed rain after a drought, *The Philadelphia Story* continued to fill the Shubert even through the summer doldrums. Naturally, the subscription cities had been promised their taste of Philip Barry's sophisticated diversion, but not before the appetites of New Yorkers had been appeased. Hence, the Guild's American Theatre Society offered for the road such specialties of the 1938–39 Broadway scene as Herman Shumlin's production of Lillian Hellman's study of Southern venality, *The Little Foxes,* its cast headed by Tallulah Bankhead; or a revival of Sutton Vane's sentimental voyage into the hereafter, *Outward Bound,* directed by Otto Preminger and starring Laurette Taylor. This restoration, incidentally, had caused several critics to recall nostagically the original 1924 New York showing with its roster composed of Alfred Lunt, Leslie Howard, Dudley Digges, Beryl Mercer, and Margalo Gillmore among others.

Langner's and Miss Helburn's most pressing concern, however, was how to provide New Yorkers a season without too much financial risk involved. They needed to stem the tide of audience indifference, yet have a series of plays that would repair the organization's battered image. One logical solution seemed to be co-production with up and coming managements who possessed good scripts. After all, the organization had shared its facilities with others before, as in the case of *Escape Me Never, Call It A Day, But for the Grace of God,* and the later Lunt-Fontanne vehicles. During the previous season it had been forced to supply its home subscribers Shumlin's rendering of Thornton Wilder's *The Merchant of Yonkers,* as well as the Group Theatre's presentation of William Saroyan's *My Heart's in the Highlands.*

Saroyan, the story goes, met actor-manager Eddie Dowling at the 1939 Drama Critics' Circle Award Dinner. Saroyan attended because

My Heart's in the Highlands had been accorded several votes as "best play of the year." George Jean Nathan had been especially taken with the offering's novelty (as he wrote in *Newsweek*):

> Lit with the gleam of a smiling fancy and stirred with a humorous compassion, this loose and gently jovial mixture of almost everything . . . simultaneously squeezes the laughter and tears out of you with some of the seemingly most carefree playwriting it has been my surprised pleasure to have experienced. . . . One of the season's few treasures.

Dowling attended the award banquet because his presentation of Paul Vincent Carroll's *The White Steed* had been selected by the Critics' Circle as the year's "best foreign play." He was also remembered for his production of Philip Barry's *Here Come the Clowns* in which he had taken over the leading role of Clancy, plus his work with *Sally, Irene, and Mary,* Maurice Evans' *Richard II,* and *Shadow and Substance.* The outcome of this meeting was that Saroyan agreed to let Dowling prepare whatever works for the stage that he might complete in the future, and he furnished the former musical comedy star with a new script titled *The Light Fantastic.* Dowling then became allied with Langner and Miss Helburn, an action that caused critic Arthur Pollock to question the wisdom of this energetic producer, "always eager to take a chance," joining forces with a seemingly moribund institution:

> He is the opposite of the Guild's directors. Why, then, does he want to huddle under the wing of the Guild? Because, perhaps, he lacks confidence in himself, worries about whether or not he really knows what his instincts tell him, is still afraid to trust his own Irish intuitions; perhaps because he wants the Guild's prestige. But he has prestige of his own and the Guild has lost what it had. [*Brooklyn Daily Eagle,* Oct. 11, 1939]

Langner and Miss Helburn must have labored prodigiously with their new playwright and co-producer during the summer, because the script reportedly was in complete disarray. Robert Lewis, who had directed *My Heart's in the Highlands* for the Group, was hired to perform the same function for *The Light Fantastic.* The premiere at New Haven's Shubert Theatre on October 5, 1939, was somehow gotten through, but at Boston's Plymouth a few days later the critics seemed frankly bewildered and one or two were even antagonistic.

Lewis was forced to resign, and several changes were made in the cast: Martin Ritt was replaced by a young dancer named Gene Kelly, and other roles were assigned to newcomers Celeste Holm, William Bendix, and Tom Tully. Dowling and Saroyan took over the directorial chores, and the play's name was changed to *The Time of Your Life.*

When Saroyan's funny yet baffling piece opened at New York's Booth Theatre on October 25, 1939, the critics found it "appealing," "tender," "fascinating," and full of hokum, "a sort of compelling unreality that is real only on the stage. Joseph Wood Krutch attempted to summarize the play's theme:

> Its moral is simply that nearly everybody is either good or would like to be if he had not got confused in a society full of problems too hard to solve, and that once you have grasped this fact the world is so full of delightfully surprising things that we should be quite a good deal happier than kings. [*The Nation,* Nov. 4, 1939]

Nearly everyone connected with the production was complimented in one way or another: designer Watson Barratt for his atmospheric San Francisco barroom, Dowling, who played a champagne-sipping philosopher, Julie Haydon, who played a world-weary prostitute, and Bendix, a beetle-browed, fatalistic policeman. Later, Saroyan's relative, Ross Bagdasarian, became somewhat of a celebrity for his whooping portrayal of a pinball machine addict. It seemed a happy venture for all concerned, including a young understudy named Dorothy McGuire.

Saroyan dedicated the published version of the work to George Jean Nathan, his staunch supporter, and later in the year *The Time of Your Life* was accorded both the Pulitzer and Drama Critics' awards, the first time a play had been so honored. Saroyan, for a number of well-publicized reasons, spurned the Pulitzer citation.

It might be added parenthetically that the Repertory Theatre of Lincoln Center's revival of *The Time of Your Life* after thirty years made Saroyan seem a trifle dated, yet still possessing an undeniable eccentric charm. In a review which ignored whatever historical interest the production may have contained, Clive Barnes wrote that the author was rather too willing to explore "the poisonously cyclamated sweetness of life." Walter Kerr, despite Barnes' "basically trivial and pretentious" write-off, spotted in the play a deep streak of pessimism which somehow increased its acceptability for today's audiences. It is revealing to read these disparate opinions from the *New York Times* in tandem.

Meanwhile, the Guild offered its subscribers Paul Osborn's *Morning's at Seven,* as produced by another manager, Dwight Deere Wiman, and directed by Joshua Logan. Osborn's sensitive comedy of character set in a small American community suggested to some the tone previously evoked by Thornton Wilder's *Our Town.* It lasted little longer than the subscription period allowed at the Longacre Theatre.

Since it had two well-received attractions playing, the Guild waited until spring to bring its next offering into New York, with Billy Rose its silent partner. This was to be Ernest Hemingway's only published play and it was adapted for the stage by Benjamin Glazer, a movie scriptwriter. As a matter of fact, the published version of *The Fifth Column* was little more than a fragment, and had been written by Hemingway while he was a correspondent in Spain during 1937. The adaptation took a number of liberties with the intent of the original text. It was concerned, of course, with the Spanish Civil War and took its title from the claim of Franco's rebel forces that while there were four columns advancing on the besieged Loyalists in Madrid, there was also a Fifth Column of sympathizers who fought the embattled defenders from within the city. The script had already been turned down by a number of producers before the Guild took out its option. In the Hemingway version the story concerns a Vassar graduate, slumming in Spain, who is a tramp addicted to wild doings. An English reporter and an American reporter engage in a drunken brawl to win her favors. She bestows her affections on the victor, the Englishman, because she becomes annoyed with the American for always talking about his wife and children. In the adaptation, however, Philip Rawlings, an American member of the Loyalist intelligence staff, and Max, his German comrade, attempt to ferret out Fifth Column spies. Dorothy Bridges, an American girl making a pathetic search for a young brother fighting with the Lincoln Brigade, and Anita, a Moorish maiden "intensely pro-loyalist, but otherwise no better than she should be" become involved with them.

After the premiere in New Haven on January 26, 1940, the *New Haven Evening Register*'s reviewer believed that "for theatrical purposes and otherwise, the original manuscript has been padded by propaganda which, for the most part, fails to enhance its value despite the fervor of accompanying declarations that there is a Fifth Column in every nation and that Spain is merely 'the front line' against Fascism." The production next moved to Philadelphia, where the *Philadelphia Record*'s Edwin H. Schloss wrote that *The Fifth Column* had been transformed into a sort of "neo-Bronson Howard war melodrama complete with spies, counter-spies, shell fire, third degrees, letters, uniforms, a palpitant heroine, and excellent Hollywood prospects."

As the production moved to other cities, Frances Farmer felt it necessary to drop the prettied-up part of Dorothy, and the Guild brought her up on charges before Equity for evasion of contract. The role was then given to Katherine Locke, who had been the dewy-eyed Ophelia in Maurice Evans' *Hamlet*. The politics of the play also became somewhat muddled, because the Russians, who supported the Spanish Loyalists against the German and Italian Fascists, suddenly signed a pact with the Nazis and began fighting the Finns. A number of well-meaning propaganda pieces were affected adversely by this turn of events.

The Fifth Column opened at New York's Alvin Theatre on March 6, 1940, and ex-Group actors Franchot Tone, as the American, and Lee J. Cobb, and his anti-Nazi German friend, were complimented for their skillful work (both had appeared in Irwin Shaw's *The Gentle People* the year before), as was ex-Group director Lee Strasberg for his adroit staging, and ex-Group designer Howard Bay for his unique, semi-constructivist setting. Ex-Belasco star Lenore Ulric did what she could with Anita, and ex-tragedian Arnold Moss made a convincing intelligence chief. Too much doctoring, however, had made whatever values the original Hemingway possessed seem anemic. The adaptation did not enjoy an extended run. But the author had had his work inexpertly adulterated by movie writers before, so probably felt resigned to the inevitable changes. During *The Fifth Column*'s preparations he was reported to be fishing off Bimini and using a tommy-gun on sharks that threatened his province. Besides, the Guild did have three productions occupying Broadway theatres, something that had not happened for quite a while.

In early February, the Lunts brought their company into New York to present *The Taming of the Shrew* for eight Finnish War Relief Fund benefit performances. This was the conclusion of the "Festival of Comedy" tour that had lasted the better part of two years. At the end of the week, Robert E. Sherwood delivered a script to their dressing room entitled *Revelation*. The playwright had conceived the basic idea while listening to a Christmas broadcast made by William L. White (son of the eminent Kansas editor) from Finland's Mannerheim Line. The acting pair was so taken with it that they wanted to put it into rehearsal immediately. Mainly out of loyalty, they asked Langner and Miss Helburn if they wished to co-produce it with Sherwood's

Playwrights' Company. The Guild's managers agreed.

Less than seven weeks later, the Lunt-Fontanne company gave its premiere performance of *There Shall Be No Night,* as the anti-Fascist piece came to be known, under Lunt's direction; its urbane drawing-room settings were supplied by Richard Whorf. When the production was taken from one tryout city to another, it garnered an outstanding set of notices. It is true that *Variety's* out-of-town reporter felt that the average playgoer would experience difficulty in following its lofty dialogue, "as it ascends into the higher branches of intellectualism and shadows the primary interest engendered in the play by its timeliness." Elliot Norton of the *Boston Post* was inclined to challenge some of Sherwood's assumptions. He felt, for instance, that to brand Russia as merely Hitler's tool in the Finnish war lacked credibility. The critical consensus, however, termed the Lunt-Sherwood undertaking "magnificent and inspired." Norman Clark of the *Baltimore News-Post* thought that it had

> . . . a tragic, Ibsen quality that shakes one's soul; leaves him in a state closely akin to fear and trembling. . . . Mr. Sherwood has written his play in words of fire; Dr. Valkonen is one of the most impressive characters in modern drama. Not only is he a scientist, but a religionist and a philosopher. . . . In portraying this man, Alfred Lunt does the very finest acting of his career.

There was some mention of postponing polling for both the Pulitzer and the Critics' Circle awards until New Yorkers had had a chance to see Sherwood's newest achievement. By the middle of April the vote in both cases had gone to Saroyan's *The Time of Your Life,* as previously mentioned, but when *There Shall Be No Night* did open to replace *The Fifth Column* at the Alvin on April 29, 1940, the metropolitan critics were all very much impressed. Brooks Atkinson found that "it honors the theatre and the best parts of it speak for the truth with enkindling faith and passionate conviction." Richard Watts, Jr. believed that even if it was a bitter, brooding tragedy, "it is not without its dogged traces of wry optimism." Sherwood, who had seemed to despair of the modern world in such peacetime works as *The Petrified Forest* and *Idiot's Delight,* had "begun to hope again in the midst of war and encroaching barbarism." Burns Mantle in the *Daily News* seemed startled to perceive

> dramatic values in the recital that are not obscured by the weightiness of the theme. . . . The moving appeal of this little family's destruction is poignantly real. It follows the pattern of drama without once succumbing to the cheaper conventions of the theatre.

Only Arthur Pollock of the *Brooklyn Daily Eagle* seemed troubled, as Elliot Norton had been, that Sherwood let his German, Ziemssen, declaim for the Russians as well as for Hitler: "Shaw would have let the Russians speak for themselves. Particularly since it is their invasion he is talking about."

The public's reactions to *There Shall Be No Night* varied widely, but all of them testified to the play's eloquence. Some wondered if it could be called "art," or simply slanted journalism. Raymond Clapper, a Washington columnist, thought that it deeply influenced national sentiments about the war, and named it "a rank, inflammatory job, pleading for intervention." A group called The Theatre Arts Committee picketed it with pamphlets declaring "The warmongers capture the Alvin!" and urged its audiences to sign peace petitions addressed to President Roosevelt. Soon after the opening Hitler's troops invaded in several directions; they swarmed into Holland, and Belgium surrendered soon thereafter. Then came the Battle of France that swiftly tore apart the Republic. During the middle of June, Sherwood wrote a plea to Americans headed "Stop Hitler Now!" which appeared as a full-page ad in several New York papers. In it he asserted that because of the play's significance, *There Shall Be No Night* would be sent on tour the following September, regardless of attendance at the Alvin. So, after contending for some of the crowds that came to see the 1940 World's Fair, the drama was sent on a tour which was to include forty-two cities in nineteen different states and two Canadian provinces. Through all this, of course, the Battle of Britain raged, and later the Lunts courageously took the play to London. There they performed it to the accompaniment of air-raid sirens and bursting bombs. Grimly, the world situation took a series of corkscrew turns, until early in 1942, following Pearl Harbor, Lunt, still made up to resemble anti-Nazi expatriate Thomas Mann, and the Playwrights' Company had to conclude that because Russia had joined the side of the allies and Finland had sided with Germany, Sherwood's original premise had lost much of its validity. A later version dealt with the Italian invasion of Greece.

Nevertheless, *There Shall Be No Night* was awarded the 1941 Pulitzer Prize for drama. It was the third time Sherwood had received the award, tying Eugene O'Neill's thirteen-year-old record. (The Drama Critics' Circle that year chose another anti-Fascist play—Lillian Hellman's *Watch on the Rhine.*) Although the Guild had only about a one-third share in its Lunt-Playwrights' Company partnership, taking into account the organization's almost total lack of artistic participation, such a portion might have been considered either gravy or wormwood, depending upon how one viewed the situation.

Through the late winter and early spring Lawrence Langner and Theresa Helburn continued their negotiations to force a new financial arrangement with bondholders controlling the Guild Theatre. The managers had indicated that they would relinquish the 52nd Street playhouse, then valued at $500,000, unless some new rental agreement could be reached. The friction that had developed between the Guild's producing unit and the bondholders in recent years came about chiefly through the managers claiming that $80,000 yearly rental and operating costs were almost double those of the average Broadway house. During the season, Sidney Kingsley's production of his adaptation, *The World We Make,* had occupied the Guild Theatre for about two and a half months. After that, *The Time of Your Life,* which had opened at the Booth, was moved there.

In March, the presentation closed for a week so that Eddie Dowling could devote full time to co-directing a new Saroyan work, *Love's Old Sweet Song,* which he was scheduled to do, with Armina Marshall listed as production assistant. After George M. Cohan had turned down the leading role in the play, the producers and playwright considered themselves lucky to secure the services of Walter Huston and Jessie Royce Landis. When its premiere took place in Princeton during early April, *Variety*'s reviewer claimed that despite *Love's Old Sweet Song*'s moments of wonderful nonsense, "a running description of it somehow defies analysis." When it moved to Philadelphia, the critics declared it a "surrealistic comedy" or "anything but well made." Henry T. Murdock of the *Philadelphia Ledger* tried to tell his readers something about its subject:

> "It does touch on life, love's Cosmos (or four white roses and two red ones) . . . California's climate, 'Time' magazine and its staff, the inadvisability of selling a house in a down market, the theory that each infant is a potential genius, and kindly take a card from the deck. What is it? Ah, the nine of clubs. We're not completely mad—the nine of clubs is in it, too."

In Baltimore, the play created much puzzlement plus a mixture of raves and outright panning.

Both Miss Helburn and Langner wanted Saroyan to tighten his script, abridging its three acts to two. The writer sought out George Jean Nathan, however, who probably pointed out that the managers' once heralded ability to fix plays had lately been in question. Whatever the reason, Saroyan remained adamant about his three acts, and *Love's Old Sweet Song* reached Broadway in a less than harmonious condition.

Actually, Saroyan's opus does have a simple melody running through it, a lilting duet between an attractive spinster and a glib-tongued patent medicine salesman, who she believes has come to woo her. The trouble was that too many discordant elements also ran through it. For instance, novelist John Steinbeck's *The Grapes of Wrath* had been the literary sensation of the year (and received the Pulitzer prize), and the sad plight of the Okies was very much on everyone's conscience. But in Saroyan's play the enormous ill-begotten brood of a migratory couple ravishes a halcyon California setting like a plague of locusts. Another far-fetched element is the domestic upheaval of a Greek wrestler's household. When the vaudeville-like comedy opened at the Plymouth Theatre on May 2, 1940, John Mason Brown of the *New York Post* seemed unable to make up his mind about the playwright's lyrically extraneous subplots: "Much as I hate to confess it, his newest offering has about it all those slipshod, slightly balmy qualities which those who do not admire Mr. Saroyan are fond of ascribing to his plays." When all the reviews had been assessed, Saroyan apparently regretted his intransigence. Unfortunately, an irrevocable verdict had already been pronounced.

A few years later, after Saroyan had been in Hollywood working for Metro-Goldwyn-Mayer, Langner wrote him concerning one of his revamped scripts entitled *Afton Waters*. The producer also asked about Ross Bagdasarian—then stationed with the Army in California—whom he remembered from both Guild-Saroyan ventures. The playwright replied that he would forward a copy of the script, but stated he was also sending it to other organizations, asking for better terms than the Guild offered. His letter concluded:

> . . . Of course I think you are away behind the times as far as the theatre is concerned, but that's O.K. too. You probably don't realize that this sort of Philip Barry-Famous Actress in the Leading Role kind of playwriting is so much nonsense [the Guild was presenting Katharine Hepburn in Barry's *Without Love*] and

what's more that it is the sort of mischief that is likely to postpone the arrival of the real theatre—but what of it, if the play will make money? Maybe it won't, though—or wouldn't without the famous actress, or maybe it won't, even *with* the famous actress. You've been in a position to make the American theatre greater than ever for a good long time, but you haven't done it. You ought to feel very unhappy about that. I hope you do. . . .

Langner's considered reply stated that he would be happy to reread *Afton Waters,* and continued:

> As to your lecture on the subject of "What I should do to make the American theatre greater," etc. etc., if it hadn't been for the Philip Barry—Famous Actress kind of playwriting we would not have had the money to put on the "Time of Your Life" and "Love's Old Sweet Song," which leaves us and our backers about $27,000 in the hole. If I like the play, the only terms I will be interested in are those which we put on the other two plays, and if this is not satisfactory, let's forget it. Like everybody else, the people in the Guild have to live—perhaps you don't see any reason why they should—but I feel differently. They work hard and conscientiously and try to play the game on the level. There isn't one of us that couldn't make a very good living in the motion pictures, if we'd wanted to sell our soul for money.

The 1939–40 Broadway season had been noteworthy for its series of light, collaborative comedies, notably Russel Crouse and Howard Lindsay's adaptation of Clarence Day's short stories, *Life With Father,* George Kaufman and Moss Hart's study of egomania, *The Man Who Came to Dinner,* as well as James Thurber and Elliott Nugent's evocation of Ohio college days, *The Male Animal.* International tensions were felt, however, in Clare Boothe's comedy, *Margin for Error,* concerning a German Consul in the United States, which caused the Nazi government to protest vigorously, or Maxwell Anderson's tragedy, *Key Largo,* in which Paul Muni portrayed a disenchanted American, tired of fighting Fascism abroad but aroused by finding its seeds sprouting on his own doorstep. One luminous event of the waning season had been the Old Vic's revival of *Romeo and Juliet* starring Laurence Olivier and Vivien Leigh. The Guild's managers determined to mount a star-studded Shakespearean revival of their own.

A number of producers were planning revivals for the approaching season. Obviously, there was just not enough decent new material available for presentation. Many playwrights felt they could not cope with the rapid shifts in current history—what seemed like an intriguing dramatic premise one moment might become hopelessly dated the following month. Therefore, restorations were prominently available: Maugham's *Our Betters* with Constance Collier, Synge's *Playboy of the Western World* with Burgess Meredith and Barry Fitzgerald, as well as Judith Anderson's return in her jazz-accompanied 1934 opus, *Come of Age.* The resurrected *Kind Lady* and *Charlie's Aunt* were already considered hits. The Guild did have several proposed original scripts to announce, nevertheless, supplied mainly by Theresa Helburn's movie-sponsored Bureau of New Plays. These included Norman Rosten's *First Stop to Heaven* and Morley Callaghan's *Turn Home Again.* In fact, the Bureau had been instrumental recently in awarding grants to several young writers who showed definite promise, including Tennessee Williams and Arthur Miller, as well as other enrollees in a playwriting seminar conducted by the producer and John Gassner at the New School of Social Research.

The Guild began its 1940–41 season, however, by reinstating prize-winning *The Time of Your Life* at its home theatre for a month's airing. Cast changes gave Fred Kelly his brother Gene's role as Harry the Hoofer, and Arthur Hunnicutt, who had portrayed the shiftless Okie father in *Love's Old Sweet Song,* the part of the loquacious Kit Carson. *The Time of Your Life* was then scheduled to go on tour, as were *There Shall Be No Night, The Fifth Column,* and *The Philadelphia Story,* as soon as Katharine Hepburn had completed its filming. Langner and his wife, Armina Marshall, had finished writing a rural situation comedy based partly on New York State's Oneida community, *Suzanna and the Elders,* and after its New York showing at the Morosco Theatre, under the aegis of producer Jack Kirkland, it too was sent trouping as an American Theatre Society subscription bill. *Suzanna,* directed by Worthington Miner, featured Lloyd Bridges, Haila Stoddard, Philip Coolidge, and Morris Carnovsky.

In the meantime, Detroit and Buffalo had been re-added to the Guild's road tour, which would now include two-week stopovers in Chicago, Boston, and Philadelphia, plus a week each in Washington, Baltimore, and Pittsburgh, and a split week in New Haven. This Connecticut city, according to tryout custom, was to view the premiere showing of the newest Guild attraction—a colorful production of Shakespeare's *Twelfth Night.*

The organization's managers had prevailed upon Helen Hayes early in the summer to play the boy impersonator Viola (or was it the other way around?), and because of the star's long-standing association with Gilbert Miller, it was necessary to include him as their partner. A search began for a Malvolio of sufficient stature, with Robert Morley and Cedric Hardwicke being fleetingly considered. Finally, Maurice Evans was officially invited, and with him his director of many lauded Shakespearean presentations, Margaret Webster. Stewart Chaney was elected to design the gaily beribboned costumes and scenery, and Paul Bowles was commissioned to compose neo-Elizabethan incidental music for the production.

Just prior to *Twelfth Night*'s New Haven opening, British actor Robert Speaight withdrew from the role of Orsino. Speaight explained that as a reserve officer he was liable to recall by his government and felt he might soon have to return to England for active service. This prodded one snappish commentator to conclude:

> It must be admitted Laurence Olivier started the whole business off on a very sour note last spring when he announced that his production of "Romeo and Juliet" must be closed at the 51st St. Theatre because he and Vivien Leigh had been sent for in a terrific rush to help save England for the English. . . . The story was apparently just a modern war-time variation of the old gag about why the show had to close. Olivier and Leigh went West, not East, and are still in this country, busily making movies. [Wilella Waldorf, *New York Evening Post*, Jan. 5, 1941]

Westley Addy, who had appeared as Hotspur in Evans' *Henry IV* production, took over as the Duke of Illyria.

Rehearsals as well as the preview period were complicated by preparations for the Helen Hayes Theatre that had been scheduled by radio station WABC to offer Sunday night competition to Edgar Bergen and Charlie McCarthy, then the most popular team on the air. Miss Hayes initiated her broadcast series with her ever popular *Victoria Regina*, which incidentally served to introduce Viennese Paul Henreid to Americans as the Prince Consort Albert.

Twelfth Night received a cordial reception when it opened in New Haven. A week later in Boston, John H. Hutchens of the *Boston Transcript* concluded that "one of the happiest of comedies still belongs in the theatre, assuming that the theatre can give it such a performance as this." His colleague, Elliot Norton, mentioned the production's delicate balancing of wry wit and broad humor. Philadelphia, too, responded with overall approbation for such featured players as Mark Smith, June Walker, and Donald Burr. When the comedy opened at Broadway's St. James Theatre on November 19, 1940, however, a number of critics, while enthusiastic, did recall the *Twelfth Night* that had been performed in 1930. In Brooks Atkinson's Sunday tribute, he quoted all the nice things his fellow reviewers had written, only to conclude:

> If I did not have the pleasantest sort of recollections of Jane Cowl's Viola of ten years ago, I should not attach so much importance to the romantic beauties of the part. Miss Cowl lacked humor to a marked degree. She is a romantic and decorative actress. [But] as Viola she captured the grace and music of the poet. . . . Her Viola suggested the high breeding to which Shakespeare makes more than one reference in the lines. This is what I miss in the lack-lustre acting of Miss Hayes.

Atkinson continued by praising Maurice Evans' Malvolio, stressing the keenly edged satire he had brought to his slightly Cockney conception of the role:

> He knows the theatrical importance of little things, like a pair of glasses that accent his sense of self-importance. . . . He knows how to project character through subtleties of walk and carriage, how to speak the spacious and savory dialogue of the Elizabethans.

Twelfth Night continued to fill the house until mid-February; then it was sent to Buffalo, Washington, Cincinnati, and other stopovers on the road. In Helen Hayes' autobiography, *On Reflection,* she states that it was not until the last week of the tour that she "found the key" to her part, but that somehow the long search had been absolutely worthwhile.

As its second subscription bill, the Guild endorsed a new play by Ferenc Molnar entitled *Delicate Story,* which was adapted, produced, and staged by Gilbert Miller while he had been acting as co-administrator for *Twelfth Night. Delicate Story* starred Edna Best, and it appeared at the Henry Miller Theatre on December 4, 1940. Its lifespan hardly lasted through the subscription period.

Meanwhile, Westley Addy had been replaced in the *Twelfth Night* cast because he was to be employed in the Guild's presentation of a new playwright's first professional production. Margaret Webster was asked to direct Tennessee Williams' *Battle of Angels,* starring Miriam Hopkins and Doris Dudley. Both women still nurtured movie ambitions.

Battle of Angels was sent to Boston and had its premiere at the Wilbur Theatre between Christmas and New Year's Day, admittedly not the best time to open a controversial piece in a parochial city. The substance of the reviews filtered back and was reported in the *New York Times*:

> The play is one more of talk than of action, except for melodramatic flourishes and a wild climax. There appear to be symbolic implications, but they are obscure in meaning, and there are episodes that seemed more shocking to the first-night audience than effective in the dramatic development.

The plot of *Battle of Angels* (which did reach Broadway later as *Orpheus Descending*) is familiar to anyone who has seen Williams' screen version, *The Fugitive Kind*, which stars Marlon Brando, Anna Magnani, and Joanne Woodward. Its two acts take place in a Mississippi Delta mercantile store, where the unloving wife of the owner conducts the business during what is believed to be his last illness (his presence being indicated by thumps for assistance from an invisible room). A youth wearing a snakeskin jacket wanders into this simmering environment. He is driven by vague longings: he wants to write a book; he has a fatal attraction for women. The play ends in an all-consuming fire—literally. In fact, smoke from the stage drove audiences into the street.

If the Boston reviewers were not greatly impressed by Williams' work, the Boston censors most certainly were. They sued to close the production, as the Guild's managers might have suspected they would. However, the organization did circulate the following letter among its Boston subscribers:

> In view of the unfortunate publicity caused by the Boston censor's protest about *Battle of Angels*, we feel it is only fair to give you the Guild's reasons for producing the play. We chose it because we felt the young author had genuine poetic gifts and an interesting insight into a particular American scene. The treatment of the religious obsession of one of the characters, which sprang from frustration, did not justify, in our opinion, the censor's action. It was, we felt, a sincere and honest attempt to present a true psychological picture.
>
> We admit that the attempt to portray the influence of the young outsider on the lives of the three different small-town women of the play did not come off successfully in dramatic

> terms. It was more of a disappointment to us than to you. Still, we feel that we should be able to expect our members to be indulgent toward an occasional experimental play and even bear with its failure, since it is only by experimentation that we can feed new authors into the American theatre. An experimental play like *The Time of Your Life,* for instance, was badly received in Boston, but was later awarded the Pulitzer prize as well as the Critics' Circle award, and was felt to have an important influence on the American theatre.
>
> *Battle of Angels* turned out badly, but who knows whether the next one by the same author may not prove a success. Incidentally, Mr. Williams was recently awarded a Rockefeller Foundation fellowship in playwriting for his ability and promise.

The demise of *Battle of Angels* naturally left a gap in the organization's schedule of subscription presentations, soon filled by Lynn Riggs' *The Cream in the Well,* as produced by Carly Wharton and directed by Martin Gabel. Its cast included Martha Sleeper, Leif Erickson, and Myron McCormick, and it opened at the Booth Theatre on January 20, 1941—for twenty-four performances. Even though its plot had to do with incest, the Guild obviously considered it more suitable for New Yorkers than Williams' play about misguided passions.

With a less than inspired track record for the season behind them, Miss Helburn and Langner consented to produce an allegorical musical that conveyed a patriotic message. This was Philip Barry's *Liberty Jones,* with music supplied by Paul Bowles. It portrays "Miss Liberty" sick abed. Doctors, nurses, stuffed shirts (blown-up shirts were characters actually seen on stage), and friends can do nothing for her. Can Tom, Dick, and Harry? Can her "Uncle"? Possibly, if they show enough faith in her recovery. The Guild owed Barry a great deal—its very existence, according to most estimates. It put on his salute to American democracy, and spared nothing; it got the services of ex-Mercury director John Houseman (who earlier had prepared Paul Green and Richard Wright's *Native Son*), fashionable designer Raoul Pène Du Bois, and a chorus of the most beautiful girls to be seen on any stage, anywhere, ever.

Liberty Jones made her initial bow in Philadelphia, then was quickly brought into New York's Shubert February 5, 1941, to repose languidly on Du Bois' highly decorated bed. Brooks Atkinson could not deny the sincerity of her various squires' motives. His considered opinion contained a number of "buts," however:

> . . . but the scenes of beauty that frequently break through in the last half of the evening do not clarify the fantasy as a whole. Most of it, also, is weighted down with symbolism which this column frankly does not understand. It is very much to Barry's credit that he is not content with writing smart comedies like "The Philadelphia Story." But his frequent attempts to rise above realism into subjective expressions of faith and ideals get their wings clipped in the theatre. In spite of its incidental beauties, "Liberty Jones" seems like a complicated way of saying something that ought to be intelligible to all of us.

The reviewer then humbled himself by adding that his were "ungrateful comments" to fling at such a high-minded attempt to provide something of a virtuoso style of playmaking. His confreres were not so gentle. *Liberty Jones,* which had cost the Guild a pretty penny, expired after twenty-two subscription performances.

As noted, few authors that season cared to write with the fierce advance of world events as their backdrop. Broadway producers were operating at considerable distance from the battlefronts, and the American public could still afford the luxury of comparative serenity. Two current comedy melodramas vied for popularity: Joseph Kesselring's *Arsenic and Old Lace,* which had been originally projected as a straight play but had its grim ingredients amusingly altered by the team of Lindsay and Crouse, and Owen Davis' adaptation of a sophisticated murder mystery, *Mr. and Mrs. North,* which lacked a measure of the other's drawing power. Other hits included Moss Hart's musical extravaganza, *Lady in the Dark,* which had been fortunate to have its dream-obsessed lady editor played by versatile Gertrude Lawrence, and Rose Franken's inconsequential *Claudia,* in whose title role Dorothy McGuire rode to stardom. Another esteemed offering had been a former Guild reject, Emlyn Williams' autobiographical *The Corn Is Green,* which provided Ethel Barrymore with the part of a no-nonsense spinster schoolmarm that many thought was the best role of her career. Yet another biographical remembrance was Joseph Fields and Jerome Chodorov's dramatization of Ruth McKenney's *New Yorker* stories, *My Sister Eileen,* in which Shirley Booth contended with life in Greenwich Village as animated by George S. Kaufman. The Guild's home had had comedy tenants for part of the year, F. Hugh Herbert and Hans Kraly's *Quiet, Please,* produced by Jesse L. Lasky and Henry Duffy. Notable exceptions to Broadway's escapist tendencies were the pieces provided by Lillian Hellman and the membership of the Playwrights' Company. Sherwood had already insisted that his *There Shall Be No Night* tour the country. Next, Elmer Rice offered *Flight to the West* with Paul Henreid portraying its "superman" villain; then, Rice directed S. N. Behrman's *The Talley Method* in which Ina Claire protests Fascist encroachments on her civilized domain. Reportedly, Maxwell Anderson, with a role for Helen Hayes in mind, was reworking a script condemning the spread of barbarism. Although none of these plays would be considered imperishable additions to the world's storehouse of dramatic literature, they revealed a trend toward propaganda that the Guild determined to follow.

Karl Zuckmayer was an émigré German dramatist whose fame rested to a certain degree on *The Captain from Koepenick,* in which he satirized Prussian obedience to the uniform. Another play by him, *The Devil's General,* portrayed realistically the Nazi mentality. The Guild began to prepare, under the direction of Worthington Miner, Zuckmayer's *Somewhere in France* (originally *The Last Round*), as it had been adapted by the playwright's fellow refugee, Fritz Kortner. *Somewhere in France* opened at Washington's National Theatre rather late in the spring of 1941. Westley Addy, who had not been enjoying especially long runs with the organization, was cast again, this time as a sympathetic Frenchman, and Dudley Digges, who played his father, gave up a lucrative part he had in Kaufman and Hart's *George Washington Slept Here* to join in this tribute to the fortitude of a sundered nation. In fact, the cast list read like a "Who's Who" of the acting profession, for it contained, besides Addy and Digges, Walter Slezak, Alexander Knox, Art Smith, Jerome Thor, Robert H. Harris, Zachary Scott, Herbert Berghof, plus actresses Arlene Francis, Kathryn Givney, and movie star Karen Morley among many others. Unfortunately, all this talent could not bring the rambling narrative to life:

> The story which the Messrs. Zuckmayer and Kortner undertake to tell of these people is one that was told many times last summer after the fall of France and before the imminent fall of other countries changed the focus [of world events]. It still has in it those appalling elements of warning which are more impressive than ever to the dwindling democracies. It deserves a better, less confused telling. [Jay Carmody, *Washington Star,* April 29, 1941]

Director Miner was advised that if he could find a way to silence a few characters, eliminate a few others, and galvanize still others into purposeful action, he might indeed reassemble a presentable structure for Broadway. The Guild, however, decided to put off such needed carpentry "till later."

Seemingly, the Guild had learned a lesson. At the end of August, as the 1941–42 season approached, Langner wrote an editorial entitled "The Case for Revivals":

> The situation today is not unlike that which faced the Guild in its first formative years. At present, the supply of first-rate American drama has fallen off rather alarmingly. . . . One cannot blame the playwright of today for being confused and bewildered, and for wondering what is worth writing about save the war and the insane present. During the past few years, our younger playwrights have dealt increasingly with social drama and pro-war and anti-war sermons, submerging the theatre in propaganda and missionary fields which are not primarily the theatre's function.

He continued by pledging that the Guild would restore great classics to the stage from a variety of periods and countries "to encourage and inspire" younger writers by giving them, as the Guild had given their predecessors, the stimulus of goals worthy of emulation. Also,

> by reviving the finest plays available, we fulfill our responsibility to an audience satiated with the grim problems of today's headlines and seeking in the theatre some new hope, some small faith in the future as well as a welcome escape from the chaos of the moment. . . . And, of course, there is a vast young audience to whom these plays will not be revivals at all, but great plays seen for the first time. [*New York Times,* Sept. 28, 1941]

The Guild obviously cared to provide something for everyone. But would everyone be grateful? The organization elaborated on its proposed series. One of its primary aims was to bring actors back from Hollywood "who either won't gamble on a new, untried script, or are unwilling to find themselves tied to a hit for a year or more." This part of the plan had been agreed to "with the warmest enthusiasm" by a number of luminaries. According to advertisements, the projected series would include, with luck, such enticements as Shaw's *The Devil's Disciple* with Spencer Tracy (when his film commitments permitted), Ibsen's *John Gabriel Borkman,* with Charles Laughton (ditto) and Elsa Lanchester, *Alice in Wonderland,* based on the 1932 Civic Repertory Theatre's production, Andreyev's *He Who Gets Slapped,* with Raymond Massey in the title role of the clown, and *Desire Under the Elms* with Walter Huston in the part O'Neill wrote for him. Earlier,

O'Neill had written that he approved the idea of Tallulah Bankhead appearing opposite Huston in *Desire Under the Elms,* and that he thought Ingrid Bergman would make a good Anna Christie, although he did not much care for this "stale" play.

Another aim of the series called for allotting a number of $1 and fifty-cent seats to enable potential customers of modest means to see great plays done on the stage. The first part of the plan most certainly belonged to the Guild's managers, but the second part sounded like an Eva Le Gallienne brainchild, as indeed it was. The actress was quoted in the advance publicity:

> American custom dooms so many modern classics to oblivion after their short season of life on Broadway; and so many classics of an older day are revived only once in a generation that our theatre is confined almost entirely to current hits. And this, as Miss Le Gallienne put it, "is as if the Philharmonic limited its programs to music being written today." . . . The Theatre Guild, recognizing that the American theatre is the only active theatre left in the world, realizes the responsibility its producers must shoulder.

Miss Le Gallienne was named director in charge of the revivals. The first presentation was to be *Ah, Wilderness!.*

This recollection of life in 1906 opened exactly eight years from the time it had been first presented at the Guild Theatre to inaugurate the organization's sixteenth season. George M. Cohan then had been its star. On this occasion, Harry Carey of the Western movies would play small-town editor Nat Miller, William Prince, whose experience had been gained in Maurice Evans' productions, would be his impressionable son Richard, and Tom Tully, who had been last seen in the posthumous Sidney Howard play, *Madam, Will You Walk,* portrayed tippler Uncle Sid. The reviews were good, although not good "box office." Richard Lockridge thought the production captured "all the play's gentle warmth and all its quiet laughter." John Mason Brown felt it was now possible "to appreciate more fully the depth, the wisdom, and the many human excellences of Mr. O'Neill's comedy," and Brooks Atkinson wrote that although it was not quite so fine grained there was "no reason for revising the first high impression" he had received from the original presentation. Only Wolcott Gibbs sounded a disapproving note:

> I have now seen "Ah, Wilderness!" twice and read it once, and I am still obliged to confess that it affects me unfavorably. In the first place, old songs, old slang, old motoring costumes, and even old Swinburne fill me with no special nostalgia. . . . In the face of a considerable and handsome barrage of adjectives from my colleagues, I would like to add that the scene in which an embarrassed father tries to explain sex to his son strikes me as one of the leading clichés of the English-speaking theatre, that of all the stage drunkards the character known as Sid Davis is probably the least persuasive. [*New Yorker,* Oct. 11, 1941]

Gibbs' comments seemed closest to the temper of the times, unfortunately. New Yorkers would have none of the O'Neill classic, even at popular prices. It closed after twenty-nine lean performances. It was then sent the subscription route, which that year had been increased to include Toronto, Columbus, Indianapolis, and Cincinnati, with several additional cities likely to be added in the near future. The scheme for a revival series, however, was almost shelved.

Even before *Ah, Wilderness!* opened, the Guild's managers found themselves enticed once more to join forces with the Playwrights' Company, this time to co-produce another propaganda piece, Maxwell Anderson's *Candle in the Wind.* Helen Hayes was to be its star, and Alfred Lunt, on leave from *There Shall Be No Night,* its director. Jo Mielziner, who recently had provided the settings for such diversified presentations as *Watch on the Rhine, Too Many Girls, Mr. and Mrs. North,* the musical *Pal Joey,* as well as various Playwrights' Company offerings, was responsible for its mood-inducing scenery, which reminded some of the striking sets he had created for Anderson's *Winterset.* Miss Hayes' wardrobe was designed and "executed" by Valentina.

Candle in the Wind chronicles an American actress' travails in Germany and occupied France. She is in love with a hero of the Resistance, and tries vainly to secure his release from a concentration camp. After a year passes, and such speeches as, "In the history of the world there have been many wars between men and beasts, and the beasts have always lost and the men have won!" she finally succeeds in freeing her lover. Many felt it smacked of "kitsch." John O'Hara, who reviewed the play for *Newsweek,* summarized his colleagues' misgivings:

> In the past the critics have been kind and more than kind to Maxwell Anderson. He no doubt is one of our important play-

> wrights, but I think we are right—the majority of us—in declaring that "Candle in the Wind" is, well, *lacking* something. . . . I am being timidly careful of my words, and I will let it off easily by suggesting that it is a bit of a bore, that it is inept, amateurish, and unworthy of all concerned. Beyond that I will not go.

But, somehow he could not restrain himself (and after all, the precedent-setting Rodgers and Hart musical, *Pal Joey*, based on some of his *New Yorker* stories concerning the affairs of an unregenerate gigolo, had not received exceptionally kind treatment either):

> That Frenchman hero had me believing that he had been written by Colette, who, you recall, is good about women and cats but not so good with men; and that in one sentence Miss Hayes pronounced it "can't" and then "cawn't." That, of course, may have been subtle direction by Alfred Lunt, who must be all too well aware that many American actresses in real life have the same difficulty, but if Mr. Lunt did that deliberately it was the only subtlety in his directing.

Candle in the Wind played at the Shubert for about three months. Unfortunately Pearl Harbor was bombed during that period, which did not exactly improve Broadway's fortunes. The following March, while the production was on tour, critic Ashton Stevens of Chicago's *Herald-American* claimed it lacked "not only sincerity, but showmanship. It is not good anti-Nazi propaganda because it is a bad play." The only attraction it had, he felt, belonged to the "names" associated with it: Helen Hayes, Maxwell Anderson, Lunt, the Guild-Playwrights' combine. The production did include a number of interesting "firsts," however. Lotte Lenya made her initial American appearance in it playing a maid. Also, it contained prototype performances of the stereotype Gestapo man created by actors fortunate enough to have German accents, such as John Wengraf, Tonio Selwart, Knud Krueger, and others who can still be seen in late wartime movies on television. Canadian Joseph Wiseman, who had appeared briefly in Anderson's *Journey to Jerusalem* the season before, was given the role of a menacing German corporal: " Ja wohl, Herr Lieutenant, dese schwine vill pay dearly. . . !"

The Guild's managers next presented on their own a plea for preserving America's ideals and virtues in time of stress, and doubtless they hoped it would duplicate the critical acclaim accorded Kaufman and Hart's 1939–40 salute to democracy, *The American Way.* In fact, the same stars would be used for Sophie Treadwell's "comedy," *Hope for a Harvest.* This play cautioning against deterioration of the national character has to do with a worldly woman (Florence Eldridge) returning from bombed-out Paris to her ancestral home in California's San Joaquin Valley. She hopes to find all the sturdy American values intact. Instead, she finds a relative (Fredric March) living on the land, who is totally discouraged by years of depression. He no longer delves into the good earth for spiritual, as well as physical, sustenance. An Italian immigrant neighbor (Alan Reed) believes America is a great land of opportunity, and he restores her faith in her homeland. The play does contain a number of overly theatrical plot complications, which the New York critics did not find to their liking. For instance, the relative's teen-age daughter is going to have a baby, fathered by her cousin, whose mother tends to excuse his complicity. The immigrant's son (Arthur Franz) nobly offers to marry the girl because he has always loved her. The opening was scheduled for the Guild Theatre, regarded by some as an unlucky omen.

Few people may have read the drama selections of the Sunday papers on December 7, the "day of infamy"; in them Brooks Atkinson and Richard Watts, Jr. expressed the view that like most of Treadwell's work, *Hope for a Harvest* was heartfelt but lacked dramatic incisiveness (the great exception to this rule was her impressionistic *Machinal* of 1928, in which Clark Gable achieved stardom). Interestingly enough, cities outside New York liked *Hope*'s contrived story line as well as its inspirational message. It lasted only thirty-eight performances at the Guild's home, however. The Marches would fare better the following season in a play Thornton Wilder had promised, to be known as *The Skin of Our Teeth.* Again, the Guild lost out, this time to producer Michael Myerberg.

Meanwhile, *Life With Father* was enjoying an unprecedented run on Broadway. After two years, and innumerable changes in its cast, this comedy of a family ruled by a crusty tyrant still appeared as robust as ever. Most managers hoped to duplicate such a bonanza. The Guild was no exception. Having failed to recapture a longevity record with *Ah, Wilderness!*, it decided to attempt the family situation genre once more. Patterson Greene's *Papa Is All* has many of *Life With Father*'s ingredients, namely, an irascible, dominating paterfamilias whose wife and children must resort to humorous strategems to gain their rightful goals. It has a Pennsylvania Dutch milieu, and Carl Benton Reid played its Mennonite father like a "despotic, bad-tempered

Old Testament prophet." Acting honors, however, belonged to Jessie Royce Landis, Celeste Holm, and Emmett Rogers, who portrayed the rest of the badgered clan. The Guild gave them plenty of opportunity to practice the play's "quaint labyrinth of customs, vernacular and idiom." In fact, a special dialect coach traveled with the cast during its numerous stopovers before arriving in New York. The road most cordially received their endeavors. And New York was not precisely unfriendly, but there were questions raised as to whether or not fun was being made of an ethnic group. Brooks Atkinson set about to dispel this notion:

> Since the Theatre Guild is offering "Papa Is All" as pure entertainment, it naturally has to be defended. Pure entertainment is difficult to interpret correctly. . . . On opening night the Guild Theatre was filled with unaccustomed laughter, and most of the subscribers trudged home under the impression that they had had a pleasant evening. This . . . may indeed be immoral. . . . It is written without guile to be entertaining, a thing that is apparently hard to understand. [*New York Times,* Jan. 18, 1942]

While possessing a certain charm, Greene's play lacked elements that create theatrical history. It did not have the kind of appeal, for instance, that belonged to another "family comedy" which opened about the same time, the pace-setting *Junior Miss* that the team of Chodorov and Fields had fashioned from Sally Benson's sub-deb magazine stories. This guileless genre piece concerning groggy parents trying to cope with bewildering offspring would set a style to be exploited with great success in F. Hugh Herbert's *Kiss and Tell* (remember Corliss Archer?) and other similarly colored baubles. The Guild had engaged Frank Carrington and Agnes Benton, directors of New Jersey's enterprising Paper Mill Playhouse, to stage *Papa Is All;* but, even this lustre by association did not seem to materialize as hoped.

Fortunately, Eva Le Gallienne and the managers had not given up completely on the idea of a Guild revival series. Her presentation that the organization would next bring into New York was considered by many its best of the year. With a bold stroke of theatre acumen, Richard Brinsley Sheridan's farcical *The Rivals* had been converted into broad slapstick. Ingenious casting transformed Shakespeare's interpreter Walter Hampden into a hammy, blustering Sir Anthony Absolute, and maniacally energetic Bobby Clark (of burlesque's Clark and McCullough) into a skitterish, capering Acres. Regrettably, Mary

Boland, grande dame of the movies, who seemed so *right* for language-murdering Mrs. Malaprop, could not properly adjust her comedy techniques to the demands of eighteenth-century English vernacular. Advanced publicity stressed the "now and then" aspects of Sheridan's venerated revel. For instance, Mrs. John Drew had once played Mrs. Malaprop, Haila Stoddard was to impersonate Lydia Languish, a part that had once been graced by Julia Marlowe, and Joseph Jefferson had been an admirable nineteenth-century Bob Acres. Mrs. Fiske had also mounted an impressive production of the play.

The Guild's cast was competent, but it was Clark who received most of the attention as he strutted, whistled, posed, leaped, and leered through his scenes. It was said that Miss Le Gallienne's job was mainly to keep others out of his way during rehearsals. Clark modestly declared Philip Bourneuf's performance as Lucius O'Trigger was easily the equal of his own, but critics and audiences alike were not convinced. *The Rivals* only played fifty-four times at the Shubert, and then took to the road. In Chicago, a few weeks later, Mary Boland quit the cast complaining of "illness." Possibly her malaise was aggravated by the continuing acclaim accorded Clark. After all, she had her movie reputation to consider. The Guild charged she had run out on her contract, and filed suit against her. First Rosalind Ivan, then Margaret Anglin took over as Mrs. Malaprop, but something vital had gone from the production. It never lived up to its hoped-for commitments.

Two revivals did make a profound critical impression that season, however. One was Cheryl Crawford's restaging of the Guild's 1935 offering, *Porgy and Bess*, with Todd Duncan and Anne Brown in their original roles. This time most of the "operatic" elements were removed, and the presentation flowed a good deal more smoothly. Another revival was Guthrie McClintic and Katharine Cornell's near perfect re-examination of Shaw's *Candida* with Raymond Massey as Morell, Burgess Meredith as Marchbanks, Mildred Natwick as Prosperpine Garnett, and Dudley Digges as Burgess. The Guild's managers were a trifle annoyed by this glowing *succès d'estime* that had been promoted with the easy acquiescence of their "patron saint." They indicated that were it not for the fact that everyone connected with the superlative production had worked for practically nothing (the proceeds going to the American Theatre Wing War Service Fund), such an array of talent could never be assembled on a paying basis, that a "good cause" had served only to raise critical expectations completely above the realm of commercial practicality. This made some recall the Guild's equally satisfying casts that had once adorned such plays by the same author as *The Doctor's Dilemma* and *Pygmalion.*

The last Guild production of the 1941–42 season was to be Emlyn Williams' *Yesterday's Magic,* which has to do with an aged actor, now fallen on hard times, reliving his former triumphs. One cannot doubt what attracted the Guild to such a story. The piece, moreover, had played two years in London, and the managers, remembering *The Corn Is Green,* did not want another possibility by the Welsh playwright to escape them. Paul Muni was cast as the actor, and this exercise in futility opened out of town. In Washington, Nelson Bell of the *Washington Post* thought it was "warmly human, bravely gay, tender and poignant," but Jay Carmody of the *Washington Star* thought otherwise:

> In authoring this wobbly piece of sentimentality, Mr. Williams joins a long list of other distinguished dramatists who have been writing more thickly than well recently. Neither he nor Mr. Muni is able to get conviction into the story that right before your eyes a great genius is being dissolved in alcohol.

Critics in Philadelphia liked Jessica Tandy's portrayal of the actor's crippled daughter, but little else. When the production reached the Guild Theatre, the critics felt as if they had been through it all before:

> The chief thing Mr. Williams' new play makes one hope is that before long a good actor will get around to playing Lear and stop bothering about those grease-paint valentines in which an old actor is always shown as being ready to play the king in the unchallenged safety of the wings. [John Mason Brown, *New York World-Telegram,* April 15, 1942]

Expatriate English director Reginald Denham had been brought in hopefully to inject a note of authority, as had some English players, but *Yesterday's Magic* barely lasted through fifty-five subscription performances.

The tendency to follow the leader, the nostalgia, and the pessimism that had marked the Guild's twenty-fourth season almost finished it for good. It would be the last time the organization would have an active hand in producing all six of its subscription presentations, in New York as well as on the road. Not that 1941–42 had been all that outstanding elsewhere on Broadway. The country's involvement in the war undoubtedly hurt the theatre, and the demand for escapist entertainment was painfully evident. For instance, it was the time for such easily digested imports as Noel Coward's spoof of spiritualism, *Blithe Spirit,* and such neo-Victorian melodramas as Patrick Hamilton's *Angel Street,* or Thomas Job's *Uncle Harry,* in which former Guild actors Joseph Schildkraut and Eva Le Gallienne found profitable employment, after her directorial chores with the Guild had been completed. Samson Raphaelson had given the year his sophisticated *Jason,* which purportedly delved into the home life of a drama critic (although few New York critics could identify with it). There were a few new plays concerning the war, such as John Steinbeck's *The Moon Is Down,* which presumably showed what happened when the Nazis invaded a neutral country, and *Letters to Lucerne,* which believably showed what happened in a neutral country's girls' school when tyranny destroyed most of the students' homelands. It was the first year that the Pulitzer committee refused to award a prize for the drama, however, as nothing shown on Broadway had been considered worthy. Things were going badly everywhere. The Guild's situation was no exception.

The Guild, nevertheless, had taken certain steps to insure its continuance. One was that it could now boast of over 85,000 subscribers in sixteen U. S. and Canadian cities. Another was that it hoped to achieve much-needed fiscal stability from a fresh Philip Barry comedy, which was to be done as nearly like *The Philadelphia Story* as possible. Robert Sinclair was again to direct, Robert Edmond Jones to provide its exquisitely refined suburban milieu, and the glamour department, with couturière Valentina in charge, would again create a chic wardrobe for its star, Katharine Hepburn. The entire production of *Without Love* was also to be given plenty of time to ripen on the road, as had Hepburn's vehicles in the past.

The star recently had completed two acclaimed motion pictures, the Oscar-winning film of *The Philadelphia Story,* and the first of a well-received series she was to make with Spencer Tracy entitled *Woman of the Year.* The movie possibilities of *Without Love,* of course, were not to be overlooked. The new Barry comedy told the story of a couple who marry not for love but because it suits their mutual convenience (both have been married before). Naturally, deep affection develops before the final curtain, but the complications the playwright had sewn into the three-act fabric were not the sort that produce critical excitement, or record-breaking revenues, for that matter. *Variety,* with its finely honed money instincts, sensed that the box-office report from New York would be rather muffled, even as the production was doing exceptional business during its thirteen-week pre-Broadway tour:

> Barry grows concerned over the state of affairs existing between Britain and Free Ireland . . . for too long a stretch in "Without Love" . . . definitely not his metier. . . . He uses the thesis as a springboard for his play, but before the inevitable third-act analogy is drawn between the protagonist's stirring plea for a brotherhood-of-nations and his own precarious marital relationship, much of the action is permitted to sag.

The extensive tour was interrupted for the summer, during which time director Sinclair, who had joined the Armed Forces, was replaced by Arthur Hopkins, who restaged many of the scenes. It seemed all tinkering had been in vain. When *Without Love* opened at New York's St. James Theatre to begin the Guild's twenty-fifth season, many felt that they were observing a dressmaker's field day, in which a fine supporting cast and an otherwise superb production had been lavished on a piece that showed only very occasional flashes of the expected Barry wit and perceptions. Elliott Nugent and especially Audrey Christie were praised for their precise handling of their often sterile high comedy roles, and it was generally conceded that the show would run for as long as its star cared to play in it (although it contained far from her best work). It did continue at the St. James for a little more than three months (through the holidays to let the ladies see the latest Valentina fashions), and then it was sent on tour with Constance Bennett and Steve Cochran as its leads. It was later made into an undistinguished, verbose movie by Miss Hepburn and Spencer Tracy.

The Guild's next offering with which it helped celebrate its twenty-fifth anniversary appeared only three evenings after *Without Love*'s opening. The whole undertaking would best be forgotten were it not that it had a fairly large and interesting cast and set a record by being presented *fewer* times than the subscription minimum allowed (if that was possible). It was an ill-advised attempt at the fantastic adapted by movie scenarist Ketti Frings from a story by Robert Ayre titled *Mr. Sycamore,* and even the derisive Wolcott Gibbs seemed to gasp for breath as he strove to demolish it:

> "Mr. Sycamore" presents a little more than the spectacle of Stuart Erwin, of the films, standing ankle-deep in a small pile of dirt for five interminable scenes and then turning into a remark-

> ably unconvincing tree. He wants, he says, to get away from the human race (though not, I bet, as passionately as I wanted to get away from the Guild Theatre, where I found myself slowly turning into granite). There isn't much to be added to this synopsis. The other characters, ranging from Mrs. Sycamore to a batty poetess, discuss the impending miracle at considerable length and extract from it, I suppose, whatever drama, pathos, and humor lie in the author's singular hypothesis. Mr. Erwin and his associates deliver a good many thoughts about life, but probably the principal lesson to be learned at the Guild is that whimsy and fantasy are by no means the same thing, and that there is nothing like a fancy production on the stage to prove it. [*New Yorker,* Nov. 21, 1942]

The Guild Theatre went dark after nineteen performances of *Mr. Sycamore*'s unusual accomplishment.

That season Theresa Helburn had taken over most of the Guild's managerial chores. Business manager Munsell was in the Army, and Langner, remembering that he was allied with creative minds outside the theatre in his capacity as patent attorney, was spending most of his time in Washington helping organize the National Inventors' Council whose members were dedicated to uncovering technical means hopefully to diminish the potency of the Rome-Berlin-Tokyo axis. So Miss Helburn was responsible for visiting the Lunts on their Wisconsin farm to reaffirm the possibilities of an old satirical comedy by German dramatist Ludwig Fulda. She was also instrumental in persuading S. N. Behrman to adapt it as a vehicle for the pair.

Most of the Lunt-Fontanne repertory troupe had become dispersed during the extensive tour of *There Shall Be No Night.* Some had gone into the service, while others, including Sydney Greenstreet, Richard Whorf, and Thomas Gomez, had gone to Hollywood. Of the rest, Montgomery Clift would appear that season with Fredric March, Florence Eldridge, and Tallulah Bankhead in Thornton Wilder's *The Skin of Our Teeth,* an Elia Kazan-directed offering destined to bring its author his third Pulitzer prize (his others being for *Our Town* and the novel *The Bridge of San Luis Rey*).

The Pirate, as Behrman's carefully-tailored script was called, received no such critical plaudits. Sadly, the reverse was true. It concerns a noble lady who is wooed by the head of a band of itinerant acrobats. He himself is a nondescript tightrope performer, but he pretends to be a famous buccaneer for reasons of prestige. There is much swirling color visible (wartime restrictions made obtaining decorative costume materials a problem), and some light-hearted complications audible as the real pirate makes his presence felt. Lunt directed this contrived fairy tale with the help of John C. Wilson, and the Guild co-produced it with the Playwrights' Company; all managements shared about a third in the proceeds. *The Pirate,* after various experiments on the road, as was customary, was brought into the Martin Beck. While the content of the never-never-land story was thought puerile (considering the impressive talent engaged in its production), the reception given the Lunts' performance was quite up to expectations in terms of personal popularity. The pair played through the season, but the Guild's road-subscription lists were never used, for in the spring Miss Fontanne became ill, and the farce closed prematurely. Later *The Pirate* became the basis for a run-of-the-mill M-G-M musical extravaganza which starred Gene Kelly and Judy Garland. And later still a similar story was used by Samuel Goldwyn as a vehicle for Bob Hope's antics entitled *The Princess and the Pirate.* Seemingly, some film properties never die, to say nothing of gracefully fading away.

Another Playwrights' Company production enjoyed more popular and critical acceptance that season, however. This was Maxwell Anderson's salute to the citizen soldier titled *The Eve of St. Mark,* which ran for about three hundred performances. The Guild's need for worthwhile scripts, however, continued to be crucial. Eugene O'Neill had allowed the managers to see a draft of *The Iceman Cometh,* but he had taken it back for further polishing. He had also been working for many years on a cycle of nine plays that was to trace an American family through several generations, but his absorption in this task was broken by the emotional chaos created by the war, and he was determined not to let any of the cycle be produced until it could be done in one marathon stretch which he felt would take at least two whole seasons. Even had the scripts been ready, the Guild was certainly in no position to tackle such a demanding assignment. Its bank balance at the beginning of the 1942–43 season had been barely $30,000, and such misadventures as *Mr. Sycamore* had reduced its resources alarmingly. In December 1942, Stalingrad was under heavy siege. The Guild felt it had enough left for one more propaganda stroke, this time to be pro-Russian. The war had warped any number of critical intuitions.

Clifford Odets, who the previous December had provided Broadway with *Clash By Night* in which Tallulah Bankhead portrayed a bourgeoise Jewish femme fatale, now had prepared an adaptation of Konstantin Simonov's *The Russian People,* which reportedly had been inspirationally performed by over two hundred theatrical companies attached to the Red Army. The Guild asked former Group director Harold Clurman to direct this opus and former Group designer Boris Aronson to provide its settings. The episodic piece had its American premiere at the National Theatre in Washington on December 14, 1942, and it was attended by Soviet Ambassador Litvinov as well as other governmental dignitaries. The capital's critical consensus, unfortunately, found it to be a bit naive, and disjointed. Two weeks later *The Russian People* moved into the Guild's home theatre. Previously, New York had been receptive to a play of similar persuasion, but *Counter Attack* had been blessed with a unified story line. The critics all were convinced *The Russian People*'s heart was in the right place; they just complained of its discursiveness, and of too many unrelated characters wandering throughout. Lewis Nichols declared in the *New York Times* that the Guild had provided it with an excellent production, "But the fact remains that, barring a few scenes, the play does not rise to the heights of the spirit of the people it represents, and almost all of its earlier passages are confused and sluggish." *The Russian People* lasted but thirty-nine performances.

As *The Russian People* limped along, the Guild seemed to go into an eclipse. Actually, the time was being used to prepare, as frugally as possible, what came to be known along Broadway as "Helburn's folly." The vicissitudes leading to the Guild's production of *Oklahoma!* have already been reported in voluminous detail: how for years Theresa Helburn and others had been searching for the right story to turn into a new sort of musical play; how she had considered longingly *Lysistrata, Marco Millions,* and *Reunion in Vienna;* how she persuaded composer Richard Rodgers to work with a new collaborator (because of Lorenz Hart's declining health), and how he teamed with Oscar Hammerstein II to prepare without compensation a unique amalgam from the modestly successful 1931 Guild undertaking, Lynn Riggs' *Green Grow the Lilacs;* how, because of the organization's financial straits, she had been forced to beg outside capital to produce the new venture (usually denied because Hammerstein had been previously associated with ten failures in a row); how the doughty little lady asked Agnes de Mille of the classical Ballet Russe, which had just performed her *Rodeo* using Aaron Copland's music, to do a new type of choreography (for Broadway) for this new type of play with fully integrated score; how Lemuel Ayres, who had worked on *The Pirate,* had to improvise many of its settings to stay within the limitations of its strict budget, and how Miles White, who had created sumptuous costumes for the Lunts' show, had been happier with his new assignment because gingham was much easier come by that season than were laces and taffetas; how director Rouben Mamoulian, a fugitive from Hollywood, was luckily "at liberty"; how established musical comedy stars, such as Mary Martin and Wilbur Evans, turned down roles in the seemingly doomed undertaking (successful musicals did not have murders in their second acts)—even Shirley Temple was advised against participating by her parents because the leading role seemed to be "too mature" for the former child actress' tender talents; how ultimately the casting had to be done primarily from a list of "unknowns," including Alfred Drake, who had been a supporting player in *Yesterday's Magic*, Joseph Buloff, who was remembered from *To Quito and Back*, and Celeste Holm, who had portrayed the harried daughter in *Papa Is All;* how the out-of-town tryout notices of *Away We Go* (earlier titles: *Yes-sirree* and *Swing Your Lady*) were a good deal less than enthusiastic. One description of the New Haven premiere read:

> Not always interesting. . . . As for the dancing, the modernists are having their day . . . . To enjoy conservative music, the dance moderne, and to make no demands for the quip brand of humor is essential for its appreciation. [M. Oakley Christoph, *Hartford Courant*, March 12, 1943]

Armina Marshall, a native Oklahoman, had been helping Theresa Helburn with the preparations, and suggested that the name be changed to "Cherokee Strip," but this was vetoed because it brought to mind a burlesque routine. A few days later in Boston, a reviewer for the *Christian Science Monitor* remembered that the previous Guild musical, *Parade*, had leaned well toward the left. He thought that the new offering indicated that the organization had somehow "righted" itself:

> . . . the story supplies folksy romance with . . . tunes in folk style from the fecund pen of Richard Rodgers. At present, the piece is too long for its matter, and contains too much rural humor and homely sentiment. Mr. Rodgers has been careful to make his songs simple . . . in keeping with the time and place, but unfortunately their simplicity, in common or in waltz time, becomes tiresome as the first scene drags on . . . . a less faithful treatment of the disposition of Jud would make a better prelude to the departure of the bridal couple.

Variety found it a "pretty-ditty, fancy-prancing combo . . . with better than average tunes and terps," but seemed bewildered as to why the girls did not appear for fully thirty-five minutes. The show's title was changed again, with an exclamation point inserted after the home state's name, and it moved to New York. There it stayed for well over five years. National companies were formed and they criss-crossed the land. It played in England, setting an all-time record at London's Drury Lane Theatre with 1,548 performances. It was also done in Germany, South Africa, Sweden, Denmark, Australia, France, Italy, for American troops stationed abroad, and who knows where else. When it celebrated its tenth birthday in Washington, D. C., the lucky few who had invested $1,500 had been paid back in excess of $50,000. This last became a dominant concern in future thinking.

As noted, there are numerous accounts concerning the dismal prophecies ("Instead of a chorus line, the thing starts off with this fella singing about what kind of a morning it is!") and the ultimate accolades accorded *Oklahoma!*. Two of the better ones are contained in Helburn's *A Wayward Quest* and Helene Hanff's *Underfoot in Show Business,* but there are many others.

Irving Berlin's famous song warns that there is no business like show business. How true. Most businesses base their predictions, their hopes, on the "average" year, the "average" sale, the "average" product. They tend to discount great peaks or dips in their production quotas or their inventories. They look rather at the "norm" for a true indication of their progress. Theatrical enterprise is very different. It always looks toward, and counts on, the big critical success, the great personal triumph, the record-breaking performance. Without these it languishes and dies. It thrives on the excitement caused by the exceptional. Modest achievements or "pretty good" reactions devitalize the theatre. Block-busting accomplishment is what invigorates a theatrical organization, encourages its personnel toward better efforts, adds purpose to its direction. A philosophy results which is based on the fantastic hit—or the resounding flop. Unlike other businesses, theatrical commerce is a series of incredible gambles, with the odds heavily favoring failure, even annihilation. Nothing substantial can be built on a "safe middle ground," because there is no such thing. "Not too bad" is just not good enough. The uninvolved observer is forever amazed at the personal courage, the eternal optimism, and the tenacious devotion the professional theatre inspires with its demonstrable record of forlorn hopes, shattered dreams, and enervating bankruptcy.

A revivifying miracle for the Guild occurred with *Oklahoma!*. Theatregoers again experienced the exhilaration of the unexpected, as they had in the past with *Liliom, He Who Gets Slapped, The Doctor's Dilemma, Strange Interlude,* and other pace-setting Guild triumphs. *Oklahoma!* not only supplied energy for survival to the benumbed organism, but gave the whole American theatre scene a substantial lift. It caused the then predictable giddy musical book to achieve greater dimension and purpose, a direction later followed so satisfactorily by Lerner and Lowe, Leonard Bernstein, Frank Loesser, and others. Every "serious play with integrated score" for the next quarter century reflected qualities of *Oklahoma!*.

But, what of the legitimate drama, supposedly the Guild's first and foremost concern? Was it affected adversely by the acclaim *Oklahoma!* received? Yes and no. Without *Oklahoma!*, Lawrence Langner and Theresa Helburn could scarcely have mustered sufficient resources to launch a new Guild season. The impetus of *Oklahoma!* allowed them next to provide American audiences with Margaret Webster's provocative interpretation of *Othello* featuring Paul Robeson, José Ferrer, and Uta Hagen. Undoubtedly the favorable commercial indications of this critically debated production persuaded a number of entrepreneurs, including Langner, that Shakespearean tragedy could be done advantageously using actors whose speech intonations were American rather than British. Undoubtedly this had direct bearing on the founding of the American Shakespeare Festival at Stratford, Connecticut, in the early 1950s, which led to the formation of similar festivals from Oregon to Ontario to Ohio. Conceivably, all of America's culture conscious summers of classical drama stem from the vitality generated by *Oklahoma!*. This is no farfetched theory. Such chain reactions stemming from a successful theatrical enterprise are quite common in our theatre's history; witness the proliferation of touring repertory companies before and after the Civil War, the Klaw-Erlanger-Shubert syndrome, the "little theatre" movement, the formation of groups espousing this or that presentational method, the spread of off- and off-off-Broadway producing ventures, and similar wide-ranging phenomena.

Following *Othello,* the Guild continued to offer plays, naturally, but the output was uneven, often sporting an ornate façade to cover philosophic hollowness. After a valiant attempt to duplicate *Oklahoma!* with Walter Kerr's dramatic setting for authentic American folk music, *Sing Out, Sweet Land!*, the organization's next substantial hit came from another Rodgers and Hammerstein musical based on an established work. *Carousel,* which transplanted Molnar's *Liliom* to Maine's rocky soil, employed most of the creative talents from *Oklahoma!*, including Mamoulian, Agnes de Mille, and Miles White; it also turned out to be a stunning transmutation. *Carousel*, however, caused many to wonder about this quite uncharacteristic deployment of the Guild's energies. Was the organization going to continue as handmaiden to the better drama? If not, what then? The answer, even to the staunchest Guild supporter, was obvious, and a bit saddening.

In 1944, the Guild made a long-awaited decision to rid itself of its burdensome playhouse, and the offices were moved to 23 West 53rd Street. Their present location is at 226 West 47th Street, where the walls are lined with placards and other memorabilia recalling the triumphs of yesteryear.

From 1945 to 1953, under the supervision of Armina Marshall and others, the "Theatre Guild of the Air" performed what was in effect a forty-week season, using many of the organization's stage presentations skillfully adapted to the requirements of radio, usually replete with outstanding casts. From 1953 to 1963, the Guild created an important contribution to what is now recognized as television drama's golden age with its television series, "The United States Steel Hour."

The Guild's original Board of Managers are gone, departed for Hamlet's "undiscovered country." Helen Westley, the first to leave, died in 1949; Simonson, the last, died in 1967. They left a lasting legacy, and much to ponder. One wishes their youthful shades were around today to launch with zest and imagination new battles in defense of decent theatre. One questions if the redoubtable six upon reflection would consider it their first duty to cultivate out-of-town subscription lists for offering the mediocrities of others, if they would deny American creativity by importing productions from the London stage intact, or if they would feel that much can be gained artistically by dabbling in debasing motion-picture manipulations. Instead, one hopes, they would feel chastened enough to start again by hiring a modest work arena in some metropolitan area where they would set about assembling a company of actors and directors who would not consider flight to the mass media necessarily the best way to advance careers. This ensemble would encourage as many stimulating playwrights as possible by performing their works with discernment and taste, free from commercial pressures and "something for everyone" considerations. (Besides, the record shows that the American audiences are highly fragmented, and what pleases one group certainly will not please another; it is useless trying to find a formula to serve everyone, for none exists.) The only true criteria is *excellence*, and if excellence is not available, then one should wait for it, or, better yet, seek it out.

But what of finances? How should this ideal company deal with the professional theatre's most insidious problem, excessive costs? Would it ask for minimum subsidies, divorced from institutional strings or political patronage, a modest investment in a continuing culture to be expected so long as integrity and creativity and growth are indicated? Or, would it insist that everything be done on a cooperative basis, with everyone sharing the work and the costs as well as the proceeds? From the Guild's experience, one realizes that the worthiest achievements in the theatre seldom flourish at the box office. Nevertheless, superiority invariably pays handsome dividends, in experience, prestige, and pride of accomplishment, if nothing else.

But, haven't these methods of organization been tried in the past? Aren't they being employed right now by university theatres, non-profit regional theatres, off-off-Broadway experimental theatres, and the like? Yes, and they must be tried again and again, *if* the United States is to have a theatre worthy of the name.

APPENDIXES

THEATRE GUILD PRODUCTIONS THROUGH *OKLAHOMA!*

FIRST SEASON

		Opened
The Bonds of Interest	Jacinto Benavente	April 19, 1919
John Ferguson	St. John Ervine	May 12, 1919

SECOND SEASON

The Faithful	John Masefield	Oct. 13, 1919
The Rise of Silas Lapham	Lillian Sabine	Nov. 25, 1919
Power of Darkness	Leo Tolstoy	Jan. 19, 1920
Jane Clegg	St. John Ervine	Feb. 23, 1920
The Dance of Death	August Strindberg	May 9, 1920

THIRD SEASON

The Treasure	David Pinski	Oct. 4, 1920
Heartbreak House	Bernard Shaw	Nov. 10, 1920
John Hawthorne	David Liebovitz	Jan. 23, 1921
Mr. Pim Passes By	A. A. Milne	Feb. 28, 1921
Liliom	Ferenc Molnar	April 20, 1921
The Cloister	Emile Verhaeren	June 5, 1921

FOURTH SEASON

Ambush	Arthur Richman	Oct. 10, 1921
The Wife With a Smile	Denys Amiel and André Obey	Nov. 28, 1921
Bourbouroche	Georges Courteline	Nov. 28, 1921
He Who Gets Slapped	Leonid Andreyev	Jan. 9, 1922
Back to Methuselah	Bernard Shaw	Feb. 27, 1922
What the Public Wants	Arnold Bennett	May 1, 1922
From Morn to Midnight	Georg Kaiser	May 21, 1922

FIFTH SEASON

R. U. R.	Karel Capek	Oct. 9, 1922
The Lucky One	A. A. Milne	Nov. 20, 1922
The Tidings Brought to Mary	Paul Claudel	Dec. 25, 1922

Peer Gynt	Henrik Ibsen	Feb. 5, 1923
The Adding Machine	Elmer L. Rice	March 18, 1923
The Devil's Disciple	Bernard Shaw	April 23, 1923

SIXTH SEASON

Windows	John Galsworthy	Oct. 8, 1923
The Failures	H. R. Lenormand	Nov. 19, 1923
The Race With the Shadow	Wilhelm von Scholz	Dec. 14, 1923
Saint Joan	Bernard Shaw	Dec. 28, 1923
Fata Morgana	Ernest Vajda	March 3, 1924
Man and the Masses	Ernst Toller	April 14, 1924

SEVENTH SEASON

The Guardsman	Ferenc Molnar	Oct. 12, 1924
They Knew What They Wanted	Sidney Howard	Nov. 24, 1924
Processional	John Howard Lawson	Jan. 12, 1925
Ariadne	A. A. Milne	Feb. 23, 1925
Caesar and Cleopatra	Bernard Shaw	April 13, 1925
The Garrick Gaieties	Richard Rodgers and Lorenz Hart	June 8, 1925

EIGHTH SEASON

Arms and the Man	Bernard Shaw	Sept. 14, 1925
The Glass Slipper	Ferenc Molnar	Oct. 19, 1925
The Man of Destiny	Bernard Shaw	Nov. 23, 1925
Androcles and the Lion	Bernard Shaw	
Merchants of Glory	Marcel Pagnol and Paul Nivoix	Dec. 14, 1925
Goat Song	Franz Werfel	Jan. 25, 1926
The Chief Thing	Nicholas Evreinov	March 22, 1926
At Mrs. Beam's	C. K. Monro	April 26, 1926
The Garrick Gaieties	Richard Rodgers and Lorenz Hart	May 10, 1926

NINTH SEASON

Juarez and Maximilian	Franz Werfel	Oct. 11, 1926
Pygmalion	Bernard Shaw	Nov. 15, 1926
Ned McCobb's Daughter	Sidney Howard	Nov. 22, 1926
The Silver Cord	Sidney Howard	Dec. 20, 1926
The Brothers Karamazov	Jacques Copeau, based on Dostoevsky's novel	Jan. 3, 1927

Right You Are If You Think You Are	Luigi Pirandello	March 2, 1927
The Second Man	S. N. Behrman	April 11, 1927

TENTH SEASON

Porgy	Du Bose and Dorothy Heyward	Oct. 11, 1927
The Doctor's Dilemma	Bernard Shaw	Nov. 21, 1927
Marco Millions	Eugene O'Neill	Jan. 9, 1928
Strange Interlude	Eugene O'Neill	Jan. 23, 1928
Volpone	Stefan Zweig's version of Ben Jonson's play	April 9, 1928

Complete cast listings of the above productions appear in Walter Prichard Eaton's *The First Ten Years.*

ELEVENTH SEASON

GOETHE'S FAUST (PART I)

ENGLISH VERSION BY GRAHAM AND TRISTAN RAWSON
PRODUCED BY FRIEDRICH HOLL
Settings and costumes by Lee Simonson
Music by Wolfgang Zeller
Dances arranged by Bernard Day

CAST

Raphael .... Martin Wolfson
Gabriel .... Douglass Montgomery
Michael .... Edward Hogan
The Voice .... Maurice Cass
Mephistopheles .... Dudley Digges
Faust .... George Gaul
Wagner .... Walter Vonnegut
Voice of the Earth Spirit .... Martin Wolfson
A Young Peasant .... Edward Hogan
An Old Peasant .... William T. Hays
A Student .... William Challee
Siebel .... Stanley G. Wood
Frosch .... Edward Hogan
Brander .... Martin Wolfson
Altmeyer .... Herbert J. Biberman
She-Ape .... Christine Putnam
He-Ape .... Eric Linden
The Witch .... Gale Sondergaard
Margaret .... Helen Chandler
Martha .... Helen Westley
Valentine .... Douglass Montgomery
Voice of the Ignis Fatuus .... Rita Vale
Lilith .... Rita Vale

Peasants, Burghers, Witches, Singers, Dancers, etc.:
Maxine Arnolde, Adelaide George, Marcella Henry, Helen Ann Hughes, Elza Moses, Helen Steers, Frances Stock, Kathleen Sternberg, Ruth Steward, Mary Ellen Vorse, Kitty Wilson, Esther Rosoff, Avis Phillips, Martha Gale, Anatole Bendukov, Bernard F. Day, George W. Ballard, Leonard Perry, Maurice Soble, Alan Wallace.

Stage Manager: George Greenberg
Ass't Stage Managers: Herbert J. Biberman, Jack Coombs, and Agnew T. Horine

Guild Theatre, October 8, 1928
(48 PERFORMANCES)

MAJOR BARBARA

BERNARD SHAW
DIRECTED BY PHILIP MOELLER
Designed by Redington Sharpe

CAST

Stephen Undershaft	Maurice Wells
Lady Britomart Undershaft	Helen Westley
Morrison	Isidore Marcil
Barbara Undershaft	Winifred Lenihan
Sarah Undershaft	Gale Sondergaard
Adolphus Cusins	Elliot Cabot
Charles Lomax	Charles Courtneidge
Andrew Undershaft	Dudley Digges
Rummy Mitchens	Alice Cooper Cliffe
Snobby Price	Edgar Kent
Peter Shirley	A. P. Kaye
Bill Walker	Percy Waram
Mrs. Baines	Edythe Tressider
Bilton	Ralph Sumpter

Stage Manager: Herbert J. Biberman
Ass't Stage Managers: Jack Coombs and Ralph Sumpter

Guild Theatre, November 20, 1928
(88 PERFORMANCES)

WINGS OVER EUROPE

ROBERT NICHOLS AND MAURICE BROWNE
DIRECTED BY ROUBEN MAMOULIAN
Setting by Raymond Sovey

CAST

Members of the Cabinet Committee:
Walter Grantley, Prime Minister .... Ernest Lawford
Lord Sunningdale, Lord Privy Seal .... John Dunn
Lord Dedham, Lord High Chancellor .... Frank Elliott
Matthew Grindle, Chancellor of the Exchequer ...... Joseph Kilgour
Humphrey Haliburton, Secretary of State
for Home Affairs .... Nicholas Joy
Evelyn Arthur, Secretary of State
for Foreign Affairs .... Frank Conroy
Richard Stapp, Secretary of State for War .... Hugh Buckler
Lord Cossington, Secretary of State
for the Dominions .... Thomas A. Braidon
Esme Falkiner, Secretary of State for the Air ...... Charles Francis
Sir Romilly Blount, First Lord of the Admiralty ..... Grant Stewart
Lord Vivian Vere,
President of the Board of Education .... Robert Rendel
St. John Pascoe, Attorney General .... George Graham
H. G. Dunne, First Commissioner of Works ...... Gordon Richards
Francis Lightfoot .... Alexander Kirkland
Sir Berkeley Rummel .... Edward Lester
Sir Henry Hand .... A. P. Kaye
Hart-Plimsoll .... Wheeler Dryden
Taggert .... Charles Cardon
Two Cabinet Messengers .... Lionel Bevans
Walter Scott

Stage Manager: Lionel Bevans
Ass't Stage Manager: Jack Coombs

Martin Beck Theatre, December 10, 1928
(91 PERFORMANCES)

CAPRICE

SIL-VARA

ADAPTED AND STAGED BY PHILIP MOELLER

Settings by Aline Bernstein

CAST

Von Echardt .... Alfred Lunt
A Delicate Lady .... Geneva Harrison
Minna .... Carolina Newcomb
The Doctor .... Ernest Cossart
Clerk .... Leonard Loan
Amalia .... Lily Cahill
Ilsa Von Ilsen .... Lynn Fontanne
Robert .... Douglass Montgomery

Stage Manager: Leonard Loan
Ass't Stage Manager: Geneva Harrison

Hollis St. Theatre, Boston, December 17, 1928

Guild Theatre, December 31, 1928

(186 PERFORMANCES)

DYNAMO

EUGENE O'NEILL

STAGED BY PHILIP MOELLER

Settings by Lee Simonson

CAST

Hutchins Light .... George Gaul
Amelia Light .... Helen Westley
Reuben Light .... Glenn Anders
Ramsey Fife .... Dudley Digges
May Fife .... Catherine Calhoun-Doucet
Ada Fife .... Claudette Colbert
Jennings .... Ross Forrester
Rocco .... Edgar Kent

Stage Manager: Herbert J. Biberman
Ass't Stage Managers: George Freedley, Rupert Carr

Martin Beck Theatre, February 11, 1929

(50 PERFORMANCES)

MAN'S ESTATE

BEATRICE BLACKMAR AND BRUCE GOULD
STAGED BY DUDLEY DIGGES
Settings by Cleon Throckmorton
CAST

Joseph Jordan, Jerry's uncle .... Edward Favor
William P. Jordan, the Father .... Dudley Digges
Caroline Jordan, Jerry's aunt .... Florence Gerald
Minnie Jordan, the Mother .... Elizabeth Patterson
Jerry Jordan, the Son .... Earle Larimore
Emily Bender, their daughter .... Armina Marshall
Dr. Frank Bender, their son-in-law .... Edward Pawley
Sesaly Blaine, a Guest .... Margalo Gillmore
Rev. Dr. Eustace Potter .... Louis Veda
Cousin Grace .... Maria Ziccardi

Stage Manager: Albert Cowles
Ass't Stage Manager: Frances Herriott

Biltmore Theatre, April 1, 1929
(48 PERFORMANCES)

THE CAMEL THROUGH THE NEEDLE'S EYE

FRANTISEK LANGER
ADAPTED AND STAGED BY PHILIP MOELLER
Settings by Lee Simonson
CAST

Mrs. Pesta .... Helen Westley
Pesta .... Henry Travers
Street Urchin .... Norman Williams
Susi .... Miriam Hopkins
Counselor Andreja .... Joseph Kilgour
Director Bezchyba .... Morris Carnovsky
Marta Bojok .... Catherine Calhoun-Doucet
Alik Vilim .... Elliot Cabot
Servant .... Percy Waram
Lilli Bojok .... Mary Kennedy
Joseph Vilim .... Claude Rains
A Medical Student .... George Freedley
Servant Girl .... Rose Burdick

Stage Manager: Herbert Biberman
Ass't Stage Managers: Walter Scott and George Freedley

Martin Beck Theatre, April 15, 1929
(196 PERFORMANCES)

TWELFTH SEASON

KARL AND ANNA

LEONHARD FRANK
TRANSLATED BY RUTH LANGNER
DIRECTED BY PHILIP MOELLER
Designed by Jo Mielziner

CAST

A Guard	Charles C. Leatherbee
Karl	Otto Kruger
Richard	Frank Conroy
First Prisoner	Claude Rains
Second Prisoner	Philip Leigh
Supervisor	Herbert J. Biberman
Another Guard	Robert Norton
Marie	Ruth Hammond
Anna	Alice Brady
Marie's sister	Gale Sondergaard
The Husband	Larry Fletcher
People in the surrounding action	Lionel Stander
	Helen Gunther
	Laura Straub

Stage Manager: Herbert J. Biberman
Ass't Stage Managers: George Freedley, Charles Leatherbee

Guild Theatre, October 7, 1929
(49 PERFORMANCES)

THE GAME OF LOVE AND DEATH

ROMAIN ROLLAND

TRANSLATED BY ELEANOR STIMSON BROOKS

DIRECTED BY ROUBEN MAMOULIAN

Settings and costumes designed by Aline Bernstein

CAST

Sophie de Courvoisier .... Alice Brady
Claude Vallée .... Otto Kruger
Jérôme de Courvoisier .... Frank Conroy
Lazare Carnot .... Claude Rains
Denis Bayot .... Edward Rigley
Lodoiska Cerizier .... Laura Straub
Chloris Soucy .... Anita Fugazy
Crapart .... Charles Henderson
Horace Bouchet .... Allan Willey
Soldiers and Citizens ....

Robert Norton, William Earle, Lizbeth Kennedy, Katherine Randolph, Kitty Wilson, Clinton Corwin, Frank DeSilva, Paul Farber, Henry Fonda, Leopold Gutierrez, Daniel Joseph, Charles C. Leatherbee, P. Lapouchin, Hughie Mack, Lionel Stander, Mike Wagman, J. E. Whiffen.

Stage Manager: Cheryl Crawford
Ass't Stage Managers: George Freedley, Charles Leatherbee

Guild Theatre, November 25, 1929
(moved to Biltmore Theatre, December 23, 1929)
(48 PERFORMANCES)

RED RUST

V. KIRCHON AND A. OUSPENSKY

TRANSLATED FROM THE RUSSIAN BY VIRGINIA AND FRANK VERNON

DIRECTED BY HERBERT J. BIBERMAN

Scenery built and painted by Cleon Throckmorton

CAST

Bezborodov .... Lionel Stander
Lutikov .... George Tobias
Andrei .... Harry M. Cooke
Petrossian .... Elliot Sullivan
Pimples .... Lee Strasberg
Besseda .... Albert Angell
Terekhine .... Herbert J. Biberman
Voznesienski .... Spencer Kimbell
Piotr .... Luther Adler
Supervisor .... Charles Peyton
Vassili .... Theodore Fetter
Nina .... Gale Sondergaard
Fenia .... Florence House
Varvara .... Virginia Berry
Lenov .... William Challee
Lisa .... Ruth Nelson
Fedor .... Franchot Tone
Olga .... Ruth Chorpenning
First Old Woman .... Helen Plant
Second Old Woman .... Lizzie Rechelle
1st Passerby .... Wells Richardson
2nd Passerby .... Charles Peyton
3rd Passerby .... Frank Verigun
Youth .... Joseph Kleima
Beggar .... Thomas Fisher
Peddler .... George Shoemaker
Mania .... Eunice Stoddard
Loukitch .... Curtis Arnall
Secretary .... Charles Peyton
Zaviatov .... Harry Wilson
Nikolai .... Boris Korlin

Students and Laborers:

Leo Carroll, Julian Garfield, M. Fishman, Lawrence Hart, Frank Stringfellow, George Bratt, Bruce Cameron, Robert Caillé, Jack Elder, Bert Stuart, Ackland Powell, Rose Keane.

Stage Manager: Louis M. Simon
Ass't Stage Manager: Elizabeth Shaffer
Production Committee: Herbert Biberman, Cheryl Crawford, Harold Clurman

Martin Beck Theatre, December 17, 1929

(65 PERFORMANCES)

METEOR

S. N. BEHRMAN

Staged by Philip Moeller

Settings by Raymond Sovey

CAST

Ann Carr .... Lynn Fontanne
Douglas Carr .... Alexander Kirkland
Phyllis Pennell .... Shirley O'Hara
Sherman Maxwell .... Martin Berkeley
Curtis Maxwell .... Lawrence Leslie
Dr. Avery .... Edward Emery
Raphael Lord .... Alfred Lunt
Mullin .... Leonard Loan
A Butler .... Charles McClelland

Hollis St. Theatre, Boston, December 2, 1929

Guild Theatre, December 23, 1929

(92 PERFORMANCES)

THE APPLE CART

(A Political Extravaganza in Two Acts and an Interlude)

BERNARD SHAW

Staged by Philip Moeller

Settings by Lee Simonson

CAST

Pamphilius } Private Secretaries to King ...... { Thomas A. Braidon
Sempronius } { Rex O'Malley
Boanerges, President of Board of Trade .... Ernest Cossart
Magnus, the King .... Tom Powers
Alice, the Princess Royal .... Audrey Ridgewell
Proteus, Prime Minister .... Claude Rains
Nicobar, Foreign Secretary .... Morris Carnovsky
(Edgar Kent)
Crassus, Colonial Secretary .... George Graham
Pliney, Chancellor of the Exchequer .... John Dunn
Balbus, Home Secretary .... William H. Sams
Lysistrata, Powermistress-General .... Helen Westley
Amanda, Postmistress-General .... Eva Leonard-Boyne
Orinthia .... Violet Kemble-Cooper
The Queen .... Marjorie Marquis
Mr. Vanhattan, the American Ambassador ...... Frederick Truesdell

Stage Manager: Ferdinand Hast

Ass't Stage Manager: George Coulouris

Ford's Theatre, Baltimore, February 17, 1930

Martin Beck Theatre, February 24, 1930

(88 PERFORMANCES)

A MONTH IN THE COUNTRY

A Comedy in Four Acts
IVAN TURGENEV
TRANSLATED BY M. S. MANDELL
ACTING VERSION BY ROUBEN MAMOULIAN
PRODUCED UNDER THE DIRECTION OF MR. MAMOULIAN
Settings and costumes by M. S. Dobuzinsky
Executed by Raymond Sovey

CAST

Herr Shaaf .... Charles Kraus
Anna Semenova (Islaev's mother) .... Minna Phillips
Natalia Petrovna (Islaev's wife) .... Alla Nazimova
Mikhail Aleksandrovich Rakitin .... Elliot Cabot
Lizaveta Bogdanovna (a companion) .... Eda Heinemann
Kolia (Islaev's son) .... Eddie Wragge
Aleksei Nikolaevich Bieliaev (Kolia's tutor) ..... Alexander Kirkland
Matviei (a servant) .... Louis Veda
Ignati Ilich Spigelski (a doctor) .... Dudley Digges
Viera Aleksandrovna (Islaev's ward) .... Eunice Stoddard
Arkadi Sergieich Islaev (a landowner) .... Douglas Drumbrille
Katia (a maid servant) .... Hortense Alden
(later Katharine Hepburn)
Afanasi Ivanych Bolshintsov ....Henry Travers

Stage Manager: Earl Redding

National Theatre, Washington, D. C., March 11, 1930
Guild Theatre, March 17, 1930
(71 PERFORMANCES)

HOTEL UNIVERSE

Philip Barry

DIRECTED BY PHILIP MOELLER

Setting by Lee Simonson

CAST

Ann Field .... Katherine Alexander
Lily Malone .... Ruth Gordon
Pat Farley .... Glenn Anders
Tom Ames .... Franchot Tone
Hope Ames .... Phyllis Povah
Norman Rose .... Earle Larimore
Alice Kendall .... Ruthelma Stevens
Felix .... Gustave Rolland
Stephen Field .... Morris Carnovsky

Stage Manager: Leonard Loan
Ass't Stage Manager: Philip Foster

Broad Street Theatre, Newark, N. J., March 31, 1930
Erlanger Theatre, Buffalo, N. Y., April 7, 1930
Martin Beck Theatre, April 14, 1930
(81 PERFORMANCES)

THE GARRICK GAIETIES (3RD EDITION)

DIRECTED BY PHILIP LOEB

Settings by Kate Drain Lawson

Costumes by Kate Drain Lawson and Louis M. Simon

Orchestra directed by Tom Jones

Dances arranged by Olin Howland, assisted by Stella Block

Sketches by Sally Humason, Gretchen Damrosch Finletter, Leo Poldine, Albert Carroll, Benjamin M. Kaye, Newman Levy, Ronald Jeans, Landon Herrick, Louis M. Simon, Sterling Holloway

Music by Richard Meyers, Charles M. Schwab, Willard Robinson, Everett Miller, Vernon Duke, Thomas McKnight, Kay Swift, Marc Blitzstein, Ned Lehak, Peter Nolan, Harold Goldman

Lyrics by Eddie Eliscu, Henry Myers, John Mercer, E. Y. Harburg, Ira Gershwin, Paul James, Allen Boretz, Josiah Titzell

CAST

Albert Carroll, Edith Meiser, Philip Loeb, Sterling Holloway, Nan Blackstone, Ruth Chorpenning, Hildegarde Halliday, William Tannen, Roger Sterns, James Norris, Otto Hulett, Cynthia Rogers, Thelma Tipson, Edith Sheldon, Imogene Coca, Donald Stewart, Ray Heatherton, Theodore Fetter, Edwin Gilcher, Evelyn LaTour

(Fall, 1930)

Additional material by Richard Rodgers, Lorenz Hart, Herbert Fields

CAST

Philip Loeb, Albert Carroll, Doris Vinton, Sterling Holloway, Katherine Carrington, Neal Caldwell, Otto Hulett, Edgar Stehli, William Holbrook, Neila Goodelle, Donald Burr, Imogene Coca, James Norris, Rosalind Russell, Ruth Chorpenning, Bobby Roberts

Guild Theatre, June 4, 1930

THIRTEENTH SEASON

ROAR CHINA

A play in two acts and nine scenes
S. M. Tretyakov
Translated by Ruth Langner from the German version of Leo Lania
Directed by Herbert J. Biberman
Settings and costumes by Lee Simonson

CAST

Coolie .... Y. W. Woo
Wang Fu, a commission man .... Seungman Ahn
Li Tai, a merchant .... Von Wang
Hall, an American exporter .... William Gargan
Burns, a reporter .... Harry Cooke
Ama, a procuress .... Grace Chee
Mrs. Tourist .... Eva Condon
Mr. Tourist .... Erskine Sanford
Chang, a boatman .... H. L. Donsu
Pei Fu, an old boatman .... Lee Tung-Foo
A Fo, the eldest of the boatman's guild .... Frank Sinne
Ho Sung, a boatman .... Paul Fung
1st Boatman .... Ivan Achong
2nd Boatman .... H. T. Tsiang
3rd Boatman .... Henry Leong
4th Boatman .... Richard Wang
Bonze .... Arthur Leon
Low Ba, the police captain .... Charlie Fang
Mate of H. M. S. Europa .... Edward Trevor
Mrs. Smith .... Winifred Hanley
Cordelia, her daughter .... Sanchia Robertson
Lieutenant Cooper .... Eric Blore
Mr. Smith .... Reynolds Denniston
Captain of H. M. S. Europa .... Edward Cooper
Chinese boy .... Oeter Kwan
Johnson, a lieutenant .... Charles Cardon
Ist policeman .... James Lee
Ho Chin Ling, Ho Sung's wife .... Irene Wong
Ho San San, her daughter .... Elsie Wu
The Missionary .... Edwin Brandt
Mme. De Brochell .... Adrienne Lachamp

M. De Brochell .... Athy Dmitrieff
The Daoyin of the city of Wan Hsien .... Sam Kim
A student interpreter for the Daoyin .... Y. Y. Hsu
Chang Yuen, Chang's wife .... Helen Kimm
Ho Sung's son .... James Yoon
A Fo's daughter .... Siang Pan
Chang's son .... Dorothy Woo

Chinese coolies, policemen and boatmen:

Harry Yee, Choy Mok, Julius Yee, Paul Tang, Lo Tai, Sic Lee, Moon Lyo, Paul Lee, James Lee, Jhu Fung, Chok Mok, Low Fid, Thomas Wing, Low Hoo, Low Sing, B. H. Gee, M. Chang, Lee Wah, T. F. Lee, Yong Kim, Raymond Sumpong, Nick Curing, Chang Ting, Kong Sing, Raymond Quins, Jack Oda, Leo S. Lee, Jack Chow, F. C. Low, Yung Sin, S. A. Limb, Ah Limb, Low Mo, Chang Ming, Chan Chun, Jack Lou, Kam Tong, King Ah-Foo, Low Ling, Christy Low, M. E. Yang, T. H. Hong, Philip Euyang, Robert Jhoe

Sailors from H. M. S. Europa:

Clifford Odets, Harry Wise, Forrest Boone, Malcolm Anderson, Peter Howell, Jack King, Frederick Raymond, John Bethell, John Moran, Joe Savers

Stage Manager: Felix Jacoves
Ass't Stage Managers: Anatol Dendukov, George Freedley, James Jolly

Martin Beck Theatre, October 27, 1930
(72 PERFORMANCES)

ELIZABETH THE QUEEN

A Play in Three Acts
MAXWELL ANDERSON
DIRECTED BY PHILIP MOELLER
Settings and costumes by Lee Simonson

CAST

Sir Walter Raleigh .... Percy Waram
Penelope Gray .... Anita Kerry
Captain Armin .... Philip Foster
Sir Robert Cecil .... Arthur Hughes
Francis Bacon .... Morris Carnovsky
Lord Essex .... Alfred Lunt
Elizabeth .... Lynn Fontanne
Lord Burghley .... Robert Conness
The Fool .... Barry Macollum
Mary .... Mab Anthony
Tressa .... Edla Frankau
Ellen .... Phoebe Brand
Marvel .... Royal Beal
A Man-at-arms .... John Ellsworth
A Courier .... Charles Brokaw
A Captain of the Guards .... Edward Oldfield
A Courtier .... Robert Caille
A Herald .... Vincent Sherman
Burbage .... Whitford Kane
Heming .... Charles Brokaw
Poins .... Curtis Arnall
Ladies-in-Waiting: Annabelle Williams, Louise Gerard Huntington
Courtiers, Guards, Men-at-arms: Michael Borodin, George Fleming, Stanley Ruth, Nick Wiger, Henry Lase, Guy Moore, James Wiley, James A. Boshell, Thomas Eyre, Perry King, Curtis Arnall

Stage Manager: Leonard Loan
Ass't Stage Managers: Bretaigne Windust, Jerome Mayer

Guild Theatre, November 3, 1930
(later transferred to Martin Beck)
(147 PERFORMANCES)

MIDNIGHT

A Melodrama in Three Acts
CLAIRE AND PAUL SIFTON
DIRECTED BY PHILIP MOELLER
Setting by Woodman Thompson

CAST

Joe Biggers	Harold Vermilyea
Ada Biggers	Harriet MacGibbon
Mrs. Weldon	Josephine Hull
Stella Weldon	Linda Watkins
Arthur Weldon	Clifford Odets
First Reporter	Tom H. A. Lewis
Messenger Boy	Charles Powers
Edward Weldon	Frederick Perry
Second Reporter	Harold Bolton
Third Reporter	Samuel Rosen
Bob Nolan	Glenn Anders
Gar Boni	Jack LaRue
Richard McGrath	Francis Pierlot
Elizabeth McGrath	Maude Allan
Edgar Ingersoll	Fred Sullivan
Policeman	Neal Stone
Dr. Mannheim	Royal Dana Tracey
Woman Reporter	Zena Colaer
Photographers	Louis Veda, James Parker
Plunkett	Robert Strange
Treadwell	William R. Kane

Stage Manager: Louis Simon
Ass't. Stage Manager: Samuel Rosen

Guild Theatre, December 29, 1930
(48 PERFORMANCES)

GREEN GROW THE LILACS

A Folk-Play in Six Scenes

LYNN RIGGS

DIRECTED BY HERBERT J. BIBERMAN

Settings by Raymond Sovey

CAST

Curley McClain .... Franchot Tone
Aunt Eller Murphy .... Helen Westley
Laurey Williams .... June Walker
Jeeter Fry .... Richard Hale
Ado Annie Carnes .... Ruth Chorpenning
A Peddler .... Lee Strasberg
Old Man Peck .... Tex Cooper
A Cowboy .... Woodward Ritter
Another Cowboy .... Paul Ravell
An Old Farmer .... William T. Hays
A Young Farmer .... A. L. Bartolot
Marthy .... Jane Alden
Fiddler .... William Chosnyk
Banjo Player .... Everett Cheetham

Other Farmers: Carl Beasley, Joe Wilson, Roy Ketcham, Gordon Bryant, Everett Cheetham, Elmo Carr, Tommy Pladgett

Cowboys: Slim Cavanaugh, Chick Hannan, Norton Worden, Jack Miller, Pete Schwartz, J. B. Hubbard

Girls: Jean Wood, Lois Lindon, Orlanda Lee, Alice Frost, Faith Hope, Eleanor Powers, Peggy Hannan

Stage Manager: Anatole Bendukov

Ass't. Stage Manager: Hugh Rennie

Tremont Theatre, Boston, December 8, 1930

Guild Theatre, January 26, 1931

(64 PERFORMANCES)

MIRACLE AT VERDUN

A Play in Seven Scenes
HANS CHLUMBERG
with Screen Accompaniment
DIRECTED BY HERBERT J. BIBERMAN
Settings designed by Lee Simonson
Incidental music by Aaron Copland
Translated by Julian Leigh
Screen
THE WAR—1916

Scene 1
Petit Cimetière at Verdun—1934

CAST

Americans

Smith .... Caryl Gillin
Jackson .... Robert Middlemass

English

Sharpe .... J. W. Austin
Marshall .... Thomas A. Braidon
Miss Greeley .... Shirley Gale
Dorothy .... Valerie Cossart
Violet .... Hilda Chase

French

Verron .... Owen Meech
Mme. Verron .... Marion Stephenson
Remusat .... Jules Epailly
Lerat .... Carlos Zizold
Mme. Lerat .... Miriam Elias
Mme. Duvernois .... Germaine Giroux

German

Dr. Paetz .... Edward Arnold
Frau Paetz .... Helene Salinger
Von Henkel .... Con Macsunday
Frau Von Henkel .... Joan Grahn
Fritzchen .... David Gorcey
Brohl .... Max Willenz
Spaerlich .... Sydney Stavro
Heydner .... Claude Rains

Pillwein, an Austrian .... John Hoysradt
Old Italian .... Salvatore Zito
Young Italian .... Ari Kutai
Old Japanese .... J. C. Kunihara
Young Japanese .... Hanaki Yoshiwara
First Priest .... Juan de la Cruz

Second Priest .... Douglas Garden
Mazas, tourist guide .... Georges Magis
Vernier, cemetery attendant .... Edouard La Roche
Messenger .... Claude Rains

Part 2

A Company of the Resurrected

Wittekind .... Hans Hansen
Hessel .... Alexander Ivo
Weber .... Jacob Bleifer
Sonneborn .... Walter Dressel
Schroeder .... George Brant
Lehmann .... Michael Rosenberg
Schmidt .... Anthony Baker
Vaudemont, the Captain .... John Gerard
Andre Verron .... Peter Wayne
Morel .... Clement Wilenchick
Dubois .... Ali Youssoff
Roubeau .... Akim Tamiroff
Baillard .... Percy Woodley
General Lamarque, French War Minister .... Carlos Zizold
General Von Gadenau, German War Minister .... Max Willenz
French Officers .... Alexander Danarov
John Hoysradt
German Officers .... Joseph Lazarovici
Francis Schaeger
Vernier, cemetery attendant .... Edouard La Roche

Screen

Scene 2

Celebrations in Paris and Berlin—1934

Cast

Premier Delcampe .... Jules Epailly
Interrupter .... Georges Magis
Radio Announcer .... John Hoysradt
Reich Chancellor Overtuesch .... Edward Arnold
Interrupter .... Jacob Bleifer

Scene 3

Bedrooms in Paris—Berlin—London

Cast

Premier Delcampe .... Jules Epailly
Odette Lefevre .... Germaine Giroux
Reich Chancellor Overtuesch .... Edward Arnold
Frau Overtuesch .... Helene Salinger
Lord Grathford, English Prime Minister .... J. W. Austin
Leeds, his valet .... Thomas A. Braidon

Screen
THE RESURRECTION

Scene 4
A Field in the Suippe
Screen
THE RESURRECTED LOOK UPON THE WORLD
Scene 5
Shop of the Cobbler, Paul Vadinet—A Village on the Marne

Cast

Paul Vadinet .... Carlos Zizold
Mme. Vadinet .... Miriam Elias
Jacques, an apprentice .... John Hoysradt
Jeannette .... Germaine Giroux
Policeman .... Georges Magis
Pastor .... Juan de la Cruz
First Villager .... Edouard La Roche
Second Villager .... Hilda Chase
Third Villager .... Martin Cravath
Morel .... Clement Wilenchick
Villagers, Townspeople

Screen
THE WORLD LOOKS UPON THE RESURRECTED

Scene 6
Quai d'Orsay

Cast

Lord Grathford, Prime Minister of England .... J. W. Austin
Michel Delcampe, Premier of France .... Jules Epailly
Dr. Overtuesch, Chancellor of the German Reich ... Edward Arnold
Lamparenne, Prime Minister of Belgium .... Claude Rains
General Lamarque, French War Minister .... Carlos Zizold
General Von Gadenau, German War Minister .... Max Willenz
Clarkson, American Ambassador .... Robert Middlemass
Bertolotti, Italian Ambassador .... Salvatore Zito
Yoshitomo, Japanese Ambassador .... Kuni Hara
Cardinal Dupin, Archbishop of Paris .... Juan de la Cruz
Superintendent General Palm .... Douglas Garden
Chief Rabbi Dr. Sorgenreich .... Sydney Stavro
Professor Dr. Steppach, scientific authority .... Con Macsunday
The Secretary .... Thomas A. Braidon
A Young Prelate .... Ari Kutai
Tsatanaku, Japanese Premier .... Hanaki Yoshiwara
Yoshitomo .... J. C. Kunihara

Representatives of various nations:

Roumania		Robert Deviera
Yugo-Slavia		Joseph Green
Poland		Lucien Girardin
Czecho-Slovakia		Mario Lajeroni
Trolliet	of Lamparenne's group	Edouard La Roche
Charrier	of Lamparenne's group	Georges Magis

Screen
THE RETURN

Scene 7
Petit Cimetière at Verdun
(ten minutes after Scene 1)

Stage Manager: James Jolley
Ass't. Stage Managers: Sam Rosen, Jerome Mayer

Martin Beck Theatre, March 16, 1931
(49 PERFORMANCES)

GETTING MARRIED

A COMEDY BY BERNARD SHAW
DIRECTED BY PHILIP MOELLER
Settings by Aline Bernstein

CAST

Mrs. Bridgenorth	Margaret Wycherly
William Collins	Henry Travers
The General (Boxer)	Ernest Cossart
Lesbia Grantham	Irby Marshall
Reginald Bridgenorth	Hugh Buckler
Leo	Dorothy Gish
The Bishop	Reginald Mason
St. John Hotchkiss	Hugh Sinclair
Cecil Sykes	Romney Brent
Edith Bridgenorth	Peg Entwistle
Oliver Cromwell Soames (Anthony)	Ralph Roeder
Mrs. George Collins	Helen Westley
The Beadle	Oscar Stirling

Stage Manager: Ferdinand Hast
Ass't. Stage Manager: Oscar Stirling

Guild Theatre, March 30, 1931
(48 PERFORMANCES)

FOURTEENTH SEASON

HE

A COMEDY BY ALFRED SAVOIR
ADAPTED BY CHESTER ERSKIN
DIRECTED BY CHESTER ERSKIN
Setting by Aline Bernstein

CAST

Bartender .... Leslie Hunt
Elevator Man .... Claude Rains
Monsieur Matard, hotel proprietor .... Cecil Yapp
Professor Coq .... Eugene Powers
The Invalid, his daughter .... Viola Frayne
Miss Scoville .... Edith Meiser
Commander Trafalgar .... Edward Rigby
He .... Tom Powers
Princess .... Violet Kemble Cooper
Bell Boy .... Lester Salkow
Monsieur Ping .... William Gargan
Hotel Doctor .... Le Roy Brown
First Porter .... Lawrence Hurdle, Jr.
Second Porter .... Charles W. Adams
Doctor .... Robert Le Sueur

Stage Manager: George Fogle
Ass't. Stage Manager: Lawrence Hurdle, Jr.

Guild Theatre, September 24, 1931
(40 PERFORMANCES)

The Group Theatre, Inc.
presents

THE HOUSE OF CONNELLY

PAUL GREEN

Under the Auspices of the Theatre Guild, Inc.
PRODUCTION DIRECTED BY LEE STRASBERG AND CHERYL CRAWFORD

Settings designed by Cleon Throckmorton

CAST

Big Sis .... Fanny de Knight
Big Sue .... Rose McClendon
Patsy Tate .... Margaret Barker
Will Connelly .... Franchot Tone
Jesse Tate .... Art Smith
Geraldine Connelly .... Stella Adler
Evelyn Connelly .... Eunice Stoddard
Robert Connelly .... Morris Carnovsky
Mrs. Connelly .... Mary Morris
Duffy .... J. E. Bromberg
Virginia Buchanan .... Dorothy Patten
Essie .... Ruth Nelson
Jake .... Lewis Leverett
Charlie .... Walter Coy
Alec .... Clement Wilenchick
Ransom .... Philip Robinson
Reuben .... Clifford Odets
Isaac .... Friendly Ford
Tyler .... Gerrit Kraber
Alf .... Robert Lewis
Henry .... Herbert Ratner

Serenaders: Phoebe Brand, Walter Coy, William Challee, Virginia Farmer, Friendly Ford, Sylvia Feningston, Gerrit Kraber, Lewis Leverett, Gertrude Maynard, Paula Miller, Robert Lewis, Clifford Odets, Philip Robinson, Clement Wilenchick, Sanford Meisner, Harry Bellaver.

Stage Manager: Alixe Walker
Ass't. Stage Manager: Robert Lewis
Music under the direction of Max Weiser
Martin Beck Theatre, September 28, 1931
(91 PERFORMANCES)

MOURNING BECOMES ELECTRA

A TRILOGY BY EUGENE O'NEILL
PRODUCTION DIRECTED BY PHILIP MOELLER
Settings and costumes designed by Robert Edmond Jones

HOMECOMING

A Play in Four Scenes—Part One of the Trilogy

CAST

Seth Beckwith .... Arthur Hughes
Amos Ames .... Jack Byrne
Louisa, his wife .... Bernice Elliott
Minnie, her cousin .... Emily Lorraine
Christine, Ezra Mannon's wife .... Alla Nazimova
Lavinia Mannon, their daughter .... Alice Brady
Capt. Peter Niles, U. S. Artillery .... Philip Foster
Hazel Niles, his sister .... Mary Arbenz
Captain Adam Brant, of the
clipper ship, "Flying Trades" .... Thomas Chalmers
Brigadier-General Mannon .... Lee Baker

THE HUNTED

A Play in Five Scenes—Part Two of the Trilogy

CAST

Mrs. Josiah Borden .... Augusta Burgeon
Mrs. Everett Hills .... Janet Young
Dr. Joseph Blake .... Erskine Sanford
Josiah Borden, Manager of the
Mannon Shipping Company .... James Bosnell
Everett Hills, D.D., of the first
Congregational Church .... Oliver Putnam
Christine Mannon .... Alla Nazimova
Hazel Niles .... Mary Arbenz
Peter Niles, her brother, Captain of Artillery .... Philip Foster
Lavinia Mannon, Christine's daughter .... Alice Brady
Orin Mannon, her brother, First
Lieutenant of Infantry .... Earle Larimore
A Chantyman .... John Hendricks
Captain Adam Brant .... Thomas Chalmers

THE HAUNTED

A Play in Five Scenes—Part Three of the Trilogy

CAST

Abner Small .... Erskine Sanford
Ira Mackel .... Oliver Putnam
Joe Silva .... Grant Gordon
Amos Ames .... Jack Byrne
Seth Beckwith .... Arthur Hughes
Peter Niles .... Philip Foster
Hazel Niles, his sister .... Mary Arbenz
Lavinia Mannon .... Alice Brady
Orin Mannon, her brother .... Earle Larimore

Production Committee: Theresa Helburn and Maurice Wertheim
Stage Manager: Ferdinand Hast
Ass't. Stage Manager: Grant Gordon
Music Under the Direction of Max Weiser

Guild Theatre, October 26, 1931
(150 PERFORMANCES)

REUNION IN VIENNA

ROBERT E. SHERWOOD

PRODUCTION DIRECTED BY WORTHINGTON MINER

(Through the courtesy of Ray-Miner Corp.)

Settings designed by Aline Bernstein

CAST

Kathie .... Mary Gildea
Laundryman .... Stanley Wood
Elena .... Lynn Fontanne
Dr. Anton Krug .... Minor Watson
Ilse .... Phyllis Connard
Emil .... Lloyd Nolan
Herr Krug .... Henry Travers
Frau Lucher .... Helen Westley
Countess von Stainz .... Virginia Chauvenet
Count von Stainz .... Edward Fielding
Poffy .... Edouardo Ciannelli
Bredzi .... Bela Lublov
Strup .... Otis Sheridan
Torlini .... Bjorn Koefoed
Police Inspector .... Murray Stevens
Chef .... Joseph Allen
Rudolph Maximilian von Hapsburg .... Alfred Lunt
Baroness von Krett .... Cynthia Townsend
General Hoetzler .... Frank Kingdon
Talisz .... Owen Meech
Sophia .... Justina Wayne
Koeppke .... William R. Randall
Valet .... Joseph Allenton
Bellboy .... Noel Taylor
Busboys .... Ben Kranz
Hendrik Booraem
Waiters .... Charles E. Douglas
George Lewis

Production Committee: Theresa Helburn and Lawrence Langner

Stage Manager: Leonard Loan

Ass't. Stage Manager: Samuel Rosen

Music under the direction of Max Weiser

Martin Beck Theatre, November 16, 1931

(264 PERFORMANCES)

THE MOON IN THE YELLOW RIVER

A Play in Three Acts by
DENIS JOHNSTON

EPITAPH

Li Po
"And Li Po also died drunk.
He tried to embrace a moon
in the Yellow River."
—Ezra Pound

PRODUCTION DIRECTED BY PHILIP MOELLER
Settings designed by Cleon Throckmorton

CAST

Agnes	Josephine Williams
Blanaid	Gertrude Flynn
Tausch	Egon Brecher
Aunt Columba	Alma Kruger
George	Edward Nannary
Captain Potts	John Daly Murphy
Dobelle	Claude Rains
Willie	Barry Macollum
Darrell Blake	Henry Hull
Larry, one of Blake's men	Wylie Adams
Another of Blake's men	John O'Connor
Commandant	William Harrigan
A Soldier	Paul Stephenson
Another Soldier	Desmond O'Donnovan

Production Committee: Helen Westley and Lawrence Langner
Stage Manager: Milano Tilden
Ass't. Stage Manager: Paul Stephenson

Guild Theatre, February 29, 1932
(40 PERFORMANCES)

TOO TRUE TO BE GOOD

BERNARD SHAW

(A Collection of Stage Sermons by a Fellow of the Royal Society of Literature.)

PRODUCTION DIRECTED BY LESLIE BANKS

Settings and costumes designed by Jonel Jorgulesco

CAST

The Monster .... Julius Evans
The Elderly Lady .... Minna Phillips
The Doctor .... Alex Clark, Jr.
The Patient .... Hope Williams
The Nurse .... Beatrice Lillie
The Burglar .... Hugh Sinclair
Colonel Tallboys, V.C., D.S.O. .... Ernest Cossart
Private Meek .... Leo G. Carroll
Sergeant Fielding .... Frank Shannon
The Elder .... Claude Rains

Production Committee: Theresa Helburn and Philip Moeller

Stage Manager: Julius Evans

Ass't. Stage Manager: Harold Thomas

Guild Theatre, April 4, 1932

(57 PERFORMANCES)

THE GOOD EARTH

DRAMATIZED BY OWEN DAVIS AND DONALD DAVIS
FROM THE NOVEL BY PEARL S. BUCK
PRODUCTION DIRECTED BY PHILIP MOELLER
Settings designed by Lee Simonson

CAST

Wang Lung, a farmer	Claude Rains
Wang Lung's father	Henry Travers
Gatekeeper of the House of Hwang	Homer Barton
A Peach Vendor	Conrad Cantzen
A Beggar	William Franklin
The Old Lord	Harold Thomas
His Son	A. Francis Karll
The Fifth Lady	Marel Foster
A Slave	Joan Hathaway
Cuckoo	Marjorie Wood
Ancient Mistress of the House of Hwang	Kate Morgan
O-Lan, a slave	Alla Nazimova
Wang Lung's Uncle	Sydney Greenstreet
Wang Lung's Aunt	Jessie Ralph
Ching, a neighbor farmer	Clyde Franklin
Wang Lung's son	Freddy Goodrow
Two Strangers, business men from the town	Harold Thomas Vincent Sherman
A Tall Beggar	Harry M. Cooke
A Poor Man	Albert Hayes
Another Poor Man	Conrad Cantzen
A Young Speaker	Vincent Sherman
The Rich Man	Homer Barton
The Fool Child	Helen Hoy
Lotus	Gertrude Flynn
A Slave	Nola Napoli
A Doctor	Mark Schweid
Yi Ling, the maker of coffins	Donald Macmillan
Wang Lung's Eldest Son	Harry Wood
The Bride	Geraldine Kay
A Taoist Priest	Philip Wood
Priests from the Temple of Buddha	Harry Barfoot M. W. Rale

Slaves and Servants in the Great House of Hwang, Villagers, Soldiers and Citizens in the city, Mourners, etc.

Leota Diesel, Marel Foster, Claire Greenwood, Joan Hathaway, Jonatha Jones, Geraldine Kay, Dorothy Lacey, Eleanor Lynn, Stella Mark, Nola Napoli, Caroline Newcombe, Frances Propper, Harry Barfoot, Albert Brush, Austin Coghlan, Edward Favor, George Fleming, William Franklin, Tan Klas, Lester Lonergan, A. Francis Karll, Donald Macmillan, Edward Oldfield, Charles M. Palazzi, Charles Peyton, M. W. Rale, William Seltzer, Robert Sidney, Harold Thomas, Frank Verigun, Harry Walsh, Walton Warden, Harry Wood, and Larry Wood.

Production Committee: Lawrence Langner and Lee Simonson

Stage Manager: Julius Evans

Ass't. Stage Managers: Jack Daniels, Harold Thomas, Dorothy Lacey

Chestnut Street Opera House, Philadelphia, September 19, 1932

Guild Theatre, October 17, 1932

(56 PERFORMANCES)

BIOGRAPHY

A COMEDY BY S. N. BEHRMAN

PRODUCTION DIRECTED BY PHILIP MOELLER

Setting designed by Jo Mielziner

CAST

Richard Kurt .... Earle Larimore
Minnie, Marion Froude's maid .... Helen Salinger
Melchior Feydak, a Viennese composer .... Arnold Korff
Marion Froude .... Ina Claire
Leander Nolan .... Jay Fassett
Warwick Wilson .... Alexander Clark
Orrin Kinnicott .... Charles Richman
Slade Kinnicott, his daughter .... Mary Arbenz

Production Committee: Theresa Helburn and Lawrence Langner

Stage Manager: George Fogel

Ass't. Stage Manager: Robert Shayne

Guild Theatre, December 12, 1932

(283 PERFORMANCES)

AMERICAN DREAM

A TRILOGY BY GEORGE O'NEIL
PRODUCTION DIRECTED BY PHILIP MOELLER
Setting designed by Lee Simonson

CAST

1650

Roger Pingree .... Lee Baker
Martha, his wife .... Josephine Hull
Daniel Pingree .... Douglass Montgomery
Luke Pingree .... Wilton Graff
An Indian .... Frank Verigun
Lydia Kimball .... Gale Sondergaard
Celia .... Gertrude Flynn

1849

Daniel Pingree .... Stanley Ridges
Susannah, his wife .... Leona Hogarth
Abbie Pingree, his mother .... Helen Westley
Ezekial Bell .... Claude Rains

1933

Daniel Pingree .... Douglass Montgomery
Gail Pingree, his wife .... Gale Sondergaard
Hanri, a pianist .... Sanford Meisner
Vladimir, a butler .... Manart Kippen
Beth Harkness, a divorcee .... Edith Van Cleve
Richard Biddle, a gentleman .... Philip Barber
Eddie Thayer, a professor .... Stanley Ridges
Sarah Culver, a novelist .... Helen Westley
Mrs. Schuyler Hamilton, a lady .... Josephine Hull
Lindley P. Carver, a Negro .... Spencer Barnes
Julius Stern, a banker .... Lester Alden
Murdock, an economist .... Erskine Sanford
Amarylis, a dancer .... Gertrude Flynn
Tessa Steele, a sculptress .... Mary Blair
Lincoln Park, a manufacturer .... Wilton Graff
Mrs. Harry Tsezhin .... Mary Jeffery
Harry, an Indian .... Frank Verigun
Jake Schwarz, a communist .... Samuel Goldenberg

Production Committee: Lee Simonson and Helen Westley
Stage Manager: Julius Evans
Ass't. Stage Manager: Philip Barber
Guild Theatre, February 20, 1933
(Press opening, February 21, 1933)
(39 PERFORMANCES)

BOTH YOUR HOUSES

A PLAY IN THREE ACTS BY MAXWELL ANDERSON
PRODUCTION DIRECTED BY WORTHINGTON MINER
Settings designed by Arthur P. Segal

CAST

Marjorie Gray .... Aleta Freel
Bus .... Mary Philips
Eddie Wister .... Robert Shayne
Solomon Fitzmaurice .... Walter C. Kelly
Mark .... Oscar Polk
Simeon Gray .... Robert Strange
Levering .... Morris Carnovsky
Merton .... John Butler
Dell .... William Foran
Sneden .... Jerome Cowan
Miss McMurtry .... Jane Seymour
Wingblatt .... J. Edward Bromberg
Peebles .... Russell Collins
Farnum .... John F. Morrissey
Alan McClean .... Shepperd Strudwick
Ebner .... Joseph Sweeney

Production Committee: Theresa Helburn and Lee Simonson
Stage Manager: Norris Houghton
Ass't. Stage Manager: Quentin Anderson

Nixon Theatre, Pittsburgh, September 25, 1933
Royale Theatre, March 6, 1933
(104 PERFORMANCES)

THE MASK AND THE FACE

TRANSLATED FROM THE ITALIAN OF LUIGI CHIARELLI
BY W. SOMERSET MAUGHAM
PRODUCTION DIRECTED BY PHILIP MOELLER
Setting designed by Lee Simonson

CAST

Alisa Zanotti .... Shirley Booth
Giorgio Alamari .... Donald McClelland
Marta Setta .... Dorothy Patten
Cirillo Zanotti .... Leo G. Carroll
Wanda Sereni .... Alice Reinheart
Marco Miliotti .... Ernest Cossart
Piero Pucci .... Charles Campbell
Savina Grazia .... Judith Anderson
Count Paolo Grazia .... Stanley Ridges
Luciano Spina .... Humphrey Bogart
Andrea .... Manart Kippen
Giacomo .... William Lovejoy
Teresa .... Joan Marion

Production Committee: Theresa Helburn and Helen Westley
Stage Manager: Ferdinand Hast
Ass't Stage Manager: William Lovejoy

Colonial Theatre, Boston, May 1, 1933
Guild Theatre, May 8, 1933
(40 PERFORMANCES)

SIXTEENTH SEASON

GEORGE M. COHAN IN

AH, WILDERNESS!

EUGENE O'NEILL

PRODUCTION DIRECTED BY PHILIP MOELLER

Settings designed by Robert Edmond Jones

CAST

Nat Miller, owner of the *Evening Globe* .... George M. Cohan
Essie, his wife .... Marjorie Marquis
Arthur, their son .... William Post, Jr.
Richard, their son .... Elisha Cook, Jr.
Mildred, their daughter .... Adelaide Bean
Tommy, their son .... Walter Vonnegut, Jr.
Sid Davis, Essie's brother,
reporter on the *Waterbury Standard* .... Gene Lockhart
Lily Miller, Nat's sister .... Eda Heinemann
David McComber, dry-goods merchant........... Richard Sterling
Muriel McComber, his daughter .... Ruth Gilbert
Wint Selby, a classmate of Arthur's at Yale .... John Wynne
Belle .... Ruth Holden
Nora .... Ruth Chorpenning
Bartender .... Donald McClelland
Salesman .... John Butler

Production: Theresa Helburn

Nixon Theatre, Pittsburgh, Pa., September 25, 1933
Guild Theatre, October 2, 1933
(289 PERFORMANCES)

Molière's Comedy

THE SCHOOL FOR HUSBANDS

IN AN ADAPTATION IN RHYME BY
ARTHUR GUITERMAN AND LAWRENCE LANGNER
Music composed and arranged by Edmond W. Rickett
Lyrics by Arthur Guiterman
Settings and costumes by Lee Simonson
PRODUCTION DIRECTED BY LAWRENCE LANGNER

CAST

Sganarelle .... Osgood Perkins
Esgaste .... James Jolley
Street Vendor .... Parker Steward
Lisette .... Flora Le Breton
Ariste .... Stuart Casey
Valere .... Michael Bartlett
Leonor .... Joan Carr
Isabelle .... June Walker
Lysander .... George Macready
Sylvester .... Lewis Martin
1st Lackey .... Francis Tyler
2nd Lackey .... William Miley
Street Dancers .... Doris Humphrey
Charles Weidman
Bear .... Marcus Blechman
1st Girl .... Janice Joyce
2nd Girl .... Dorothea Petgen
3rd Girl .... Lee Whitney
4th Girl .... Virginia Marvin
Pierrot .... Parker Steward
Columbine .... Doris Humphrey
Harlequin .... Charles Weidman
Magician .... Robert Reinhart
3rd Lackey .... John Cherry
1st Bravo .... George Macready
2nd Bravo .... Lewis Martin
Magistrate .... Stanley Harrison
Notary .... Horace Sinclair
Link Boy .... Kenneth Bostock

Ballet Interlude

THE DREAM OF SGANARELLE

ADAPTED FROM THE BALLET "LE MARRIAGE FORCÉ"

(originally danced by His Majesty Louis XIV
and his court, the 29th day of January, 1664.)

Choreography by Doris Humphrey and Charles Weidman

CAST

Sganarelle .... Osgood Perkins
Athenée .... Janice Joyce
Shepherdess .... Doris Humphrey
Solomon .... Lewis Martin
Socrates .... Horace Sinclair
1st Egyptian .... Ada Korvin
2nd Egyptian .... Eleanor King
Dancing Master .... Charles Weidman
Tircis .... Stuart Casey

Olympians: Ernestine Henock, Ada Korvin, Katherine Manning, Hyla Rubin, Marcus Blechman, George Bockmann, Kenneth Bostock, Jack Cole, Francis Reid, Cleo Athenees.

Production: Philip Moeller
Musical Conductor: Edmond W. Rickett
Stage Manager: Julius Evans
Ass't. Stage Managers: Joan Hathaway, Eleanor Eckstein
The Max Weiser String-Wood Ensemble

Empire Theatre, October 16, 1933
(116 PERFORMANCES)

MARY OF SCOTLAND

MAXWELL ANDERSON
WITH
HELEN HAYES PHILIP MERIVALE
HELEN MENKEN
PRODUCTION DIRECTED BY THERESA HELBURN
Settings and costumes designed by Robert Edmond Jones

CAST

Jamie, a Guard .... Cecil Holm
Monk, a Guard .... William Jackson
John Knox .... Moroni Olsen
Tammas, a Guard .... Jock McGraw
James Hepburn, Earl of Bothwell .... Philip Merivale
A Page .... Maurice F. Manson
Chatelard .... Edward Trevor
Mary Stuart .... Helen Hayes
Duc de Chatelherault .... Leonard Willey
Mary Beaton .... Mary Michael
Mary Seton .... Helen Shea
Mary Livingstone .... Deane Willoughby
Mary Fleming .... Cynthia Rogers
Elizabeth Tudor .... Helen Menken
Lord Burghley .... George Coulouris
Lord Darnley .... Anthony Kemble-Cooper
Lord Douglas .... Edgar Barrier
David Rizzio .... Philip Leigh
James Stuart, Earl of Moray .... Wilton Graff
Maitland of Lethington .... Ernest Lawford
Lord Huntley .... Charles Dalton
Lord Morton .... Stanley Ridges
Lord Erskine .... George Coulouris
Lord Throgmorton .... Ernest Cossart
Lord Ruthven .... Leonard Willey
Lord Gordon .... Philip Foster
Graeme, a Sergeant .... Maurice F. Manson
A Warder .... Quentin Anderson

Production Committee: Lawrence Langner and Philip Moeller

National Theatre, Washington, D. C., October 23, 1933
Alvin Theatre, November 27, 1933
(248 PERFORMANCES)

DAYS WITHOUT END

A Modern Miracle Play

EUGENE O'NEILL

PRODUCTION DIRECTED BY PHILIP MOELLER

Settings designed by Lee Simonson

CAST

John .... Earle Larimore
Loving .... Stanley Ridges
William Eliot .... Richard Barbee
Father Baird .... Robert Loraine
Elsa, John Loving's wife .... Selena Royle
Margaret .... Caroline Newcombe
Lucy Hillman .... Ilka Chase
Herbert Stillwell .... Fredrick Forrester
Nurse .... Margaret Swope

Production Committee: Lawrence Langner and Lee Simonson

Stage Manager: George Greenberg

Ass't. Stage Manager: Warren Goddard

Plymouth Theatre, Boston, December 27, 1933

Henry Miller's Theatre, January 8, 1934

(57 PERFORMANCES)

THEY SHALL NOT DIE

JOHN WEXLEY

PRODUCTION DIRECTED BY PHILIP MOELLER

Settings designed by Lee Simonson

CAST

Cooley .... William Lynn
Henderson .... John L. Kearney
Red .... Tom Ewell
St. Louis Kid .... Fred Herrick
Blackie .... Frank Woodruff
Deputy-Sheriff Trent .... Ralph Theadore
Jeff Vivian .... Ralph Sanford
Lewis Collins .... Bob Ross
Jackson .... C. Ellsworth Smith
Charley .... George C. Mantell
Hillary .... Derek Trent
Smith .... Hugh Rennie
Walter Colton .... William Norton
Virginia Ross .... Linda Watkins
Lucy Wells .... Ruth Gordon
Luther Blakely .... Hale Norcross
Benson Allen .... L. M. Hurdle
Roberts .... George R. Hayes
Purcell .... Alfred Brown
Walters .... Bryant Hall
Warner .... Grafton Trew
Heywood Parsons .... Al Stokes
Roy Wood .... Allan Vaughan
Andy Wood .... Joseph Scott
Morris .... Joseph Smalls
Killian .... Eddie Hodge
Moore .... Frank Wilson
Oliver Tulley .... Robert Thomsen
Doctor Thomas .... George Christie
Captain Kennedy .... Frederick Persson
Sergeant Ogden .... Ross Forrester
Mrs. Wells .... Helen Westley
Tommy .... Edward Ryan, Jr.
Young Man .... Tom Ewell
Russell Evans .... Dean Jagger
Guard .... James Young

Principal Keeper .... Charles Henderson
Lowery .... Carroll Ashburn
William Treadwell .... Brandon Peters
Rev. Wendell Jackson .... Fred Miller
Warden Jeffries .... Leo Curley
Rokoff .... Louis John Latzer
Cheney .... St. Clair Bayfield
2nd Guard .... Robert Porterfield
Mrs. Parsons .... D. Browne Cooke
Mrs. Wood .... Georgia Burke
Mrs. Purcell .... Cecil Scott
Mr. Purcell .... Robert J. Lawrence
Mrs. Williams .... Catherine Francis
Nelson .... Erskine Sanford
Constable .... Albert West
Nathan G. Rubin .... Claude Rains
Johnny .... Hugh Rennie
Mr. Harrison .... Frank Wilson
Frank Travers .... Douglas Gregory
Judge .... Thurston Hall
Doctor Watson .... Robert J. Lawrence
Attorney-General Dade .... Ben Smith
Jury Commissioner Crocker .... Ralph Sanford
Clerk of Court .... Albert West
Seth Robbins .... Harry Hermsen
Circuit Solicitor Slade .... Carl Eckstrom

Mob, Hoboes, Soldiers, Court Guards, Court Audience, Jurymen, Reporters, Messenger Boys, etc.

Irene Bevans, Orrin Burke, George A. Cameron, Angus Duncan, Jack Flynn, Vallejo Gantner, Marshall Hale, Eddie Hodge, Alexander Jones, William H. Malone, Edward Mann, George C. Mantell, Grace Mills, Frank Phillips, Robert D. Phillips, Dorothy E. Ryan, Phil S. Michaels, Jack Stone, Jerome Sylvon, Ben Vivian, Charles Wellesley, John Wheeler, Betty Oakwood, George Carroll, Phillip Carter.

Production Committee: Theresa Helburn and Lee Simonson
Stage Manager: Adams Rice
Ass't. Stage Managers: Norris Houghton, H. B. Lutz

Royale Theatre, February 21, 1934
(62 PERFORMANCES)

RACES

FERDINAND BRUCKNER
WITH EARLE LARIMORE, MADY CHRISTIANS,
AND STANLEY RIDGES
ENGLISH VERSION BY RUTH LANGNER
DIRECTED BY THERESA HELBURN
Settings by Lee Simonson

CAST

Karlanner .... Earle Larimore
Tessow .... Harvey Stephens
Siegelmann .... Zvee Scooler
Hans Hinz Rosloh .... Stanley Ridges
Helene Marx .... Mady Christians
State's Attorney .... Fuller Mellish
Change .... William Williams
Teacher .... Ellen Hall
Secretary .... Leo Hoyt
Forester .... Frederick Roland
Boy .... Freddie Goodrow
Marx, Helene's Father .... Clarence Derwent
First Student .... Van Heflin
Second Student .... David Thurman Krupp
Magistrate .... Con MacSunday
Third Student .... Philip Barber
A Voice .... C. Norman Hammond
First Student Leader .... George Cotton
Second Student Leader .... Shepperd Strudwick

Chestnut Street Opera House, Philadelphia, March 19, 1934
(closed after Philadelphia engagement)

JIG SAW

A COMEDY BY DAWN POWELL
WITH
ERNEST TRUEX SPRING BYINGTON
PRODUCTION DIRECTED BY PHILIP MOELLER
Settings designed by Lee Simonson

CAST

Ross .... Virginia Tracy
Porter .... Albert Berg
Bell Boy .... James York
Mrs. Letty Walters .... Cora Witherspoon
Del Marsh .... Ernest Truex
Claire Brunell .... Spring Byington
Nathan Gifford .... Eliot Cabot
Frank Mason .... Charles Richman
Julie .... Gertrude Flynn
Mrs. Finch .... Helen Westley
Ethel Mason .... Mabel Kroman
Simpson .... Shepperd Strudwick

Production Committee: Lee Simonson and Helen Westley
Stage Manager: George Greenberg
Ass't. Stage Manager: James York

Ethel Barrymore Theatre, April 30, 1934
(49 PERFORMANCES)

SEVENTEENTH SEASON

A SLEEPING CLERGYMAN

A PLAY IN TWO ACTS BY JAMES BRIDIE
PRODUCTION DIRECTED BY PHILIP MOELLER
Settings and Costumes designed by Lee Simonson

CAST

A Sleeping Clergyman .... Frank Kingdom
Dr. Cooper .... J. Colvil Dunn
Dr. Coutts .... Harry Mestoyer
Wilkinson .... Harry Joyner
Charles Cameron, the first .... Glenn Anders
Mrs. Elspeth Hannah .... Helen Westley
Dr. William Marshall .... Ernest Thesiger
Harriet Marshall, his sister .... Ruth Gordon
Aunt Walker .... Alice John
Cousin Minnie .... Gertrude Flynn
Wilhelmina Cameron .... Ruth Gordon
John Hannah .... Theodore Newton
A Sergeant .... Walter Lawrence
A Constable .... Donald Campbell
Charles Cameron, the second .... Glenn Anders
Donavan .... J. Malcolm Dunn
Sir Douglas Todd Walker.......................... A. P. Kaye
Lady Todd Walker .... Charlotte Walker
Hope Cameron .... Ruth Gordon
A Prostitute .... Sheila Trent
Lady Katherine Helliwell .... Florence Britton
Dr. Purley .... Malcolm Soltan
A Medical Student .... Robert Haig
Doctors, Nurses, etc.: John Taylor, Frank Henderson, Elizabeth Valentine, Phoebe Gilbert

Production Committee: Lawrence Langner and Lee Simonson
Stage Manager: George Greenberg
Ass't. Stage Manager: John Taylor

Guild Theatre, October 8, 1934
(40 PERFORMANCES)

VALLEY FORGE

A PLAY IN THREE ACTS
BY MAXWELL ANDERSON
WITH
PHILIP MERIVALE
PRODUCTION DIRECTED BY HERBERT J. BIBERMAN
AND JOHN HOUSEMAN
PRODUCTION DESIGNED BY KATE DRAIN LAWSON
Costumes designed by Carroll French
Music arranged by Max Weiser

CAST

Andrew .... Thaddeus Clancy
Spad .... Alan Bunce
Alcock .... Victor Kilian
Teague .... Grover Burgess
Mason .... Charles Ellis
Jock .... Jock McGraw
Oscar .... Hans Hansen
Nick .... Robert Thomsen
Minto .... Harry Hermsen
Marty .... Alexander Mirsky
Tavis .... Frances Sage
Auntie .... Florence Gerald
Neil .... Hendrik Booraem
Lieutenant Cutting .... George Coulouris
Rover .... Bingo
Lieut. Col. Lucifer Tench .... Stanley Ridges
An Aide .... Philip Robinson
General George Washington .... Philip Merivale
Marquis de LaFayette .... Edward Trevor
Sir William Howe .... Reginald Mason
Mary Philipse (Mistress Morris) .... Margalo Gillmore
Major André .... John Hoysradt
A Brigadier .... Charles Drummond
A Captain .... John Ryder
Fielding .... Stephen Appleby
"The Washington" (masquerade) .... George Cannon
First Soldier .... Alan Bandler
Second Soldier .... James Roader
Third Soldier .... Wallace Acton

A Civilian .... George Spaulding
General Varnum .... Harold Gould
General Stirling .... Harold Elliot
Rafe .... John Sennott
Mr. Harvie .... Harold Tucker
Mr. Folsom .... Erskine Sanford
General Conway .... Charles Francis

Ladies and Officers: Cora Burlar, Eleanor Eckstein, Jean Sennott, Cynthia Sherwood, Katherine Standing, Helen Shea, Guy Monypenny, Joseph Romantini.

Musicians: Max Weiser, Nicolai Pesce, Maurice Sackett
Production Committee: Theresa Helburn and Lawrence Langner
Stage Manager: Julius Evans
Ass't. Stage Managers: John Taylor, Joan Hathaway

Listed in Nixon Theatre opening night program:
The minuet staged by Martha Graham
(the author was co-director instead of Biberman)
(Mary Philipse was played by Ruth Weston,
Major André by Lowell Gilmore)
Nixon Theatre, Pittsburgh, November 19, 1934
Guild Theatre, December 10, 1934
(58 PERFORMANCES)

RAIN FROM HEAVEN

S. N. BEHRMAN
WITH
JANE COWL
AND
JOHN HALLIDAY
PRODUCTION DIRECTED BY PHILIP MOELLER
Setting designed by Lee Simonson

CAST

Joan Eldridge .... Hancey Castle
Mrs. Dingle .... Alice Belmore-Cliffe
Rand Eldridge .... Ben Smith
Hobart Eldridge .... Thurston Hall
Lady Violet Wyngate .... Jane Cowl
Hugo Willens .... John Halliday
Sascha Barashaev .... Marshall Grant
Phoebe Eldridge .... Lily Cahill
Clendon Wyatt .... Statts Cottsworth
Nikalai Jurin .... José Ruben

Production Committee: Theresa Helburn and Lee Simonson
Stage Manager: George Fogle
Ass't. Stage Manager: Robert Woods

Plymouth Theatre, Boston, December 10, 1934
Golden Theatre, December 24, 1934
(99 PERFORMANCES)

(In association with Charles B. Cochran)
ELISABETH BERGNER
IN

ESCAPE ME NEVER

A PLAY IN THREE ACTS BY MARGARET KENNEDY
PRODUCTION DIRECTED BY KOMISARJEVSKY
Settings designed by Komisarjevsky

CAST

Sir Ivor McClean .... Leon Quartermaine
Lady McClean .... Katie Johnson
Fenella McClean .... Eve Turner
Woman Tourist .... Sheila Taylor
1st Tourist .... Cyril Horrocks
2nd Tourist .... John Boxer
Caryl Sanger .... Griffith Jones
Butler .... Bruno Barnabe
Herr Heinrich .... William F. Schoeller
Gemma Jones .... Elisabeth Bergner
Sabastian Sanger .... Hugh Sinclair
Waiter .... Peter Bull
1st Spinster .... Joan Blair
2nd Spinster .... Muriel Johnston
Mrs. Brown .... Joan Blair
Wilson .... John Boxer
Petrova .... Nina Bucknall
Dresser .... Muriel Johnston
Pianist .... Cyril Horrocks
Messenger .... William Mills
Miss Regan .... Susan Brown
1st Man .... Peter Bull
2nd Man .... John Boxer
3rd Man .... A. J. Felix
Stallkeeper .... Cyril Horrocks
Man .... Bruno Barnabe
Woman .... Muriel Johnston
Girl .... Jane Vaughan

Music arranged by Leslie Bridgewater
Stage Manager: Ernest W. Parr
Ass't. Stage Manager: William Mills
Technical Director: J. W. Rivers

Sam S. Shubert Theatre, January 21, 1935
(96 PERFORMANCES)

THE SIMPLETON OF THE UNEXPECTED ISLES

GEORGE BERNARD SHAW
WITH
NAZIMOVA AND ROMNEY BRENT
PRODUCTION DIRECTED BY HARRY WAGSTAFF GRIBBLE
Settings and Costumes designed by Lee Simonson

CAST

The Emigration Officer .... Rex O'Malley
Wilks .... Lionel Pape
The Young Woman .... Patricia Calvert
The Station Master .... Reginald Malcolm
The Priest, Pra .... McKay Morris
The Priestess, Prola .... Nazimova
The Lady Tourist .... Viola Roache
Sir Charles Farwaters .... Lawrence Grossmith
The Clergyman .... Romney Brent
Janga .... Leon Janney
Kanchin .... Franklin Gray
Maya .... Alma Lloyd
Vashti .... Rita Vale
The Angel .... Louis Hector

Production Committee: Lawrence Langner and Lee Simonson
Stage Manager: George Greenberg
Ass't. Stage Manager: Stephen Appleby
Guild Theatre, February 18, 1935
(40 PERFORMANCES)

PARADE

A SATIRICAL REVUE
WITH
JIMMY SAVO

Sketches by Paul Peters, George Sklar,
Frank Gabrielson and David Lesan
Lyrics by Paul Peters, George Sklar, Kyle Crichton
Music by Jerome Moross
Musical and dance numbers supervised and staged by Robert Alton
Settings designed by Lee Simonson
Orchestra under the direction of Max Meth

ACT I

THE POLICE STATION
(by Paul Peters and George Sklar)

The Sergeant .... Ralph Riggs
The Desk Officer .... David Lesan
A Man .... J. Elliot Leonard
A Girl .... Evelyn Dall
Commissioner O'Brien .... Charles D. Brown
Policemen .... Parade Octette

ON PARADE
(Lyrics by Paul Peters and George Sklar)

Sung by .... Edgar Allan

THE LAST JACKASS
(by Paul Peters and George Sklar)

The Jackass .... George Ali
Farmer Brown .... Ralph Riggs
Mrs. Brown .... Eve Arden
Baby Brown .... Lois Leng
Mr. Butterspread .... Charles D. Brown
Manfred .... David Lawrence
Ethelbert .... David Lesan
Ronald .... Leon Janney

"I'm Telling You, Louie!"
(Lyrics by Paul Peters and George Sklar)
Sung and danced by Vera Marshe and Earl Oxford

Specialty Dance
Charles Walters and Dorothy Fox

THE CRISIS
(by Frank Gabrielson, David Lesan and Michael Blankfort)

The Pickets .... Parade Octette
The Radio Announcer .... Earl Oxford
Lester M. Puffle .... Jimmy Savo

"SELLING SEX"
(Lyrics by Kyle Crichton)

Sung by .... Evelyn Dall

THE DEAD COW
(by Alan Baxter and Harold Johnsrud)

Paw .... Charles D. Brown
Maw .... Eve Arden
Johnny .... Leon Janney
Mary .... Lois Leng
The Official .... J. Elliot Leonard

"DECADENCE"
(Music by Will Irwin)

Danced by .... Charles Walters and
Dorothy Fox

"LIFE COULD BE SO BEAUTIFUL"
(Lyrics by Paul Peters and George Sklar)

Sung by .... Jean Travers and
David Lawrence
Solo Dance by .... Esther Junger

"SEND FOR THE MILITIA"
(Music and Lyrics by Marc Blitzstein)

Sung by .... Eve Arden

COLLEGE DAZE
(by Frank Gabrielson and David Lesan)

The Secretary .... Vera Marshe
The Freshman .... Jimmy Savo
The Dean .... Charles D. Brown

"YOU AIN'T SO HOT"
(Lyrics by Paul Peters and George Sklar)

Sung by .... Avis Andrews

SUGAR CANE

Leader of the Revolt .... Esther Junger
Workers .... Modern Dance Group
The Overseer .... Irvin Shurack

HOT DOG
(by Paul Peters and George Sklar)

The Wayfarer .... Jimmy Savo
The Chestnut Vendor .... Ralph Riggs
The Hot Dog Vendor .... J. Elliot Leonard
The Hot Dog Customer .... Leon Janney
Policeman .... Parade Octette

OUR STORE
(by Turner Bullock)

Mr. Fisher .... Charles D. Brown
Miss Jessup .... Jean Travers
Miss Howard .... Eve Arden
Dr. Carruthers .... Ralph Riggs
Miss Mason .... Lois Leng

THE TABLOID REDS
(by Paul Peters and George Sklar)

Leader of Bomb Throwers .... Esther Junger
The Bomb Throwers .... Yisrol Libman
André Cherise
The Girl Communist .... Modern Dance Group
The Policeman .... Bob Long
The Communist Leader .... Jean Travers
The Communist Newsy .... Leon Janney
The Communist Baby .... Polly Rose
Comrade No. 1 .... Earl Oxford
Comrade No. 2 .... J. Elliot Leonard
Comrade No. 3 .... David Lawrence
Mr. Capitalist .... Roger Logan
Mrs. Capitalist .... Evelyn Monte
Junior Capitalist .... Ezra Stone

ACT II

"FEAR IN MY HEART"
(Lyrics by Paul Peters and George Sklar)

Sung by .... Earl Oxford, Jean Travers
Specialty Dance .... Dorothy Fox and Charles Walters

"MY FEET ARE FIRMLY PLANTED ON THE GROUND"
(Lyrics by Emanuel Eisenberg)

Sung by .... Jimmy Savo

THE HAPPY FAMILY
(by Frank Gabrielson and David Lesan)

Mother .... Eve Arden
Father .... Charles D. Brown
Willie .... Ezra Stone
Egbert .... Leon Janney
Big Brother .... J. Elliot Leonard
Sister .... Lois Leng

"MARRY THE FAMILY"
(Lyrics by Michael Blankfort)

Sung by .... Vera Marshe, Earl Oxford
The Family:
Grandma .... Susanne Remos
Grandpa .... Yisrol Libman
Papa .... Melton Morre
Mama .... Stella Sanders
Sister .... Polly Rose
Brother .... Leon Janney
Three Aunts .... Ruth Ross, Ethel Axel, Ida Bildner
Three Uncles .... Jerome Thor, Norman Emburgh, William Houston

HOME OF THE BRAVE
(by Frank Gabrielson and David Lesan)

The Announcer .... Earl Oxford
Mr. John Smith .... Charles D. Brown
Mrs. John Smith .... Eve Arden
Joe .... Jimmy Savo
The Inspector .... Ralph Riggs

"I'M AN INTERNATIONAL ORPHAN"
(Lyrics by Paul Peters and George Sklar)

Sung by .... Evelyn Dall

THE FREE CLINIC
(by Frank Gabrielson and David Lesan)

The Nurse .... Vera Marshe
First Man .... Charles D. Brown
Second Man .... Jimmy Savo
Dr. Lewis .... David Lesan
Dr. Jenkins .... Earl Oxford
Dr. Broadly .... David Lawrence

"LETTER TO THE PRESIDENT"

Sung by .... Avis Andrews

THE PLAGUE
(by Frank Gabrielson and David Lesan)

Mr. Brown .... Charles D. Brown
Mrs. Brown .... Eve Arden
The Visitor .... Ralph Riggs

BOURGEOIS PROCESSIONAL

The Laborers: Harry Smith, Jerome Thor, Clyde Walters
The Dowagers: Susanne Remos, Ethel Axel, Ruth Ross
The Salvation Army Girl: .... Doris Newcombe
The Politicians: Jos. Lennon, Jack Ross, Bob Gray, Roger Logan
The Ballerina .... Eunice Thawl
The Debutantes: Lillian Moore, Beverly Hosier, Marguerite White
The Minister .... J. Elliot Leonard
The Street Walker .... Lulu Morris
The Boy Scout .... Leon Janney
The Cheerleader .... Yisrol Libman
The Collegians: Stella Sanders, Doris Ostroff, Ethel Selwyn, Ida Bildner
The Chorus Girls: Stella Claussen, Grace Kaye, Katherine Dougherty, Polly Rose, Wanda Allen
The Banker .... André Charise
The Professor .... Bob Long
The Widow .... Evelyn Monte
Leading Politician .... Ralph Riggs

FLIGHT FROM THE SOVIET

(by Paul Peters, George Sklar and Kyle Crichton)

The Announcer .... Ralph Riggs
The Lecturer .... Eve Arden

BON VOYAGE

(Lyrics by Kyle Crichton)

The Reporter .... David Lawrence
The Soldier .... Charles D. Brown
The Cleric .... Ralph Riggs
The Statesman .... Jimmy Savo

FINALE
"PARADE"

(Lyrics by Paul Peters and George Sklar)

Sung by Edgar Allen
and the Entire Company

"Parade" Girls: Wanda Allen, Stella Claussen, Miriam Curtis, Mary Katherine Dougherty, Beverly Hosier, Eunice Thawl, Grace Kaye, Evelyn Monte, Doris Newcombe, Polly Rose, Lillian Moore, Marguerite White.

Modern Dance Group: Doris Ostroff, Stella Sanders, Ethel Selwyn, Ethel Axel, Ida Bildner, Lulu Morris, Ruth Ross, Susanne Remos.

"Parade" Octette: Norman Lind, John Weidler, William Houston, Geoffrey Errett, Melton Moore, Bradley Roberts, Ernest Taylor, Norman Van Emburgh.

Orchestrations by Conrad Salinger, Russell Bennett and Jerome Moross

Production Committee: Lee Simonson and Philip Moeller

Stage Manager: Dennis Murray

Ass't. Stage Manager: H. Gordon Graham

Guild Theatre, May 20, 1935

(32 PERFORMANCES)

IF THIS BE TREASON

REV. DR. JOHN HAYNES HOLMES AND
REGINALD LAWRENCE

PRODUCTION DIRECTED BY HARRY WAGSTAFF GRIBBLE

Settings designed by John Root

CAST

Duncan, Secretary to the President .... Hunter Gardner
Robert Gordon, the President's Son.................... John Stark
Turner, Press Secretary to the President .... Walter N. Greaza
John Gordon, President of the United States .... McKay Morris
Miss Folwell, Private Secretary to the President ..... Kathryn Givney
Mrs. Gordon, the President's Wife .... Armina Marshall
Mansfield, a young diplomat .... Robert Williams
Mrs. Bane .... Kathleen Comegys
British Ambassador .... Edgar Kent
French Ambassador .... Marcel Journet
Bright, Senator from Massachusetts .... Donald Mackenzie
Fitzgerald, Representative from Wyoming .... Leo Curley
Dickinson, Secretary of State .... Boyd Davis
Hill, Senator from California .... Mitchell Harris
Smith, Representative from Georgia .... Lawrence M. Hurdle
Fulton, Secretary of War .... Frank Dae
Jarvis, State Department Messenger .... Tom Neal
Wilmot, Representative from Illinois .... Robert Lowe
Admiral James .... James Spottswood
Aldrich, Secretary of the Navy .... Harland Tucker
Brainard, Ex-President of the United States ...... Thomas Chalmers
Todu, Secretary-Aide to General Nogatu ...... Biacouren Yoshiwara
General Nogatu, Conference Delegate .... Edgar Kent
Dr. Fujimoto, Conference Delegate .... Takashi Ohta
Lord Carrington, British Ambassador to Japan ...... Charles Bryant
Yato, Premier of Japan .... Tom Powers
Baron Ishiwara, Conference Delegate .... George Hiroshe
Koye .... Arthur Hughes

Guests at the Reception, Messengers, Japanese People and Soldiers: Gretchen Barclay, Bianca Bond, Ruby Gordon, Rita Johnson, Jane Keith, Maoe Kondo, Cynthia Sherwood, Ruth Stevens, E. Takamoto, Nellie Thorne, Barbara Adams, David Morgan, William Galloway, Peter Galvan, Lewis Hall, Regis Joyce, Thomas Neal, Russell Sage, Edwin Vickery, Bert C. Wood.

Production Committee: Lawrence Langner and Philip Moeller

Assistant: Carly Wharton

Stage Manager: Lawrence M. Hurdle

Ass't. Stage Managers: Eleanor Eckstein, Barbara Adams

Music Box Theatre, September 23, 1935

(40 PERFORMANCES)

(in association with John C. Wilson)
WILLIAM SHAKESPEARE'S COMEDY

THE TAMING OF THE SHREW

with
ALFRED LUNT AND LYNN FONTANNE
PRODUCTION DIRECTED BY HARRY WAGSTAFF GRIBBLE
Scheme of production devised by Mr. Lunt and Miss Fontanne
Production and costumes by Claggett Wilson
Settings by Carolyn Hancock

CAST
(In the Induction)

Christopher Sly .... Richard Whorf
A Lord .... Lowell Gilmore
First Huntsman .... John Balmer
Second Huntsman .... Gilmore Bush
Third Huntsman .... Winston Ross
Bartholomew, a page .... William Clifford

(Actors in the Play)

Lucentio .... Alan Hewitt
Tranio .... Bretaigne Windust
Two Townswomen .... Jacqueline DeWitt
Ernestine DeBecker
Pantaloon .... Le Roi Operti
Baptista .... Sydney Greenstreet
Gremio .... George Graham
Hortensio .... Barry Thomson
Bianca .... Dorothy Mathews
Biondello .... George Meader
Petruchio .... Alfred Lunt
Grumio .... Horace Sinclair
Widow .... Doris Rich
Maid .... Jacqueline DeWitt
Katherine .... Lynn Fontanne
Curtis .... Alice Belmore Cliffe
Servants to Petruchio:
Nathaniel .... Gilmore Bush
Joseph .... Thomas Coley
Gregory .... William Gray
Philip .... Winston Ross
Cook .... Stephen Sandes

Haberdasher .... S. Thomas Gomez
A Tailor .... Le Roi Operti
A Pedant .... Robert Vivian
Vincentio .... David Glassford
Officer .... S. Thomas Gomez
A Prisoner .... Stephen Sandes
Horses .... Harry Be Gar
Arthur Chester

Acrobats: Roy Rognan, George Snare, Stuart Barlow
Dwarfs: John Ballas, Freddie Goodrow, Ray Holgate, Ray Schultz

Music composed and arranged by Frank Tours

Production Committee: Lawrence Langner and Helen Westley

Stage Manager: George Greenberg

Ass't. Stage Managers: Elizabeth Chester, Phyllis Connard

Nixon Theatre, Pittsburgh, April 22, 1935
Guild Theatre, September 30, 1935
(129 PERFORMANCES)

PORGY AND BESS

AN AMERICAN FOLK OPERA

(Founded on the play *Porgy* by Du Bose and Dorothy Heyward)

Music by George Gershwin

Libretto by Du Bose Heyward

Lyrics by Du Bose Heyward and Ira Gershwin

Production directed by Rouben Mamoulian

Settings designed by Sergei Soudeikine

Orchestra conducted by Alexander Smallens

CAST

Mingo	Ford L. Buck
Clara	Abbie Mitchell
Sportin' Life	John W. Bubbles
Jake	Edward Matthews
Maria	Georgette Harvey
Annie	Olive Bell
Lily	Helen Dowdy
Serena	Ruby Elzy
Robbins	Henry Davis
Jim	Jack Carr
Peter	Gus Simons
Porgy	Todd Duncan
Crown	Warren Coleman
Bess	Anne Brown
Detective	Alexander Campbell
Two Policemen	Harold Woolf
	Burton McEvilly
Undertaker	John Garth
Frazier	J. Rosamond Johnson
Mr. Archdale	George Lessey
Nelson	Ray Yeates
Strawberry Woman	Helen Dowdy
Crab Man	Ray Yeates
Coroner	George Carleton

Residents of Catfish Row, fishermen, children, stevedores, etc.

The Eva Jessye Choir: Catherine Jackson Ayres, Lillian Cowan, Sara Daigeau, Darlean Duval, Kate Hall, Altonell Hines, Louisa Howard, Harriet Jackson, Rosalie King, Assotta Marshall, Wilnette Mayers, Sadie McGill, Massie Patterson, Annabella Ross, Louise Twyman, Helen R. White, Musa Williams, Reginald Beane, Caesar Bennett, G. Harry Bolden, Edward Broadnax, Carroll Clark, Joseph Crawford, John Diggs, Leonard Franklin, John Garth, Joseph James, Clarence Jacobs, Allen Lewis, Jimmie Lightfoot, Lycurgus Lockman, Henry May, Junius McDaniel, Arthur McLean, William O'Neil, Robert Raines, Andrew Taylor, Leon Threadgill, Jimmie Waters, Robert Williams, Ray Yeates.

Choral Director: Eva Jessye

Children: Naida King, Regina Williams, Enid Wilkins, Allen Tinney, Herbert Young.

The Charleston Orphan's Band: Shadrack Anderson, Eric Bell, Le-Verris Bilton, Benjamine Browne, Claude Christian, Shadrack Dobson, David Ellis, Clarence Smith, John Strachan, George Tait, Allen Tinney, William Tinney, Charles Williams, Herbert Young.

Production Committee: Lee Simonson and Warren Munsell

Assistant Conductor: Alexander Steinert

Assistant Coach: J. Rosamond Johnson

Stage Manager: Harold Woolf

Ass't. Stage Managers: Frances Herriott, Burton McEvilly

Colonial Theatre, Boston, September 30, 1935

Alvin Theatre, October 10, 1935

(124 PERFORMANCES)

(In association with Lee Ephraim)
Dodie Smith's Comedy

CALL IT A DAY

WITH
GLADYS COOPER AND PHILIP MERIVALE
PRODUCTION DIRECTED BY TYRONE GUTHRIE
Settings by Lee Simonson

CAST

Dorothy Hilton .... Gladys Cooper
Roger Hilton .... Philip Merivale
Vera .... Valerie Cossart
Ann Hilton .... Jeanne Dante
Martin Hilton .... John Buckmaster
Catherine Hilton .... Florence Williams
Cook .... Florence Edney
Mrs. Milson .... Lillian Brennard Tonge
Paul Francis .... Glenn Anders
Ethel Francis .... Frances Williams
Muriel Weston .... Viola Roache
Frank Haines .... Lawrence Grossmith
Elsie Lester .... Esther Mitchell
Beatrice Gwynne .... Claudia Morgan
Alistair Brown .... William Packer
Joan Collett .... Mary Mason

Administration Committee: Theresa Helburn and Lawrence Langner
Company Manager: Max A. Meyer
Stage Manager: Leonard Loan
Ass't. Stage Managers: Franklin Downing, Margot Stevenson
National Theatre, Washington, D.C., January 20, 1936
Morosco Theatre, January 28, 1936
(194 PERFORMANCES)

END OF SUMMER

S. N. Behrman

WITH

INA CLAIRE AND OSGOOD PERKINS

PRODUCTION DIRECTED BY PHILIP MOELLER

Setting by Lee Simonson

CAST

Will Dexter	Shepperd Strudwick
Mrs. Wyler	Mildred Natwick
Paula Frothingham	Doris Dudley
Robert	Kendall Clark
Leonie Frothingham	Ina Claire
Sam Frothingham	Minor Watson
Dr. Kenneth Rice	Osgood Perkins
Dennis McCarthy	Van Heflin
Dr. Dexter	Herbert Yost
Boris, Count Mirsky	Tom Powers

Production under the general supervision of
Theresa Helburn and Lawrence Langner
Stage Manager: Margaret Linley

Bushnell Memorial, Hartford, Conn., January 30, 1936
Guild Theatre, February 17, 1936
(153 PERFORMANCES)

IDIOT'S DELIGHT

ROBERT E. SHERWOOD
WITH
ALFRED LUNT AND LYNN FONTANNE
DIRECTED BY BRETAIGNE WINDUST
PRODUCTION CONCEIVED AND SUPERVISED BY
MR. LUNT AND MISS FONTANNE
Setting designed by Lee Simonson
Dances staged by Morgan Lewis

CAST

Dumptsy .... George Meader
Signor Palota .... Stephen Sandes
Donald Navadel .... Barry Thomson
Pittaluga .... S. Thomas Gomez
Auguste .... Edgar Barrier
Captain Locicero .... Edward Raquello
Dr. Waldersee .... Sydney Greenstreet
Mr. Cherry .... Bretaigne Windust
Mrs. Cherry .... Jean Macintyre
Harry Van .... Alfred Lunt
Shirley .... Jacqueline Paige
Beulah .... Connie Crowell
Edna .... Frances Foley
Francine .... Edna Ross
Elaine .... Marjorie Baglin
Bebe .... Ruth Timmons
1st Officer .... Alan Hewitt
2nd Officer .... Winston Ross
3rd Officer .... Gilmore Bush
4th Officer .... Tommaso Tittoni
Quillery .... Richard Whorf
Signor Rossi .... Le Roi Operti
Signora Rossi .... Ernestine De Becker
Major .... Joseph Della Malva
Anna .... Una Val
Irene .... Lynn Fontanne
Achille Weber .... Francis Compton

Musicians: Gerald Kunz, Max Rich, Joseph Knopf
Company Manager: Lawrence Farrell
Stage Manager: George Greenberg
Ass't. Stage Managers: Le Roi Operti, Tommaso Tittoni
National Theatre, Washington, D.C., March 9, 1936
Sam S. Shubert Theatre, March 24, 1936
(300 PERFORMANCES)

AND STARS REMAIN

Julius J. and Philip G. Epstein
WITH
CLIFTON WEBB AND HELEN GAHAGAN
Staged by Philip Moeller
Setting by Aline Bernstein

CAST

Lucy Trenchard .... Claudia Morgan
Overton Morrell .... Clifton Webb
Faith Feible .... Mary Sargent
Perry Feible .... Richard Barbee
Grandfather Trenchard .... Charles Richman
Mrs. Trenchard .... Suzanne Jackson
Cynthia Hope .... Helen Gahagan
Fredrick Holden .... Ben Smith
Nichols .... Edgar Kent

Production in charge of Theresa Helburn,
Lawrence Langner, and Philip Moeller
Stage Manager: John Haggott
Ass't. Stage Manager: Alfred Atcheverry

Nixon Theatre, Pittsburgh, September 28, 1936
Guild Theatre, October 12, 1936
(56 PERFORMANCES)

PRELUDE TO EXILE

William McNally
WITH
WILFRED LAWSON   EVA LE GALLIENNE
LUCILE WATSON
PRODUCTION DIRECTED BY PHILIP MOELLER
Settings and costumes designed by Lee Simonson

CAST

Countess Marie D'Agoult .... Lucile Watson
Adolph (servant to the Wagners) .... Roland Hogue
Cosima Liszt von Bulow .... Miriam Battista
Richard Wagner .... Wilfred Lawson
Mathilde Wesendonck .... Eva Le Gallienne
Otto Wesendonck .... Leo G. Carroll
Malwina Schnorr .... Beal Hober
Ludwig Schnorr .... Arthur Gerry
Minna Wagner .... Evelyn Varden
Gotfried (footman to the Wesendoncks).................. Henry Levin

Production under the supervision of Theresa Helburn,
Philip Moeller, and Lawrence Langner
Stage Manager: Charles Holden
Ass't. Stage Manager: Henry Levin

Chestnut Street Theatre, Philadelphia, November 16, 1936
Guild Theatre, November 30, 1936
(48 PERFORMANCES)

(By arrangement with Sidney Harmon)

BUT FOR THE GRACE OF GOD

LEOPOLD ATLAS

PRODUCTION DIRECTED BY BENNO SCHNEIDER

Settings designed by Stewart Chaney

CAST

Josey .... James McCallion
Eddie .... Gene Lowe
Petey .... Joe Brown, Jr.
Bosco .... Leslie Klein
Snowball .... Paul White
Uncle Louis .... Harry Levian
Fotzo .... Robert Mayors
Mooch .... Arthur Bruce
Sharkey .... Edgerton Paul
Bugsey .... Jack Arnold
Ralphy .... Melbourne Ford
Charley .... Robert J. Mulligan
Frank Adamec .... James Bell
Mrs. Sullivan .... Beatrice Moreland
Hannah Adamec .... Kathryn Grill
Wilson .... Anthony Ross
Rusek .... Clem Willenchik
Stanley .... Maurice Burke
Kababian .... Joseph Greenwald
Zhlub .... Stanley Povitch
Julius .... John Call
Rosey .... Gilda Oakleaf
Bertha .... Harriet Caron
Berg .... P. A. Xantho
Whitey .... Lester Lonergan III
Marty .... Robert Reeves
Mac .... Clem Willenchik
George Shay .... Frank Gabrielson
Bert .... Phil Sheridan
First Woman .... Dorothy Scott
Second Woman .... Norma Chambers
Interne .... Sidney Packer
Steve .... Phil Sheridan
York .... Robert Gordon

Production under the supervision of Theresa Helburn,
Lawrence Langner, and Sidney Harmon

Stage Managers: P. A. Xantho, Harold Hecht

Ass't. Stage Manager: Robert Reeves

Guild Theatre, January 11, 1937

(42 PERFORMANCES)

MAXWELL ANDERSON'S

THE MASQUE OF KINGS

WITH

HENRY HULL   MARGO

DUDLEY DIGGES   PAULINE FREDERICK

PRODUCTION DIRECTED BY PHILIP MOELLER

Settings and costumes designed by Lee Simonson

CAST

The Countess Larisch .... Claudia Morgan
A Maid .... Catherine Lawrence
Count Taafe .... Herbert Yost
The Emperor Franz Joseph of Austria-Hungary ...... Dudley Digges
A Servant .... Pierre Chace
Koinoff .... Glenn Anders
The Empress Elizabeth of Austria-Hungary ...... Pauline Frederick
Count Larisch .... John Hoysradt
Marie .... Bijou Fernandez
Fritz von Bremer .... Alan Hewitt
Louise .... Elizabeth Young
D'Orsy .... Benjamin Otis
Loschek .... Edward Broadley
The Crown Prince Rudolph of Austria-Hungary .... Henry Hull
Bratfish .... Henry Hull, Jr.
The Baroness Mary Vetsera .... Margo
The Archduke John of Tuscany .... Joseph Holland
Sceps .... Wyrley Birch
An Officer .... Franklin Downing
A Soldier .... Charles Holden
A Soldier .... Hobart Skidmore
County Joseph Hoyos .... Leo G. Carroll

Production under the supervision of Theresa Helburn, Lawrence Langner, and Philip Moeller

Stage Manager: Charles Holden

Ass't. Stage Managers: Franklin Downing and Henry Hull, Jr.

Montclair Theatre, Montclair, N.J., January 18, 1937

Sam S. Shubert Theatre, February 8, 1937

(89 PERFORMANCES)

STORM OVER PATSY

A COMEDY BY BRUNO FRANK
ADAPTED BY JAMES BRIDIE
WITH
SARA ALLGOOD   ROGER LIVESEY
CLAUDIA MORGAN   IAN McLEAN
PRODUCTION DIRECTED BY PHILIP MOELLER
Settings designed by Aline Bernstein

CAST

Victoria Thomson .... Claudia Morgan
Maggie .... Valerie Cossart
Mr. Burdon .... Roger Livesey
Mrs. Honoria Flanagan .... Sara Allgood
Lisbet Skirving .... Brenda Forbes
William Thomson, Provost of Baikie .... Ian McLean
Joseph McKellar .... Francis Pierlot
Horace Skirving .... J. W. Austin
Court Usher .... Clement O'Loghlen
Clerk of the Court .... Farrell Pelly
The Judge .... Leo G. Carroll
Mr. Fraser, the Prosecutor .... Louis Hector
Mr. Menzies, K. C. .... John Hoysradt
Junior Counsel .... Kendall Clark
Stenographer .... Jack Burley
Policeman .... Herbert Standing
Dr. Cassidy .... Jack Byrne
Patsy .... Colonel

Court Spectators: Frances Kidner, Elizabeth A. Jones, Seymour Gross, Dan Rudsten, Carrie Bridewell, Harry Hermsen, Phyllis Langner

Production under the supervision of Theresa Helburn,
Lawrence Langner, and Philip Moeller
Stage Manager: Edward Goodnow
Ass't. Stage Manager: Kendall Clark

National Theatre, Washington, D.C., March 1, 1937
Guild Theatre, March 8, 1937
(48 PERFORMANCES)

JANE EYRE

A dramatization of Charlotte Brontë's novel

By Helen Jerome

DIRECTED BY WORTHINGTON MINER

Settings and costumes by Lee Simonson

CAST

Mrs. Fairfax .... .Viola Roache
Leah .... Phyllis Connard
Jane Eyre .... Katharine Hepburn
Mr. Rochester .... Dennis Hoey
Adele Varens .... Patricia Peardon
Grace Poole .... Teresa Dale
Mason .... Irving Morrow
The Maniac .... Theresa Guerini
Lady Ingram .... Katherine Stewart
Lord Ingram .... Wallace Widdecome
Briggs .... Wilfred Seagram
Reverend Wood .... Boyd Davis
Diana Rivers .... Barbara O'Neil
Hannah .... Marga Ann Deighton
St. John Rivers .... Stephen Ker Appleby
Blanche Ingram .... Shirley Dale

Production under the supervision of Theresa Helburn and Lawrence Langner

Shubert Theatre, New Haven, Dec. 19, 1936
(given an extensive tour, but not shown in New York)

TWENTIETH SEASON

TO QUITO AND BACK

BEN HECHT

WITH

SYLVIA SIDNEY AND LESLIE BANKS

PRODUCTION DIRECTED BY PHILIP MOELLER

Settings and costumes designed by Aline Bernstein

CAST

Railway Official .... Joseph M. deVillard
Howard Evans .... Francis Compton
Lola Hobbs .... Sylvia Sidney
Alexander Sterns .... Leslie Banks
Zamiano .... Joseph Buloff
Officer .... Walter Armin
Francisca .... Virginia Holden
Tomasa .... Eugenia Rawls
Florinda .... Isobel Donald
Maria .... Virginia Gregori
Alfredo .... George J. Lewis
Captain Stewart .... Horace Sinclair
Fifi Stewart .... Lena Peters
Harold Frazer .... Walter Greaza
Countess Rivadavia .... Evelyn Varden
Dr. Duquesne .... Jack Soanes
Manuella .... Natalia Danesi
A Soldier .... Manuel De Moya
Colonel Pizarro .... Manart Kippen
Diaz .... Charles H. Pinkham
An Officer .... Albert Allen
Fortune Teller .... Sidonie Espero
Dr. Borodin, Minister of the Interior .... Henry Levin
Sanchey, a Guitarist .... Alfonso Chavez
Comrade Santoya, Minister of Transportation .... Jan Ullrich
Comrade Patayo, Minister of Finance .... Harry Bellaver
Comrade Rienza, Minister of Education .... Samuel Brown
Comrade Gonzalez, Minister of Agriculture .... Fred Clegg
Muggsie .... Himself
Natives, Soldiers, etc.

Mildred Levin, Michael Lackman, Louis Halprin, Don Kelly, Lone Mountain, Fredricka Fortello, Juan DeAguenta, Manuel Risto, Sheila Richart, Tommi Bissell, Edilberto G. Burgos, Tuan Garcia, Jose Ramirez.

Production under the supervision of Theresa Helburn, Lawrence Langner, and Philip Moeller

Colonial Theatre, Boston, September 20, 1937

Guild Theatre, October 6, 1937

(46 PERFORMANCES)

THE ALFRED LUNT AND LYNN FONTANNE PRODUCTION OF
JEAN GIRAUDOUX'S COMEDY

AMPHITRYON 38

ADAPTED BY S. N. BEHRMAN
DIRECTED BY BRETAIGNE WINDUST
PRODUCTION CONCEIVED AND SUPERVISED BY
MR. LUNT AND MISS FONTANNE
Settings designed by Lee Simonson
Costumes designed by Valentina
Music composed and conducted by Samuel L. M. Barlow

CAST

Jupiter .... Alfred Lunt
Mercury .... Richard Whorf
Sosie, Servant to Amphitryon .... George Meader
Trumpeter .... Sydney Greenstreet
Warrior .... Alan Hewitt
Alkmena .... Lynn Fontanne
Amphitryon .... Barry Thomson
Nenetza .... Kathleen Roland
Kleantha .... Jacqueline Paige
Echo .... Ernestine De Becker
Leda .... Edith King

For the Theatre Guild–
Company Manager: Lawrence Farrell
Stage Manager: George Greenberg
Ass't. Stage Managers: Jacqueline Paige, David Selva
Curran Theatre, San Francisco, June 23, 1937
Sam S. Shubert Theatre, November 1, 1937
(153 PERFORMANCES)

GASTON BATY'S DRAMATIZATION OF FLAUBERT'S NOVEL

MADAME BOVARY

WITH

CONSTANCE CUMMINGS

ADAPTED AND DIRECTED BY BENN W. LEVY

Settings and costumes designed by Lee Simonson

(adapted from the original production of Gaston Baty)

CAST

Emma Bovary .... Constance Cummings
Monsieur Rouault .... Arthur Griffin
Charles Bovary .... Harold Vermilyea
Homais .... Ernest Cossart
Mme. Lefrançois .... Alice Belmore-Cliffe
Hippolyte .... John O'Connor
Binet .... Robert Vivian
Leon Dupuis .... Carl Harbord
Mme. Caron .... Hazel Hanna
L'Heaueux .... Ernest Thesiger
Félicité .... Valerie Cossart
Justin .... O. Z. Whitehead
Mme. Homais .... Viola Roache
Rudolphe Boulanger .... Eric Portman
Girard .... Maurice Manson
Mme. Bovary, Senior .... Eda Heinemann

The Companions .... { Ann Freschmann, Frances Harison, Jacqueline De Wit, Lilyan Miller, Mary McCormack, Gladene Parr }

Production under the supervision of Theresa Helburn, Lawrence Langner, and Benn W. Levy

Company Manager: Max Meyer

Stage Manager: John Haggott

Ass't. Stage Managers: John O'Connor and Irving Morrow

National Theatre, Washington, D.C., October 5, 1937

Broadhurst Theatre, November 16, 1937

(39 PERFORMANCES)

THE GHOST OF YANKEE DOODLE

A Play in Two Acts by
SIDNEY HOWARD
WITH
ETHEL BARRYMORE AND DUDLEY DIGGES
PRODUCTION DIRECTED BY JOHN CROMWELL
PRODUCTION DESIGNED BY WOODMAN THOMPSON

CAST

Sara Garrison	Ethel Barrymore
John Garrison	Frank Conroy
Patience Garrison	Marilyn Erskine
Michael Garrison	Jack Kelly
Senator Callory	George Nash
Doris Garrison	Kathleen Comegys
Roger Garrison	John Drew Devereaux
Joan Garrison	Barbara Robbins
Robert Garrison	Eliot Cabot
Martin Holme	Richard Carlson
Mary	Ethel Intropidi
James Madison Clevenger	Dudley Digges
Ockleford	Don Costello
Steve Andrews	Russell Hardie
Buck Anson	Donald Black
A Police Sergeant	Edward Butler
Policemen	Arthur Davidson
	George Goss
Burke	Lloyd Gough
Dr. Miller	Howard Roberts

Production under the supervision of Theresa Helburn,
Lawrence Langner, and John Cromwell
Stage Manager: Edward McHugh
Ass't. Stage Manager: Kendall Clark

The Auditorium, Rochester, N.Y., October 27, 1937
Guild Theatre, November 22, 1937
(48 PERFORMANCES)

S. N. Behrman's

WINE OF CHOICE

WITH

LESLIE BANKS CLAUDIA MORGAN

ALEXANDER WOOLLCOTT

PRODUCTION DIRECTED BY HERMAN SHUMLIN

Setting designed by Lee Simonson

CAST

Charles Dow Hanlon .... Herbert Yost
Togo .... Akihiko Yoshiwara
Binkie Niebuhr .... Alexander Woollcott
Wilda Doran .... Claudia Morgan
Dow Christophsen .... Theodore Newton
Laddy Sears .... Donald Cook
Ryder Gerrard .... Leslie Banks
Leo Traub .... Paul Stewart
Collins .... John Maroney

Production under the supervision of: Theresa Helburn and Lawrence Langner

Stage Manager: Charles Holden

Ass't. Stage Manager: John Maroney

For the opening in Montclair:

Production directed by Philip Moeller

Binkie Niebuhr .... Harry Wagstaff Gribble
Wilda Doran .... Miriam Hopkins
Leo Traub .... John Cranwell

Montclair, N. J., Theatre, December 11, 1937

Guild Theatre, February 21, 1938

(43 PERFORMANCES)

The Alfred Lunt and Lynn Fontanne
production of Chekhov's

THE SEA GULL

Translated by Stark Young
DIRECTED BY ROBERT MILTON
Settings and costumes designed by Robert Edmond Jones
CAST

Irina Arkadina, Madame Trepleff, an actress .... Lynn Fontanne
Constantine Trepleff, her son .... Richard Whorf
Peter Sorin, her brother .... Sydney Greenstreet
Nina, a young girl, daughter of a wealthy landowner .... Uta Hagen
Shamreyeff, a retired lieutenant, Sorin's steward ...... Harold Moffet
Pauline, his wife .... Edith King
Masha, his daughter .... Margaret Webster
Boris Trigorin, a literary man .... Alfred Lunt
Eugene Dorn, a doctor .... John Barclay
Semyon Medvedenko, a schoolmaster .... O. Z. Whitehead
Yacov, a laborer .... Alan Hewitt
Cook .... S. Thomas Gomez
Housemaids .... Jacqueline Paige
Ernestine De Becker

Company Manager: Lawrence Farrell
Stage Manager: George Greenberg
Ass't. Stage Manager: Jacqueline Paige

Ford's Theatre, Baltimore, Md., March 16, 1938
Sam S. Shubert Theatre, March 28, 1938
(41 PERFORMANCES)
(limited engagement)

The Theatre Guild and the Actors' Repertory Company present

WASHINGTON JITTERS

A Comedy in Two Acts by John Boruff and Walter Hart
Based on the novel of the same name by Dalton Trumbo
DIRECTED BY WALTER HART
Settings designed by Lawrence L. Goldwasser

CAST

Radio Announcer .... Erik Walz
Harvey Upp .... Anthony Ross
Miss Preston .... Rose Keane
Mrs. Dwight .... Lesley Stafford
Senator Marple .... Francis Pierlot
Hamilton Dill .... Forrest Orr
Photographer .... Douglass Parkhirst
Senator Briggs .... Will Geer
Congressman Fusser .... Bertram Thorn
Mehafferty .... Harry Shannon
Sam Dawson .... Robert Porterfield
Poindexter .... Robert Williams
Henry Hogg .... Fred Stewart
Mrs. Nelson .... Kathryn Grill
Eula Keefer .... Helen Shields
Guide .... David Clarke
Tourist .... Norma Chambers
Waiter .... Edwin Cooper
1st Senator .... David Clarke
2nd Senator .... Kendall Clark
Jerry .... Kendall Clark
Clerk .... John O'Shaughnessy
Perigord .... Robert Thomsen
Manager .... Erik Walz
Waiter .... Kendall Clark
Senator Ransom .... John O'Shaughnessy
McGinty .... David Clarke
General Smedley .... Edwin Cooper
Lieutenant .... David Clarke
Coward .... George Oliver Taylor
Jenny Bronson .... Dorothy Brackett
A Sign Painter .... Edwin Cooper
Reporter .... Kendall Clark
Hostess .... Norma Chambers
Jed .... David Clark

Production Committee: Theresa Helburn, Lawrence Langner, Philip Moeller, Rose Keane, John O'Shaughnessy and J. Edward Shugrue

Theatre Manager: Max A. Meyer

Technical Director: J. Edward Shugrue

Stage Manager: John Haggott

Ass't. Stage Manager: Kendall Clark

Guild Theatre, May 2, 1938

(Previews for subscribers and "benefit parties" beginning April 11)

(24 PERFORMANCES)

TWENTY-FIRST SEASON

DAME NATURE

by André Birabeau

Adapted by Patricia Collinge

DIRECTED BY WORTHINGTON MINER

Settings designed by Norris Houghton

CAST

Max .... Thomas Coffin Cooke
Beer, a Schoolboy .... Charles Bellin
Second Schoolboy .... Frederick Bradlee
Third Schoolboy .... Edwin Mills
Concierge .... Edward Cooper
Doctor Faridet .... Harry Irvine
Leonie Perrot .... Lois Hall
André Brisac .... Montgomery Clift
Batton .... Morgan James
Fourth Schoolboy .... Peter Miner
Nanine .... Kathryn Grill
Marie .... Grace Matthews
Madame Brisac .... Jessie Royce Landis
Monsieur Brisac .... Onslow Stevens
Uncle Lucien .... Forrest Orr
Paul Marachal .... Wilton Graff

Production under the supervision of Theresa Helburn, Lawrence Langner, and Worthington Miner

Stage Manager: John Haggott

Ass't. Stage Manager: John O'Connor

Westport Country Playhouse, July 4, 1938

Booth Theatre, September 26, 1938

(48 PERFORMANCES)

(As produced by Herman Shumlin)

THE MERCHANT OF YONKERS

A farce in three acts by Thornton Wilder
(Based on a comedy by Johann Nestroy; taken from an English version)

STAGED BY MAX REINHARDT

Settings by Boris Aronson

CAST

Horace Vandergelder .... Percy Waram
Ambrose Kemper .... Bartlett Robinson
Joe Scanlon .... Philip Coolidge
Gertrude .... Carrie Weller
Cornelius Hacki .... Tom Ewell
Ermengarde .... Frances Harison
Melchoir Stack .... Joseph Sweeney
Mrs. Levi .... Jane Cowl
Barnaby Tucker .... John Call
Mrs. Molloy .... June Walker
Minnie Fay .... Nydia Westman
A Cabman .... Edward F. Nannary
August .... Peter Struwel
A Cook .... Maida Reade
Miss Van Huysen .... Minna Phillips

Guild Theatre, December 28, 1938
(39 PERFORMANCES)

JEREMIAH

by Stefan Zweig
Translated by Eden and Cedar Paul
WITH
ARTHUR BYRON EFFIE SHANNON KENT SMITH
Acting version prepared by John Gassner and Worthington Miner
STAGED BY WORTHINGTON MINER
Settings and costumes designed by Harry Horner
Music composed and arranged by Chemjo Vinaver
Lyrics composed by Ruth Langner
Choreography staged by Felicia Sorel

CAST

Jeremiah .... Kent Smith
Mother .... Effie Shannon
Zebulon .... Hannam Clark
Baruch, his son .... Alfred Ryder
Lesh, his sister .... Elizabeth Royce
Issacher .... Ernest Rowan
Rebecca, his daughter .... Katherine Murphy
Laban, his son .... Robert Thomsen
Jochebed .... Kathryn Grill
Her Husband .... Robert Malcolm
Her Older Son .... Paul Tripp
Her Younger Son .... Vincent J. Donehue
Ruth, her daughter .... Joan Adrian
A Huckster .... Henry Levin
Uriah, a peddler .... Mark Schweid
His wife .... Kay Wilt
Zephania .... Charles Furcolowe
His Wife .... Mary Fischer
Micha, his father .... John McKee
His Mother .... Nell Harrison
A Merchant .... David Rosen
His Wife .... Virginia Gregori
His Nephew .... Cameron Mitchell
Solom, another merchant .... Gordon Nelson
His Wife .... Roberta Bellinger
His Daughter .... Katharine Bard
His Son-in-law .... Theodore Paul
The Elder .... John Hendrick
His Niece .... Betty Young

Her Husband	George H. Lee
Gad, the strident one	Charles Jordan
His Wife	Marian Rudley
Zilpah, his sister	Mary Perry
Hananiah	Harry Irvine
Pashur	Benedict McQuarrie
Abimelech	Robert Harrison
First Sentry	John O'Connor
Second Sentry	Byron McGrath
First Guard	Arthur Sachs
Second Guard	Harold Hoha
Third Guard	Alexis Tcherkassky
Zedekiah	Arthur Byron
Herald	Philip Lewis
Ahab	Byron Russell
His Father	Arthur Villars
Nahum	St. Clair Bayfield
Imre	Henry Bennett
Joab	Morgan James
Nehemiah	Cornell Wilde
Aaron	Tom Morrison
Shephan	George Petrie
Assyrian Captain	Mervin Williams
Second Assyrian Officer	Byron Russell
Third Assyrian Officer	David Rosen
First Assyrian Soldier	Theodore Paul
Second Assyrian Soldier	Vincent J. Donehue

Production under the supervision of Lawrence Langner
and Philip Moeller

Theatre Manager: Max Meyer
Stage Manager: John Haggott
Ass't. Stage Manager: John O'Connor

Guild Theatre, February 3, 1939
(35 PERFORMANCES)

(A Guild-sponsored Mercury Theatre production)

FIVE KINGS (PART I)

Condensation by Orson Welles of Shakespeare's Chronicles
DIRECTED BY ORSON WELLES
Technical supervision by Jean Rosenthal
Scenery designed by James Marcom
Costumes by Milla Davenport
Incidental music composed by Aaron Copland

CAST

Chorus .... Robert Speaight
Bolingbroke .... Morris Ankrum
Prince Hal .... Burgess Meredith
Clarence .... Richard Baer
Gloucester .... Guy Kingsley
Hotspur .... John Emery
Northumberland .... Eustace Wyatt
Worcester .... Macgregor Gibb
Westmoreland .... John Adair
Warwick .... Lawrence Fletcher
Exton .... William Bishop
Vernon .... John Straub
A Lord .... William Mowry
Archbishop of Canterbury .... Edgar Barrier
Bishop of Ely .... George Duthie
Lord Chief Justice .... Erskine Sanford
Salisbury .... Stephen Roberts
Bracy .... John Willard
Falstaff .... Orson Welles
Bardolph .... Gus Schilling
Poins .... John Berry
Peto .... William Alland
Page .... Edgarton Paul
Gadshill .... Sanford Siegel
Wart .... Gerold Kean
Pistol .... Eustace Wyatt
Shallow .... Edgar Kent
Silence .... Fred Stewart
Bullcalf .... Stephen Roberts
Mouldy .... William Herz
Feeble .... John Willard

Shadow	James Marcom
Davy	Francis Carpenter
Court	Fred Stewart
Bates	John Willard
Williams	Richard Wilson
Gower	John Straub
Finellen	Edgar Kent
Servant to Hotspur	Stanley Poss
French Queen	Ellen Andrews
Montjoy, Ambassador of France	Gerold Kean
Lady Percy	Lora Baxter
Mistress Quickly	Alice John
Mistress Doll	Grace Coppin
Katharine	Margaret Curtis
Alice	Rosemary Carver
French Lady	Ann Saks

(After opening in Boston on February 27, 1939, the production traveled to Washington, then to Philadelphia—where it closed before its scheduled New York showing.)

Katharine Hepburn in

THE PHILADELPHIA STORY

by Philip Barry

DIRECTED BY ROBERT B. SINCLAIR

Designed and lighted by Robert Edmond Jones

CAST

Dinah Lord .... Lenore Lonergan
Margaret Lord .... Vera Allen
Tracy Lord .... Katharine Hepburn
Alexander Lord .... Dan Tobin
Thomas .... Owen Coll
William Tracy .... Forrest Orr
Elizabeth Imbrie .... Shirley Booth
Macaulay Connor .... Van Heflin
George Kittredge .... Frank Fenton
C. K. Dexter Haven .... Joseph Cotten
(courtesy of the Mercury Theatre)
Edward .... Philip Foster
Seth Lord .... Nicholas Joy
May .... Myrtle Tannahill
Elsie .... Lorraine Bate
Mac .... Hayden Rorke

Production under the supervision of Theresa Helburn and Lawrence Langner

Company Manager: Herman Bernstein

Stage Manager: Karl Nielson

Ass't. Stage Manager: Hayden Rorke

Shubert Theatre, New Haven, February 16, 1939

Sam S. Shubert Theatre, March 28, 1939

(417 PERFORMANCES)

(A Group Theatre Production)

MY HEART'S IN THE HIGHLANDS

A play in one act by William Saroyan
STAGED BY ROBERT LEWIS
Settings and costumes by Herbert Andrews
Music by Paul Bowles

CAST

The Boy	Jackie Ayers
Ben Alexander, the Poet	Philip Loeb
Johnny, his Son	Sidney Lumet
Jasper MacGregor, the Actor	Art Smith
Mr. Kosak, the Grocer	William Hansen
Johnny's Grandmother	Hester Sondergaard
Rufe Apley	James O'Rear
Philip Carmichael	Loren Gage
Henry	Phil Brown
Mr. Wiley	Harry Bratsburg
Real Estate Agent	Nicholas Conte
Husband	John O'Malley
Wife	Catheryn Laughlin
Ester Kosak	Mae Grimes
Two Guards	Peter Leeds
	Charles de Sheim

Good Friends and Neighbors:
Edna Reis, Eileen Detchon, Undine Forrest, Charles Henderson, Mary Liles

Guild Theatre, April 13, 1939
(44 PERFORMANCES)

TWENTY-SECOND SEASON

(In Association with Eddie Dowling)

THE TIME OF YOUR LIFE

BY WILLIAM SAROYAN

DIRECTED BY EDDIE DOWLING AND WILLIAM SAROYAN

Settings by Watson Barratt

CAST

Newsboy .... Ross Bagdasarian
Drunk .... John Farrell
Willie .... Will Lee
Joe .... Eddie Dowling
Nick .... Charles De Sheim
Tom .... Edward Andrews
Kitty Duval .... Julie Haydon
Dudley .... Curt Conway
Harry .... Gene Kelly
Westley .... Reginald Beane
Lorene .... Nene Vibber
Blick .... Grover Burgess
Arab .... Houseley Stevens, Sr.
Mary L. .... Celeste Holm
Krupp .... William Bendix
McCarthy .... Tom Tully
Kit Carson .... Len Doyle
Nick's Ma .... Michelette Burani
Sailor .... Randolph Wade
Elsie .... Cathie Bailey
A Killer .... Evelyn Geller
Her Side Kick .... Mary Chaffey
A Society Lady .... Eva Leonard Boyne
A Society Gentleman .... Ainsworth Arnold
First Cop .... Randolph Wade
Second Cop .... John Farrell

Stage Manager: John Haggott
Ass't. Stage Manager: Randolph Wade

Shubert Theatre, New Haven, October 5, 1939
Booth Theatre, October 25, 1939
(185 PERFORMANCES, plus revival during following season)

THE FIFTH COLUMN

From the published play by Ernest Hemingway
ADAPTED BY BENJAMIN GLAZER
STAGED BY LEE STRASBERG
Setting by Howard Bay

CAST

Anita	Lenore Ulric
Philip Rawlings	Franchot Tone
Max	Lee J. Cobb
Antonio	Arnold Moss
A Soldier from New York	Wendell K. Phillips
Another Soldier	Henry Levin
Hotel Manager	Emile Boreo
Dorothy Bridges	Katherine Locke
Preston	A. J. Herbert
Petra	Hilda Bruce
A Sentry	Henry Levin
Another Sentry	Michael Sage
A Thin Officer	John Gerard
A Man in Civilian Clothes	David Leonard
A General from Germany	William F. Schoeller
An Orderly	Philip Lewis
Doyle	Charles Jordon
Holt	Don MacLaughlin
Hotel Electrician	Sid Cassel
An Assault Guard	Michael Sage
Private Wilkinson	Kendall Clark
A Man in a Brown Leather Coat	John Gerard
Another Assault Guard	Raoul Henry
The Butterfly Man	Harry Davis
First Waiter	Sid Cassel
Second Waiter	Philip Lewis
An Artilleryman	Michael Sage
Two Assault Guards	Fred Catania Peter Knego

Shubert Theatre, New Haven, January 26, 1940
Alvin Theatre, March 6, 1940
(87 PERFORMANCES)

(Co-produced with the Playwrights' Company)

THERE SHALL BE NO NIGHT

BY ROBERT E. SHERWOOD
STAGED BY ALFRED LUNT
Settings by Richard Whorf
Costumes by Valentina

CAST

Dr. Kaarlo Valkonen .... Alfred Lunt
Miranda Valkonen .... Lynn Fontanne
Dave Corween .... Richard Whorf
Uncle Waldemar .... Sydney Greenstreet
Gus Shuman .... Brooks West
Erik Valkonen .... Montgomery Clift
Kaatri Alquist .... Elisabeth Fraser
Dr. Ziemssen .... Maurice Colbourne
Major Rutkowski .... Edward Raquello
Joe Burnett .... Charles Ansley
Ben Gichner .... Thomas Gomez
Frank Ormstead .... William Le Massena
Sergeant Gosden .... Claude Horton
Lempi .... Phyllis Thaxter
Irma .... Charva Chester
1st Photographer .... Ralph Nelson
2nd Photographer .... Robert Downing

Stage Manager: Charva Chester
Ass't. Stage Managers: Ralph Nelson
Robert Downing

The Playhouse, Providence, March 29, 1940
Alvin Theatre, April 29, 1940

(Produced in association with Eddie Dowling)

LOVE'S OLD SWEET SONG

BY WILLIAM SAROYAN

STAGED BY EDDIE DOWLING AND WILLIAM SAROYAN

Settings designed by Watson Barratt

Music by Paul Bowles

CAST

Ann Hamilton, 44, a beautiful, unmarried small-town woman		Jessie Royce Landis
George Americanos, a Postal Telegraph messenger		Peter Fernandez
Barnaby Gaul, 51, a pitchman		Walter Huston
Tom Fiora, another messenger		James S. Elliott
Demetrios, an American citizen		Angi O. Poulos
Cabot Yearling, a family man		Arthur Hunnicutt
Leona Yearling, 44, his wife		Doro Merande
Newton Yearling, 19, their half-wit son		Eugene Fitts
Velma Yearling	their twins	Barbara Hastings
Selma Yearling	their twins	Ardele Hastings
Al Yearling	their other children	Thomas Jordon
Henry Yearling	their other children	Eric Roberts
Jesse Yearling	their other children	Jackie Ayers
Lucy Yearling	their other children	Patsy O'Shea
Ella Yearling	their other children	Mae Grimes
Susan Yearling	their other children	Patricia Roe
Maud Yearling	their other children	Carol Esa
Lemmie Yearling	their other children	Bob White
Mae Yearling	their other children	Eleanor Drexler
Harry Yearling	their other children	Michael Artist
Wilbur Yearling	their other children	Gerald Matthews
Richard Oliver, a novelist		Lloyd Gough
Elsa Wax, a photographer for Life Magazine		Beatrice Newport
David F. Windmore, a college man		Alan Hewitt
Daniel Hough, a farmer		John A. Regan
Mr. Smith, a representative for the West Coast Novelty Amusement Company		Nick Dennis
Mr. Harris, his associate		George Travell
Sheriff		Howard Freeman
Stylianos Americanos, 41, Georgie's father, a wrestler		Alan Reed
Pericles Americanos, 61, Stylianos' father		John Economides

Production assistant: Armina Marshall

Stage Manager: Tom Bate

Ass't. Stage Managers: Bettina Cerf, Henry Dowling, Ross Bagdasarian

Forrest Theatre, Philadelphia, April 8, 1940

Plymouth Theatre, May 2, 1940

(44 PERFORMANCES)

(Produced in association with Gilbert Miller)
HELEN HAYES AND MAURICE EVANS
In William Shakespeare's Comedy

TWELFTH NIGHT

DIRECTED BY MARGARET WEBSTER
Settings and costumes by Stewart Chaney
Music by Paul Bowles

CAST

Orsino, Duke of Illyria .... Wesley Addy
Curia / Valentine } gentlemen attending the Duke .... { George Keane / Philip Huston
Viola .... Helen Hayes
Sea Captain .... Anthony Ross
Sir Toby Belch, uncle to Olivia .... Mark Smith
Maria, Olivia's gentlewoman .... June Walker
Sir Andrew Aguecheek .... Norman Lloyd
Feste, a clown .... Donald Burr
Olivia .... Sophie Stewart
Malvolio, steward to Olivia .... Maurice Evans
Antonio .... Ellis Irving
Sebastian, brother of Viola .... Alex Courtnay
Fabian, servant to Olivia .... Raymond Johnson
Attendant to Olivia .... June Brehm
Officer .... Anthony Ross
Soldier .... Irving Morrow
Sir Topas, a priest .... Wallace Acton
A Page .... Osbert Chevers

Watchman, Sailors, Soldiers, Musicians, and Attendants to Olivia and Orsino:

Jacqueline Paige, Larry Gates, Donald Buka, Max Leavitt, Guy Spaull, Lauren Gilbert, William Hansen

Stage Manager: John Haggott
Ass't. Stage Manager: Jacqueline Paige

St. James Theatre, November 19, 1940
(129 PERFORMANCES)

MIRIAM HOPKINS

in

BATTLE OF ANGELS

BY TENNESSEE WILLIAMS

DIRECTED BY MARGARET WEBSTER

Setting by Cleon Throckmorton

Music by Colin McPhee

CAST

Dolly Bland	Dorothy Peterson
Beulah Cartwright	Edith King
Pee Wee Bland	Robert Emhardt
Sheriff Talbott	Charles McClelland
Cassandra Whiteside	Doris Dudley
Vee Talbott	Katherine Raht
Valentine Xavier	Westley Addy
Eva Temple	Hazel Hanna
Blanche Temple	Helen Carewe
Myra Torrance	Miriam Hopkins
Joe	Clarence Washington
Small Boy	Bertram Holmes
Bennie	Ivan Lewis
Jabe Torrance	Marshall Bradford

Stage Manager: John Haggott

Ass't. Stage Manager: Elaine Anderson

Wilbur Theatre, Boston, December 30, 1940

(Closed in Boston, January 11, 1941, after a censorship fight.)

LIBERTY JONES

A Play with Music by
PHILIP BARRY
STAGED BY JOHN HOUSEMAN
Music by Paul Bowles
Scenery and costumes designed by Raoul Pène Du Bois
Dances by Lew Christensen

CAST

Liberty Jones	Nancy Coleman
Liberty's Uncle	William Lynn
Liberty's Aunt	Martha Hodge
Tom Smith	John Beal
Dick Brown	Tom Ewell
Harry Robinson	Howard Freeman
Nurse Cotton	Katherine Squire
Nurse Maggie	Ivy Scott
The Two Reporters	Don Glenn, Graham Denton
The Two Dancers	Lew Christensen, Elise Reiman
The Three Shirts	Victor Thorley, Louis Polan, Richard Sanders
The Four Doctors The Committee of Four The Four Policemen	Norman Lloyd, Murray O'Neill, Allan Frank, William Mende
The Five Singers	William Castle, Roy Johnston, Eva Burton, Ruth Gibbs, Alyce Carter
The Seven Friends	Lew Christensen, Joseph Anthony, Vincent Gardner, Craig Mitchell, William Castle, Roy Johnston, Jack Parsons
The Eleven Friends	Elise Reiman, Bedela Falls, Caryl Smith, Honora Harwood, Ellen Morgan, Helen Kramer, Barbara Brown, Constance Dowling, Eva Burton, Ruth Gibbs, and Alyce Carter

Shubert Theatre, February 5, 1941
(22 PERFORMANCES)

SOMEWHERE IN FRANCE

BY CARL ZUCKMAYER AND FRITZ KORTNER

WITH

DUDLEY DIGGES ARLENE FRANCIS ALEXANDER KNOX

STAGED BY WORTHINGTON MINER

Setting by Watson Barratt

CAST

Gustave Marignac .... Dudley Digges
Olympe Marignac .... Kathryn Givney
Papa Memechose .... Art Smith
Beaumont .... Robert H. Harris
Buerzenich .... Walter Slezak
Mercier .... Alexander Knox
Marin .... Henry Levin
Stenographers .... Varvara Thery, Anna Minot
Rigolette .... Elaine Anderson
Marie .... Karen Morley
Jocelin .... Arlene Francis
Fleur .... Flora Campbell
André Marignac .... Wesley Addy
Jacques de Laboureur .... Clay Clement
Ordonnance Corporal .... Victor Christian
Filou .... Nick Conte
Guard .... Harry M. Cooke
Adjutant .... Zachary Scott
General Duffort .... Robert Harrison
German Colonel .... Jack Mylong-Muenz
German Lieutenant .... Harald Bromley
Major Himmelmann .... Victor Thorley
Lieutenant Mehlmann .... John Hacker
Captain Milder .... Herbert Berghof
Workmen .... Sid Cassel, Paul E. Wilson, Donald Lee, Jerome Thor, Don Glenn, Peter Boyne
French Soldiers .... Jerome Thor, Henry Levin, Sid Cassel, Don Glenn, Peter Boyne
German Soldiers .... William Rykey, Paul E. Wilson, Donald Lee, Brian Connaught

Stage Manager: John Cornell

Ass't. Stage Manager: Elaine Anderson

National Theatre, Washington, April 28, 1941

(Closed before being brought into New York City.)

AH, WILDERNESS!

A Comedy of Recollection
BY EUGENE O'NEILL
STAGED BY EVA LE GALLIENNE
Settings designed by Watson Barratt

CAST

Nat Miller, owner of the *Evening Globe* .... Harry Carey
Essie, his wife .... Ann Shoemaker
Arthur, their son .... Victor Chapin
Richard, their son .... William Prince
Mildred, their daughter .... Virginia Kaye
Tommy, their son .... Tommy Lewis
Sid Davis, Essie's brother, reporter on the *Waterbury Standard*
Tom Tully
Lily Miller, Nat's sister .... Enid Markey
David McComber, dry-goods merchant .... Hale Norcross
Muriel McComber .... Dorothy Littlejohn
Wint Selby, classmate of Arthur's at Yale .... Walter Craig
Belle .... Dennie Moore
Nora .... Philippa Bevans
Bartender .... Zachary Scott
Salesman .... Edmund Dorsay

Administrative Directors: Theresa Helburn, Lawrence Langner
General Production and Casting Direction: John Haggott
Assistant to Administrative Directors: Armina Marshall

Guild Theatre, October 2, 1941
(29 PERFORMANCES)

(Co-Produced with The Playwrights' Company)
HELEN HAYES
in

CANDLE IN THE WIND

BY MAXWELL ANDERSON
DIRECTED BY ALFRED LUNT
Settings and lighting by Jo Mielziner
Miss Hayes' clothes designed and executed by Valentina

CAST

Fargeau .... Philip White
Henri .... Benedict MacQuarrie
Deseze .... Robert Harrison
Charlotte .... Leona Roberts
Mercy .... Nell Harrison
Madeline Guest .... Helen Hayes
Maisie Tompkins .... Evelyn Varden
Raoul St. Cloud .... Louis Borell
German Captain .... Harro Meller
German Lieutenant .... Knud Krueger
Colonel Erfurt .... John Wengraf
Lieutenant Schoen .... Tonio Selwart
Corporal Behrens .... Mario Gang
Madame Fleury .... Michelette Burani
Monsieur Fleury .... Stanley Jessep
First Guard .... Brian Connaught
Second Guard .... Ferdi Hoffman
Cissie .... Lotte Lenya
Corporal Mueller .... Joseph Wiseman
Third Guard .... George André
Fourth Guard .... Guy Monypenny
Corporal Schultz .... William Malten
Captain .... Bruce Fernald

Stage Manager: John Haggott
Ass't. Stage Managers: Jacqueline Paige,
Guy Monypenny

Shubert Theatre, October 22, 1941
(95 PERFORMANCES)

FREDRIC MARCH, FLORENCE ELDRIDGE,
AND ALAN REED
in

HOPE FOR A HARVEST

BY SOPHIE TREADWELL
STAGED BY LESTER VAIL
Settings by Watson Barratt
Miss Eldridge's costumes designed by Valentina

CAST

Mrs. Matilda Martin	Helen Carew
Antoinette Martin	Judy Parrish
Elliott Martin	Fredric March
Carlotta Thatcher	Florence Eldridge
Nelson Powell	John Morny
Victor de Lucchi	Arthur Franz
Billy Barnes	Shelley Hull
Bertha Barnes	Edith King
Joe de Lucchi	Alan King
A Woman	Doro Merande

Stage Manager: Maurice McRae
Ass't. Stage Manager: Anna Minot
Guild Theatre, November 26, 1941
(38 PERFORMANCES)

PAPA IS ALL

BY PATTERSON GREENE
STAGED BY FRANK CARRINGTON AND AGNES MORGAN
Setting and costumes by Emeline Roche

CAST

Mama	Jessie Royce Landis
Jake	Emmett Rogers
State Trooper Brendle	Royal Beal
Emma	Celeste Holm
Mrs. Yoder	Dorothy Sands
Papa	Carl Benton Reid

Dialect Coach: Robert Scheffer
Stage Manager: Wylie Adams
Ass't. Stage Manager: Hathaway Kale
Guild Theatre, January 6, 1942
(63 PERFORMANCES)
(played in six cities before being brought into New York)

MARY BOLAND, BOBBY CLARK, AND WALTER HAMPDEN

in

THE RIVALS

BY RICHARD BRINSLEY SHERIDAN

Prologue by Arthur Guiterman

STAGED BY EVA LE GALLIENNE

Settings and costumes by Watson Barratt

Musical setting by Macklin Marrow

Orchestra under the direction of Macklin Marrow

CAST

Lydia Languish .... Haila Stoddard
Lucy .... Helen Ford
Julia .... Frances Reid
Mrs. Malaprop .... Mary Boland
Captain Absolute .... Donald Burr
Fag .... Raymond Johnson
Faulkland .... Robert Wallsten
Acres .... Bobby Clark
Boy .... Walt Draper
Sir Lucius O'Trigger .... Philip Bourneuf
David .... Roland Hogue
Sir Anthony Absolute .... Walter Hampden
Footman .... George Boots
Footman .... William Whitehead

Company Manager: Max Mayer
Lecturer: Sam Pearce
Stage Manager: John Fearnley
Ass't Stage Manager: Elaine Anderson

Shubert Theatre, January 14, 1942

(54 PERFORMANCES)

PAUL MUNI

in

YESTERDAY'S MAGIC

BY EMLYN WILLIAMS

STAGED BY REGINALD DENHAM

Scenery designed by Watson Barratt

CAST

Mrs. Banner .... Brenda Forbes
Barty .... Patrick O'Moore
Fan .... Cathleen Cordell
Bevan .... James Monks
Maddoc Thomas .... Paul Muni
Cattrin .... Jessica Tandy
Robert .... Alfred Drake
Mrs. Lothian .... Margaret Douglass

Guild Theatre, April 14, 1942

(55 PERFORMANCES)

TWENTY-FIFTH SEASON

KATHARINE HEPBURN

in

WITHOUT LOVE

BY PHILIP BARRY

STAGED BY ROBERT B. SINCLAIR

Designed and lighted by Robert Edmond Jones

Miss Hepburn's clothes by Valentina

CAST

Patrick Jamieson .... Elliott Nugent
Quentin Ladd .... Tony Bickley
Anna .... Emily Massey
Martha Ladd .... Ellen Morgan
Jamie Coe Rowan .... Katharine Hepburn
Kitty Trimble .... Audrey Christie
Peter Baillie .... Robert Shayne
Paul Carrel .... Lauren Gilbert
Richard Hood .... Paul Chisholm
Robert Emmet Riordan .... Neil Fitzgerald
Grant Vincent .... Royal Beal

(The Theatre Guild gratefully acknowledges the assistance of Mr. Arthur Hopkins in re-staging the play, Mr. Sinclair having joined the Armed Forces.)

Shubert Theatre, New Haven, February 26, 1942

St. James Theatre, November 10, 1942

(113 PERFORMANCES)

MR. SYCAMORE

The Saga of John Gwilt in Eight Verses
BY KETTI FRINGS
Based on a story by Robert Ayre
with
LILLIAN GISH STUART ERWIN ENID MARKEY
DIRECTED BY LESTER VAIL
Settings designed by Samuel Leve

CAST

Tom Burton .... Harry Townes
Ned Fish .... Harry Sheppard
John Gwilt .... Stuart Erwin
Myrtle Staines .... Leona Powers
Abner Coote .... John Philliber
Estelle Benlow .... Enid Markey
Julie Fish .... Louise McBride
Albert Fernfield .... Buddy Swan
Mr. Fernfield .... Walter Appler
Fletcher Pingpank .... Franklyn Fox
Rev. Doctor Doody .... Russell Collins
Jane Gwilt .... Lillian Gish
Fred Staines .... Otto Hulett
First Milkman .... Ernest Theiss
Second Milkman .... Kenneth Haydon
Third Milkman .... Rupert Pole
Mr. Oikle .... Albert Bergh
Emily .... Mary Heckart
Mr. Hammond .... Jed Dooley
Daisy Staines .... Pearl Herzog
Mr. Hoop .... Ray J. Largay
Mr. Fink .... Harry Bellaver
People of Smeed .... Peggy Opdycke, Albert Vees,
Helen Dodson

Stage Manager: Mae MacAvoy
Ass't. Stage Manager: Peggy Opdycke

Guild Theatre, November 13, 1942
(19 PERFORMANCES)

(In association with the Playwrights' Company)
THE ALFRED LUNT–LYNN FONTANNE PRODUCTION OF

THE PIRATE

BY S. N. BEHRMAN

(Suggested by an idea in a play by Ludwig Fulda)

STAGED BY MR. LUNT AND JOHN C. WILSON

Settings by Lemuel Ayers

Costumes by Miles White

Music by Herbert Kingsley

Dances by Felicia Sorel

CAST

Manuela .... Lynn Fontanne
Pedro Vargas .... Alan Reed
Isabella .... Lea Penman
Mango Seller .... Juanita Hall
Fisherboy .... Albert Popwell
Ines .... Estelle Winwood
Capucho .... James O'Neill
Lizarda .... Muriel Rahn
Estaban .... Robert Emhardt
Don Bolo .... Walter Mosby
Trillo .... Maurice Ellis
Serafin .... Alfred Lunt
Viceroy .... Clarence Derwent
Maids to Manuela .... Ruby Greene, Anna Jackson, Louvinia White
Maid to Isabella .... Inez Matthews
Viceroy's Guards .... Guy Monypenny, Peter Garey
Members of Serafin's Troupe, Soldiers and Townspeople:
David Bethea, Bruce Howard, Martha Jones, Jules Johnson

Martin Beck Theatre, November 27, 1942

(177 PERFORMANCES)

THE RUSSIAN PEOPLE

BY KONSTANTIN SIMONOV
AMERICAN ACTING VERSION BY CLIFFORD ODETS
DIRECTED BY HAROLD CLURMAN
Settings designed by Boris Aronson
Musical direction by Lan Adomian

CAST

Martha Safonova .... Margaret Waller
Maria Kharitonova .... Eleonora Mendelssohn
Kozlovsky .... Eduard Franz
Valya .... Elizabeth Fraser
Vasili .... Robert Simon
Wounded Man .... Ernest Graves
Safonov .... Leon Ames
Borisov .... Randolph Echols
Shura .... Anna Minot
Vasin .... Victor Varconi
Panin .... Herbert Berghof
Lieutenant Vasilyev .... Peter Hobbs
Globa .... Luther Adler
Old Man .... Joseph Shattuck
Second Old Man .... Jefferson Coates
Rosenberg .... William Malten
Werner .... Harold Dyrenforth
Kharitonov .... E. A. Krumschmidt
Unknown Man .... Harro Meller
Red Army Man .... Ad Karns
Sentry .... Jon Dawson
Captain Gavrilov .... Roger Beirne
Krause .... Walter Kohler
German Soldier .... David Koser
Semyonov .... Mark Schweid
Major General Lukonin .... Robert Simon
Signal Man .... Michael Strong
Red Army Men, German Soldiers ....David Koser, Ad Karns, Ernest Graves, Harro Meller, Jon Dawson, Michael Strong
Russian Singers: David Tuchinoff, Leo Resnik, Boris Belostozky, Michael Greben, Lucian Arnold Ruttman, Seymour Osborne

Production Manager: John Haggott
Ass't. Stage Managers: Bettina Cerf, Elaine Anderson

National Theatre, Washington, D. C., December 14, 1942
Guild Theatre, December 29, 1942
(39 PERFORMANCES)

OKLAHOMA!

(A Musical Play based on "Green Grow the Lilacs" by Lynn Riggs)
Book and Lyrics by Oscar Hammerstein 2nd
Music by Richard Rodgers
(Orchestrations arranged by Robert Russell Bennett)
PRODUCTION DIRECTED BY ROUBEN MAMOULIAN
Choreography by Agnes DeMille
Settings by Lemuel Ayers
Costumes by Miles White
Orchestra conducted by J. Schwartzdorf

CAST

Aunt Eller .... Betty Garde
Curly .... Alfred Drake
Laurey .... Joan Roberts
Ike Skidmore .... Barry Kelley
Fred .... Edwin Clay
Slim .... Herbert Rissman
Will Parker .... Lee Dixon
Jud Fry .... Howard da Silva
Ado Annie Carnes .... Celeste Holm
Ali Hakim .... Joseph Buloff
Gertie Cummings .... Jane Lawrence
Ellen .... Katharine Sergava
Sylvie .... Ellen Love
Andrew Carnes .... Ralph Riggs
Armina .... Kate Friedlich
Aggie .... Bambi Linn
Cord Elam .... Owen Martin
Jess .... George Church
Chalmers .... Marc Platt
Mike .... Paul Schiers
Joe .... George Irving
Cowboy .... Jack Harwood
Sam .... Hayes Gordon
The Girl Who Falls Down .... Joan McCracken

Laurey's Friends: Ann Newland, Rosemary Schaefer, Nona Feid, Maria Harriton, Marian Horosko, Billie Zay

Cowboys: Gary Fleming, Jack Claus, Jack Miller, Rem Olmstead, Pat Meany, Jack Baker, Ken LeRoy

Jud's Postcards: Louise Fornaca, Vivian Smith, Margit DeKova, June Graham, Muriel Gray, Kate Friedlich

Shubert, New Haven, March 11, 1943
St. James, March 31, 1943
(Over 5 years in New York)

LETTER FROM LEE SIMONSON TO THE GUILD'S BOARD OF MANAGERS

Hotel Winthrop
Lexington Ave. & 47th St.
New York City

December 1, 1937

Dear Bored:

What the Guild is obviously suffering from is a chronic inability to judge the dramatic and theatric values of the scripts it selects, and an almost equal inability to make up for weaknesses of its scripts by tricking them over in performance—in the manner of the Messrs. McClintic, George Kaufman or George Abbott. In former seasons our financial failures were often succés d'éstime. They are now not even that. Our revisions of plays are academic—they are always obvious improvements and leave the essential weakness of the script (except in the case of Sam Behrman) exactly where it was at the beginning. Our casting is equally ineffective. When it doesn't handicap a play as in "Quito" it isn't the kind that puts a play over.

Bovary is an example. It was obviously never anything but a vehicle for a virtuoso actress of the first order. But on the strength of a personal success that Cummings had had in "Mme Conti," which was not enough to put that play over, the Steering Committee plumped for her. Why? She had neither the experience, the technique, nor the virtuosity to be a safe bet. The Guild has held plays before that it couldn't cast, even for several seasons and then dropped them. Why the rush to do a $30,000 production in the beginning of a season before we knew how the season was going? Most of us liked the quality of Baty's script, and Maurice raved about the quality of the French performance. The steering committee plumped for a director who cordially disliked both and said so. He was, nevertheless, given carte-blanche to make a version of his own and practically no time at all was left between the date when the Guild saw the version—which naturally took out of the script everything we believed gave it a chance—and the date when rehearsals had to begin. Naturally, the steering committee didn't want to admit it had blundered and call the whole thing off at a cost of $10,000, so, in self defense, it hoped against hope and tried to muddle through.

If that is sound theatre management, I am the Shah of Persia. We take a synthetically made "star" of very limited experience—(her one success was in a comedy where she was supported by one of the most skillful English comedians, "Beau" Hanan) and without leaving ourselves any leeway, commit ourselves to a script we didn't like and a director whose point of view we don't believe in.

I am not out to make scapegoats of Terry and Lawrence. They have worked very hard and had some bad breaks. But I do think I am not out of order when I state my opinion that they, as a steering committee in executive control, are not the solution to the Guild's problems. As a steering committee they are obviously no shrewder theatrically and less shrewd financially than the Guild operating as a whole. Their one obvious success was sending Kit Hepburn on the road in "Jane Eyre." But the play, even after endless revision on the road and months of extra salary for Tony Miner, was still so lousy as a script that we didn't dare bring it into New York. And after another revision by Sidney Howard, Hepburn has just refused to come in with it for the same reason.

I have always believed that any value the Guild had came as a result of its group expression. The hammer and tong arguments, the exhausting sessions, may have seemed a waste of time. But they were much less so than the procedure we are following now. We give ourselves no time and no opportunity for critically considering or controlling what we are doing. Take "Yankee Doodle." I saw it at a dress rehearsal. And I was never asked nor evidently expected to see it again until the opening performance in New York. Neither was Phil although his critical reaction to it (as events have proved) was sounder and more penetrating than anybody else's. It simply doesn't follow that Terry and Lawrence have the only ideas about a production that matter.

Moreover our crazy, forced schedule which jams almost an entire season of production into the first three months—ignoring the howls of our subscribers—divides our energies and exhausts everyone, including Terry and Lawrence, so that we cannot do a proper job. It is financially reckless as well. We gamble on everything simultaneously. In the old days after two flops we could reconsider, and often changed our program, and put on a play we had not planned to do because it seemed financially or artistically the thing. Or we waited until one success had begun to turn in earnings and help run the organization before risking a spectacular and elaborate production. On our present schedule we risk our capital and our subscription cash simultaneously. To date we have lost in three months' operation 85% of the first and slightly over 50% of the second. This is no way to run any business.

I also wish to point out, as I wrote to Lawrence's lawyer last year while the present financial arrangements were under discussion, that the maximum salaries set are unsound from a business point of view, and out of all sound proportion to our capital, our other expenses, and the present earning powers of the Guild. When they are paid they are merely unemployment insurance and have to be paid back in one form or another. A financial crisis follows. This is also due to the fact that $100,000 capital is obviously not enough since a single $30,000 production that can incur $10,000 running losses on the road can reduce our capital to the point where salaries have to be cut automatically ½ or even ¾. I feel it has been proved that the only safe capital reserve is $150,000 and that nothing but normal salaries (of 10,000 and 12,000 dollars) should be paid until this is earned. Operating losses wouldn't then almost immediately bring on a financial crisis. If we can't rearrange this with our bond holders it ought to be made an agreement among ourselves.

In closing, I have one more concrete suggestion to make: the present operating control of the steering committee of two should be abandoned. There should be a single Guild executive representative for each production, Terry and Lawrence taking turns. That representative should call on any member or members of the Board for special help in any field, casting, re-writing, designing, etc., and incidentally get over the notion that only Terry or Lawrence are capable of revising a play. He or she should report back to the Guild fully and at frequent intervals, and be responsible for creating the opportunities for the Board to react to our productions regularly and frequently as a group at special meetings if necessary. And our perfunctory and hasty board meetings instead of delegating vital decisions to others will have to be long enough to thresh out our policies and our decisions in detail even if we have to meet twice a week. I see no other way that will give us a chance to keep going.

Yours,

Lee

BIBLIOGRAPHY

BOOKS

Atkinson, Brooks. *Broadway.* New York: Macmillan, 1970.

Binns, Archie. *Mrs. Fiske and the American Theatre.* New York: Crown Publishers, 1955.

Blake, Ben. *The Awakening of the American Theatre.* New York: Tomorrow Publishers, 1935.

Blum, Daniel. *A Pictorial History of the American Theatre.* New York: Greenberg, 1951.

Brown, John Mason. *Dramatis Personae.* New York: The Viking Press, 1965.

———. *The Worlds of Robert E. Sherwood.* New York: Harper & Row, 1965.

Clark, Barrett H. *European Theories of the Drama, with a Supplement on the American Drama* (2nd ed. rev.). New York: Crown Publishers, 1947.

Clurman, Harold. *The Fervent Years.* The Group Theatre and the 1930's. New York: Hill and Wang, 1957.

Coad, Oral S. and Edwin Mims, Jr. *The American Stage.* New Haven: Yale University Press, 1929.

Coward, Noel. *Play Parade.* New York: Garden City Publishing Co., 1933.

De Mille, Agnes. *Dance to the Piper.* Boston: Little, Brown, 1952.

Eaton, Walter Prichard. *Plays and Players.* Cincinnati: Steward and Kidd, 1916.

———. *The Theatre Guild, The First Ten Years.* New York: Brentano's, 1929.

Faulkner, Harold Underwood. *The Quest for Social Justice, 1898-1914.* New York: Macmillan, 1931.

Freedley, George. *The Lunts.* New York: Macmillan, 1958.

Freedley, George and John A. Reeves. *A History of the Theatre.* New York: Crown Publishers, 1941.

Gassner, John. *Form and Idea in Modern Theatre.* New York: Dryden Press, 1956.

———. *The Theatre in Our Times.* New York: Crown Publishers, 1955.

———, ed. *Twenty Best European Plays on the American Stage.* New York: Crown Publishers, 1957.

Gelb, Barbara and Arthur. *O'Neill.* New York: Harper and Brothers, 1962.

Gould, Bruce and Beatrice Blackmar Gould. *American Story.* New York: Harper & Row, 1968.

Guthrie, Tyrone. *A Life in the Theatre.* New York: McGraw-Hill, 1959.

Hacker, Louis M. and Helene S. Zahler. *The United States in the 20th Century.* New York: Appleton-Century-Crofts, 1952.

Hanff, Helene. *Underfoot in Show Business.* New York: Harper and Brothers, 1962.

Hartnoll, Phyllis (ed.). *The Oxford Companion to the Theatre.* New York: Oxford University Press, 1951.

Hayes, Helen. *On Reflection.* New York: M. Evans, 1968.

Helburn, Theresa. *A Wayward Quest.* Boston: Little, Brown, 1960.

Hewitt, Bernard. *Theatre U. S. A.* New York: McGraw-Hill, 1959.

Himelstein, Morgan Y. *Drama Was a Weapon.* The left-wing theatre in New York, 1929–41. New Brunswick: Rutgers University Press, 1963.

Hughes, Glenn. *A History of the American Theatre, 1700–1950.* New York: Samuel French, 1951.

Komisarjevsky, Theodore and Lee Simonson. *Settings and Costumes of the Modern Stage.* New York: Studio Publishers, 1933.

Langner, Lawrence. *G. B. S. and the Lunatic.* New York: Atheneum, 1963.

———. *The Magic Curtain.* New York: E. P. Dutton, 1951.

MacGowan, Kenneth and William Melnitz. *The Living Stage.* Englewood Cliffs, N. J.: Prentice-Hall, 1955.

Mantle, Burns. *Best Plays of 1928–29.* New York: Dodd, Mead, 1929. See Burns Mantle's "Best Plays" series through the 1943 season.

———. *Contemporary American Playwrights.* New York: Dodd, Mead and Co., 1938.

Morehouse, Ward. *Matinee Tomorrow—Fifty Years of Our Theatre.* New York: Whittlesey House (McGraw-Hill), 1949.

Morris, Lloyd. *Curtain Time, The Story of the American Theatre.* New York: Random House, 1953.

Nadel, Norman. *A Pictorial History of the Theatre Guild.* New York: Crown Publishers, 1969.

Nathan, George Jean. *Since Ibsen.* New York: A. A. Knopf, 1933.

Parker, John, ed. *Who's Who in the Theatre.* New York: Pitman Publishing (ninth edition, 1939; tenth edition, 1947).

Quinn, Arthur Hobson, ed. *Representative American Plays.* New York: Century, 1917.

Rice, Elmer. *The Living Theatre.* New York: Harper and Brothers, 1959.

Saylor, Oliver M. *Our American Theatre.* New York: Brentano's, 1923.

Shannon, David A., ed. *The Great Depression.* Englewood Cliffs, N. J.: Prentice-Hall, 1960.

Simonson, Lee. *Part of a Lifetime.* New York: Duell, Sloan and Pearce, 1943.

———. *The Stage Is Set.* New York: Harcourt, Brace, 1932.

Sobel, Bernard, ed. *The Theatre Handbook and Digest of Plays.* New York: Crown Publishers, 1948.

Stagg, Jerry. *The Brothers Shubert.* New York: Random House, 1968.

Sullivan, Mark. *Our Times, the United States.* New York: Charles Scribner's Sons. Vol. III (Pre-War America), 1930, Vol. IV (1909–1914), 1932.

Terkel, Studs. *Hard Times.* New York: Pantheon, 1970.

The Theatre Guild Anthology. New York: Random House, 1936.

Thorp, Willard. *American Writing in the Twentieth Century.* Cambridge, Mass.: Harvard University Press, 1960.

Toohey, John L. *A History of the Pulitzer Prize Plays.* New York: The Citadel Press, 1967.

Webster, Margaret. *The Same Only Different.* Five Generations of a great theatre family. New York: A. A. Knopf, 1969.

Zolotow, Maurice. *Stagestruck: The Romance of Alfred Lunt and Lynn Fontanne.* New York: Harcourt, Brace & World, 1964.

UNPUBLISHED DOCTORAL DISSERTATIONS

Arbenz, Mary Hedwig. "The Plays of Eugene O'Neill as Presented by the Theatre Guild." University of Illinois, 1961.

Gasper, Raymond Dominic. "A Study of the Group Theatre and Its Contribution to Theatrical Production in America." Ohio State University, 1956.

Gordon, George N. "Theatrical Movements in the *Theatre Arts* Magazine, 1916–1948." New York University, 1957.

Handley, John Guy. "A History of *Theatre Arts* Magazine, 1916–1948." Louisiana State University, 1960.

INDEX

This book was set in ten point Caledonia, and was composed by
Modern Typographers Inc., Clearwater, Florida.
It was printed and bound by
Benson Printing Company, Nashville, Tennessee.
The paper is
New Era Matte manufactured by the Mead Paper Company.
The design is by Edgar J. Frank.